MW00567084

The Pigheaded Soul

Essays and Reviews on Poetry and Culture

Jason Guriel

THE PIG

HEADED

SOUL

ESSAYS AND REVIEWS
ON POETRY & CULTURE

The Porcupine's Quill

Library and Archives Canada Cataloguing in Publication

Guriel, Jason, 1978–, author
    The pigheaded soul : essays and reviews on poetry and
culture / Jason Guriel.

ISBN: 978-0-88984-368-4 (pbk.)

    1. Canadian poetry (English)—History and criticism.
2. American poetry—History and criticism.   I. Title.

PS8143.G87 2013   c811.009   c2013-904522-8

Published by The Porcupine's Quill, 68 Main Street, PO Box 160,
Erin, Ontario N0B 1T0. http://porcupinesquill.ca

Readied for the press by Carmine Starnino.

Represented in Canada by Canadian Manda.
Trade orders are available from University of Toronto Press.

We acknowledge the support of the Ontario Arts Council and the
Canada Council for the Arts for our publishing program. The financial
support of the Government of Canada through the Canada Book Fund
and the Government of Ontario through the Ontario Media Development
Corporation is also gratefully acknowledged.

Canada

Ontario
Ontario Media Development
Corporation

Canada Council   Conseil des Arts
for the Arts   du Canada

ONTARIO ARTS COUNCIL
CONSEIL DES ARTS DE L'ONTARIO

for Sonya Tomas
for putting up with my pigheadedness

and for Carmine Starnino
for encouraging it

Table of Contents

Introduction

When I was younger, I had the habit of imagining what I'd say, were I a rock critic, about this or that album. But such grey literature, dreamed up for the back pages of music trades, was almost always left untyped at the back of my mind. (The one review that escaped my skull: a letter to the editor of *Mojo*, in which Radiohead is taken to task by a pigheaded twentysomething.) My first real reviews were commissioned by a literary magazine, now defunct, that had requested to see some poems, but found nothing to its liking. Several submissions were dispatched; nothing took. In what was surely a last-ditch attempt to get something of mine into print (and save all parties any further embarrassment), the editors wondered if I might like to try reviewing a collection of poetry. That might shut me up.

New assignments resulted in commissions from other magazines: book review begat book review. In the generally dull world of poetry criticism, a remotely sharp judgment will tend to perk the ears of editors who like a little edge, even if some readers elect to call the noise they hear a 'hatchet job'. Those conspiracy theorists who assume I have an axe to grind should be assured that the whetstone was usually someone else's idea.

Put another way, *The Pigheaded Soul* was written largely by accident, under the radar of even its author, who apparently couldn't bring himself to turn down too many gigs. The few times I vowed to get out of the game and back to poems, some editor always pulled me back in. Before I could reconsider, I had embarked on yet another criticism spree.

As a result, the many mercenary parts of *The Pigheaded Soul* have been assembling just beyond the borders of my attention for years now. They wanted only for someone to walk their ragtag ranks, dust an epaulette or two, haul off by the earlobe the runts. Some of my subjects I was free to choose; others were suggested to

me. I couldn't have composed—wouldn't have *wanted* to compose—
The Pigheaded Soul some other, more deliberate way.

Why the piecemeal approach? Why let the content needs of editors—surely the obsolete gatekeepers of another era—set the pace of
writing? Technology, after all, has made it tantalizingly easy to air a
windy, unsolicited opinion about a book, a poem (even if Twitter,
thankfully, limits the character count). But I have preferred being
asked for mine and, when possible, paid for it. (If you're to hang
yourself, someone else ought to subsidize the rope.) Plus, the wait
between gigs—I didn't realize I was waiting at the time; I simply
didn't assume there'd always be another gig—kept a useful sort of
gag in place. I wrote, when I wrote at all, with a healthy respect for
the silence I was about to break—and a hunch that most who shatter
it, shouldn't. Anyway, even when I was the one pitching the piece,
there was almost always an exacting editor on the other end whom I
could trust to be as tough on me as I felt it was my duty to be on the
books under review. I wanted structure: to write for an editor I
respected and to write to deadline.

My brief stint as a paid blogger was fun for a time, and I've preserved some of the posts in these pages. But it also permitted the
young critic too much of the wrong kind of freedom: freedom to go
on at length; freedom to qualify; freedom to moisten an otherwise
wick-crisp phrase for fear it might inflame the comment stream;
freedom to take the real-time responses of those kind enough to read
one's writing—and by extension, to take one's writing—too seriously. I gathered I was expected to set a tone: to stay on top of the
comment stream by pouring into it enough courtesy to ensure the
poisonous comments were merely parts per million. (Thank you,
reader; may I have another?) But in the utopian interest of dialogue
and community, I often made like the failing teacher who has to put
up with a certain amount of petulance if he's to keep the class moving along. What Christian Wiman says about teaching—'The chief
difficulty is the sound of your own voice, the assuredness that
inevitably creeps in, the sheer volume of talk that, after a few weeks,
you feel flabbing around you like a body gone bad'—is what I want
to say about our endless, editorless, online adventure. Except it's not
even 'assuredness' that's the real problem in the poetry world (flame

wars, sparked by the self-assured, can be trusted to flame out); it's the low hum of hedging, a commitment to consensus, that high-speed Internet encourages. In moderation, of course, social media can make for a useful tool. Still, I was grateful to return to scattered, old-school assignments.

My goal in composing these pieces has been to honour gut reactions, however acidic, and to be entertaining about it. I have tried to assume that readers of poetry are smart grown-ups with overscheduled lives, who might appreciate a vigorous opinion. I haven't felt especially hemmed in by the Canadian border; I have scarcely noticed it. The first half of this book is about Canadians; the other half, about others—Americans, mostly. Surely we've reached a moment when critics who happen to possess a Canadian passport shouldn't need to feel compelled to gin up more interest in the national poetry than they want to.

My take on Oscar Wilde's epigram about life—that *art* is too important to be taken seriously—is an operative principle. Make 'em laugh is another. Pauline Kael's description of those acerbic journalists who, transplanted to Hollywood in the 1930s, transformed its screenplays—'they brought movies the subversive gift of sanity'—would characterize the poetry critics who've meant the most to me, including Carmine Starnino, Clive James, Michael Hofmann, William Logan, the late Thomas Disch, and, when she's cared to write prose, Kay Ryan. These are critics who return to me some of my very own rejected thoughts—they surely had been mine, hadn't they?—about the screwball state of poetry. But they also do so with *sprezzatura*, with a reader in mind and a deadline to meet, seemingly failing again and again to consider the impact their sharp sentences might have on their own careers, none of which were inflated enough to require bursting in the first place.

The truly helpful poetry critics can't help themselves—and can't help but frustrate some (maybe even many) of the very readers they hope to serve. These are the readers who tend to want too much and, paradoxically, too little from poetry. 'It seems to me we have enough distraction,' writes one such reader, Sina Queyras, proprietor of the Lemon Hound blog. 'Ideas are what is lacking. I have always turned to poetry to think.' This sure sounds great, but it makes the sayer (a

poet herself, natch) sound even greater. (It also suggests—disingen-
uously—that a blog proprietor is above the business of distraction.)
By overburdening poems with so noble a purpose (making thoughtless readers think) we over-ennoble their authors. To be sure, a person might acquire a fact or two from poems, but the best poetry is
first and foremost what T.S. Eliot would call a 'superior amusement'. When one such amusement, by Robyn Sarah, describes a
sneeze as

> going where it takes us,
> brakeless,
> making the noisy noise
> it makes us make

it's hard not to be amused by the repetitions and internal rhymes
that so expertly seize and bear us along. When another amusement,
by Pino Coluccio, describes how a man

> tried to keep, in what he wrote—
> each word composed, each word remote,
> each word a tooth in turning gears—
> the time reliably for years

it's hard not to be tickled by the way this stalled but staggering time-
piece of a poem winds us up as we wait for the payoff. Sarah and
Coluccio are far too intelligent to try to teach us anything, to condescend. Yes, their poems make us more alert, but the authors make no
great claim to cracking open some mindless reader's middlebrow
and terraforming her consciousness. As with the best kind of 'experimental' poets, the adjective is implicit. Entertainment, escapism—
these are feats enough.

But far too many readers of poetry prefer to flatter themselves
with the splendid thought that the thoughtful work they read (and
write) is food for thought. For them, poetry is lifestyle, career,
scented candle. Think of the professors who've invested too much of
their selves (and CVs) in poetry—hybrid, eco, conceptual, what
have you—to take the stuff less seriously than they do. How to break

it to them that the following lines, by the much-celebrated Dionne Brand,

> you feel someone brush against you,
> on the street, you smell leather, the lake,
> the coming leaves, the rain's immortality
> pierces you, but you will be asleep when it arrives

are so vague and solemn as to be ridiculous? That such raspberry-ready poetry ought to inform a YouTube bit on coffee houses? What is obvious to the music nerds in one scene of *High Fidelity*—that latter-day Stevie Wonder is laughable—isn't always so obvious to readers when faced with the wobbly wonders of the poetry world. The subculture simply hasn't evolved, as pop music has, a collective taste that can be counted on to parse the truly cool Coluccio from the humorously Bland. Only a few scattered critics stubbornly insist on holding court, which is to say putting their own careers on trial with every opinion they hand down. Is this foolishness? Late in life, reflecting on why he chose to stay in inhospitable Hollywood, Orson Welles sighed: 'I was going to show them that they were wrong, and I've spent the rest of my life *showing* people, trying to *prove* that what is said is wrong, and that's been an enormous waste of spirit and of energy.' Is this the fate of poets who too much enjoy the pose they strike, writing critical prose?

I realize only now that the first critics I admired wouldn't have identified as critics. I still recall the white-haired woman who taught me—by way of nothing more than her own capacity for wonder—the craft that had surely gone into the first verse paragraph of T.S. Eliot's 'The Hollow Men'. We'd been engaged, Grade Eleven Advanced English, in some quiet work at our desks, when she'd unceremoniously taken up some chalk and started copying out the lines, which looked so much better buoyed on green slate:

> We are the hollow men
> We are the stuffed men
> Leaning together
> Headpiece filled with straw. Alas!

Our dried voices, when
We whisper together
Are quiet and meaningless
As wind in dry grass
Or rats' feet over broken glass
In our dry cellar....

Pointing out the economy, the assonance, the similes, she was convinced this handful of lines had taken Eliot a month. It didn't matter that her guess was probably just that—guesswork; the real lesson was the example of a grown woman (she would have been nearing retirement, actually) finding herself floored in front of a blackboard, a grown woman who felt it was *okay* for a handful of lines to be worth a month's labour. (What were the accounting students, in some other room of the school, learning about balancing ledgers, about time and money?) I didn't set out to be a critic, but on some unconscious level, I was filing away certain encounters with enthusiasm that now seem to me, well, critical. They are almost the only moments with certain teachers I remember.

Other pearls, however, were the product of irritation. My senior-year writing teacher—a gaunt, sharp woman—could muster no patience for the Beat poet who finds his utterances too inevitable to revise. This wasn't 'conservatism', that label a conservative mind will pin on those it decides aren't liberal enough; this was concern for language. Anyway, what's more conservative than a rigorously regulated subculture of rebels—you could opt in any number of avant-gardists, pre- and post-Beat—for whom innovation amounts to the same old pileup of talking points? (For a list of talking points, skip ahead to 'The Spectric Poets' or 'Going Negative'.) In short, my teacher's irritation was instruction. Negativity, as I suggest later in these pages, isn't a very practical term for capturing what can be a very practical emotion, especially when modelled to minors with potential. I encourage those entrusted with the education of impressionable minds to direct their charges to the chapters on Charles Bernstein, e. e. cummings, and Dennis Lee before it's too late—before they lose these youngsters to the snares of UbuWeb.

At university—where I took and, for a time, taught creative

writing courses—most of the instructors practised something called 'constructive criticism': they peeled poems apart gently, for the purpose of building up their fragile young authors. (The one exception: Richard Teleky, a straight-talking American-Canadian who taught with a pug on his lap and whose syllabus assigned a book of actual book reviews, Philip Marchand's *Ripostes*—the perfect riposte to those of us who persisted in believing that Michael Ondaatje was any good.) Meanwhile, over in the English department, authors were considered 'dead', and poems, 'texts', the better to bring them down to some idealized earth where, all bards being equal, the concrete poetry of bpNichol (hollow stuff) could share syllabi with sturdier material like, well, 'The Hollow Men'. I was never so reactionary that I could dispense entirely with Barthes and Foucault, who have become, like the dead white men they helped stuff and mount, convenient straw men. But these particular dead white theorists—and the many zealots to whom they supplied a tongue—presented a dead end to the young man with aspirations to write lucid, entertaining prose. Hence the double life as a book reviewer who has failed, again and again, to evolve beyond evaluative judgments.

Many others who have meant a lot to me were not—are not—poetry critics *per se*: David Foster Wallace on location, Fran Lebowitz on modern life, Dorothy Parker on everything. (I have long hoped a publisher would collect the pieces Stephen Metcalf—*Slate*'s critic-at-large—has filed for his Dilettante column over the last decade.) I've subtitled this book 'Essays and Reviews on Poetry and Culture' because, while most of the pieces are devoted to poetry, many of them betray a promiscuous interest in other cultural products that are every bit as compelling as poems and sometimes more so: movies, music, and the like. 'The key to being a TV critic without losing one's mind,' writes Troy Patterson, 'is to not watch too much television, or so I hope.' Stealing away from the poetry world for short (and sometimes not-so-short) stretches has been critical to maintaining a sound mind, if not a pigheaded soul.

—J.G.
Toronto, 2013

ONE

How I Learned to Survive
without Margaret Atwood

I'm drawn to desert island lists, and I suspect Harold Bloom is, too. It's a certain-kind-of-guy thing: men who are better with their books than their hands can still enjoy imagining the provisions they would require were they displaced to some atoll, even if the provisions amount to little more than collections of poems—kindling by which to warm the mind as opposed to the extremities. But they don't, these shipwrecked men of letters, go overboard; a *short* list of essentials is preferred, a sign of frugality, thrift. And the more esoteric the list, the better. Declaring that one would stow a Complete Shakespeare (a sensible choice, like canned meat) wastes a perfectly good opportunity to display one's knowledge of the arcane. Bloom's own list of the best American works of the twentieth century itemizes such perversely specific stuff as Bud Powell's song 'Un Poco Loco' and the Byron the Light Bulb set piece in Thomas Pynchon's novel *Gravity's Rainbow*. It's a doctor's note for the survivalist with particular dietary needs.

Bloom's book, *The Western Canon*, by contrast, goes long. At the back there's even a country-by-country breakdown of the best writers of all time. The American list takes up over six pages, and deservedly so. The Canadian list, on the other hand, is small enough to fit the *back* of the hand: it runs to a mere eight names. More remarkable than the Canadian list's concision, however, is its content. Although the usual suspects—Alice Munro, Margaret Atwood—are present and accounted for, there's no sign of Al Purdy, Earle Birney, bpNichol, Robert Kroetsch, Lorna Crozier, Patrick Lane, or Susan Musgrave. Non-Canadian readers should be apprised that up here the aforementioned are big fish, considered among the best we've got by those who can't see the smallness of the pond for its puffed-up fauna. But they don't make Bloom's list. And while I don't want to cede *too* much authority to the old aesthete's opinion, it was instructive, if not humbling, to discover what a prominent non-Canadian (an island of one at Yale) thought of my country's accepted canon—which was not very much. It was particularly instructive to discover on Bloom's list a Canadian poet of whom I'd never heard, a poet who'd never been discussed in any of the Canadian literature courses I'd taken at university, nor featured in *15 Canadian Poets x 2*, the flag-red and rigorously dull handbook with which one was apt to be equipped in such environs.

Perhaps, though, Bloom should have marooned Daryl Hine (1936–2012) offshore, in the blank, geopolitically neutral margins of *The Western Canon*'s pages. (He certainly should have heaved Atwood overboard altogether.) Born in British Columbia, Hine left Canada in 1958 and describes himself as 'stateless' in the tart introduction to his *Recollected Poems*. With a hint of curmudgeonly triumph, Hine observes:

> At first temporary, my Eurocentric exile metamorphosized into an alien residency in the United States when opportunities denied in my native land opened, first in New York and then in Chicago.
>
> I compensated for my lack of a B.A. (which I thought correctly that I should never need) by taking a Ph.D. at the University of Chicago, and instead of the work in a bookshop that I had been offered in Montreal, found myself editor of *Poetry*.

I wince at the uniquely Canadian foresight that offered a future editor of *Poetry* no more than a retail job. But our loss was Chicago's gain, and anyway, in Canada's defence, Hine's dense poetry, with its piquant wordplay and cosmopolitan allusions, would have conflicted with the nationalist project that took hold of my country in the 1960s, embodied in lines like these, by Al Purdy, from his poem 'At the Quinte Hotel':

> I am drinking
> I am drinking beer with yellow flowers
> in underground sunlight

and you can see that I am a sensitive man
And I notice that the bartender is a sensitive man too
so I tell him about his beer
I tell him the beer he draws
is half fart and half horse piss
and all wonderful yellow flowers ...

'Song of Myself', this ain't. And yet some consider Purdy to be
Canada's Whitman, and 'At the Quinte Hotel', a classic, a Song of
Themselves. The poem was even made into a short film, starring a
Canadian 'rock star'—one Gord Downie—as the pathetic, half-
soused speaker, a recurring figure in CanLit. In fact, Atwood's industry classic, the 1972 survey, *Survival: A Thematic Guide to Canadian
Literature*, argues that the central Canadian character is basically a
loser, a victim of British and American imperialism, struggling to
survive a hostile, perpetual winter. The book doubles cleverly as self-
help manual, designed to help Canadians acknowledge their status
as victims. It's as dreary as it sounds and now quite dated. Nevertheless, as recently as the late 1990s, *Survival* was still being distributed
among Canadian high school students like some sort of grim, state-
sponsored inoculation.

Daryl Hine, who published his first two collections in Canada, is
nowhere to be found in *Survival*, nor are these vigorous, almost joy-
ous stanzas, fished from a 1967 poem of his called 'The Trout':

I lean on air as prisoners on time
Not to let them down. My impetus,
In the interest of my kind sublime,
Appears in person merely perilous:

To climb the stair of stone where I was spawned,
Where ponds are oceans and the rapids give
Gasps of an unreachable beyond
I try, I fail, I wriggle loose, I live

Drop by drop against the stream I am,
And in death's shallow waterfall belong

Forever to the torrent and the dam
As defunctive music and recurrent song.

Spilt in sperm the mating pair ignore,
Caught in each other's scales as in a net,
I hung about above the ocean floor,
Part of the liquid pattern of the carpet ...

The speaker may be a survivor, struggling upstream, but Hine's language sure doesn't struggle. It gleams with what sonneteers used to call *sprezzatura*, the confident, making-it-look-easy gloss that greases great art: note the gamy alliteration of 'give/Gasps', the almost aquatic rhyme of 'spawned', 'ponds', and 'beyond'. Flung upon a scale and left to flip for itself, the slick thing scans.

But if 'The Trout' practically pops out of the water with vigour, the Canadian poetry I grew up reading and assuring myself I liked—some of which *Survival* preserves—exhibits an almost embarrassed aversion to virtuosity as well as an uncritical, if not calculated, anxiety about the sort of rough northern country on which only a small percentage of Canadians ever make their homes. Bodies of water in poems like Gwendolyn MacEwen's 'Dark Pines Under Water' and Atwood's 'This Is a Photograph of Me' are almost violently still, the better to appear to run deep. (Dragging such depths will tend to turn up a drown victim and, worse, a mood.) In the latter half of the Atwood, for instance, the speaker says coolly out of the corner of her parentheses,

(The photograph was taken
the day after I drowned.

I am in the lake, in the center
of the picture, just under the surface.

It is difficult to say where
precisely, or to say
how large or how small I am:
the effect of water
on light is a distortion

but if you look long enough
eventually
you will be able to see me.)

But you won't see her; you will see only Atwood's passé point: the signified has died, and words—the invigorating kind we go to poems for—won't bring her back. As poet-critic Carmine Starnino explains,

> The Canadian voice, under the tenure of nationalist influence, became a reduced thing—effete, etiolated—rather than an instrument marked by a prodigious expressive range, a rich breadth of capability.

Even Canada's few virtuosos, like A.M. Klein and P.K. Page, were less celebrated for aesthetic achievements than for card carrying. It's not hard, then, to get why poems like 'The Trout' didn't much appeal to the generation of poets, critics, teachers, and journalists whose search for an authentic 'Canadian' poem was qualified by a wariness of *too much* breadth, *too much* capability. Canadian poetry, it was felt, should be a survivor, scoured clean of foreign influence: a gaunt, washed-up underdog. Hine, though, cuts a very capable figure and, as a consequence of at least one country's literary fashions, has suffered for it.

Not that Hine was embraced with bunting at the 49th parallel; editorship of *Poetry* aside, Hine the poet remained square-peggish in the United States of the sixties and seventies, where free verse was form of choice for many social movements, and formal verse, a conservative anachronism. But the so-called 'New Formalism' that emerged in the eighties hardly claimed Hine as heroic forefather. If he belongs to a lineage, it's that of gay American poets like James Merrill, Richard Howard, and Howard Moss. Like the poetry of his peers, Hine's work demonstrates a lifelong investment in language—not, mind you, language in the L=A=N=G=U=A=G=E sense (or language as Atwood's speaker understands it: a murky medium), but good old-fashioned words that just might, if they're the right ones, strike us as inseparable from the things they describe. Here's the first

stanza of 'Don Juan in Amsterdam', a poem of exile from 1960, two
years into Hine's own exile:

> This also is a place which love is known in,
> This hollow land beneath a lifeless sea,
> Remote from whatever region he was born in,
> How far it is impossible to say.
>> The brackish water as I crossed
>> A bridge was delicately creased
> And stained and stale, like love-disordered linen.

A virtuoso, Hine cuts the near-naive rhyme of 'known in'/'born in'
with the unnerving off-rhymes 'sea'/'say' and, even better, 'crossed'/
'creased', the stanza maturing and souring as it slumps, via the assonance of 'stained and stale', toward its exquisitely musty final image.
'Love-disordered linen' easily tops my desert island list for Best
Image of Polluted Canal Water Ever (or Best Image of Soiled Post-
coital Bed Sheets Ever).

But although he would've likely hated the label, Hine was not
just a poet's poet (Richard Howard, John Hollander, and Mark
Strand have all praised his work), but a formalist's formalist, whose
poems sometimes feel like feats pulled off for the sake of their having
been pulled off. In other words, virtuosity has its downsides, and in
1991's 'Canzone', the rhyme scheme first distracts, then irritates,
transforming the opening stanza into an echo chamber:

> Such grainy elements of the obvious would
> Make up the basic building-blocks of matter,
> Which our ancestors understood as wood,
> Whatever the primitive root-word for wood,
> That substance time and energy will weather.
> Unlike earth and air and water, wood,
> A material to do with what one would,
> More often overlooked than understood,
> May misrepresent the stuff for which it stood—
> The world is after all not made of wood,

As you will notice if you look around,
Any more than the earth is obviously round.

I tend to favour a rich, rhyme-saturated lyric (especially since I was
reared on the impoverished, self-consciously 'Canadian' free verse of
poets like Purdy), but Hine's verbal effects can sometimes drown out
his verse.

To be fair, Hine defines a poem as 'a verbal object capable of giving a specific kind of aesthetic pleasure in itself. As such it is like a
painting or a sculpture, more than merely representational…'
Richard Howard says as much when he suggests that, for Hine,
'the poem is always the statement of itself.' Poetry is not a means
to an end; poetry *is* the end, just as 'the lines and masses of a
statue'—according to Wyndham Lewis (an exile to Canada)—'are
its soul'. Indeed, 'art has *no inside*', writes Hugh Kenner (also
Canadian), 'nothing you cannot *see*'. But Hine's descriptive chops
remain considerable, and when he strikes the right balance between
sound and sense, as in the latter half of 'Panta Rhei', he achieves a
state that critics sometimes shy away from judging and no longer
much believe in—aesthetic perfection:

But what if all this flim-flam simply means,
Ourselves apart, that nothing moves at all?
        So all commuters know
The disconcerting, transient sensation,
As a train begins to leave the station,
        Of stationary motion,
Refreshment- and shoeshine-stand, newspaper stall
And platform appearing to slide away, although
In fact the world stands still and still we flow.

The recurring themes that animate Hine's poetry are hardly as
unfashionable as its methods. Exile, adolescence, fraught love—
poetry's classic concerns are also Hine's. In fact, although Hine dated
the poems in *Recollected Poems*, the book eschews chronology in
favour of old-school thematic sections (like art, love, place, and
time) that seem aimed at the sort of mythical general reader who
buys Bloom's books or occasionally needs to look up a Valentine's

Day verse—and fast. And yet such readers may find themselves surprised. 1979's 'Letting Go' exposes an unusually naked vulnerability,
apt to make us uncomfortable when it describes how

>   you lay
> Candid as a cadaver on the couch
> I could have slept on, but I went away
> Ashamed to stay, afraid almost to touch.

Those prepared to follow the book's dates (to jump back and forth,
as in one of those old 'Choose-your-own-adventure' stories) will discover that Hine's work, over time, grows increasingly intimate, especially compared to his earlier language experiments. For example,
1991's 'Splendidior Vitro' shifts its focus from love to the deeply
unsexy subject of friendship, which,

>   tempering the grim extremes
> Of fire and ice, thrives at room temperature;
> Patient and forgiving, it disdains
> Love's ecstasies, anxieties and pains
> In shaky equilibrium, secure
> From ever being recognized in dreams.

Friendship is hardly popular fodder for poetry, but Hine reminds us
that such a 'room temperature' subject—'secure/From ever being
recognized in dreams'—may ultimately be more valuable than we
ever dreamed. Friends, after all, pick up where distraught sonnets
and slam performances leave off; they bring poets, and all of us regular lovesick civilians, back from our various brinks of despair.
Friends rarely make it into poems, though, and Hine's unfashion-
ably brave recognition of friendship's value is all but avant-garde in
our culture.

Hine can also treat usually solemn themes like exile with an
unexpected and slangy energy. You wouldn't guess he had it in him if
you had read only the erudite critical attempts by Howard and
Northrop Frye to disentangle Hine's many themes and allusions—
attempts that leave his poems more knotted and forbidding than

they were in the first place. In Hine's poem 'Ovid's Sorrows of Exile', however, the speaker is but an iPod away from resembling an ironic, post-everything Ovid when he observes

> the steep, seaweedy stairs
> Where I braved the brutal, stupid stares
> Of hairy bystanders bundled up in bear-
> Skins, beneath a broad and bare
> Sky light. These hicks can't speak a word of Latin!

These fun, slightly funky lines from 1999 succeed because they marry their potentially gimmicky conceit to genuine rigour—in this case, the risky but rewarding structure of rhyming couplets. Even as early as 1975, in the anapestic *In and Out: A Confessional Poem*, Hine can explain a 'truth' of Heraclitus through pop imagery that would make Camille Paglia proud:

> Instantaneous Spring had attacked
> Montreal overnight like a laxative,
> loosening snow from the slopes
> of the mountain, from rooftops and sidewalks
> and streets, where it piled up in barricades
> during our annual siege,
> till the city began to resemble
> a dissolute snowball dissolving.

My favourite example of Hine loosening up, though, is a love poem from 1979 that compares a departed lover to a mythic god and concludes with the damning couplet: 'Is he visiting with the Hyperboreans? God/Forgive me, what made me think he was a god?' Serious stuff, right? The poem is called 'What's His Face'.

In his later years, Hine devoted his time to translation. But his collection &: *A Serial Poem*, the first new book of his own poems in nearly two decades, was shortlisted for the Governor General's Award, which suggests that Canadian readers may finally be ready to embrace him. At the very least, the nationalist activists of yesteryear have begun to give way to a newer, more globally minded generation of Canadian poets increasingly dissatisfied with defeatist verse about a defeatist colony. Evan Jones has been a particularly brave champion; he edited Hine's recent books, and included the poet in *Modern Canadian Poets*, which finds no room for Atwood or Purdy—a first for such an anthology. (Will these survivors of the *Survival* era, minor poets each, be voted off *other* desert islands in the future? Will Canadians see the courage in Jones's evictions?) When asked if it's even correct to think of his work as Canadian, Hine was diplomatic: 'Not really; I've never been self-consciously Canadian, as a writer at least. By default, perhaps.' Even if poets like Hine make our desert island lists merely by default, we should embrace our tired, our poor, our huddled masters.

The World's Not-So-Secret Admirer

Several springs ago, *This Is Not a Reading Series*—the humane Toronto reading series in which writers are encouraged to do anything but actually read their own work—hosted a discussion on poetry and the environment. Towards the end of the evening, the moderator read a poem to a panel of poets from Gaspereau Press. It wasn't his, and it went like this:

> The stately ripple of the garter snake
> In sinuous procession through the grass
> Compelled my eye. It stopped and held its head
> High above the lawn, and the delicate curve
> Of its slender body formed a letter S—
> For 'serpent,' I assume, as though
> Diminutive majesty obliged embodiment.
>
> The garter snake reminded me of those
> Cartouches where the figure of a snake
> Seems to suggest the presence of a god
> Until, more flickering than any god,
> The small snake gathered glidingly and slid,
> But with such cadence to its rapt advance
> That when it stopped once more to raise its head,
> It was stiller than the stillest mineral
> And when it moved again, it moved the way
> A curl of water slips along a stone
> Or like the ardent progress of a tear
> Till, deeper still, it gave the rubbled grass
> And the dull hollows where its ripple ran
> Lithe scintillas of exuberance,
> Moving the way a chance felicity
> Silvers the whole attention of the mind.

The moderator asked the panel of poets if the poem—'Garter Snake', by Eric Ormsby—could be considered an 'environmental poem'. It was a neat move, an attempt to right a discussion (that had been veering more and more into trendy politics) by reminding the panel that a poem's prime responsibility is to be excellent. At least, I thought it was a neat move. I didn't anticipate George Elliott Clarke's swift showman's quip a well-timed beat later. '"Garter Snake",' he said, 'is about the poet's penis.'

Give credit where it's due: Clarke's crack was funny. It drew its laugh from the audience, myself included. But there was a slightly knowing, even self-righteous note to the laughter. The audience laughed because it knew (as Clarke, a competent comedian, gambled it would) that Ormsby had committed a laughable *faux pas*, at least for a male poet: he had written a sincere, reverential poem about a phallic-shaped reptile, minding its own business in nature. Apparently no one had told Ormsby that it's no longer acceptable for a male poet to exercise his 'othering gaze', his 'patriarchal power', his 'colonizer's language'—there's an M.A.'s worth of clichés to choose from here—on a poor, defenceless garter snake.

We've reached an odd moment when a poem as exquisite as 'Garter Snake' can be so crassly, but craftily, dismissed. It's into this moment that Biblioasis has delivered the delicately dust-jacketed *Time's Covenant: Selected Poems*, which compiles Ormsby's first five collections, plus the usual uncollected rarities, and a new sequence, 'Time's Covenant', for the completists. (I like to pretend Ormsby has a rabid cult following; he certainly deserves one.)

But before turning to the first poem in *Time's Covenant*, newcomers should check the date of Ormsby's first collection, *Bavarian Shrine and other poems* (1990), against his date of birth (1941). Ormsby has taken his time as a poet; he has had a busy career as a noted Islamic studies scholar and contributor of expert opinion to periodicals. At a time when poets publish early and often (with what David Solway gauges to be 'CV-driven velocity'), Ormsby moves at the kind of unhurried, understated, underwater pace that would have suited Elizabeth Bishop—or one of the sea creatures an Ormsby poem frequently nets with well-knit lines.

I write 'nets' because Ormsby is not an environmentally friendly poet. That is, his poems don't scrutinize the relationship between interloper-human and interlopee-nature. In the typical Ormsby poem, the players and props enjoy fairly fixed positions: the speaker (usually an 'I') looks, while some object (usually an animal, or bit of bric-a-brac, or hunk of Florida real estate) gets good and looked at. Ormsby, clearly, is one of our most voyeuristic poets. And in our more moralistic moments, we might be troubled by the way the speaker in an Ormsby poem blames his gaze on his chosen object, as if the object was just asking to be objectified. Indeed, like good feminists, we might not agree with the Ormsby speaker who claims that 'mannequins/Sport ... alluring alcoves of thigh' and conch-shells 'draw/The eye, and then the fingertips, inside'. We might even (reasonably) balk at the recurring adjective 'virginal', or one speaker's insistence that an old woman's 'Old/Velvets insisted on being felt'. With a bit of theory under our belts, it would take little effort to diagram the way an Ormsby speaker first appropriates and then composts nature into convenient truths. For example, in 'Grackle', an oblivious grackle does its thing, but the speaker thinks the grackle's 'repertoire seems meant to flatter/Us by mimicry and so exonerate/Our grosser faults ...'. Elsewhere, a similarly oblivious scorpion 'made [the speaker] dream of voyages', while yet another poem asks, 'Is gazing a favour that gazed waves bestow?' And then there's that garter snake, which, Clarke suggests, exists to celebrate the size of something else. Again and again, the natural world seems to provide Ormsby with an opportunity to celebrate his own capacity for seeing and, by extension, his self. If properly primed by an angry professor, some of us might feel inclined to heave that cinder block of a word, 'humanist', at the poet. (Not too long ago the cinder block would have been 'bourgeois'.)

But to flail Ormsby to the row-in-unison beat of the latest, already out-of-date theory is not only to ignore an inconvenient truth (good writing is good voyeurism), but to ignore the fact that Ormsby *is* an activist—an activist for what he calls 'all negligible things'. The speaker in an Ormsby poem can usually be found peering into cracks, crevices, corners and alcoves, or loafing about abandoned foundries, neglected gardens, and the less touristy stretches of the beach. While the poetry of an Adrienne Rich often campaigns for the sort of marginalized groups that have mandates, Ormsby's poetry sets up camp on actual, physical margins—the edges and baseboards to which skin flakes of all colours are eventually swept. Like the mullein weed, his poetry 'domesticates/Small desolations and … pinches place/From peripheries where places cannot be …'. He then populates these 'peripheries' with 'negligible things' like combs, pebbles, nails pried '[o]ut of a powdery corner', and just about anything that can stick to the sole of a shoe. (Had Ormsby been the hapless motorist stranded between highways in J.G. Ballard's cult novel, *Concrete Island*, I suspect he would have been perfectly happy amid the debris.)

He collects animals, too, but he's poetry's most liberal zookeeper since Marianne Moore. Like Moore, he's not after big game; his poetry consistently sides with the underdogs and squatters who occupy all of those aforementioned cracks, crevices, corners and alcoves: garter snakes, moths, spiders—critters few hunters would want to bag and stuff. Ormsby, then, is no hunter; he's a pack rat, and his body of work is a richly musty flea market of poetic curios and near-obsolete words, lovingly collected. 'The refrain in his poems is not "I am",' observes Amanda Jernigan, 'but "I like". He is a verbal spendthrift, a connoisseur of the actual, the mortal world's not-so-secret admirer.'

Some of us might prefer a more explicitly outraged poem that exposes, say, the squalid environmental conditions in a sweatshop. Ormsby prefers to consider how perfume bottles 'showed their clumsy seams/—mere factory casts!—running up their backs/Like a wind-stunned thread of tears'. Such stunning lines posit a principal reason for reading Ormsby: to be privy to extraordinarily precise (but original) feats of verbal description. If Auden was right and poetry is basically just 'memorable speech', then Ormsby has given us much to remember. As a 'verbal spendthrift', he may sometimes send us to the dictionary, but the trip is usually worth it. Like the cellar in his poem of the same name, Ormsby 'gives/Reluctant nobility to … disowned things' in language that deserves to be memorized:

We saw the lightning lace the school's façade
With instantaneous traceries and hairline fires,
Like a road map glimpsed by flashlight in a car.
                              —from 'Rain in Childhood'

The conch is the trumpet of solemn festivals
And its pinnacle—auger-threaded,
Spire-sleek, piquant as lance-
Tip or the brass casque of a khan—
Scalpels the roughened currents asunder.
But the russet life that hides inside,
Whose flesh tastes good in broths,
Flinches from the light.
                              —from 'Conch-Shell'

I thought of the kingdoms it had crept
Through under the ground, spud-
Smug, amid the dust of the bones of shahs
And eunuchs, those generations of the Flood,
The Colossi and the Accursed,
The Great Hunger and the hegiras,
Telemons and ostraca and, worst,
Immense anti-archives of dirt.
                              —from 'Episode with a Potato'

The rails that stretch away in parallel
Abraded brightnesses dismay, like those problems
In your old mathematics book at school ...
                              —from 'Railway Stanzas'

But here, before the open waves, where beach
umbrellas bloomed in tulip rows ...
                              —from 'My First Beach'

'[T]hese are just a few of the things I can't bear not to quote,' Randall Jarrell once wrote, in an essay on Moore's poetry. 'I haven't yet come to the things I want to quote—I may never get to them.' The same can be said of Ormsby's oeuvre, where brilliant image follows brilliant image with such frequency the reader is left blinking. At their worst, Ormsby's poems can seem like mere catalogues of description, with little in the way of narrative or argument to tie the riches together. Even Ormsby's fine book, *Araby*—devoted to the misadventures of Jaham and his sidekick Bald Adham—works less as a coherent, book-length narrative than as a collection of individually excellent lyric poems that just happen to star the same cast.

At their best, however, Ormsby's poems form a body of work that doubles as a primer on poetic perception. There's little in the way of typographical hijinks; the poems align themselves responsibly with a left margin that, in turn, confers on the first word of each line the dignity of a capital letter. And their matter-of-fact titles like 'Nose', 'Grackle', and 'Rooster' are only apparently banal. Such titles seem to constitute a self-imposed challenge, forcing Ormsby, time after time, to rise above banality and deliver the best poem we'll ever read about a nose, a grackle, a rooster. Elizabeth Bishop was great at this game. Nevermind that her mentor, Moore, wrote a fine poem called 'The Fish'; Bishop's 'The Fish' has the last word just as Ormsby's poem, 'Rooster', has the nerve to take a shot at supplanting Bishop's own 'Roosters'. Certainly no poet, not even Bishop, has better recorded the rooster's 'dark, corroded croak/Like a grudging nail tugged out of stubborn wood …'.

Ormsby, then, may just be another poet's poet, but that's no label to sniff at. Although not much recognised in her lifetime, Bishop—famously described as a 'poet's poet's poet'—has since eclipsed many of her contemporaries. And though we may laugh at the easy joke of one of Ormsby's less-accomplished peers, it's worth noting that 'Garter Snake' originally appeared in *The New Yorker*. Ormsby's poems, in other words, have reached beyond the boundaries that have consigned so much verbally humdrum Canadian poetry to its narrow but deserved place, next to the vacuum cleaner. Poems like 'Garter Snake', 'Grackle', 'Rooster', 'Song for an Ironing Board', 'The Song of the Whisk', 'Childhood House', and a growing handful of others, are built to last—just in case we stop laughing long enough to recognize them for what they are: classics, daring us to supplant them with our own.

New-Fangled, Old-Fangled

The poems of George Johnston and Jeramy Dodds are so apparently dissimilar one could print the poets' names at the top of the foolscap to delineate duelling, impermeable columns. Johnston, who passed away in 2004, wrote poems about children at play, domestic goings-on, and marriage announcements; Dodds, who is still young, has poems about a pin-up, a theremin quartet, a tractor beam, and other exotica. Johnston's poems often scan, defer to a rhyme scheme; Dodds's favour free verse, dense paragraphs of the stuff. Johnston's poems are restrained, which means they work their magic quietly, like magicians in straitjackets; Dodds's are pyrotechnic, which means they make great displays of lions, rabbits, and other props plucked from hats, from out of nowhere. In Johnston's poems, the pronoun 'I' is relatively transparent, a clear phone booth in which a coherent someone seems to be standing; in Dodds's poems, the pronoun seems both transparent *and* empty, the sort of sci-fi booth into which anyone could be beamed.

Caroming from column to column is fun work for a time, until, that is, one makes the mistake of taking a tally and drawing a conclusion—and you can imagine (maybe already *have* imagined) the conclusion: Johnston's poems are old-fashioned, rickety; Dodds's poems are new-fangled, radical. But as Robyn Sarah has it, in her brief preface to *The Essential George Johnston*, Johnston is 'a radical poet—radical in the truest sense of one who made the language new by going to its roots'. So even though Johnston would seem to present a placid lyric poetry about domestic goings-on, the poetry is more 'daring', Sarah proposes, than what she calls 'the linguistic antics of the avant-gardists'—and there *is* plenty of proof to pull and quote. In an example of Sarah's, Johnston can rearrange a sentence's words to bracing effect, giving the reader a deep hit of pre-storm air:

Airs through windows yet
and through the downstairs let
that over pastures come
thunder from.
                    —from 'Firefly Evening'

He can also strip away the commas and sound as breathlessly
ecstatic as an e. e. cummings:

I do not like anything the way I
like you in your underwear I like you
and in your party clothes o my in your
party clothes and with nothing on at all
you do not need to wear a thing at all
for me to like you ...
                    —from 'Us Together'

He can also strand a pronoun on a stanza's periphery, painting a picture of a marginal life with little more than type itself:

His eyes are warm with love and death,
Time makes a measure of his breath;
The world is now profound and he
Fearful, on its periphery.
                    —from 'The Pool'

And he can sample colloquial talk, and loop dull words like 'did',
and splice the spools together smoothly:

Them hunters, it aint safe. Bang
bang bang go end of summer flies
in the lampshades, bang around the room
dying lazy. Eva dies at last.
...
End of summer chime
in the aftergrass, did did, did did,
almost done. Overhead

looms the redtail
for the little ones …

—from 'Onset'

But when Johnston writes in more traditional forms—which is much
of the time, at least in his early work—the results can be just as
unsettling as his later, more formally mischievous achievements.
Here are four quatrains called 'War on the Periphery':

Around the battlements go by
Soldier men against the sky,
Violent lovers, husbands, sons,
Guarding my peaceful life with guns.

My pleasures, how discreet they are!
A little booze, a little car,
Two little children and a wife
Living a small suburban life.

My little children eat my heart;
At seven o'clock we kiss and part,
At seven o'clock we meet again;
They eat my heart and grow to men.

I watch their tenderness with fear
While on the battlements I hear
The violent, obedient ones
Guarding my family with guns.

'War on the Periphery' is neither pro- nor anti-war, and the tension
between the sing-song form and the grim, matter-of-fact subject matter stays nice and taut to the very end, like a hangman's rope. Johnston's speaker lives, as many Westerners do, in a peaceful enough
place, insulated by walls, their soldiers, 'a little booze'. But it's a hard-
won haven and maybe not even that. 'They eat my heart and grow to
men,' the patriarch says of his hungry children (barely concealed
cannibals) with whom he's walled in. 'War on the Periphery' was

published in *The New Yorker* in 1951 and thought pretty riveting by its
first readers; today, one can imagine the poem's study of a world in
which wars cannot be separated out from the suburbs they purport to
protect—a world in which rough men are said to stand ready to do
violence on behalf of the drowsy—being cited by the devotees of a
Dick Cheney as much as those of a George Orwell. But the study of a
world in which even 'ordinary' relationships between parent and off-
spring are exercises of power would resonate with readers who are up
on their Foucault, too.

Many of the poems in *The Essential George Johnston* are similarly ambiguous and ever so slightly unsettled. Sarah is a dab hand;
she has avoided Johnston's longer verse and his translations. Only a
couple of poems starring his troupe of everymen—homier takes on
T.S. Eliot's Prufrock and Weldon Kees's Robinson, which appeared
in Johnston's early collections—have been included. What's left are
some forty-eight pages of the poet's better poems: the slightly darker,
richer stuff. Not that Johnston's body of work was in dire need of
pruning. Johnston took poetry seriously enough not to publish very
much of it, and put out a collection something like every six years.
Plus, each instalment in the Porcupine Quill's Essential Poets series
tops out at a humane forty-eight pages or so, which one can not only
get through but imagine rereading. Sarah's sharp editing simply
brings a series of unsentimental set pieces into vivid relief: a suicide's
hat makes its way out to sea; a cat toys with a baby bird; a man, con-
sidering straw smoke, imagines his cremation.

Perhaps, then, Johnston is less a 'radical poet' and more the
author of a clutch of poems that come to no easy conclusions and in a
wide enough range of forms that we can save the fellow the indignity
of classifying him. And anyway, the adjective 'radical', when applied
to the noun 'poet', is redundant. Any person worth calling a poet
(and there are far fewer of these than we might prefer) writes poetry
because more basic modes of communication (like the emoticon-
caulked prose of texting, say) just won't do—because basic communication isn't the point. 'All poetry is experimental poetry,' wrote
Stevens. In other words, all poets are always already 'radical' or
'experimental' or 'innovative'. This isn't to suggest that good poets
haven't occasionally huddled around some hub, mimeographed or

emailed out a manifesto, and declared themselves an avant-garde; this is only to suggest that *all* poets are mavericks, whether they, or their circle, choose to brand themselves as such or not. Johnston, for his part, didn't much think of himself as a poet, let alone a maverick. His seems to have been a vintage strain of modesty, which, if it resisted the title 'poet', did so out of a healthy respect for the title. Johnston had other interests, too, from bell-ringing to beekeeping, and other titles, as esteemed translator of the Icelandic sagas and beloved teacher (though he avoided, what he called with almost Poundian comedy, 'creyative workshops').

Nevertheless, one of the presses apparently preferred by those who self-brand or are branded as 'mavericks' is Toronto's Coach House Books, which, its website boasts, 'has been publishing and printing high-quality *innovative* fiction and poetry since 1965' (italics mine, but just barely). To fancy one's maverickness too much is to risk seeming as dated as Dada or as self-mythologizing as Sarah Palin. But there's nothing dated or self-mythologizing about Dodds's debut collection, *Crabwise to the Hounds*, which has got to be the best book of poems its publisher has typeset in years, though not because Dodds is some 'radical poet' but rather because he is, like Johnston, simply (though not *merely*) a poet. (If anything, he seems to have an interest, as Johnston most definitely did, in tracing roots; Dodds has been translating the *Poetic Edda*, that cache of poems in Old Norse.)

Still, some will want to claim Dodds for the revolution, and not necessarily those professional avant-gardists looking to fill their ranks. A recent review of *Crabwise to the Hounds*, by an otherwise sensible reviewer, insists, 'if this book can be characterized it must be considered part of the avant-garde.' But must it? And which avant-garde? (There seem to be so many of the things, tramping bravely forward.) Perhaps the assertion ought to be: if this book *must* be characterized it *can* be considered part of *an* avant-garde. And yet Dodds, for his part, doesn't appear to have imposed upon his poems the duty of prodding the reader out of passivity, by scrambling the order of words for the sheer sake of scrambling it; nor does he wheelbarrow in and dump at the reader's feet all of the clauses it was *his* responsibility to organize. Boring as this may sound, a genuine jolt requires careful planning, and in the first two lines of the book's first piece—a ruthlessly scant six words—Dodds's planning pays off:

A bed
  robbed of its river.

With those first two words, 'A bed', Dodds sets up the reader, gets her picturing something to sleep on. With the next four, 'robbed of its river', Dodds startles the reader, pulls the bed out from under her. Also, by robbing a familiar word, 'riverbed', of its river, Dodds enables the reader to see the metaphor anew—to recognize, for the first time, that the word 'riverbed' *is* a metaphor, that a river is like any other body stretched out on bedding, that its tossing and turning is not unlike a dreamer's. And 'robbed' is a smart choice (perhaps the only choice) not just because it alliterates with 'river' but because it conceals that stolen 'bed'.

A poem—whether fixed or free, lyric or language, traditional or experimental, name the deadlock—assures the reader that there's a sound reason for most, if not all, of its words. Even if it has been channelled via meditation or hallucinogens or randomizing computer program, the poem will somehow account for the quality of the meditation or give some assurance that the hallucinogens have been well spent or the lines of code well programmed. Assurance is not reassurance, and Dodds, like Johnston, doesn't comfort (a verb that's far too maligned anyway). His talent is for using a minimum of well-chosen words to plant expectations which can then be teased, toyed with:

            You can't shoot
  your mouth off if you're out of earshot.
  Let bylaws be bygones, don't mind
  your own business into the ground,
  all that glitters is not cold to the touch.
  You're only human once. If you've taken
  the American way down a one-way street,
  you've got to wipe your nose with the heart
  on your sleeve.
                    —from 'The Epileptic Acupuncturist'

This is stimulating matter, and always one step ahead of the paying customer: constantly estranging but never, finally, frustrating or alienating. Dodds is too much the *courteous* showman (to nick an adjective from Adam Kirsch), and the reader, though much entertained, is no less critical for enjoying herself. 'I'm not a huge fan of the non sequitur style of some surrealism,' Dodds says, in a recent interview. 'I do want to make leaps, but I'd like the stunts to be well-planned, the landings as smooth as I can get them. More like a short-sighted and washed-up Evel Knieval [sic] than a Dadaist monk shot from a rabbit.'

Dodds is having a moment in Canada. One news site recently named him one of the top ten best poets in the country. He's not, but he's a good poet, and *Crabwise to the Hounds* deserves a good fraction of the attention it has gotten even if one senses that it's too much a young man's book, that some of its pieces seem to do little more than stockpile startling images, that some of its pieces seem to end where they end because the poet ran out of startling images to stockpile. Still, 'short-sighted' as this young man's well-planned stunts may be, how many of us can manage even one image as startling as any of these:

> You'll hand-shade
> your eyes as you pilot your lighter-than-air
> craft, making pylons of the factory stacks.
> Balletic birds will crumple the quiet
> with a conniption of trills over your lofting
> bladder of boiled draft. By the seashore,
> you'll see an octopus catcher plug his trident
> into the beach as an abandoned bathysphere
> pitches and bobs like last night's last pub dancer.
> Downwind, two lovers will breathe in the cave
> of a capsized dory, beneath the squall that will soon
> toss your hand-blown bulb and basket off course,
> touching it down on a crop-circled bull's eye,
> a hork's distance from the rehearsal hall.

> —from 'Modulated Timbre and Cadence for Baby Grand'

'New-fangled, old-fangled,/in, either way,' wrote George Johnston in a poem for another poet. Johnston, it's safe to say, has never
really been 'in'. Dodds, however, is very much 'in', though this
shouldn't be counted against him. (If anything it ought to worry
him; as television's Abraham Simpson half-laments, half-warns, 'I
used to be with it. Then they changed what "it" was.') Johnston and
Dodds are both new-fangled and old-fangled, which is only to say:
each is a good poet, which *itself* is a redundancy and only to say:
each is a poet, carrying out his respective offices, and needs no more
boosterism than that.

Flaking Off Beautifully

Twelve years ago, a woman visited my writing class and delivered a talk, something to do with sleep and Odysseus. I can't remember much of what the woman said; to my undergraduate ears, she sounded like a muted trombone murmuring away: an adult out of *Peanuts*. Folk legend has it that Canadian poet Irving Layton once hollered at Margaret Atwood, 'Your reading is so boring it's putting me to sleep!' But I have no good excuse for not recalling more about the giant of literature who visited herself on my class and must've seemed pleasant enough. (I certainly can't blame Hypnos, Greek God of Shut-Eye.) In the manner of the historian at a loss for words: so much for the day I didn't quite hear Anne Carson speak.

But inside of a year or two (a tipping point of a moment) we were, all of us, from the widest-eyed to the sleepiest, buying up and talking about the books of this Carson woman, a Canadian-born poet and classicist. The turn of events was a source of bemusement for the professor of mine who'd organized the talk. He'd been reading Carson when no one in Canada seemed to care about her. Canada came around, but not before Carson, like many of its native-born stars, had looked south, to the United States, for a firmament to light up.

If Carson's pairings of such disparate figures as Augustine and Hopper or Keats and Duchamp now seem familiar, it's a function of the extent to which the reading public embraced an idiosyncratic taste that couldn't have been invented in a boardroom. Consumers, for the mysterious reasons that keep A&R men up at night, simply *liked* Carson's commingling of the archaic and the contemporary. They liked the idea of a poem in which Virginia Woolf interviews Thucydides on the set of a production called *The Peloponnesian War*. They liked the idea of a gay red monster who falls in love and aspires to be a photographer. Carson came to embody a set of incongruous nouns that—a certain cross-section was surprised to discover—

weren't incongruous at all: Greek mythology, McLuhan-era media, volcanoes, post-structuralism, the mysteries of desire, Canada.

Taking stock, I'm surprised to discover that I own as many books by Carson as I do. For awhile there, they appeared at a goodly clip, every two years or so, drawing prizes and praise, beginning in 1992, when Carson herself was 42. With regular folk willing to fork over for her poetry, retailers stocked up, erring on the side of impractical quantities. But if, like me, you prefer your bookstore maintain as many different poets as it can on the one shelf it grudgingly loans them, then you might've felt, as I did, vaguely scandalized at the sight of remaindered hardbacks of *Men in the Off Hours*. This wasn't Carson's fault; this wasn't necessarily a judgment on the worth of her work. (If anything, it presented a moral about the limits of speculation and a symptom of a market hopped up on hype.) Still, it's hard not to suspect that a relatively modest unit-shifter like Carson's *Autobiography of Red*—or Allen Ginsberg's *Howl and Other Poems* or Christian Bök's *Eunoia*—is less read than recycled: purchased for its apparent novelty, inspected for a time, and finally released into the wilds of the used bookstore, the graveyard of undergraduate enthusiasms. My earlier, indifferent self might've had the correct response to the Carson phenomenon. Ignorance of trends can be liberating.

And yet I wouldn't like to part with Carson's *Glass, Irony and God*, mostly because of 'The Glass Essay', an early long poem which the poet hasn't bettered. Like the narrator of Carson's later book, *The Beauty of the Husband*, the speaker of 'The Glass Essay' has demonstrably bad taste in the beloved. She's reeling from a break-up and recovering at her mother's, which is situated 'on a moor in the north'. The mother strikes us as an opinionated type, given to remarking on the cut of bathing suits in the Sears Summer Catalogue. She thinks the speaker ought to toughen up, not dwell in the past; the speaker, for her part, thinks about the Brontës, navigates the moor, drops in on a father with dementia. The poem exhibits many of the tics that have come to characterize Carson's work:

- the blending of seemingly discrete genres like the essay, the poem;
- scholarly interjections on art, literature, history, philosophy;

- a wormhole that warps time and space, enabling the spirit of earlier figures, like the Brontës, to shade the present; and
- a presiding intertext or two.

At times, it can seem as if Carson does little more than pour sentences into a mould of long and short lines, allowing the sentences to assume the edges and contours of the sort of flinty, serrated thing we usually call, on sight, poetry:

> My father lives in a hospital for patients who need chronic care
> about 50 miles from here.
> He suffers from a kind of dementia
>
> characterized by two sorts of pathological change
> first recorded in 1907 by Alois Alzheimer.
> First, the presence in cerebral tissue
>
> of a spherical formation known as neuritic plaque,
> consisting mainly of degenerating brain cells.
> Second, neurofibrillary snarlings
>
> in the cerebral cortex and in the hippocampus.
> There is no known cause or cure.

Big words from a fancy discipline like neuroscience look especially neat when slipped into lines of poetry, where one doesn't expect to find them. It's a trick as old as the great Brooklyn Dodgers fan Marianne Moore, who liked herself a poem with an esoteric lexicon and dollops of quotation; it's a trick that leads the late critic Guy Davenport to defend, in Carson, the natural innocent who seems 'unpoetic'. (In general, it's sound practice to stick the stuff you want to disparage with the pejorative 'poetic' and the stuff you want to promote with the counterintuitive superlative 'unpoetic'.)

But when Carson, to borrow a line from Frost, is content to be new in the old-fashioned way—when she works at her similes, when she arranges for some alliteration—she's far more compelling than the poet who transcribes an exchange between Woolf and

Thucydides, or compiles a list of scatological synonyms for the anus, or stretches a line to the right margin, only to let it go, like a waist-band mischievously snapped. Indeed, there may be no more shocking effect in all of Carson than the moment in 'The Glass Essay' when the speaker—in lucid, linear language—revisits some bad sex:

> When nude
> I turned my back because he likes the back.
> He moved onto me.
>
> Everything I know about love and its necessities
> I learned in that one moment
> when I found myself
>
> thrusting my little burning red backside like a baboon
> at a man who no longer cherished me.
> There was no area of my mind
>
> not appalled by this action, no part of my body
> that could have done otherwise.

'[N]ude' and 'moved', like our lovers, don't quite rhyme. The repetition of 'back' mechanizes the speaker, reducing her to rote movements and reasoning. The 'b's lend a lightness, even buoyancy, which is duly popped by brute thrust of simile: that 'burning red backside' is *all* of our burning red backsides after the fall, tarred with the one blush; that 'baboon', cartoon of a word, bulges toward us in funhouse proportions.

Carson has a cinematographer's eye for the image that sticks and disturbs. 'My face in the bathroom mirror/has white streaks down it', the speaker of 'The Glass Essay' tells us at the outset. 'I rinse the face and return to bed.' Carson's use of the definite article—'*the* face'—severs a self from its image. (It's the stuff, that free-floating visage, of mirror stages, horror movies.) Later, same poem, a 'videotape jerks to a halt/like a glass slide under a drop of blood', an incredibly specific sort of analogue motion, recorded with the precision of an unblinking aperture. 'What are the imperatives,' the speaker goes on to wonder, 'that hold people like Catherine and Heathcliff/together and apart, like pores blown into hot rock/and then stranded out of reach//of one another when it hardens?' Before the question's up, Carson has all but answered it, demonstrating by way of terrific simile a thermodynamic law of doomed romance: smouldering things tend to cool. (Later, in *Autobiography of Red*, Carson demonstrates another law, this one of adolescent attraction: 'They were two superior eels/at the bottom of the tank and they recognized each other like italics.')

I have kept up with Carson because, once upon a time, she wrote poetry like 'The Glass Essay', in which the bad is tolerable and the good unforgettable. But if Carson is something of a Vesuvius, from which much of worth has bubbled up, the pockets of poetry—those aforementioned 'pores blown into hot rock/and then stranded out of reach'—have grown fewer and farther between. In her last collection, *Decreation*, the poetry appears to have been dashed off with the relaxed hand of an artist whose least effort is sure to be overvalued by the critical consensus, if not the marketplace:

> First line has to make your brain race that's how Homer does it,
> that's how Frank O'Hara does it, why
> at such a pace
> Muses
> slam through the house—there goes one (fainting) up the rungs
> of your strange BULLFIGHT, buttered
> almost in a nearness
> to skyblue
> Thy pang—Pollock yourself!
> Just to hang on to life is why....

If this thing, which Carson has seen fit to label 'Gnosticism III', wasn't generated in a fit of free association, it still gives the impression of a brain making poor choices rapidly. The caps lock key has been depressed for no apparent reason beyond, perhaps, the pleasure of depression; 'buttered', a bizarre adjective, looks like it has been prompted less by necessity than neighbouring syllable 'BULL'; 'almost in a nearness' is awkward; two fine words have been coerced into cliché ('skyblue'); an archaism has been reactivated ('Thy'); a new verb tried out ('Pollock'); a final period eschewed. The late Davenport might've admired 'Gnosticism III'. 'As with Matthew Arnold,' Davenport wrote, in the preface to *Glass, Irony and God*,

> truth and observation are more important than lyric effect or coloring. If a good line happens, it happens. Anne Carson's poems are like notes made in their pristine urgency, as fresh and bright as a series of sudden remarks. But they are the remarks of a speaker who remains silent until there's something to be said, something that has been processed in the heart and brooded over in the imagination and is not to be further processed in rhyme or meter.

Davenport couldn't have known that Carson, poised for near-universal acclaim, would have little need for his pre-emptive defence. He surely couldn't have known that this apparently 'silent' speaker, poised to publish a lot, would not be so frugal with her voice. But he overrates the inherent value of 'sudden remarks', which has been driven down in the age of texting. And he seems to cop to (by not being bothered by) the duller stretches in Carson: 'If a good line happens, it happens.' But seemingly unprocessed poetry like 'Gnosticism III', and some of the earlier work which Davenport esteems 'fresh and bright', merely record, as so much of our poetry has done for decades, a smart mind warming up. Carson's, I think, is so much better bearing *down*—on some moment of domestic terror (a woman rinsing a face) with all the hoary poetic devices at its disposal, a book of ancient thought at hand, a TV flickering in the background.

* * *

Nox, Carson's latest, is a reproduction of a scrapbook the poet made after her brother, an elusive type, died in 2000. More precisely, it takes the form of one very long sheet of paper, folded many times over, like an accordion. The accordion comes in a beautiful box that opens like a book—a 'fuck you' in the face of the Kindle and other such devices meant to streamline life? It's probably easiest to place the open box on a desktop and, as each pleated 'page' is read, shift it from one side of the box to the other. (You can try reading *Nox* like a paperback, but you need to maintain a firm grip on the thing or it's apt to spring away.) Some will insist that *Nox* challenges the way we read texts by calling attention to the sheer stuff of texts. Such is the nature of the pleated, interconnected pages that you can't turn one down without bringing up the next: each new page presents itself tautly—dog-eared in the literal sense. In other words, you can't just turn a page and be done with it; you have to wrestle with *Nox*, the way you would grief. It's an object of mourning, an elegy made material. But it also belongs to a class of cumbersome novelties that includes the jack-in-the-box, the string of paper-dolls-holding-hands, and the McDLT. (Some other critic already took 'Slinky'.) Describing *Nox* will busy colloquia for years to come.

The text itself alternates between definitions of a particular word (proposed by an elegy of Catallus's, which kicks off *Nox*) and facing fragments (of poetry, photos, letters, art). Sometimes, word has something to do with fragment, as when Carson provides a list of entries for 'mutam' ('saying nothing, silent', etc.) and, on the other side of the pleat, points out that the brother 'had nothing to say' after the death of their mother. But the connection between a given set of definitions and the facing fragment isn't always readily apparent. The reader, then, is pressed into service, poring over the ruins of the brother's life. In fact, early on in *Nox*, Carson refers us to Herodotos, the first historian. (No Carson production is truly complete without its classical intertexts.) She describes the historian as a figure with 'authorial power'—a valid point in borrowed language, as musty as that Foucault reader you once brought to the book exchange. The historian, it's now generally accepted, presents a conspicuous fellow, a closet novelist in the business of disfiguring the past by imposing a shape on it: a beginning, middle, and end. He ought to learn to make do with scraps, as does the protagonist's mother in *Autobiography of Red*, scrutinizing photographs of shoes and socks; as does the reader of *Nox*, squinting at the brother's leavings. 'A brother never ends,' Carson notes. 'I prowl him. He does not end.'

But *Nox*'s scraps are predictably scrappy: 'scrappy' in the sense of stuff one presses between the leaves of a high-end scrapbook, and 'scrappy' in the sense of the underdog artifact: weather-beaten, but gorgeously so. The art is primitive, precocious—the sort of child's play that's made poignant by a sneaking feeling that the inner child who did the fingerpainting is done for. The photographs depict the denizens of a simpler time (a young Carson, her mother, the brother) who occupy the centre of the shots, facing up to the lens, to posterity, without irony or hedonism. (What will scrapbookers of the future do now that photographs, the indestructible evidence of spring breaks gone wild, are digital fodder for Facebook and no longer condemned to decay to a pleasing sepia tint?)

In short, the scraps move us, but in the easy way of the object of spoilt innocence: the brittle sprig you forgot you preserved in a book; the bedraggled baby's shoe you stumble upon in a storm drain. It's pretty hard not to feel for Carson's brother or, at least, the kid in swim trunks on the cover of *Nox*, who faces the reader of the future in charmingly oversized goggles; the reader learns, after all, that this same kid (with so much of the soon-to-be-wasted potential implied by such photographs) will grow up and have a run-in with the law; will have to skip town (and Carson's life) to avoid jail time.

If *Nox* is a sincere expression of grief, it's also a commodity, serving up a particular satisfaction: the sense that we can't entirely explain a messy, decaying past, but we can, at least, contain its more photogenic elements in a beautiful box; the sense that we can have our ruins and gentrify them, too. Many of *Nox*'s scraps appear to be pasted or stapled in—until, that is, one runs a palm across the smooth, rich stock on which *Nox* is printed. A charcoal rubbing appears to have dirtied its facing page—but, of course, the charcoal is smoke and mirrors. (Your fingertips, which your inner fetishist will want to rinse before handling *Nox*, have nothing to worry about.) Carson's reproduction is not unlike the Victorian furniture that's mass-produced and carefully distressed for yuppies of the twenty-first century, its white paint flaking off beautifully.

Nox continues a trend that started with *The Beauty of the Husband* and Carson's translations of Sappho, *If Not, Winter*: the use of blank space to confer an aura on scant traces of type. Carson devotes whole pages to faux-profundities like 'In small white sleep mits your hands protrude' (sic) and 'Repent means "the pain again"' and

'Places in the world where you and I saw things'. The fragment should suit Carson, a poet of moments. But *Nox*'s have none of the crispness of the epigrammatic or the concentration of the Imagistic—and they don't need to. Like driftwood, they are excused, if not ennobled, by the shipwreck in whose wake they float: the awful occasion of an actual person's death. How else explain Carson's use of clichés like 'it made my heart sink' and 'out of the blue'? The poet that Davenport defended for appearing 'unpoetic' is sounding more poetic than ever. 'I wanted to fill my elegy with light of all kinds,' she tells us. Later: 'I am curious about the season of coldness you have there.' Still later: 'There is no possibility I can think my way into his muteness.'

At its best, *Nox* records some curious detail of the past in Carson's cool deadpan:

> Now by far the strangest thing that humans do—
> [Herodotos] is firm on this—is history. This asking. For
> often it produces no clear or helpful account, in fact people
> are satisfied with the most bizarre forms of answering, e.g.
> the Skythians who, when Herodotos endeavours to find out
> from them the size of the Skythian population, point to a
> bowl that stands at Exampaios. It is made of the melted
> down arrowheads required of each Skythian by their king
> Ariantes on pain of death. Herodotos describes the bowl,
> what else can he do?

Carson, we're reminded, is one of our more entertaining scholars, given to the colloquial phrasing: 'So let's say in general Odysseus and sleep are not friends.' Like the filmmaker Quentin Tarantino, reliable connoisseur of the pulp fictions of the 1970s, Carson has an eye—set higher on the brow than Tarantino's—for the classical curio worth preserving. That talk she gave to my writing class, twelve years ago, can be found in *Decreation* and, it turns out, is a good read; my earlier, indifferent self doesn't know what it missed.

If I were an editor, looking to advance an idea of Carson-as-poet, I would preserve all of 'The Glass Essay'; some of her *Short Talks*; a few things from sequences like 'The Life of Towns' and 'TV Men'.

I would promote a couple of the shorter lyrics like 'Hokusai' and 'Father's Old Blue Cardigan'; a very few excerpts from *Autobiography of Red* and *The Beauty of the Husband* in a section called 'Fragments'; and, in its entirety, the late, lush success, 'Guillermo's Sigh Symphony'. I would append 'Appendix to Ordinary Time', an elegy for Carson's mother, which does more in two conventional pages than *Nox* does in its one really long page. I would preserve these selections between no-nonsense covers in, say, garish pink: something to ward off the consumer who would keep *Nox* on a coffee table and enjoy stealing glances of the thing. For a blurb, I would ignore much of what's been written about Carson in recent years and merely carry forward Davenport's early observation that 'Anne Carson's powers of invention are apparently infinite.' I think I would call the book *Volcanoes*, and I would urge the discerning reader to read this slim volume by a little-known talent who deserves more attention. Anne Carson, the Phenomenon, has had enough of the other kind of reader.

Autobiography of Reader

The first thing I notice, flipping through the new Anne Carson, is fancy lining: the Canadian poet and classicist has centre-justified the bulk of the text, leaving it to the word processor (not for the first time a collaborator) to work out the spacing—and leaving a strip of aerated text down the middle of most pages. Is this poetry? Prose? Like other recent Carson productions, *Red Doc>*, the sequel to 1998's verse novel, *Autobiography of Red*, is a feast for first glances.

But when I finally resolve to turn away from surface pleasures and reckon with the words, I encounter nothing less than the voice of, well, Anne Carson!—learned, deadpan, commaless, and frequently carried away by tangent. In other words, I encounter page after page of this sort of thing:

> Gathering   swim
> gear in the bathroom he
> glances at the mirror.
> Sharp stab his face no
> longer young no more
> beauty impact. Get used
> to this. Other ways to
> navigate the world. Did
> Daniil Kharms have this
> particular rug pulled out
> from under him one day in
> a bathroom in Leningrad it
> seems unholy to ask....

A consistent, distinctive voice isn't usually a problem. (Most poets should be so lucky.) But I'm not very far into reading *Red Doc>* when I find myself wondering why a voice so unperturbed by its latest packaging—long and short lines, rival columns, the screenplay, the essay, opera—needed such packaging in the first place. It's hard to think of another, more restless poet, whose adventures in form and genre, from book to book, have left less of a mark on her sensibility. Is it that the medium isn't so much the message as the marketing strategy? Carson poems, I'm convinced, will soon come packaged in Cornell box—but they will sound like Carson.

I'm also not very far in when I find myself wondering what's going on. Already I'm leaning far too much on a rather slim crutch, near to buckling: the advance copy's blurb. It explains that Geryon, the red-winged monster from *Autobiography of Red*, has reached manhood and now goes by 'G' (we should be grateful; a savvier poet, sensing an opportunity, would've selected the Twitter handle '@Geryon'). The blurb also identifies some of the supporting characters and their professions (artist, war veteran). This is most helpful; pronouns in *Red Doc>* don't always have obvious owners, and dramatic dialogue doesn't always earn the backslashes the poet seems to feel are sufficient to parse the speakers. Indeed, doesn't this rapid-fire deadpanning between Ida (the artist) and Sad (the war veteran)—

        why'd   you
enlist/oh people thought
I'd be better off/off/I was
getting   into   mischief/
people

like   who/Dad/mischief
like   what/is   this   an
interview/I like to close all
the loops ...

—sound a lot like this rapid-fire, deadpanning between G and one Lieutenant M'hek—

      you're   the
team/

small   team/you're   the
guy   who   comes   every
evening with the drugs/
no   my   team   is
nonpsychotropic/so

what do you do/talk /
does that help him/one
test   for   this   question/
what test/did he   cap
himself yesterday ...

Are these the voices of four characters talking?—or is Carson merely in talks with herself?

Far scarier than keeping the characters straight: the blurb hints that *Red Doc>* is 'haunted by Proust'. Carson books typically have truck with an intertext or two, and I typically do okay. I know enough about *Wuthering Heights*, Keats, Duchamp, and the like to have gotten by in the past. But Proust? I empathize with G's mom who, early in *Red Doc>*, declares, 'well I'm not fond of those multi-volume things' and '[it] could be too late for me to appreciate Proust on the other hand I'm at a loss I've read all the Len Deightons in the library.' *Oh, moms and their middlebrows!* Carson's text seems to sigh. But I empathize with G's; this review is her autobiography, too.

* * *

I want to write something like, 'When last we left Geryon, he was lighting out for the territories'—but *Autobiography of Red* wasn't that kind of book, with characters you especially cared about and a hairpin plot to organize them. It was more a weave of loose ends: set pieces in which an arty teenager lives among humans who aren't terribly concerned he's a red monster out of myth. (To wit: his mother 'neaten[s] his little red wings' before sending 'him out the door.') In one kind of early Carson poem, the past exerts its pressures on the present; for instance, *Wuthering Heights* weighs on a forlorn woman. In another kind, the past breaks cleanly through; Hektor writes his wife from the set of a TV shoot. *Red* was the cartoony culmination of that other kind of poem. The original Geryon is slain for his herd by Herakles; Carson's mythic red monster goes to school, works a library's stacks, pines for Herakles (now more asshole than hero), inscribes postcards with 'bits of Heidegger', and produces an autobiography in 'the form/of a photographic essay'—begun, as such things are these days, at a young age (five!). Think highbrow *Hellboy*, and you're not far off; *Red* would've appealed to a readership aging out of an enthusiasm for Anne Rice or Neil Gaiman and into seminars on deconstruction, queer theory, and classical mythology. It even came equipped with an apparatus of playful scholarship— grad school made cool. But the cover's cursive ('A Novel in Verse') and strategic stain (suggesting the book had been steeped in Earl Grey) called out to old souls everywhere.

In a verse novel of moments, some of *Red*'s were masterfully engaging, but only to the extent that they made an original observation (a new simile, say) with precision: 'Passengers streamed/on board like insects into lighted boxes and the experiment roared off down the street.' Other, less visionary moments, however, were conspicuously opaque: 'The instant of nature / forming between them drained every drop from the walls of his life/leaving behind just ghosts/rustling like an old map.' Was that mixed drink of a metaphor, layered over four lines, the sort of thing Michael Ondaatje was drunk on when he announced, 'Anne Carson is, for me, the most exciting poet writing in English today?' Was Ondaatje, himself a master of overwriting, anointing a successor?

Carson is too successful to be condescended to; she doesn't need my help. But the autobiography of any reader will betray its weak spots, moments of humanity (or vanity) in which the reader wishes he could protect the author from, well, all her other readers! Some of these enablers—otherwise reasonable critics—defend Carson's unevenness. 'If a good line happens, it happens,' wrote Guy Davenport back in the 1990s. 'What you get is the over-all action of the mind rather than the high-shine lacquer of the apt image,' wrote Meghan O'Rourke in 2010. Carson as uncooked savant—that's one way of explaining away the *longeur* between her better lines. It also establishes two bars of commitment: a low one for the poet (who's an innocent anyway, a flake adrift on her breeziness, on autopilot) and a high one for the reader (who should be grateful merely for the work of interpreting the innocent's utterances). If *Red* didn't present Carson's best (that would be the *Wuthering Heights* poem), it did provide, as commercial successes will do, a version of Carson that's convenient to recall: uneven, but daringly—necessarily—so. It takes slightly more effort to imagine a poet who can capture the insects in lighted boxes, but who can't keep (or *won't* abide) an editor to corral her other, flightier impulses.

* * *

A particularly amiable group of misfits has gathered itself around G, now a mature herdsman of musk oxen. Carson has headhunted the quirkier elements of some quad: these include Sad (the afore-mentioned war veteran, who seems to have PTSD), Ida (the artist, who takes no shit), 4NO (some guy who thinks he's a god), and Io (an ox who will get high on a hallucinogen and take flight with G—monster's best friend). As in *Autobiography of Red*, the characters live from set piece to set piece. Nothing else—such as voices of their own—conspires to give them life. By *Red Doc>*'s midpoint, some of the misfits have made fast friends, observed oxen, and travelled to a glacier. The text takes occasional, scholarly sidebar to hash out the nature of polar exploration, the principles of flight, the role of oxen in military history. Near the glacier is another chilly place: a psychi-atric clinic where G's entourage holes up for a time and encounters authority figures like CMO, which would seem to be short for 'Chief Medical Officer'. This particular cartoon (Ida calls him 'Pig Doc') 'laughs horribly' and believes in, natch, 'Rationality.... A pre-scribed amount at a prescribed time. It's how you keep animals in line it works for people too....' When we first meet CMO, he is fix-ing a car. Will the menacing mechanic also try to fix the minds of G and co.?

For every gleamingly exact image in *Red Doc>*—

> Each [ox] head
> has two horns that part as
> neatly as a boy about to

> play the piano wets his
> hair and hopes it stays
> flat for the whole recital.

—there are many more vague, unrealized ones: 'A little zipper whine that runs along the convolutes of his ear licking in under every bone like a bad emotion'; 'Night's bones are still forming'; 'A bright smell streams into the car'; 'the entire cold sorrow acre of human history'. Of course, I'm over the moon for crescent-crisp similes like, 'The moonlit ironing boards grandstanding like steeds' (even if Eric Ormsby's poem 'Song for an Ironing Board', which predates *Red Doc>*, broke in the ironing board-as-horse conceit). And I'm all for economical solutions like, 'He sits up suddenly drenched in ringing. Phone.' But what do we make of a book that also finds room for the following: 'His heart sinks'; 'stop on a dime'; 'her nerves are already tingling'; 'right on the money'; 'come at her with murder in his black eyes'; 'who had the heart'; 'a smile that dazzles'; 'a stab of envy'; 'clean as a whistle'. Surely even a daringly uneven talent shouldn't be permitted as many clichés as Carson is?

* * *

Halfway through the book, I seem to be getting by without the background in Proust. I'm sure I'm missing resonances; but Carson has assumed I share enough of her knowledge to ask a rhetorical question, while also ensuring the reference, if it escapes me, is self-explanatory:

> What a scamp that Proust.
> That Albertine. Does
> anyone really believe the
> girl stays asleep for four
> pages in volume V while
> Marcel roams around her
> prostrate form and
> stretches out beside it on
> the bed....

Other kindred souls—that flapper-era reader of *The Waste Land*, say—didn't have it half as good. (Can you imagine Eliot deigning to clarify themes in the colloquial: 'What a mess this modern world. That fisher king. Does anyone really believe the scamp can make the thing rosy again?') Is this, then, part of Carson's appeal—that she allows amateurs a little bit of light contact with literature they might not otherwise read? Those of us who don't have our Proust have already been encouraged to identify with G's well-meaning mom. If we press on to the end of the section, we discover that the sleeping girl, prostrate in the eyes of Proust, is 'a sleep plant that cannot tell him lies or escape his knowing. Poor Marcel. What is there to know.' Not much, it turns out. I don't need to lug around 'multivolume things'; I just need to linger a little in a seminar on the male gaze.

To what extent is Proust—or Beckett, or whomever a Carson book recruits—an interchangeable signifier of hefty, high culture? Discussing the typical Paul Auster novel, James Woods elegantly describes the manoeuvre: 'A visiting text—Chateaubriand, Rousseau, Hawthorne, Poe, Beckett—is elegantly slid into the host book.' Whom, I've started to wonder, will Carson host next. What is there to quote.

* * *

In one scene of *Autobiography of Red*, young Geryon, gazing out a car window, 'thought about thoughts'. Is Carson's ideal reader the sort of person who enjoys the thought that he or she is the sort of person who thinks about thinking?

* * *

In the latter half of *Red Doc>*, Carson's misfits help put on a play, spring one of their own from the clinic, and pick up by the side of the road—who else?—Hermes in a 'silver tuxedo'. A slightly stiff lieutenant, a colleague of Sad's, pitches in and learns to tend oxen (and, I suppose, his soft, springy side; instead of being pilfered by some violent hero, some Herakles, the herd is seen to). Someone always seems to be weeping in *Red Doc>*: 'G weeps thinking of Proust'; '[Sad] weeps in a sort of fury'; '[Sad] starts to cry'; 'Tears pour in Ida's heart'; '[G] grips his arm and weeps'; 'The weeping has been arriving about every seven minutes.' Is it that characters who are types are typically given to tears? Carson's are given to breaking into song, waltz. They find themselves befriended by bats, who swoop in to lend a wing, the way small critters will do at cartoon's crescendo. Their antecedents would seem to be J.D. Salinger's Glass family, Wes Anderson's moody prodigies—creative, misunderstood souls. Ida, for one, 'often gets lost in basements well in fact Ida often gets lost. Despite map or compass.' I would expect no less than aimlessness from Carson's right-brained heroes.

And then there's G, already an autobiographer, about whom the text observes:

> Writing itself is what he
> loves now the mental
> action the physical action.
> He thinks about writing all
> the time while doing other
> things or talking to people
> he is forming sentences in
> his head it keeps the white
> away....

In the life of every reader comes a moment, maybe several, when he thinks, hey, maybe he should try his hand at poems. But passages like the above are insidious to the extent that they portray writing as painless, pleasurable 'action'. 'I hate writing, I love having written,' said Dorothy Parker, who had the love-hate balance about right. The genius of G's ongoing saga—and surely one reason for the first book's success—is the silent appeal it makes to the alienated adolescent in all of us: we, too, can be memoirists of our own monstrosity. We would be better off heeding Elizabeth Bishop's observation: '[I]t's true, children sometimes write wonderful things, paint wonderful pictures, but I think they should be *dis*couraged.' We would be better off clipping G's wings.

* * *

In the last act, G arrives at his mother's deathbed, and the reader arrives at the best writing in all of *Red Doc>*. It may be that a person starved for verse is primed to receive even the slightest noise as music—but Carson has written beautifully about parents before: 'The Glass Essay', 'Father's Old Blue Cardigan', *The Beauty of the Husband*. Here, she writes so well about G's dying mother, you wonder why she felt she needed the preceding picaresque, the Proust-dropping, the oxing around. Check out, instead, Carson's eleventh-hour meditation on time, a poignant page of doggerel on mothers, and these other, assorted epiphanies:

When he is there they
lift the stones together.
The stones are her lungs.

How
strange his mother is lying
out there in her little
soaked Chanel suit....

At home they
all seemed caught in a
badly blocked play and
faces put on wrong....

Were this a true autobiography of reader (and not what it actually is: broadsides of book reviewer), I would've bailed on *Red Doc>* the moment Io, in flight, 'lets loose a great fart and poops gloriously just missing [G's] head'. That was the real end of me. The death of the reader. But given the nature of the gig, I had to resurrect my resolve and push onward; I had no choice. Those who *have* the choice may wonder, not unreasonably, whether a few late fragments—that hint at some better book, set at a hospital: *Red at a Death Bed*—are worth their effort. It's a valid question, though one that probably doesn't occur much to classicists. Or archaeologists.

Or the sort of person who takes solace in a scene that would seem to be about Proust but is, in fact, about a much more Sisyphean figure—the Anne Carson fan:

> this lost city
> whose smashed clues and
> indecipherable   evidence
> poor Marcel has to dig
> through   each   evening
> feverish for a real shard.
> How was your day? this
> question on which so much
> hangs. You don't really
> want to know. Yet he
> keeps digging....

Godno

The back cover copy of Dennis Lee's latest collection, *Yesno*, describes the Toronto poet as 'beloved', and it's hard—it's against civic bylaw—to disagree. Yet I've often wondered if the word's a kind of backhanded compliment. Like pink insulation, 'beloved' protects those poets too soft and cuddly to otherwise survive in the harsh climes of criticism. (It also ensures the copywriter feels warm and fuzzy about his own capacity to love.) Who would be so cruel as to criticize new work by the 'beloved' author of *Alligator Pie* and *Fraggle Rock* lyrics, the 'beloved' icon who co-founded House of Anansi Press, won a Governor General's Award, and became Toronto's first Poet Laureate? An institution like Lee (or, say, bpNichol) surely qualifies for heritage site status.

Just above that 'beloved', *Quill & Quire*'s blurb asserts, '[f]rom Yeats through *Finnegans Wake*, from Dylan Thomas to Samuel Beckett, Lee hints at a long lineage of inventive writers whose work appeals to the ear as well as the mind.' In addition to the fact that *Finnegans Wake* is not an 'inventive writer', note that Lee is not a part of that 'long lineage'; he merely 'hints' at it, which is hardly a praiseworthy feat. (Someone who defaces subway posters 'hints' at a tradition that includes Marcel Duchamp.) The blurb spares the rod but cuffs the childlike poet backhandedly.

At least the cover, which carries forward the design of Lee's 2003 companion volume, *Un*, is consistent with the branding. Boasting an embossed title (*'Yes'* in white, *'no'* in black) set against a bold red, the book resembles the sort of self-help guide that tops non-fiction bestseller lists. Indeed, a good subtitle for *Yesno* would have been *The Power of Positivenegative Thinking*. Lee's newest, you see, straddles the impasse marked by binary oppositions, those rigid, black-and-white distinctions we use to structure and limit our lives. More specifically, *Yesno* asks, 'How hew to the/pushpull?

How/straddle the twain of what is?' By asking those questions, *Yesno* not only suggests that life is—who would have thought?—too complex to be reduced to binaries; the book also decentres traditional structures of linguistic meaning, its poems becoming sites for 'pushpull' or the free play of signifiers.

Anyway, that's what I might have written if I was a graduate student in the 1980s. Because those Derrideanesque buzzwords are now dated, if not derivative, Lee's 'pushpull' of meaning prompts only my bewilderment—and not because that 'pushpull' is so unusual, but, rather, because it's business as usual. For example, in 'galore' (the title mind-bendingly lowercased and placed at the bottom of the page, the better to knock us on our heads), Lee asks:

How can the
tonguetide of object/sub-
jection not garble what pulses in
isbelly?

I have another question: how can a poet as allegedly inventive as Lee serve up such stale, garbled pie? The ingredients include reheated work by the usual suspects: bpNichol, Daphne Marlatt, Language poets, and deconstructionists (or 'poststructuralists', which, as David Foster Wallace points out, is what you call deconstructionists who don't want to be called deconstructionists). It's hard, then, to see Paul Celan's supposed influence on *Yesno*; lines like

Grammars of outcome,
twin-
twined in collision/collusion

have been par for course in Canadian poetry for years, and can be found, in some variation, in any number of books regularly churned out by our more 'experimental' practitioners. The cliché, 'Grammars', can easily be exchanged with the equally cliché 'Vocabularies', 'Alphabets', 'Lexicons', 'Geographies', 'Taxonomies', or 'Arithmetics'. Even more predictable, however, is Lee's use of the backslash to both weld and separate two words that, despite their differences, are (steady yourself) one letter away from each other.

Again, if I were that graduate student, late of the 80s and fresh off a theory seminar, I would assure you that Lee's use of the back-slash emphasizes the slippery nature of words, words that might, any moment, turn themselves (and your consciousness) inside out. But there's nothing risky about Lee's backslash, which, far from an agent of liberating ambiguity, communicates a meaning ('This is daring stuff!') quite comfortably. Such pseudo-experimental gestures abound in *Yesno*, like the wry, mass-produced buttons on a hipster's jacket, all-too-familiar signs of rebellion, and thus no longer signs of rebellion. (*Yesno*'s 'Whacked grammar' pitches Lee somewhere between an embarrassing uncle, trying to be 'hep', and Poochie, the disastrous cartoon dog without a cause, dreamed up by marketers on an episode of *The Simpsons*.) In fact, how easily Lee's nice phrase, 'things wriggle free of their names', successfully names things wriggling free of their names. In other words, the overstated gap between a word and its meaning may be theoretically valid, but a good poet renders the gap irrelevant.

Indeed, when Lee keeps the clichés in check, *Yesno* is capable of offering lovely lines like 'Still itching to//parse with a two-tongued heart, shambala/scrapings. To/praise with a broken art.' Else-where, one salvages jazzy riffs like 'Giddyap, ganglia'. Still, those are moments, not poems, and too much of *Yesno* reads like shapeless nonsense—although perhaps 'nonsense' is not the right word. As the American poet Kay Ryan reminds us,

> nonsense is *always* shaped. You can distinguish real non-sense from garbage because nonsense is shaped and tense.... Nonsense, like poetry, is a kind of game, with rules or requirements. Neither is pointless play like that endless horsies whinnying and prancing thing girls do, or that strange martial arts sequence by which small boys advance through rooms. Play assumes that there is no end. Games (nonsense and poetry) assume there is—if only for the sake of seeing it thwarted.

Lee, the author of such garbage as 'How surd a blurward stut. How/peewee thingsong,/surfing the plenary killcurve', is not unlike Ryan's small boy moving through the house, making a 'pointless' but tolerable noise. There is little shape or tension in *Yesno*'s poems. Lines and verse paragraphs often break with arbitrary logic ('How can the/tonguetide'), and the overall slapdashness absolves the reader of committing to, or caring about, Lee's project.

Some will insist that the reader must become an active participant in the process of making *Yesno*'s meaning. But a reader (at least one not working on a dissertation or working to prop up a 'beloved' reputation) is under no obligation to engage with a poem, especially if that poem seems to be standing at a distance from its words, indifferent, paring its fingernails. Ultimately, *Yesno* fails to corral its wordplay into a contract with the reader, the sort of contract that produces a payoff by either exceeding or inventively thwarting the expectations it sets up. 'How/peewee thingsong' establishes no expectations for Lee to exceed or thwart. Lee's play is unbounded by any walls a reader can recognize, the sort of 'rules or requirements' found in work as diverse as Shakespeare's sonnets, Emily Dickinson's hermetic hymns, or even the concentrated language squeezed out by Oulipo constraints. I offer such diverse examples not because I want Lee to start writing in pentameter. But Lee might raise his game by inviting the reader into one: the sort of game Frost called 'prowess—something to achieve, something to win or lose'. This 'prowess' seems to me especially important if Lee wants one of *Yesno*'s messages, 'blue planet, hold on', to reach some of the people on that planet.

Yesno, after all, is not just the latest act in a familiar tragicomedy (Esteemed Poet Gets Down with the Kids and Goes Avant-Garde, but Not Too Down or Too Avant-Garde); it provides further evidence that Lee, like Leo and Oprah, has gone green, a noble if somewhat fashionable metamorphosis seemingly inaugurated by his previous collection. *Un*, which solidified Lee's late pseudo-experimental style, represents a more pessimistic (i.e., its cover is black) version of the updated, optimisticpessimistic *Yesno*. Nevertheless, both books exhibit a similar anxiety about the state of the world and the environment. Reviews of Lee's current project have gone so far as to describe it as a 'howl', and indeed *Yesno* contains many polemical howlers like 'Who but a bupkus/quixote would tilt at the corporate mindmills?' Of course, Lee, whose children's books have done good business for a few of those 'corporate mindmills', is no 'bupkus/quixote', and anyway, 'corporate mindmills' is not just an easy shot; it's the propaganda one would expect from an amateur activist, and belongs in front of an open mic or in *Adbusters*' slush pile. But while magazines like *Adbusters* attempt to offer constructive solutions, *Yesno* takes on no such responsibility. Abandoning the conventional language of earlier Lee books like *Civil Elegies*, *Yesno* goes avant-garde, but not too avant-garde. It goes green, but not too green. If it was a traffic light, I suppose it would be red and green. Whatever else it is, *Yesno* is PC poetry for our gridlocked age.

Manufacturing Conceit

The Rush to Here is George Murray's first collection of poetry in four years. But for awhile there—2000 to 2003—Murray was averaging 0.75 collections a year, prompting David Solway to suggest Murray slow down the assembly line. If poetry is wine, and should be, as Solway put it, '*chambréd* for a spell', then Murray had been cranking out boxed juice. On first glance, Murray seems to have absorbed the advice. He has bided his time and released a book that sure looks slim. But don't let *The Rush to Here*'s long gestation and compact dimensions fool. The book uploads fifty-seven sonnets into the tradition. That's a lot of poetry for anyone to write, let alone the individual talent behind the once-popular, now-defunct *Book Ninja* website, which a generation of writers, looking to procrastinate, bookmarked.

Still, whatever you may think about Murray's productivity, this is all surely good news for the sonnet. Long after it swept Renaissance Europe, the product that was eventually imported into England, and which Shakespeare found useful, hasn't been much improved upon. In the last two centuries alone, its patrons have included vegetarians, Jesuit priests, urban hipsters, doomed soldiers, chicken farmers, Nobel Laureates, and even those mavericks who insist on their name in the lower-case (Shelley, Hopkins, Millay, Owen, Frost, Heaney, and cummings, respectively). Anthologies of the stuff keep on coming. If consumer satisfaction is any indication of longevity, then the sonnet looks poised to outlast Uno, Oulipo, and many other modern fads.

The sonnet persists, of course, because it's so much more than mere Tupperware, fourteen lines deep. It's certainly more than a rhyme scheme, which Murray has ditched here, favouring 'thought rhymes' (the 'rhyme' between 'ladders' and 'chute', for example). The sonnet is a living laboratory for testing out conceits—extended metaphors in which one thing, what your English teacher would've called the 'tenor', is seen in terms of something else, the 'vehicle'. A good sonnet usually depends on the strength of its metaphors, a good *metaphor*, on a connection between tenor and vehicle that's surprising (we didn't anticipate it) but also logical (we *could've* anticipated it—if we'd had the poet's vision). 'The soft applause of snow on the window' may be surprising, but is it logical? Does 'snow' sound like 'soft applause'? Or is the pair of ears behind the mixing board of that metaphor a little tone deaf? Surely 'rain', which actually does sound like soft applause, would've been the more appropriate tenor. But another metaphor, one that detects the arc of someone's 'brow bone' in a 'proscenium', boasts good eyesight; brow bones and prosceniums look alike, but their resemblance hadn't really been apparent—at least until Murray pointed it out.

These two metaphors—the first a flop, the second a success—can be inspected in the opening quatrain of the opening sonnet of *The Rush to Here*. And the quatrain itself can be viewed as a microcosm of an overall collection whose metaphors are sometimes bracing, but often baffling. Take, for example, the opening line of 'The Audience': 'Weather the shape of eggs, colour of knitting.' Forget, for a moment, that weather is already a vague word; in what ways is it egg-shaped? Just what colour is knitting? Isn't it just the colour of whatever yarn you're using? Other poems prompt similar questions. How do you 'unbuckle your face like a belt after/a holiday dinner'? When the woman in 'Tackle Box'

> works the bar like it's a tackle box,
> hooks and weights against the wild's best wiles,
> hands loose as though driving a wood cart on
>
> a dirt road in the late light's trickery

what on earth is she actually *doing*? The poem is thought-rhyming 'wiles' with 'trickery', but what about the woman? Is she fishing for a tip or fending off some sharks? Is she making a mixed drink or is Murray merely mixing his metaphors? These aren't the productive questions—Who *is* Prufrock? What *exactly* depends on a red wheelbarrow?—that a richly ambiguous poem with clear syntax can prompt. In other words, my queries aren't drilling for deeper meaning. They're gut reactions of bafflement to poems that don't seem to make enough of the right kind of surface sense. Maybe bafflement is Murray's goal, but I doubt it, and just a dram of doubt over whether a poem is intentionally baffling or unintentionally bad usually means the poem's rotten. Too often, readers direct their doubts against themselves—'*I* just don't get poetry'—but they can be assured that faces aren't like belts. Bars aren't like tackle boxes. These are *Murray's* failures: failures of matchmaking, failures to smoothly marry tenor to vehicle.

But sometimes a Murray metaphor can't arrange that marriage because one of its terms isn't a specific, concrete thing that can be visualized. The night, for example, is a time of day. It holds no physical dimensions. It's not tactile. It's surely not, as Murray's poem 'Go' insists:

> a bull
> with six banderillas in its flank, a mad
> wolverine caught in the corner and harassed
> a dog stumbling in the last moments of rabies.

We are bored by this because there was never a possibility for us to have come up with the wounded bull, the mad wolverine, the dying dog. (The night is simply not like these things.) Over and over, Murray's metaphors bottle foggy, abstract tenors inside clear, specific vehicles. And the results are not good:

> ... [T]he mind a parking lot for desire.
> —from 'All the Standard Candles'

> ... [Y]our memories unmoor ...
> —from same

> God is fear's ghost ...
> —from 'Plain Jane'

The future floats foetal ...
—from 'The Wide Tropic'

Panic's gearwork ...
—from 'The Averages'

I can cite more. But for now, consider how effortlessly any of the aforementioned tenors can be slotted into that last vehicle, 'gear-work':

The mind's gearwork

Memory's gearwork

Fear's gearwork

The future's gearwork.

Because ethereal ideas like memory and future and fear can't really be *seen*, Murray is free to see them in any way—and in terms of any vehicle—he chooses. Neglecting the good poet's self-imposed obliga-tion to the difficult work of precise observation, *The Rush to Here* is a sweatshop, churning out metaphors that look original but are actually quite easy to mint. (My editor, by the way, points out that my matchmaking metaphor works better than my bottling metaphor. But hopefully he'll keep them both in, if for no other rea-son than to demonstrate that deregulated metaphor production afflicts even book reviewers.)

Murray's poetry, then, doesn't really *discover* logical connections between seemingly unrelated but distinctly perceivable things—which Christian Wiman's poetry does when it describes a 'dark/doorway' as the 'wall's yawn', or which Bruce Taylor's does when it calls a coast a 'ragged ... salt line on a boot'. Murray's son-nets *manufacture* connections between unrelated things, many of which are airily abstract. In doing so, they suffer from the same Renaissance-era problems that Shakespeare diagnosed when he wrote, 'My mistress' eyes are nothing like the sun.' (Recall Murray's 'soft applause of snow on the window', and now cock your ear at Wiman's simile 'leaves shush themselves like an audience.')

Murray's poems also suffer from artlessness. A pattern of beats has been maintained, but according to an interview, the more sonnets Murray wrote, the more he found he 'didn't like the faux Elizabethan sing-song sound that comes from the linguistic acrobatics necessary to complete the rhyme contract'—which sounds an awful lot like laziness. 'Linguistic acrobatics' only look like acrobatics when the poet in question lacks skill. Good sonnets conceal the effort behind them; their rhyme schemes come off naturally.

But sometimes the sonnets in *The Rush to Here* suffer from plain old grammatical imprecision. The simile, 'humanity opening/like nesting dolls', from 'Spilling Through the Break', should be 'humanity opening/like *a* nesting doll'; though once again, an abstract concept, 'humanity', seems not quite right. Maybe the simile should be '*humans* opening/like nesting dolls', but even then, do humans do this? 'The errors rain down like rocks to the head', from 'Wilt', would work better as 'The errors rain down like rocks *on* the head', but once again, the decision to work with a fluid noun allows any number of options (whereas a coastline's rigid contours must be reckoned with). Errors could also rain down like, well, rain. Murray's language here is about as watery as it gets.

'Call it precious and go to hell,' Truman Capote told *The Paris Review*, 'but I believe a story can be wrecked by a faulty rhythm in a sentence—especially if it occurs toward the end—or a mistake in paragraphing, even punctuation.' The same can be said of a single, deal-breaking word in a poem. And *The Rush to Here* contains far too many deal-breakers. The book's not quite a disaster; that's not the right word. Outside of slam contests, poetry's failures are quiet and usually hinge on a few creaky words. And while words may be no more than warped windows that can never fully swing open onto reality, writers—especially poets—would do well to keep those windows as clean and clear as possible. They might even begin by not describing words as windows. That's just lazy.

Full of It

Nick Thran's *Every Inadequate Name* was recently shortlisted for Canada's Gerald Lampert Memorial Award, which goes to a best first book of poems. Certainly, Thran's is first-bookish, a mixed messenger bag of seemingly well-workshopped moments, including:

- the requisite poem about a grandparent ('Club Amnesia');
- the requisite reference to Pablo Neruda ('Thoughts While Driving a Stretch of Mountain Road, Listening to a Tape of Pablo Neruda Reading "Las Alturas de Machu Picchu"');
- the requisite prose poem ('Gurdeep's Brain');
- the requisite found poem (some salsa instructions);
- a demonstration of chops (via quatrains in 'Isolation Camp, a Letter');
- a demonstration of stamina (via the fourparter, 'Bird Time');
- a thruline to glue it all together (a series of 'Coastline Variations,' caulking the book's joints); and
- a laundry list of arsonist-mentors (lurking around the Acknowledgements) who apparently 'lit' and 'fanned the early flames' for Thran.

Actually, there are lists throughout the book. Thran's come disguised as poems, but they're not fooling. Rather, they pass off unmemorable, prosy repetition as incantation:

This is for all the proprietors
who close up late, know laundry is often done
when there is nothing left to do.

This is for the Coin O'Rama
after it empties.
　　　　　　—from 'The Coin O'Rama Laundromat, a Dedication'

Say, *yellows, greys, dark blues,*
and dress yourself in them.

Say, *my bones are the fortress that will not fall,*
and scrub-shine those teeth with vigour.
                    —from 'Morning Routine, with Shadow'

The poem won't ever save the world.
The poem won't even raise you up
from your sickbed and make you feel better.
                    —from 'The Poem You've Been Waiting For'

Because lists are easy to generate, their success—that is, their ability to compel our attention beyond a first reading—depends on the success of their individual entries. (Anaphora, the repetition of phrases like, 'This is for', at the starts of lines, will only get a poet so far—to the beginning of her next line.) But do the following lovely enough lines—

A sigh at the end
of each word that she whispers:

La playa. Las estrellas. Mira. Mira.

A sigh at the end
as she draws you in closer:

Ahora.

There is a man who will dive.

—really merit isolation on an entire page? Do they merit more than that first reading? Do they (and perhaps this is the only question that matters) delight us?

I'm with the American poet August Kleinzahler, who reminds us (because we usually do need to be reminded) that 'art's exclusive function is to entertain, not to improve or nourish or console....'

Thran *is* capable of entertaining us, at least in small doses. When his poetry sidles up to the demands of devices as rudimentary as rhyme, the results really are quite good, as in the latter half of 'Monday in the World of Beauty':

> She tries to sell you blonde highlights.
> *Tsks* your current unkempt style,
> and decides it would be easiest
> to just go on and do
> what it is that we normally do.
>
> Cold sheers trim the neckline clean.
> She promises you'll leave this place
> a brand new you.
> The jar
> of sanitizer glows.
> Electric. Unreal. Blue.

The almost singsong 'oo' rhyme not only sharpens the dullness of the salon experience; the expectation of a rhyme scheme helps to ensure the reader will finish and maybe even reread the poem, as I did. Indeed, it's the little things like alliteration that recommend a description of a dream in which 'I am a cymbalist,//bare palmed, back row, and we're working/through a rendition of Beethoven's twenty-fifth Sonata.' And when Thran abandons low-grade incantation—in favour of something clear to say, something streamlined by good old cause and effect—his poetry earns that second reading:

> As it stands, the cricket's size grows in the telling,
> spreads like the news, years ago, of abandoned stacks
> of dirty magazines stowed at the creek behind
> the street where I grew up. When my bicycle tires
> edged over the lip, boys were already clutching the rain-
> soaked pages in their fists, the ink of my first
> glimpses of flesh were already starting to pale,
> to bleed into the leaves. Seriously, we'd say
> in the schoolyard, it was the coolest. Later, actual

clothing would melt off actual flesh; yes, melt,
not just fall to the floor, because, seriously, she
was the hottest.

As the alliteration of 'st-' stacks up, as 'hottest' follows 'coolest', as
pornography gives way to puberty, these lines from Thran's poem,
'Seriously, It Was the Biggest Cricket', hitch the device of repetition
(so previously gimmicky) to some driving force. Indeed, Thran's better poems avoid the aimless surrealism of his worst—

I think I'll split a pomegranate
and display the halves like dentists' x-rays
to a patient, star-filled night.

—by having a plot, an argument, some parsable point.

That point *can* be a little ponderous, though. In 'Club Amnesia',
Thran's speaker measures a group of trashed club-goers against the
example of his miner-soldier-grandfather. The club-goers, of course,
don't stand a chance, and the poem sounds an awful lot like a moral.
(But then they should have recognized that an establishment by the
name of 'Club Amnesia', when patronized in a poem, serves more
than shooters; it serves cultural amnesia. Get thee to a library!) Is
the wisdom resulting from a mine or a bullet really preferable to getting trashed with friends? Does Thran's speaker find the sanitizer
'unreal' because he's a hopeless Romantic with pastoral visions of
some more authentic life beyond the smog of salons?

Thran's poems, if we're to consult the back cover copy, are
'about the risks we take in our struggle to remain passionate about
something (anything) in an age when an ingrained cynicism
attempts to keep genuine passion at arm's length.' Which 'age' does
the copy mean? Even a century ago, poets like Yeats felt compelled
to observe, 'The best lack all conviction, while the worst/Are full of
passionate intensity.' But Yeats was full of it. Let the worst have their
passionate intensity. There's surely too much of it in certain of
Thran's poems, like 'Club Amnesia' and 'How Pop Sounds'. In the
latter, the second person wants to hammer a friend for badmouthing
some pop song, and comes off as more than a little heavy-handed:

I'm sick of this song, your friend says.
This must be the worst music
ever invented. When was the last time
the sugar wore off? The last time
you looked him straight in the eye
and told him how you heard this same song
sung by a boy
at the edge of a candlelit dock
over the lake where his best friend drowned?

You don't know shit, you want to say.
You don't know how Pop sounds.

The poem practically grabs the poor reader by the lapels, but as the American poet Kay Ryan argues, 'poems are to liberate our feelings rather than to bind them. If a poem sticks you to it, it has failed.' *Every Inadequate Name* shouldn't make us cynics and amnesiacs feel quite so inadequate, especially if the book would like us to remember it.

Primordial Muse

The pre-poem moment has to do with inspiration, inhalation: the moment that precedes, and maybe even overlaps with, the poet's writing of the poem; the moment when, loafing in the grass, the poet is struck with an urge to compose something and strips the Moleskine of its shrink wrap. The pre-poem moment is of the highest order of pregnant pause, tape hiss, silence. It's the moment before a Coleridge is jarred out of his recollection of an opium dream by a knock on the door; it's the ingesting of the opium; it's the dreaming. (I suppose it's also the moment when a person sets about programming the algorithm that enables a computer to spew out stanzas.) The idyll in which powerful feelings get recollected (and poems get themselves written) proposes itself on subways, at desks, in Starbucks, in the midst of birdwatching, in response to perceived injustice. It's the primordial ooze, the part with the muse. These days, it often overlaps with the filling out of grant applications.

The pre-poem moment can produce more than just poetry; it can produce—where there'd been, only moments before, a mere person—a poet. One day, in the seventh century, an illiterate cowherd could be seen to be lurking at the edge of a conversation. He was not good, the cowherd felt, in social situations. When the lyre or conch shell or speaking spliff (or whatever gave a body the right to put its two cents in) was passed to the cowherd, he declined it. But when he retired to the altogether less demanding company of his cows, he fell asleep and was visited by an angel. The angel bestowed on the cowherd the chops of a poet, plus a mandate: to talk up God in song. The cowherd went on to compose a hymn, which is reproduced at the front of the *Norton Anthology of Poetry*. But he's far more famous, the cowherd, for *becoming* Caedmon, the first English poet; he's far more famous for a pre-*poet* moment.

This phenomenon—in which a vacuum suddenly blossoms, Big Bang-like—is still observed, centuries later. The American poet Samuel Menashe claims to have gone to bed one night in 1949, having never thought of himself as a poet, only to wake up inspired to bang out some lines. (A sociologist might suggest that a Caedmon or Menashe has been inspired alright—with the sufficient amount of educational capital needed to want to compose such specialized stuff as poems.)

Still, in '[t]he moment before a poem, there's often nothingness,' says poet Evie Christie, one of the contributors to *Approaches to Poetry: The Pre-poem Moment*, edited by poet-critic Shane Neilson. *Approaches to Poetry* is a book about the loafing in the grass, the visitations of angels, the waking up to wanting to write something, the nothingness. (Alas, there's no partaking of opium to report.) Neilson's book presents twenty-seven essays on the pre-poem moment by twenty-seven Canadian poets. Each poet reflects on the lead-up to one of his or her poems, which poem Neilson then prints for our inspection. Although this may sound like an easy enough gig, the term 'pre-poem moment' can be understood to refer to a whole *lot* of moment: the sum total of time the contributor lived before he or she wrote the first line: a lifetime. T.S. Eliot hypothesized that the catalyzing mind is always working on some poetry or other; it's always storing up this or that, anticipating some later date when a finished poem—its fragments shored together—will suddenly present itself. Wayne Clifford, one of Neilson's contributors, suggests that 'everything I've ever done, spoken, read, and made, everything of this whole person, can be seen to participate in the next making.' Claire Sharpe's poem 'Aperture' is, in Sharpe's words, 'the raw culmination of what goes on in my head....' 'I often joke,' says Zachariah Wells, 'when asked how long it takes me to write a poem, that the one I finished yesterday took me 32 years (or whatever my age might be on a given day).' 'Questions of origin,' says Brian Bartlett in his diligent play-by-play on the creation of his splendid 'All the Train Trips' '—maybe they could be comprehensively answered only if the poet sat down and offered days of elaborations, or wrote a book about all the encounters with the words, other poems, other people, and many miscellaneous influences that led to the breaking forth of language

into one poem.' There's a Charlie Kaufman screenplay in here,
somewhere.

But for what I suspect are practical reasons, many of Neilson's
contributors—including Clifford, Sharpe, Wells, and Bartlett, who
eventually do narrow their focus—tend to put the time span of the
pre-poem moment at a relatively brief interval. Wells, homing in on
the genesis of his 'Achromatope', writes,

> Immediately upon finishing 'The Case of the Colorblind
> Painter' [from Oliver Sacks's *An Anthropologist on Mars*], I
> read it over again and, with a number of the more poignant
> phrases and images from the story bouncing around my
> brainpan, I started to write. In about forty-five minutes, I
> had a draft of 'Achromatope'.

In Wells' anecdote, the catalyzing mind sounds a lot more like a
squash court or lottery ball tumbler, 'bouncing' ideas around. But
the point, Eliot's, is still the same: poems accrete in poets' minds. (If,
as Bartlett suggests, poems are later helped along by editors and
readers of 'still-under-question drafts', then such charity is also part
of the pre-poem moment.)

It matters where poems come from, Neilson argues in his introduction — a few pages of prose that's smart, colloquial, some of the
finest in the book:

> Life is the poet readied, pen in hand; it is the poet creative
> by other means and moved when she is supposed to be
> moved, amidst the preliminaries, braced before the poem.
>
> There is a natural resistance to this idea. We feel that
> any dive into the murk of poem-stuff, of deriving intentions,
> is reductive, making the poet's version into an official ver-
> sion and trussing the poem in all its promiscuity into the
> missionary position.

'[T]he poet creative by other means'—this also applies to the poet
who composes terrific introductions to anthologies. Neilson, at the
very least, seems ready for his detractors, but then, they predate him

by decades. The New Critics of the first half of the twentieth century eschewed questions of intention and concerned themselves with the poem alone, which, they argued, acquires its meaning from a larger tradition in which the poem has its tendrils. Later, Roland Barthes, in his infamous essay-cum-obituary 'The Death of the Author', declared that 'it is language which speaks, not the author....' (If the New Critics had flushed the author out of the brambles of his work, Barthes had picked him off coolly, a shot heard round the world or, at least, its graduate seminars.) Romantic types such as Harold Bloom and Camille Paglia, meanwhile, have kept a vigil for an author whose death they've refused to accept. Geoffrey Cook, one of Neilson's contributors, seems to hint at something like middle-ground when he notes that

> whatever the author's intention(s) may have been in its writing, a poem is completed when it has become independent of authorial intention and consciousness. At least I have had no other experience of my own work: 'my' poem is 'done' when it is *not* mine.

For the most part, though, Neilson's book locates itself on the unfashionable side of origins, intentions—the 'murk of poem-stuff', as he puts it. It's surely brave of him to have asked of twenty-seven poets, '*What went into that?*', poets being, in my experience, hungry for the interest of others and all too happy to hold forth.

Fortunately, Neilson gathers good stories: John Barton's survival of a 'dream-time' plane crash, Jason Dewinetz's 'thing' for pocket knives. *Approaches to Poetry* is fascinating, entertaining. But in offering up the reflections of twenty-seven active Canadian poets, it risks including a few who are not obvious stylists of prose. For instance, Sue Sinclair's poem, 'I Am My Body', isn't greatly illuminated by its precious preface. 'Often I begin a poem when some quality of the light strikes me,' intones Sinclair. 'I sometimes think in light; light comes weighted with emotion and meaning for me. I suspect I'm not alone in this.' I, too, suspect (and fear) she's not alone. But Sinclair and other light-minded poets do readers a service when they think in electrochemical signals (as opposed to emotion-weighted light) and talk specifics. She then goes on to write that

> The experience that calls for something like a poem is an especially intense engagement: senses, feelings, thought, all sharpened, focussed. Unified. But I think it would also be safe to say that something intense in the sensuous world usually calls up a rush of feeling that leads me toward a thought.
>
> This poem is a new kind of poem for me. I very rarely begin in the mode of thought. But in this case there was a thought: if the self is the body, what about the times when my body gives out on me, when it doesn't feel like it belongs to me?

One wishes that a person with special knowledge of 'especially intense engagement[s]' and 'rush[es] of feeling' could find some less banal way of communicating them to those of us who've resigned ourselves to operate in what Sinclair calls (as if it were entirely too rational and regrettable a practice) 'the mode of thought'.

Elsewhere, several of Neilson's contributors, lit from below by flashlight, confess to feeling haunted. 'I was haunted by it, certainly,' says Harold Rhenisch of a Robin Skelton poem. 'That moment of the invisible becoming visible through some acquired character has always haunted my poems as an image,' says Crispin Elsted of a memory. I would like to arrange an exorcism of some of the phrases that haunt some of the sentences in *Approaches to Poetry*:

My heart raced. (Sara Tilley)

... I began to walk around the city, eyes wide. (Mark Abley)

... *thousands* of caribou, maybe ten or twelve thousand, spread out as far as the human eye could see. (Alison Pick)

I would also like to think I could know nothing of the experience of someone who has gone through a civil war. But when Goran Simic, in the preface to his poem, observes that 'the war scars carved on our skin were deeper than we thought', I'm all too sure I know what he means. (In wars—and clichés—scars are rarely just skin deep.) Still, even a war-torn poet couldn't manage to muster as solemn an air as the aforementioned Sharpe, who

> can only suggest, then, that [her poem] 'Aperture' forms no more than the articulation of, or 'opening' onto, a profound, perhaps perceived, isolation; an attempt to offer some tangible clutch of the clarity which comes by word at times as a drip from confusion, and at others as a natural cascade of relief; proof of the journey in an offering of that which I am unable to extend through conversation; that which may be impossible to translate into conventions of meaning.

This paragraph, too, 'may be impossible to translate into conventions of meaning.'

I admire Sinclair's and Amanda Jernigan's notions that poems are less 'creations' than 'responses'. These admit some hubris, some sensitivity to a larger social world that has a hand in poems. Bravado's good, too. David Solway's delightful essay, 'Finding a Voice', documents a literary hoax that dates back to 1969: Solway's ginning up of an alter ego, a Greek poet named Andreas Karavis. How immodest of the young Solway, who gets himself fired from a teaching job in Crete for spouting 'anti-junta sentiments'; who, thinking himself invulnerable, swaggers into a police station and demands that his visa be 'processed before lunch'; who receives lines from Karavis in his dreams; who understands the value of the aesthetic. 'After the birth of my son,' recalls Solway, 'I spent the last few drachmas I had diligently scrimped together and hired a horse and carriage to escort my new family back from the hospital in style, to the cheers of our neighbours in the old quarter who crowded their windows and balconies.' Such wasteful, if not reckless, behaviour—such indifference to the needs of those loved ones who might need the drachmas—all in pursuit of a little 'style' makes for good memoir, even if it's an unsustainable career strategy, long term. As he gets older, Solway sees, in Karavis, the means to develop a new style.

Solway's wife, meanwhile, worries that she's become a 'bigamist, never knowing who she was waking up beside', and Solway's son phones 'from Edmonton to express his concern that the boundaries of [Solway's] personality were starting to waver and grow porous'. This is most excellent soap opera, the best essay in Neilson's book. Has the Solway-Karavis entity optioned the screen rights?

Wayne Clifford's may be the second best essay. It bespeaks an important characteristic of the successful poet: a healthy interest in the rest of the world:

> Long before I begin, or am even aware I will begin, I don't read poetry. I read science, now mostly on-line. I read *The Economist*. I read histories and compilations, learn about looms, the manufacture of needles, the fossil record, stromatolites, sawyering (an especial interest of mine made difficult by the paucity of easily come by information), the goings-on inside cells, the quantum foam at the tiny, tiny frontier between our observable universe and the arrivals and departures among the almost-there realities of the utmost small. I try to get my head and heart around 13.6 billion years, the approximate, but assured, age of this cosmos of which I'm such a very small but somehow significant part.

Clifford 'learns about looms', a line that alliterates nicely. But he suggests—by phrases like 'goings-on' and 'easily come by' and 'almost-there'—an easy, stylish way with difficult material. He gently torques clichés ('I try to get my head and heart around 13.6 billion years') and so makes good use of them. One may not read *The Economist*, but one sort of trusts a poet who stoops to such unromantic behaviour.

In his introduction, Neilson writes that 'the poet who shrugs his shoulders in response to "How did you get here?" abdicates his responsibility. One would never bother asking him for directions again.' The latter sentence is nicely put and probably true: a shrug is usually enough to shut down a line of inquiry. But I would submit that poets have no responsibilities in excess of those required by law. And I would add that the shrug, when executed properly, can be a calculated but useful form of self-defence, if not self-mythologizing. Here's Bob Dylan, on *60 Minutes*:

Q: I've read somewhere that you wrote 'Blowin' in the Wind' in ten minutes. Is that right?
A: Probably.
Q: Just like that?
A: [pause] Yeah.
Q: Where did it come from?
A: It just came. It came from ... uh ... like uh ... right out of that wellspring of, uh, creativity, I would think, you know.

Dylan is much more revealing about what drives the artist when he describes destiny as

> a feeling you have that you know something about your-self—nobody else does—the picture you have in your mind of what you're about will come true. It's kind of a thing you kind of have to keep to your own self, because it's a fragile feeling. And if you put it out there, somebody will kill it. So, it's best to keep that all inside.

There can be a danger in *not* keeping it all inside, in reflecting *too* much on ambitions, intentions. Solway is one of the contributors to Neilson's book who seems to have understood the importance of strategic silence. 'A fiction,' he writes in his piece on the Greek alter ego, 'cannot at first be recognized as fictitious if it is to do the practical work for which it was designed.' A poet's most important fiction may be the placard of herself she fashions for others. She should want to be careful about how she presents it.

For instance, in her prose account of a pre-poem moment, Monica Kidd, a young doctor, tries to help a keeled-over woman (fellow poet Amanda Jernigan, who also writes about the incident and who would turn out to be okay). Kidd recalls how, after the arrival of the paramedics, 'a man grabs me by the elbow and says, *I guess you'll have more to write about,* and I briefly hate him for it. *This night is not over yet,* I think.' Kidd's heated response to the crass comment would seem to be a matter of principle; using a friend's keeling-over as fodder for a poem should be the furthest thing from her mind. Still, why am I dismayed by a poet who appears to make a virtue of *not* wanting to exploit an experience for the sake of a poem? Kidd didn't need to tell us about her correct internal response to the crass comment; she didn't need to tell us about the comment at all.

This went down at a St. John's pub in April of 2009, which means the resulting poem, 'Anything I Can Touch and Everything that Haunts' (again with the haunting!) must've been composed shortly before *Approaches to Poetry*, a 2009 release, came out. Did Kidd seize on the first moment of tranquility that presented itself post-pub and start recollecting? After presenting a few relatively precise images of nature ('this torn ice,/these fir trees, their turpentine sighs'), the poem relaxes into soft focus and obliges the reader to squint:

> Anything I can touch and
> everything that haunts.
> Don't think of last night; you on the floor
> and the spin of questions, the deep silence
> I pushed through to find your circled sentries.
> The empty place that silts with words
> of closure, comfort
> and other lesser fictions.

The 'circled sentries', I'm guessing, were suggested by the pub-goers who surrounded Kidd as she tried to attend to the keeled-over Jernigan. But it's not clear that the reader is supposed to get this from the poem. In fact, it's not clear *what* the reader's supposed to get, what with Kidd's easy abstractions and hollow nouns—the 'sentries', the 'everything that haunts', the 'deep silence', the 'empty place that silts with words'. Read without its preface, the latter half of the poem could just as easily refer to a round of spin the bottle, party-crashed (and buzz-killed) by Kidd. Kidd's prose account of a young doctor's insecurities in the face of bystanders' expectations is far more compelling a piece of writing. The poem it means to introduce—which hasn't cleared its pre-poem moment, fully formed—still needs professional attention, incubation, a heat lamp.

I'm also dismayed by the poet who appears to make a virtue of not contriving to impress or entertain me. Simic claims that, 'I didn't write poetry to impress anybody because circumstances already impressed me.' Sharpe boasts that, 'I can say with confidence that the content of what I write is never calculated, and that it has difficulty adhering to a clearly expressed goal or action or theme.' This is all too noble. Tim Bowling, thankfully, does seem to have a reader in mind:

> [Donald Hall's] argument—that too many contemporary poets expend no effort to hook the reader or to give him a pay-off—struck me as lamentably true.... In brief, I generally begin a poem only when an emotion or idea encounters an out-of-the-ordinary linguistic expression, and I generally end a poem in the same manner. This method has nothing to do with imagined readers and everything to do with myself: if I'm not engaged and rewarded, why write at all? And if what engages and rewards me fails to do so for others, then surely my poems will meet the fate of 99% of all poems: they'll be immediately forgotten.

Bowling's is one of the more reader-sensitive of the approaches tried out in Neilson's anthology: poets (at least those who mean for their work to be read by others) should do more than engage and reward themselves (especially if the reward is the self-righteous sense that their poems don't need to appeal to others). Bowling himself is one of the more honest poets; he would prefer his poems be remembered. 'I try, always, to be as clear as I can,' writes another poet, Elsted. 'That is my part of the contract with the reader. If a poem of mine is difficult, complex, it is still as clear as I could make it.' Good for the poet who deigns to observe a contract with the reader—who deigns to want to be clear. The pre-poem moment surely can involve, if only unconsciously on the part of the poet, some divining of a distant, destined audience. This is assuming the poet is crass enough to dream about *post*-poem moments.

Travel Writing

At the time of writing—it's early 2009—Canadian poet Elise Partridge can claim to enjoy a daily audience of many tens of thousands of readers. These aren't just any old readers; they are those most fantastical and coveted of literate creatures: general readers. They are also the commuters, myself included, who take public transit in Toronto, where Partridge's poem 'Vuillard Interior' has been on display, adjacent to ads for community college and debt management.

Is the Toronto Transit Commission trying to nudge the city's poets to consider their options? Is a large audience for their work possible only when the audience, cornered in a subway car, has no choice but to consider what it's presented, like that restless youth in *A Clockwork Orange*, forced to watch films that are good for him? In any case, I've been reading and rereading Partridge's poem for months now—looking at it, living with it, the way one looks at and lives with a painting, if one could afford one.

Or perhaps the poem is rather more like some artist's dream of a mobile exhibition, which follows and won't give up on beguiling its audience. And I don't think 'beguiling' too strong a word; like any artwork at which one stares for long stretches—of subway track, of time—the poem, a triolet, starts to play its tricks.

> Against brown walls, the servant bends
> over the coverlet she mends—
> brown hair, brown flocking, a dun hand
> under the lamp, the servant bends
> over the coverlet she mends
> draped across her broad brown skirts;
> knotting, nodding, the servant blends
> into the coverlet she mends.

On first glance, a tired commuter—and not necessarily the sort of domestic the poem is about, but perhaps a worried financial worker or graduate student—may find in Partridge's poem some gorgeous ekphrasis. To be sure, it paints a picture that's worth its forty-five well-chosen words.

But one should pay attention—literally pay this free poem with attention—because the laws that govern the world of *Waiting for Godot* also govern the world of 'Vuillard Interior'. Life repeats with subtle, sinister changes: neutral 'brown' fades to duller, shittier 'dun', and the creative act of 'knotting' collapses into 'nodding', which suggests the servant is 'nodding' off or, voiceless and power-less, nodding to order. The sly slipping of a fifth consonant into the verb 'bends' dissolves the servant in paint and 'blends' her into background, where she's less an object of what feminist film criti-cism calls the 'gaze' than an object that's glazed, even glossed, over. The top-heavy starts of lines—including trochees ('under', 'knot-ting') and dactyls ('over the', 'into the')—reinforce the rote, hunched-over labour.

The subway doors open. They disclose some of us, absorb others.

Unlike Aunt Jennifer, who sews her panel of tigers in Adrienne Rich's feminist classic, 'Aunt Jennifer's Tigers', Partridge's servant is no artist. She mends, does her duty, adds nothing much that's new to the world. If anything she subtracts from the world, subtracts her-self. Or, more accurately, *is* subtracted—and by art, of all things. Vuillard's paintings—which blend together, or so the poet suggests through her refusal to name a specific one—present us with domestic scenes. But they also risk, as all representations do, the obscuration and obliteration of the figures who populate them. Unbeknownst to her, the servant holds more than literal thread; she holds a line, a line against her obliteration, a line that's lost line by line as Partridge's ruthless poem unravels or, more terribly, cinches tight.

Moon Dreams

Real estate is on a lot of minds these days, but it's in them, too; isn't
the mind (read: the imagination) a kind of low-rent housing to
which we can retreat, however briefly, when startled by the silver-
fish? I write 'low-rent' because the only price the imagination exacts
is our attention to what's going on around us, in the real world,
which isn't always very interesting (or encouraging) under its bare
bulb. But why limit ourselves to *our* imaginations when we can live
comfortably in those of others? (Why create when we can read?)
Here is Don Coles's poem, 'On a Caspar David Friedrich Painting
Entitled "Two Men Observing the Moon"':

> They have been standing here, tiny hands
> clasped behind tiny backs, gazing upwards
> at a full moon ever since their arrival 179
> years ago. My heart swells with—with what?—
> envy, not much but some, also with admiration,
> looking at them. So small and so undemanding—
> this patch of stony ground has always contented them.
> How full their heads are with moon-thoughts!
> Though there is more to be said. I for instance
> who all my life have been discarding
> patches of ground, stony or picturesque makes
> no difference, have of late begun gazing upwards
> fairly often, more than I used to, I would say,
> thinking harmless thoughts. If I had been glimpsed
> even one of those times, just then, or then, or
> that other time, by someone who walked on past
> and never turned to look again,
> I'd live in that one mind forever serene as these,
> a thought I'll keep. I could say more

but they show me there's no need.
How the moon shines! How the two men observe!
And how willingly would I have spent my life
as they have, murmuring small comments
to my friend as the years pass!

To live in someone else's mind forever—this is not exactly what the
music critic Lester Bangs means when he suggests that the session
musicians on Van Morrison's *Astral Weeks* seem to be '*dwelling
inside of* each other's minds'. (Bangs seems to be talking about the
sort of relationship which we sometimes say, 'shares the same wave-
length', and for which we now reserve the uglier term, 'synergy'.)
No, to live in a mind is to be kept alive by it, to be as delicate as data,
but as retrievable, too. It is to be the woman in *Citizen Kane*, the one
in the white dress, glimpsed for a moment by Everett Sloane's character but called to mind, unbeknownst to her, once a month for the
rest of Sloane's character's life. In the age of Internet stalkers, who
copy and paste our images onto hard drives more permanent than
memory banks, such behaviour may sound creepy; to many fans of
Kane it probably sounds romantic. (Sloane's character is kind of a
sweetheart.)

Coles's speaker would certainly be content to linger in the mind
of 'someone who walked on past/and never turned to look again'.
Sure, the speaker's wish is narcissistic in that 'I-am-thought-of-
therefore-I-am' sort of way. But the thought that one could be
housed and nourished in someone else's thoughts is, as the speaker
suggests, an attractive one, especially in a world where Descartes is
dead. It's a thought the speaker will 'keep'—and a thought the poet
has had before. In Coles's poem, 'Codger', a man

remembers a woman
getting out of a car in winter, must be fifty years ago,
wore a little fur coat and looked him
straight in the eye when he came up.
He kept right on going, of course....

Coles himself, though very much alive, is a specimen of poet's poet who seems to live mostly in the minds of a too-meagre few; he avoided a recent launch of a new selection of his poems, although he did send a gracious note to be read aloud at the event: reason enough to remember him at a time when many of us poets, so quick to network, are all a-Twitter.

But there's another place we can live, the poem proposes, and that's a painting, a work of art. It's a romantic notion, if not an original one; the songwriter Paul Buchanan once wished he could inhabit the first sixteen bars of Marvin Gaye's 'Inner City Blues'. Buchanan is on to something—have you heard those sixteen bars?—and so is Coles's speaker. It would be nice to have a 'patch of stony ground', to have a friend to murmur 'small comments' to, even if one senses the speaker, unlike the moon gazers, could never be content with such modest real estate. '[H]ow willingly would I have spent my life/as they have,' are the words of someone at the end of a nomadic life.

I myself am no nomad, and could settle in any number of works of art: Miles Davis's 'Moon Dreams'; Patrick Leigh Fermor's travelogue *A Time of Gifts*; the Viennese rubble of the film *The Third Man*; the leafier stretches of *Astral Weeks*; the lost world that Louis Armstrong's 'West End Blues' trumpets; the brief crescendo that opens up, like some clearing, at the end of I think it's Tom Verlaine's long, winding solo in the Television song 'Marquee Moon'. Maybe in a poem or two by Coles.

I would certainly enjoy spending time with Coles's speaker, who can be forgiven his use of cliché because he lives so fully in the moment—from dash to comma, but with none of the professional beatnik's programmatic approach to improvisation. 'My heart swells with—with what?' the speaker asks, searching it. (He comes up with 'envy, not much but some, also with admiration …'.) His genius is also his courage: counter to what's taught in the world of MFA workshops, he tells instead of shows, and isn't anxious about the fact that Friedrich's picture is worth more than a thousand words. Moreover, he knows when he can call on cliché and allow a heart to swell. 'So small and so undemanding—/this patch of stony ground has always contented them,' he explains, like some gallery guide tasked with giving the same tour over and over, but with no loss of enthusiasm and no resort to metaphor. ('How full their heads are with moon-thoughts!' is somehow filling, isn't it?) He would be a good friend, this guide who, having given us the moon, doesn't give us the slip and slink off to some other wing of the gallery.

Child's Play

One word that gets a lot of play in our critical writing—since the dawn of Derrida, anyway—is 'play' itself. We're often wanting more of it, not less, and the freer the play, the better. But I wonder if Eliot's old saw about free verse—'no verse is free for the man who wants to do a good job'—can be extended to the more general concept of play: no play is free for the man who wants to play well. Which is only to say: it's nice, maybe even necessary, to have some rules in which to wriggle, even if the rules are arbitrary and amount to little more than a Houdini's self-imposed straitjacket. The children at play in Suzanne Buffam's poem 'Play', from her debut book, *Past Imperfect*, have the fun they have because of the rules they set for themselves. They don't escape from this play unscathed—and neither does the reader—but then, play doesn't always end in pleasure. The poem, in other words, only *looks* like child's play:

> He has put his shirt on backwards and allowed her,
> just this once, to touch his face. Her arms
> reach through the empty sleeves and in
>
> this game, they've become his. His hands
> hang empty at his sides. They share the body
> of one child. The mirror gives back one body
>
> of two minds. One sees the other's fingers
> find his eyes and knows to hold them closed
> until she's finished with the lids. Because
>
> she's seen it done before, she knows to still
> the chin while filling in the other's lips, although,
> this time, she's working blind. She stills him

with a finger and he feels his own chin quiver
when she laughs. And since she can't see
where she's been, the colour thickens in some places

and in others doesn't take. They name this face.
They dream up something ugly and it sticks.

The girl in this poem can't just do whatever she pleases. She
can't look to see if she's colouring within the lines of her co-player's
eyelids and lips—and the co-player, the boy, can *only* look at what
she's doing, can only offer up the lines in which to colour: the template, the field of play. How boring this game would be if she could
see him or he could guide her; how boring if they were free and this
was no game but, rather, one kid scribbling away on another, oblivious to the borders proposed by eyelids and lips. Anarchic scribbling
is giddy fun for a time—remember the feeling when, as a child, you
exceeded a colouring book's suggested boundaries?—but it can
quickly exhaust itself and result in chaos. The kids in Buffam's
poem, however, create and manage a controlled chaos.

Further, the face they fashion startles not because it's smeared all
over with lipstick, but because the lipstick (or whatever they're using)
'thickens in some places//and in others doesn't take'—because the
face they paint comes *close* to some standard of beauty (albeit an arti-
ficial standard, set by the kids or the society working through them).
Maybe this is merely how such Frankensteins work: they startle us not
because they are formless, like the horror movie mist that will produce a tentacle; they startle us because they cleave close to, even as
they fail to realize, a norm. Social norms, of course, are slightly different than a game's rules, which can be altered easily enough; social
norms are the rules that have atrophied and calcified and assumed a
sinister crust of normalcy. They have the gall to judge the things that
fall short of them, 'ugly'.

The poem itself cleaves close to, even as it fails to realize, a metrical norm, a rough pattern of iambs—'the ghost', to steal from Eliot
again, 'of some simple metre [that] should lurk behind the arras in
even the "freest" verse.' Buffam can play with our expectations only
by first establishing them. Or, put another way, she can pull the rug

out from under the reader only by first weaving one. Or, put yet *another* way, she can break the rules only by first observing some. For example, when Buffam ends the first tercet by describing how the girl's 'arms/reach through the empty sleeves and in', the sense is so seemingly self-sufficient, many readers may momentarily hear an end-stopped line that describes a completed motion of 'wriggling through and in'. But the word 'in' also comes to serve a phrase in the next tercet—'this game'. In other words, that line we may have heard as end-stopped—if only for a microsecond—turns out to be enjambed. The reader of Buffam's poem, like its 'blind' girl, enjoys the feeling of being slightly off balance, of lacking some crucial byte of information, such as the word 'two' in line seven, a surprise after the previous repetitions of 'one'. Buffam's thoughtful line breaks get inside of, and play with, the reader's head.

Appropriately, Buffam keeps the basic building blocks of her poem, the words, simple; they're a lot like the sort of blocks with which a lot can be done when someone at play is left to her own devices. Deceptively dull words like 'still' and 'chin' and 'filling' and 'lips', when placed in careful sequence, strengthen one another. They are the pieces that go together. They interlock.

The poem ends and the child's play turns ugly—the poem's last trick on us. Perhaps these kids have disturbed a previously dormant ugliness within themselves, the monster that's released whenever well-mannered children are stranded on islands and left to their own government for too long. Buffam's poem's kids were smart to follow the rules of their game for a time—the game does look fun!—but in giving their creation an ugly name, they seem only to reinforce some more insidious norm.

Or perhaps in birthing a body of two minds, they've undergone a growth spurt, and attained, unintentionally, a newer, darker notch of maturity. Is this what being in love will be like? The question doesn't occur to the kids, but perhaps it occurs to us and suggests a much different thread of readings of 'Play'. More likely and literally, Buffam's poem traces—masterfully so—the general arc of the play of children, which can end abruptly (and often in tears, even bruises, though not just the physical kind). Whatever else this startling poem does, it assures us that the pleasures of play are not free.

Lost and Found

In the audio commentary for his film *Two-Lane Blacktop*, cult director Monte Hellman notes the great advantage of working with 'non-actors' like James Taylor and Dennis Wilson, innocent amateurs who don't try to act. The great advantage of the speaker in Brian Bartlett's recent poem, 'Dear Georgie', is the fact that he doesn't know he's in a poem. If only more poems' speakers sounded like him, a natural who's not angling for Academy recognition. Poems' speakers usually sound like poets.

But Bartlett's guy probably never expected to be heard by the likes of us. In this sense, he's less heard than overheard, less addressing a world than working out a worldview, his only audience, his sister Georgie, even if his questions lack question marks and the 'dialogue' between the two looks like it's one way—his way. He's no narcissist, though. He is—was—a very real person, named Hermon Lawrence, and 'Dear Georgie' is a found poem, made up of sentences recovered from his letters to Georgie. We don't have her responses; not here, anyway. But let's listen in to the half we do have—one side of a once-lost exchange, which is now left-justified:

Dear Georgie

(From letters written in October 1918 by Hermon Lawrence of Bayside, New Brunswick, to his older sister, Georgie Bartlett, while he was training—as he detailed at the end of each letter—in 'the 3rd Heavy Canadian Battery, Composite Bridge, Witley Camp, Surrey, Eng.')

The war news have been good for quite awhile
but I dont think it can be fought
to a finish this fall.

I havent yet got that box you mailed Aug 10
and was about giving it up until today
when Tom Walker told me he just received

a box mailed July 7th, a jar of strawberries in it.
They hadnt put the wire clip over the cover—
well the strawberries had run all through

and spoiled it. A shame to throw it all away.
The first of the week I saw a play,
'Lucky Durham.' The main thing is to have

the parts well acted. I suppose I wont
be satisfied to see moving pictures.
Plays will be apt to spoil me.

I heard a fine illustrated lecture on Pompeii,
Rome and Naples. The lecturer had a lantern
with slides, views all down the west coast of Italy,

Vesuvius. Nearly all the beauty of Europe
isnt natural, but the work of man. Very different
from the beauty of America. I want to see

more of America, if I can arrange to
without too much trouble.
The Hotels Cecil and Savoy on the Strand

are the best hotels in London. I wasnt in them
but on the grounds around them.
I would like to spend about 24 hours

in one. When we get to our new camp
we will all have heavy horses.
The worst part is cleaning the harness,

all the steel will have to be kept shining.
One is apt to have a few tumbles at first
over the jumps. The weather changes very quick—

one can never tell in the morning what kind of day
it will be. Oh how are the apples this year.
Have they had a very large crop.

Sometimes I sit in one of the chairs
in front of the fireplace—they have been keeping
a fire lately—and go over the times we had

in my mind. I would like to farm just as we did
but there will have to be some change.
It wont do for Dwight and I to go on working

together. That will have to be settled later.
The first thing for me to take a hand in settling
is this business over here.

It would be nice to think we've tuned in to some pure signal here. But Bartlett's speaker—let's call him, but not confuse him too much with, Hermon—is a composite, edited together by Bartlett from different letters. But edited with care. Too often, found poetry functions like a forwarded email, which foists some bit of text upon us as if the mere fact of the foisting is reason enough to read the text. The 'finding' of a successful found poem, however, is comparable to the writing of a more traditional lyric—it takes serious effort since the poet, in seeing poetry where no one else does, is essentially creating, is freeing a shape from its shaggy, obscuring context (as sculptors do; as Yeats, lining Pater's prose, did).

This takes taste, and Bartlett, a born sampler, has done us a favour by identifying and salvaging only the choicest bits in Hermon's letters. In the process, he has hit upon a winning mix: for example, the alliteration of 'fought', 'finish', and 'fall'. But it's not just about finding the words that go together. Bartlett calls 'Dear Georgie' a 'found-reconstructed' poem, which means he has made interventions. His well-judged lining in the first tercet enacts a cascade of ever-shorter lines, as well as a quiet tension: the tercet manages the 'finish' the war can't seem to. Further, the choice of 'fought' anticipates the choice of other, upcoming words, including 'got', 'box', 'Aug', and 'Tom', giving Hermon's voice some assonance, some coherence. Good choices gird this poem.

But Bartlett's to be commended for his apparent restraint, too, for not touching up lines like:

I havent yet got that box you mailed Aug 10
and was about giving it up until today
when Tom Walker told me he just received

a box mailed July 7th, a jar of strawberries in it.

It would be hard for someone who is consciously *after* a poem to come up with constructions as subtly disruptive as Hermon's. Even the typical Language poet, in disrupting the sentence, probably goes further than necessary. In the above example, the word 'giving' (replacing some more appropriate choice like 'to give') is snag enough, and Bartlett lets it do its estranging work on us. Consider, too, the awkward but natural beauty of lines like: 'Nearly all the beauty of Europe/isnt natural, but the work of man.' As *Two-Lane Blacktop*'s director says of one of his non-actor's improvisations, 'You can't write dialogue like this.' You can't write dialogue like Hermon's either, or anyway, it would be hard. Bartlett, I'm guessing, knows the gift he's got in these letters.

What's telling (and maybe alarming) about Hermon's European travelogue is how seemingly unconcerned it is with the political theatre of its day, preferring instead a more escapist theatre. The war is hinted at, and cleanly contained, in the ominous phrase, 'this business over here', which Bartlett cleverly withholds until the very end where it casts its shade backward, dimming the more trivial moments, including the theatre criticism, the lecturer's talk. Also, a less bloody blood-drama (a drama for bit players, brothers on farms the world over) is buried between lines like 'It won't do for Dwight and I to go on working//together. That will have to be settled later.'

But Hermon isn't Stevens, the butler-let-out-on-a-road-trip in *The Remains of the Day*, oblivious to the news of the day. (He's not even *Two-Lane Blacktop*'s drag racers, Taylor and Wilson, motoring across an America to which they remain unconnected.) Hermon wants to see America. He's a sensitive, curious young man, the sort who sits by fires and goes over the times he's had in his already-nostalgic mind. 'I suppose I wont/be satisfied to see moving pictures,' he writes, resigned to the only culture he has known—the only culture he *may* know if he doesn't make it through the last October (not to mention November) of the war. Or maybe he's just a vinyl man with slight pretensions—as young men can be—and has no time for the newfangled. He's certainly painstaking as he puts his life in order. Consider the laboured repetition in the lines, 'I wasnt in them/but on the grounds around them,' which emphasizes a touching struggle for inconsequential precision.

Hermon, it turns out, is the poet's great uncle. But had Hermon been a hoax, Bartlett still could claim the creation of something human, a creation whose queries—'Oh how are the apples this year./Have they had a very large crop'—are made all the more poignant by their lack of question marks. (It's as if history puts a period on questions that can no longer be answered.) 'Dear Georgie' is no mere conceptual stunt; it's a great Canadian war poem. As for Hermon, he ought to be left in peace for the poem he didn't write and, paradoxically, praised for the one he did. Consider him both lost and found.

Griffin Poetry Prize Field Notes

'We're just casing the thing,' says the very short and very old woman. She's standing with a slightly taller, slightly younger woman in front of a growing line of ticket holders. We have assembled at the Macmillan Theatre for the 2008 Griffin Poetry Prize reading, where nine poets are scheduled to read from shortlisted books. Tomorrow, two of them—one Canadian and one non-Canadian—will each receive a $50,000 cheque at a gala dinner. I ask the next person in line, a middle-aged woman, who she's come to hear. 'All of them!' she replies.

'I don't know any of the poets,' confesses a well-dressed woman as we file into the theatre. But she figures this is a good place to discover them. Her confession is a reminder that John Ashbery, the evening's star reader, may be a household name, but maybe only in households that subscribe to *The New Yorker*. I grab a seat close to the stage and settle in.

On stage, tasteful lighting picks out a podium as well as a few chairs and a couple of sofas. Six pillows, divided between the sofas, spell out 'P-O-E' and 'T-R-Y' in the same multicoloured font as the Griffin logo. Above the sofas, vertical banners, one for each nominee, hang wafting gently. I ask the young lady on my left who she's here to see. Before she can reply, the old woman on *her* left, who gathers that I'm 'press', leans across and informs me that this young lady is not only her granddaughter but a poet in her own right. This forces the young lady into a fit of denial.

The grandmother, wearing a black blouse and single strand of pearls, has a habit of steadying her hand on her granddaughter's knee and leaning towards me so that she can point out celebrities in the audience, like Michael Ondaatje and Susan Swan. I think the grandmother senses that I'm new at this and need a scoop. I pretend like I've already spotted them and feign boredom. Of course, when the grandmother's not looking, I hustle over to ask Ondaatje who he likes tonight. He replies, almost before I can finish the question, 'All of them!'

I thought you might say that, I say. He pauses to reconsider. 'None of them?' He laughs. Then, more seriously: 'All of them.'

I try Susan Swan, who, thankfully, has an opinion. She's backing David McFadden. 'He's been overlooked for years as a poet and a prose writer,' she explains. She adds that she hasn't actually *read* any of the nominated books yet, but she plans to in the next few days, which is a bit of a relief since I haven't read the books either. The nominees now take the stage all at once, like members of a folk-rock supergroup. I head back to my seat.

John Ashbery goes first. He's wearing olive pants, a navy blazer, a blue shirt, and a red tie. His famous description of himself (just 'like everybody else') is dramatically sharpened by his age (he's an octogenarian) and visible frailty (he's slow to the podium). As he reads poems from his shortlisted book, *Notes from the Air: Selected Later Poems*, he inhales audibly after every line or two. But the twinkle in Ashbery's eyes still resembles the one I've seen reproduced on book jackets—somewhere between mischievous and mildly startled. He's also sharp enough to sense the sort of church this is.

'I grew up listening to the radio, especially the CBC,' he says, drawing murmurs of approval. 'So I've always felt close to Canada even though I haven't been here very much.' He then banters with the audience over the correct pronunciation of 'Newfoundland' before deciding, with charming stubbornness, 'I won't change my pronunciation tonight,' which gets a big laugh. His poems are okay, but their titles—'Interesting People of Newfoundland'—are the real crowd-pleasers. He should just read those.

The biggest laughs of the night go to American poet Elaine Equi, who reads next from her selected poems, *Ripple Effect*. She has short, shorn hair and approaches the podium wearing a baggy black T-shirt and black slacks. I'm bracing myself to learn about some politically disadvantaged group, but then she opens her mouth and declares—'Ohmigosh, this is completely awesome!'—which oxygenates the room wonderfully. She proceeds to offer up matter-of-fact facts like: 'When I try to write longer poems sometimes I just paste shorter ones together' and 'I don't often rhyme but in this poem I made up for it because every line rhymes.'

The poems themselves are so short and shorn of effect they're basically jokes. 'Perversely Patriotic', for instance, goes like this—

Terrorism has ruined
S&M for me.

Now it just seems
like watching
the news.

—and absolutely *kills*. Equi's the Sarah Silverman of this crowd but, like any comic, she's only as good as her last joke. Still, I suspect she would make more money doing stand-up and horsing around in her hometown of NYC than playing 'dark horse' next to Ashbery, the favourite tonight.

Scott Griffin introduces a last-minute stand-in for Clayton Eshleman, who's been shortlisted for his translations of César Vallejo. Eshleman is apparently guiding people to a cave in France. I don't know what this means, nor do I catch the stand-in's name, and Griffin offers no blurb. The stand-in reads with passion, but the performance is undercut by his sporty sweater, a red number that zips at the neck. It's a nice top, but he still looks like he was roped in off the street.

After reading a poem from his nominated book (yet another career retrospective) and drawing some weak applause, the next reader, David Harsent, tells the audience, 'If you want to, you can save those little ones for a big one at the end,' which is a nice thing to say and makes us laugh. Harsent, a bespectacled white-haired Brit, reads another one and draws more weak applause. 'Okay, so don't hold back,' he says dryly.

After the intermission, American poet Robert Hass pays tribute to Korean poet Ko Un, the recipient of the Lifetime Recognition Award, though given the mean age of the nominees on stage (57.7) and the fact that all but one of the shortlisted books are career retrospectives, the Griffin *itself* kind of feels like a lifetime recognition award this year. Ko Un is short and wears a large, powder blue blazer, which really brings home the enduring repercussions of trade embargoes. With Hass serving as translator, Ko Un recites some lines about maple leaves, before proclaiming: 'I've come to this country and want to become a maple leaf, too.' This brings the house down. Like good touring showmen, the international nominees seem obliged to reassure the locals that they have a nice town.

Canada's Robin Blaser is up next. He wears khakis, a brown blazer, and a pink dress shirt. Blaser is eighty-three, so it's another slow trip to the podium. He mumbles that he feels 'drunk', asks, 'Is it evening yet?' and says that George Bowering, one of the judges, told him not to 'mumble'. It's the sort of shtick available only to the really old, those who've earned the right to make fun of their well-meaning minders. His voice is great, too, a ravaged baritone that I'm told comes from years of smoking. It has a lulling effect, though, and the poems from his *Collected Poems*—full of vague words like 'earth' and 'water' and 'grief'—blur together.

The penultimate readers—Nicole Brossard along with her two translators, Robert Majzels and Erin Mouré—appear to have coordinated. All three wear dark colours, though Brossard works a red top and, flanked by the other two, gives the impression of an ex-politician still important enough to merit a security complement. At any rate, Majzels is the severe one, Mouré, the charmingly awkward one with great bangs, and Brossard, the calm axle. The three poets take turns in front of the mike, talking over one another, overlapping French with English. It's a neat trick but, as with Blaser's voice, it's hard to concentrate on the poetry: the performance both lulls and distracts.

David McFadden, the last poet, seems the most nervous. He's a short man—the mike's almost eye level—and wears a dark suit, a red dress shirt, and an oversized yellow flower pinned to his lapel. His voice quavers a bit, but his poems sound nice enough, with crowd-pleasing references to doughnut shops, Toronto's Bloor Street, and rooftop dancing. A lot of the poetry tonight has been introduced as 'avant-garde', which, given the examples on hand, must mean mildly disjunctive imagery in the form of free verse or prose. Such poetry is surely preferable to what 'avant-garde' poetry usually means (funny noises), though much less entertaining.

Finally, Ondaatje takes the stage to present the nominees with leather-bound versions of their books, and before he opens his mouth, I duck out to beat the rush for Ashbery's autograph. (I don't even *like* Ashbery's poetry, and I have Ashbery fever.) I wind up at the head of a long line of people with bags of books they've brought to have signed, some by the Canadian nominees, which is a heartening sight. I have to repeat my request, but Ashbery does personalize my book.

* * *

'This is a private party,' says the very tall and very thick bouncer. I've just asked him if the door he's blocking is 55 Mill Street, but his reply is ambiguous. I walk down a door, where an art show appears to be underway. But the smokers outside send me back the way I came. This is the Distillery District, a block of converted warehouses by the lakeshore, which, in Toronto, means the middle of nowhere. The bouncer seems annoyed to see me again.

'What are you looking for?'

I say that I'm covering the Griffin Poetry Prize awards for *Maisonneuve* and is this it? He still looks annoyed, which may just be The Effective Bouncer's way, but then he disappears inside only to return, a moment later, with a woman in evening wear. This *is* the Griffin, then. But the woman in the evening wear says that things are running late and dinner hasn't been served yet and would I mind coming back in forty minutes when the awards will be announced. Since I was nice enough (I thought!) to arrive after dinner, as instructed, and since this is the middle of nowhere, a neighbourhood from which even the homeless appear to have fled, the woman in the evening wear's news is a little distressing. I must look a little distressed, too, because, on second thought, she wonders if there *is* an extra seat at the media table, which, it turns out, is half-empty, and will pretty much stay that way for the rest of the night.

And once I do make it to that seat, the wait staff, a very professional lot, bombard me with attention and wine and super-tender veal, which is pleasantly confusing, given the vaguely hostile greeting at the door. But then the room itself is pleasantly confusing. One of the journalists I'm sitting with likens it to a thirties cabaret and half-expects a chorus line to snake around some corner. I think it's closer to the kind of party a film mogul would've thrown during the silent era. There are palm fronds in one corner of the room, multi-coloured ribbons dangling like seaweed from the walls, a precariously tall flower in a slender vase sprouting from the centre of each table, and a giant feather on each plate, which, on closer inspection, is actually a pen. The lights overhead keep changing, working through the rainbow, or the Griffin brand's colour scheme, and this means my super-tender veal keeps changing colour, too, which is a bit disorienting. On stage, the podium resembles a fibreglass harp without strings.

I ask the nice, short-haired blonde from the Canada Council, sitting next to me, if she'll give me a quote about the Griffin, and after some soul-searching, she seems to decide it probably can't hurt too much. It's a good quote, by the way—optimistic, on-message, full of praise for the Griffin's international scope—but would look better posted on the Griffin's Web site. The journalists at my table, from the big newspapers, have already written their articles and are really just waiting for two pieces of information—i.e. the winners—which they'll plug into their 'copy'. (One of them will do this on-site, retreating with his laptop to a corner.) Then, they'll do something to the 'copy' called 'massaging'. They seem to regard me and my Moleskine as cute. (They won't open *their* notebooks until right before the awards are announced.) One of them asks me when my 'filing date' is. I think that means 'deadline', so I tell him two weeks. Another journalist, wearing circular frames and a pinstripe dress shirt, guesses that I must be doing an 'atmosphere piece'. I tell him, yes, that's right (though I'll have to Google 'atmosphere piece' when I get home).

When the awards finally begin, a short film starts up on the room's multiple projection screens. The film represents the only low-budget concession of the whole event. It begins with grainy, black-and-white images of a forest, like the one in *The Blair Witch Project*, scored with a creepy melody, picked out on what sounds like a marimba. A harmonium (I think) enters the mix, and then an electronic 2/4-ish beat kicks in. The film's montage cycles through images of brooks babbling and hands typing and, finally, a lone hand writing out the names of the Griffin trustees (e.g. 'Atwood',

'Ondaatje', etc.) with a brush. It's nice, but does look like it was edited on some film student's laptop.

Before the awards are given out, though, the team of Ko Un and Hass takes the stage. The very prolific Ko Un wants to read some poems he has spontaneously composed at his table, and Hass is going to translate. One of the poems goes: 'As soon as I got here I got drunk. This place used to be a distillery.' Then he reads an excerpt from an older poem: 'Going down/I saw the flower/that I hadn't seen going up.' He finishes with a longer piece, in Korean, called 'Time with Dead Poets'. The poem goes on some, so if you don't know Korean, you kind of have to politely wait it out. David Harsent has taken to playing with his giant feather pen.

Next, Liverpool's Paul Farley, one of last year's nominees, gives a witty speech on the struggles of the poet. Given the way poets are so lavishly treated at the Griffin, Farley wonders if Canada's screen-writers are, as in a certain Martin Amis story, the ones who have to send their work to little magazines. He wears a dark suit with an open-necked white dress shirt and no tie. A bit of stubble roughens up an otherwise cherubic face. He seems kind of cool, actually.

But then George Bowering takes the stage to announce the inter-national winner. Wearing a dark blazer over a yellow shirt and brown pants, he consults a slip of paper and reads, 'Make sure you feed the dog before you …' and then makes a bumbling show of hav-ing the wrong slip, which gets a weak laugh and does seem a little vaudevillian after Farley's genuinely funny speech.

John Ashbery wins, as expected, and has to be physically helped onto the stage. The thunderous applause causes my table's tall flower to fall on me, which I'm hoping Ko Un witnessed and will duly trans-form into a few lines of folk wisdom. Thankfully, the other journal-ists pitch in to lift the flower off of me. Ashbery wears an outfit simi-lar to last night's—navy blazer and olive pants—and once again mentions that he grew up listening to CBC radio.

'I'm really very fond of Lake Ontario,' he adds, among other nice things.

Robin Blaser wins, too, and, like Ashbery, has to be helped onto the stage (this isn't your kids' Griffin). He consults a piece of paper—'I wrote this out just in case'—and seems to get choked up.

He tells the crowd, 'You don't get to be a winner very many times in your life.' Even if you can't keep a line of Blaser's poetry in your head, it's still a touching moment. I try my luck at mingling.

One prominent US poet in attendance, a regular contributor to *Poetry* magazine, wonders if the applause for Ashbery sounded louder than the applause for Blaser. But then the poet's wife reminds him that he's talking to a journalist, and I lose the quote. Still, I'm secretly thrilled someone thinks I'm a journalist. I snoop around some more.

'I was very happy that Ashbery won,' says the poet A.F. Moritz, sitting at a table. 'The choices seemed to represent a certain freedom of creativity and association, and could be seen as a riposte to formalist notions.' Of course, James Lasdun, on behalf of his fellow judges, had previously assured the crowd that 'none of us was looking to promote any particular style or aesthetic.' The judges—Lasdun, Bowering, and the Mexican poet Pura López-Colomé—were just looking for 'good poetry'. But I don't have to snoop around too much further to overhear some very reasonable questions like: how could three judges realistically read, in any depth, the 509 books that were submitted to the Griffin?

I ask Barry Callaghan, the publisher of Exile Editions, if he has an opinion about the night. His partner, the artist Claire Weissman Wilks, seems to think my asking the question isn't a good idea. Callaghan bows his head nearly to the table, in apparent distress. Then, he lifts his head and says, crisply, 'I best keep my opinions to myself.'

Can I quote you on that?

'Yes.'

The dance floor's open, but no one's on it. Dinner ran late, and it *is* eleven on a work night. Last year, rumour has it, some of the nominees danced to music by bands like Rage Against the Machine. I'm hoping (but also kind of betting) that that's not going to happen this year, and so I go find my cab.

War of the Words

The other night, your correspondent found himself—geographically, but spiritually, too—in Toronto's financial district. It was rush hour, and professionals in suits and business casual were streaming past. Only one busker (on alto sax) and a few scalpers held their ground; the rest were off to other pleasures: home, dinner, *Cougar Town*. You can feel a little silly in such bustling company, especially when you're on your way to a poetry reading. But you can feel a little superior, too, like the speaker in that great report of rush hour, 'Crossing Brooklyn Ferry' by Walt Whitman: a sensitive soul stuck in traffic.

Down by the Harbourfront Centre—where twenty poets were set to read in what was being called a quote Battle of the Bards—were actual ferries, with names like Mariposa Belle and Empress of Canada splashed on their hulls. But they didn't appear to be going anywhere, these lashed-up hulks. A box office for boat tours was shuttered. There were new condominiums everywhere, which is to say: no signs of life. It was nearly April, the cruellest month. It seemed hard to believe that fun could be had down here.

But then a grown woman walked by, wearing black boots, a black skirt, a striped purple hoodie and, for good measure—a poet's measure—a beret. And your correspondent knew that he was in the right place for a good time.

* * *

The Battle of the Bards also goes by the name 'Poetry NOW', in deference to one of its sponsors, Toronto's NOW magazine. But most people in the know have elected to call it 'Poetry Idol', in deference to its spiritual forefather, the motherland's Simon Cowell. Twenty published poets, randomly selected by lottery, read for five minutes each, before a panel of three judges and an audience of some two hundred. (When poets pool their resources—that is, when twenty of them guilt their friends and family *en masse*—they can get up a healthy number.) Unlike those on *American Idol*, the judges of Poetry Idol don't offer their charges the reality check of immediate feedback. There's no retired Abdul to tear up at the turn in your sonnet; no caustic Cowell, wearing Armani and his best scowl, to suggest you try your hand at haiku. There are certainly no phone lines for the audience at home to tie up. (There's no audience at home.) The judges convene in closed session and anoint a winner the next day. It may be that they wish to spare published poets the indignity of a dressing down in public, one that might include frank notes on wardrobe, presentation, beret; it may be that teenagers who aspire to be pop stars are more emotionally mature than published poets, and thus better equipped to take constructive criticism.

Your correspondent took part in the Battle of the Bards a couple of years ago, and his stomach recalls the churning. But when he got up on stage, he was blinded by the lighting rig, which left him with the sense that he was weirdly—wonderfully!—alone. That's how professional performers do it, he thought. They arrange to have stars in their eyes at all times.

* * *

The woman with the striped purple hoodie and beret was a one-off; most of the people milling about before the reading, in the lobby of the Harbourfront Centre, could dress themselves. The older couples favoured dark sweaters and jeans, and the men had their arms crossed, as if bracing for an art film. The younger attendees pulled off skinny jeans and smart side-bags. A trapped bird was flitting about the exposed beams of the lobby ceiling. By now, it's probably been captured by quatrain.

What brought you out tonight? your correspondent asked an older couple.

'We're going to do the wave later,' the husband said. The wife laughed.

A young brunette with bangs and pink barrettes—sitting on the floor of the lobby, next to her knapsack—seemed out of place. Do you go to these events often? your correspondent asked.

'No.'

Are you into poetry?

'No.'

Just off the lobby, in the Brigantine Room, your correspondent stole a look at the judges' tables. On each was something called a 'Score Sheet', with the names of the competing poets running down the left side, and two blank columns down the other: one with the heading 'score out of 5', the other, 'comments'. The five-star system surely beats the inverted thumb by which ancient, imperial Eberts condemned the talent to the lions. But how does a poet earn her five stars? Your correspondent asked one of the judges—Toronto's Poet Laureate, Dionne Brand, who came topped with a 180° spray of grey hair—what she was looking for that night.

'Something surprising,' the Poet Laureate said. 'A reading in which the poem's intentions are fully regarded. And maybe something where the different layers of meaning in the work are evident.'

Are you looking to be entertained?

'I don't really like that word,' the Poet Laureate said. Indeed, she seemed puzzled by the premise of the question.

* * *

Before the Common Era, most of the poets who read at the Battle of the Bards would've made good lunch for lions. But in AD 2011, they had mere cubs to fear, a pack of young poets and editors, sitting at the back of the Brigantine Room, exchanging snickers and a flask of something.

Your correspondent tried to focus on the stage. A recurring, pan-poet reference to the tongue reassured the audience that it was attending to something like poetry or, at least, something sensual, oral. Gloria Alvernaz Mulcahy described 'tongues ready/for sweet juices' and a 'longing for your tongue/to slide into sea salt and sweat'. Another poet talked about being 'untethered by tongue'. Still another, about the 'unfading tongues of old women'. Still *another*, about 'the tack of saliva between tongue and reed'. Still *another*, about a 'fault-finding tongue'.

A few poets did more than speak in tongues, though. The English-born Jill Battson copped to the appeal of *Martha Stewart Living*, then read her poem, 'Why You Should Be Jailed, Martha'.

David Groulx absolutely killed with the line, 'John Wayne is trying to kill me.' (Groulx is part Ojibwe.) Heather Cadsby—a prim, older poet who held forth on feeding ducks—let fly the phrase 'it's fucking whole grain', which worked like the report of a rifle to wake up the audience. Kildare Dobbs read a thing about Giacomo Casanova that actually scanned and rhymed, a first for the night. 'He washes well and shaves his cheek,' said Dobbs,

> and changes stockings once a week
> but nothing masks the pheromone
> special to Giacomo alone.
> Two nuns a hundred yards away:
> one whiff—they're in the family way ...

In other words, some entertainment—by way of witty couplets or the stray bullet of a killer line—can be had when nineteen randomly selected poets gather. But to what extent did the audience respond to the performances, as opposed to the poetry? Would the poetry have been as funny had the audience encountered it on the page? Although people laughed at the bit about the nuns, it was hard not to feel that Dobbs—like his witty couplets—was a curio from some other epoch, carried forward and rooted for on principle. (Dobbs served in World War II and needed to be helped on stage. These days, he serves to personify the State of Formal Poetry.) It was also hard not to feel that the prim, older poet—the one who held forth on feeding ducks and said 'fucking'—got the laugh she got because one doesn't expect such language from prim, older poets who hold forth on feeding ducks. Your correspondent worried about separating the Poetry from its Idol, the couplets from their context, the swears from the sweet lady. He worried that the Poetry wouldn't survive on its own, on the page, without the heat lamp of a human mouth.

At times, an electric personality defibrillated some flat lines, kept them beating. Gary Barwin, the second reader to take the stage, was podium-ready and launched straightaway into a persona that couldn't help but hiss, over and over, 'I make it rain!' He had long grey hair, a beard to match, an untucked dress shirt; he looked a bit like the actor who played Bob in *Twin Peaks*, a feral hepcat. But when he got to the end of the poem, where the speaker notes that he's 'set his hair on fire', Barwin turned to the audience and said calmly, smoothly, 'Thank you, I'm a travel agent....' The audience laughed, put at ease. It's okay if you felt weird about all that, Barwin's one-liner assured them. But that travel agent, sitting across from you on the subway at rush hour? Beware. He has inside himself a Whitman or, at least, Wereman.

Your correspondent was surprised to discover that Robyn Sarah, whose work he'd read and liked, had agreed to perform. Sarah—a sixty-two-year-old Montreal poet, born in New York—has put out many collections; has had work all over, in *Jacket*, *The Hudson Review*, *The New Criterion*, *The Norton*; even published early books by the likes of August Kleinzahler and A.F. Moritz. Although your correspondent participated in a previous Battle of the Bards and found it a positive experience, he felt that a poet of Sarah's stature should have better things to do on her Wednesday p.m. Indeed, the night before, another poet, about the same age as Sarah, had confided that he'd instructed his publisher *not* to submit his name to the draw for the Battle of the Bards.

Your correspondent tried to talk to Sarah, before the reading, but she was suffering from a headache. When she took to the stage and confronted the bank of lights, she winced. (Some people aren't disposed to stars in their eyes.) 'I have a migraine,' she told the crowd, with a slight laugh. She had on a grey scarf; her silver hair was pulled back.

'I'm reading from *Pause for Breath*—which is *not* a yoga book.' The audience had heard a lot of banter that night; this was pretty much all of Sarah's. She had good poems and the good sense to get out of their way. One piece, about going to an emergency room for a splinter, got laughs, not because she'd dressed a painful anecdote or brought a bandaged thumb to the podium; it got laughs because lines like these make a funny noise all their own:

> [W]e are here
> with our fiery-hot fingertip, red
> as a pepper (whose taut shiny pad
> feels like to burst open, to split
> like a sausage casing and spit

out its meaty insides)—as we wait
for a doctor to rule on our splinter:

all told, full five hours of fidget
for the sake of a digit.

And another poem, an exquisite sonnet, drew a murmur from the
audience. It begins with a speaker removing from her wall a friend's
gift of a 'sprig of unknown bloom ... mounted on black'. Later, at
the start of the sestet, the speaker informs us that,

after months of fearing to walk past
in case the stir should scatter it to bits,
I took it out to scatter it at last
with my own breath, and so to call us quits.
—Fooled! for the fluff was nothing but a sheath,
with tiny, perfect flowers underneath.

* * *

Sarah didn't win—that honour was shared by the 'I make it rain!' guy
and Groulx, he of the killer line. They secured readings of their own
and publicity for their books in the sponsoring weekly, which also carries ads for adult massages. A few others received invitations to return
to the Harbourfront Centre. But is it petty to want to know which
number, out of the five, Brand and the judges scored Sarah, this jour-
neyman poet? Is it boorish to want to demand a recount or lob the
stone of a 'boo'? Or is it merely entering into the spirit of an event that,
enjoying the brand identity, 'Battle of the Bards', would seem to
encourage a desire to see certain bards vanquished and certain others
crowned with braided sprigs of laurel, the way the ancients did it up?

Your correspondent fell to chatting with Sarah after the reading.
She was still suffering from the migraine. He and several others
guided her back to the nearest subway station, in the financial district, where she would be ferried away. By the station, the saxophonist and scalpers had long since decamped. Like Sarah, they'd offered
what entertainment they could.

TWO

All Ears: Phone Calls to an Old Poet

It was usually Mondays I spoke to the poet Samuel Menashe. We had a ritual: I would call to let him know I was ready for our talk; then he would call me back. I was a graduate student in Toronto, and Samuel—well, he was hardly well off either; he'd lived in a rent-controlled New York walk-up, with the bathtub in the kitchen, for fifty years. But the poet had a long-distance plan.

Sometimes our ritual broke down. I would sit there holding the phone, for one minute, two, waiting for Samuel's call. He would've entered my number wrong or been searching scraps of paper for it. (There wasn't yet the YouTube video of his apartment, but I had a notion the place was an affable mess.) Eventually, I would eat the long-distance charge and dial New York. The connection re-established, Samuel almost always sounded distressed. He would take my number down for the umpteenth time and repeat it to me slowly. (You would think I was a journalist for the *Times*.) I couldn't bring myself to ask him to try calling me back.

He was eighty-two by then. I was trying to interview a poet for a chapter of a dissertation. The year before, I'd gotten in touch for permission to reprint one of his poems in an anthology. I admired his work, but at that point, I figured I was going to do a dissertation on the San Francisco cult poet Weldon Kees. Samuel, a cult poet in his own right, pointed out that others had already written about Kees. 'Young man, why don't you work on *me*?' Samuel wondered aloud. *Letters to a Young Poet*, this wasn't. Still, he asked a good question. (Why *didn't* I work on him?) Plus, the nakedness of the appeal was somehow more honest than a poet's usual, more subtle angling for attention. It was sort of charming, even.

Samuel was guileless when it came to his career. After surviving World War II, he completed a doctorate at the Sorbonne and published his first book of poems in England, to some note. But he had a hard time securing a publisher in New York, where he spent the rest of his life in the walk-up. He taught a bit early on at Bard College, but was never a citizen of the creative writing world. Nor did he especially ingratiate himself to people with power. I don't think he went out of his way to make trouble. (He certainly didn't have the professional avant-gardist's feel for the strategically public salvo.) He probably just couldn't help himself. This one time, Samuel was walking down the street when he happened upon a poetry editor of *The New Yorker*. Now, your typical poet is going to want to be friendly, if not deferential, toward this powerful person. Samuel greeted her by reciting a poem of his. He was a great reciter of poetry.

'Didn't we publish that?' the editor is said to have asked.

'No, you didn't publish that,' Samuel replied. 'Moreover, you didn't publish my poems in the table of contents.' The editor stormed away. 'I was just trying to give her a flower,' he told me innocently.

As Samuel talked, I typed, the receiver between my neck and shoulder. At first, I think I felt I was doing something good: for an old man who could use the conversation and, more importantly, a flailing scholar (and fledgling poet) who could use an original topic. I was living at home then, working out of my sister's old bedroom, which I'd converted into a makeshift office. It was just me and my mother in the house; my father had suffered a paralyzing stroke and was laid up in long-term care. Heaps of books and paper rose from the floor. Some of the papers were handwritten drafts of poems that Samuel had sent. It only occurs to me now, typing this, that my sister's bedroom wouldn't have looked terribly different from Samuel's living space, except the walls were the pink of her childhood. (Samuel's walls were white and flaking, his furniture distressed beyond the point that a young, chic couple with money would find acceptable.) The rest of the house was pretty messy, too. My mother and I had surrendered it to the dust.

Beyond the clutter, the similarities stopped. My home was a bungalow in a suburb of Toronto—an unlikely place to be receiving calls and mail from a New York bohemian who'd once supplied Allen Ginsberg with addresses to visit in Europe, which the author of 'Howl' duly entered into what Samuel described to be 'a very well-ordered address book, the opposite of what I have.' That detail—

when it was delivered up—made me straighten a bit. (I'd often been skeptical of the rebel pose that poets like Ginsberg struck.) Samuel then told me about attending a reading of Ginsberg's. The famous Beat poet read a poem that he assured the assembled would be finished in heaven. 'I raised my hand,' Samuel said, 'and asked, "Why do you call it a poem on earth?"'

We talked in the morning, which was better for Samuel. He preferred to spend the rest of the day walking about New York, perhaps working out a poem in his mind—if there was a poem to be worked out. Central Park was a favourite destination, which he revealed to be the source of some of his splendid poems, like 'Forever and a Day':

> No more than that
> Dead cat shall I
> Escape the corpse
> I kept in shape
> For the day off
> Immortals take.

Actually, Samuel had seen a dead *squirrel*; 'cat' was merely the poet's elegant, one-syllable solution. (An amateur would've been faithful to the fact of the squirrel; Samuel's deference to the philosopher's trusted prop was a sign of faith in iconic forms.) But cat or no, you wouldn't guess the poem, so pared of particulars, had been proposed by a walk through Central Park. Samuel was an inveterate whittler of detail, and the Library of America's recent selection of his work—in an edition that's as smart and spare as one of those iconic Salinger paperbacks—conceals a tourist's guide of New York and its ghosts.

Samuel never married nor had children. I suspect that for New Yorkers of a certain generation, he was a kind of constant, an institution on foot, the neighbourhood *flâneur*. It's tempting to romanticize such a life. 'Are you attracted in any way to the image of Blake as a kind of outsider?' I asked him once. 'No, I would love to have been an insider,' he sighed without hesitation and (it should be recorded) an eye to his image: a good thing for a young poet to witness. Several times, he told me he wished he'd married, gotten a steady job at a college, and moved out of the walk-up that, he recalled all too often, his father had called a 'hovel'. My interview notes are silent on what I said in reply. 'You shouldn't say that,' is probably all I mustered. There isn't much else to say to a person who traded a life for poetry and maybe regrets the trade. (If there is, Canadian graduate school doesn't teach it.) My visions of a feel-good bestseller—*Mondays with Menashe*—were dissipating. I looked out the window of my sister's bedroom, as I often did when talking to Samuel, there to find two lawn ornaments, a plastic swan and rabbit, floundering in uncut grass.

Still, I don't think Samuel was depressed, as we often understand the term. ('I liked his precise use of the word hovel,' he said brightly of his father's dark comment.) Moreover, he was the sort who could say he'd be fine never waking up again, and *still* present as energetic, even positive, to use a much-abused word. He often launched into our conversations by observing that he was 'all ears', at which point he'd never fail to explain that he'd first heard that exotic expression on the lips of the late Russian poet Joseph Brodsky, with whom he sometimes had a 'friendly acquaintance'. But if Samuel circled back to some of the same well-trodden ground, it's because it was, in part, the turf on which he'd built his life. Time and again, he would tell of being seized by this or that phrase—some stray line of the Old Testament, Simone Weil, a relative long dead. He liked telling me about a particular visit from an aunt and a cousin. On parting, he'd tried to give his cousin a hearty farewell. His aunt, however, had leaned in.

'Don't waste your words,' the aunt whispered to Samuel. 'They fall to the ground/And there is no wind/To pick them up.'

'Isn't that unbelievable?' Samuel would exclaim to me, marvelling at his aunt's 'complete poem' (which he'd taken the liberty of lining through his emphatic pauses). It was that generous sense of wonder that led him to reproduce the sayings of his parents as epigraphs for a couple of his own poems. These parents, he said, were so far up the slope—of Parnassus, I think he meant—that he himself had to take but a step to plant a boot on the peak and become a poet. 'They weren't philistine clods, and I was the young poet. Nonsense. My father insisted that I had to be a misfit.'

Usually, though, Samuel didn't like talking influences. When I asked him which poets he read, he said, 'I glance at the poems in *The New Yorker*. Blake.... I used to know a lot of Hopkins by heart.' (A Hopkins had hauled him out of a funk, once.) In terms of contemporary poets, he mentioned Kay Ryan and Billy Collins. When I pressed him on specific poems, he conceded a Franz Wright in some number of *The New Yorker*. 'It was wonderful to me,' he said. But when I asked if he remembered the title, he said, 'No, no, but the point is it was "one poem." One poem can nourish me.' There was a time when he would throw a sheet over his bookcase to discourage guests from checking up on his reading. It may be that, having been neglected for so long, Samuel was wary of losing the attention of his interlocutors to other, more securely shelved poets.

He was certainly quiet on the war, especially the Battle of the Bulge, which took place in the Ardennes forest in the winter of 1944–45. It was some months of talking to Samuel before he got into specifics. I'll let him take over:

> The artillery was incessant, it was like a storm where the lightning never stops. And I was nineteen. You have to imagine what children we were. You were less mindful. And I came into this farmhouse where a remnant of some of the platoon was. And I'd never seen an earthen floor. I didn't know the term 'shock.' I sat down with my back against the wall. And my eyes met the sergeant's eyes. Our eyes met momentarily. And we looked away. And I knew then that I looked away because I knew that I was looking at somebody who was going to die very soon, and he looked away for the same reason.
>
> I've given you the background, but I don't provide that material in the poem 'Warrior Wisdom.' It's not necessary.

Then, he recited the poem:

> Do not scrutinize
> A secret wound—

Avert your eyes—
Nothing's to be done
Where darkness lies
No light can come.

Samuel didn't go in for confessional poetry, with its grievances, laundry lists, and one or two carefully curated details. (It wouldn't have occurred to him to remember the sergeant's name to us or assign his hair a colour.) This is sometimes the case with people who might have something worth confessing.

But Samuel wasn't an unconscientious man. He always asked about my father, who wasn't looking like he was going to recover the ability to walk. Plus, those drafts of poems he sent were a weekly wonder. I framed a couple of them; I have dozens more. In Neal Stephenson's novel *The Diamond Age*, one character's tossed-off and handwritten messages—Chinese characters done in brush stroke—are deemed priceless. Samuel, too, could will a work of art into being merely by copying out four or five lines in his elegant cursive.

Not that Samuel was a prolific letter writer. (He often declared that if his posthumous reputation depended on correspondence, he'd be done for.) He was more of an inveterate self-editor who, having altered a poem, often worried that the earlier, obsolete version would endure if he dropped dead before he could alert anyone to the edit. On more than one occasion, I received two or three drafts of the same poem in the space of a few days, each arriving separately and labelled with the time and date, overriding the last version. His notes, scrawled beneath the poems, hinted at a contest that occupies the aging artist—the race against time:

March 10, 2009

Dear Jason,

The attempt above was done quickly—a few hours between two days—and sent to you in haste

With my thanks
and my best wishes—
Samuel

9:10 AM, June 6, 2009

Dear Jason,

Is the merger [of two poems] above possible. It occurred five
minutes ago. I had to unseal the envelope & put it in.

Years ago I said all escapes are narrow.

Best wishes,
Samuel

4:35 PM, June 30, 2009

… 'Time Out of Mind' was finished a half hour ago—after a
week or two. (It will probably change by tomorrow.[)]

Best wishes,
Samuel

I hope we speak very soon

The drafts arrived with the frequency and force of gusts from Parnassus. Reading them—and imagining the octogenarian already racing to a mailbox to dispatch their replacements—I would absorb
some of Samuel's anxiety. I had better care for these, I thought; the
soldier-poet's struggle had recruited me.

But that was the war that had posted all that hard copy. It had
put a bayonet point on Samuel's sense of mortality. Many claim to
live as if each day was the only day: a boast. But Samuel really did
live that way. He wrote somewhere that he was amazed when confronted with the curiosity of people who carried on about their plans
for, say, the following summer; he was amazed they assumed they
would survive to see it.

The handwritten poems and revisions he sent weren't just
hedges against death; many of them were gifts, too. Having discovered that I especially liked a particular poem, he would reproduce it

for me. He would also dispatch poems to mark occasions. When I got married, he sent a beautiful lyric as a benediction:

Eaves at dusk
beckon us
to peace
whose house,
espoused,
we keep.

He even produced a fair copy of 'Forever and a Day', one of my favourites, and mailed it off. He was frank about his writing career, but he knew enough to please the fans he found. Noting his book was out of stock in some store, he would return with copies of his own. What's marvellous is not that he did this—don't we all front-face our accomplishments periodically?—but that he volunteered the fact to others.

The younger reader will have wondered why Samuel didn't just send his work—or answer my questions—by email. 'Young man,' he might've replied, 'I've never mastered more than the telephone, which is very handy.' Once or twice, I had the honour of transcribing some new poems for Samuel. He would've had these photocopied and mailed to *Poetry* magazine, which had recently given him the Neglected Masters Award, or *First Things*, the Catholic periodical that had taken a sudden interest in his work, much to his surprise. Sometimes he even wondered what I thought of a particular work in progress. He seemed genuinely interested in my opinion, this poet who had once earned the admiration of Robert Graves, Hugh Kenner.

I wonder now if Samuel found it odd, even dispiriting, that he was recounting his life to a young Canadian with limited influence and not, say, a crack interviewer from *The Paris Review*. But he never let show that he was anything less than grateful to be talking to me. Months after he'd answered all my questions, we continued to talk. In time, though, we fell out of touch. (I was still a couple of years from writing my chapter.) But I called in the summer of 2011 to let him know I was finally drafting it. By this point, Samuel was

living in a nursing home. He sounded frail, but elected to take down
my number and address dutifully. He asked about my father, as he
always had. (My father had passed away a few weeks before, which I
hated telling Samuel, given his own age and state.) He also asked, as
he often did, when I was coming to New York. I said, as I did too
many times, I was going to try for the fall. Would more drafts of new
poems arrive? He passed away a couple of weeks later.

On occasion, Samuel would try to pass off some line or image
out of which he'd never been able to make poetry. ('I never am concerned with originality,' Samuel often affirmed.) I hardly knew
what to do with these castoffs, though I was flattered to be
entrusted with them. Is this how an apprentice felt, when his
Renaissance mentor, thrusting some vellum his way, said, 'Here, see
what you can do with this sketch?' I was no apprentice, and
Samuel, no mentor. To be sure, students of literary history could lap
up some juicy anecdotes at his feet. He was a sharp observer of the
poetry world, and the sheer observation of such artifacts as Allen
Ginsberg's orderly address book confirms the keenness of Samuel's
eye. Indeed, in another life, he might have made a fine literary journalist. (After the war, he entertained aspirations to be a 'foreign
correspondent'.) But mentor? If Samuel had lessons to impart, they
weren't the sort the industrious MFA workshop, hammering away
at poems, wants to hear. There's a podcast in which Samuel steps
outside of his apartment and declares, 'I have nothing to add to this
day.... An old friend of mine, we're admiring the sunset, and she
says, "You should make a poem out of it." I said, "No! The sunset is
enough."'

One time, as he talked, I watched a snowfall build up in my
backyard. After I got off the phone—Samuel having signed off with,
'Good morning, my dear', the way he did—I noticed that the plastic
swan and rabbit were very nearly buried. All you could make out of
the rabbit were its ears. It was all ears.

The snowfall should have been enough, of course; but I couldn't
help but write up the moment anyway. There was even a line from
one of Samuel's letters that would make a perfect epigraph. I figured
I would show the poem to the old poet when I got it just right (and
maybe even typeset in a decent magazine). I would make the trip to

New York and thrust the publication into his hands. If only he had known what I was up to, he might have laughed. It's not always worth what you lose, getting poems right.

Two Minds

What would the critic William Logan make of the other William Logan, the poet who shares his brainpan? This is the sort of fantasy bloodsport the Internet likes to think on. Logan 'commits offenses for which he'd pillory any other poet,' says one website. '[I]f his critic ever reads his poetry, he's done,' says another. 'William Logan once wrote a review of William Logan's poetry that made William Logan cry,' submits a third.

Even an advocate can't help but see double. David Barber, dividing Logan in two, predicts that 'the baleful poet ... is bound to outlast the malevolent critic....' But an odd idea has stuck: to strike a poet-critic where it hurts (or to hit his sweet spot), one should aim at someone close to his heart—his inner bard. In other words, Barber takes for granted what Michael Hofmann peels off the underside of the critical consensus on another poet-critic: 'the callow, unexamined assumption' that a poet will always prefer his poems to his critical prose.

The talking heads should know better. Reflecting on his own reviews, Hofmann says, 'A lot of the articulacy and the connections and the nerves that might have gone on poems, have gone on these pieces.' To be sure, critical prose that's as stylish as Hofmann's may even *be* a form of poetry; here's the music critic Greil Marcus on a collection of writings by his late peer Lester Bangs: 'Perhaps what this book demands from a reader is a willingness to accept that the best writer in America could write almost nothing but record reviews.' You don't have to agree about Bangs to accept the idea that a writer can make art out of the minor genre he makes do with. There was a time when T. S. Eliot's canonical essay 'The Metaphysical Poets' was but a lowly book review, in an old number of the *Times Literary Supplement*. Now it's the stuff that Nortons are made of.

Still, the 'callow, unexamined assumption' persists. And those critics who go after William Logan—who's been called 'the most hated man in American poetry' for hating on some of America's most beloved poets—sometimes do so in the manner of a Mafia: they go after his loved ones. Indeed, I have read accounts of chilly, impersonal poems. But these adjectives can't possibly apply to warm, personal poems like 'The Ghost' and 'Wrapping Up' from *Strange Flesh* (2008), Logan's best book. They sure don't apply to the poem that *Poetry* printed in 2010, called 'The Box Kite':

> The lift, the very lift and pull of it!
> They'd wasted the summer morning,
>
> father and son in the devil's
> breath of July—gnats wheeling
>
> madly above the drive—pasting Sunday comics
> across the struts, like the canvas skin
>
> of a Sopwith Camel. Into the close-gnawn yard
> with its humpback boulder,
>
> they dragged it triumphantly, unreeling the twine
> until the contraption yanked itself
>
> from bald earth, high above
> the matchbox houses on the verge
>
> of woods and the sweet-smelling bog,
> to a height where a boy might peer over the horizon
>
> to Boston—and beyond, the ocean.
> The son was my father. I tottered at his legs,
>
> having borrowed his name and my grandfather's.
> They payed out the ramshackle affair

until it became a postage stamp. The line
burned a bloody groove into my palms,

the last time they stood at ease with each other.

Arriving as late as it does, the sentence 'The son was my father'
sends a jolt. The line 'The line burned a bloody groove in my palms'
leaves the brain with rope burn. The poem is not perfect (that
'sweet-smelling bog' could give off a more precise whiff) but the
afterglow of its brightest moments remains on the inside of one's eyelids: the 'Sunday comics … like the canvas skin//of a Sopwith
Camel', the 'postage stamp' of a faraway kite. 'The Box Kite' is the
work of a Jarrellian lightning strike.

But Logan seems to have accepted that live wires like 'The Box
Kite' may, because of his critical candour, be grounded for a time.
Asked if he thinks his 'criticism has hurt the reception of [his]
poetry,' Logan tells the interviewer, poetry-critic-may-care,

> I certainly hope so. Why write criticism if it's so trivial it
> doesn't have a cost? I've been warned, often enough, that
> writing criticism is suicide … yet I can't say my poetry has
> suffered in reviews, can't say I've faced real disfavour.
> Because criticism rouses passions, because it has more cur-
> rency (and is sometimes easier to understand), there are
> readers who think of me only as a critic. The poet mildly
> objects.

Logan then splits from the split personality metaphor: he shores
himself up and goes on to observe, like an Emersonian patriarch,
that his 'poetry must make its own way.' The loved ones have to fend
for themselves, no matter how hard their father has made it for
them. Before you've even read one, you can feel about Logan's
poems the way you might feel about the children of a celebrity; they
have a lot of chill and shadow to drag themselves out of.

You can also feel no inclination to offer these children a hand,
especially if you've been on the business end of their creator's judgments. Because the readership for poets is mostly other poets, it's

likely that some of Logan's poems have been read, when read at all, through those most wobbly and barely balanced of bifocals: the prism of tears. But Logan may also be poetry's Joan Rivers, whose ritual savagings of her peers' sense of style have lost their teeth precisely *because* they amount to ritual: a rite of initiation that every Nobody, with the hopes of being Somebody, hopes to endure. (I despaired recently when Logan set his sights on Michael Dickman and found the poet 'off in the corner drawing burning houses and pulling the wings off insects'; the description was dead-on, but I'm dismayed the minor Dickman is now conspicuous enough to merit such major attention; I'm dismayed Logan has felt obliged to 'do' Dickman.) So when a Logan attacks, we should be of two heads and hope the cooler one prevails. Thank you, reviewer. May I have another?

* * *

Logan's *Deception Island: Selected Early Poems 1974–1999* offers those of us who need it an opportunity to be our better selves and give his poetry a chance. But what is Sean O'Brien up to on the back cover when he insists that 'Logan's are never going to be the Nation's Favourite Poems, but their presence reminds us of what poetry can include?' What about Robert McDowell, who declares, '"The most hated man in American poetry", a title one could be proud of in this time of fawning and favour-trading?' Are the back cover blurbists covering their backsides? Even the publisher's copy appears aware of its PR problem when it states that Logan's 'poems … do not fit comfortably with the work of most of his contemporaries, and perhaps do not want to fit at all.' *Deception Island* could be renamed *Defensive Island*; it's a prickly production, the drawbridge drawn up.

But then even the poems have been stamped with titles like 'This Island' and 'Ice', and come from books called *Sullen Weedy Lakes* and *Sad-Faced Men*. ('Deception Island' itself is the name of a place in Antarctica.) Many of the poems open a stark view on a natural world in which people are perfunctory, a world in which poems would have no choice but to make their own way, poor things. 'Men are walking on the harbor!' exclaims the speaker of 'Ice', that exclamation point an impure mix, part wonder, part irony. (He goes on to ask, 'What has kept us from falling?' and will concede a grim point by way of gorgeous alliteration: 'Our inner charts are navigators' guesses://white floes, flaws, flyaway islands.') In another poem, the speaker notes that, 'Without binoculars,/we are diminished forms, figures/in a figurative scape.' 'Soon the gosling and the goose/will attempt to reproduce,' begins one quatrain, 'and will pardon dead Parnell's/small affairs in grand hotels.' If 'The Box Kite' provides a worm's-eye view of a kite (which looks like postage), Logan's early poems provide a kite's-eye view of us worms (who look like ants).

That gosling and goose aren't the only animals having at each other. *Deception Island* makes an especially useful gift for, say, the fifth grader who's been tasked with flow-charting the food chain. A crab spider sizes up its gecko. A male mantis is 'eaten by his mate'. A lizard 'uncurls its tongue/around a fly'. Another lizard 'stalks and stalks'. 'A small hawk swerves/to claw the sparrow its alchemy deserves.' *Deception Island* is a little like the island in a reality television show: a place that matches predator to prey with the ruthless precision of some executive producer.

Or is it a little like the island in *Lord of the Flies*: land on which a writer can conduct his controlled trial, on which he can deposit, unpoliced, the weak and the strong, thereby putting civilization on trial. ('All animals act cruelly/toward each other,' concludes one Logan poem. 'We are no different.') For example, the tour de force with the deceptively banal title, 'The Secession of Science from Christian Europe', takes a grand tour of atrocities made possible by civilization, including:

- 'monks//bending to goatish debaucheries';
- 'nodding philosophers' observing a 'captive pigeon suffocate';
- 'the broken backs of coal fields conjuring up/thin tubes of ether and glass'
- 'the naked horror of the bronze flayed horse';
- 'children gutted in the ditch'; and
- 'great humps/of horses, flies clogging their throats'.

I could go on, but I won't, because I'm merciful—or so I think! Turns out people are predators. (They, too, have an inner critic—a Dr Johnson, if not Dr Jekyll.) As one poem suggests, only the prey has changed: 'now the panther learning the edge of the axe,/now a Persian kneeling—then a knife in the neck'. Where's the Logan critique of the classroom scroll that depicts various beta versions of *Homo sapiens*, on their way to straightening their posture?

Elsewhere in *Deception Island*, within mere pages of one another: thieves choke to death in 'a termite-ridden house', 'fish are rising to the maggoty hook', a 'blood-stained mattress dries/in the Vacancy Motel', and 'nine dead cats//[hang] drooling from a wooden altarpiece'. By the time you come across a poem called, 'Animal Actors on the English Stage after 1642', ninety-six pages in, you're apt to cry, 'What fresh hell is this?' Imagine the *SNL* character Debbie Downer had held a doctorate: the voice in Logan's early poems is often that of the learned, sullen partygoer who's never met a conversation he couldn't kill by introducing into it some grisly fact about the civilized human's capacity for cruelty.

Still, some of the best poems in *Deception Island* seem to be the result of time well spent in the archive. These are the ones that give a glimpse of a lost tradition and the silly, self-styled literary types who inhabited it. (These are the ones on which Logan the Poet *and* Logan the Critic appear to have collaborated.) In 'Flower, of Zimbabwe', a pair of 'old-school types', the sort who 'dined Thursdays in the Army and Navy Club', reflects on war crimes and buggery, the 'fat one' observing at the poem's end, 'You had to know your Ovid in those days.' A short, lined letter in the voice of Lewis Carroll frets about the problems of the writer ('I'm so *awfully* busy!'), but then cracks an ugly joke, revealing a crack in Carroll:

One of my pupils this term is a negro,

with a tiny face black as a coal,
and frizzly wool for hair. I have had to keep
a label on the skuttle,
and a label on him, marked in large letters,

in black ink, 'THIS IS THE COAL-SKUTTLE'
and 'THIS IS HIM,' so as to know which is which.

The unoriginal simile redeemed by slightly archaic use of the
indefinite article ('black as a coal'), the enjoyably convoluted
grammar ('I have had to keep'), the garish caps ('THIS IS THE
COAL-SKUTTLE') —awful as the speaker is, you believe in Logan's
sketch, and maybe even marvel at it, too; less than a pair of pages in
length, it gives the impression of having been set down quickly, but
confidently, with a few slashes of charcoal, mined from a vein of
what Eliot once called the 'unexplored resources of the unpoetical'.

The monologue, 'Keats in India', finds the poetry in another
slightly archaic and seemingly uncooked voice—'seemingly',
because the voice pulses to the pentameter. Drawing from letters and
memoirs, the monologue imagines a Keats who survives to see 1848
and tour the Ganges, where he logs his observations and reveals the
period racism. But it follows the development of a poem, too:

> Some fakirs swam aside to beg for alms;
> but one stood on the bank, a raw-boned devil
> like Shakespeare's Edgar topped by a filthy turban,
> a mad array of rags and wretchedness—
> two satchels flung across his narrow shoulders,
> the shredded length of a scarlet cummerbund,
> a palmetto leaf he held like a lady's fan,
> waving it coyly the while he laughed at us.
> . . .
> The camels followed like a caravan!
> The country from Allahabad is jungul,
> uncultivated, flat and wild, broken
> by marsh, impassable in rain. Poor Wordsworth,
> I think, would button up his collar and huff
> at all these casual miles, no walk in sight,
> and scarce a bush of which to make a poem.
> We have to wrap our heads in turban cloth
> while our bearers try to whistle up a wind,
> like English sailors. The sun has blistered us,

though dawns are freezing cold, and the shade chills.
My servant is insensible to weather—
he sleeps all night on the gharry's open roof
while we catch shivers in the smoky carriage.
One eve I dragged a blanket up to him
and asked next morn whether it gave him comfort.
'Oh, very, sir,' said he. 'It was my pillow.'

The insufferable poet is in the details: the resort to Shakespeare; the feminization of the 'raw-boned devil' he fears; the judgment on some 'jungul'; the pity for the elder poet; the white Romantic's burden. And yet it's hard not to be awed when, at the close, having discovered 'the city of your dreams is but a fraud', the imaginary Keats comes to

an elephantine gateway, Room-ee-Durwazu,
the most complacent arch I'd ever seen.
Room-ee-Durwazu, called the Gate of Rome,
by which these strangers mean Byzantium.
Like Alexander, there I was at last,
come continents to face the long road home.
I have begun the 'Ode to Darkness' now.

Keats, like the elder poet he pities, has been making poetry out of bushes all along! Worse, that last line can't help but reduce the Romantic, however briefly, to the status of the tourist (who can't help but reduce his experiences to the dimensions of an ode). And yet we forgive him these trespasses because the poet (I mean Logan now) has been making poetry as well—masterful poetry, at that.

Indeed, in 1991, the Poetry Society of America gave 'Keats in India' the John Masefield Memorial Award. But why isn't this poem better known? In a counterfactual universe, the conceptual poet Kenneth Goldsmith has just published 'Keats in India' to wide acclaim. People with surnames like Silliman and Bernstein are praising Goldsmith his derring-do. They are saying, these avant-gardists, that in cobbling together a composite of Keats based on letters and memoirs, Goldsmith has let the air out of the self-contained

Romantic voice—that Goldsmith has made a masterpiece of found poetry. Marjorie Perloff is working up a monograph called *Ode to a Grecian Knock-Off*. Post-colonial courses are assigning the poem to graduate students. Magazines are assigning their journalists to Goldsmith. But back in our universe, 'Keats in India' is merely a long lyric poem by the guy who says the mean things in *The New Criterion*.

Logan also satirizes the grant-seeking artist, the old woman clutching 'the portfolio/of her novel, unfinished yet'. Even the storyteller who holds our attention fast (with a yarn about his wife receiving a bedside visit from Death) is merely a salesman on a sales call. 'Love lies, and so does art,' goes one poem that should've made the cut—'Nocturne Galant' from *Vain Empires* (1998). This is nasty but necessary work, Logan's ongoing vivisection of the artist. Entertaining, too. People may be animals, having at one another, but at least Logan sometimes allows that his readers are pigs for pleasure.

He sure doesn't spare the scalpel during self-examinations. In the poem 'Dear DD', a speaker who appears to be Logan approaches his grandmother's deathbed and is forced to face something like the death of the author:

> Your eyes had that thousand-yard stare.
> 'It's William,' I said. 'William, the poet.'
> Your eyes cleared,
> and then, in a hoarse, hunted whisper,
>
> 'You only think you are.'

There's 'William, the poet', and there's the William who *thinks* he's a poet; of all the vivisections in *Deception Island*, this last is the most disturbing—and far more courageous a criticism than Logan is often given credit for. It's as close as we may come to getting Logan the Critic on Logan the Poet.

But that Critic *can* go a little easy on his Poet at times, as the worst of the early poems attest. In a recent book like *Strange Flesh*, glass-blown sea creatures are described with gleaming precision: 'jellyfish like upended chandeliers', 'a feathery starfish like an armature/of delicate fir branches'. But such quality control is clearly absent in the younger Logan's efforts to capture, say, a lizard. He assures us it has 'sinister/manners' and a 'scale coat', then proceeds to flatten it into abstraction as surely as if he'd run it over. Indeed, this lizard

> lives in observation of the moment's
> flicker, the watched ascendancy of night:
> it is the sharp minute in which he breathes.
> To live beneath things supernal,
>
> in that muted harmony that is eating and taking,
> taking and giving back, his composition of pause,
> where time is a weight and moment nothing.
> The absent dark: his movement is silence.
> —from 'The Lizard in His Medium'

You have to dig around in Logan's early work to turn up a description as delightfully exact as a 'caterpillar of coast'; the poems often date themselves with phrases like 'muted harmony', 'absent dark', 'muted mathematics', 'philosophies of bone', 'an awful geography'. They always seem to be taking shots at some caricature of a tourist—'self-important', 'childish', 'demanding', 'coughing', her gaze 'almost cruel'—an easy target for young poets and other such terrorists. But these indiscretions don't aggravate as much as they should. If anything, they prove a poet's selected isn't simply a product of natural selection. That is, they prove Logan the Critic's fallible humanity, which can't help but indulge the Poet his imprecision. In these moments, the Critic is least useful—but kind of lovable.

Perfect Contempt

T. S. Eliot's *The Waste Land*, like Matthew Weiner's *Mad Men*, isn't terribly optimistic about the male/female (or is it male/administrative-assistant) relationship. In one episode (of the poem, not the telecast), our hero, a certain 'young man carbuncular', visits with his lady friend, a 'typist'. He's after a joyless assignation, which is the wont of harried men in early Eliot (and hollow men—admen—on booty calls); she's playing easy to get, which is to say not defending herself against his 'assaults'. On finishing his business, the young man departs, and the typist

> turns and looks a moment in the glass,
> Hardly aware of her departed lover;
> Her brain allows one half-formed thought to pass:
> 'Well now that's done: and I'm glad it's over.'
> When lovely woman stoops to folly and
> Paces about her room again, alone,
> She smooths her hair with automatic hand,
> And puts a record on the gramophone.
>
> 'This music crept by me upon the waters'....

The Oliver Goldsmith number, which Eliot is sampling here, has it that the only art available to women who stoop to folly is the art of dying. But *modern* women, Eliot suggests, are too benumbed to dabble in the arts; they smooth their hair and put on records—the comforting sort of 'music' that 'crept by' Ferdinand in *The Tempest*. These aren't records to think on; Eliot's typist hasn't exactly reached for the Stravinsky or her prized acetate of Dadaist racket. She has the CPU of a jukebox, and moves—grooves—accordingly, which is to say automatically. (She might as well be dead.) The episode comes couched in pop comforts like rhyme and meter. It's as if a crackling gramophone is grinding out some trifle, square in the middle of a collage of classier ruins.

But there must be other responses than the automaton's available to modern women who prefer not to be mauled by young men carbuncular and who enjoy their gramophones. Eliot's typist could buck herself up and, instead of merely playing a song, sing one, an original. Let's call it 'Résumé':

Razors pain you;
Rivers are damp;
Acids stain you;
And drugs cause cramp.
Guns aren't lawful;
Nooses give;
Gas smells awful;
You might as well live.

In other words, Eliot's typist could be more than a nameless typist, more than a type. She could be something other than an extra in an Eisensteinian montage, a model member of the masses, a petal on a wet black bough. She could be allowed a *complete* thought, instead of just the half. (She could be a complete wit, instead of a halfwit.) In general, she could have more of a mouth on her. She could be Dorothy Parker.

Parker, for her part, could be hard on the singing that makes up this, the new edition of her *Complete Poems*, which first appeared in 1999 and, through legal wrangling, has been expanded to include a few more poems. 'My verses are no damned good,' she told an interviewer in 1956. 'Let's face it, honey, my verse is terribly dated—as anything once fashionable is dreadful now. I gave it up, knowing it wasn't getting any better, but nobody seemed to notice my magnificent gesture.' Parker had a point, but only because by the time she made it—that time of life when an old writer's thoughts turn to her *Paris Review* interview—she had enough distance on her younger self to be able to remove the younger self to the wrong side of history. To be sure, the worst of the younger self's poems (and this is a lot of them) would've sounded 'terribly dated' to the mature woman who'd committed herself to causes and come to be blacklisted. They confront the contemporary reader first and foremost as firmly end-stopped metrical patterns, which is what formal poems do when we have no great reason to concentrate on their words, when their words have, over time, revealed themselves to be the go-to words of a bygone world: the stock content another era's professional—an adman, say—could generate and manipulate at will, in a pinch. When reading a stanza of 'Hearthside', for one, it takes an effort not to glaze over and count stresses:

> If I seek a lovelier part,
> Where I travel goes my heart;
> Where I stray my thought must go;
> With me wanders my desire.
> Best to sit and watch the snow,
> Turn the lock, and poke the fire.

In general, Parker came up with no surprising images or similes or metaphors of her own. The odd telephone makes an appearance and keeps things up-to-the-minute. But for the most part, she made do with lads, suns, stars, things, tears, time. The heart is so frequently reached for and handled in Parker's poems it's as worn and polished a prop as Yorick's skull. Eliot wrote that it was the poet's business 'to make poetry out of the unexplored resources of the unpoetical'. Parker worked the exhausted resources of the poetical.

But Parker was wrong to discard her efforts in verse *en masse*, even if the gesture made for good interview and was, in keeping with her general aesthetic, wickedly economical. (Her first collection of poems was reluctantly retrieved from magazines and titled *Enough Rope*, which means, of course, the bare minimum of verse required to make a book and hang a poet.) She was wrong to discard her efforts not because she 'was her own worst critic', as *The Paris Review* put it, but because her best poems are already the best critics of the worst. For instance, the knowing sensibility behind the follow-ing stanzas from 'One Perfect Rose' has inhaled enough of the bad stuff to be allergic to a florid sign system:

I knew the language of the floweret;
   'My fragile leaves,' it said, 'his heart enclose.'
Love long has taken for his amulet
   One perfect rose.

Why is it no one ever sent me yet
   One perfect limousine, do you suppose?
Ah no, it's always just my luck to get
   One perfect rose.

Joan Acocella, writing in *The New Yorker*, argues that Parker's ambition is narrow, her mode deflation: Parker pumps up the expectations of readers, and then, with the tack of a final line or stanza—with no tact at all—sticks it to them (the expectations, not the readers; Parker is reader friendly or, at least, the friend of yours who knows how to needle you). But it can also be said that Parker inflates the deflated; she aerates the often claustrophobic confines of poems (what with their perfect, perfumy roses), letting in oxygen, helium, limousines.

'Light verse precisely lightens,' wrote John Updike, in a piece on the rather more heavy *Cantos of Ezra Pound*. '[I]t lessens the gravity of its subject.' Parker's best poems are the lightest, which means the smallest, the ones that, just this side of the aphoristic, have acquired the most buoyancy. (It may even be that Parker's aphorisms—'Brevity is the soul of lingerie'—*are* the poems.) But in her introduction to *Complete Poems*, the biographer Marion Meade suggests that the Great Depression leavened a light touch for the better:

> In [Parker's] third book of poetry, *Death and Taxes* [1931], can be noticed a distinct shift in mood, a maturity and reflection, less mockery, fewer knee-jerk responses to people who got under her skin.... Instead of Parkerlite, audiences were given sad, solemn lyrics that seemed ripped from the dark reaches of her unconscious.

Death and Taxes certainly contains a few classics: 'The Flaw in Paganism', 'Sanctuary', 'Cherry White', and 'Sweet Violets'. But if there's a mature and reflective Parker, she should take the label 'Parker-lite'; we remember the other one, the Parker of the first two collections, *Enough Rope* and *Sunset Gun*, precisely *because* of the 'mockery' and 'knee-jerk responses'. Parker got her start pushing product, writing captions for clothes in *Vogue* in the 1910s; later, as a member of the Algonquin Round Table, she frequented the famous hotel where the various lives of various parties would shore up and try out their wit. One had to be quick with one's comebacks and stylish about viciousness. In time, Hollywood would require her services on screenplays. Economy, for Parker, wasn't just a matter of aesthetics, of making sure that every word contributes; it was a matter of economic survival. Like the finest of Updike's, her poems hold to an archaic idea of accountability to mythic figures: smart general readers who don't read a lot of poetry and are mostly looking to pass a moment in stylish company. They're funny, too. Unlike so many contemporary poems— all punchline all the time—Parker's have a comedian's sense of structure and timing; the punchlines, when they come, are as crisp as tapped cymbals (even if the downbeat drummer strikes us as a potential suicide).

Put another way, poems like 'One Perfect Rose' want no great gloss. Like the Marianne Moore of the line, 'I, too, dislike it', Parker sides with the morose skeptic, if not philistine, who's wary of symbolism, of what sneaky things (roses and poems) might really mean. But 'One Perfect Rose' is more than metapoetry of a kind that stretches back, past Gertrude Stein, to the Shakespeare of 'Sonnet 130', and reaches forward to the Andy Warhol of Marilyn Monroe paintings and the mid-century world of advertising; it's another response to young men carbuncular the world over, with a not-so-subtle subtext: the size of your empty sign matters. Like 'Résumé', like so many others, 'One Perfect Rose' proposes wit and pragmatism as a way of life for the modern depressive who might otherwise be tempted to take her life or, worse, make a collage. Indeed, in 'A Well-Worn Story', Parker's inner-environmentalist worries that she has 'spoil[ed] a page with rhymes'. In 'Bohemia', she savages those of us who've an installation to ready, an opening night to get ready for, a subscription to *The Believer* to renew:

Playwrights and poets and such horses' necks
Start off from anywhere, end up at sex.
Diarists, critics, and similar roe
Never say nothing, and never say no.
People Who Do Things exceed my endurance;
God, for a man that solicits insurance!

Perhaps, then, what Parker made, out of the exhausted resources of
the poetical, was less poetry than anti-poetry. In doing so, she anticipated the anti-matter of Joycelin Shrager, the late Tom Disch's parody of a wanting poet. 'i don't think it's vanity,' writes the parody,

> i'm just
> a very visual personality type
> my eyes are hungry all the time which is why
> i've been obsessing over the fact
> that i can't see my feet making
> a bump in the blanket since they were
> amputated victims of mastectomies....
> —from 'before he killed himself donald'

Shrager reminds us of the lower-case dangers a 'visual personality
type', left to her own devices—her laptop or Moleskine—can get up
to.

In addition to Disch, Parker anticipates the tough love of
another spiritual heir, the contemporary wit Fran Lebowitz, who
gets a laugh by giving an audience the truth in style, in a cascade of
clauses: 'There are too many *books*, the books are *terrible*, and this is
be*cause* you have been *taught* to have self-esteem.' Parker, too, is
one of the great critics of that transhistorical human spirit that's
always wanting us to read its poems and, after World War II, comes
to concentrate itself in college classrooms and comment streams. In
'Bohemians: A Hate Song', she writes, 'They are always pulling
manuscripts out of their pockets,/And asking you to tell them, honestly—is it too daring?' In a May 1958 piece about Jack Kerouac, for
Esquire, Parker remarks on (even as she demonstrates by example)
the dangers of too much typing:

Like many a better one before me, I have gone down under
the force of numbers, under the books and books and books
that keep coming out and coming out and coming out,
shoals of them, spates of them, flash floods of them, too
blame many books, and no sign of an end. And this at the
time of what is recognized as the slack season in the publishing industry!

By 'publishing industry', she means the mid-century businesses that
put out too much product and aren't letting up. But she could just as
easily be misunderstood to mean the Twitter feeds of today, or the
workshops of Dana Gioia's gentle ire, or the open mic that comes in
for scorn in an episode of *Mad Men* ('Too much art for me,' says one
character), or the hacks of Alexander Pope's *Dunciad*, emboldened
by the convenience of the latest publishing platform, the printing
press; what worries Parker is the deluge.

But Parker, like Noah, sort of needed the deluge, if only to
emphasize her own buoyancy, her being above it all. In fact, alien-
ation is a secret source of pleasure in some of her speakers, setting
them apart from their less joyfully alienated peers—the armoured
animal of a Marianne Moore poem, say, or the emotionally armoured
speaker of an Edna St. Vincent Millay sonnet (the one who learns
about the death of a loved one from the back of a fellow commuter's
paper but can do little more than compose her face and focus on the
subway ads for fur storage, modern life being what it is and all). The
second part of Parker's foray into free verse, 'Oh, Look—I Can Do It,
Too: Showing That Anyone Can Write Modernist Verse' parodies the
blighted cityscape of the Millay sonnet and something like Eliot's
'Preludes':

A litter of newspapers
Piled in smothering profusion.
Supplements sprawling shamelessly open,
Flaunting their lurid contents—
'Divorced Seven Times, Will Re-Wed First Wife',
And, 'Favorite's Account of Escape from the Harem'.
Unopened sheets of 'help' advertisements;

Editorials, crumpled in a frenzy of ennui;
Society pages, black with lying photographs.
Endless, beginningless heaps of newspapers....
Outside, a thin gray rain,
Falling, falling hopelessly,
With a dull monotony of meaningless sound,
Like the voice of a minister reading the marriage service.

Perhaps you had to be in the employ of a magazine, as Parker usually was, to make light of the despair that other moderns felt in the
presence of a 'litter of newspapers', which *could* be thought a sign of
a robust mass media. But still, even if one had to be alienated, one
could at least enjoy oneself. In 'Frustration', a perfectly sane American psycho imagines the 'pleasure' of 'Speeding bullets through the
brains/Of the folk who give me pains'. In 'Sanctuary', a quatrain of
folk art so familiar it could be credited to Anonymous, an island of
one surveys the countryside:

My land is bare of chattering folk;
    The clouds are low along the ridges,
And sweet's the air with curly smoke
    From all my burning bridges.

The island of one has none of the Facebook user's fear of de-friend-
ing and its consequences; she's cheerful about blowing up connections, blowing social capital. She doesn't brood in her bedroom,
playing Smiths records, like Eliot's typist. Parker's speaker, in
'Indian Summer', will 'do the things I do,/And if you do not like me
so,/To hell, my love, with you!' She finds the grim joy in a nasty
business, as most of her peers don't—save, perhaps, the Virginia
Woolf who records of herself, 'My real delight in reviewing is to say
nasty things.'

Like Disch, like Lebowitz, Parker's spiritual heirs aren't merely
poets; they're scrappy professionals, living by their wits and wit in
equal measure; the unfashionable sorts of outcast; the geniuses of the
system. I'm put in mind of Cary Grant's world-weary cat burglar, in
To Catch a Thief, who boasts to Grace Kelly, with whom he'll shortly

consummate a cool flirtation, that he doesn't care for 'modern poetry'. I'm also put in mind of *Mad Men*'s Peggy Olson, the secretary-turned-quick-study-turned-copy-writer, who has to hustle to get her haiku-sized ad copy into shape, even as she learns her way around a drink cart. (For Peggy—for Parker—the world of work isn't entirely a waste land.) Indeed, a Parker poem like 'News Item'—'Men seldom make passes/At girls who wear glasses'—could've been a caption in *Vogue*. In any event, it's as durable and viral as a commercial jingle. I don't mean the jingle of the serious artist's scorn; I mean the jingle that should be accorded the respect of a poem because it was produced by what Camille Paglia is right to call 'folk artists, anonymous as the artisans of medieval cathedrals'. Parker's spiritual ancestors, on the other hand, include the Samuel Johnson of the line, 'No man but a blockhead ever wrote, except for money', and the Oscar Wilde of all of the epigrams. She'll never replace the major poets of her era, which we're right to take more seriously, even if we wish some of them would lighten up; she's too busy angling for a laugh and killing. She's that gramophone, crackling away among the moderns, cutting the discord with a tune, something you can hum.

The Pigheaded Soul

The matter-of-fact title of the new collection of poems by Kay Ryan tweaks a theme with which the poet, history suggests, has grown pretty comfortable. In 2010 this book was called *The Best of It: New and Selected Poems*; now it's called *All of It: Collected Poems 1965–2035*. But then, Ryan has never been terribly precious about the titles of her books. These tend to be donated by the lead-off poems, none of which have seemed especially inevitable in the role. In fact, thanks to recent insights into alternate universes, science can now confirm that Ryan's breakout collection, *Flamingo Watching*, has been variously titled, *Slant*, *Say It Straight*, *Extraordinary Lengths*, *The Things of the World*, and *A Certain Kind of Eden*. In each universe, the book has always enjoyed the same reception. (*Life Studies*, on the other hand, has been far less influential when called *Skunk Hour*, and *The Waste Land* all but bombs in the universes where it's known as *He Do the Police in Different Voices*.) Ryan's lead-off poems are less born-leaders, establishing a theme, than reliable grunts who would seem to do and so get tapped for promotion to the front line. One is as able as another, and the books they add up to are never the point.

Most American poets now follow Ryan's example. The titles of their books are borrowed from randomly deputized poems, and the books themselves—ever slim—abstain from irrelevant epigraphs, over-determined section dividers, and showy endnotes. But the distaste for what Ryan calls 'vogue shapes for poetry books' used to be counterintuitive, if not subversive, back when poetry collections were organized by narrative arcs, those starchy structures that feel to us, in the 2030s, as odd and constricting as the undergarments of an earlier, more decadent age.

It was a weird time, the turn of the century. A majority of poets still taught in MFA programs as opposed to MBA programs (that's

Master of Blogging Arts, of course). Weirder still, the Association of Writers and Writing Programs Annual Conference (AWP) was not yet virtual but, rather, a real-world destination to which poets actually travelled, in-flesh. Ryan's account of a trip to one such conference—the much-anthologized 'I Go to AWP'—preserves, as time capsules do, some of the period detail, including the anxiety experienced by poets and editors who were made to actually mingle with one another, physically. At one point in this classic of gonzo journalism (not to mention anthropological fieldwork) Ryan finds herself surrounded by a pack of poets, one of whom indicates that he hasn't yet discovered the arc of his new manuscript. Ryan's baffled response—'What *is* an arc?'—seems to have been innocent enough. But given its eventual impact on American poetry, she may as well have asked a band of hunter-gatherers why they felt compelled to sacrifice their virgins. With a single question, one that would go on to supply the first major study of Ryan's work with its title, Ryan had inadvertently killed off the arc as organizing principle, just as the old Apple platform iTunes killed off the long-player.

If it's now an age of poems and 45s, then it's an age in which most poems look and sound a lot like Ryan's—so much so that her concise, linear style (heavy on the abrupt enjambment and internal rhyme) is the default setting for versifiers, the way ABAB was the default for the Georgians, and free verse, the default for the Modernists, and disjunction, the default for the Ashberians (or the Sillimen or the Dean Youngians—the scholars are still deciding). Ryan is a giant of letters, which means merely that her least gesture ('What *is* an arc?') can rattle foundations and get a culture to questioning itself. But 'I Go to AWP' was commissioned at a time when Ryan looked like enough of an outsider to all but guarantee that her visit to a poetry conference would result in the filing of a funny report about a fish out of water. The fish, it turns out, would become even more conspicuous. With reluctance, she would accept the role of Poet Laureate of what was then the United States and, in the decades after, the more significant role of Poet of Her Generation. And yet it's easy to forget the way in which her poems first infiltrated American culture—quietly, covertly, in the manner of things that tend to last.

Ryan didn't teach creative writing. Worse, she made her home in Northern California, far from centers of literary power, with their schmoozing and book-launching and elbow-rubbing. (This was the eighties, before the days of social networking, when one had to actually live near a literary party in order to attend it; to be in close proximity to a body in order to poke or friend it.) Struggling to publish, at a low point, she considered a trip (by motorized vehicle, of all things) to meet *The New Yorker*'s poetry editor in person and so obtain an audience for her poems. But at the last minute, she decided not to go. She was too proud, and her poems, it seems, were going to get little help—even from Ryan. Instead, they would have to help themselves; they would have to endure what the poet called, not without a kind of affection, 'the slow old mail': the cumbersome and publicly run postal system by which paper copies of poems were submitted to blogazines (and by which people in general texted one another). The long waits, often followed by rejection, toughened the poet and improved the poetry. In time, accomplished poems began to distinguish themselves to editors who owed Ryan exactly nothing but still couldn't help being won over by the things. Discreetly, these poems crept into magazines, anthologies, the milieu. They were small, sure—'as small as those animals which save the foolish heroes of fairy tales—which can save only the heroes, because they are too small not to have been disregarded by everyone else.' Actually, that's Randall Jarrell describing Marianne Moore poems. And when Kay Ryan describes the flamingo in her classic 'Flamingo Watching'—

> unnatural by nature—
> too vivid and peculiar
> a structure to be pretty,
> and flexible to the point
> of oddity

—she is describing Kay Ryan poems, whether she means to or not. It doesn't matter that the flamingo is 'too exact and sinuous/to convince an audience/she's serious'; the Kay Ryan poem convinces.

And it does so by encouraging its audience to feel like the one anatomized in another Ryan classic, 'Ideal Audience':

Not scattered legions,
not a dozen from
a single region
for whom accent
matters, not a seven-
member coven,
not five shirttail
cousins; just
one free citizen—
maybe not alive
now even—who
will know with
exquisite gloom
that only we two
ever found this room.

Ryan's relatively clear language and quick turnaround of rhyme (a rhyme one is never quite prepared for) had the effect of smelling salts. Thus did her skinny columns of type, with their unexpected kinks, create an alert consumer (and out of tough-to-thaw types like Dana Gioia and Charles Kinbote—literally tough-to-thaw since both have since been cryogenically frozen for posterity). But the point is, the poems never sacrificed their entertainment value. They were too smart *not* to please.

They were also too smart to appear to bother much with the ideas of their day. They weren't oblivious to the ideas and maybe even accepted some of them. The notion that our most unique expressions are only ever remixes of, or responses to, the expressions of others—the notion that nothing is original—was merely a given in Ryan's poems, which often salvaged some cliché of language or another's words as epigraph, and then proceeded to make small talk with the salvaged scrap; to open, as they used to say, a dialogue. The notion that the meaning of an image like lime light is only ever provisional and depends on context—that a 'bowlful' of limes

right at
one's elbow

produces no
more than
a baleful
glow against
the kitchen table

—was another given which her poetry accepted but never condescended to make explicit. Even the lyric 'I'—for which so much
twentieth-century poetry served as a bullhorn and which so much of
the rest of the century's poetry sought to muffle—was casually
absent in many of Ryan's poems. Her poetry could take humanism
and leave it.

Many academics came late to Ryan's work, despite the fact that
poems like 'Shift', in which 'Words have loyalties/to so much/we
don't control', were as critical of our attempts to represent the world
through language as any old Language poem. (The poems' only sin,
really, was readability.) Also, Ryan's advocacy for underdogs of all
stripes obscured the fact that she had a cause: underdogs of all
stripes. As a result, critics were slow to claim lines like these, from
her poem 'Turtle', for the Left, for ecopoetry, what have you:

> With everything optimal,
she skirts the ditch which would convert
her shell into a serving dish. She lives
below luck-level, never imagining some lottery
will change her load of pottery to wings.

Other poems, such as 'A Certain Meanness of Culture', excerpted
below, weren't aggressively anti-globalization or whatever, but they
did take their swipes at yuppies like T.S. Eliot, on behalf of those
who dwell in pre-gentrified deserts,

before the mythology,
... in the

first tailings of industry,
and [who are] of course lonely
and susceptible to
the opinions of donkeys
since donkeys are the
main company out here
among the claims.
Snakes and wild things
skitter off too fast
for conversation.
You can get an appreciation
for why a donkey is
fussy about books
since she carries them.
You start to value culture
like you would water.

In short, her poems could be transgressive, a word that once enjoyed
a currency and which some academics liked to say of the literature
they liked. But the transgression was never obvious, and anyway,
Ryan's suspicion of buzzwords (like 'transgressive', for one) was
never going to endear her to a certain set, at least in the early days of
her career. 'It's funny how writers will all want to jump on the same
bed till the springs pop out,' Ryan famously wrote of that word
'transgressive'. 'Then they go jump on another one.'

Despite the subtlety of their, yes, transgressions (and despite
the poet's own apparent wariness of herds) Ryan's poems always
seemed to angle for something like the ideal audience of a universal
reader. They weren't overheated; they understood, as the poet herself liked to say, that only a properly chilled poetry can draw heat,
life forms, readers. They certainly didn't limit their readership by
making specific references to, say, a popular culture the readership
might not share. Topical events were left uncommented on, and at
least one poem that could've been mistaken for commentary was
held back for a spell. '["Home to Roost"] was sitting on the desk of
an editor in New York at the time of 9/11,' Ryan once told *NPR*,
'and it suddenly took on this terrible added significance, and I had

to withdraw it because it seemed cruelly appropriate.' Ryan's poems didn't aim to be cruel. Nor did they assume the poet's personal traumas would necessarily interest a discerning reader. Nor did they succumb to the fragment, which lured so many of the previous century's poets down a dead end, where thoughts need not be completed. Rather coolly, Ryan's poems completed their thoughts, following unforeseen lines of thinking, roads less travelled, a fork's most slanted tine. They showed their work and obeyed a logic, but not the logic of a Mister Spock, a logic feeling around for firm footing. The Ryan poem often concealed a loose plank in its reasoning, through which a reader was apt to plunge. Indeed, many of the pithier responses to the Ryan poem—the blurbs on her books—are really just confessions of vulnerability to an underestimated power: the scrawny kid who pins the stronger arm (David Yezzi); the changeup that freezes its batter (Kate Moos). 'People come up and say, "Oh, your poems are so funny",' Ryan would recount. 'I tell them, wait until you get home.'

All of It will interest the completists who feel that they must have every last poem, the least B-side, the grainiest demo. But it's a bulky book, and those curious about the poet's early work might be better off consulting *The Rest of It: Uncollected (and Repudiated) Poems*, which collects banished books like *Dragon Acts to Dragon Ends* and *Strangely Marked Metal*, and is available for download on iVerse. I myself still return to the first retrospective, *The Best of It*, from 2010, an altogether more user-friendly affair than later and increasingly comprehensive selections. I also return to the book as a form of penance, self-flagellation of which I hope Ryan approves. As your search engine may recall, I entertained some reservations with *The Best of It*, in a review for the blogazine *Poetry*, twenty-five years ago, a moment when Ryan, heaped with honours, must've seemed due for backlash. I wondered if she had published too many poems and, in doing so, had diluted her body of work. We now know she hadn't. That collection, at least, holds up. And its one imperfection, its one amateur effort—an early poem for her father, set off from the rest—turns out to be the perfect touch of sentiment, the perfect off-note.

Still, after decades of living in this, the Age of Ryan, one can start to long for some of the sprawl of late-twentieth-century poetry—those book-length projects and, stuffed inside them, almost to bursting, the long lines and shaggy verse paragraphs and confessions of dredged-up stuff and photojournalistic set pieces and collages of this and that. Ryan, to be sure, has too many imitators, turning out competent poems like 'Bendable Straw', by one Frank Hoaks, which recently appeared in *The New Yorker*:

> Long repressed
> it reveals its inner
> accordion and
> with a little pressure
> breaks
> down like the back
> of the camel
> it comes to
> resemble—
> a wrinkle in
> some spine's plan.
> Extracted from
> its malted
> it would make
> for buoyant bedding
> for the exalted—
> for example
> in his manger
> some son of man.

The blogazines are glutted with this sort of lean, clever thing, so much so that it may be time to revisit those former giants—specialists in sprawl like John Ashbery and Anne Carson—who have been long forgotten. Or, better yet, it may be time to just plain visit poets like Samuel Menashe, Peter Van Toorn, Don Coles, Robyn Sarah, Arturo Belano, Bruce Taylor—singular poets who never achieved the material success of Ryan (or Ashbery or Carson) but were her quirky peers and continue to persist in certain memory banks, like viruses that can't quite be wiped clean.

Will Ryan still be a giant of letters in another twenty-five years? It's wonderful that she ever *was* one, that she became so central, that Gioia's early hope—'Ryan's magnificently compressed poetry ... signals a return to concision and intensity' (1998!)—even came to pass. But perhaps, as some critics contend, she has had her day. Many of these same critics assure me that the Neo-Flarfists (who 'make' their poetry out of the transmissions of extraterrestrials) are the next big thing. Others insist that the future of poetry belongs to the bow tie-sporting Robots, many of whom are fairly dominating the blogazines (or *The New Criterion*, anyway) with their machine-tooled sonnets and sestinas. Still *others* argue that the great poet of the twenty-first century—the last poet, really—is Facebook, which is to say: all of us.

It would be easy to ignore these predictions for the simple fact that they are predictions. But then even Jarrell was not above making a prediction, which is only science fiction for exactly as long as it takes to come true. Here's Jarrell again, on one future in particular:

> Sometimes when I can't go to sleep at night I see the family of the future. Dressed in three-tone shorts-and-shirt sets of disposable Papersilk, they sit before the television wall of their apartment, only their eyes moving. After I've looked a while I always see—otherwise I'd die—a pigheaded soul over in the corner with a book; only his eyes are moving, but in them there is a different look.
>
> Usually it's Homer he's holding—this week it's Elizabeth Bishop. Her *Poems* seems to me one of the best books an American poet has ever written: the people of the future (the ones in the corner) will read her just as they will read Dickinson or Whitman or Stevens, or the other classical American poets still alive among us.

In time, the pigheaded soul swapped out Bishop for Ryan. Will he still be reading Ryan, over in the corner, in 2060? Maybe not. It's probably pointless to bet on the next big thing, especially when you're not Jarrell and especially when cultures are fragmenting and poetries are replacing poetry and the next big thing is likely just a lot of little things. Perhaps you should only blog your enthusiasms and make a case for your favourites (even if it can't hurt *too* much to imagine a future in which you wouldn't entirely mind living).

The Poetry in the Prose

In Stephen King's novel, *The Waste Lands*, the character Jake, a teenager with one Chuck Taylor in another dimension, channels onto paper an incantation, which his teacher mistakes for a precociously poetic response to a humdrum homework assignment. The incantation, 'My Understanding of Truth', is not great, at least by the standards of a *Poetry* magazine, but it's good enough to earn an A+. The teacher is impressed—'Younger students are often attracted to so-called "stream-of-consciousness" writing, but are rarely able to control it'—and even suggests Jake's work be published in the student magazine. Jake laughs. He thought he was losing his mind. It turns out the teen is merely a Romantic poet, gawky antenna receiving lines like these:

> The way station is the truth.
> The Speaking Demon is the truth.
> We went under the mountains and that is the truth.
> There were monsters under the mountain. That is the truth.
> One of them had an Amoco gas pump between his legs and was
>   pretending it was his penis. That is the truth.

I remember admiring Jake's weird poem when I first read King's novel—when I was a teenager and thought poems ought to be weird. Now, I enjoy the harmless fun of it all: as ultimate sovereign over the world of *The Waste Lands*, King gets to play poet, via Jake, but critic, too, judging his poem an A+. How very human of the deity, whose bestselling works about the inhuman have often left the critical establishment horrified.

Ours is a pantheistic universe; many writers, not just critics, like to play God. They populate their writing with poets who don't exactly exist, and they pass judgments on the poetry: works of art

within works of art. Sometimes these writers will christen a character a poet, the better to humanize a monster. I have in mind another
seminal text in my education: that issue of *Archie* in which Moose,
the intemperate jock, puts an avant-garde poem for his girl, Midge,
up on the blackboard. The Internet assures me it went something
like this:

> Taller than the tallest tree is,
> Wider than the widest sea is,
> That's how much in love we is!

It shouldn't surprise us—though it surprises Moose's peers—when
their teacher finds herself taken with the tercet, and suggests the jock
pursue publication in some little magazine; the poem is a specimen
of what art critic Roger Cardinal would call 'outsider art', a category
that includes the work of 'mediums and innocents'. Moose presents
as the primitive who has just discovered fire—the flame of creativity
that flickers in the *Homo sapiens* heart.

Like Moose, other fictional innocents have pushed the limits of
poetry: an act of innovation that's far easier to outsource to one's
characters than to actually do oneself. Here is television's Edith
Bunker, redefining American poetry in an episode of the sitcom *All in
the Family* (1968–1979). To recap, Edith has taken an interest in
Catholicism, and her husband, Archie, wants to know what for:

> Archie: You ain't yet explained to me what's all the attrac-
> tion with the Catholics?
>
> Edith: They have lots of interesting things, like those con-
> fessionals right in the church. They're like telephone booths
> to God.
>
> Gloria: Ma, that's very poetic.
>
> Archie: What the hell's poetic about it, I didn't hear nothing
> rhyme?

THE POETRY IN THE PROSE

Terminally misguided patriarch or Terminator machine sent back in time by the Tea Party to terrorize the 1970s? Whatever Archie is, he believes that poetry ought to rhyme. But Edith observes no such rule; she is, on the surface, the untutored savant, and her daughter, Gloria, her ideal critic: Edith's the Whitman, Gloria, the Emerson. And that sound of applause? That's the writing team, off camera, patting itself on the back.

Nabokov plays both poet and exegete on a much larger scale in his *Pale Fire*, which consists of a 999-line poem (by a character named John Shade) and its endnotes (a novel by other means). Shade isn't real, but he's real enough; he possesses a biography, a bibliography, and, of course, the 999-line poem, which is quite good for a poem that doesn't exactly exist in the world outside of *Pale Fire*—as good, one might add, as a poem by Nabokov himself. The real-world critic Ron Rosenbaum may be living on another planet when he suggests that '"Pale Fire", the poem within the novel, may well come to be looked upon as the Poem of the Century,' but perhaps extra-planetary residence is prerequisite to judging the out-of-this-world.

Thomas Pynchon's novel, *The Crying of Lot 49*, slim as it is, nevertheless finds room to house its own works of art, plus their commentators. Here, have a listen to what Pynchon's characters are hep to: 'Miles's Song', a British Invasion knock-off by an American beat group calling itself the Paranoids:

Too fat to Frug,
That's what you tell me all the time,
When you really try'n' to put me down,
But I'm hip,
So close your big fat lip,
Yeah, baby,
I may be too fat to Frug,
But at least I ain't too slim to Swim.

'It's lovely,' says one of the song's auditors, politely, 'but why do you sing with an English accent when you don't talk that way?' Pynchon's characters also enjoy a performance of a Jacobean revenge play, *The Courier's Tragedy*, the sort of snuff drama in which a man can be observed to wave around a rapier (tipped with, what else, an impaled flaming tongue) and can be heard to scream in iambic pentameter:

> Thy pitiless unmanning is most meet,
> Thinks Ercole the zany Paraclete.
> Descended this malign, Unholy Ghost,
> Let us begin thy frightful Pentecost.

The lights go out, the act ends, and someone in the audience—perhaps anticipating the response of Pynchon's real-world reader—says, 'Ick.' In Pynchon's prose, there's always a little song, and everyone's a critic.

Our real-world playwrights have long enjoyed the convention of the play within a play, which can be an easier, more manageable production to pull off than the plain old play itself. I like to think Shakespeare enjoyed imagining his most famous play within a play, *The Mouse-Trap*, a remake of *The Murther of Gonzago*, which premieres in *Hamlet* and kick-starts the murderous Claudius's conscience, sending him out of the theatre and off to prayer. If only all plays could be so literally moving. And if only all productions had a resource like Hamlet, who not only tweaks the script but offers constructive criticism and acting tips to the troupe of players, just before curtain.

There's a canon of these works of art within works of art (with their attendant criticism) just waiting to be constructed by some budding Harold Bloom (Yale's all-too-real critic). The canon might include the acclaimed assemblages in William Gibson's *Count Zero*—counterfeit Cornell boxes by a Canadian science fiction novelist—and the fake discography music critic Lester Bangs forges for the real-world garage band, Count Five. (An example of a fake Count Five record? *Snowflakes Falling on the International Dateline*, which Bangs assigns the catalogue number Columbia MS 7528, and which, the critic reminds us, 'featured the unparalleled "Schizophrenic Rainbows: A Raga Concerto", which no one who's sat through its entire 27 minutes will ever be able to forget, especially

the thunderous impact of the abrupt and full-volumed entry of
George Szell and the Cleveland Orchestra in the eighteenth minute.')

Or maybe this canon wants a community of Blooms, who will
offer more diverse examples than I do, including ones by non-white,
non-male writers. (Imaginary cultures are not immune to culture
wars.)

Writers rarely have much control over how their works are
received, but they do have control over the worlds their writing
frames. Granted, the laws of these worlds can be disconcerting. The
critic Philip Marchand, who once took an inventory of Margaret
Atwood's novels, discovered that her male characters tend to be
mediocre artists, fated to preside over 'inane', 'farcical' works. Basically, he discovered the diplomat for CanLit is a bit of a dictator. We
can be authoritarians, erecting our utopias.

Still, I'm charmed by the very human impulse to smuggle into
some writing some amateur poetry—to imagine an art that doesn't
need to work too hard, that can be greeted as a ready-made success
or dismissed with a single damning 'Ick', depending on the mood of
a King or a Pynchon. These works within works don't need pub-
lishers, and don't need to be in good taste. They don't obey our
laws, and don't have to. They don't even have to be any good!
These works need merely be imagined. As the main character in
J.M. Coetzee's novel *Disgrace* observes, while composing his touch-
ingly tasteless opera about Byron's mistress, with parts for banjo
and singing dog, 'Surely, in a work that will never be performed, all
things are permitted?'

A Big Star Implodes

Rock star and ne'er-do-well Alex Chilton (1950–2010) gave good non-interview: he knew how to wriggle free of a line of questioning like almost no one outside of elected office. '[F]or you to write about me would be the *best* way for me to begin to have something against you,' he told *Mojo* magazine on one occasion. 'I have to rest my voice,' he told *Rolling Stone* on another (*after* a show, mind, as he brandished a cigarette, which could've doubled as a makeshift middle finger). In these, our Heisenbergian times—when the sheer observation of an event, it's accepted, can't help but change the event—a thwarted journalist will know enough to make her failure to land the story a part of the story itself. Gay Talese's account of a near-meeting with an ailing Frank Sinatra is one such early classic of this sort of amateur astronomy, in which the close call with the shooting star is regarded as better than nothing and duly logged. Encounters with the Memphis-born Chilton (including those in which he actually answers questions) are probably better described as close calls.

Perhaps Chilton, who could lay claim to the authorship of some five or six legitimate pop standards, sensed that he should safeguard his legacy by not exhausting their meanings in conversation with tape recorders. Or perhaps he had little to say about these standards, which it was perfectly in his rights to feel weren't worth getting worked up about. Or perhaps he had an advanced understanding of the showman's injunction to always leave an audience wanting more: give them nothing much in the first place. Chilton could resemble a kind of performance artist, hermetically sealed off from his patrons, who must be content with their mumbled asides to one another because the artist, preoccupied with his fretwork, has turned away— turned inward—as if protesting an abstract, unspecified injustice. (Chilton has been compared to Melville's legal copyist Bartleby, a performance artist in his own right. Bartleby, students of American lit will recall, refuses to work—'I would prefer not to,' he repeats calmly—and, like some avant-garde exhibit, stands stock-still in the middle of his workplace.)

Chilton could resemble such an artist and still draw the crowd he drew because of the two or three pivotal contributions he'd once managed: the production of early tracks for the Cramps; the cutting of the aforementioned five or six standards, including especially 'Bangkok' (1978), a postcard's worth of travel writing (or an excuse for a lascivious pun) set to two-plus minutes of frenetic music, with Chilton on guitar and, double-tracked, some other Chilton working the drum kit; and, finally, the recording of Chilton's own solo long-player, *Like Flies on Sherbert* (1979, 1980), which an astute minority (with flawless taste, I might add) rates among the very best of our rock 'n' roll.

Chilton was born in Memphis and, as a teenager, enjoyed an early success—his whole fifteen minutes of allotted fame—with a boy band of the 1960s called the Box Tops. (Even then, Chilton appeared to be drawn to the lascivious pun.) He drifted in and out of bands, a songwriting partnership, women, eventually making his way to New York, where he got 'Bangkok' on tape. (The B-side, a cover of an old chestnut by the Seeds, was every bit as nutty as the A-side.) He was the punk we most prefer but would never want to be ourselves: a punk by necessity. As one critic clarified, 'The fact that pictures of him in New York from this period make him look like Richard Hell was simply down to the fact that he couldn't afford to buy clothes or shoes.'

In 1979, he released—I want to say 'unleashed'—*Sherbert*. A slightly different version came out in 1980. Nobody bought it at the time, and I mean 'Nobody' in the Odyssean sense: that transhistorical traveller who may have been an absent husband, but was present to purchase the first pressing of *The Velvet Underground and Nico*, the first edition of *Howl*, the first issue of *transition. Sherbert* certainly didn't sound promising, at least for the opening few bars of songs like 'Boogie Shoes', on which Chilton's band sounds hard-pressed to rouse itself and Chilton, whom someone has foolishly entrusted with the vocals, comes in prematurely on the wrong beat.

The false start is left in, but then it doesn't matter; the track has won over, if not made you aware of, that perverse part of yourself that enjoys a pileup (and anyway you find you rather prefer the redundancy; later, same song, Chilton will hold the plosive 'p' of the lyric 'I want to do it 'til I can't get it up' a farty microsecond too long, the way a saxophonist will exceed his instrument's natural limits).

Sherbert—like Thomas Pynchon's novel *Gravity's Rainbow*, that era's other great work of detumescence—is all about rockets at the ends of their arcs, fuselage at its most flaccid, big stars imploding. Songs are started and scrapped abruptly, Chilton isn't always near the required mic, guitars are slashed at arbitrarily, and primitive electronics are prone to gurgle, die. (It's a record in the passive voice.) The music, a blend of covers and originals (the covers befouled by sheer proximity) fairly lurches through its genres: refried R&B, brokeneck rockabilly, torched country, punk schlock, and girl-group bubblegum, the chewed-up kind—all of this in the Lynchian mode, which had yet to be worked out formally. Producer and pianist Jim Dickinson, of the Rolling Stones' 'Wild Horses', presided over the mayhem. In surviving black-and-white footage of the sessions, a hooded man (a figure out of snuff films) beats the strings of a double bass with a drum stick. Chilton's eyeballs can be observed to bulge as he affects a comic, Transylvanian accent. Others caper about, into range of the camera, Bacchanalian-like. It's the footage that's shot by those carefree types who still feel safe in their excesses; the footage that's later recovered by the authorities in horror movies.

To the chagrin of his fans—a long-suffering lot—Chilton didn't pursue the *Sherbert* sound too much further; in the 1980s and 90s, he reinvented himself as a washer of dishes and interpreter of standards, which is to say he was washed up. But if he sometimes seemed to be phoning in his live performances, then he was also communicating, as Andy Warhol did, from a calculated distance (Warhol, recall, loved the telephone). And if Chilton, the interpreter, seemed to be defacing the Great American Songbook, then he could also be said to be annotating it, scribbling in its margins. (His take on something called 'The Oogum Boogum Song', from the 1999 covers album *Loose Shoes and Tight Pussy*, restores a dusty classic to its rightful gleam.) Like Peter Buck (guitarist for REM and, more importantly, professional music nerd) and the Cramps (who've done their share of restoration themselves), Chilton is an archivist of the already-decided-against: dusty classics, yes, but also the songs Oedipa Maas, from another Pynchon novel, *The Crying of Lot 49*, finds herself listening to: 'songs in the lower stretches of the Top 200, that would never become popular, whose melodies and lyrics would perish as if they had never been sung.' Chilton taught a generation of hipsters how to acquire their acquired tastes, and if they couldn't always make sense of his—he had a penchant for such stuff as 'Volare'—then they missed what might have been a point of his career: taste makes no sense (that is, cents; Chilton's investment in the meanderings of his taste was not a lucrative one).

In his later years, and among his more nonsensical career moves, he unearthed a cache of obscure songs, which he co-wrote in the early seventies with someone named Chris Bell. (Chilton and Bell briefly co-helmed a band or something.) Chilton began to perform these songs again and even cut a new album with an improvised lineup, including surviving members of the original arrangement and some choice ringers. Fans of *Sherbert* couldn't appreciate Chilton's renewed interest in these obviously minor songs, dashed off in his twenties, if not adolescence. But then, Chilton often seemed to have a perverse understanding of his own historical importance. (Indeed, he'd have us remember the minor works at the expense of his actual achievements.) Funnily enough, Fox's sitcom-cum-Bildungsroman, *That '70s Show*, employed one of these minor songs, 'In the Street', over its opening credits. The song must have struck the creative minds behind the show as sufficiently naïve, but at least they had taste enough not to use the original version, commissioning instead a superior cover by something called Cheap Trick.

Critics who must come up with copy to write about a cult figure like Chilton will list the far more successful artists on whom the cult figure—against good sense, all odds, the marketplace—left a clear impression. Chilton, we're informed over and over, inspired the likes of Buck as well as the Replacements, Teenage Fanclub, the Bangles, This Mortal Coil, Jeff Buckley. His is a respectable list of protegés, but it's smaller than some want to admit and always about the same in composition, give or take. (No one who values her time would bother to undertake a list of those entities influenced by, say, a Bob Dylan; like the sun's, Dylan's influence over whole hemispheres of peoples is merely assumed.) Chilton, too, is often credited with patenting an energy drink called 'powerpop', from which others made the fortune Chilton should have.

Chilton's real and lasting influence has been on the aforementioned hipster. His music is the sort of fetish item the 'flawless taste' is expected to cite. It's part of the curriculum, and to have come to an understanding as to why one should opt for an Alex Chilton over, e.g., a Bob Dylan is to have achieved the hipster's equivalent of the Bachelor of Arts: the bare minimum required to make one's way in the rarefied world of the record store and the soon-to-be-gentrified neighbourhood. Hipsters owe him not a little for their sense of slovenly cool and ought to pay his estate the appropriate royalties. They might start by buying another copy of *Sherbert*, this one for an unenlightened loved one. Or, even better, they might buy one of the rarely bought late albums. Of course, we don't owe it to Chilton to remember the music *he* would like remembered. In the long run, it's probably best we remember the music that matters to us—the 'Bangkoks' and *Sherberts*—in the interest of other sides of stories.

Lovable Losers

Kevin: Yeah, well I thought a little joke might be a good idea, just to sort of, I dunno, kick off the proceedings as it were, you know. What do you think? Good idea?

Band: Does anyone know one?

Kevin: Yeah, you ever hear the one about the middleclass idiots who sort of spend all their time analyzing their own emotions and writing bullshit poetry, you know, that we're supposed to read? I mean, as if we're fucking interested.

Band (laughs): That's a good one.

Kevin: You like that one?

Band: Where did you hear that one? Did you make it up yourself?

Kevin: No, no, it's a true story, that one.

Band (incredulous): No!

Kevin: Honestly, it's true, I didn't make it up.
                                        —Dexys Midnight Runners

Every so often, a subculture, especially an insecure one, likes a reflective surface held up to its mug, if only to confirm that it does, in fact, exist. Surely many readers of Nick Hornby's novel, *High Fidelity*—specifically, those who fancied themselves connoisseurs of their popular music—enjoyed seeing their record-store world represented in print as much as they enjoyed the novel itself. At the very least, *High Fidelity* had therapeutic benefits. It allowed a notoriously difficult type—the usually young, usually white, and invariably male record collector—an insight into certain of his own tendencies: the obsession with obscure vinyl, the making of the mixtape for purposes of mating, the compilation of the top-five list in the event of exile to some desert island. By identifying his tendencies, the novel was also gently satirizing them, but no matter; *High Fidelity* was still a pleasure, if only because it enabled that most satisfying kind of voyeurism: the prolonged peek at oneself.

A good deal of the excitement that greeted Nicholson Baker's novel *The Anthologist* in 2009 issued from the poetry world, which recognized in the novel something like its own *High Fidelity*. *The Anthologist* concerns a middle-aged poet named Paul Chowder, one of a few fictional characters in an otherwise real world—*our* world, the one in which a man named Paul Muldoon serves as poetry editor for *The New Yorker* and a Ted Kooser has 'sticky outy ears'. Chowder, we're to understand, is a bit of a has-been; it's been years since he got his Guggenheim (the 'Old Gugg', as he puts it), and the appearances of his poetry in *The New Yorker* have tapered off (not that there were many to begin with). He ought to be applying the finishing touches to an anthology, *Only Rhyme*, that he's been editing, but he can't quite bring himself to write the introduction. Instead, he has holed up in his barn and taken to kibitzing with the reader; in fact, for long stretches, the novel assumes the form of an improvised primer on poetry. (When Chowder says, 'Woops—dropped my Sharpie', ten pages in, we realize he's been diagramming something.) It's as if he's running an MFA workshop in an empty room. He's not wrestling voices or anything; he's merely rehearsing his ideas to the drywall, as lonely poets are apt to do. 'What I thought was that I could practice talking through the introduction as if I were teaching a class,' Chowder explains. (He no longer can bear to teach the real kind of class, with live students.) He's also weathering a breakup, although the romantic subplot, as in *High Fidelity*, seems a little incidental. But then so does the main plot, such as it is. Poet pines, poet procrastinates, poet serves on panel at conference.

Much of the novel's pleasure derives from Chowder's musings on poetry and anecdotes about the subculture. And yet the many names of living, breathing poets dropped by Chowder are mostly ends unto themselves. If you're hoping for a showdown between, say, Franz Wright and William Logan, for some fisticuffs between aggrieved poet and ruthless reviewer, your blood lust won't be sated. If you're agreeably scandalized when Chowder calls Billy Collins a '[C]harming chirping crack whore', you're let down a sentence later when Chowder withdraws the cheap shot. ('I know nothing about him,' he says, like a good adult. 'I know only my own jealousy.') Robert Pinsky, another big name, strikes Chowder as 'a pretty smooth dude. He used to be the poetry editor of *The New Republic*. Rejected some things of mine and more power to him.' And yet it's unclear what Chowder means by 'smooth'—an artist's *sprezzatura*, a careerist's crassness, a Don Juan's slickness? For a thwarted poet addressing an empty room, Chowder can be remarkably ambiguous, if not cagily diplomatic, about his contemporaries; he names names, but to no great effect. Only Muldoon appears (very briefly) as an actual character with something like narrative business to carry out: by encouraging Chowder to send new work to *The New Yorker*, he does double duty as *deus ex machina*, whose purpose it is to impose upon the novel a happy ending.

But then it's no simple feat to set a living, breathing poet down in a novel and concoct words for him to say or business for him to carry out; after all, he might not appreciate the words, the business. The poets who grace novels as characters tend to be selected from the ranks of the long dead. Some recent examples include Hopkins in Ron Hansen's *Exiles*, Dickinson in Jerome Charyn's *The Secret Life of Emily Dickinson*, and Marceline Desbordes-Valmore in Anne Plantagenet's *The Last Rendezvous*. Novelists especially like to exhume Byron. Perhaps the long dead, like most inanimate things, are just easier to get a grip on than the far more active and slippery and lawyer-retaining poets who, for good or bad, are still with us (though, in truth, the unacknowledged legislators of the world don't retain lawyers—their heirs do).

When writing about the long dead, the novelist can consult letters, diaries, biographies, bills of sale, marginalia: all manner of scrap. And where these fail, where the papyrus crumbles or gives way to gaps, the novelist's imagination, far from being hindered, is liberated. The exchanges between Wilfred Owen and Siegfried Sassoon, as the two poets revise Owen's work in Pat Barker's *Regeneration*, are so vivid you might think they're based on transcripts. Barker, to be sure, did her research; some of the fictional Sassoon's remarks appear to have been inspired by the *real* Sassoon's written comments, which survive on a draft of Owen's poetry. But for the most part, Barker must imagine. And what she imagines—the nudging along of the naïve talent (Owen) by the reluctant mentor (Sassoon)—is unsentimental enough to be believable:

Sassoon picked up the next sheet. Craning his neck, Owen could just see the title of the poem. 'That's in your style,' he said.

'Yes. I ... er ... *noticed*.'

'No good?'

'Starts and ends well. What happened in the middle?'

'That's quite old, that bit. I wrote that two years ago.'

'They do say if you leave something in a drawer long enough it'll either rot or ripen.' [...] Sassoon was shuffling Owen's papers together. 'Look, why don't you have a go at ...' He peered at the title. '"The Dead Beat"? Work at it till you think you've made some progress, then bring it back and we'll have a go at it together. It's not too traumatic, is it? That memory.'

'Good heavens, no.'

'How long do you spend on it? Not that one, I mean generally?'

'Fifteen minutes.' He saw Sassoon's expression change. 'That's *every day.*'

'Good God, man, that's no use. You've got to sweat your guts out. Look, it's like a drill. You don't wait till you *feel* like doing it.'

'Well, it's certainly a new approach to the Muse. "Number from the left! Form fours! Right turn!"'

It may be that Barker has recovered some sense of the pre-Iowa poetry workshop, when the student (there was but the one) was an imposition, and the teacher (a cranky aesthete) had to be won over, and the workshop doubled as somebody's living quarters (Sassoon and Owen have been working in Sassoon's room at Craiglockhart War Hospital). Or it may be that Barker understands a bygone world and its protocols: how a poet once dealt with his protegé through Socratic patience ('What happened in the middle?'), indignation ('Good God, man, that's no use'), and military simile ('Look, it's like a drill'). Or it may just be that Barker understands poets, in which case what she doesn't know about the actual Owen and Sassoon doesn't matter; she knows enough to present, in an accurate way, the putting together of two heads to make a poem better.

Nicholson Baker understands poets, too, and some of his anecdotes, I'm happy to report, are of a slightly scandalous nature. At one point we're informed that Theodore Roethke and Louise Bogan 'really liked each other. So they had their lost weekend together, drinking quarts of liquor and doing every wild fucky thing that you can imagine that two manic-depressive poets might do.' Wild fucky bits aside—and there aren't many of them—*The Anthologist* gets many other details about the American poetry world just about right. For example, Chowder's love-hate relationship with *The New Yorker*—a fine magazine with which many poets still find fault, at least until their poetry appears in it—would be note-perfect if Chowder didn't appear to have a subscription and, instead, was imagined at a Borders, paging through an unpurchased copy, wondering whether he should buy the thing. As it is, Baker has his poet thinking how he'll

> flip through the newest issue, walking back from my blue
> mailbox, hunting for the poem [Muldoon] chose over mine,
> and it'll be the same thing as always. The prose will have
> pulled back, and the poem will be there, cavorting, saying,
> I'm a poem, I'm a poem. No, you're not! You're an imposter
> [sic], you're a toy train of pretend stanzas of chopped
> garbage. Just like my poem was.

Elsewhere, the questions of Chowder's well-meaning neighbour—'So why did poems stop rhyming? Were all the rhymes just used up?'—register the layperson's ignorance of, and mild curiosity about, an alien and seemingly anachronistic art form. (In a novel about opera, the neighbour would be heard to wonder why those Viking-helmeted singers have to sing so darn *loud* all the time.) The noisy cash register that goes off during Chowder's poetry reading at a book-store is another perceptive detail, as is the poet's optimistic bit of accounting, which considers the dozen or so attendees—including 'several bookstore employees'—a 'good crowd'. (Had the reading been set in a bar, the noise would have come from a bartender clink-ing glasses or customers racking up a pool table.)

More generally, Baker allows Chowder the sort of observations that a poet may feel are true but is probably better off not commit-ting to in print. This, for instance:

> ... translations are never good.
>   Well, wait—that's not fair. That's ridiculously unfair. I've read some wonderful translations. Translations of Tranströmer, for instance. But my heart does droop when I see that it's a translation.

And this:

> And we all love the busy ferment, and we all know it's non-sense. Getting together for conferences of international poetry. Hah! A joke. Reading our poems. Our little moment. Physical presence. In the same room with. A community. Forget it. It's a joke.

For these passages alone (and there are others like them), *The Anthologist*, which is as much a study in honesty as poetry, should be handed out, shrink-wrapped, from a barrel, to aspiring poets as they enter the workshop.

And yet, as some critics have pointed out, something is slightly off in *The Anthologist*; its universe resembles a kind of Twilight Zone that falls just short of approximating reality. In *The New York Times*,

David Orr expressed bafflement at Chowder's scant references to literary magazines that aren't *The New Yorker*. David Kirby, in *The Washington Post*, raised an eyebrow at the $7,000 that Chowder will be paid on delivery of his anthology. One wonders if $7,000 is a successful novelist's idea of the kind of capital that changes hands in the poetry world. One also wonders about the business acumen of bookstores in Baker's Twilight Zone. Do they typically invite poets who, like Chowder, have no new book to promote to give readings? Poets, like touring bands, tend to gig in support of recent product. Perhaps Baker simply wanted his poet to give a reading. Perhaps a novel about a poet is supposed to feature a set piece with a reading.

More problematic is Chowder's taste in poetry. His hobby horse is something he calls four-beat poetry, stray lines of which he's apt to plump for: Raleigh's 'Give me my scallop-shell of quiet', for instance. But Chowder's hand-picked lines don't always convince. (Is the excellence of Roethke's 'Ye littles, lie more close' so self-evident it need merely be quoted? Is it really good enough to be anthologized on its own, as Chowder suggests, in some hypothetical book devoted to 'single lines'?) Worse, Chowder has a weakness for chestnuts. He subjects us to a four-page exegesis of Elizabeth Bishop's 'The Fish', a poem that even Bishop herself grew tired of seeing chewed over; and he refers us to 'The Raven', 'Ozymandias', 'Kubla Khan', 'Musée des Beaux Arts', 'The Charge of the Light Brigade'. It's not that these aren't classics worth rereading; it's that they're staples of survey courses. (Perhaps a novel about a poet is supposed to make multiple references to 'Ozymandias' and 'The Raven'?) I'm put in mind of Michael Hofmann's comments on the difference in taste between Bishop and Robert Lowell, as revealed in their correspondence:

> [H]e comes to her, at various times, with Faulkner, Pope, *Middlemarch*, Chaucer, Dryden, Tasso, Shakespeare, Carlyle, Macaulay, *Dr Zhivago*, 'all of Thucydides. Isn't Molière swell!'; she counters with such things as *Marius the Epicurean*, Frank O'Hara, Captain Slocum, Mme de Sévigné ... Sergey Aksakov. It's not that her writers are impressively obscure or *recherché*—though they are that, too!—they

bespeak a taste as his, frankly, don't. They are the product
of longer and more grown-up searching.

When it comes to contemporary poetry, Chowder's 'favorite poet at
the moment' is Mary Oliver, whose poems, he reflects, are 'very
simple. And yet each has something.' He also thinks highly of W.S.
Merwin, who, like Oliver (not to mention Bukowski, Angelou,
Neruda, and Rumi), takes up far too much of the space the typical
bookstore will cede to poetry. They're the overstocked poets that an
amateur—Chowder's neighbour, for instance—will encounter first.
Such bland, predictable taste, from a supposed insider, suggests
that the insider hasn't done enough 'grown-up searching'. We're not
surprised when he implies that it's *de rigueur* to 'crack open next
year's *Best American Poetry*' or when he receives *The New Faber
Book of Love Poems* from Amazon.

    Chowder, for all his love of four-beat poetry, has little sense of
contemporary poets who work in, as gets said, traditional forms.
Baker goes to the trouble of inventing a 'Renee Parker Task, who's a
hotshot among young formalists', but why invent a hotshot when
you can simply refer to a real one like A.E. Stallings or David Yezzi
(or an established formalist like Marilyn Hacker or Annie Finch),
especially when the novelty of your novel is, partly, its name-drop-
ping? A jab or two is thrown at the likes of Charles Olson, John Ashbery, and Allen Ginsberg, but Chowder's cudgelling of long-dead
avant-gardists, such as the 'young bully' Ezra Pound, borders on the
flogging of dead horses, especially in these target-rich times. (Ron
Silliman, Charles Bernstein, and Anne Carson are alive and well and
ready to be reviled by a sensibility like Chowder's.) His sense of
active critics and reviewers doesn't extend much beyond Helen
Vendler and Charles Simic. Where's the musing on Adam Kirsch or
Dan Chiasson, both of whom review poetry for *The New Yorker*? Or
Marjorie Perloff? Clive James? Dana Gioia? Michael Hofmann?
Ange Mlinko? If we're to have a novel about a failed poet—Chowder
once enjoyed a 'reputation as a bad-boy formalist' but can no longer
rig up a decent rhyme scheme—he surely should have suffered a
withering notice from William Logan in *The New Criterion*.

    Unlike those of the record store clerks in *High Fidelity*—whom you can trust to recommend an album you've never heard of—Chowder's range of reference is suspiciously narrow. He's rather like the hapless customer who, inquiring after some mid-period and middle-of-the-road Stevie Wonder, gets pilloried for it by a clerk. Chowder may well be intended as a parody of the middle-aged curmudgeon, out of touch with recent doings, but are most readers—the ones who know little about poetry and just want to read the new Nicholson Baker novel—going to get the parody? These readers, even if they recognize Chowder's curmudgeonliness, are apt to take him for knowledgeable, a sound guide to the American poetry world. They might even buy his conspiracy theories about iambic pentameter. (Chowder insists that what gets labelled iambic pentameter is really just a three-beat line in disguise.) They might even buy a book by Mary Oliver.

It's possible that this Paul Chowder character is little more than a special effect: the lifelike avatar of an amateur enthusiast named Nicholson Baker, who writes a stylish novel but hasn't much of a clue about poems. One can only imagine the novel the late Tom Disch, presented with the same material, would've come up with. Disch's Muldoon, I like to think, wouldn't have invited a middling mid-careerist to enlarge the slush pile of *The New Yorker*; he would have been, instead of a mere cameo figure, a fully realized, high-wattage superstar who knows enough to be wary of the moths he draws at public events. (The poetry editor of a major East Coast magazine is a god in a machine precisely to the extent that he bats away those pesky bugs that gum up the works.) And Chowder, in Disch's hands, might have been less soupy than his Pynchonesque surname leads us to believe. He might have worked the poetry editor a bit, cornered him at a party, slipped a manuscript under a bathroom stall. Or else he might have snubbed the superstar altogether, preferring his own darkness to the dizzying light. A brave novelist, I like to think, would have risked some speculation, and even a lawsuit or two. He would have arranged a duel between a Wright and a Logan. He would have told us what he really thinks about this or that big name. He would have named names, alright—in the manner of the Congressional witness who leans toward the microphone and does in careers.

If Baker's hollow hero, a bit of a dummy, gives voice to one great, troubling truth, it's the truth of another, a ventriloquist named Amy Lowell—the real-world poet and professional bane in the life of Ezra Pound. Chowder is struck by Lowell's observation that 'Poetry seems to be, for some strange reason, a young man's job'; the apophthegm, he tells us, 'slapped me in the head like a big heavy cold dogfish. Poetry is a young man's job. What a frighteningly true thought.' Chowder is a good study in middle-aged competence; he's old enough to know he'll never write a great poem but still might manage a good one. He's feeling his age and daydreaming, too. 'The wind comes over, *whssssew*,' he says,

> and it's cold, and the ladder vibrates, and I feel very exposed and high up. Off to one side there's Helen Vendler, in her trusty dirigible, filming our ascent. And I look down, and there are many people behind me. They're hurrying up to where I am. They're twenty-three-year-old energetic climbing creatures in their anoraks and goggles, and I'm trying to keep climbing. But my hands are cold and going numb. My arms are tired to tremblement [sic].

An improbable energy—cold fusion that's better left unquestioned—often powers the young poet: a yet-to-be-justified belief in the value of her own work. Kay Ryan hypothesizes that '[t]he most important thing a beginning writer may have going for her is her bone-deep impulse to defend a self that at the time might not look all that worth getting worked up about.' But it can be hard to sustain this 'bonedeep impulse' as a poet ages; as 'energetic climbing creatures', with impulses of their own, begin to accumulate behind. (In the movie, the climbing creatures will be scored to LCD Soundsystem's 'Losing My Edge'.)

* * *

If Chowder has lost his impulse, the young poets in Roberto Bolaño's novel, *The Savage Detectives*, are intensely animated by theirs. Bolaño's poets, who make up an avant-garde in Mexico City, would seem to be the sort of young men who, according to Lowell, are up to the job. How they love poetry, these energetic climbing creatures.

How much energy they have for the loving of poetry, for the churning out of 'two-handed writing, three-handed writing, masturbatory
writing (we wrote with the right hand and masturbated with the left,
or vice versa if we were left-handed), madrigals, poem-novels, sonnets always ending with the same word'—the litany runs on. Because
self-respecting avant-gardists need a brand identity all their own,
Bolaño's poets call themselves 'visceral realists' (a name that recalls
the real-world Infrarealists, of which Bolaño was a co-founder). The
visceral realists abhor canonical Octavio Paz and revere obscure
Cesárea Tinajero, the mythic fount of visceral realism. They have
but one of Tinajero's poems to go on, from the only surviving issue of
a defunct little magazine, *Caborca*, which libraries have preferred
not to remember. Nevertheless, they strike out in search of her. These
aren't the most avant of gardists; they're oriented less toward a
future destination and more toward headwaters, some source that
might explain their present foaming.

　　And foam they do: early in the novel, with the zeal of revolution-
aries, they storm a poetry workshop and denounce the instructor's
'critical system'; later, a lone visceral realist challenges a critic to a
duel with swords. (We finally get that match-up between a Wright and
his Logan.) And yet the visceral realists can't always articulate a clear
rationale for their aversions. Challenged by an editor to write a review
of Paz, they accept but don't follow through. In time, their 'childishly
stubborn' refutation of poets like Paz loses resolve. Late in the novel,
one of their leaders, Ulises Lima, who seems to have once flirted with
the notion of kidnapping Paz, stumbles on the great poet in a seedy
park—or, rather, Paz stumbles on Lima, who has taken to mucking
about in seedy parks. The meeting is amiable, anticlimactic, but then
the revolutionary energy of the visceral realists has long since dissi-
pated, let out by ellipses. 'We kept moving ...', sighs one member. 'We
kept moving.... We did what we could.... But nothing turned out
right.'

　　The quest for Tinajero takes place in 1976 and is narrated by
Juan García Madero, the youngest of the visceral realists and a late
addition to their ranks. Madero's account of the quest frames a long
series of eyewitness accounts—the bulky middle of the book—in
which different narrators, in the years following 1976, recall the

visceral realists and, in particular, their leaders, the aforementioned Lima and his friend, Arturo Belano. Because they mostly live in the minds of others, Lima and Belano can start to seem like the tissuey stuff of legend. These others (including supporters, but also editors, ex-lovers, and other professional detractors) try out all sorts of opinions about the visceral realists, and the reader is free to take sides. Bolaño's prose, as translated by Natasha Wimmer, is pleasingly functional where it could have been disastrously purple: it mostly aims to get down the voices of the narrators and then get out of their way. For a novel about poets, *The Savage Detectives*, like *The Anthologist*, gives the impression of putting a lot of stock in the power of the good old human voice at its least rehearsed and most conversational. (Fortunately, one can only *imagine* the purple prose a Michael Ondaatje or Anne Michaels, presented with the same material, would have slathered on.)

In general, the many narrators of *The Savage Detectives* don't have good news to report. In the 1980s and 90s, Lima and Belano, who often appear bedraggled, cast about the globe, passing in and out of other, more settled lives, leaving their impressions. There's a vague sense that they've gotten some stuff published, made some inroads. But the effect of the book's calculated bulk on its reader is akin to that of MLB's gruelling 162-game season; over time, as minor gains are erased by accumulating losses, the reader starts to experience the baseball fan's creeping sense of doom as sheer mathematics takes over and a beloved team is squeezed out of contention. (Or is the effect like that of, say, the mounting rejection slips that come to bury a middling mid-careerist, despite his having attained such peaks as *The New Yorker* once upon a time?) Eventually, Lima and Belano part ways, fade away. Lima, a 'real spectacle', is last eye-balled in Mexico City; Belano, a makeshift journalist, in war-torn Liberia, on the eve of some battle in which he's gotten himself mixed-up: one final windmill at which the visceral realist intends to tilt.

As for Madero, toward the end of the novel we're encouraged to believe he never existed by the 'only expert on the visceral realists', some scholar with a 'little book' on the movement. By the time Madero's narration resumes and the quest of 1976 reboots, we know that we can't quite believe in him, and that nothing much could have come of the quest; we have already heard tell of Bolaño's poets in their later years, losing steam like James Joyce's Stephen Dedalus, Thomas Pynchon's Tyrone Slothrop, and David Foster Wallace's Hal Incandenza, the great protagonists of our great novels of entropy. Indeed, *The Savage Detectives* belongs to a lineage that includes *Ulysses*, *Gravity's Rainbow*, and *Infinite Jest*, big books about exhaustion, cycling down. And the target reader of such books belongs to a lineage that includes the aforementioned record collectors. Usually young, usually male, and invariably obsessive, this reader enjoys clambering across vast tracts of the craggiest narrative turf, knowing full well there's no destination, no resolution at the end. Like Sisyphus, he enjoys the mastering of the hopeless, cyclical task.

The visceral realists, I suspect, wouldn't care much for Baker's Chowder; and Chowder, his head in the latest Oliver, wouldn't have heard of the visceral realists. Still, in spite of their superficial differences in taste (superficial because bad taste is bad taste) they have something in common: they're underdogs. As such, they refer us to earlier breeds of underdog, including the aforementioned Dedalus as well as J.D. Salinger's Seymour Glass. These underdogs may be, like Dedalus, on the cusp of forging in the smithies of their souls the uncreated conscience of their race, but they remain underdogs. We're meant to root for them. But we're not meant to read their poetry, or much of it, anyway. We're presented with just enough of Chowder's to wonder about its worth—

> I walked upstairs behind her
> Staring at her stitched seams
> Normally she wore black pants
> But it was the last day of the year
> That she could wear the white ones
> So she did

—and we're presented with none by the visceral realists, beyond Tinajero's one poem. This missing poetry probably doesn't amount to much, but the fact of its absence allows it to stay mythical:

unmade but unmarred. Our libraries are poorer for having only scraps of Sappho's body of work, but our imaginations aren't. (Pynchon's novel *Vineland* was much better during the seventeen years when it was a mere rumour going viral.) Cleverly, Bolaño—who was also a poet and could easily have ghostwritten some poems for his visceral realists—leaves the poems between the lines, where they can only raise expectations, especially in the young.

And it *is* often the young who invest the most in the *idea* of art, which doesn't always return a profit. Bolaño's poets invest so much in the idea of the poetry of Tinajero (a modern-day Sappho with even fewer scraps) they fail to notice the idea is a Ponzi scheme that will never pay off. But in following their quest for Tinajero, I, too, got caught up in the sheer adventure of it all. Just what will happen, I found myself wondering, if they actually find Tinajero? Will she recite a poem so spectacular that everyone in earshot, myself included, will spontaneously combust? Probably not, since the only extant poem of hers is a concrete poem meant to be seen, not heard. But when Bolaño knocks off Tinajero almost as soon as she's found, and, worse, denies the reader access to her notebooks (the Dead Sea scrolls of visceral realism), he knows what he's doing: preserving, by cruel twist of plot, the myth of Tinajero. Who wants her actual poetry? Her life is poetry enough.

The short life of Seymour Glass is poetry enough, too: a haiku. Salinger's beloved character serves a sentence as a child radio star; later, he serves in World War II as a combatant. He winds up as an English professor and, finally, a suicide. But what Seymour really was, his brother Buddy insists, was a poet. 'And I mean a *poet*. If he never wrote a line of poetry, he could still flash what he had at you with the back of his ear if he wanted to.' The poet, we learn, did stoop to actually write some lines—184 poems' worth, to be precise— but the reader is privy to just four, a quatrain of charming juvenilia:

John Keats
John Keats
John
Please put your scarf on.

In the wake of Seymour's suicide, Buddy is entrusted with the job of securing a publisher for the poems. Until Buddy does so, the poems can't be shared with the reader—they can only be paraphrased, by order of Seymour's widow. It's a neat trick on Salinger's part: We *have to* take Buddy's word that Seymour's 'un-Western' and 'lotusy' poems are as good as he claims—so good, so pure, their publication will be their soiling. In fact, the publisher he has in mind—a jaded mind—will inevitably

> bear them away, right off to his *shady* presses, where they'll very likely be *constrained* in a two-tone dust jacket, complete with a back flap featuring a few curiously *damning* remarks of endorsement, as solicited and acquired from those *'name'* poets and writers who have *no compunction* about commenting in public on their fellow-artists' works.... [italics mine; cynicism his]

But having talked up his brother's poetry, Buddy has the presence of mind to ask, 'Do I go on about my brother's poetry too much? Am I being garrulous? Yes. Yes.' And in a tangent on Shelley's 'Ozymandias' (that classic of survey-course curricula to which Chowder refers us), Buddy wonders, 'Is it conceivable that [Shelley's] life is outliving much of his best poetry?' Buddy, singing his brother's praises, seems to suspect that poets must do more than cultivate what he calls 'Racy, Colorful Lives'; they must either sing or, as Buddy puts it, 'give us one good field mouse, flushed by the heart, in every stanza.'

At least Joyce's Dedalus squeaks out some song in *Portrait of the Artist as a Young Man*: he labours over a villanelle, and the reader even gets to read it. ('Your eyes have set man's heart ablaze', goes one line.) But, as critic Seamus Deane suggests, the villanelle is hardly worth the effort: '[Dedalus] forsakes everyone, he goes off armed with a half-baked aesthetic theory that, after mountainous labour, has only produced a little mouse of a poem; he dedicates himself solemnly and humorlessly to an absurdly overstated ambition.' (Deane, unlike Buddy, demands more of a poem than mere mousiness.) Dedalus's next attempt at song has its premiere in *Ulysses*:

On swift sail flaming
From storm and south
He comes, pale vampire,
Mouth to my mouth.

It's the juvenilia of a goth—an Irish one who doesn't favour eyeliner, but a goth just the same.

Dedalus, to his credit, *does* suspect that he's a bit ridiculous. Walking along a beach, he recalls his younger self:

You bowed to yourself in the mirror, stepping forward to applause earnestly, striking face. Hurray for the God-damned idiot! Hray! No-one saw: tell no-one. Books you were going to write with letters for titles. Have you read his F? O yes, but I prefer Q. Yes, but W is wonderful. O yes, W. Remember your epiphanies on green oval leaves, deeply deep, copies to be sent if you died to all the great libraries of the world, including Alexandria?

Dedalus is only slightly more productive an epiphanist than Little Chandler, the newly married father of one in Joyce's short story 'A Little Cloud'. Little Chandler would like to 'write a book and get it published, that might open the way for him.' In fact, '[t]here were so many things he wanted to describe: his sensation of a few hours before on Grattan Bridge, for example. If he could get back again into that mood....' But Little Chandler has a crying child to rock. He stands for every aspiring poet who has ever tried to settle into a rhythm of work, only to be interrupted by progeny, domestic duties, the white noise of family life.

Joyce's poets aren't as productive as Bolaño's Madero, who, at the age of seventeen, can take the following inventory:

How many poems have I written?
    Since it all began: 55 poems.
    Total pages: 76.
    Total lines: 2,453.
    I could put together a book by now. My complete works.

Still, Dedalus and Madero share a fantasy: they want to possess an oeuvre, without having to give too much thought to what it might consist of. (The reader certainly never gets to inspect Madero's metastasizing body of poetry, which remains as abstract a proposition as Dedalus's trilogy, 'F', 'Q', and 'W'.) Dedalus, I suspect, would have found kindred spirits among the visceral realists; and they, in turn, would have found a solid travelling companion in Dedalus, who, by the end of *Ulysses* (which constitutes a virtual walking tour of Dublin) has demonstrated he has the legs for entropic quests. Indeed, in another time—the 1940s, say—the visceral realists would have journeyed to Manhattan in the hope of reading (or, better, coming *close* to reading) one of Seymour's 'lotusy' poems. They would have loved to learn that Seymour is dead, the fact of his suicide a bonus; and they would have preferred arriving late to the furnace where Buddy has only *just* rosebudded the last of Seymour's unread poems, the notebooks buckling, crackling. These are young men more interested in playing poet than writing poetry, more interested in the idea of poetry than the matter itself. Poetry, after all, is merely fodder for their own inner fires.

Even those fictional poets who would appear to be successful—who have actually written good poetry and been acclaimed for it—can seem like lovable losers. John Shade, the subject of Nabokov's *Pale Fire*, is one of the great fictional poets, perhaps the greatest. The proof is in the poetry that Nabokov, a genius, donates to Shade:

> I was the shadow of the waxwing slain
> By the false azure in the windowpane;
> I was the smudge of ashen fluff—and I
> Lived on, flew on, in the reflected sky.
> And from inside, too, I'd duplicate
> Myself, my lamp, an apple on a plate:
> Uncurtaining the night, I'd let dark glass
> Hang all the furniture above the grass,
> And how delightful when a fall of snow
> Covered my glimpse of lawn and reached up so
> As to make chair and bed exactly stand
> Upon that snow, out in that crystal land!

These, the opening couplets of Shade's last poem, aren't the work of a young poet whose gaze is turned inward, but rather the assured output of an old man who, as a child, peered at windowpanes in which the reflections of furniture were made, by a poet's emerging vision, to stand on snow. (The young Shade gazing at glass wasn't posing in mirrors; he was working at poetry.) Shade is no Tinajero, living in obscurity, awaiting the pilgrimage of young followers, literary executors-to-be. His work has been recognized; he and his wife can tune in to a televised debate about poetry with the reasonable expectation that Shade will be mentioned. If anything, he has *too* devoted a following; after Shade is murdered, a mad scholar, Dr Charles Kinbote, absconds with the manuscript of Shade's last poem and—fitting it with a commentary—imposes his own meanings on it. Shade becomes a victim of violence, both physical and scholarly. He is riddled with bullets and, worse, endnotes.

If not always charming, poets like Chowder and Madero are surely easier to like than the Speedo-wearing caricature of a Nobel Laureate in David Foster Wallace's short story 'Death Is Not the End'. The unnamed Laureate, having been 'thrice rejected' by the Guggenheim Fellowship Committee,

> had decided that he'd simply be damned, starve utterly, before he would ever again hire a graduate assistant to fill out the tiresome triplicate Guggenheim Foundation Fellowship application and go through the tiresome contemptible farce of 'objective' consideration ever again.

The visceral realists are definitely easier to like than the right-wingèd monsters in Bolaño's encyclopedia of imaginary writers, *Nazi Literature in the Americas.*

Ultimately, one's reaction to the visceral realists reveals something about one's tolerance for the sort of fiery, youthful rebellion that doesn't require a lot of fuel—the sort that runs on plumes of smokescreen. As John Updike suggests—in a review of a book by, coincidentally, Nicholson Baker—'out of the books of others we sift a book of our own, wherein we read the lessons we need to hear.' Some will see, in *The Savage Detectives,* a loving portrait of the necessary pretensions of young poets. Those with a soft spot for the sheer idea of the avant-garde may just see a loving portrait, period. Experts on Mexican literature and historians of the 1970s, tapping gently, will detect some real people behind Bolaño's characters. Myself, I'm pretty sure I see some of the poets with whom I once shared workshops: kids who weren't especially sharp but still fancied themselves edgy; who felt that a poem about a spider ought to assume the shape of a spider; who organized themselves with the fervour of guerrillas, usually against those elements they deemed conformist; who were suspected of defacing a display case of faculty books, in protest against their exclusion from some official event at the university, some bit of pomp. (So-called 'avant-gardists' never pout more than when they've been denied the very swag that they, as ascetic rebels, ought to spurn.) These, my peers, harboured what they believed to be a healthy mistrust of authority; they are the reason I now harbour a healthy mistrust of a healthy mistrust of authority.

And yet I do detect, in Bolaño's poets, a younger version of myself, daydreaming about the stories I imagined Salinger was stockpiling in secret. In truth, I didn't really want the stories; his hermit's life was story enough. But to this day it's a safe bet to buy me a record if the musician who made it is a reclusive perfectionist. It's even safer if the musician is dead, and her one release, a murky demo, a mere hint at what could have been. (I tend to feel, like the audiophiles in *High Fidelity*, the pull of the obscure.) So when Bolaño, without blinking, kills off Tinajero and closes the book on her oeuvre forever, some small, sentimental part of me is indulged. But we ought to be wary of overindulging our small, sentimental parts. Bolaño—and this is true of Baker and certainly Salinger—entertains not a little love for his fictional poets. And because these poets are modeled on actual people who once comprised Bolaño's circle, the love can amount to self-love. (Belano, his name suggests, is really just a stand-in for Bolaño.)

Whatever we feel about Chowder or the visceral realists, we could probably use more representations of poets who aren't lovable losers; who have enjoyed some success in areas outside of literature, such as medicine or insurance—poets for whom poetry is not the only obsession, not a means to revolution. We could do with more poets who, like T.S. Eliot, consider poetry a 'supreme amusement'; more poets who, in taking poetry less seriously than, say, a visceral realist, just might wind up taking it more seriously. We could do with more poets who will assure us that they, too, dislike poetry. In general, we could stand to read about fewer adolescents, fewer failures, fewer white guys. We could stand to read about more cult figures— not the fetish objects of some avant-garde's perpetual questing, but craftsmen, poets' poets, inveterate scribblers in margins, on receipts. And we could stand more dry wits, more Sassoons, editing the work of the wet-behind-the-ears. We've had a lot of fictional poets who are easy to love; we need more who actually deserve it.

The Kindness of Second Readings

Frederick Goddard Tuckerman wrote poems too weird to be much appreciated in his own milieu, the United States of the nineteenth century, and not weird enough to distinguish the poet to many of his later readers who, failing to squint, saw little more than an accomplished sonneteer. Those contemporaries of Tuckerman's who might've otherwise enjoyed the poems tended to quibble and find his handling of form a bit 'rough'. Nathaniel Hawthorne, an admirer of the 1860 edition of Tuckerman's *Poems*, a privately printed affair, appears to have had a grasp of the problem. '[I]f you could be read twice,' Hawthorne wrote to Tuckerman, 'the book might be a success; but who reads (in a way that deserves to be called reading) so much as once, in these days?' Hawthorne reminds us that holding the attention of the distracted is a social problem that predates the hyperlinked web page.

Selected Poems of Frederick Goddard Tuckerman, edited by Ben Mazer and introduced by Stephen Burt, offers current readers an opportunity to pass over the passed-over poet all over again. They really shouldn't; this is a crisp edition of some pretty fine verse. Still, a frustrated well-wisher may wish the poet had thought ahead and taken pains to include a few more surface novelties—a few more em dashes, maybe—to push the modern angle and scare up an audience.

But then, as his biographer of 1966 put it, 'Tuckerman never thought of himself as a pioneer; he went his solitary way exploiting the sonnet form, experimenting with diction and imagery to satisfy only himself.' At the age of ten, Tuckerman, already the anti-rebel, would author a memorandum in which he pledged 'to try to behave better at table and to try to break myself of being so set and always wanting to have just what I like best all the time.' The adult would go on to find the sonnet a sturdy enough structure for weird poetry about decaying New England houses. He would also become something like a recluse. 'Critics sometimes wonder about the reason for this,' observes the critic Yvor Winters, 'but I am sure that the isolation was caused merely by intense boredom—it could not have been otherwise.' This is the humane speculation of an advocate. It frees the serious artist—who has withdrawn from his society—from the image of the neighbourhood crank, that loner who keeps snakes and enlivens the folklore of the locals.

Tuckerman's poems, especially the ones composed in the wake of his wife's death in 1857, grieve and grieve. They fess up to a powerlessness in the face of a larger, incomprehensible force we might call variously God, Time, Nature. In 'Sonnet V', from the third of his terrific sonnet sequences, the centrepiece of Tuckerman's achievement, the speaker recalls an anxious trot which he and a little sister took through a 'burial place':

> The stones that grudgd us way, the graveside weed
> The ominous wind that turn'd us half about.
> Smit by the flying drops, at what a speed
> Across the paths, unblest, & unforgiven
> We hurried homeward when the day was late
> And heard with awe that left no place for doubt
> God's anger mutter in the darken'd heaven.

The stones make up a half-alive hoard, shuffling aside to let interlopers through. (The alliteration of 'gr' emphasizes the reluctance with which nature grindingly gives way to our timid trespasses.) The thunder isn't mere Gothic effect; it's the inexplicable muttering of an inexplicable deity—the speaker's younger self's sure of it and duly awed.

Tuckerman's early work can be vague, even clichéd. But where the immature poet saw 'pine-trees weep' and 'pining woodland ways', the mature poet of the sonnet sequences notes

> Dank fens of cedar; hemlock-branches gray
> With tress and trail of mosses wringing-wet;
> Beds of the black pitch-pine in dead leaves set
> Whose wasted red has wasted to white away.

It's as if the bout of glaucoma that impaired the younger poet has reversed, and a foggy landscape can now assert its alien and complex self in HD, augmented by sparkling sound. Here is a 'low brook drawling by'. There is a 'worm, that touch'd, a twig-like semblance takes'. Tuckerman elected to see out his years among the flora and fauna of his New England; rarely have flora and fauna enjoyed the privilege of such precise attention.

But Tuckerman is good about giving some definition to abstract stuff, too. Scandal, which a lesser poet would be tempted to personify, is positively pungent: 'bleeding-new, or journal dank', as a nineteenth-century sensibility would've experienced it. In another sonnet, the speaker, with a mind to describe his terrible, roiling grief, pictures the rock in which 'the sea/Has worm'd long caverns, like my tears in me'. In yet another,

<blockquote>
the sea
Went back & forth upon its bar of shells,
Wash'd & withdrew, with a soft shaling sound,
As though the wet were dry, & joy were grief.
</blockquote>

In Tuckerman, a pleasant visit to the beach can turn like a sonnet; a New England home can turn derelict. Civilization, ever provisional, is mostly a matter of front-facing. Light falls on a mantelpiece, on a 'vase of violet', but Tuckerman is privy to what once occupied the same spot: 'the forest-heart, hung blackening/The wolf-bait on the bush beside the spring.'

It's the curse of a Tuckerman—like the toy monkey who won't stay buried—to be rediscovered over and over. Critics looking to promote the poet will bring up run-ins with the likes of some Hawthorne or Tennyson. It may be that they want to provide some historical context, or that they hope the dandruff of fame will rub off on the wanting figure. Tuckerman has also been enlisted in the service of lost causes. Yvor Winters, who nursed a thing against Romanticism, thought Tuckerman one of the best American poets of the nineteenth century, and Tuckerman's 'The Cricket', 'the greatest poem in English of the century' and 'a greater poem than *Sunday Morning* [sic]'. Burt's sensible, sober introduction to Mazer's selection, however, appeals to a sense of perspective. 'The most ambitious claims that have been made for Tuckerman,' writes Burt, '(Winters's in particular) are more against other American poets than for him; he deserves to be remembered instead for what he did well.' This is probably true, even if one can't help but secretly enjoy ambitious, if not perversely untenable, claims. Winters's opinion of Tuckerman blooms within the critical consensus like an insoluble tonic: a column of kicked-up sand, compelling in its own right.

Tuckerman has always relied on the kindness of second readings. (He has already been reappraised a few times in the last century or so.) Perhaps the best one can hope for Tuckerman is that this new edition arranges for the professional oblivionist a fresh cohort of devotees who will give his poems their next second reading.

Chain of Fools

When I was invited to review *Human Chain*, the twelfth collection of poems by some Seamus or other, I was like, sure; I felt certain I'd heard of the author before. Nevertheless, I consulted a learned expert, which is to say the Google homepage, and started typing. As soon as I reached the 'm' in the subject's given name, the mind of Google not only knew who I was after; it filled in the rest of his name. (It also supposed I might have an interest in 'seamonkey', 'seamus o'regan wedding', and the state of being 'seamless'.) A person's importance, we've come to learn, is a function of the minimum number of keystrokes it takes for an Internet search engine to have heard of him. Seamus Heaney comes to mind, the mind of Google, very quickly.

I'm kidding, of course; a person's importance is also a function of his celebrity. Heaney did the adaptation for an Angelina Jolie vehicle called *Beowulf*. He has received the odd prize, too. But he first acquired a name as long ago as the 1970s, for certain poems about nooks and crannies and digging up dirt on Ireland's natural history. In 'Bogland', 'The Tollund Man', 'Bog Queen', and others, Heaney, a kind of forensic anthropologist, pokes around the bogs of his country, stumbling upon prehistoric bodies and, worse, the template for *CSI*. (The speaker in 'The Glanmore Sonnets', from 1979's *Field Work*, calls himself an 'etymologist of roots and graftings'. But the very turf of Ireland, wracked by the Troubles, also presented the poet with a palimpsest of violence—a crime scene to squat near and brood on.) Other, more personal poems of the period make an *artistic* virtue of nosing about and burrowing; amateur archaeology, these poems insist, is a form of writing. Indeed, in the final quatrain of the remarkable 'Personal Helicon', a child who once got into crevices and up to no good—who could not be kept 'from wells / And old pumps'—has grown up to become a poet, with an *Ars Poetica* that explains his childish behaviour:

> Now, to pry into roots, to finger slime,
> To stare, big-eyed Narcissus, into some spring
> Is beneath all adult dignity. I rhyme
> To see myself, to set the darkness echoing.

Elsewhere, in something called 'Digging'—Heaney's greatest hit apparently, his 'Come On Eileen'—the spade with which earlier generations of Heaney men cut through turf is repurposed as a pen, and the pen, the one that's mightier than the sword, as a peace-time implement: 'snug as a gun' but not, in fine, a gun. It's a neat conceit—the conceit of a lifetime, really. In the elegy 'Mid-Term Break', the speaker puts conceit to use and digs a hole, this one for a four-year-old's earth-bound coffin: '[a] four-foot box, a foot for every year'. (If only the line was made of four iambic feet, instead of the five! Still, is there a more memorably measured grave in English verse?) Your Internet browser offers the earnest student of Heaney all manner of resources related to these beautiful early poems, especially 'Digging', including web sites that make available the term papers of other earnest students, for a fee. Poems are classics when they power an industry: the educators who assign them and the students who are required to have an original thought about them.

Poems are also classics when their own author can't help but plagiarize the things. Indeed, if *Human Chain*, which reflects on different stages of Heaney's life, was submitted for extra credit, I'd want to ask the author to come in for a meeting and explain himself or, at least, the origin of lines like

> me in broad daylight
> On top of a cartload
> Of turf built trig and tight,
> Looked up to, looking down,
> Allowed the reins like an adult ...

and

> Run your hand into
> The ditchback growth

And you'd grope roots,
Thick and thin.
But roots of what?

and

She took me into the ground, the spade-marked
Clean-cut inside of a dugout
Meant for calves.

Dung on the floor, a damp gleam
And seam of sand like white gold
In the earth wall, nicked fibres in the roof.

These passages—with their 'turf' and 'roots' and 'spade'—are perhaps intended to tease, like the few bars of a hit song a reunited band would rather not play but feels compelled to acknowledge when performing live. You've got to throw the dog a bog, they seem to suggest.

One new poem, 'The Conway Stewart', even plays like a sequel to 'Digging'—a misguided sequel with a bigger budget than the original, but a sequel all the same. (Never mind that 'The Pitchfork', from Heaney's 1991 collection *Seeing Things*, took a stab at extending the franchise, comparing the plain old pitchfork to the javelin of an athlete or warrior.) The poem's young speaker, in the market for a luxury pen and on the eve of 'parting' from his family, gazes upon a

'Medium', 14-carat nib,
Three gold bands in the clip-on screw-top,
In the mottled barrel, a spatulate, thin

Pump-action lever
The shopkeeper
Demonstrated,

The nib uncapped,
Treating it to its first deep snorkel
In a newly opened ink-bottle,

Guttery, snottery,
Letting it rest then at an angle
To ingest,

Giving us time
To look together and away
From our parting, due that evening,

To my longhand
'Dear'
To them, next day.

That 'first deep snorkel ... Guttery, snottery' gets the gulp of a
fountain pen perfectly. (It also suggests the sniffling, if not stiff
upper-lipping, of a golden lad about to leave for school.) But the
Conway Stewart's not the modest, 'snug as a gun' implement of
'Digging' or even the 'small runny pen' of a later poem in *Human
Chain*, 'Colum Cille Cecinit'; the Conway Stewart is serious
artillery—a deluxe 'Pump-action' affair. There's nothing wrong, of
course, with composing a paean to a luxury good. (Frederick Sei-
del, the great bard of Ducati racing bikes, does so all the time.)
Indeed, Heaney's poem might've been better off concentrating
solely on pen-as-fetish-object. But by turning away from the Conway Stewart abruptly, by turning the shopping trip into a backdrop
for a 'parting', for an emotional moment, the poem suggests that
the reader of 2010 (the reader for whom the recent economic crisis
has already provided more than enough emotional moments)
should care about an event that, as described, doesn't do enough to
earn her interest and might even annoy: a slightly melancholic kid
receiving a pen with a '14-carat nib', for the writing of homesick letters and, I'm guessing, a master's juvenilia. If 'The Conway Stewart' was accompanied by harpsichord and done in stop-motion, it
would be a Wes Anderson picture.

'The Conway Stewart' also presents evidence of a master on automatic: a memory is selected, an object fingered, some larger point triggered. So, too, does the book's title poem, which concerns a literal human chain: a line of labourers passing bags of meal along. 'Nothing surpassed//That quick unburdening,' the speaker tells us, before pivoting toward the final tercet and a grand finale: the 'unburdening', the letting go of the bags, is 'backbreak's truest pay-back,/A letting go which will not come again./Or it will, once. And for all.' The lines are accomplished, if a little tossed-off: the poem throws in with some internal rhyme, stands guard against cliché by cleaving one in two. But the overgeneralization seems easy: 'Nothing surpassed//That quick unburdening....' (Really? Nothing?) And the abrupt, implied epiphany—we're all connected until we're not; there's letting go and *then there's letting go*—socks us like a bag of meal. Why must poems insist on converting grunt labour into a greater, transcendent sum? Is it that, in looking for a quick way out of poems, the easiest direction is up?

The poem, 'The Butts', on the other hand, gets a grip on so much more than a pen and a parting, a bag of meal and a cooked-up con-clusion: the impenetrable mysteries of a dying man and, finally, the man himself—the body that wants sponging. At the beginning of the poem, Heaney maps out the musty ecosystem of an elder's wardrobe—a different breed of bog—as defamiliarized by trespass-ing speaker, a child, probably:

His suits hung in the wardrobe, broad
And short
And slightly bandy-sleeved,

Flattened back
Against themselves,
A bit stand-offish.

Stale smoke and oxter-sweat
Came at you in a stirred-up brew
When you reached in,

A whole rake of thornproof and blue serge
Swung heavily
Like waterweed disturbed.

Like the 'snottery' pen of 'The Conway Stewart', the suits are personified—tailored to human proportion—expertly. But unlike the
pen, they're 'stand-offish'; they've got character and compel attention. The wardrobe itself is less obvious a symbol than the human
chain or bag of meal, and more murky; the suits 'Swung heav-
ily/Like waterweed disturbed.' Later, the 'chaff cocoons' of the
suits' 'cold smooth pocket-lining' prove to be

A paperiness not known again
Until the last days came

And we must learn to reach well in beneath
Each meagre armpit
To lift and sponge him,

One on either side,
Feeling his lightness,
Having to dab and work

Closer than anybody liked
But having, for all that,
To keep working.

That long, penetrating line—'And we must learn to reach well in
beneath'—digs in, painfully; if you've had to handle one, you'll
know that a frail body in its 'last days' has too much give to it. It
draws us close, 'closer than anybody liked', and requires 'work'.
The epiphany, then, packs in none of the title poem's wallop—the
'once. And for all'; it gets at a more human-scale discomfort with
decay and death. Moreover, it precedes a three-part sequence on
Heaney's 2006 stroke, the second part of which avoids epiphany
altogether and sticks to the stunning facts, like the

hand that I could not feel you lift
And lag in yours throughout that journey
When it lay flop-heavy as a bellpull

And we careered at speed through Dungloe,
Glendoan, our gaze ecstatic and bisected
By a hooked-up drip-feed to the cannula.

Having 'careered at speed' in an ambulance myself—my father the victim of the stroke—I can attest to the fact that the facts—the 'hooked-up drip-feed', for one—are estranging enough.

But between the accomplished poems spills the stuff of, well, stuffing. *Human Chain* is a mixed bag of meal: remembrances, covers of Irish lyrics, a bit of translation. 'Derry Derry Down' comes on as the kind of folk tune a musician calls to mind and reels off at sound check, so that the engineer can check the levels; the kind of trifle that belongs to the public domain and means more to the musician who recalls it than the audience that endures it. The first section of the trifle ogles at

The lush
Sunset blush
On a big ripe

Gooseberry:
I scratched my hand
Reaching in

To gather it
Off the bush,
Unforbidden,

In Annie Devlin's
Overgrown
Back garden.

This sort of thing would be precious if it wasn't so literally cheeky. 'Annie Devlin's/Overgrown/Back garden' isn't just any garden; it's all such secret nooks and crannies—that is, fannies—into which ventures some whippersnapper and out of which emerges dewy-wet Man. The poem winks, and the reader, fairly fanned, winces. (At least in 'Nesting Ground', from 1975's *Stations*, the sentry has the good sense not to plunge his arm into 'sandmartins' nests', where it might get clawed up. And in 'The Skunk', from *Field Work*, the speaker is more direct and adult about his ogling of the beloved's 'head-down, tail-up hunt in a bottom drawer/For the black plunge-line nightdress.')

Other moments in *Human Chain* seem downright parodic of an earthy, folksy poetry, knocked together in a shed. We hear tell of 'a van/Roadblocking the road'; a 'speed-merchant ... Hard-rounding the corner'; a 'sun-admitting door'; a 'letting go'; an 'alms-collecting mite-box', a 'shortcutting to the buses'. Elsewhere, prepositions jut like splinters, as if the poet has been breaking lines across a cor- duroyed knee, thus keeping the lines honest and putting a rustic edge on some otherwise well-made poetry. In 'The Baler', summer is 'Fork-lifted, sweated through/And nearly rewarded enough//By the giddied-up race of a tractor/At the end of the day/Last-lapping a hayfield.' In 'Eelworks', the speaker describes a 'first encounter with the up close/That had to be put with.' He goes on to note 'The butt of the freckled/Elderberry shoot//I made a rod of', 'the blue- black/Slick-backed waterwork/I'd live to reckon with.' I know peo- ple who can't get enough of chewing over this roughed-up stuff. (Sometimes, for brief moments, I'm one of them.) But after awhile it does discolour the teeth.

Heaney is at his best when, like the forensic anthropologist of the early poems, he's got his eye on the details: the way an 'oil-fired heating boiler comes to life/Abruptly, drowsily, like the timed col- lapse/Of a sawn down tree'; or the sound of Walter de la Mare as he pronounces bark—'*ba-aak*'—'in his rare, recorded voice'; or the way 'a gross of nibs', in a dream, 'Spills off the shelf, airlifts and links/Into a giddy gilt corona.' One wants to tell folks not to try this sort of precise, memorable description at home—and one means it. Still, the diehards (which is a lot of us, apparently, linked arm-in-arm) will opt to love *Human Chain* and make it—have made it!—an unqualified success. (It's tussling, even as I get this down in Word, with Mary Oliver's *Swan* for the top of the charts—the charts that track sales of poetry, but still.) The rest of us, when we have to, will admire it publicly with muted words—if only because the wider world's praise is so ringing—even as we scratch our heads privately, and think, 'I want to like this more than I do.' These rest of us would be well-advised to look into the older poems, which the Web, the true human chain, can be counted on to keep at hand. I'm not pulling your chain.

Sub-Seuss

Young people encounter many temptations on their way to adulthood: vampires, *Atlas Shrugged*, Pink Floyd, the acoustic guitar. Of course, such stuff, designed to indulge one's sense of oneself as a unique individual, must eventually be repudiated. It's not easy, growing up.

But I had no trouble saying no to the relentlessly quirky e.e. cummings. Thank the high school teacher who required me to get cummings's 'anyone lived in a pretty how town' by heart. I laboured over the poem for an afternoon, recited it to the wall, gave up. What was at stake if I misremembered the order of words like 'up so floating many bells down'? Does it really matter it's not 'up so *many* floating bells down'? Would cummings himself have applauded the mistake as a heartening sign of a maverick mind at play?

The poetry, I concluded, wasn't just sub-Seuss; it was tantamount to a teaching tool of the most condescending kind: the last resort. (*No, really, poetry is crazy fun* was the point one was meant to internalize.) cummings seemed to have been invented to convert that stubborn student the syllabus has failed to win over to verse—or, at least, to reacquaint the kid with his inner child, the id whose appetite for nonsense and nursery rhymes has been socialized away. When it came to cummings (or unstructured playtime) resistance was supposed to be futile.

Randall Jarrell nearly said as much when he noted that, 'No one else has ever made avant-garde, experimental poems so attractive to both the general and the special reader.' He should've said that, 'No one else has ever made a *formula* for avant-garde, experimental poems so attractive to people who don't actually read poetry but would like to think they can write it.' Even today, it's enough to reject an institution or two—capitalism, grammatical English—to be mistaken for an innovator. Rebel, misspell, repeat:

v

o

i

c

  eo

    ver

(whi!tethatr?apidly

legthelessne sssuc kedt oward

black,this

)roUnd ingrOundIngly rouNdar(round)ounDing

                       ;ball

                       balll

                       ballll

                       balllll

The message that cummings communicates here—and which langpo types and concrete poets continue to internalize—is remarkably unambiguous: words are toy blocks, and poems, child's play. No one else has made making it new look so easy.

But cummings's poems themselves were only superficially 'new'. Beneath the tattoo-thin signifiers of edginess—those lowercase 'i's, those words run together—flutters the heart of a romantic. (Is there a correlation between typographically arresting poetry and emotional arrestedness?) He fancies himself an individual among masses, finds the church ladies have 'furnished souls', opposes war. He's far more self-righteous, this romantic, than any soldier or gossip—and far deadlier: he's a teenager armed with a journal.

Recording his thoughts about sex or the female body, however, cummings's speaker is less a teenager than a child trapped in a man's body, which is to say a man-child: a boob blinking at a pair of breasts. In poem after poem, he can't help but notice such curiosities as 'sticking out breasts' and 'uttering tits' and 'bragging breasts' and 'ugly nipples squirming in pretty wrath' and breasts that are 'firmlysquirmy with a slight jounce' and 'wise breasts half-grown'. (Hands off, ladies! He's spoken for.) And when he shifts his attention to other parts of the beloved—and, worse, gropes for only

the weirdest words to describe them—the boob makes an ass of
himself:

> i bite on the eyes' brittle crust
> (only feeling the belly's merry thrust
> Boost my huge passion like a business
>
> and the Y her legs panting as they press
>
> proffers its omelet of fluffy lust)

How does one excuse such lines? Is it that you can't write a poem
without breaking some eggs? That you can't make it new without
making a mess?

> boys w!ll be boyss, i guess....

The Spectric Poets

'Among recent poets in English, we have noted few who can be regarded in a sure sense as Spectrists'—so sniffed Anne Knish, in the preface to an anthology too exclusive to admit more than a couple of poets: Knish and her colleague Emanuel Morgan. It was a coterie that could fit inside a foxhole. Nevertheless, from 1916 to 1918, the Spectrists had the attention of figures like Edgar Lee Masters and editors of magazines like *Poetry*. Harriet Monroe accepted Spectric poems; Alfred Kreymborg kitted out an issue of *Others* with the stuff. Knish and Morgan's anthology, *Spectra: A Book of Poetic Experiments* (1916), was covered in the papers and, like all novelties perceived to be cutting edge, divided readers. An impromptu fan base dispatched letters to Pittsburgh, the improbable locale where the movement's masters made camp. Even William Carlos Williams struck up a correspondence. Knish was said to be Hungarian, the prized object of suitors' duels. Morgan was said to be one of the duellists. That the Spectrists have largely been forgotten shouldn't be counted against contemporary memories, however, or some vision of Stubborn, Steamrolling History; oblivion is the proper fate of figures who never quite existed in the first place.

Knish was really Arthur Davison Ficke, and Morgan, Witter Bynner. Ficke and Bynner were a pair of poets who composed the sort of competent poetry that would come to be displaced by the efforts of more experimental modernists like T.S. Eliot, Ezra Pound, and the rest. But the pair of poets was also a pair of jokers; and Ficke and Davison, when remembered at all, are remembered for the mock-modernist poems they whipped up and attributed to their Spectric alter egos—poems like Knish's 'Opus 50', which kicked off the anthology. Having imagined 'a dusk/Where rich amber lights/Quiver obscurely' and 'the depths of a tropic forest', Knish concludes, 'I think I must have been born in such a forest, / Or in the tangle of a Chinese screen.'

What—beyond the sheer fact of Amy Lowell—were Davison and Bynner mocking? 'Our intent in publishing [*Spectra*],' Bynner wrote *Poetry* in 1918, 'was not to question the use of free verse and not to "bait the public", but to satirize fussy pretence....' By this point, the hoax had been exposed; the Spectric poems Monroe had accepted would not appear in her magazine. But if they *had*, they wouldn't have looked especially out of place alongside the work of a Lowell or Stevens. (But then even today, the opening lines of Knish's 'Opus 40'—'I have not written, reader / That you may read'—would rouse the guy (it's usually a guy) who finds, say, Kenneth Goldsmith's ambition to author unreadable books provocative: the masochist who takes pleasure in being told to fuck off.) When Knish describes her entanglement in a 'Chinese screen', she might as well be describing generations of rebels who, in supposing they've wriggled free of mainstream habits, find themselves entangled in an entirely new set: the tendency to want to stump readers, turn a nose up at the bourgeois, reject the rational, prioritize immediacy, and appropriate the work of those others who seem sufficiently Other.

Funny thing about the Spectric hoax, though: it resulted in some poems that, well, *wouldn't have looked out of place alongside the work of a Lowell or Stevens!* Some of it was offensive, much of it silly. But in panning with such perverse abandon for only the most convincing fool's gold, Ficke and Bynner couldn't help but turn up a few nuggets of the real stuff:

> Its mighty roof
> Is copper rivering with the rain.
> —from 'Opus 76', by Knish

> And in the dawn, lava ... rolling down ...
> Down-rolling lava on an up-pointing town.
> —from 'Opus 7', by Morgan

A thousand round-red mouths of pain
Blaring black,
A twisting comrade on his back
In a round-red stain,
Clotted stalks of red sumac,
Discs of the sun on a bayonet-stack....
—from 'Opus 29', by Morgan

Knish's preface to *Spectra* identifies the 'theme of a poem ... as a prism, upon which the colorless white light of infinite existence falls and is broken up into glowing, beautiful, and intelligible hues'—nonsense to us, but not necessarily to a generation still trying to reckon with Vortices and Images. And prankish preface aside, the Spectric anthology *is* flecked with poems that gleam: opuses 40 and 80 by Knish, and opuses 9, 16 and 29 by Morgan. These are marred only by their anti-titles, which satirize the tendency of poets to feel that their fleeting perceptions—their dream songs and cantos—are too precious to label properly and so better be tagged and logged quickly. Grant them proper titles, affix Stevens's name, and they would look like the minor works of a master.

In the wake of the hoax, armchair psychologists opined that Ficke and Bynner, by taking up masks, had actually unmasked their true selves. (Inside every stuffy formalist writhes a straitjacketed experimentalist!) Nowadays, in our post-whatever world, we're apt to make the banal point that there are no true selves, just the masks. (But then, we've known for centuries that all the world's a masque, haven't we?) The Spectric hoax hints at other, better lessons, not least: it's easy to concoct poems that *appear* to be innovative—and, by extension, easy to convince oneself that one is avant-garde. How else explain the fact that the perpetrators of such latter-day hoaxes as Language poetry and flarf have yet to fess up to their frauds? They are hucksters conning themselves.

What would Ficke and Bynner, were they with us today, call their alter egos? Would they fashion the spectre of a professionally indignant poet-blogger who, believing too much in the zest of her bark, appoints herself the Lemon Pug? A mad scientist by the moniker Kristoff Book, who has taught himself the finer points of

DNA so that he may teach bacteria to be bardic? A plagiarist who composes by Google search and gets tenure? A poet-professor of witness on holiday? Most poets would be too preposterous to believe in if they didn't already exist. We are already our own best parodies.

Rosy-Fingered Yawn

Alice Oswald's *Memorial* is a translation of the *Iliad* that chucks the dull stuff (the plot points, all that talking) and retains the choice bits (the violence, the similes). It is Homer cutting to the chase—Homer cut to the quick. Thin, with a blood-red cover, you can read it in an hour. Swear.

Had I a young ward in my charge, one who could do with some culture, that's how I'd pitch Oswald's book to him. He would want to return to his *World of Warcraft*, his *Game of Thrones*. But I would counter him his entertainments by reading aloud the following verse paragraphs, from pages nineteen through twenty of the Oswald:

> Beloved of Athene PHERECLES son of Harmion
> Brilliant with his hands and born of a long line of craftsmen
> It was he who built the cursed fleet of Paris
> Little knowing it was his own death boat
> Died on his knees screaming
> Meriones speared him in the buttock
> And the point pierced him in the bladder
>
> And PEDAEUS the unwanted one
> The mistake of his father's mistress
> Felt the hot shock in his neck of Meges' spear
> Unswallowable sore throat of metal in his mouth
> He died biting down on the spearhead....

'That's fucked up!' my ward would have no recourse but to observe. 'Lemme see that.' I would yield the book to him, thereby launching an amateur on a life of poetry.

He would be right to say so, too; Oswald's book *is* 'fucked up'. It starts with a long roll call of soldiers who get killed in the *Iliad*, a narrow column of names—

PROTESILAUS
ECHEPOLUS
ELEPHENOR
SIMOISIUS
LEUKOS
DEMOCOON
DIORES
PIROUS [etc.]

—that runs down the left-hand side of the page, for seven whole pages, which some might judge boring, a waste of paper. They can't, these philistines, appreciate the aura contrived by unused space in books, nor do they recognize that the names accrete to form a kind of concrete poem *and* war memorial—the sort of slab that squats in parks and is meant to overwhelm you with a sense of many lives wasted, provided you linger on it.

Traditionally, the *Iliad* has been understood to be about the Trojan War, which was triggered when Helen ditched her husband, Menelaus, King of the Argives, for Paris of Troy. (We are more sophisticated now; we understand Homer's epic poem to be about a battle between the forces of good and evil—a scapegoat and her oppressive patriarchy.) But while Homer's poem dwells on the parrying of patriarchs—heroes packing spears—Oswald's zeroes in on many of the wasted lives: the grunts on the receiving end of the spears, the small print on the slab in the park.

Following the opening roll call, *Memorial* alternates between what Oswald calls 'short biographies of soldiers', which tend to be violent, and Homer's nature similes, which the translator tends to repeat. So after the bit where the guy bites the spearhead, the book offers up the following, for counterpoint:

Like suddenly it thunders
And a stormwind rushes down
And roars into the sea's ears

And the curves of many white-patched waves
Run this way and that way

Like suddenly it thunders
And a stormwind rushes down
And roars into the sea's ears
And the curves of many white-patched waves
Run this way and that way....

The book then lurches to the next scene of violence—and so on. (Oswald calls *Memorial* 'bipolar'.) Towards the end, it isolates a lone simile per page, for twelve pages. War is hell, the book seems to say. Give poetry a chance.

You should certainly give *Memorial* a chance. It contains some memorable formulations—'flower-lit cliffs', for instance, and 'a huge birdfair a valleyfull of voices'. At its sharpest, the poetry is as serrated as one of Wyndham Lewis's *Timon of Athens* illustrations; detailing the death of Agelaos, the poet observes, 'When a spearshot pushed through his shout and out through the chest/He fell made of metal banging on the ground.'

But sometimes Oswald relies, for effect, on a kind of willed breathlessness. The first red flag is waved in the very first sentence of the preface. 'This is a translation of the *Iliad*'s atmosphere,' Oswald asserts, 'not its story.' For the sake of 'atmosphere', she proceeds to drop commas, run sentences together, go for the gross-out:

Then Socus who was running by now
Felt the rude punch of a spear in his back
Push through his heart and out the other side poor Socus
Trying to get away from his own ending
Ran out his last moments in fear of the next ones
This is black wings coming down every evening
Bird's feathers on your face
Unmaking you mouthful by mouthful
Eating your eyes your open eyes....

Oswald says she's stripped away Homer's narrative to 'retrieve the poem's *enargeia*', which she translates to mean 'something like "bright unbearable reality"'. Surely the run-ons and lack of punctuation have been deployed to blind us with brilliance or, at the very least, get all up in our helmets. But these are the sort of easy, go-to solutions a poet will grab for when she's after some violent spontaneity. They assure some fantasy of a complacent reader that what he's supposed to be experiencing is discomfort, what with all the Brutal Hyperreal Lyricism going on.

If I call *Memorial* 'Anne Carson-lite', it is not to suggest that Carson, the Canadian poet and classicist, is especially weighty; it is to suggest, rather, that *Memorial* updates the classical world with but a touch of the weirdness that is often attributed to the not-very-weird poetry of Carson. Oswald, less radical than rascal, slips in references to 'parachutes', 'god's headlights', and 'astronauts'. Near the end, Hector is compared to a man 'in full armour in the doorway' who leaves 'his motorbike running'. The problem is not just that Hector was a convertible man; it's that there's something predictable, even calculated, about Oswald's choices. *Of course* the book is subtitled 'An Excavation of the *Iliad*'; archaeology would be the appropriate metaphor for a post-Foucauldian project that seeks to recover a subjugated narrative—that 'bright unbearable reality'. *Of course* Oswald describes her 'approach to translation' as 'fairly irreverent' and notes that she's 'aiming for translucence rather than translation'; what translator today is declaring her goal a stuffy, cautious fidelity? We're supposed to be irreverent now, aren't we?

Don't get me wrong; as the bodies pile up and the similes diffuse between them like so much battlefield dust, *Memorial* isn't without the power to compel. But the book-length stunt grows a bit boring by the end, and I would hope those novices who start with *Memorial* (a notch on a bookworm's spear) would eventually find their way to the *Iliad*—perhaps Robert Fagles's translation, which has all of the violent energy of Oswald's and none of the fashionable manoeuvres. Until then, Oswald's book should help conscript a few novices into a cause that's at least as old as Homer: trying to get folks to appreciate an oral art that's always dying, which is to say only as alive as its last breath.

Not Just Poetry

'Our most honored poets are gifted and prolific,' writes Camille
Paglia in her recent anthology *Break, Blow, Burn*, 'but we have
come to respect them for their intelligence, commitment, and the
body of their work. They ceased focusing long ago on production of
the powerful, distinctive, self-contained poem.' Clive James makes a
similar point when, criticizing Charles Olson's viral influence on free
verse, he praises Frost's 'aspiration to self-containment', to the
'choppily well-separated thing', to 'writing a poem, not just writing
poetry'. This shortage of choppily well-separated things is, it seems,
pandemic. 'We forget that a single poem is an independent work of
art, no less than a painting,' observes the Canadian poet Robyn
Sarah, diagnosing the tendency of poets to fatten their collections
with empty carbs, plumping manuscripts up to the forty-eight-page
minimum that makes them eligible for awards and publishing subsi-
dies.

A poem, not just poetry. That's what our era is lacking, claims a
growing chorus of pundits; and what these four takes are hunting.

* * *

Never mind the subtitle; there are no poems in Jorie Graham's
twelfth collection, at least not in Paglia, James, and Sarah's sense of
the word. 'As always,' Graham recently observed, 'I feel I am writing
a book rather than a collection, so speaking about one poem out of
context is hard.' A concept album rather than a compilation of sin-
gles, *Sea Change* is unified by apocalyptic worry, or what the back
cover describes as the 'once-unimaginable threshold at which civilization as we know it becomes unsustainable'. The ambition to create individually realized poems has been washed away by a tidal
form that alternates between the long lines of Whitman and the
shorter lines of Williams. Here's the beginning of 'This':

Full moon, & the empty tree's branches—correction—the tree's
branches,
expose and recover it, suddenly, letting it drift and rise a bit then
swathing it again,
treating it like it was stuff, no treasure up there growing more
bluish and ablaze....

Like waves, the lines surge forward, foam against the middle of the
page, and then retreat to the left margin. And like waves, they don't
discriminate between bottled messages and old boots; they carry all
manner of psychic refuse and fragmented perception ashore for the
reader's inspection—both the faulty first impressions ('the empty
tree's branches') and the corrected second glances ('the
tree's/branches').

And why not? Many theorists now assure us that the self *itself* is
fragmented, confined to the warped pane of its subjective gaze and
burdened with a language that can never fully represent its environment. Favouring process over product, the churning *Sea Change* is,
in its own words,

blurring the feeling of
the state of
being. Which did exist just yesterday, calm and
true.

But at what point does the desire to represent the imprecision of perception become an excuse for imprecise writing? Or is our gaze so
hopelessly subjective that we can comfortably abandon the struggle
for precision, as Graham does when she describes

the bent back ranks of trees
all stippled with these slivers of
light like
breaking grins—infinities of them—wriggling along the walls....

One doesn't stipple with 'slivers'. One stipples with dots and points
of paint. Slender things like door cracks, crescent moons, and, yes,

'breaking grins' are slivered. Seurat canvases and Lindsay Lohan
are stippled. Is Graham being imprecise to underscore the imperfection of the self's perceptions, or just sloppy? The question cannot be
answered because the idea underlying this sort of poetry—language
is always already inadequate—always already inoculates it against
charges of obscurity.

Readers with a gut worth trusting, however, might observe that,
when it comes to the business of actually reading *Sea Change*, 'it is
as much an effort to attend to the words one by one as to pronounce
them one by one.' That's Hugh Kenner on the verse of Arthur
Symons, but Kenner's words can be applied, just as easily, to Graham's twenty-first-century slush:

> Honor exists. Just punishment exists. The sound of
> > servants not being
> set free. Being told it is postponed again. Hope as it
> > exists in them
> now. Those that were once living how they are not
> > here in this
> moonlight, & how there are things one feels instantly
> > ashamed about in it, & also, looking at it,
> the feeling of a mother tongue in the mouth....

The vague nouns ('it', 'things'), the passive voice ('is', 'are'), and the
awkward, almost undergraduate grammar ('ashamed about in
it')—all conspire to a criminal indistinctness. This is a shame since
Sea Change wants to address real crimes like environmental degra-
dation and Guantanamo. But these crimes require a clarity that can
only be strengthened by the struggle for the right words, not weakened by it.

After all, there *are* elegant ways to express our inability to
express ourselves. Memorable lines from 'Prufrock'—'That is not it
at all,/That is not what I meant, at all'—come to mind because
that's what memorable things do. And there are crisp, epigrammatic
ways to confront our incoherence, too. Recall Mark Strand's 'Wherever I am/I am what is missing', or Dickinson's 'I'm Nobody! Who
are you?', or Iago's 'I am not what I am'. Faced with such verbal

triumphs, how can selves as incoherent as ours ever hope to keep
Graham's damper-pedalled lines—'Who is one when one calls one-
self/one?'—straight in our minds? No one doubts Graham's intelligence and commitment. She has assembled a body of work that
demands respect. But it's becoming easier to assure ourselves that
she's an important poet than to remember the specific, well-crafted
reasons why.

* * *

Descartes' Loneliness, the title of Allen Grossman's latest collection,
is a fitting one for our times. It's lonely, after all, to be a humanist
when so many poets are 'blurring the feeling of/the state of/being'.
Grossman, however, seems unfazed, as demonstrated in this excerpt
from the book's afterword, a quaint appendage to find in a collection
of poetry:

> Poets are persons aware of aloneness and *competent to
> speak in the space of solitude*—who, by speaking alone,
> make possible for themselves and others *the being of per-
> sons*, in which all the value of the human world is found.

This belief in '*the being of persons*' is so unfashionable it's almost
refreshing. But if Graham's speaker is too incoherent, Grossman's is
all too coherent, the voice of someone who—having long ago decided
that he's a poet—apparently feels no need to revise awful proclama-
tions like this one, from 'The Famished Dead':

> Now look! That other shadow is Pat, my
> old nurse.
> She had no body even then. She wore what
> nurses wore *instead of bodies* in those days.
> That's why her being dead now makes no difference
> to me. What's important is still her body.
> 'Take it off, Pat.
> Instead of breasts to suck, you wore two pins.
> Instead of a cunt, God knows what you had there.'

There are humanists, and then there are hams. Grossman, here, isn't after the choppily well-separated thing, the self-contained poem. Rather, he's a good example of those contemporary poets who, to quote Paglia, 'treat their poems like meandering diary entries and craft them for effect in live readings rather than on the page.' Certainly, Grossman's use of exclamation points, italics, and lurid words makes his work ready-made for the podium.

Of course, whether Grossman actually reads *Descartes' Loneliness* at live readings is beside the point; throughout the book, the speaker, frequently referred to as 'Allen', booms his voice outward as if the reader's skull were an auditorium. He begins one piece with the proclamation, 'O Kid!' Another one starts with 'Look!' Here's a megaphone of a stanza, from 'The Invention of Night':

> *Song is extreme work.* Help me, river sister!
> It's getting dark. Hey, sweet water! Flow fresh
> through ocean's salt. Give me some words for him
> I love, so he can give words to someone else.
> Start love's gift once more:—WORDS FOR ANOTHER.
> So everybody will have something to give someone.
> If not, I'll drown you in oceans of salt tears.
> Then you'll be indistinguishable from tears.
> This is Arcadia.

Song is only '*extreme work*' to the wide-eyed person who overvalues his perceptions. *Good* song, on the other hand, takes hard work, the sort of toil that, over time, drains poems of clichés like 'oceans of salt tears'. Grossman, however, absolves himself from such toil, and forces the clichés and capital letters to do double duty, single-handedly raising the ordinary to the oracular. And despite evidence of metre, much of the writing in *Descartes' Loneliness* sounds like flat, conversational prose, to which Grossman has added various stock props: sun, mind, birds of no specific species, their warbling, and Death personified.

Extreme singing certainly has its patrons. J.D. McClatchy, on the back cover, observes that Grossman's 'is the austere inward gaze, and the oracular voice of the prophet and seer.' But the blurb ends there, implying that just being a prophet and seer is enough. A poem, though, needs more of its maker than a big mouth.

* * *

Reading Davis McCombs's second collection, *Dismal Rock*, after Graham's and Grossman's books is a little like putting on your first pair of corrective glasses: language sharpens and well-defined things—not just minds and birds—suddenly come into focus. Imprecision is, after all, a luxury of late style. Younger poets still making a name for themselves, like McCombs, know that they must be clear and compelling and not take up too much of our time—'for time,' as August Kleinzahler points out in a recent talk, 'has vanished with inflated rents and the blitzkrieg of what's cheerfully called information, information to be attended to, and I'm talking right now.'

McCombs gets this and—in the first section of *Dismal Rock*, a sequence on tobacco farming—gets down to business, describing a world with the rigour of an anthropologist in the field:

> The people are talking about budworms; they are talking
> about aphids and thrips. Under the bluff at Dismal Rock,
> there where the spillway foams and simmers,
> they are fishing and talking about pounds and allotments;
> they are saying white burley, lugs and cutters.
> Old men are whittling sticks with their pocketknives
> and they are saying Paris Green; they speak of topping
> and side-dressing; they are whistling and talking
> about setters, plant beds and stripping rooms.

In these lines, from 'Lexicon', McCombs's speaker, a good listener, has catalogued his environment's recurring sounds—the 'u' in 'bluff', 'lugs', and 'cutters'; the 'w' in 'white', 'whittling', and 'whistling'—and organized them into a brief, cohesive sound loop that captures the aural energy of a rural landscape. *Dismal Rock* reassures us that words, when used well, can work. They can record the world and, at their best, transform it, as McCombs's do when they describe a bat 'crossing/the water on the boat of its reflection', or 'a bulb of gnats [that] flickers on/above the damp leaves'.

But while words can be made to work, they can also become workmanlike. And while much of the poetry in *Dismal Rock* is precise, much of it is also unmemorable nature poetry, opting for the obvious over the transformative:

>   ...[E]ach moment flaring up
> like a match, consuming itself...
>   —from 'Gnomon'

>   ...[T]his is the river's
> whorled thumbprint, the water's surface dark as ink.
>   —from 'The Tobacco Economy'

>   ...[T]he storm that, far beyond him, was purpling
> like a bruise...
>   —from 'Hobart'

>   ...[W]hen the storm spread
> like a bruise along the coast...
>   —from 'Bob Marley'

This is the sort of poetry in which things unspool (see 'Salts Cave Revisited' and 'Northtown Well'), in which stuff is compared to 'ash' (see 'The Tobacco Economy' and 'Stripping Room')—poetry, in other words, that's teetering on the cliff of our era's clichés.

McCombs, a Yale Younger Poet, *is* capable of some fine moments—but then who isn't in an era that valorizes the bite-sized fragment over the fully realized narrative, the poetry over the poem? Instead of working through the implications of a neat idea—that bat 'crossing/the water on the boat of its reflection', for example— McCombs merely moves onto the next idea—'it is squeaking/like a rusted hinge'—which is far less startling. The poems in *Dismal Rock*, then, are less poems than lists of description that never quite cohere into the self-contained pieces that need every one of their words. Like worms and double albums, they can be sectioned and still survive.

* * *

The author of this next book, a semi-finalist for Yale Younger Poet, committed suicide last year. Her poems are about flowers and mental health; they have titles like 'Dried Flowers' and 'Night Nurse', and brandish sharp lines like

> Don't talk to me of Paris;
> I have duties.
> Don't talk to me of loss;
> I bury pills in applesauce.

Given those facts alone, it would be easy to write off Sarah Hannah through a single, obvious comparison. But the most amazing—and consequently tragic—fact about her second—and last—collection, *Inflorescence*, is that its poems (and they *are* poems, choppily well-separated and varnished with formal finish) are very, very good. Whatever the poet was going through, it didn't hinder the production of small, complete masterpieces like 'The Riddle of the Sphinx Moth':

> An enormous body kamikaze-dives
> At me from behind the eaves of a summer
> Shack: a sudden blow between the eyes,
>
> A hybrid whirr—half bird, half bee—she hovers,
> Helicopters to the grass, and sparks: Long-short-long,
> Morse code in creature-speak for *Get you gone*.
>
> I run inside. What was she? A pair of dragonflies
> Combined to mate like biplanes in a blitz
> Seem cordial in comparison to this—the eyes,
>
> Two narrows, solid black, or should I say,
> Twin Stygian pools of fixedness,
> Her torso thick, a pattern throbbing in the fur,
>
> And what was that prodding in front of her?
> A stick, a thin proboscis, twice as long as she,
> Insinuates itself in jimsonweed—

Sucks out all the juice. Twenty quiet minutes pass
Until I hear a rattle on the glass;
The window's shaken out of frame—she's in!

She fouls the bed—the whole room's a sty.
I should flee. I shudder in my chair instead.
She owns this house, not I.

A buzz and feint, and with a glare
She's out the door. She owns the house,
Not me. I've solved the riddle:

All skirmishes aren't fatal;
All metaphors don't fly.

Like McCombs, Hannah has a knack for images, but unlike
McCombs, she's careful not to overload the poem with too many,
showcasing only the special ones. She's also careful—as 'Ariel'-era
Plath wasn't always—to unify them. The staggering description of a
'pair of dragonflies/Combined to mate like biplanes in a blitz' is
supported by references to kamikaze planes, helicopters, and Morse
code, so that when the reader comes to 'a pattern throbbing in the
fur', the sphinx moth has already been transformed, in the reader's
mind, into furry fuselage, capable of rattling windows. The deft use
of rhyme and alliteration further unifies this subtle, anti-war psy-
chodrama, lending an aura of inevitability to words like 'throbbing',
'prodding', 'proboscis', 'sucks', 'pass', and 'glass'. The poem can't
afford the loss of any of them.

But while Hannah expertly moves the reader, word by word, to
the poem's finish, she's careful not to craft *too* tidy an ending. She
solves her riddle with a bit of folk wisdom—'All metaphors don't
fly'—but in doing so, subverts the very art, metaphor-making, that
she has mastered, suggesting the limits of poetry. She completes a
final rhyme, but also drops a line from what would have been the
final tercet, introducing a note of anxiety that's far more subtle than
the self-consciously fragmented work of Graham. Indeed, many of
Hannah's poems set up consistent patterns of stanzas only to deviate

from them at the last moment. Life, Hannah seems to have recognized, is closer to coherence than chaos, which makes it all the more troubling when it falls just short of gelling.

The pieces in *Inflorescence* add up to a memoir about Hannah's care for her terminal mother. But the best ones—'Greenbrier', 'Common Creeping Thyme', 'The Leaded Windows', 'Night Nurse', and 'Eternity, That Dumbwaiter'—are anthology-bound and easily transcend the collection's overall arc. Hannah has not left a body of work that, through sheer bulk, demands our grudging respect. She has left us poems, each its own testament.

Words Fail Him

In senior year of high school, my friend Tom discovered the works of Marilyn Manson and took up the vestments: hair dye, torn nylons, Doc Martens. He insisted I borrow his *Heart of Darkness*, his *Darkness at Noon*. (He preferred his fiction dimly lit.) We convened in Ms. B——'s creative writing class and toyed with the idea of putting together our own literary magazine, which we planned to stack in place of the school newspaper: a blow struck against hegemony.

One day, Ms. B—— assigned the class a poem to write. I still have Tom's by heart, but only because the frigid response it received from our teacher, when she made her way around to him, freeze-dried it for posterity. (Critics often embalm the art they mean to bury.) This is the poem Tom read aloud:

This
is
a
poem.

Tom had meant to startle Ms. B——, but she just frowned and said, 'This is too easy.' She had a point: Tom had dashed off the poem in seconds. He might have defended himself by pointing out that it had taken Marcel Duchamp even less time to sign the name 'R. Mutt' to a urinal. But unlike Duchamp, Tom had the example of Duchamp to go on. And unlike Duchamp's first (and more reactionary) audiences, Ms. B—— seemed to have no quarrel with the rebel who ropes off any old thing (a urinal, four minutes and thirty-three seconds of room tone), declares it art, and dares you to say otherwise. She hadn't failed to regard Tom's poem as a poem; it had merely failed to startle her.

* * *

If he'd been familiar with the movement, my friend could have labelled his effort 'Language poetry'. Language poetry, which took shape in the 1970s, is poetry that calls attention to itself as language. In fact, it's sometimes spelled 'L=A=N=G=U=A=G=E poetry', an act of masochism before the era of copying and pasting. Still, if you had to type them out, the equal signs, like speed bumps, would have slowed you down and maybe even gotten you thinking about the materiality of words, letters.

Note that those equal signs aren't plus signs: Language poets aim to thwart our yen for language to add up to some larger point, to provide closure, takeaway. (These dubious satisfactions, they point out, can already be had in the offerings of what Charles Bernstein calls, 'Official Verse Culture'.) Some Language poets, like Ron Silliman and Lyn Hejinian, work the prose poem. Here's an excerpt from Hejinian's book-length *My Life* (1987):

> Are we likely to find ourselves later pondering such suchness amid all the bourgeois memorabilia. Wherever I might find them, however unsuitable, I made them useful by a simple shift. The obvious analogy is with music. Did you mean gutter or guitar. Like cabbage or collage. The book was a sort of protection because it had a better plot. If any can be spared from the garden.

The title of the poem toys with us: if this is memoir, it's memoir by way of paper shredder. Its basic unit is the fragment, or what Silliman calls the 'new sentence'. And the fragments are intended to be 'nonabsorbable'—Bernstein's coinage for disruptive writing that 'prevents an initial/"illusionistic" reading'.

Language poets also lineate their fragments, crafting such quatrains as these, from Bob Perelman's 'Chronic Meanings' (1993):

> The impossibility of the simplest.
> So shut the fucking thing.
> Now I've gone and put.
> But that makes the world.

The point I am trying.
Like a cartoon worm on.
A physical mouth without speech.
If taken to an extreme.

The phone is for someone.
The next second it seemed.
But did that really mean.
Yet Los Angeles is full.

Who is the speaker? What point is he or she trying to make? It's hard to say, though that may be the point of a poem in which a mouth is 'without speech' and a phone call has no obvious recipient: it's hard to say what one means, especially when one speaks in sentences that stop short, five words in. Anyway, in both Hejinian and Perelman, the result is the same: the reader can't relax into reverie, so frequent and jarring are the jolts.

But what's so bad about kicking back with a poem that conjures the illusion of a speaker serving up a clear message in a linear way? (What's so bad about a good read?) And why do these curious peoples, the Language poets, want to take the reader by the lapels and jostle her so? I have a hunch the French are to blame. In 1968, Roland Barthes declared the author dead. I think he got the Language poets to thinking. Like those characters on *The Twilight Zone* who emerge from a coma only to find themselves in a comatose world (a suburb, say), the Language poets seem to believe they are awake to the fact that the rest of the populace is asleep. They want the reader to wake up already and see that words aren't portholes to the author's soul. Poems are socially constructed. They are the expressions of a society, its ideologies. You don't curl up with Robert Lowell; you curl up with humanism.

Maybe by writing in a fragmentary way, then, Language poets are trying to break the illusion that poems are people talking. They are trying to land one on the chin of humanism and, while they're at it, the kisser of capitalism. After all, if the reader can't figure out what the author is saying, then she can't affirm the author's existence as an individual property owner (the property being the poem's meaning). Once roused, the reader can take back the language from the clutches of the patriarchy or Corporate America or what have you. As Bernstein puts it in an early essay, 'Writing and Method',

> The text calls upon the reader to be actively involved in the process of constituting its meaning.... The text formally involves the process of response/interpretation and in so doing makes the reader aware of herself or himself as pro-ducer as well as consumer of meaning. It calls the reader to action, questioning, self-examination....

Instead of feeling like a frustrated consumer, the reader can endeav-our to make her own meaning out of the fragments. In fact, she can explain to her sleepier peers why Language poems need to be so fragmentary; she can become a graduate student.

Surely, though, there are readers who share the Language poets' philosophical assumptions but don't want to read writing shot through with disruptions. And surely there are those who aren't much startled by the disruptions, having encountered them before. They might not be able to distinguish a Language poem from, say, the automatic writing of the Surrealists. But they know a poem that jerks a thumb at itself when they see one.

Indeed, these readers might point out that the work of different avant-garde poets from different periods can sound very similar. Consider the following passage from Bernstein's 1994 book *Dark City*:

> Where are those fades (arcades, shades)
> when you need them? Who
> was that text I saw you with
> last night? Is there life after
> grammar (glamour)? The Czech
> is in the jail (the wreck is
> in the wail, the deck is in the
> sail, the Burma-Shave's shining over the
> starry blue skies, Waukegan, New Jersey,
> 1941).

Doesn't it sound an awful lot like this, from 1964, by Jackson Mac Low?

> This makes meat before heat,
> putting in languages other than English.
>
> This gets leather by language
> while discussing something brown.
>
> Finally being a fly
> & forcing someone to see something,
> this ends by going over things.

Or this, from 1914, by Gertrude Stein?

> Out of kindness comes redness and out of rudeness comes
> rapid same question, out of an eye comes research, out of
> selection comes painful cattle. So then the order is that a
> white way of being round is something suggesting a pin and
> is it disappointing, it is not, it is so rudimentary to be ana-
> lysed and see a fine substance strangely, it is so earnest to
> have a green point not to red but to point again.

The Language poet's Seuss-like doctoring, his gumming up of gram-mar, his juxtaposition of words that are a typesetter's slip away from one another: these are reliable licks in a repertoire, the ones you play if you want to count yourself part of Official Avant-Garde Culture.

* * *

All the Whiskey in Heaven, Bernstein's selected poems, gathers work that goes back to 1975. There are short lyrics, prose poems, a riddle, a ballad, found poems, excerpts of longer things. Few of the pieces in the book lend themselves to paraphrase. The typical Bernstein poem is not the transcript of a coherent voice with something on its mind; it's a collage of fragments of voices, advertising-speak, detritus. To the extent that it has one, the subject matter is usually the opacity of words.

Still, something like a recurring point of view often surfaces through the flotsam. A Bernstein poem tends to be wary of walls and boundaries. It doesn't much care for institutions that, in a bygone era, normalized behavior, like mental health facilities or summer camps. (It has not aged as well as its targets.) It looks askance at the corporate world and the myth of the self-determining individual. (It finds the individual a rather more socially-determined creature, and fair enough.) But it's not without a sense of humour. A Bernstein poem is a pig for puns, punch lines, and one-liners. It's a ham with a left-wing axe to grind.

For example, here are the opening lines of the very first poem in *All the Whiskey in Heaven*, 'Asylum', from Bernstein's 1975 book *Asylums*:

rooms, suites of rooms, buildings, plants

in line. Their encompassing or total character

intercourse with the outside and to departure

such as locked doors, high walls, barbed
wire, cliffs, water, forests, moors

conflicts, discreditings, failures

of assimilation. If cultural change

the outside. Thus, if the inmates stay

victory.

The poem's a cut-up of Erving Goffman's *Asylums*, a 1961 study that argues the psychiatric hospital produces the patient. The first line of Bernstein's poem comes from the first page of Goffman's book, the second, from the second. But the pattern doesn't last. It's as if Bernstein took a pair of scissors to the book, made a heap of the scraps, and left us with the task of making the meaning.

What might this task entail? The poem begins by listing spaces and structures that are 'in line'. (It's as if the poem, having been granted a visitor's pass, is roaming the grounds of some asylum, logging the stuff that's under control.) But 'rooms, suites of rooms, buildings, plants' aren't just 'in line', they're also words *in a line*—a line of poetry! So Bernstein borrows some images from Goffman, of bounded spaces. But he also cracks wise with a pun, reminding those of us bookworms who might otherwise relax into the reverie of reading that the images, far from being firm representations of the things of the world, are made of words, words, words. Bernstein goes on to call up more of Goffman's images, these of containment: 'locked doors, high walls'. But he leaves his sentences in tatters, ironically enough.

In other words, it's hard to get a grip on 'Asylum', which is always unravelling, like some restless, self-reflexive weave of loose ends. (Bernstein could be likened to Penelope, if only Homer's cooped-up prisoner of patriarchy had undone her needlework every few seconds, as opposed to every evening, and thrust it in her suitors' faces: 'See? The macramé is the message!') 'Asylum' certainly doesn't have a coherent speaker; Goffman's voice has been shredded. In fact, the poem doesn't even acknowledge its source. You have to know your sociology, or at least have the presence of mind to run 'Bernstein' and 'Asylum' through your search engine, to come up with Goffman's name.

And yet there are plenty of words and phrases in 'Asylum' that have the buzz of academic thought about them—'failures/of assimilation', 'cultural change', 'outside', 'power', 'boundary'. So although the poem is a pileup of sentence fragments, the fragments do suggest a meaning: people are separated from the 'outside' world by a 'boundary' and turned into 'inmates' when institutions with 'power' force them to 'assimilate' to norms and rules of decorum. Perhaps, then, that's why the poem is so fragmented: it's fomenting an uprising against the institution of grammar!

But we've only just gotten started. In another poem, the collage-like 'Standing Target', from Bernstein's 1980 book *Controlling Interests*, the reader would seem to have even more work to do. (Are Bernstein's poems public works projects, meant to provide able-

bodied readers with the bricks and mortar?) There are passages of
punning, self-reflexive lyricism to reckon with:

> How sad lines are, crisscrossing
> out the hopes of an undifferentiated
> experience, the cold sweeps
> past, eyes tear, the night begins
> again.

There's corporatese:

> As President and Chief Executive Officer
> of Sea World, Inc., David DeMotte is
> responsible for managing all aspects
> of the Company's operations at Sea
> World parks in San Diego, Aurora,
> Ohio, Orlando, Florida, and the Florida
> Keys. A native Californian, DeMotte,
> and his wife Charlotte, enjoy hunting,
> fishing, and tennis in their spare time.

There's advertising-speak that interrupts the poem like a commercial break:

> *Note the exclusive right-side-up feature.*

There's a camp counsellor's assessment of a 'pretty frisky little boy',
who might be a young Charles Bernstein:

> Charlie has grown to enjoy our organized games
> His interest carries throughout the
> period, as a rule. He pulls his share in
> team set ups and cheers loudly for
> his team.

And, toward the end, there's an explosion of words, as if the poem's
gone haywire:

```
fatigue
        of      of
            openfor
     to              , sees
doubles
glass           must....
```

What to make of a President of Sea World who 'enjoy[s] hunting,/fishing'? A camp counsellor who refers to one of his charges as a 'pretty frisky little boy'? Reader, that's up to you. But it would seem that Bernstein finds people with power inherently creepy. They manage 'operations' and organize the world into 'games' and 'team[s]'. More generally, they draw 'sad lines' in 'undifferentiated/experience', which is to say they presume to make sense of chaos. They are also, these creeps, associated with the most criminally banal examples of language in Bernstein's poem. If only little Charlie were left to his own devices and allowed to play freely in the muck of pure language—instead of being harangued into 'organized games' where he has to side with a 'team'—he might avoid a career in advertising or, worse, turning out like DeMotte. He might become a Language poet, given to explosive outbursts.

In Terry Gilliam's movie *Brazil*, Sam Lowry, a Chaplinesque everyman in a fedora, lashes out at his world, a kind of art deco dystopia that's mired in bureaucracy. One day at work, in his cell of an office, he puts a kink in the pneumatic tubes that serve as the building's communication system. The tubes bulge as messages begin to build up. Eventually, a gasket blows and a blizzard of paperwork swirls down from the ceiling. His co-workers stagger about, stunned. I think that Bernstein's goal—especially in early poems like 'Asylum' and 'Standing Target', but also in later ones like 'The Klupzy Girl' and 'Palukaville'—is basically Lowry's: to blow up the language (of mainstream institutions, in particular) and jolt us drones into some more critical mode of thinking. '[O]bviously/it's startling to see contexts changed on you,' figures one Bernstein poem. 'This is the way to start a sentence about startling a sentence,' boasts another.

* * *

Bernstein seems to be trying to blow up the language of poetry, too—
or, at least, blow smoke in its face. He's certainly not after original
metaphors that evoke the world in memorable ways. Every so often,
though, he writes what he seems to think is a conventional poem, if
only for jokes. Here's 'The Measure', a poem from the early 1980s:

> The privacy of a great pain enthrones
> itself on my borders and commands me
> to stay at attention. Be on guard
> lest the hopeless magic of unconscious
> dilemmas grab hold of you in the
> foggiest avenue of regret.

Piling on the metaphors, the speaker describes 'a great pain' as
something regal, 'unconscious/dilemmas' as some kind of 'hopeless
magic', and 'regret' as a foggy 'avenue'. His language is as vaporous
as that of a nineteenth-century Symbolist. It parodies the sort of
poetry in which a gasbag works out his feelings, in which the word
'lest' is lathered on sincerely.

Here's another parody, 'Castor Oil', from Bernstein's recent collection *Girly Man*:

> I went looking for my soul
> In the song of a minor bird
> But I could not find it there
> Only the shadow of my thinking
>
> The slow sea slaps slow water
> On the ever farther shore
> And myself pulled under
> In the uneven humming
> Of the still wavering warps
>
> Tuneless, I wander, sundered
> In lent blends of remote display
> Until the bottom bottoms
> In song-drenched light, cradled fold.

The speaker seems to be the Romantic type; he's got his ear out for some sign of himself in nature. But it turns out there isn't a 'soul' to be found in birdsong, 'Only the shadow of my thinking.' And the speaker's quatrains, over-the-top alliteration ('slow sea slaps slow', 'wavering warps'), and hackneyed poeticisms ('I wander, sundered', 'song-drenched light') are meant to be taken in jest; the poem's lax (and laxative) title tells us so.

Here's an observation: whenever Bernstein appears readable, whenever he resorts to traditional devices like alliteration and rhyme, he's likely having us on. For instance, 'Verdi and Postmodernism' begins by trying to get at the beauty of some stately, swan-like beloved. But the title might as well be 'Verdi vs. Postmodernism' or 'Verdi o, Postmodernism I'; by the fourth line of the poem, a glut of half-rhymes and alliteration has scotched the attempt to describe the beloved, converting a delicate (if conventional) lyric into nursery rhyme:

> She walks in beauty like the swans
> that on a summer day do swarm
> & crawls as deftly as a spoon
> & spills & sprawls & booms.

Insofar as Language poetry can say anything, this seems to say that we do women a disservice when we try to represent them or compare them to swans. (It wasn't just Zeus who defiled Leda; Yeats, by writing his poem, got in on the action, too.) Better to revel in word-play—'spills & sprawls & booms'—than rape a natural wonder with precise description. And better to revel ironically. If you must use a hoary old device like rhyme or alliteration, make sure you *over*use it. If you must write about beauty, work in some ampersands. 'Verdi and Postmodernism' ends with impotent griping: the speaker—who is presumably meant to be identified, at least in part, with the composer—wishes he could 'overturn a state, destroy a kite'. But he also remarks, paradoxically, that he has 'no wishes'. Words fail him— he's been transplanted to the postmodern world, the operatic fool!

I have a feeling I ought to find these poems funnier than I do. The very title of *All the Whiskey in Heaven* suggests the book's a barrel of celestial laughs, and in his back cover blurb, Paul Auster exclaims about the poems, 'good Lord, can they ever make you laugh.' But Bernstein's sense of humor often amounts to little more than relentless sarcasm. I had occasion to recall my high school friend's salvo—'This/is/a/poem'—when I read these, the opening lines of Bernstein's 'Thank You for Saying Thank You' (2001):

> This is a totally
> accessible poem.
> There is nothing
> in this poem
> that is in any
> way difficult
> to understand.
> All the words
> are simple &
> to the point.
> There are no new
> concepts, no
> theories, no
> ideas to confuse
> you. This poem
> has no intellectual
> pretensions. It is
> purely emotional.
> It fully expresses
> the feelings of the
> author: *my feelings,*
> *the person speaking*
> *to you now.*
> It is all about
> communication.
> Heart to heart.
> This poem appreciates
> & values you as
> a reader.

I get that the Language poet has to be seen as above 'accessibility'. But does he have to be so passive-aggressive about it? In its extreme coolness, 'Thank You for Saying Thank You' seems a little too hot. It reads like the venting of someone who was jilted by a *New Yorker* poet.

Unlike, say, Tom Disch, who had the nerve to write his mock-elegy 'At the Grave of Amy Clampitt' while Clampitt was still alive, Bernstein tends to be remote and vague in his anti-poems. He has been called 'the undisputed master of atmospheric doggerel', but it's no great act of iconoclasm to snicker at some neo-Romantic who goes looking for his soul in 'the song of a minor bird' or who objectifies women. I mean, who *doesn't* hate that guy?

* * *

Here's another observation: the more fragmentary Bernstein's poetry, the less explosive. The startling moments, such as they are, tend to occur in the staid stretches on which Bernstein has visited but the slightest, most tailored acts of violence. For example, in a prose poem called 'Foreign Body Sensation', the speaker carries on coherently for nearly two pages in the course of listing his accomplishments. (We could be reading one of his cover letters.) But the accomplishments start to make for an insoluble mix. Is this, in fact, a single speaker, or several? Is this a monologue of many? Near the end, the speaker notes:

> For a while, I served in the Peace Corps in Guatemala as a nurse working with cancer patients. After two years in Met State, I became increasingly eager to work with severely disturbed children. I am beginning to dabble in writing screenplays, humor, and poetry. What time is left I devote to coursework at the Divinity School, where I am studying for the priesthood. It seems I have done other things also, but maybe not. I guess I. In the future, I look forward to the private practice of pathology. Just when that will occur is uncertain. I am now administering substances to others to alter or obliterate their consciousness.

How could it be that the speaker is a nurse, a child care worker, a writer, *and* an aspiring priest? Unaware of how strange he sounds, the speaker keeps going: 'It seems I have done other things also, but maybe not.' But then he seizes up, as if someone's cut the power: 'I guess I.' (You can almost picture his head lolling forward.) Is this the robotic voice of capitalist ambition breaking down before our eyes? Whatever it is, it rights itself and soldiers on. The speaker expresses an interest in diagnosing disease ('the private practice of pathology') and doping people up ('administering substances to others to alter or obliterate their consciousness'). Are we back in the asylum?

If only the speaker could hear himself, he'd realize that he's not an individual but a whole culture speaking: a culture of gormless go-getters. And Bernstein, for his part, is less an author in the traditional sense (an individual dragging the depths of his soul for *le mot juste*) than what Barthes calls a 'scriptor', a socially-situated someone who knots together pre-fabricated strands of language, cadged from the culture. In other words, Bernstein enjoys a certain distance from the language he arranges. Because it's not his—because the idea of an author who owns his words is worm food—he can take an ironic, even superior attitude towards its sources: for example, those bourgeois types who are always expressing an earnest desire 'to dabble in writing screenplays, humor, and poetry'. *Don't humanists say the darndest things?* the poem seems to ask.

But if the Bernstein of 'Foreign Body Sensation' is a scriptor, at least he's one with a sense of restraint, even craft. Like the director of a slasher flick, he withholds the hatchet for a goodly time before lopping a sentence short ('I guess I'), which snaps us to attention. He provides enough tension to make the cut count, enough coherence to keep the chaos crisp. Not so in 'Dysraphism', a six-page poem so thoroughly chopped up the reader has no chance to relax into reverie, that state the Language poet disdains but into which we must first lapse in order to be startled:

Pump ass! A wash
of worry (the worldhood of
the whirl). Or: 'Nice being here with anybody.' Slips
find the most indefatigable invaginations, surreptitious

requiems.
Surfeit, sure fight.
Otherwise—flies,
detergent whines, flimflam psychosis. Let's:
partition the petulance, roast
the arrears, succor the sacred. 'If you don't keep up
with culture, culture will keep up
with you.' Sacral dosing, somewhat
hosting. Thread
threads the threads, like
thrush.

Even when faced with the not unfunny and perfectly compre-
hensible 'Solidarity Is the Name We Give to What We Cannot Hold'
(from the 1999 collection *My Way: Speeches and Poems*), the reader
may reasonably wonder why she should persist with it, for if she
reads enough of the opening—

I am a nude formalist poet, a sprung
syntax poet, a multitrack poet, a
wondering poet, a social expressionist
poet, a Baroque poet, a constructivist poet,
an ideolectical poet. I am a New York poet in
California, a San Francisco poet on
the Lower East Side, an Objectivist poet
in Royaumont, a surrealist poet in Jersey,
a Dada poet in Harvard Square,
a zaum poet in Brooklyn, a merz poet
in Iowa, a cubo-futurist poet in Central Park.

—she may sense that she can safely skim (if not skip) the next two
pages of what seems to be another curriculum vitae, and settle finally
on the end:

& I am none of these things,
nothing but the blank wall of my aversions
writ large in disappearing ink—

She may even sense that she can skip the pedestrian epiphany (poets like Bernstein are tough to pin down) and dwell on the em dash alone—a tongue stuck out, or party favour unfurled, in the face of closure. (Really, the em dash is all the poem Bernstein's point needs.) The *responsible* reader, of course, should try not to skim. But even the most diligent will do so when she's not being provided for, when the maze of the poem isn't dispensing enough pellets.

'Let's Just Say', a listless list from the 2003 chapbook of the same name, also encourages skimming. So little is at stake that one can slide down the poem the way one might a ladder, the lines blurring by like rungs. Here are some of them, should you care to concentrate:

> Let's just say that sleep is the darker side of dreams
>
> Let's just say that sometimes a rose is just a read flower
>
> Let's just say that every step forward is also a step nowhere
>
> Let's just say that the thirst for knowledge can only be quenched
>   if one learns how to remain hungry
>
> Let's just say that green is always a reflection of the idea of green
>
> Let's just say that I encounter myself not in the mirror but in the
>   manure....

The first line has a lovely logic. (It's the pellet of the poem.) But the second insists on reminding us, in the manner of so much of Bernstein's poetry, that the word 'read' is only a letter away from 'red', that its meaning is a social matter, that we 'read' the 'rose' into the 'flower'. (In other words, the second line makes us groan.) The third line is a koan that clears the mind. The fourth should be declaimed into a hands-free microphone headset in a hotel conference room. The fifth? More koan. The sixth suggests that none of this should be taken too seriously; the speaker has shit on his face. But if we're feeling a little lost, the anaphora in 'Let's Just Say' reassures us that all lines are created equal—save for the last one, of course, which is more equal than the rest by virtue of its lashing up the loose ends: 'Let's just say that the lie of the mind is the light of perception.'

I'm guessing that Bernstein would like the reader 'to be actively involved in the process of constituting [the] meaning' of poems like 'Solidarity Is the Name We Give to What We Cannot Hold' and 'Let's Just Say'. But how much work *is* there for the reader? Isn't the reader only free to create—which is to say repeat to teacher—the pre-approved meanings that the poem funnels her toward? What advance has Bernstein made over, say, Kenneth Koch's 'Alive for an Instant'? Written all the way back in 1975, the poem runs, in part:

I have a man in my hands I have a woman in my shoes
I have a landmark decision in my reason
I have a death rattle in my nose I have summer in my brain water
I have dreams in my toes
This is the matter with me and the hammer of my mother and father
Who created me with everything
But I lack calm I lack rose
Though I do not lack extreme delicacy of rose petal
Who is it that I wish to astonish?

* * *

Here are some more questions. How does a Language poet know when her poem is finished, or at least ready for the typesetter? (It strikes me that a non-linear and non-representational poetry of fragments that resist closure could go on forever.) Does a Language poem end where it does because its author got winded and, well, a poem has to end *somewhere*? What does her revision process look like? Why is it 'Surfeit, sure fight', and not 'Sure fight, surfeit'? Why couldn't the lines in 'Solidarity Is the Name We Give to What We Cannot Hold' and 'Let's Just Say' be shuffled into a different order and still enable the reader to come up with the same point about the wobbliness of words? And if the lines *can* be shuffled into a different order, why should the reader read the poems at all? And why does the Language poet keep writing them, once she's got a few under her belt? How many Language poems does it take to unscrew the signified from the signifier? Does the Language poet feel a duty to keep producing product? Is it that, in a fallen world, where meaning is endlessly deferred, someone has to be brave and selfless enough to keep on rearranging the language the rest of us take for granted, thereby creating the startling poems that reflect our postmodern reality? Is rearranging language really enough to startle the kinds of readers who would be inclined to wrestle with a Language poem? Haven't these readers already read the Koch poem? How many more like it do they need? To repurpose that last line of Koch's, who is it that Language poets wish to astonish?

In an early essay, Bernstein writes:

> By rotating sentences within a paragraph (a process analogous to jump cutting in film) according to principles generated by and unfolding in the work (rather than in accordance with representational construction patterns) a perceptual vividness is intensified for each sentence since the abruptness of the cuts induces a greater desire to savor the tangibility of each sentence before it is lost to the next, determinately other, sentence.

But isn't that a tall order? Language poetry would seem to depend on the existence of readers who are *initiated enough* to be game for these rotations but, paradoxically, *innocent enough* to find the rotations vivid. I don't doubt that there are readers who believe that they find lines like 'Pump ass! A wash/of worry (the worldhood of/ the whirl)' terribly disruptive to their person. But my inner lab technician worries about the placebo effect. It may be that those readers who have boned up and know what Language poetry is supposed to do to them have deceived themselves into giving it the benefit of the doubt.

Or it may be that Bernstein is not unlike the late director Sam Peckinpah, who thought that if he presented violence in slow motion, with lots of abrupt cuts, he would disturb the moviegoer, make her more critical. The well-meaning Peckinpah didn't count on the possibility that in slowing down violence—in showing a shot-up body's slow tumble off the roof of a saloon—he was also aestheticizing it, and anaesthetizing the viewer. In much the same way that moviegoers have gotten used to the sight of a body riddled with bullets, readers have adjusted to poetry shot through with disruptions; indeed, they fairly expect them.

They expect self-reflexivity, too. By the mid-1980s, when Bernstein was writing essays like 'Artifice of Absorption', the mainstream media was already busily co-opting postmodern strategies of self-reflexivity, the better to captivate its audiences. David Foster Wallace wrote about the phenomenon in 1993, fingering such culprits as 'the ironic '80s' true Angel of Death Mr. D. Letterman' and TV commercials that called attention to their conventions. By the late 1990s, 'going meta' was no longer a weapon exclusive to the quiver of Official Avant-Garde Culture; it had fallen into the hands of the teenager who means to be a nuisance to his creative writing teacher.

* * *

Of course, if you want to count yourself a part of Official Verse Culture, you could do worse than sell your book to Farrar, Straus and Giroux, the publisher of *All the Whiskey in Heaven*. Back in the day, Bernstein was the co-editor of a bimonthly little magazine called *L=A=N=G=U=A=G=E*, which ran for thirteen saddle-stitched issues from 1978 to 1981, and appears to have been banged out on a typewriter. (Inspecting an online reproduction of an issue, you can almost picture one of its editors typing manically, the other pacing the room, free-associating.) These days, however, Bernstein does business with FSG, which publishes the editor of *Poetry* and the poetry editor of *The New Yorker*. Has he sold out? Is selling out even *possible*? Pierre Bourdieu says that 'the artist cannot triumph on the symbolic terrain except by losing on the economic terrain (at least in the short run), and vice versa (at least in the long run).' In other words, there are no sellouts, just sell-by dates. By appearing to repudiate the mainstream, Bernstein banked plenty of capital—the symbolic kind. The Language poet who did without, but has come to be consecrated, can now cash in, trading the coinage of cool he earned by appearing to resist the commercial world for such goods as late-career hardbacks with FSG. (Avant-garde poetry is never an innocent dalliance, free of the marketplace. It's a bet against the present, a bet on future appreciation.)

Bourdieu also says that

> works and artists which have 'left their mark' are destined to fall into the past, to become *classic or outdated*, to see themselves thrown *outside* history or to 'pass into history,' into the eternal present of consecrated *culture*, where trends and schools which were totally incompatible 'in their lifetime' may now peacefully coexist, because they have been canonized, academicized and neutralized.

Is it possible that Bernstein has been 'canonized, academicized and neutralized'? He has come to hold a chair at a university. He has cameoed in a commercial (opposite Jon Lovitz), even a big Hollywood movie (*Finding Forrester*). His work has appeared in *Poetry*, *Harper's*, *The Nation*, *The Best American Poetry*, and *The Norton Anthology of Poetry*. Language poets, we might conclude, lead an ascetic existence early in the life cycle, but later grow fat and happy. More power to them, I say! Still, I wonder what Bernstein's younger self would make of all that power?

* * *

There's a university library in Toronto that boasts an art installation: a glassed-in bank of dead light bulbs on a wall next to an escalator. If, while riding the escalator, you happen to make some noise—for example, if you ask someone, 'What's the deal with the bulbs?'—the bulbs will flicker to life briefly. (There are microphones among them, and they're triggered by sound.) The installation is apparently meant to remind us that we always play a role in establishing the meaning of a work of art, even if that role involves little more than asking a question in earshot of it.

The thing about those bulbs, though: they haven't worked in the fourteen or so years I've been going to the library. They're now a dusty curiosity, about which first-time visitors will ask exactly once, if at all. What the bulbs used to be able to make you feel like you could do—'Let there be light!'—is but folk rumour.

The poems in *All the Whiskey in Heaven* are like the bulbs: inert period pieces that once made a show of inviting the reader to participate (as though up until then she'd been a thoughtless bystander). If anything, by aiming to startle an innocent out of her reverie, they condescend to her; they assume that she, like patrons of escalators the world over, is living too straight and narrow and mechanized a life. But why condescend when you can manage a sentence as clear and genuinely startling as 'The alphabet is frozen sound'? That metaphor—'content with the old-fashioned way to be new', as Frost once put it—can be found in Bernstein's recent essay collection, *Attack of the Difficult Poems*. I would trade his entire selected poems for it.

Going Negative

The negative review is a curiosity, unique to anxious enclaves like the poetry world. It's not that people who review movies don't say harsh things—they do. But when a book of poetry receives a tough verdict, we often label the review 'negative', and speculate about the reviewer's motives, the agenda behind the takedown. Indeed, behind words like 'negative' and 'agenda' and 'takedown' lurks the sense that the reviewer is the one making the trouble and the book of poetry—whether it deserves a kicking or not—is being bullied. We're far less paranoid about motives when, say, a movie receives a tough review in *The New Yorker* or *Slate* or *Rolling Stone*, even when we disagree with the verdict—even when we're so outraged we fire off an email to some editor's inbox. This is because negative reviews of movies (and LPs and TV shows) represent the norm, and aren't usually labelled 'negative'. Movie critics with whom we disagree are merely wrong; poetry critics (and politicians) go negative.

Maybe poetry is so marginal, so fragile a commodity, we worry about kicking it when it's already pretty clearly down. Whatever the reason for our anxiety, the negative review, when it appears in magazines like *Poetry*, is often more of an event than it ought to be. But negativity, I'm starting to think, *needs* to be the poetry reviewer's natural posture, the default position she assumes before scanning a single dactyl. Because really, approaching every new book of poetry with an open mind is as well-meaning but ultimately exhausting as approaching every stranger on the street with open arms; we'll meet some nice people, sure, but our charming generosity won't be reciprocated most of the time. What's worse, a tack-sharp taste, dinged by so much sheer dullness, will in time become blunted (into blurb-writing, no doubt). When parting any new book of poems—particularly by an author we're not too familiar with—it's best to brace ourselves and expect the worst. This needn't involve cynicism. Indeed, we probably shouldn't be opening the book in the first place if we aren't, on some deep level, already hoping for the best—that is, the discovery of a great poem. But hope should remain on that deep level, well-protected, until the shell that shields it is genuinely jarred.

After all, how many volumes of new poetry, published in the last calendar year, will still be jarring us in five years? In *one*? Shouldn't the negative review, if we're honest and adult about it, be the norm? And if so, shouldn't we retire the adjective 'negative' in favour of something far more accurate, if a little awkward, like 'necessarily skeptical', as in, 'Man, William Logan sure has gone necessarily skeptical on that poet?'

These are not purely rhetorical questions. If you're frequently having the top of your head taken off—Emily Dickinson's description of what authentic poetry does—I'm glad for you. But you're reading better books than me. And Dickinson, too. After all, the gist of her metaphor, it seems, is that such head injuries are by definition exceptional. Rare. Don't expect any in the next few pages, from the poets under review, or from me (there just isn't enough of that kind of writing around). And, for the love of poetry, be skeptical.

* * *

On the back cover of *The Usable Field*, the third collection by Jane Mead, Ira Sadoff proclaims: 'Jane Mead's our Emily Dickinson, our most ambitious solitary.' But come on. The sheer fact that Mead has a book with blurbs—published in her lifetime and supported by Guggenheim money—should cast doubt on her cred as a recluse, at least of Dickinson's kind (Dickinson, recall, published but ten poems in her lifetime, all anonymously). Mead, of course, is only the latest poet to be named the next Emily Dickinson. Anne Carson held the post, briefly. Kay Ryan, too. Nowadays, we understand a recluse to be someone who doesn't want a JPEG of herself on her dust jacket, or to teach an MFA seminar. Even our most skittish writers—the holed-up-in-a-panic-room types like Thomas Pynchon—have made cameos on *The Simpsons*. If there is a recluse of Dickinson's genius and originality out there, we likely won't know about her until much later, for the simple reason that we can't yet imagine her or the language in which she'll speak to us (if we could, she wouldn't be a reclusive genius; she would probably have a blog or something). One thing's for certain: she'll be nothing like Emily Dickinson. Emily Dickinson wasn't even *her* era's Emily Dickinson.

We can imagine Jane Mead's language all too well. It's the Language of Our Time, a verse that's free (though not too free), with a dash of Ashbery and a hint of Jorie (though not too much of either), a verse that's aimed squarely at a woodlot. There are no valves of attention, or dots on a disc of snow, or nerves sitting ceremonious as tombs in *The Usable Field*. Rather, Mead, less poet than stenographer, substitutes a vague, blurry shorthand for the specific, vivid images one finds in the work of visionaries like Dickinson, but also in the lines of our better, less celebrated contemporaries. For example, the poet Eric Ormsby, a specialist in the specific, vivid image, describes a rooster's 'dark, corroded croak/Like a grudging nail tugged out of stubborn wood', a simile that nails it. But Mead, faced with a similar challenge, describes the sound of cowbirds as, well, 'the sound of cowbirds/in sudden excellence'. Ormsby's simile carefully transcribes the complexities of bird-sound; Mead opts for (surrenders to?) shorthand and, in another poem, actually writes, 'complexities/of bird-sound'. Instead of recording (and, via memorable simile, amplifying) some bit of birdsong, Mead muffles it with meaningless gauze like 'sudden excellence' and 'complexities'. Her poetry, then, doesn't so much describe its objects as obscure them with prefabricated language as airy as bubble wrap:

The waves between us—
house light and transform motion
into the harboring of sounds in language.
        —from 'The Origin'

All manner

of knowing pushes up, out of
visibly nowhere . . .
        —from 'It Was Not Anything After All?'

I wanted to know
about the earth and the sea—about
the unleashed moments.
—from 'Same Audit, Same Sacrifice'

...[S]ome great thing
is crossing our path, into dusk.
—from 'The Flesh Is Fear'

In retrospect, those hazy titles—which 'Origin'? whose 'Flesh'?—
should've been the tipoff to the lazy shorthand they label.

The objects of this shorthand, however, are themselves limited.
The periodic table from which Mead mines the basic elements of her
poetry includes light, river, wind, wing, heart, bird, and grass. But
even when Mead gets precise and identifies a specific kind of bird or
plant, her ultimate goal is not clarity but mystery. One of her go-to
gimmicks is the question—not, mind you, the sort of question a
poem will propose for the purpose of puzzling out an answer. Mead's
questions—'What/can one person say to another?' or 'What//do the
weeds know ...'—are unanswerable, smoke machines that pump dry
ice into her lines, leaving them (and us) in the fog.

'[T]he sub-arguments of the moving mind are endless,' observes
one of Mead's speakers, toward the end of *The Usable Field*, and it's
a valid point. But it's an old point, too, and the poetry it sometimes
produces—vague, disjunctive, inconclusive—doesn't so much track
the movements of our minds as reflect them at their muddiest. And
anyway, I already know that my mind is unreliable, meandering,
fucked up; why would I want to see it represented on the page? The
minds I want to watch at work—Dickinson's, Frost's, and, more
recently, Samuel Menashe's, the late David Foster Wallace's—these
minds understand the costs of careful thought too much to devalue
it. These are minds struggling to cut a crisp path through the dry ice.

* * *

'That title is so good you shouldn't even make the picture—just
release the title!' So declared Orson Welles when his protégé, Peter
Bogdanovich, asked Welles what he thought of the title, *Paper Moon*.

Bogdanovich didn't know what a paper moon had to do with the movie he was planning; he knew only that he liked the title. But a good title—e.g. *Snakes on a Plane*—can generate excitement even when the work in question turns out to be kind of questionable.

Many of the titles of the poems in D.A. Powell's fourth collection, *Chronic*, are so catchy they constitute events in and of themselves, micro-masterworks of wit. In his earlier books, the first lines usually doubled as the titles, lending the poems an offhand cool; here were poems so self-sufficient they spoke for themselves. Four books in, Powell's poems now have proper titles, some of which threaten to upstage the main acts. They include: 'lipsync [with a nod to lipps, inc.]', 'chia pet cemetery', '[not the musical:] south pacific', 'scenes from the trip we didn't take to the antarctic', and—echoing that hilariously abbreviated obit from *Lolita* ('picnic, lightning')—'plague year: comet: arc'. It's a bit disappointing, then, to read the poetry that follows these titles—poetry that, in a sense, can't possibly fulfil the promise of such brief but brilliant openings. For instance, while the title, 'coit tower & us', is taut and clever, the slack poetry it's attached to—

some nights I feel that loss as if my own trembling musculature
lies concealed under a rubbled city, listening to the mission bells

you pull me from this collapsed architecture, you too a kind of pillar
you almost have that same heft, as we climb, I see you stronger

—is stock footage, so familiar you'd swear it was filmed on modernism's backlot, the rubble trucked in from some crank's canto. In the playfully titled, 'meditating upon the meaning of the line "clams on the halfshell and rollerskates" in the song *good times* by chic', the speaker confesses the sort of unplayful sentiments that make audiences squirm at open mics, like 'who could have guessed love's a palpable thing', and 'touch: that sensation I'd almost lost', and

it's still 1980 somewhere, some cornerof your dark apartment
where the mystery of the lyric hasn't faded. and love is in the chorus
waiting to be born.

You might expect *some* fun from a poem called, 'the expiration date on the world is not quite the same as the expiration date on my pro-phylactic', but the poem collects maudlin paraphernalia such as 'old phone nos.', 'all the unused appliances', and a 'grim barge to obliv-ion'. Like the author of dull academic studies, whose only joy is com-ing up with the titles—'He's a Maniac, Maniac: The Effects of High-Energy Caffeine Drinks on Youth Ages 12–18' (title mine)—Powell front-loads flat writing with frothy wit.

Initial hijinks aside, Powell's poetry is mostly serious stuff, and contains references to disease, decay, ruin, a dodgy environment, and one 'mangy green triangle where two freeways form a crotch', a striking, maybe superb image, even if one wonders what civilization *can* do to dress up a graveyard abutted by freeways. But civiliza-tion—seemingly embodied in what one poem calls the impulse to 'master nature'—is, as usual, the problem. So, too, is referentiality. As another poem insists, 'clarity never arrives, it is a spar in a far mine, it cost us dearly.' Indeed, *Chronic*'s poems avoid clarity (which, Powell's right, *does* 'cost us'—the time and effort required to achieve it) for a more easily attained opacity (although opacity is always easily attained). The title poem itself tallies up some of the book's, and contemporary poetry's, more fashionable gestures, including:

- reliance on buzzwords ('the profession of absence, of being absented');
- mistrust of order ('white and red perimeters where no perimeter should be');
- mistrust of linearity and having a point ('here is another in my long list of asides:/why have I never had a clock that actually gained time?');
- anxiety over what words mean ('and by *resilient* I mean *which holds*');
- Romantic bluster ('this wondrous swatch of rough');
- imprecision ('this wondrous swatch of rough'); and
- sympathy for small critters ('I saw that heron I didn't wish to disturb').

The clichés are compounded by Powell's now-familiar style, which includes a long, fragmented line, colons followed by gaps of white space, and a refusal to capitalize the starts of sentences. These stylistic tics must've seemed risky once. Perhaps the refusal to capitalize was a sign of quirky, anti-humanist modesty. Perhaps white space was supposed to clear the reader's head, give her pause, a chance to pitch in and help the poem make some of its meaning (whatever that means). But such tics have long since become codified shortcuts to mild shock, like those t-shirts that claim their owners to be 'PUNK'.

Still, the sensibility behind titles like 'hepatitis ABC' and 'democrac' (sic!) and 'clown burial in winter' is clearly so sharp it could laser off tattoos. I only wish it was the one writing the poetry.

* * *

John Poch's second collection, *Two Men Fighting with a Knife*, contains the sort of poetry that confronts most reviewers most often: poetry that's not especially bad but not especially good either—poetry, in other words, that should be guarded against at all costs. After all, we can spot and reject the awful easily enough. Books of poetry that are merely okay constitute a much more insidious norm that, over time, wears reviewers down, filing away initial gut reactions which, since taste is subjective, are always right, but also always in danger of being second-guessed. The result is the gutless review—a non-review, really—in which mild praise cancels out mild reservations, leaving the reader without a clear verdict and the poet, if he's lucky, with a blurb-able quote.

And yet: there are some fine moments in *Two Men Fighting with a Knife*, and if I have reservations with the bulk of the book—and I do—they aren't meant to mitigate my praise. The opening sonnet, 'Ghost Town', appeared in *The Paris Review* and probably deserved to, which surely can't be said of most poems composed in any given quarter:

> It need not be a desiccated wreck
> of boards, completely uninhabited,
> adobe bricks regressed to mud, hay. Heck,
> It might be verdant and jackrabbited.

The wind might not lament; the gift shop door
could jingle bells, the jasmine candles wafting.
Beyond some seniors at the convenience store,
you might observe a fisherman shoplifting.

But say it's vacant and bunch grass gray. Then torch
an image, scent, or song from your present life
to reconstruct the step, the stairs, the porch,
the house, town, two men fighting with a knife.

Much like the architecture of a sonnet:
a step, and suddenly you die upon it.

The robust alliteration ('hay', 'Heck') and chewy imagery ('bunch
grass gray') offer instant pleasures, but the self-reflexive payoff—a
risky move for a formal poem—succeeds in running the reader
through on its final line. 'Independence Day' is another keeper,
which ends with these exquisite lines:

> Small children tamed
> by night looked out from family cars, leaning
> toward sleep. We parted without touching on
> what family means or meant: our fathers gone,
> our mothers scrubbing through a collar stain.
> The sky gone black; the stars were intervening.

Most of Poch's poems, though, aren't up to the standards set by
these examples. There are no out-and-out disasters; Poch's commitment to craft—to ensuring that his lines scan and rhyme—guarantees that the slightest of his works are always readable, even enjoyable (an advantage that mediocre formal verse has over mediocre
free verse). However, it's this same commitment to craft, to satisfying a pre-imposed pattern, that can lead Poch's verse into subtle but
costly contortions. The resulting limbo never falls on its face but
nevertheless looks awkward, as demonstrated by the opening of
'John Poch':

A smaller Jackson Pollock, my polar blues
in cursive curse and scratch. A wasted fire
to write myself lies scribbled, smolders. Moods
instead of house-high flames' emotion mire
a vision. Ink, they lie.

Frost's great innovation—a voice so natural you don't notice the
iambs—remains much impersonated but, as Poch proves, rarely
possessed. Poch simply doesn't make it look easy.

But even that fine sonnet 'Ghost Town' has its flaws. A couple of
the lines I just quoted—'Then torch/an image, scent, or song from
your present life'—do sound a little awkward. And the first few lines
of the previously praised 'Independence Day'—

My father's birthday—how could I forget?
A friend and I had come to where, at sunset,
a band plays Sousa marches every year.
Thousands on the green, and children orbiting
antique family blankets. Steadfast, or slipping
to outer shells, held by the nuclear ...

—sound a little clunky, too. Perhaps the critic Yvor Winters was
right: poems are either great or not. We can charitably point out the
pros of those flawed poems that make up the middle-ground—
where, let's face it, most of us, including yours truly, reside—but it's
a safe bet posterity won't be as tolerant as us in mapping out a grey,
demilitarized zone between the durable and the perishable. So I
guess I'm mitigating my praise.

But really, the real failing of *Two Men Fighting with a Knife*—a
failing, to be fair, shared by most of the collections which smart,
well-meaning editors, even now, are FedExing to their rosters of
reviewers—is the lack of game-changing metaphors. Pan the verse
of John Poch long enough and you'll uncover glints of gold, like his
description of a fork lying in 'the shadow of a napkin's knee'. But in
the absence of such brilliant images, Poch's clever quatrains are just
that—clever:

Dear Doctor, don't get me wrong. I adore my wife,
but you looked inside me. Maybe it's the morphine
talking, but love abounds in the surgeon's knife.
Expect a card on February Fourteen.

Certainly Poch's subjects—desiccated Americana, the stepladder at
Strand Bookstore, spinal surgery—brim with potential, but his
actual language—'I'm dead/yet want to open, close, and surprise/
like a heart or sunset'—is dead on arrival.

'I sometimes think there is no good news about translation,
ever,' wrote Michael Hofmann recently in *Poetry*. I sometimes think
there is no good news about poetry, ever. Or today, anyway. That's
negative, maybe, but that's how I know poetry exists: when I'm least
expecting it, when everything's dross, when I've given up hope and
have my head down—that's when the real stuff, like so much low-
hanging plumbing, clocks me. Or takes the top of my head off. Or
whatever poetry does to us, those rare, rare times we run into it. Stay
positive.

Acknowledgements

Grateful acknowledgement is made to the following magazines and websites, where earlier versions of these essays and reviews—sometimes with different titles and in different form—first appeared:

Books in Canada: 'Godno', 'The World's Not-So-Secret Admirer'.
Canadian Notes & Queries: 'Full of It', 'Primordial Muse'.
Harriet: 'Child's Play', 'Lost and Found', 'Moon Dreams',
    'The Poetry in the Prose', 'Travel Writing'.
Maisonneuve: 'A Big Star Implodes', 'Griffin Poetry Prize Field Notes',
    'War of the Words'.
The New Criterion: 'The Kindness of Second Readings'.
Parnassus: 'Lovable Losers', 'Words Fail Him'.
PN Review: 'Chain of Fools', 'Flaking Off Beautifully',
    'Rosy-Fingered Yawn', 'Two Minds'.
Poetry: 'Autobiography of Reader', 'Going Negative', 'How I
    Learned to Survive without Margaret Atwood', 'New-Fangled,
    Old-Fangled', 'Not Just Poetry', 'Perfect Contempt', 'Sub-Seuss',
    'The Pigheaded Soul', 'The Spectric Poets'.
Riddle Fence: 'Manufacturing Conceit'.

Small parts of the introduction are adapted from pieces that first appeared in *Contemporary Poetry Review* and *The New Quarterly*.

Thanks to Jeremy Axelrod, Mark Callanan, Ben Downing, Evan Jones, Herbert Leibowitz, Michael Lista, Drew Nelles, Jason Ranon Uri Rotstein, Michael Schmidt, Don Share, Carmine Starnino, Zachariah Wells, Christian Wiman, and David Yezzi.

'Going Negative' and 'Not Just Poetry' received the Editors Prize for Book Reviewing from *Poetry*.

About the Author

Jason Guriel is a poet and critic whose work has appeared in such influential publications as *Poetry, Reader's Digest, The Walrus, Slate, Parnassus, Canadian Notes & Queries, The New Criterion,* and *PN Review.* His poetry has been anthologized in *The Best Canadian Poetry in English,* and in 2007, he was the first Canadian to receive the Frederick Bock Prize from *Poetry* magazine. He won *Poetry*'s Editors Prize for Book Reviewing in 2009. Guriel lives in Toronto, Ontario.

MW00567688

IMMIGRATION SERVICE
- 4 OCT 1988
DEPARTED
(1095)
HONG KONG

DEPARTMENT OF IMMIGRATION
PERMITTED TO ENTER
AUSTRALIA
24 APR 1986
on
For stay of 12 Month
SYDNEY AIRPORT 54

IMMIGRATION DIVISION BANGKOK THAILAND
A 72 DEPARTED
- 9 FEB 1987
SIGNED

ETHNIC AFFAIRS
.........Person
30 OCT 1989
DEPARTED
AUSTRALIA
SYDNEY 32

中华人民共和国
广东省公安厅

上陸許可
ADMITTED
15. FEB. 1986
4
Status: 4-1-4
Duration: 90 days
NARITA(N)
Immigration Inspector

ADMITTED
20 OCT. 1988
Status: 4-1-16
Duration 180 days
Port: HANEDA
Signature
出入国管理局
日本国
Narita Air Port
USED

T R A V E L E R ' S
HAWAII
C O M P A N I O N

№ 011278

THE UNITED STATES
OF AMERICA
NONIMMIGRANT VISA
ISSUED AT
U.S. IMMIGRATION
170 HHW 1710
JUL 2 0 1998

HONG KONG
(1038)
- 7 JUN 1987
IMMIGRATION
OFFICER

The 1998–1999 Traveler's Companions
ARGENTINA • AUSTRALIA • BALI • CALIFORNIA • CANADA EAST • CANADA WEST • CANADA •
CHINA • COSTA RICA • CUBA • ECUADOR • FLORIDA • HAWAII • HONG KONG • INDIA • INDONESIA •
JAPAN • KENYA • MALAYSIA & SINGAPORE • MEDITERRANEAN FRANCE • MEXICO • NEPAL •
NEW ENGLAND • NEW ZEALAND • PERU • PHILIPPINES • PORTUGAL • RUSSIA • SPAIN •
THAILAND • TURKEY • VENEZUELA • VIETNAM, LAOS AND CAMBODIA

Traveler's HAWAII Companion
First Published 1998
The Globe Pequot Press
6 Business Park Road, P.O. Box 833
Old Saybrook, CT 06475-0833
www.globe.pequot.com

ISBN: 0-7627-0236-2

By arrangement with Kümmerly+Frey AG, Switzerland
© 1998 Kümmerly+Frey AG, Switzerland

Created, edited and produced by
Allan Amsel Publishing, 53 rue Beaudouin
27700 Les Andelys, France. E-mail: aamsel@aol.com
Editor in Chief: Allan Amsel
Editor: Laura Purdom
Original design concept: Hon Bing-wah
Picture editor and designers: Laura Purdom and David Henry

ACKNOWLEDGMENTS
The Publisher would like to thank Aloha Airlines of Hawaii for their assistance in the
compilation of this book. The author would like to acknowledge the following
organizations and individuals who helped in this project: Hawaii Visitors
Bureau, Sheraton Hotels, Kona Village, Bonnie Tuell, Connie Wright Glenn
and Dean Myatt, and Wayne Glenn for his insights on Hawaiian culture.

Printed by Samhwa Printing Co. Ltd., Seoul, Korea

TRAVELER'S HAWAII COMPANION

by Carl Myatt

Photographed by Nik Wheeler

Kümmerly+Frey

The Globe Pequot Press

OLD SAYBROOK

Contents

TRAVELER'S HAWAII COMPANION

KAUAI

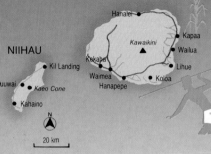

NIIHAU

- uuwai
- Kaeo Cone
- Kahaino
- Kil Landing

N

20 km

Hanalei

Kawaikini ▲

Kekaha

Waimea
Hanapepe

Kapaa

Wailua

Lihue

Koloa

OAHU

Waimea

Laie

Wahiawa

Makaha

Kaneohe

Kailua

Honolulu

Ewa

Waikiki

Koko Head
Regional Pk

CANADA

- Vancouver
- Seattle

UNITED STATES

Salt Lake City ●

San Francisco ●

Los Angeles ●

San Diego ●

PACIFIC OCEAN

HAWAIIAN ISLANDS

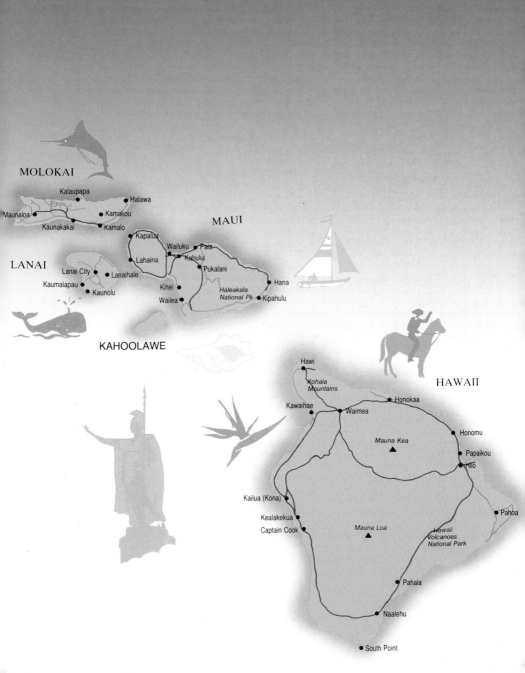

MOLOKAI

Kalaupapa
Halawa
Maunaloa
Kamakou
Kaunakakai
Kamalo
Kamalo

MAUI

Kapalua
Wailuku Paia
Lahaina Kahului
Pukalani

LANAI

Lanai City Lanaihale
Kaumalapau
Kaunolu
Kihei
Wailea
Hana

Haleakala
National Pk
Kipahulu

KAHOOLAWE

Hawi
Kohala
Mountains
Kawaihae
Waimea
Honokaa

HAWAII

Mauna Kea
▲
Honomu
Papaikou
Hilo

Kailua (Kona)
Kealakekua
Captain Cook
Mauna Loa
▲
Hawaii
Volcanoes
National Park
Pahoa

Pahala
Naalehu
South Point

TOP SPOTS

Pele's Fiery Garden

There is something strangely spiritual about **Hawaii Volcanoes National Park**. It's to be found in the silence surrounding the giant expanse of Kilauea Crater. It's there in the emerald and jade beauty of the ohia and fern forests where even the birds appear timorous of breaking the silence for fear of snapping a spell. It's there in the unseen presence of ancient warriors who walked its trails in centuries past.

Perhaps the spirituality one senses is in all of these things that make you stand and gasp in awe at the wondrous sights in this park. For this is Pele's place — the Big Island — home of the legendary fire goddess, so revered by the Hawaiians.

To the Hawaiians, the power of Pele is incalculable for Pele can both destroy and build. And as recently as 1986, she has done both.

Because the focal point of Hawaii Volcanoes National Park — the Kilauea Caldera and its fire pit, Halemaumau— are at an elevation of 4,000 ft (1,219 m), visitors to the park may be subjected to changing weather patterns. But be not dismayed. Viewing Volcanoes in all its many moods is part of the mystique of this magical place.

It is not uncommon, for instance, to race through the Stygian darkness of the lava fields on Chain of Craters Road in a blinding rainstorm, only to plunge into the valley and along the coastal plain to be greeted by a full moon. On such nights, the ribbons of magma streaking the hillsides on their downhill plunge to the ocean stand out in sharp relief. Here, as the lava enters the ocean, it glows and hisses, sputters and explodes in a display of pyrotechnics only God could have created.

Pele's garment spreads… a full skirt encompassing mountain and sea. Visitors stand transfixed, then may be moved to join in a dance of joy in the moonlight.

The entrance to the park is an easy 45-minute drive from the Big Island's principal town of Hilo. Once in the park (it costs $10 for each vehicle entering, $5 for pedestrians or bicycles), check in at the visitor center. Films and videos

OPPOSITE: A boardwalk along Devastation Trail, Hawaii Volcanoes National Park, protects the vegetation. ABOVE: The art of Pele. New lava hardens in Volcanoes National Park.

are screened daily in the auditorium. Another feature of the park is the Thomas A. Jaggar Museum, located three miles from the park entrance, which offers earth science displays and murals of Hawaiian culture. From an adjacent overlook you get different views of Kilauea Caldera and Mauna Loa.

Crater of Many Colors

If Hawaii Volcanoes National Park is a place of brooding, even slightly dangerous beauty, Maui's Haleakala — "The House of the Sun" — is its antithesis. To experience this mighty crater at its most glorious, see it at sunrise. Pack a picnic basket and a thermos of hot coffee and head off for the 10,000-ft (3,000-m) mountain, giving yourself at least two hours from the time you leave the coastal plains until you reach the summit. The road winds leisurely up the slopes and it's slow going, sometimes through thick mist, sometimes through sudden cloud bursts... until you reach the top.

At sunrise, as the fireball tips its way over the rim, the light seems to come from the very bowels of the crater illuminating the bowl and turning it into the canvas of some fiendish painter. Whereas Kilauea and its environs are all dark chocolate lava fields, Haleakala is a palette of subtle earth tones, splashed with sudden bursts of iridescent jades, blues and rose tints. You can view Haleakala from several vantage points at the summit, or you can hike its many fine trails. Tucked away in the crater are cabins and campsites. Tours on horseback are also available.

Haleakala's crater is 3,000 ft (914 m) deep and 21 miles (34 km) in circumference — large enough to hold the island of Manhattan. Its landscape, though more colorful, is often compared to the surface of the moon — so much so, that American astronauts trained here for their historic moon landing. The summit

of the mountain is part of the greater Haleakala National Park... a wondrous region, home to rare and exotic plants and wildlife.

Season of the Whales

Every year from December to May the whales return to the Hawaiian islands in a migratory ritual almost as old as the earth itself. Their traditional route takes these magnificent giants of the sea from their summer playground in the Arctic Ocean in Alaska to their winter birthing grounds in the waters off Maui. From Kauai to the Big Island, residents of the islands and thousands of visitors line

shorelines or take launches and sailing craft out to sea for a glimpse of these fascinating mammals. During the season you're almost guaranteed to see whales. Their waterspouts flash in the air, the whomp of their tails hitting the water echoes across vast expanses of ocean, and occasionally one of these huge creatures goes air borne, breaching the waters as it feeds. About 1,500 to 2,000 whales are believed to migrate to the islands each year. Some travel individually, others in pods. One winter day, whale watchers on the island of Oahu counted more than 700 whales in transit to Maui.

Marine scientists are tagging and tracking the whales by satellite in an effort to better understand their migratory movements. Researchers are particularly interested in determining the interisland movements of these mammals. The commonly held belief is that the whales approach the islands from the southwest end of the Big Island, then spend most of their time in the waters around Maui, Lanai, Molokai and Kooholawe, before cruising past Kauai on their way back to Alaska.

Experienced researchers from the Pacific Whale Foundation ((808) 879-8860 TOLL-FREE (800) WHALE-11, or Greenpeace ((808) 661-3333, on Maui; Whalewatch ((808) 322-0028, on the Big Island; or Captain Andy's Sailing Adventures

Haleakala Crater, a painter's palette of colors.

℃ (808) 882-7833, on Kauai; are among the operators that offer whale-watching cruises. Most charters guarantee sightings; if you don't see whales, you can go out again at no charge.

Window to the Heavens

The summit of Mauna Kea (Big Island) at elevations above 13,000 ft (4,000 m), with its cloud-free, dry atmosphere, is the ideal astronomical observing site. More major telescopes are located here than on any other single mountain peak. In total, there are now eight telescopes, plus the Hawaii Antenna of the Very Long Baseline Array in full operation on Mauna Kea, with other facilities still being built. Astronomers say that the percentage of clear nights at Mauna Kea is among the highest in the world. The atmosphere's stability and the location of the summit far from city lights allow for detailed studies of the faintest galaxies that lie on the very edge of the universe.

To get there from Hilo, take Highway 130 north to Highway 200, known to locals as **Saddle Road** for it traverses the "saddle" between Mauna Kea and Mauna Loa. The road is in better shape than it has been for some time, but a four-wheel-drive vehicle is required for the climb up the mountain above the visitor center. Remember, winds at these

elevations have reached 150 mph (242 kph) and temperatures can plummet to 20°F (-4°C), so make sure you have warm clothes.

A drive of 40 minutes or so along Saddle Road brings you to a crossroads and check station for hunters entering the state park. Take the right fork. The road leads to the **Ellison Onizuka Center for International Astronomy**, dedicated to the memory of the Big Island astronaut who perished in the space shuttle Challenger disaster in 1986. Onizuka, born in Keopu, Kona, was the first American of Japanese ancestry selected for the space shuttle program. Situated at an elevation of 9,190 ft (2,800 m), the facility that honors his memory includes a visitor center and accommodation for astronomers built in Swiss chalet style. The exhibits at Onizuka Center, formerly Hale Pohaku (House of Stone), range from geology to history.

The **Mauna Kea Observatory and Visitor Center** ℃ (808) 961-2180, part of the Onizuka Center, provides public star gazing programs. The visitor center is open Friday 1 PM to 5 PM, Saturday and Sunday 9 AM to noon and 4 PM to 5 PM. Children under 16, pregnant women

and those with health problems are not encouraged to proceed to the summit.

The 30-minute ride from the visitor center to the summit's observatories is a journey filled with anticipation. The stark, red-dust, lunar-like landscape has become synonymous with the mountain. The United States' space program once used this location as a training ground for astronauts.

At the summit the observatories stand in a straight line, silhouetted like domed sentinels in the clean, sharp air. The blues of the sky begin to blend into shades of orange and pink, casting a spectrum of color onto quilted clouds that seem to gently lap at the barren rock faces. As late afternoon turns to twilight, the heavens respond in a final blaze of glory, and the sun sinks into the billowy whiteness of the clouds, leaving behind a trail of color that washes the sky in a spray of purple and red. Be sure at some time to leave the sunny side of the mountain to view the eerie shadow the mountain casts onto the white clouds below, giving the appearance of an identical summit rising in the distance.

Soon the stars begin to appear so brightly, they seem to illuminate the mountain. Lavender and purple blend to black and in the darkness it will be cold. But wrap your coat a little more tightly around yourself and take in the magic of the Milky Way as few have seen it.

Tours of the summit facilities are conducted by the University of Hawaii Institute for Astronomy on weekends and holidays. Sunset and star gazing adventures are organized by **Paradise Safaris** ((808) 322-2366.

Merrie Monarch Festival

Every year in April a ritual takes place in the town of Hilo, on the eastern seaboard of the island of Hawaii, that may be unique in the annals of dance. It's called the Merrie Monarch Festival, and while it is in essence rather like a gathering of the tribes and a dance competition rolled

into one, it is also a reaffirmation of both the Hawaiian culture and a reminder of the greatness of a people.

If there's one word to describe what unfolds at the Edith Kanakaole Tennis Stadium, it is *passion*. There's passion in the coming together of so much talent, in the choreography, in the interpretation of the dance, in the costuming and in the competition itself. But more than anything else, there's passion in the bonding together of a people through their own unique art form — the hula.

For four days, the great auditorium echoes to the sounds of ancient chants, lovely, melodic falsetto singing, the strumming of guitars, ukuleles and bass guitars and the incessant beat of countless drums. There are times when as many as 50 to 80 dancers from one of the *halaus* (dance schools) appear on stage at one time, swaying in unison. And everywhere there is color... in the brilliant costumes, in the flowers that adorn the dancers, in the tropical blossoms, such as the blood-red

OPPOSITE TOP: Kukui nut necklace adorns young dancer. BOTTOM: The sounds of the ukulele are the sounds of the islands. ABOVE: Hula dancer... all sensuous grace.

anthuriums and the dazzling array of orchids that bedeck the fringes of the stage.

As befits a family gathering, there are occasional tears, but a spirit of joy pervades this place. There are many hula festivals in Hawaii during the course of a year (see FESTIVE FLINGS, page 59), but this one attracts the best. It's also the hottest ticket in town, so getting in isn't going to be easy. This calls for long-range planning — perhaps two years in advance, and you must seek assistance from a reputable travel agency if you are to lay your hands on a couple of prized tickets.

Canyon of Red Waters

As mighty as Arizona's Grand Canyon may be, for sheer beauty Kauai's Waimea Canyon is hard to beat. On days when the sun is high in the sky and clouds race across its face casting swift shadows, the canyon walls fleetingly change colors: pinks and oranges intermingle with the earthen tones already there. Somewhere high on Waialeale, already hidden in cloud, water is rushing off its steep shoulders, on the way to the ocean. The water begins its surge to the ocean, stained brown by vegetation in the Alakai Swamp in Waialeale's crater. Closer to the ocean, the water turns redder and redder as it mingles with the earth, giving Waimea its name, Reddish Water.

The high forests and valleys of Waimea are places of quiet beauty, laced with trails and isolated homesteads. Koa, ohia and eucalyptus trees grow alongside yellow ginger and other shrubs and vines. Maile vines, mokihana berries and ferns, so beloved by lei makers, add to the dazzling variety of the vegetation. Suspension bridges cross the Waimea stream at several points. It is always a dramatic place where nature can turn suddenly quixotic, and the dreamlike quality can quickly be shattered by a flash flood up the mountain that turns the stream into a torrent, causing waters to rise sometimes as high as 20 ft (six meters).

Deep in the tropical foliage of the canyon, wild boars forage, while on the inner slopes of the canyon, mountain goats feed. Beautiful birds, many of them rare, inhabit the valley floor and the higher reaches of the Alakai Swamp.

Sea Caves and Secret Coves

The sea cliffs of Kauai's Na Pali Coast drop some 4,000 ft (1,200 m) to the water's edge in almost perpendicular, serrated ridges. Waterfalls plunge from these heights to the ocean. Here and

there, a tiny cove or an enticing sandy beach beckons. Boat tour operators — whether by inflatable power boat, catamaran, sailboat or kayak —will take you up to the base of the cliffs, often into cavernous sea caves where the clarity and color of the waters will astound you. Hidden behind this natural escarpment are secret valleys where a thriving Hawaiian culture once existed. Na Pali Coast boat tours leave from harbors on the north, south and west shores of the island, but the most popular departure point is the north shore, where there are many operators from which to choose.

The best known are **Captain Zodiac Raft Expeditions** ((808) 826-9371, **A Na Pali (Eco) Adventures** ((808) 826-6804, and **Hanalei Sea Tours** ((808) 826-PALI, all situated in the north shore town of Hanalei. There's even a moonlight cruise on a catamaran that's well worth taking.

To explore the secret places of the Na Pali Coast that you can't see from the ocean, take a helicopter ride. Pilots will fly you deep into those emerald

The many hues of Kauai's Waimea Canyon leave visitors in awe.

valleys to the edges of waterfalls and give you a spectacular bird's-eye view of the razor-sharp ridges of the sea cliffs. There are several excellent helicopter tours available. Contact **Air Kauai Helicopter Tours** ((808) 246-4666, **Jack Harter Helicopters** ((808) 245-3774, or **Safari Helicopters** ((808) 246-0136.

War and Remembrance

On a serene Sunday morning, December 7, 1941, squadrons of Japanese aircraft flying out of the sun struck the American fleet at Pearl Harbor, Oahu, all but destroying it. The attack signaled America's entry into the war. Among the vessels sunk with huge loss of life was the battleship USS *Arizona*. The *Arizona* was never raised, and the warship became a tomb for those who died with it. Our nation has not forgotten the sacrifice our young men made in this terrible conflict. The site where the great ship went down is a permanent memorial, not merely to those who perished that morning, but to the senselessness of all wars. When you visit the *Arizona*, you'll see a 23-minute film of the events leading up to and including the attack on Pearl Harbor. The visitor center has a museum displaying a variety of historic photographs, news clippings and memorabilia. From the center, you'll be transported to the memorial by a shuttle boat, which leaves every 15 minutes. The Arizona Memorial is less a place of sorrow than it is of hope and pride. It is also a place of great historical significance, maintained by the **National Park Service** ((808) 422-0561.

Palette of Exotic Colors

Few can look at Oahu's Hanauma Bay for the first time and not gasp with delight. The waters glint in shades of aqua and emerald green, then darken mysteriously as huge shoals of fish make swift shifts in direction. Skin divers and snorkelers lie poised, mesmerized by a unique show of marine life.

An undersea volcanic eruption about 35,000 years ago created Hanauma Bay. Members of Hawaiian royalty are said to have used the bay for festivals and fishing. Hula competitions for both men and women and sacred wrestling tournaments were held here. King Kamehameha V and King Liholiho used the bay as their private fishing grounds.

Today its reefed waters are protected by law. This explains why Hanauma Bay is one of the best free shows in the world, guaranteeing an unforgettable ocean experience.

Beneath the magnificent colors that play on the bay's surface is a world of hidden beauty. Put on a face mask… dive and colors leap at you. Fish of all shapes and sizes flit by like moving rainbows. Proud fish with puffy chests bob in the gentle swell alongside other fish that dart and twist and leave with a flick of the tail. The waters of the bay teem with all manner of coral fish and endangered marine species such as dolphins and green sea turtles. A soft, sandy indentation in the coral bed called Keyhole is a good spot to feed the fish and swim alongside them. The marine gardens are alive with movement and color.

If you want to spend the day here, come early because the parking spaces go quickly. Bring a picnic lunch. Feed the fish (buy your fish food at the bay). Because tennis shoes worn by waders have been destroying the coral and denuding it of seaweed essential as a marine food resource, authorities have been forced to restrict visiting times to Hanauma Bay. It's the price of popularity.

Bring your suntan lotion, beach chairs, umbrella, underwater camera and plenty of extra film (snorkeling equipment can be rented at the park). And if you're too exhausted to make the steep climb back up to the car lot at the end of the day, a trolley will take you there for a small fee.

A donation is requested of those who wish to visit the marine sanctuary of Hanauma Bay.

Hanauma Bay, East Honolulu, is one of the best snorkeling sites on the island.

YOUR CHOICE

Ocean Playground

It is only natural that ocean activities make up a big part of any Hawaiian holiday. The waters around the islands are perfect for swimming, surfing, windsurfing, scuba diving and snorkeling, canoe and kayak paddling, yacht racing, and fishing.

SURFING
Historians speculate that the modern sport of surfing may be a combination of two skills brought to the islands by the earliest settlers — the Polynesians from the Marquesas Islands, and the Tahitians who followed in their wake.

A favorite pastime of the Marquesans was *paipo*, in which the person rode a wave by lying prone on a rounded board. Ten centuries after the Marquesans, the people of Tahiti brought with them a different type of water sport called *paka*, in which the participant rode the waves standing erect in a canoe (*wa'a*). It is probable that the two pastimes contributed to the sport of surfing that the kings and chiefs of Hawaii adopted as their own — a sport that eventually became so popular on the islands that even the women were participating.

By the 1800s, the popularity of surfing had waned due to pressures brought to bear on the Hawaiian lifestyle by Boston missionaries, and it wasn't until Duke Kahanamoku came on the scene in 1904 that the sport revived. The duke is credited with having done more to popularize modern surfing than any other man. This Hawaiian of noble birth went on to attain even greater fame as an Olympic swimming champion.

The duke introduced the sport to thousands around the world, inspiring young and old, men and women, to try their hand at it. Today, years after his death, his memory burns as brightly as ever on the professional circuit. Surfing carnivals are held in Australia, southern California, South Africa and South America, but some of the finest surfing still takes place in the islands, and there

OPPOSITE: Colorful surfboards await renters on a Waikiki rack. ABOVE: Pursuing a favorite island pastime, a surfer slashes through waves.

isn't a more exciting venue on earth than Oahu's North Shore, where only the bravest and the most skilled dare to confront the mountainous waves of Waimea Bay and the famed Banzai Pipeline off Ehukai Beach.

One of the first men to surf the Banzai Pipeline was Fred Van Dyke, author of *Thirty Years of Ocean Adventures with Fred Van Dyke*. He recalls the first time he set eyes on the Pipeline. "I thought at the time it would be another 2,000 years before anyone surfed it. This was in 1955. Seven years later, on a day when wave heights were reaching 20-plus, Bob Pike, Peter Cole, Ricky Gregg, Jose Angel and I, with a bunch of other guys, finally did it." After all these years, it still takes a special breed of surfer to challenge the Pipeline.

Each year thousands come to challenge that power. Some go home short of their goal, perhaps having underestimated the enormity of their task. But a lucky few feel the pride and satisfaction at having gained membership to surfing's most exclusive club.

If it is the variety of surf sites off the islands' shores which have made Hawaii the surfing capital of the world, it is the immensity of the waves which have made Oahu the mecca of surfing's aficionados. In the summer, when most storms occur in the South Pacific, the island's south shore bears the brunt of wave activity, and as a result, beaches from **Ala Moana** to **Makapuu** and **Sandy Beach** draw the wave riders. The north shore, on the other hand, is like glass at this time of year, making it a favorite with snorkelers and windsurfers.

When the storms begin to brew, however, and swells are generated in the Gulf of Alaska and the Sea of Japan, snorkelers are nowhere to be seen; surf season is here again. The transformation off the north shore is remarkable. Winter swells bring waves that average about six to eight feet (two to two and a half meters), and often reach monstrous proportions of up to 30 ft (nine meters).

For the professional surfer the north shore is the equivalent of the mountain

climber's Himalayan range, and **Sunset Beach, Ehukai Beach, Waimea Bay** and the **Haleiwa Alii** are the Everest of his ambitions. These "arenas," as they are known, are the finest in the island, and when the waves are breaking right, they are among the world's greatest surfing beaches.

Numerous competitions are held around the island, most notable among which are the Triple Crown of Surfing in December and the recently initiated Eddie Aikau "Big Wave" meet.

A word of warning about the Hawaiian waves: These are some of the largest in the world. Don't attempt to surf the north shore in winter if you're anything less than highly experienced. Be sure to pay careful attention to wave heights. They are measured from trough to crest, the "rideable" part of the wave, and give a good indication of the type of surf with which you are likely to be dealing.

The **Weather Service Forecasts** ((808) 836-0234 gives wave height reports. Follow these measurements when judging surf. Don't trust the estimations of local surfers. They have been exposed to huge surf for years and often grossly underestimate the size and awesome power of these watery beasts.

If you are totally inexperienced but wish to try your hand at this sport, rest assured that there are a number of safe areas where you can experiment. Other beaches on Oahu that are fairly calm year-round and offer perfect introductory waves are **Kuhio** and **Queen's Beaches** in the Waikiki area. Boards are usually available for rent at these areas. If you want some instruction, look no further than the "beach boys" who ply their trade on **Waikiki Beach**. Local surfing experts insist that these men provide the uninitiated with an excellent introduction to the sport. The "boys" are local, they know the waves, they know their trade

Boogie boarders TOP enjoy the curls, while surfers off the shores of Oahu BOTTOM challenge the awesome power of the sea in a spirit of adventure and risk.

and above all they are masters of public relations. So go down, rent a board and try a lesson or two — you'll enjoy it!

The west coast of Oahu features waves that break year-round from swells originating south, west and north of the islands. Popular surfing spots include **Tracks**, across from the Hawaiian Electric power plant at Kahe. This spot is a favorite of beginners.

The more experienced surfers gravitate to **Maile Point**, which protrudes into the ocean like a peninsula. Here the waves can range from two to 15 ft (one half to four and a half meters).

Makaha, however, remains the premier surfing beach on the west side. As befits its reputation, international surfing contests have been held here since 1954. On days when the waves range from small to medium, boogie boarders join the surfing elite to bounce around in the notorious "Makaha backwash", the rush of water that races back down the steeply inclined beach and out to sea. On days when the north swells are in evidence, waves can reach heights of over 25 ft (eight meters).

Near the end of the highway is Keawaulu Bay, more popularly known as **Yokohama Bay**, or Yokes. The waves in this bay break in very shallow water, creating a ride much like the **Banzai Pipeline** on the north shore.

Since all the islands possess popular surfing beaches, selection is a matter of personal taste and experience.

KAUAI
The **Hanalei** area on the north side is Kauai's answer to Oahu's North Shore. In winter, the waves are definitely for experts only. Beginners might try the waves around **Poipu Beach**.

MAUI
Maui boasts **Honolua Bay** and **Maalaea** on the west side of the island as its gift to the surfing world. The big surf on the Valley Isle is to be found at **La Perouse Bay**. Don't take a chance in these waters

Surfers and windsurfers prepare to put out to sea.

unless you know what you're doing. Beginners may wish to try areas near **Kaanapali Beach** in west Maui where board's can be rented.

HAWAII

The Big Island's main surfing challenge is in the **Hilo** area, where it can get extremely rough between September and March. If you're just starting out, most professionals recommend the Kailua-Kona side as one of the "mellowest" areas at which to catch a wave.

EXTREME SURFING

A new form of surfing has begun to emerge in Hawaii that allows the most experienced big-wave riders to catch waves in excess of 30 ft (nine meters). This new style of surfing is a blend of traditional surfing with windsurfing and water skiing. Teams of surfers ride to the outer reefs on jet skis, then take turns getting towed into a wave that is much too large to catch under normal conditions.

The surfers ride boards with straps (similar to those found on windsurfing boards) that allow the riders to launch themselves into the air to do flips. It's mind boggling to see someone riding a 30- to 40-ft (nine- to 12-m) wave and then polishing it off with a 360-degree loop.

WINDSURFING

MAUI

When talk turns to windsurfing, no matter where in the world, one of the most frequently discussed destinations is **Hookipa** on Maui.

Renowned windsurfer Mike Waltze is credited with having discovered the site. It has since become the windsurfing capital of the world and has been the setting for championship events since 1981. Hookipa, however, is not the place for novices. Waves can often reach sets of 10 to 15 ft (three to four and a half meters), and it is an intimidating prospect trying to windsurf here unless you have all the skills. For the less experienced or for those who want more fun than thrills, try **Kihei,**

Spreckelsville or **Kanaha**. If you want to rent windsurfing equipment, try the town of Paia, not far from Hookipa.

OAHU

There are several good windsurfing spots on Oahu. **Diamond Head** and **Lanikai Beach** are favorites. And **Maunalua Bay** in East Oahu is gaining popularity. The lookout at Diamond Head is a spectacular viewing site. On a clear day, with the ocean alive with myriad colored sails, and tanned bodies soaring high off the lips of waves, it's a sight to behold.

UNDERWATER ENCHANTMENT

In and around Hawaii's emerald waters exist some of the world's greatest diving sites. Tectonic activity and underwater eruptions over eons have created spectacular settings such as cathedral-like caverns, lava tubes, huge arches and towering pinnacles, all home to myriad forms of sea life.

While SCUBA diving off the islands you may see everything from sea turtles to dolphins, manta rays and sharks. If possible, try not to miss the annual migration of the humpback whales, which lasts from December to April.

Hawaii's waters contain a host of reef fish. One third of Hawaii's fish are indigenous to these waters and come in a spectrum of colors and tongue-twisting names. For instance, the official state fish is the Humuhumunukunukuapua'a, whose name is almost longer than the fish itself.

Hawaii is an underwater photographer's dream. Fish flock around you in their curiosity, especially at the more remote locations, and make perfect subjects for photos. Photography is in fact the only capturing that is recommended, as conservation of the islands' marine life is a primary concern of the dive shops and SCUBA diving organizations.

If you are planning a dive trip to Hawaii or would like to take advantage of some underwater action once you get to the islands, be comforted by the knowledge that there are no seasonal restrictions. Diving and snorkeling sites

are accessible throughout the year. Your only concern might be to plan your vacation for the tourist "off seasons"— from September to early November or April through mid-June.

When you are planning a dive, it is important to know when environmental changes may occur. Between June and August, water swells from the south sometimes result in large waves on the southern dives of the islands, and these should be avoided. From October through January, northwestern swells generate waves on the northern shores which could endanger the inexperienced diver. Water currents also stir up seabed sediments, making for poor underwater visibility. For up-to-the-minute information on weather and sea conditions, check with the United States National Weather Service.

Diving has a long history in the Hawaiian chain, but even the ancient Hawaiians realized that if their undersea masterpiece was to survive, stringent conservation methods had to be adopted. Don't disturb the many unique and beautiful creatures you will encounter. In their natural environment they are nature's gems. Remove them from it,

and their beauty dissipates rapidly (see also DANGEROUS ANIMALS, page 302).

Each island in the Hawaiian chain has its own unique undersea attractions. There are more than 200 excellent SCUBA diving sites in Hawaii.

OAHU

Dive sites are found mainly on the south and west shores. Several wrecks are viewable, including a 165-ft (50-m) minesweeper and a 196-ft (60-m) sunken barge. In addition, there are many caverns and fascinating reefs to explore. Four harbors around the island make for quick and easy access to most areas, and the major dive operations are located close to harbor launch sites. Pickup service from Waikiki hotels is available.

No diver should leave Oahu without paying a visit to **Hanauma Bay**. This scenic spot on the south coast — formed naturally when the sea eroded the edge of an ancient volcano — is enclosed by a large reef about 100 ft (30 m) offshore which provides protection against strong

Windsurfers glide over the smooth waters of Paia, near Hookipa State Park, Maui.

currents and waves, thereby creating the ideal diving location.

Hanauma Bay is one of the state's many underwater reserves and one of the most popular snorkeling and diving sites in the islands. Diving at Hanauma is like being in a huge aquarium, where the fish are tame and curious enough to eat from your hand. The calm waters afford snorkelers a chance to float in emerald splendor and admire the shifting rainbows of activity that are everywhere. Tropical sea life includes butterfly fish, parrotfish, goatfish, surgeonfish and green sea turtles. The outer reef area is just as abundant in marine life, and its gradual slope makes it perfect for introductory dives. Hanauma has something to offer everyone — from the pool-paddler to the budding Jacques Cousteau. Don't miss it!

Also on the south shore of Oahu, in Maunalua Bay, is **Turtle Canyon** which is accessible only by boat. At depths of nine to 40 ft (three to 12 m), the canyon offers vistas of lava flow ridges and huge sandy faces. The canyon derives its name from the green sea turtles which thrive in its waters. Also common are fantail filefish, parrotfish and triggerfish.

For the more experienced diver, the sinister sounding **Shark's Cove** on the north shore offers a worthwhile experience. At depths of 15 to 45 ft (four and a half to 14 m), this shore-based dive explores a series of huge caverns in which light filters down through the roof creating a breathtaking stained-glass effect. This is without doubt the most popular cavern dive on the island. Dive here only in the summer.

KAUAI

The south shore of Kauai is diveable year-round and offers a spectacular and diverse variety of marine life. The north shore, when not being pounded by winter surf, has lava tubes and caverns that can be explored.

Kauai's dive shops are found mainly in the Wailua and Poipu areas. There is a choice of four launch areas, all within 30 minutes of the major dive sites.

Some of the island's most popular diving locations are to be found off the Na Pali Coast. For the snorkeler or diver there is Oasis Reef. A feature of this boat dive, one of five in the area, is a lone pinnacle, surrounded by sand, which rises from a depth of 35 ft (11 m) to just below the water's surface. As the name of this reef implies, this is an "oasis" for thousands of beautiful fish, including false Moorish idols and porcupine pufferfish. There is also an abundance of octopi, lobsters and moray eels in the area.

SCUBA divers should try the 65- to 80-ft (20- to 24-m) cavern dive to the quaintly named General Store, which in reality is two caverns nestled under a horseshoe-shaped ledge. This is also the site of a nineteenth century shipwreck, a silent reminder of an ill-fated voyage. In the Poipu area, the Sheraton Caverns dive shows off three huge lava tubes running parallel to each other. Turtles, lobsters and the occasional white-tip shark are frequently found here.

Divers should not miss the experience of SCUBA diving around the "Forbidden Island" of Niihau which is only about 18 miles (29 km) to the west of Kauai. This area offers near-virgin diving sites, a feature of which are huge underwater caverns and amphitheater-like "rooms." If larger marine life is what you're after then look no further than Niihau waters where tuna, jacks, rays, barracuda, sharks and other large game fish are common. Note, however, that your boat must anchor offshore for no outsiders are allowed on the cultural preserve of Niihau or on the nearby island of Lehua, a seabird sanctuary.

MAUI

Maui is the organizational center for dives in the Maui County area, which encompasses the islands of Molokai,

TOP: Swimming and snorkeling in the clear waters of Hanauma Bay, Oahu. BOTTOM: A fishy scenario at Sealife Park, Oahu.

Lanai and Kahoolawe. Dive and snorkeling operations in Maui are concentrated in the main resort towns of Wailea and Lahaina, and dive trips to Molokini and the neighboring islands can be arranged from here. Maui area dive sites offer glimpses of creatures that are rarely seen elsewhere in the Hawaiian chain. Garden eels and morays are common. Docile whale sharks are sometimes seen, and those lucky enough to come across them rarely forget the humpback whales.

When on Maui, don't miss the marine preserve at **Honolua Bay** on the northern shore, where many tame fish and coral varieties can be found. This is a popular spot for introductory dives but is usually rough in the winter. There's also the splendid **Five Caves** site at Makena.

Fifteen minutes off the west coast of Maui, the top of crescent-shaped Molokini Crater, rises out of the ocean. Molokini is another marine preserve featuring a variety of dive sites and is home to shoals of multicolored reef fish, all very friendly in their protected environment.

LANAI

The Lanai coast is one of the best diving sites in the world. You'll find SCUBA expeditions and introductory dives for newcomers to the sport. **Diving expeditions** are organized at three dive sites where the waters are so clear it is possible to dive at night with underwater flashlights. Creatures that normally swim in the deep, dark waters of the ocean come closer to the surface after the sun goes down. Be sure to visit the **First** and **Second Cathedrals** on the south shore. Here several pinnacles rise from 60 ft (18 m) to the surface and roomy caverns produce an awesome effect. The many fascinating chambers are inhabited by moray eels, lobsters and shrimp.

Menpachi Cave, with its 100-ft (30-m)-long lava tube, and **Sharkfin Rock,** protruding out of the water like a shark's dorsal fin, are other favorite sites off this island.

MOLOKAI

One of the more popular diving sites off the coast of Molokai is **Mokuhookini Rock** off the east coast. This was formerly a military bombing target during World War II, and numerous artifacts from that era can still be found there. There are many pinnacles and drop-offs in this snorkeling–SCUBA diving spot and marine life includes barracuda, gray reef sharks and ulua.

BIG ISLAND

The waters off the western Kona Coast of the island of Hawaii are generally calmer and clearer than around many of the other islands. Protected from the wind and rain by the mountains of Mauna Kea and Mauna Loa, the seabed is a kaleidoscope of colorful coral and calm, silt-free beauty. Thousands of reef fish dart about in the crystal waters, and dolphins play, twisting and turning acrobatically around dive boats.

In addition to fantastic scuba diving at **Honaunau Bay** and the **Aquarium** at Kealakekua, both state preserves, local dive operators will be glad to introduce you to some of the other popular spots around the island.

The **Kona Cathedrals** is a large room created by a lava-domed roof. Beams of light from the surface penetrate and create a church-like, stained glass effect. The Cathedrals teem with tropical fish, while manta rays and white-tip sharks are not uncommon.

Fantasy Reef is a large, open cavern with a skylight and the largest collection of colorful "Christmas tree" coral in Hawaii. Varieties of tropical fish include hawkfish, saddlewrasses, pink damselfish and peacock flounders. Snorkeling is possible both here and at the Cathedrals.

The **Chimney** is another interesting site for SCUBA divers. Here, a white-sand canyon is bracketed by two lava walls that run to a height of 40 ft (12 m). The Chimney itself is actually a 40-ft (12-m)-high lava tube which can be entered at a depth of about 65 ft (20 m) and exited near the water's surface. Helmet shells are common and many red fish, including menpachi and *aweoweo* (bigeye), can be found under ledges.

For the more experienced diver, **Plane-Wreck Point**, located just south of Keahole Point, is recommended. A twin-engine Beechcraft lies broken in half on a bed of white sand at a depth of approximately 100 ft (30 m). The fuselage is penetrable and is now a playground for a variety of marine life such as damselfish, fantail filefish and menpachi, which glide silently through the many crevices.

Most Big Island dive operations are located in the Kailua-Kona area, and charter boats leave from there and from Keauhou, both of which are about 30 minutes from the major dive sites.

SUBMERSIBLE ADVENTURES

There is another way of exploring the mysteries of the underwater world — without actually getting wet — that is, from the safety and comfort of a submarine. **Atlantis Submarines** ((808) 973-9811 launched the world's first passenger submarine in 1985 and now operates in 10 locations around the world. Hawaii is the perfect environment for submersible adventures and in recognition of this, Atlantis in 1994 launched the world's largest submarine in Hawaiian waters. Operating off Waikiki, *Atlantis 2000* is 92 ft (28 m) long, displaces 150 tons and can carry 64 passengers. The *Atlantis 2000* tour includes a visit to a sunken World War II oil tanker which rests on the ocean floor and serves as a habitat for an incredible variety of fish. Submarine dives are also available on the Big Island off the Kona Coast.

Maui is served by both the Atlantis Submarines TOLL-FREE (800) 548-6262, and the *Nautilus,* a semi-submersible.

CANOEING AND KAYAKING

MOLOKAI

Three major international ocean canoeing and kayaking races take place each year from the island of Molokai to Oahu. The resort at Kaluakoi is the perfect launch site on Molokai for these events which attract contestants from the mainland

United States, Australia, South Africa and Japan.

Bankoh Kayak Challenge (May): What was once a traditional Hawaiian event has now developed into the world championship of ocean kayak racing. This is considered one of the toughest sporting events in the world. It's hours of backbreaking paddling, often against some of the most challenging currents to be experienced on any stretch of water. In recent years, the Australians and the South Africans have had a private duel among themselves for bragging rights. The race finishes in the Oahu suburb of Hawaii Kai.

Na Wahine O Ke Kai (September): This outrigger canoe paddling event for six-women crews is now regarded as the world championship of canoeing. Teams come to Kaluakoi from as far afield as Australia, New Zealand, Tahiti, Canada, and the mainland. Spectacular crew changes take place in mid-ocean, as one paddler plunges off the canoe and is replaced by another paddler, who has to scramble aboard from the water as the canoe sweeps past her. The race takes

Outrigger canoe racing is a major sport in the islands.

place over 40 miles (65 km) of the Molokai Channel, one of the roughest stretches of water in the Pacific. Crews have to contend with huge swells and riptides as they make their way to Kahanamoku Beach in front of the Hilton Hawaiian Village on Oahu.

Molokai Hoe (October): This is the men's version of the world outrigger canoe championship. The course and the hazards are the same as for the women's event. The competition, just as intense, continues to gain in international notoriety. The finishing point for this event is slightly different. It ends at Fort Derussy Beach, Waikiki, next to the Hilton Hawaiian Village where the women finish. For more information call **Ocean Promotion** ((808) 325-7400.

KAUAI

You can kayak for pleasure in most Hawaii waters, but experienced kayakers should explore the sea cliffs of Na Pali. This is a veritable wonderland of pretty coves, marvelous sea caves and grottoes. The ocean can get rough at times, so you must know what you are doing.

For a leisurely paddle, the **Hanalei River** trip is recommended. This is an easy journey down a serene river past fields of taro and thickets of hau. You don't have to take much with you except sunscreen and some light refreshments. For information, contact **Kayak Kauai Outbound** ((808) 826-9844 TOLL-FREE (800) 437-3507.

FISHING
BIG ISLAND

The waters off the **Kona Coast** on the Big Island are recognized as the mecca for big game fishing in the islands. Every year, in August, international sports fishermen from around the world congregate in this little resort town for the **Hawaiian International Billfish Tournament**. Their quarry is that magnificent game fish, the Pacific blue marlin. This fish, with its distinctive swordlike snout, has tipped the scales at 1,000 lbs (450 kg), but typically they weigh between 300 and 400 lbs (135 and 180 kg). The most coveted of the marlin family is the black marlin, but these are somewhat rare in Kona waters. When found, they can weight up to 1,800 lbs (800 kg). The marlin is a difficult fish to catch because it is fast and strong. Its meat is moist, white and superb.

LANAI

Big game fishermen on Lanai go after mahimahi, yellowfin tuna, wahoo or the prized Pacific blue marlin. Either of Lanai's two resorts, the Lodge At Koele, and the Manele Bay Hotel ((808) 565-3800

TOLL-FREE (800) 321-4666 FAX (808) 565-3868, Lanai Company Inc. P.O. Box 310, Lanai City, HI 86763 WEBSITE http://www. Lanai-resorts.com, can arrange for a boat and all the equipment to take you out on a trip. Fishing charters — shared or private — are also available on all the islands. Check local tourist publications or the concierge at your hotel for information.

Spear fishing is popular with the islanders, and the octopus or tako the favorite target. The locals bake or steam the octopus and use it for poke, a delicious octopus salad.

KAUAI
Freshwater fishing is available on Kauai at Kokee State Park. For a modest fee of $3.75 you can get a 30-day freshwater fishing license from the **Department of Land and Natural Resources** ((808) 587-0077.

Hitting the Trail

Six of the major Hawaiian islands have much to offer in terms of hiking trails

and camping sites. Whether difficult or easy, the ultimate reward is an opportunity to commune with the out-of-doors in one of nature's masterpieces.

For information on any of the state facilities contact the **Department of Land and Natural Resources** ((808) 587-0300 for camping or ((808) 587-0166 for hiking.

HIKING
OAHU
Visitors tend to regard Oahu as a mere extension of Waikiki's commercialism. This is a mistake. The island has a surprising number of remote areas of almost virginal beauty, and several trails present views that are equal to the more famous vistas on the neighboring islands.

Mount Tantalus, at 2,013 ft (614 m), was named after the mythical Greek king. Just as the legendary monarch was punished by being made to stand in a pool of water that receded each time

OPPOSITE: Hikers on Haleakala gaze out over a swirling bank of clouds. ABOVE: Looking down into the House of the Sun.

he tried to drink, so it is said that this peak seems to recede into the distance the further up you hike. In this region a series of interconnecting footpaths run in a basic south-to-north direction, from the depths of the valley to the heights of Mount Tantalus. There are trails to suit the interest and abilities of most hikers, but the cliff trails are recommended for their superior views.

Two of the more popular elevated trails that branch off from Tantalus are the **Manoa Cliffs Trail** (six miles or 10 km) and the **Puu Ohia** or **Ohia Tree Hill Trail** (four miles or six and a half kilometers). Both appeal to the hardy walker. The Puu Ohia Trail, in particular, has a wonderful view of the Nuuanu Valley and Pali Highway areas.

For those who prefer a leisurely stroll, the valley trails are recommended. What these trails lack in panoramic splendor they more than make up for by the presence of unique flora. Among the scores of flowering plants on these trails look for Job's Tears, a type of branched grass with elongated and pointed leaves. This plant attains heights of up to six feet (two meters) and produces black, blue-gray and white pea-sized beans much in demand by lei makers.

Job's Tears can be found in profusion on the **Makiki Valley Trail,** which begins at the Tantalus Drive trailhead, heads eastward, descends into Makiki Valley, then passes the Nahuina Trail to the north. After a short distance, the Makiki Valley Trail crosses Kanealole Trail to the south. It is a place of pure enchantment and natural serenity. Cool springs bubble out of the ground and Job's Tears are everywhere.

The trail winds its way through a heavily forested valley and around small gulches and tiny streams. Mountain apple trees tempt the hiker to pause and taste the delicious fruit. The trail eventually links up with other trails near the bottom of the hill. Also at the foot of the hill is the Makiki Environmental Education Center.

Aiea Loop Trail (4.8 miles or 7.7 km) is located in the **Keaiwa Heiau State Recreation Area,** site of an ancient healing *heiau* (temple) around which grow many of the medicinal plants once used by the *heiau kahunas* (temple priests). This graded trail is a favorite with residents and offers an enjoyable experience for families. Passing through a forest of Norfolk pines and several varieties of eucalyptus, the trail is a fascinating blend of non-native greenery and some samples of traditional Hawaiian flora such as ohia lehua, koa and sandalwood. The Aiea Loop branches off sharply to the right after 1.6 miles (2.5 km) and then follows the ridge above North Halawa Stream before descending through a forest where many native trees are in evidence. At the three-mile (4.8-km) mark of the hike, be on the lookout for the wreckage of a C-47 cargo plane which crashed on the ridge in 1943.

The **Wiliwilinui** and **Lanipo Trails** (three hours each way) are parallel walks to peaks located on the Koolau range, from which one obtains great views of the windward side of Oahu. Wiliwilinui can be entered from Laukahi Street on Waialae-Iki Ridge, located on the southeastern side of the island. It's a strenuous hike to an elevation of about 2,000 ft (610 m) overlooking Kapakahi Gulch to the west and Wailupe Gulch to the east.

Despite the elevation, it is a fairly gentle ascent to the summit, but the trail can get muddy and caution is advised. Notable flora includes the multicolored lantana, lavender, and the Philippine orchid. Look for interesting bird life on the trail, particularly the endemic elapaio, a gray bird which chirps a curious wolflike whistle, and the crimson apapane which can often be found feeding on the nectar of ohia flowers. The road ends at 1,800 ft (550 m) and the trail continues to the summit where the views of Waimanalo in the east and Kualoa Point to the north are magnificent.

The misty forests of Kokee State Park are a paradise for hikers.

From the top of the Wiliwilinui Trail, Lanipo extends west along the crestline. Lanipo Trail provides one of the few vantage points from which to view **Kaau Crater**. Kaau is an ash and lava cone formed within the last 150,000 years. Situated at the base of the Koolau range, this crater, as is the case with so many Hawaiian landmarks, has an origin steeped in legend. It is said that the demigod Maui, wanting to join Kauai and Oahu, threw his hook hoping to catch the foundation of Kauai, and pulled a rock loose instead. The rock is said to have fallen at Kaena Point on the North Shore of Oahu while the hook landed in the Koolaus and created Kaau Crater.

The last stretch of the Lanipo Trail is more strenuous than Wiliwilinui and great agility is required to traverse the precipitous ridge and thick brush. From the summit one can see all the way from Waimanalo to Kailua. If you're in good shape, try this one. It's worth it.

It is about an hour and a half from Honolulu to the **Sacred Falls State Park** on the windward side of the island. In order to get there, drive over the Pali on Highway 61, then take a left and proceed along Highway 83. Sacred Falls is clearly signposted.

Sacred Falls Trail is an easy hike that is very attractive and interesting. This place has many legends, the principal of which surrounds the Kaluanua, or "the big pit," into which the waterfall plunges from a height of almost 90 ft (27 m).

Almost from the instant you reach the trail, the waterfall comes into view, luring you onward like some mystic beacon. The trail crosses Kaluanua Stream and runs into a 1,600-ft (490-m) walled canyon. Guava and mountain apple trees grow in the valley. At the end of the canyon, the trail cuts through a dry stream bed once fed by a waterfall, which also is the subject of a legend. It is here that Kamapuaa, of Hawaiian mythology, and his men were trapped while fleeing

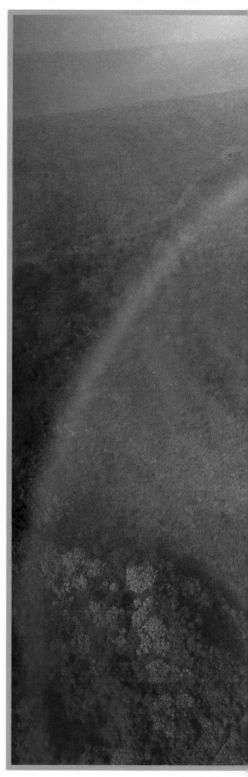

A colorful arc curves high above the West Maui Mountains. Scenes such as this are common in the Rainbow State.

an enemy force. In order to escape, Kamapuaa transformed himself into a gigantic pig, and his army climbed on his back and then onto a ledge above to safety. If you examine the usually dry waterfall, you will notice a large indentation. This is where Kamapuaa, in pig form, is said to have supported himself, his massive weight leaving behind an impression.

The Sacred Falls pool is often muddy, but it is cold and refreshing.

Camping

There are 18 campsites on Oahu. Nearly all are controlled by a county, state or federal agency, and all require camping permits. Campsites at public beach parks extend from **Haleiwa** on the north shore to **Bellows Beach** on the windward coast. The **City and County of Honolulu** ((808) 523-4525 oversees 13 beach parks. Each has a different character. Campfires are not allowed, but cooking is permitted on grills. There are no public cabins on Oahu, but several under private jurisdiction. The **State of Hawaii Campgrounds** ((808) 587-0300 are similar to the city's. Reservations are taken 30 days in advance on Oahu, but a year in advance on the neighboring islands.

MAUI

The grandeur of Haleakala is best appreciated by walking its trails on an overnight hike. It's a journey that traverses rainbow-colored splatter cones and towering cliffs. This once active volcano is also sanctuary to about 200 of the *nene*, or Hawaiian goose, and the wildly beautiful *ahinahina*, the Haleakala silversword. This member of the sunflower family is found nowhere else on the planet and was probably spawned by seeds carried across the Pacific on tradewinds. What is unique about the silversword is that it blooms only once in a five- to 20-year life cycle — and then it dies.

Hikers have several choices at Haleakala, but for the dedicated walker, the **Crater Loop Hike** (20 miles or 32.3 km) is a must. The trailhead is

located 10,023 ft (3,055 m) above sea level at the visitor center. The initial section down the **Sliding Sands Trail** to the floor of the crater is a comfortable walk and gives hikers an opportunity to acclimate to the elevation. In the early morning, views along this trail sweep across the entire expanse of the crater. The longer you spend on this trail, the more vivid the colors become. Red, ochre and shiny black sand begin to merge with stones flecked with golden hues to form rivers of colors. Another aptly named section of the trail is **Paint Pot**, the most colorful of the cinder cones in the crater. Here purples intermingle with rich grays and bright reds. The final climb to the rim of the crater at the Crater Road junction is a spectacular ascent on switchbacks that gain 1,400 ft (426 m) of elevation in 3.9 miles (6.3 km).

Day hikers can take the round-trip **Halemauu Trail** (eight miles or 13 km) to the Holua cabin area down the Halemauu Trail in approximately six hours. Very fit hikers, without the encumbrance of heavy backpacks, can cross the crater via the **Sliding Sands–Halemauu Loop** in a day (eight to 10 hours).

Because Haleakala's trails are at altitudes that never drop below 6,000 ft (1,829 m), it is important to be prepared for cold nighttime temperatures and the chance of frost. Days are often sunny, dry and hot in the shadeless hollow of the crater, but it is prudent to anticipate cold, foggy and wet afternoons when the clouds roll in.

It is necessary to check in at park headquarters located on the Haleakala Crater Road at the 7,030-ft (2,142-m) level. Backcountry permits are issued here, and cabins, if available, can be assigned.

For information contact **Haleakala National Park** ((808) 572-9306. Recorded park information can be heard on ((808) 572-7749. For other information and reservations write to Superintendent, Haleakala National Park, P.O. Box 369, Makawao, HI 96798.

Camping

The National Park Service also runs the campgrounds at Haleakala. The **Home Grove** campsite is often cool, windy and rainy. Grills, potable water and chemical toilets are available. **Kipahula** can be warm, wet and breezy. No water is available here, so bring drinking water. Chemical toilets are provided. There are cabins at **Kapalaoa** (5.8 miles or 9.5 km), **Holua** (6.3 miles or 10.1 km) and **Paliku** (9.8 miles or 15.8 km) with tent sites also at the latter two areas. Paliku and Holua have limited nonpotable water that must be treated before drinking. No open fires are permitted. The 12-bunk cabins are so popular that they are awarded on a lottery system. Apply by writing up to 90 days in advance. Hikers who do get a cabin should arrive with appropriate equipment and supplies. The rangers have detailed park maps and updated information on trail conditions.

Maui County ((808) 243-7389 has three parks for camping — **Baldwin**, near the ocean town of Paia, **Rainbow**, in the upcountry village of Haliimaile, and **Kanaha Beach Park**, near the airport.

The state has two sites — at **Waianapanapa**, near Hana (12 cabins,

tent sites and ocean views) and a lone cabin at **Polipoli Springs** at an elevation of 6,200 ft (1,890 m). Since cabin requests greatly exceed the number available, a monthly lottery is held for reservations. Only one request per group is accepted. Call ((808) 984-8109.

MOLOKAI

Kamakou Mountain, at an elevation of 4,970 ft (1,515 m), is the highest point on Molokai. Its slopes are dressed by a native Hawaiian forest. Within the 2,774 acres (1,123 hectares) of the Nature Conservancy's **Kamakou Preserve** are rare plants and animals that don't exist anywhere else on earth.

The wetter slopes of the mountain are heavily forested with ohia trees, huge tree ferns, orchids and silver lilies. In the drier areas, hardwoods, including small groves of sandalwood, thrive.

The trails of Kamakou Preserve are a source of fascination for hikers. The mountain is rich in historical sites and has a wide variety of climates and terrains. It is

OPPOSITE: Protea grow to enormous sizes in the islands' cooler climes. ABOVE: Rare silversword is found only on the upper slopes of Haleakala on Maui.

also home to five endangered species of forest birds. The *'olomao* (Molokai thrush) and *kakawahie* (Molokai creeper) live only on the island. The red i'iwi, green amakihi, and the crimson and black 'apapane are seen more frequently, as is the *pueo* or Hawaiian owl.

The **Nature Conservancy of Hawaii** ((808) 553-5236 FAX (808) 553-9870 takes hikers into the preserve once a month. Hikers are advised to seek the advice of the Conservancy about trails and trail conditions. For much of the year, the forest is a very wet place.

To reach the entrance of the preserve, go east on Forest Reserve Road to a point where it leaves Highway 46, about half a mile (one kilometer) south of the junction of Highway 46 and Highway 47 (Kualapuu Road). A 45-minute drive will bring you to the preserve's entrance at the Waikolu Lookout, provided it hasn't been raining. In wet weather, the road may be impassable.

Camping

Molokai has three campsites for tent campers. The two sites operated by the county are at **One Alii** and **Papohaku Beach Park** ((808) 553-3204. The parks have restroom facilities with showers, drinking water and barbecue pits. Fee: $3 for adults and $1.50 for children. There's also tent camping at **Palaau State Park**, which is run by the **Hawaii State Division of Parks** ((808) 984-8109.

KAUAI

Half the battle to hiking in **Kokee State Park (Waimea Canyon)** is getting there. The park is roughly 38 miles (61 km) from Lihue. Your efforts, however, will be well rewarded when you reach the park headquarters on the edge of Waimea Canyon. There are 16 trails worth exploring in Kokee, each with a unique identity and splendid panoramic views ranging from the grandeur of Waimea Canyon to the rugged beauty of the Na Pali Coast and the lush vegetation of its rain forests. The area also contains facilities for picnicking, swimming and camping by permit (issued by the Hawaii State Division of Parks ((808) 984-8109).

The 3,657-ft (1,115-m)-deep Waimea Canyon has been blessed with vibrant forests set deep in tropical valleys. Several trails branch out from the canyon floor. Of these it is the strenuous **Canyon Trail** (1.7 miles or 2.7 km), ending at the Cliff Outlook, which presents Waimea Canyon at its best.

The **Berry Flat Trail** (one mile or 1.6 km) and the **Puu Ka Ohelo Trail** (530 yards or 500 m) are two forest trails highly recommended for the casual hiker. The trails wind through areas forested with California redwoods, Australian eucalyptus, native koa and Japanese sugi pines. The sweet smell of pine refreshes

the spirit, making these two of the more enjoyable walks in the park.

Other relatively easy trails include the **Iliau Nature Loop** (530 yards or 500 m) and the **Cliff Trail** (200 yards or 180 m). The Nature Loop is akin to a walk through a botanical garden, offering a close-up view of several species of plants endemic to Hawaii, including the unusual iliau. The **Cliff Trail** gives a good view of Waimea Canyon.

Ditch Trail (3.5 miles or 5.6 km) and **Koaie Trail** (three miles or 4.8 km) are considerably more difficult to hike. The former covers some rather rough terrain, but has splendid views of Kohua Ridge

and the waterfalls that run off it. Koaie Trail is somewhat easier and more popular. At the end of Koaie is a natural pool, ideal for a refreshing swim after this vigorous hike.

Other strenuous but beautiful trails include the **Kukui Trail Loop** (2.5 miles or four kilometers) with a view of a 2,000-ft (610-m) drop into the canyon, the **Alakai Swamp Trail** (3.4 miles or 5.5 km) and the strenuous **Awaawapuhi Trail** (3.3 miles or 5.3 km) which climbs high above the Na Pali Coast.

Kauai's Waimea Canyon is often compared to the Grand Canyon.

The trails above the imposing Na Pali Coast lead to the Na Pali wilderness. They are tough and dangerous, but for those who dare, the rewards are great. The first 440 yards (400 m) of the trail lead almost straight up, but as you pause for breath, the views more than compensate your effort.

The **Haena–Kalalau Trail** (11 miles or 18 km) was the original route built by the Hawaiians who populated the beautiful hanging valleys of these regions. (To camp in Kalalau State Park you must have a permit, issued for a maximum of five nights.) Sections of the trail are only a matter of inches wide with sheer drops to the ocean below. There are no handrails to protect the hiker, so caution is urged.

You may wish to take a short hike to **Hanakapiai Beach** and waterfalls, which would give you a first hand experience of the famous hanging valleys of the Na Pali wilderness. At Hanakapiai Beach, an icy stream feeds into the ocean in an area dotted with caves. The trail into the valley, source of Hanakapiai Falls, winds through mango groves and a forest of mountain apple, breadfruit and guava trees. It also circles a deep, clear pool where you'll want to take a dip to refresh yourself before tackling the last stretch to the falls.

Finally, deep in the valley where ferns grow in wild profusion, are the three-tiered **Hanakapiai Falls**, cascading to the boulders below from a height of 2,950 ft (900 m) in a lacy sheet of water.

This place of enchantment is rarely touched by the sun. Primitive, beautiful and serene, it refreshes the soul as much as the senses.

Camping

Kauai County ((808) 241-6660 has seven oceanside beach parks ranging from **Haena Beach Park** in the north to the **Lucy Wright Park** close to the ocean near Waimea. Permits are $3 per night per adult. There's no charge for children.

The three state parks ((808) 274-3445 where camping is permitted include **Na Pali Coast, Kokee State Park** and the **Polihale State Park**, 140 acres (56 hectares)

overlooking Waimea Canyon. There are also privately owned cabins in Kokee State Park ((808) 335-6061 with rates ranging from $35 to $45 per unit. These units can also be booked through Kokee Mountain Lodge ((808) 984-8109.

BIG ISLAND

The hikes in **Hawaii Volcanoes National Park** offer dramatic contrasts. **Devastation Trail** is the site of a violent volcanic eruption that, in 1959, smothered a once beautiful forest with cinder and ash. All that remains are charred tree trunks and lava rock. Devastation Trail shows how powerful and destructive a volcano, such as Kilauea-Iki, can be. A boardwalk paves part of the trail to keep hikers from walking on the cinder fall and prevent damage to the slowly returning vegetation.

The trails in Volcanoes range from easy to difficult. Among the easier ones are **Sandalwood Trail** (1,320 yards or 1.2 km), **Sulfur Bank Trail** (600 yards or 550 m) and the **Thurston Lava Tube Trail** (550 yards or 500 m). The most exciting is the Thurston. As lava flowed through this area, the outer layers cooled and solidified while the inner flow remained molten and kept traveling, eventually emptying itself and creating a tube.

Though not as amazing as the Thurston Lava Tube, the Sulfur Bank and Sandalwood Trails have trademarks of their own, though not pleasant ones. Odors created by sulfurous fumes which escape through steam vents in the craters diffuse the air. The pungent smell may cause nausea or headaches if you stay in the area too long.

Semi-difficult trails are more abundant in the park. One such trail is **Crater Rim Trail**, made all the more difficult by recent overflows of lava onto the path. The trail begins at Volcano House and loops around the Kilauea Military Camp and the Hawaii Volcano Observatory. On a clear day you might see Mauna Loa looming in the distance. The Crater Rim Trail passes through pretty woodlands alive with ohelo shrubs that produce bright red berries, believed to be favored

by the volcano goddess Pele. The legend advises us that a quantity of the berries picked must be thrown into the crater as an offering. Other trails in the semi-difficult category include the **Halemaumau Trail** (3.2 miles or 5.1 km) which traverses the Kilauea Caldera, the **Kilauea Iki Trail** (two miles or 3.2 km) and the **Byron Ledge Trail** (2.5 miles or four km).

While it is one of the more strenuous hikes in the park, the **Hilina Pali Trail** (6.4 miles or 10.3 km) rewards those who persist with superb views of the Big Island's southeast coast. The best time to walk this trail is in the afternoon. Doing it too late is not advisable; dusk comes quickly in these mountains, and one shouldn't be caught out here unequipped in the dark. It is almost 2,000 ft (610 m) down to Halape Trail Junction.

One of the best hikes in Hawaii Volcanoes National Park is along the **Mauna Loa Trail**, which begins at an elevation of 2,032 ft (619 m), at the end of Mauna Loa Road, and terminates at 13,250 ft (4,038 m), at the summit cabin. A minimum of three days is required to complete the round trip to the summit. Four days is strongly recommended.

The trail passes through *nene* (Hawaiian goose) country and an open ohia forest. Once above Red Hill at 10,035 ft (3,059 m) — where there's an eight bunk cabin — the trail follows Mauna Loa's northeast ridge. Bring your own water for use on the trail. There is no charge to use the cabins, but hikers must register at park headquarters. At the summit cabin (12 bunks) an arrow points to water and ice in a lava crack. A word of caution: This is not a particularly dangerous climb, but if you are burdened with a heavy backpack, it could be difficult. Remember that the summit has subarctic weather and conditions can change rapidly and without warning. Winter storms can last several days and the snowpack can be from six to nine feet (two to three meters) deep.

A second trail (6.1 miles or 9.8 km) — marked with yellow blazes — to the summit of Mauna Loa begins at an elevation of 11,000 ft (3,350 m) near the Mauna Loa Observatory. It will take you from six to eight hours to complete the hike because the terrain is steeper than the other trail. The round trip may take

Halemaumau Trail traverses the inhospitable Kilauea Caldera. OVERLEAF: Fresh lava from Kilauea tumbles into the ocean, creating clouds of steam — and new land on the Big Island.

an entire day, so in order to return before dark, you must begin hiking by 10 AM. On this trail, altitude sickness is a danger because of the rapid climb from sea level. The trail must be walked at a pace that allows for acclimatization.

Camping

There are a dozen county-operated beach parks on the Big Island that permit camping. A list of these sites may be obtained by calling the Department of Parks and Recreation ((808) 961-8311. The campgrounds range from the **Waipio Valley Lookout** to **White Sands Beach Park** near Kailua-Kona. Fees are $1 a day for adults and $.50 per child.

The state oversees cabins at **Mauna Kea, Kilauea** and **Kalopa**. Each cabin contains linen, cooking facilities and utensils. Two of the cabins are for hikers attempting to climb Mauna Loa and are available at no cost on a first-come, first-served basis. They are the **Red Hill Cabin** (eight bunks) at Puu Ulaula 10,035 ft (3,058 m) and the **Mauna Loa Cabin** (12 bunks) at Mokuaweoweo Caldera rim 13,250 ft (4,038 m).

Ten housekeeping cabins are also available at **Namakani Paio**; each sleeps four. Reservations must be made at least a month in advance with the National Park Service ((808) 967-7311. Fees for these units are $24 per night.

Volcano House ((808) 967-7321 in the park also offers cabins and campsites.

LANAI

The island abounds in **hiking trails**. One of the favorites is named after the naturalist George Munro. The trail is lined with Norfolk pines and unique flora native to New Zealand, which Munro introduced to the island.

There is no potable water on the trails of this dry island, so you must carry your own. Many people treat the water before drinking it.

Camping

Hulopo's Beach campground is owned by the Koele Company ((808) 565-6661, P.O. Box L, Lanai, HI 96763. There is an

initiation fee of $5 and a $5 fee per day per person. Bordered by a spectacular white-sand beach and arid kiawe forest, the comfortable, lawned camping area provides clean restrooms, private outdoor cold showers, and cooking areas. It's necessary to make reservations well in advance, since there are only three shaded campsites. Stays are limited to seven days.

Hunting

On this island where large herds of axis deer once roamed the high slopes, hunting has been a major activity for as long as can be remembered. Hunters came during the season and nearly always used the rustic **Hotel Lanai** as their headquarters. The hotel, built by the Dole Corporation in 1927 for visiting dignitaries, retains all its old world charm. And the hunters still come.

HORSEBACK RIDING

There are a number of spots on all the islands where you can saddle up and ride the range, forest or ocean trails.

OAHU

The **Turtle Bay Hilton Golf and Tennis Resort** offers a variety of trail rides on its property. The first is a 45-minute ride that gives you a first hand experience of the beauty of the north shore. This ride takes you along the oceanfront and through a forest of ironwood trees. Rates: $35 for adults, $22 for children.

The Hilton's Evening Ride is a romantic hour and a half trail ride along a scenic route. Rates: $65 per person, or $55 per person with a group of four or more.

The Advanced Ride is a 40-minute trot and canter through the Kawela Bay trails. This outing is for qualified riders only. Rates: $50 per person.

MAUI

Adventures on Horseback ((808) 242-7445 FAX (808) 572-4996 E-MAIL peemer@aloha.net, is more than a mere trail ride. It is an opportunity to see parts of these islands that few tourists see.

A rider encounters the majestic Lanai landscape.

The rendezvous for the start of this adventure is a beautiful private ranch in Haiku on the slopes of Haleakala. Here you will be served refreshments and introduced to the horses.

Each trail ride party consists of six riders and an experienced guide. The only condition stipulated by the organizers is that guests have a love for horses and an adventurous soul.

The journey takes you along the edges of majestic sea cliffs pounded by surf, with the rolling green and golden slopes of Haleakala in the background. The destination is Haiku Falls via eucalyptus and fern forests, and secluded tropical settings fed by freshwater streams. In these lush forests, waterfalls cascade into shimmering pools.

After a morning swim, you get a picnic lunch of pita bread sandwiches, fruit, cheeses, vegetables and fresh-squeezed lemonade.

Private and exclusive rides of various types and duration may be custom-designed and reserved. But due to the limited number of guests allowed for each outing, advance reservations are usually required. Cost per rider: $175 plus tax.

Riding stables are located from Kapalua in West Maui to Makena in South Maui, and from Waihee Valley to Hana. And there are several trail rides offered by other trail companies. You can ride into Haleakala Crater, or up into the Hana highlands near Ohe'o Gulch. You can ride onto ranch lands high above the central valley or go from the beach at Makena to the winery at Ulupalakua. Operators and rides on offer include:

Ironwood Ranch ((808) 669-4991 or ((808) 669-7593 or ((808) 669-4702, 5095 Napilihau Street, Lahaina, HI 96761. West Maui Journey $75; Sunset Ride $100; Picnic in Paradise $135.

Makena Stables ((808) 879-0244, 7299 South Makena Road, Kihei, HI 96753. Introductory $99; Morning $115; Sunset $130; Advanced Winery Ride $160.

HAWAII

On the Big Island, **Kings' Trail Rides** WEBSITE http://www.interpac.net/~hit/ktr.html E-MAIL bones@interpac.net, at Kealakekua (outside Kona) offers adventure rides through forests, up the slopes of Mauna Loa volcano, and past a working Hawaiian cattle ranch with views of Mauna Kea. Or you can opt for a ride through cool, dense fern forests with stunning views of Mauna Loa and the Hualalai Mountains to the north.

Another route takes you along the Kona Coast route to the Captain Cook monument on the historic Kings' Trail. You might end the day swimming at Kealakekua Bay.

LANAI

Long before Lanai turned to pineapple cultivation, it was a ranch. Many of the tales passed down by native cowboys, or *paniolos*, tell of cattle drives by moonlight and sea roundups when cattle were driven into the surf to be loaded on barges and shipped to Honolulu. Old cattle trails exist around the Lodge at Koele ((808) 565-3800 TOLL-FREE (800) 321-4666 FAX (808) 565-3868, where the ranch house used to be, that are perfect for horseback riding. Check with the lodge for rates.

MOUNTAIN BIKING

The mountain bike, designed for off-road use, is a perfect way to see the islands. Great weather year-round makes for the

LEFT: Riders hit the trail on Molokai. RIGHT: Father Damien's grave is a place of pilgrimage.

perfect cycling environment, and the choices are tremendous. You can take the low road or trails through forests of fragrant flowers and fruit trees. Or you can take the plunge down a well-paved mountain highway escorted by tour operators who know their way around.

All islands have a range of public and private biking trails.

OAHU

Kaena Point in Northwest Oahu is a flat trail parallel to the ocean. It's an easy 10-mile (16-km) run in each direction.

Kuliouou, east of Honolulu, presents a fast four-mile (6.5-km) downhill run with plenty of switchbacks.

Mililani in Central Oahu is a 13-mile (21-km) loop that is the best trail for all types of riding — single tracks, technical uphills, and great downhills.

Maunawili Trail in windward Oahu is doubletrack riding on an 11-mile (18-km) cliffside trail with panoramas all the way.

Peacock Flats in Northwest Oahu is challenging. It starts with a three mile (five kilometer) climb on a paved road, leading to a network of jeep trails that constitutes a 13-mile (21-km) loop from Mokuleia Beach Park. From high on this

trail there are splendid views of the ocean and the activity at Dillingham Airfield, such as the gliders and small planes bearing parachute jumpers.

Pupukea is a 17-mile (27-km) loop on the north shore that first takes you uphill and then along the north shore's beaches.

You can rent bicycles and equipment on Oahu at McCully Bicycle and Sporting Goods ((808) 955-6329, Honolulu; the Bike Factory ((808) 946-8927, Honolulu; the Bike Shop ((808) 596-0588, Honolulu; Island Triathlon and Bicycle ((808) 732-7227, Honolulu; Island Cycle Center ((808) 627-0714, Central Oahu; and Barnfield's Raging Isle ((808) 637-7707, on Oahu's North Shore. Rentals rates start at $25 a day with Kona full-suspension bikes at $35 a day.

KAUAI

Here's a real thrill: a bike ride from the famed Waimea Canyon all the way down to the coast — a distance of about 12 miles (19 km). **Outfitters Kauai** ((808) 742-9667 organizes this early morning adventure which begins with a cup of hot coffee and blueberry muffins and a view of a spectacular sunrise over the canyon. Then it's a downhill rush on smooth roads to the coast.

If you do this trip in the afternoon you will be treated to soft drinks and cookies and a view of sunset over the isle of Niihau. On both cruises, you'll have opportunities to stop and take stock of one of the most beautiful stretches of country on the planet. You'll be regaled with narrative on the history, culture, legends and folklore of Kauai. It's a wonderful way to see the place. Cost per person: $65.

MAUI

For the thrill seeker, nothing beats a plummet down a mountain road on a sturdy bike. Rather like riding the mules down the trail to Kalaupapa on Molokai (see THE MULE TRAIL, page 242), the free-wheeling Haleakala downhill is an experience that shouldn't be missed. Several companies organize the bike ride down the mountain, but **Cruiser Bob's** ((808) 579-9292 claims to have been the first in the state to do so.

Riders are picked up en route and taken by van to the summit, there to be assigned a bicycle — a robust piece of equipment designed for safety, comfort and ease of handling. The little caravan begins its descent in single file with a guide at its head and the van bringing up the rear, and in constant contact by radio.

The journey takes riders from the high barren slopes of the mountain, through eucalyptus forests, and then through flower and vegetable gardens where the scented air is crisp and cool. After a picnic lunch, it's off again to the towns of **Makawao** and **Paia** where short breaks are taken for refreshments. The entire journey takes seven hours.

MOLOKAI

Because it has so little traffic, Molokai is an excellent place for a bike ride. You can take a leisurely ride through quaint plantation towns and fishing villages, or tackle a dirt road that winds through a tropical rain forest before emerging on a mountain top overlooking the ocean.

If you need to rent a bike, want additional advice on routes or wish to take a guided mountain bike tour, contact **Fun Hogs Hawaii** ((808) 567-

9292 or ((808) 552-2555, which operates out of the Kaluakoi Hotel and Golf Club's Beach Activities Center. Fun Hogs is run by Mike and Maria Holmes. Their story is typical of what often happens in Hawaii. Both had jobs in the building industry, but finally decided to turn Mike's passion for sport — he was a surfer and paddler of international reputation — into a business.

HAWAII

The **Beach Road or Wild Orchid Ride** is a 21-mile (34-km) excursion starting and ending in Hilo. A fun coastal ride, it goes through the town of Keaau and then through fields of wild orchids and a rain forest. The ride is fast and easy, starting out on red cinder and moving inland for a while on a dirt road that ends at Kapoho. Here you turn around and skirt Kalapana on the way back. This ride is recommended for both beginner and intermediate riders.

The **Kulani Trail**, also known as the **Killer Single Track**, takes you south out of Hilo onto Stainback Highway and

onward to Waiakea Arboretum. You begin the strenuous part of the ride on entering a forest of 100-ft (30-m)-tall eucalyptus trees surrounded by carpets of wild ferns. As the name of this ride suggests, it's a single-track trail full of slippery roots, rocks, mud and fallen trees. Caution is advised. How long you take to complete this ride depends on how good a rider you are. It's recommended for intermediate and expert riders.

Designed strictly for the mountain man or woman with good lungs and strong legs, **Kilohana** runs 6.6 miles (4.1 km) each way from the Kilohana Hunter Checking Station off Saddle Road. Kilohana means "lookout point" and you'll see plenty of those on this trail. Most of this ride is at elevations ranging from 5,500 to 7,446 ft (1,676 to 2,270 m). The highest point of the ride is Puu Laau, where you're advised to rest at the hunter's cabin that stands in the midst of a eucalyptus grove. The riding time is about two and a half hours; recommended for intermediate and advanced riders.

For more information about these and other Hawaii rides, contact the **Big Island Mountain Bike Association** ((808) 961-4452 and request their fine brochure.

Bicycles may be rented at Hilo Bike Hub ((808) 961-4452 or Hawaiian Pedals ((808) 329-2294.

Sporting Spree

MARATHONS
In the last decade Hawaii has become the center of major international sporting events. It began with the Honolulu Marathon, and now the state is also the center for triathlons and other endurance events that require space and interesting terrain, which Hawaii has in abundance.

Honolulu Marathon
In 1973, 162 runners competed in the inaugural Honolulu Marathon. The field has steadily grown to over 30,000, making

Bikers zip through Parker Ranch on the Big Island.

it the third largest marathon in the world and the second largest in the United States, behind the Boston Marathon.

For all its international notoriety, the Honolulu Marathon — held every December — continues to be recognized as "the people's marathon," for it attracts not only the professional, world-class athlete, but also the weekend runner who comes out to run for the fun of it and the pride of saying he or she finished.

The Honolulu Marathon is turning into the proving grounds for the great racers, especially those from the African continent. From 1985 to 1997, the Honolulu Marathon has been dominated by African runners. Ibrahim Hussein of Kenya won it three years in a row from 1985 to 1987 and set the course record in 1986 of 2 hours 11 minutes 43 seconds. (In that same year, Carla Beurskens of the Netherlands set the women's course record of 2 hours 31 minutes 1 second.)

Since 1986 only Gianni Poli of Italy (1988) and Bong Ju Lee of Korea (1993) have interrupted the African march to victory. Simon Robert Naali of Tanzania has won it twice, in 1989 and 1990, and Benson Masya of Kenya has won it three times, in 1991, 1992 and 1994. Josiah Thungwane of South Africa won it in 1995 and then went on to win the Olympic Marathon in Atlanta in 1996.

The majority of entrants now come from the mainland United States and foreign countries, with as many as 20,000 coming from Japan alone. These numbers, together with the support teams and families, mean a huge boost to Hawaii's tourist economy.

The course for the race stretches from downtown Honolulu to Hawaii Kai in east Oahu and back. The run begins at the famous Aloha Tower from where the participants wind their way down Ala Moana Boulevard, through Waikiki, and onto Kalanianaole Highway leading east. The race twists through the suburbs of Hawaii Kai, which is approximately the halfway point, before turning back down the highway, over Diamond Head, to the finish at Kapiolani Park, which marks the end of the 26-mile (42-km) course.

As runners weave their way through the streets of Honolulu, one can't help but be reminded of the ancient Hawaiian *kukini* or "swift runners".

The organizers here like to declare: "New York has the crowds, Boston has the prestige, but Honolulu has it all!" For more information contact the Honolulu Marathon Association ℓ (808) 734-7200, 3435 Waialae Avenue, Room 208, Honolulu, HI 96816.

Men and Women of Steel
The **Bud Light Ironman Triathlon** — a combination of three existing long-distance races popular on the island of Oahu — was conceived in Hawaii by John Collins, a Navy man, and now enjoys a place in sporting history.

The Ironman Triathlon is a combination of the Waikiki Rough Water Swim (2.5 miles or 4 km), the Around-Oahu Bike Race (112 miles or 180 km) and the Honolulu Marathon (26 miles or 42 km).

The first Ironman event took place on Oahu on February 18, 1978, and attracted 15 men, 12 of whom finished. Gordon Haller won that race in 11:46:58.

A year later the race attracted its first woman entrant, Lyn Lemaire, who finished in 12:55:38, placing fifth overall behind the race winner, Tom Warren of San Diego (11:15:56). *Sports Illustrated* magazine called the event "lunatic."

Lunacy must be catching. In 1983 this grueling endurance test reached epidemic proportions with over 1,000 such events taking place around the world. The Hawaiian event, now held at Kona on the Big Island, however, is recognized as the world championship and attracts the best there is. So popular has this event become that the regulations have been tightened to limit the number of participants. Qualifying meets are held around the world, and an athlete has to either win a qualifier, meet a qualifying standard time, enter as a foreign competitor or be selected by a lottery in order to be accepted to race in Hawaii.

The legendary Dave Scott, a Californian, was the first triathlete to come in under nine hours when he completed the 1984 race in 8:54:20. In 1993, Mark Allen slashed the record down to 8:07:45. But new faces from Europe are starting to be a factor in this race, notably the Germans Lothar Leder and Thomas Hellriegel.

A consistent performer in the women's division has been Paul Newby-Fraser of Zimbabwe. The 1982 women's event that brought worldwide focus to this grueling race. On that occasion, Julie Moss was leading when she collapsed 400 yards (364 m) from the finishing line. Instead of being led off the course, Moss crawled to the finish in front of television cameras, coming in second behind Kathleen McCartney. Suddenly Julie Moss had become a heroine of the world — and just as quickly the world had learned about the Ironman through an iron woman.

The Budweiser Beer Company is now the main sponsor, so prize money has soared in both the men's and women's division. The classic receives national television coverage.

Ironman week in Kona is one giant party. If you want to watch this event, book early, because accommodation becomes very tight at this time of year.

Backpacking

Backpackers can take advantage of privately run youth hostels and the state's more than 30 government-run campsites.

The hostels primarily offer dorm-style bed space. However, many also have a few private rooms at very reasonable rates. Unless otherwise noted, hostel accommodations include shared baths and communal kitchens. A few offer continental breakfasts. Most require you to bring your own linens (towels and bed sheets). The hostels usually have a steady flow of visitor traffic year-round. Guests are encouraged to book at least one month ahead to ensure that space is available.

Some of the campsites are free; others charge $3 to $5 per day. All campsites require a permit, and stays are limited (for details see HITTING THE TRAIL).

YOUR CHOICE

OAHU
Backpackers Vacation Inn and Plantation Village ((808) 638-7838 FAX (808) 638-76515, 59-788 Kamehameha Highway, Haleiwa, HI 96712, is located on Hawaii's North Shore. Dorm bed: $16.50 per day; private room: $50 to $65 per day (sleeps one to two persons); studio: $89 per day (private bath; sleeps one to two persons).

Hosteling International-Honolulu, Manoa Branch ((808) 946-0591 FAX (808) 946-5904, 2323A Seaview Avenue, Honolulu, HI 96822, in the Manoa Valley, is convenient to hiking trails. Amenities include a communal television, bus schedules, activity bulletin board, and reading room. Dorm bed: $12.50 for HIAYH members, $15.50 for non-members; private room: $35 to $57.50 (sleeps two to three), includes private bath.

Hosteling International-Honolulu, Waikiki Branch ((808) 926-8313 FAX (808) 946-5904, 2417 Prince Edward Street, Honolulu, HI 96815, is in Waikiki near the beach. Amenities include a communal television, bus schedules, activity bulletin board, and reading room. Dorm bed: $15.50 for HIAYH members, $18.50 for non-members; private room: $35 to $40 (sleeps two), includes private bath.

Island Hostel ((808) 942-8748, 1946 Ala Moana Boulevard, is located in Waikiki near the beach and has coed and women's dorms as well as private rooms. Dorm bed: $16.50 per day, $105 per week; private rooms: $45 per day, $275 per week (sleeps one to two people).

MAUI
At the **Banana Bungalow Hawaii** ((800) 8HOSTEL, 310 North Market Street, Wailuku, Maui, HI 96793, amenities include a television room, and group outings ($5 to $9 per person). Dorm bed: $15 per day; single room: $33 per day; double room: $40 per day.

Maui Hostel at the North Shore Inn ((808) 242-8999 FAX (808) 244-5004, 2080 Vineyard Street, Wailuku, Maui, HI 96793, has separate men's and women's dormitories. Dorm bed: $15 per day; single room: $30 (includes refrigerator);

double room: $40.70 (includes refrigerator); private double bunk: $37.50 (includes refrigerator).

BIG ISLAND
Arnott's Lodge and Hiking Adventures ((808) 969-7097, 98 Apapane Road, Hilo, HI 96720, has an all-you-can-eat barbecue Wednesday and Saturday ($7). Dorm bed: $17 per day; single room: $31; double room: $42.

Holo Holo Inn ((808) 967-7950 FAX (808) 967-8025, Kalainoua Road, Volcano, HI 96718, is one mile (one and a half kilometers) from Hawaii Volcanoes National Park. Dorm bed: $17 per day; private room (minimum two people): $40.

Hotel Honokaa Club (775-0678, Honokaa, HI 96727. Dorm bed: $15 per day; standard room: $35 for a single, $40 for a double (no linens provided, shared bath); mid-range private room: $45 (linens, private bath, and continental breakfast); deluxe private room: $55 to 65 (linens, private bath, television, and continental breakfast).

Don's Tropical Valley Hostel ((808) 889-0369 E-MAIL tropical@pacific-ocean.com, P.O. Box 1333 Kapaau, HI 96755, is on the northwest side of the Big Island. Rooms start at $15.50.

KAUAI
Kauai International Hostel (823-6142, 4534 Lehua, Kapaa, HI 96746, is convenient to beach trails and Sleeping Giant Mountain. Dorm bed: $16; private room: $40 (sleeps two).

YMCA Camp Sloggett (/FAX (808) 335-6060 E-MAIL KAUAIYW@PIXI.NET (no street address), is located in Kokee National Park. YMCA Camp Sloggett offers campsites, hostel accommodations and a lodge (for groups of five or more). Campsites (with communal shower and toilet): $10 per day; dorm bed: $20 per day. Lodge: June to April, (for private groups) $20 per person per day, five-person minimum and two- to three-day minimum stay; May, $20 per person per day, eight-person minimum and two- to three-day minimum stay. The lodge has a fireplace and kitchen.

Living It Up

Much of the attraction of the Hawaiian islands as a tourist destination is its natural beauty; but its other asset is its ability to provide the great escape for those caught in the crosshairs of notoriety and fame.

Those who wish to luxuriate in extravagance — and get away from it all need look no further than the Rainbow State — provided, of course, that money is no object. Almost every resort is a secret oasis unto itself. In addition to the great resorts and hotels, there are several excellent private residences for rent that can swallow you up and nurture you for as long as you wish.

KAUAI
The **Sheratioin Princeville** on Kauai's North Shore may be one of the most romantic settings on the planet. The resort sits on a plateau above beautiful Hanalei Bay. In addition to the gorgeous views of mountain and ocean, Princeville offers every luxury to its guests. Its top-of-the-line accommodations include the Royal Suite ($3,500 a night) and two Presidential Suites ($2,750 a night). The Royal Suite, at 2,400 sq ft (223 sq m) is the size of a luxury apartment. Amenities include a "royal spa" and a full butler's kitchen. Good use is made of black and white marble in the understated elegance of the interior design. Imported furniture, silk wall drapes and bedding, artwork and antiques give additional accents to the suite. The panoramic views of Hanalei Bay and the Pacific Ocean are unmatched from this vantage point.

The Presidential Suites, at 1,800 sq ft (167 sq m), offer three times the space of a standard Princeville room. There's a two-story loft with tropical decor, and a one-story suite designed with Brazilian blue quartz granite. Both suites have independent spas, butler's pantry kitchen and standard amenities.

Princeville Resort, overlooking Kauai's lovely Hanalei Bay, epitomizes Hawaiian-style luxury.

OAHU

The west side of Oahu is a land of raw beauty where a rugged stretch of coastline has been transformed into an elegant oasis. Most resorts tend to be well away from the perimeters of major cities.

The **Ihilani Spa and Resort** is a quick car ride away from Honolulu, yet it boasts all the trappings of a great resort, from a dazzling beach to a superb golf course and a spa that is decadently Roman in concept and design. If you have several thousand dollars in loose change, you can indulge your fantasy at the Ihilani.

Six deluxe Spa Suites ($550 per night) are positioned in garden settings close to the ocean. From your private whirlpool in your garden lanai, you can sip champagne while taking in the sunsets for which the leeward side of the island is so famed. Or you can rent the 4,000-sq-ft (372-sq-m) Presidential Suite that has every luxury you can possibly imagine, from deep-soaking marble baths to a butler on call. The cost for one night of fantasy: $5,000.

The Ihilani's full-service spa is equipped with Thalasso treatment hydrotherapies, which the resort claims is one of only two in existence in the country. The spa's other specialty is its herbal wraps — chamomile, linden, sassafras or peppermint are all available.

The Spa Café and Terrace, which overlooks the resort's lagoons, serves breakfast and lunch, and is one of five distinctive restaurants on the property. The resort's signature restaurant is the Azul, which captures the essence of fine Mediterranean dining.

The property on which the **Halekulani Hotel** now stands in Waikiki once housed a private residence. That residence, the **House without a Key**, remains a part of the hotel complex today. For sheer luxury and excellent service, this hotel may be the cream of the crop in Waikiki's highly competitive tourist district. It's a hotel of quiet, understated elegance and exquisite taste. The Halekulani has a range of suites that extend from the Club Suite ($700) all the way up to the Presidential ($4,000) and Royal Suites ($4,500). The Royal and Presidential Suites each have 4,066 sq ft (378 sq m) of floor space.

The Halekulani offers its patrons a choice of dream vacations called "Heaven on Waikiki Romance" packages. You have a choice of eight days and seven

nights for $3,059 double occupancy, or four days and three nights for $1,489.

Recognizing that one of the most irksome things for an international traveler to do is to hang around in the hotel lobby at the end of a long flight, the Halekulani checks guests into their rooms immediately and allows them complete the registration process in the privacy and comfort of their rooms.

The rooms at the Halekulani are superbly appointed. Its signature restaurant, La Mer, is perhaps the finest French restaurant in the islands

MAUI

Many a novelist had Hana in mind when describing the lush landscapes of the Pacific,

for Hana can be the perfect embodiment of a tropical paradise. It's a place of rushing waterfalls, exotic plant life, and luxuriant flowers in a wild assortment of colors. Here giant tree fern and flowering arbors thrive alongside a variety of tropical fruit trees in countryside that changes dramatically from forest to mountain pastures to rolling meadows to rugged shoreline whipped by raging surf.

For over half a century, one place has impressed itself on the minds of those fortunate enough to have come to Hana — the **Hotel Hana-Maui** on the Valley Isle's eastern shoreline. In recent years, this sprawling retreat has drawn the tired and weary to a tranquil 4,500-acre (1,800-hectare) cattle ranch. Here herds still graze on the gentle lower slopes of the majestic volcano, Haleakala, which dominates this side of the island.

Sea Ranch Cottage N° 216 is one of several beautifully appointed cottages on the property. What makes N° 216 so desirable is its location overlooking the turbulent ocean-battered cliffs, with views of the mystical island of Alau. Legend has it that the demigod Maui snared and drew up the island of Maui from the deep while he was on Alau. You can book this two-bedroom cottage for $795 a night, sit in your hot tub, share a glass of wine with a companion and gaze into the night sky or admire the changing hues of the ocean as the sun dives down beneath the horizon. Except for the sounds of waves crashing against the rocky edges of the shoreline, there is only the sound of your own heartbeat to break the silence of this very special place.

The **Kea Lani Hotel** resort in Wailea, Maui, latched onto something when it introduced its Grand Chefs on Tour series — an event designed to make any fine food lover's heart miss a beat. For $19,500, the hotel will provide you and your companion with a seven-night gourmet holiday, the likes of which you'll find hard to match anywhere.

The concept is simple: The resort flies in famous chefs from around the world, pairs them with some of Hawaii's best chefs, tosses in a respected vintner or two, and mixes the whole lot with guests prepared to pay for the privilege of eating, sipping and learning from the masters.

The package includes first-class air fare from the mainland to Maui; a luxury car; seven nights at the Kea Lani's beautifully appointed, two-bedroom oceanfront villa with private plunge pool; a personally escorted deep-sea fishing trip which is aptly titled "From the Hook to the Cook", followed by a lesson in the kitchen on how to prepare the freshly caught fish in the Hawaiian style. And there's more: three signature dinners prepared by the Grand Chefs; a sunset massage; and all manner of wine tastings. If you wish, one of the hotel's chefs will also cook a meal for you on the beach.

LANAI

Discriminating travelers give the **Lodge at Koele** high marks for its location and atmosphere. The real charm of staying here is being at an old-fashioned hunting lodge in foothills forested with pine trees, yet within sound of the surf. Nature provided the basics at Koele; man with his ingenuity did the rest. The grounds are graced with a large pond, flowering trees and shrubs, and a magnificent golf course out of the island's high country. The centerpiece of the lodge, its medieval Great Hall, has soaring timber ceilings, huge open fireplaces, and flowering planters. This splendid room has all the gentility of a royal European residence. Tea is served each day accompanied by sandwiches and pastries.

If you want to splurge at the lodge, book the Garden Suite. This one-bedroom suite with living room and fireplace

OPPOSITE: Reflections of the Hana-Maui Hotel.
ABOVE: The Ritz Carlton Hotel at Kapalua.

overlooks the sculptured garden and reflecting pool of this lovely property. It guarantees privacy. The cost is $1,500 per night.

HAWAII

The **Hapuna Beach Prince Hotel** is one of the newer hostelries on the Big Island's Kona Coast. Sister hotel to the famed Mauna Kea Beach Hotel, it is part of the Mauna Kea Resort. The Prince opened in 1994 on the edge of Hapuna Beach, one of the world's finest beaches.

This hotel has all the amenities you would expect from a luxury hotel and one extraordinary bit of extravagance: For comfort, service and decadent indulgence, the Hapuna Suite is hard to beat. "Suite" is something of a misnomer. It is in reality a self-contained bungalow aside from the main hotel, complete with its own swimming pool. The 8,000-sq-ft (743-sq-m) residence boasts three master bedrooms with private baths, lanais, a study or fourth bedroom, a gorgeous living room furnished in earth tones that opens onto the ground floor lanai and pool area, dining room — and, of course, butler service. Most areas of this beautiful house provide glorious views in all directions, particularly of the coastline and the mountains in the background. The price is $7,000 a night.

Down the road from the Prince is the **Orchid at Mauna Lani**, part of the International Sheraton Group's Luxury Collection of hotels. Two 18-hole championship golf courses, an Art Center and significant historic sites are part of this 32-acre (13-hectare) property.

In addition to the richness of the accommodation, the Orchid offers its patrons the Orchid Center for Well-Being which incorporates sport, culture and "mind–body synchronization" into guests' daily activities. Part of the center's program, the Spa without Walls, draws from a variety of ancient healing techniques, including those used by the Hawaiians. A two-night Spa without Walls vacation for two costs $389. The package includes a 50-minute massage

or body treatment each night near a spot where waves break over the rugged shoreline, and unlimited use of weights and exercise equipment. Other elements of the program are tai chi classes, aquatic aerobics, yoga and snorkeling. The Mauna Lani claims that the resort — like Sedona in Arizona and Lourdes in France, is considered a "power point" on the planet — a place where positive energies gather. But you will have to experience this program to find out whether these theories hold true.

There are other fantasies you can play out at the Orchid resort. For between $2,250 and $2,950 — depending on what accommodation you choose — the resort offers vacation packages that are among the best in the islands. The Executive Suite Ocean View package will get you and your partner beautiful accommodation in a luxury suite for three nights. For the price of $2,250, you are also provided limousine transportation from the airport, champagne and fruits when you arrive, a four-course dinner for two, with a bottle of wine thrown in for good measure and a private dinner for two at a beach cabana catered by Brown's Beach House Restaurant. For $2,950 you get all that, plus lodging in the super luxurious Oceanfront Suite. And if you want to splurge yet further, the Presidential Suite is yours for $3,500 per night.

Family Fun

Hawaii is a kids' paradise: Marine parks, the great volcano on the Big Island, horseback riding, helicopter excursions, and, of course, plenty of beach activities keep youngsters interested and happy and give families plenty of choices for things to do together.

The island also excels in providing grown-ups and kids a break from each other — recognizing that big people and little ones don't always agree on what constitutes a fun time. Parents who want to take a break and play some golf or tour a museum can do so knowing that their children will be entertained and looked

after. Almost every hotel in Hawaii, and certainly all the resorts, have excellent planned children's activities.

Children's programs offer everything from sports, kite flying and nature hikes, to arts and crafts activities, such as lei making and coconut painting. There's also storytelling, an art at which the locals are quite accomplished. Without exception, children's activities are supervised by well-trained, accredited hotel staff. Most programs operate from 9 AM to 3 PM.

Festive Flings

HULA FESTIVALS
HAWAII
The chant floats eerily over the hush of the enormous crater. It's an invocation to Pele, the deity of the volcano. Dancers lining the rim of Halemaumau at the Kilauea Caldera slip into motion. The chant resonates in the early morning air. Wisps of sulfur rise lazily from the crater floor. As quickly as it begins, the tribute to the fire goddess is over. One *halau*

(school) leaves. Not long afterwards, another shows up. The ritual is repeated.

It's April on the east side of the Big Island, and these annual tributes to Pele signify the approach of the **Merrie Monarch Hula Festival** at the 5,000-seat Edith Kanakaole Tennis Stadium in Hilo.

The woman who first conceived of such a festival, and remains its driving force, is Dottie Thompson. Her objective was simply this: "To gather the best hula dancers from all the islands, revive the arts and create a performance that is a rite, a celebration… and a statement about Hawaii and its people."

Thompson has succeeded beyond her wildest dreams. Her people have heeded the call, and they gather each year in the quaint capital of the island in an exuberant celebration that has made the Merrie Monarch — named in honor of King David Kalakaua — one of the world's great pageants.

A school of young boogie boarders makes a splash on Oahu, where calm waters in sheltered bays provide a safe place for family water sports.

The week-long festival begins with performing arts celebrations, arts and craft shows and culminates in two nights of friendly but fierce competition between the halau. Highlights of the festival take place on its last two nights are the *kahiko* (ancient) and *awana* (modern) competitions. These two dance forms represent two entirely different disciplines.

There is grave nobleness in the *kahiko* style which is in essence an interpretation of an ancient song or chant. It is structured and solemn. It begins with the measured entrance of the *kumu hula* (teacher) who sets the stage for the dance by chanting. Dancers enter, chanting their response. The only accompaniment, other than the chanting, is provided by traditional Hawaiian percussion instruments — gourd drums, stone clappers, bamboo sticks and rattles. The dancing is impassioned, fiery, at times breathlessly primitive and exciting.

In contrast, the *awana* hula has a gaiety to it that is wholly contagious. Guitars and ukuleles blend with the percussion instruments creating contemporary music that brings a smile to the faces of dancers and the audience. The costumes in the *awana* have a definite Western influence, a reminder in a sense of how the hula has evolved since those postmissionary days.

The audience finds itself awash in color, light and emotion. And there are constant reminders that this is an event at which one is privileged to be present.

Molokai

Unlike the Merrie Monarch, the **Molokai Ka Hula Piko** is not a competition. It is purely a celebration of the hula on the island that claims to be its birthplace. Throughout the year, Hawaiians make pilgrimages to this island in search of spiritual renewal. Most of them invariably end up at Moohelaia in Maunaloa, where hula is said to have evolved as a sacred ritual. Legend has it that Laka, sister of Pele founded the first hula school here. Kumu hula come here to chant the praises of Laka, to pass the chants onto their disciples and students, and to dance under the stars until dawn.

The Molokai Ka Hula Piko is a relatively new event for the island and may have taken its cue from the Merrie Monarch. It began in 1991 and has turned into a week-long event that takes place in May. It features art exhibits, craft fairs, lectures on Molokai's history, and Hawaiian story telling. It ends with a long day of music and dance featuring halau from around the state, as well as teams of dancers from other parts of the world, such as Japan at Papohaku Beach Park. At the heart of all this activity is kumu hula John Kaimikaua, of Halau Hula 'O Kukunaokala, an imposing figure of a man. Like Thompson, he has become the inspiration for Ka Hula Piko. Visitors to this event are growing in numbers. And accommodation is becoming tight, so book both transportation and accommodation early. For information, contact the Molokai Visitors Association ((808) 553-3876 TOLL-FREE (800) 553-0404.

Oahu

Every year, on the third Saturday in July, hula aficionados flock to Moanalua Gardens to see the **Prince Lot Hula Festival**. Each year has a different theme relating to the traditions of Moanalua.

The Prince Lot Hula Festival is not a competition. Hula halau are invited to participate on the earthen mound stage, in the open air under stately trees — the perfect setting for an event of such cultural significance. The festival provides an opportunity for kumu hula throughout the islands to demonstrate their skills in hula kahiko and hula awana. The hula mound on which the dancers perform is named after Kamaipuupaa, a favorite female *kahuna*, priestess, in Lot's household.

In any dance form, it's important to start them young — and so it is with the hula. The **Queen Liluokalani Keiki Hula Competition**, named in honor of a much beloved monarch, attracts children, or *keikis*, aged six to 12. It is not uncommon for over 500 of these youngsters from over two dozen halau to perform at this festival. Youngsters are taught that while there are winners, the true meaning of this event is the sharing and joy of the dance.

CALENDAR OF EVENTS

JANUARY

The **Traditional Japanese Mochi Pounding Festival** heralds the start of the new year. The venue is the Volcano Art Center, Volcanoes National Park, the Big Island. Japanese nationals in Hawaii also celebrate the **Cherry Blossom Festival**, when the old ways are commemorated with cultural performances and demonstrations, capped by the crowning of the Cherry Blossom Queen.

Hawaii Volcanoes National Park is the center of much athletic endeavor for the **Volcano Wilderness Marathon and Rim Run**. An energetic group runs 26 miles (42 km) through the desolate Kau Desert, while over 1,000 participants run a 10-mile (16-km) race around the Caldera Crater Rim.

The **Big Island Triathlon Invitational** is a three-day endurance event ranging all over the island that includes an overnight stay at Hawaii Volcanoes National Park.

Professional men and women compete for prize money in the annual **Maui Rusty Pro Surf Meet** ((808) 575-9264, at Hookipa Beach Park and Honolua Bay on Maui.

One of the highlights of the Chinese New Year is the **Narcissus Festival** ((808)

533-3181. Events include the Narcissus Queen Pageant and the Narcissus Coronation Ball, all leading up to Chinese New Year.

CJM Stables on the south shore of the Garden Island of Kauai hosts the **Kauai rodeo** ((808) 742-6096, with *paniolo,* Hawaiian cowboys.

Two golf events take place this month: **PGA MasterCard Championship** TOLL-FREE (800) 417-2770 takes place at the Jack Nicklaus golf course at historic Hualalai Resort at Kaupulehu in Kona. The Mauna Lani Resort's Francis I'i Golf Course hosts the annual **Senior Skins Game** ((808) 885-6622, which features top masters in professional golf.

The annual **Superkids** event ((808) 325-5339, at the Old Kona Airport in Kona, features activities and sports competitions for children six months to 12 years of age. Proceeds go to the American Lung Association.

FEBRUARY

Held at the Pawahi Street entrance of Kaikoo Mall in Hilo, the **Annual Hilo Mardi Gras Ball** ((808) 935-8850 is a

A hula dancer communes with nature.

beautiful event with royal pageantry, formal wear, gourmet catering, costume ball and live entertainment.

Chinatown on Oahu is the place to be for **Chinese New Year**, a night of celebration and feasting at restaurants and in the streets.

One of the biggest Big Island attractions of the year on the Kona Coast is the start of the rodeo season, which traditionally begins at the **Waikoloa Stables** on what once was Parker Ranch land. The rodeo opens the Hawaii Rodeo Association's schedule of seven sanctioned events on the Big Island, Maui and Kauai. The **Great Waikoloa Rodeo** attracts the finest *paniolos* (cowboys) in the region, who compete in a program of events ranging from bull riding, steer undecorating and

poo wai u, an event unique to Hawaiian rodeos in which paniolos display the technique they use to rope and tie cattle in the mountains.

Waimea Cherry Blossom Heritage Festival ((808) 961-8706, takes place on the Big Island at historic Waimea Church Row Park. The festival celebrates Japan's Hanami, which is the viewing of the flowers during spring. It presents the history of the cherry trees, a tea ceremony, cherry pie and ice cream tasting, mochi-tsuki demonstration, bonsai, oriental arts and crafts, entertainment and distribution of cherry trees for planting in the Waimea area. Also in Waimea, the **Waimea Town Celebration** ((808) 338-9957 is a party and parade on Kauai celebrating the Hawaiian and multi-ethnic history of the town where Captain Cook first set foot in Hawaii. Food booths, games, entertainment, and three-mile (five-kilometer) and six-mile (10-km) foot races, canoe and bike race make up the day and evening.

MARCH

March is kite-flying month. At the three-day **Annual Oahu Kite Festival** ((808) 735-9059, the public is invited to show off their kites at Kapiolani Park on Oahu; while at the **International Kite Festival**, Sandy Beach, Oahu, the "battle of the kites" features some of the top kite flyers in the world. The **Hawaii Challenge International Sportkite Championship** ((808) 735-9059, Kapiolani Park in Honolulu, is the venue for the longest running sport-kite competition in the world, attracting top kite pilots from all over the globe.

During **Whalefest Week on Maui** ((808) 661-3271, many events celebrating the endangered Pacific humpback whale take place in the old whaling ports of Lahaina and Wailea; it begins with Whale Day at Wailea Shopping Center. Also this month, volunteers around Maui count

ABOVE and LEFT: The Waimea Plantation Festival features children's activities. OPPOSITE: The Waikoloa Rodeo TOP on the Kona Coast. A wrangler BOTTOM sports a belt attesting to his Caucasian, *haole*, ancestry.

the humpback whales spotted in one day during the **Great Whale Count** ((808) 879-8860, sponsored by the Pacific Whale Foundation. You can call to volunteer for this five-hour project.

Three exciting events constitute **Molokai in March** ((808) 553-5215 TOLL-FREE (800) 254-8871 ((808) 552-2791: The **Prince Kuhio Celebration** honors this member of Hawaiian Royalty with dance, chant and ceremony at Kiowea Park–Kapuaiwa Coconut Grove near the town of Kaunakakai. **Paniolo Heritage Rodeo** ((808) 552-2681 is a traditional rodeo event at Molokai Ranch that features generations of Hawaiian cowboys. And **Punana Leo O Molokai** is organized by Lori Lei Rawlins.

The **Hawaiian Pro Windsurfing Competition** ((808) 575-9264, takes place at Hookipa Beach Park on Maui.

The **Honolulu Festival** ((808) 523-8802, Sky Gate, Oahu, features Japanese street performers, food booths, sumo, kite flying and bon dancing as part of this annual event to celebrate Japanese culture.

In mid-March paniolos provide lots of action during the full range of rodeo events at the **Kona Stampede** ((808) 885-7628, at Honaunau Arena, Honaunau, Kona.

The **Maui Marathon** ((808) 871-6441 is an annual run from Kahului to Whalers Village at Kaanapali with an international field of runners.

The annual **Kapalua Celebration of the Arts** ((808) 669-6200 pays tribute to

the people, arts and culture of Hawaii, with demonstrations of hula, chant, native art and food.

APRIL

Wesak, or **Buddha Day** is on the closest Sunday to April 8, and celebrates the birthday of Gautama Buddha. Ornate offerings of tropical flowers are placed at temple altars throughout Hawaii.

The **Paniolo Ski Meet** features exciting skiing atop the Big Island's Mauna Kea, conditions permitting.

Local families present a unique collection of Hawaiian quilts at the **King David Kalakaua Festival Hawaiian Quilt Show** ((808) 933-4360, which is held at the Wailoa Center in Hilo on the Big Island.

Professionals from around the world gather for the **Da Kine Hawaiian Pro Am Windsurfing Competition** ((808) 575-9264, at Hookipa Beach on Maui.

The annual fundraising event, the **Hawaii Professional Rodeo** ((808) 235-3691, takes place at the New Town and Country Stables in Waimanalo on Oahu.

Bankoh Ki-Ho Alu ((808) 239-4336 features some of the islands' foremost slack key guitar talents. Capacity crowds pack the grounds of the King Kamehameha Kona Beach Hotel, Kona.

An international food fair, live entertainment, a children's carnival and games and rides are side shows to the **Honolulu International Bed Race** ((808) 735-6092 or ((808) 696-2424 or ((808) 696-4423, where local teams are matched against competitors from as far away as Australia.

The **Kihei Sea Festival** ((808) 879-8176, features ocean sports, music, food and crafts and activities.

MAY

May 1 is celebrated as May Day in many parts of the world, but in Hawaii everyone dons a lei for **Lei Day**. Festivities abound throughout the state, including the

ABOVE: A devotee prays at the Jodo Mission, Maui. OPPOSITE: Actors portraying the royal court march in the King Kamehameha Day parade.

Brothers Cazimero Annual May Day Concert ℂ (808) 597-1888, a tradition at the Waikiki Shell for more than two decades. It's a flower-filled evening of Hawaiian music and picnics.

The **Annual Festival of the Pacific** on Oahu is a week of athletics events, music, song and dance celebrating the multi-ethnic people of the Pacific.

The **Captain Cook Festival** at Kailua-Kona offers Hawaiian games, music and fishing.

On **Japanese Boys' Day**, you'll see *koi* (paper carp) flying from rooftops. They symbolize the virtues of strength and courage, and the number of koi kites corresponds to the number of sons in the family, with the largest, highest koi for the eldest, and then down the line.

Filipino Fiesta is a month-long celebration of the islands' Filipino population. Food, various festivities, and a beauty contest are part of the event.

Costumed riders from the annals of Hawaiian history ride again at **Hawaii on Horseback**. Horsemanship and a Western flair mark these days held in and around Waimea and the Parker Ranch on the Big Island.

Annual Western Week at Honokaa on the Big Island is a fun-filled week with a Western theme. It includes a cookout, parade, rodeo and dance.

Sponsored by the Big Island Art Guild, the **Annual Spring Arts Festival** ℂ (808) 933-4360 is an art show open to all. It's held at the Wailoa Center in Hilo on the Big Island.

The **Prince Albert Music Festival** ℂ (808) 826-9644 is an outstanding classical music festival held over four days at the Princeville Hotel on Kauai. The concert celebrates the life of Prince Albert Edward Kauaikeaouli Lei O Papa a Kamehameha (1858–1862). A statewide keiki kane hula competition for boys aged 6 to 12, and a Holoku Tea, featuring traditional formal wear and a Songs of Hawaii competition, enrich the festival.

A variety of plants, including many exotic species, are on sale at the **Kona Orchid Society Orchid Show and Orchid Pant Sale** ℂ (808) 939-9760.

Experts are on hand to answer questions about how to choose and grow orchids.

During the **World Fire-Knife Dance Championships** ℂ (808) 293-3333, fire-knife dancers compete in performaces of extraordinary bravery at the Polynesian Cultural Center on the North Shore of Oahu.

Papohaku Beach Park at Kaluakoi on Molokai is the venue for **Molokai Ka Hula Piko** ℂ (808) 553-0404, a celebration of the birth of hula. There are performances by hula halau, musicians and singers from Molokai and other islands. Hawaiian crafts, including quilting, woodworking, featherwork and deer-horn scrimshaw, are demonstrated and sold.

The annual **Molokai to Oahu Kayak Challenge** ℂ (808) 239-4123 departs from the remote Maunaloa Coast of Molokai crossing 38 miles (61 km) of the Molokai Channel to Oahu.

The **Annual Big Island Bounty Festival** ℂ (808) 885-2000, at The Orchid at Mauna Lani on the Big Island, is the premier showcase for Hawaii regional cuisine. The festival, which takes place Memorial Day weekend, immerses participants in the newest food trends in Hawaii and the mainland. Top chefs unveil their latest culinary creations; and farmers, ranchers, fishermen, and specialty food producers display their wares and invite samplings of their harvests. There are grill-outs, seminars, cooking demonstrations, and a lavish Sunday brunch.

Western Days in Honokaa ((808) 775-0598 features sidewalk sales and displays all weekend, with a karaoke contest, line dancing, a parade, a rodeo, and saloon girl dinner dance.

The **50th State Fair** ((808) 595-4606, at Aloha Stadium on Oahu, is held over four weekends, beginning Memorial Day weekend. The fair features entertainment, rides and commercial exhibits.

JUNE

Many events the month of June honor King Kamehameha the Great, a Big Island native son. **King Kamehameha Day**, June 11, is a state holiday with festivities on all islands. Kailua-Kona puts on a *hoolaulea* (large, festive party),

parades, art demonstrations, entertainment and contests. The statue of King Kamehameha, across the street from Iolani Palace in Honolulu, is draped in fresh-flower leis measuring 13 ft (four meters) in length for the **King Kamehameha Statue Decoration Ceremonies** ((808) 586-0333. Music and hula performances create an excellent photo opportunity. The **Annual Honolulu King Kamehameha Floral Parade** ((808) 586-0333, features floral floats, marching bands, colorful mounted units and a King's Court participating in a four-mile (six-and-a-half-kilometer) parade from downtown Honolulu to Queen Kapiolani Park. The **Kamehameha Ski Meet** atop Mauna Kea takes place in

early June, where bikini-clad contestants compete Hawaiian style. Finally, the **Annual King Kamehameha Hula Competition** is held at the Neal S. Blaisdell Center Arena. More than 20 halau compete in both traditional and contemporary hula styles.

Three days of Hawaiian craft making workshops, hula and Hawaiian food tasting constitute the **Puuhonua O Honaunau Cultural Festival** at Hawaii Volcanoes National Park, Hawaii.

The **Annual Oahu Hoolaulea** ((808) 586-0333 is a day-long festival of Hawaiian entertainment, with hula and song, crafts and foods, at Kapiolani Park in Honolulu.

Kalakaua Avenue is the venue the **Pan-Pacific Hoolaulea "Block Party"** ((808) 923-2951, which begins with a mini-parade that includes a *mikoshi*, which is a ceremonial shrine brought from Japan just for this event. The evening includes entertainers from Hawaii and Japan and food booths.

Bankoh Ki-Ho Alu ((808) 239-4336 is a celebration of Hawaiian slack key guitar playing in all its diversity. This annual event is staged at the Maui Arts and Cultural Center.

The **Kapalua Wine and Food Symposium** ((808) 669-0244 is a gathering of wine experts for formal

OPPOSITE: Feather leis can be highly prized works of art. ABOVE LEFT: Orchids bloom wild in the damp, hot climate of the islands. ABOVE RIGHT: Participants in a children's festival.

"Pageant of Nations" in Hilo. Folk dances, complete with authentic costumes from throughout Asia and the Pacific, add a rare excitement to the festivities.

The **Ukulele Festival** takes places at Queen Kapiolani Park bandstand, Oahu.

Koloa Plantation Days ((808) 332-9831, are a celebration of sugar plantation life on Kauai, that features the culture of many immigrants, with cane cutting contests, entertainment, sports, crafts, foods and a parade in colorful Koloa Town.

The **Pineapple Festival (** (808) 565-7600 features pineapple cooking contests, and offers arts, crafts and entertainment in Lanai City on the island of Lanai.

tastings, discussions and the Chef's Kapalua Seafood Festival at Kapalua Resort on Maui.

The **Biennial Transpacific Yacht Race** ((808) 236-0940 E-MAIL schooner@lava.net, is the oldest long-distance sailboat race in the world. The distance is 2,225 nautical miles, from Los Angeles to the finish at Diamond Head Buoy in Honolulu.

Kaunakakai Wharf on Molokai is the site of the **Molokai Seafest (** (808) 553-3876, which aims to raise awareness of the sea as one of the most important cultural, recreational, and economic resources of Hawaii. The festival features an outrigger canoe regatta sponsored by the Molokai Canoe Racing Association, a sailing canoe demonstration by the Molokai Voyaging Canoe Society, a windsurfing race, food booths and entertainment by island musicians.

July

The week of the Fourth of July offers the all-American sport of rodeo along with all the parades. Don't miss the July 4 **Annual Parker Ranch Fourth of July Rodeo (** (808) 885-7311, at Paniolo Park on Parker Ranch rodeo grounds in Waimea. This is the most popular rodeo of the year on the Big Island and includes many Western festivities.

The annual **Naalehu Rodeo**, in Naalehu, includes motorcycle and dune buggy races, luaus, food booths and Hawaiian entertainment along with the traditional rodeo events.

The **Big Island Marathon** in Hilo is a full marathon and a half marathon which starts and ends at the Hilo Hawaiian Hotel.

Four-person teams consisting of one professional and three amateurs compete in the 54-hole Mauna Kea Beach Hotel's **Annual Pro-Am Golf Tournament**, held along the Big Island's Kohala Coast.

The **International Festival of the Pacific (** (808) 961-6123 features a

Join the birthday party for the Atlantic bottlenose dolphins at the **Annual Dolphin Days (** (808) 947-7817, Hilton Waikoloa Village on the Big Island. The three-day extravaganza features guest celebrities and a variety of activities.

The **Annual Concert in the Sky (** (808) 245-5006, a July 4 celebration, is held in Lihue, Kauai, at Vidinha Stadium, beginning at 3 PM. The day features food, crafts and game booths, pony rides and petting zoo, and family games, such as a watermelon eating contest, a wheelbarrow race and a coconut toss, and concludes with a spectacular fireworks show which draws more than 10,000 people each year.

ABOVE: The Atlantic bottlenose dolphin is give a birthday party at the annual Dolphin Days festivities. OPPOSITE: Workers harvest pineapple, a fruit once closely identified with the islands. The pineapple industry is now all but gone.

Makawao Rodeo ((808) 573-0090, the largest rodeo of the year in Hawaii, with more than 350 cowboys from all over the world, livens up Oskie Rice Rodeo Arena, at Kaanaolo Ranch on Maui the Fourth of July weekend. This is a Hawaiian style rodeo, with rough stock and roping events, and rodeo clowns. Before and after the rodeo, enjoy live entertainment and country western dancing.

The **Floating Lantern Ceremony** ((808) 661-0939 is a special event for the O Bon season, when the Japanese invite ancestral spirits to join in the harvest. The floating lantern ceremony, at Puunoa Point, honors the souls of the dead. Traditional Japanese dances are performed at the Jodo Mission in Lahaina, Maui.

Bayfest ((808) 254-7679, at Kaneohe Bay, is Oahu's biggest water sports carnival. This three-day event features a health and fitness fair, live entertainment, carnival rides, a military display and food booths.

Kapiolani Bandstand, Honolulu, is the site for the **Ukulele Festival** ((808) 732-3739, where top ukulele musicians perform and fine ukuleles made in Hawaii and abroad are on display.

The **Pro-Am Billfish Tournament** ((808) 329-6155 is one of the top big-game fishing tournaments in the world and includes parties and daily weigh-ins at Kona Pier.

AUGUST
The **Kona Hawaiian Billfish Tournament** ((808) 922-9708, in the waters off Kona, features American teams seeking entry to the **Hawaii International Billfish Tournament** ((808) 329-6155, held one week later. Kailua-Kona hosts this, the top billfishing tournament in the world, featuring teams from many countries, a parade and weighing in ceremonies at Kailua Pier.

Have a great time Tahitian style with the people of Kauai as they honor their Polynesian roots with the week-long **Kauai-Tahiti Fete**. Dancers from Tahiti, the Hawaiian islands and the mainland participate in intense competition in this event.

The macadamia nut harvest is celebrated with sporting events, horse racing and a harvest ball at the **Macadamia Nut Harvest Festival** ((808) 755-7792, Honokaa, Hawaii.

The **Maui Onion Festival** ((808) 667-4567, at Kaanapali Beach Resort celebrates Maui's famous agricultural product and gourmet ingredient. Displays, music and entertainment highlight the event.

At **He Olelo Hoohiki I Malama 'Ia**, the spirit of Queen Liliuokalani narrates the dynamic annual, musical drama staged by more than 200 members and friends of The Church of Jesus Christ of Latter-Day Saints, at the Kauai War Memorial Convention Hall.

The **Kenwood Cup Hawaii International Ocean Racing Series** ((808) 346-9061 is a 10-race sailing series of varying distances that is part of the Champagne Mumm World Cup international sailing series. The long-distance races finish off at Diamond Head and can be viewed from Honolulu shores and cliffs.

The **Hawaii State Windsurfing Championship** ((808) 877-2111 is a professional and amateur women's and men's competition at Kahana Beach Park in Kahului, Maui.

Cuisines of the Sun ((808) 885-6622 is an annual festival prepared by chefs and held at the Mauna Lani Bay Hotel on the Kohala Coast of the Big Island.

The largest long-distance canoe racing event in the world **Queen Liliuokalani Long Distance Outrigger Race** draws teams from around the Pacific Basin to Kailua-Kona on the Big Island. A lantern parade of competitors is a side attraction.

The annual **Maui Music Festival of Jazz** ((808) 661-3271 features jazz and contemporary music and draws enthusiasts and performers from around the world to Kaanapali on Maui.

SEPTEMBER
In early September don't miss the **Parker Ranch Round-Up Rodeo**, Paniolo Park in Waimea.

The annual **Oahu Aloha Festival** ((808) 944-8857 kicks off with opening ceremonies in Honolulu. Floral parades,

Hawaiian Royal Balls, the Steel Guitar Festival, storytelling, horse racing, paniolo hat and lei contests, fishing tournaments and ukulele performances are featured.

The **Maui Ultimate Cycling Challenge** ((808) 575-9151 is a bike ride up the slope of Haleakala Volcano that challenges professionals and amateurs alike as they pedal to the 10,000-foot (3,000-m) summit.

Many of Hawaii's top women entertainers bring their musical and dancing talents to the stage at the Bishop Museum for the annual **Bankoh Na Wahine O Hawaii** ((808) 239-4336. The concert features a range of talents, both traditional and contemporary, reflecting the richness and diversity of the Hawaiian music scene.

Top female paddling crews from around the world compete in the annual 40.8-mile (65.7-km) women's Molokai-to-Oahu world championship long-distance outrigger canoe race, **Bankoh Na Wahine O Ke Kai** ((808) 262-7567.

Run to the Sun ((808) 871-6441 is one of the world's toughest endurance runs from the town of Paia at sea level on Maui to the 10,000-ft (3,000-m) summit of Haleakala.

OCTOBER

At Cooks Discoveries ((808) 885-3633, in Waimea on the Big Island, some of the most creative lei making goes into making floral hatbands during the **Hat Lei Contest**, with ferns, nuts, flowers and other interesting materials decorating the hats of Hawaiian cowboys.

The **Annual Bankoh Molokai Men's Outrigger Canoe Race** ((808) 261-6615 is a grueling 41-mile (66-km) Molokai-to-Oahu six-person outrigger canoe championship. Nearly 100 nine-man teams of the best male outrigger canoe paddlers in the world compete for the title. The finish can be seen at Fort DeRussy Beach, Waikiki, Oahu.

The **Bankoh Talk Story Festival** ((808) 592-7029, is Hawaii's largest free celebration of storytelling and oral history.

The **Hilo Macadamia Nut Festival** ((808) 966-9301, at Nani Mau Gardens, Hilo, is a day-long festival celebrating one of the most popular nuts in the world, includes cooking demonstrations, entertainment, sporting events, contests and displays of macadamia nuts.

Hookipa Beach, Maui, is the site for the **Aloha Classic World Wave Sailing Championships** ((808) 575-9151, the final event of the Pro Boardsailing Association World Tour with an international field of competitors.

Halloween in Lahaina ((808) 667-9175, on Front Street in Lahaina, Maui, is a Mardi Gras-like celebration with all the right ingredients — outlandish costumes, great food and good times.

NOVEMBER

The **Annual King Kalakaua Keiki Hula Festival** is for children from around the state who come to Kailua-Kona to perform their hula. Plenty of fun mixed with serious competition.

Christmas in the Country, Volcano Art Center, Hawaii Volcanoes National Park ((808) 976-7676 takes place atop Hawaii's volcano. Merrymakers frolic in the crisp air or relax around a blazing fire, drinking hot toddies. There are arts and crafts, and food, and Santa puts in an appearance for the *keiki* (children).

Hat leis make fashion statements throughout the islands.

Taste the only coffee commercially grown in the United States at the **Annual Kona Coffee Festival** in Kailua-Kona. Parades, arts and crafts displays, ethnic foods and entertainment are all part of the festivities.

The Kona Coffee Festival incorporates a wide range of events: The **Farm Fair** offers displays by Kona farmers who produce fresh vegetables, tropical fruits and macadamia nuts in addition to coffee. Kona coffee farmers bring out their best coffee to be judged by an international group of coffee connoisseurs at the **Cupping Competition**. A **Festival Grand Parade**, featuring floats and marching bands and the **International Lantern Festival**, lights up Alii Drive. At **Kona Heritage Park and International Market** ((808) 326-7820, coffee roasting, tasting and coffee museum displays, ikebana floral displays, a festival of artists, Kona coffee lei contest, and a pioneer's luncheon become a big attraction in Kailua-Kona on this last day of the Kona Coffee Festival.

The **Hawaii International Film Festival** TOLL-FREE (800) 752-8193 presents films, seminars and workshops in Oahu as part of one of the world's fastest growing movie festivals.

The **Taro Festival at Honokaa** ((808) 775-0598 takes place on the Big Island's northern coast where taro was grown in giant river valleys in ancient times. This event celebrates a renewal of the culture of taro, the staple food of old Hawaii.

Located in Honokaa, an historic town on the Hamakua Coast, it features displays, food, crafts and entertainment.

The annual **Winter Wine Escape** ((808) 880-1111 invites the public to meet top wine makers from around the world and top chefs who place the perfect wine with the best of Hawaiian regional cuisine at the Hapuna Beach Prince Hotel.

The **Annual Triple Crown of Surfing Series** ((808) 638-7266 is a professional, big-wave surfing championship on Oahu's North Shore. The men's Pipe Masters signals the conclusion of the Surfing Professionals world tour after which a men's and women's world champion and Triple Crown champion are named.

There are three orchid shows in November: The Maui Orchid Society displays its best at the **Maui Orchid Show** ((808) 247-8335, with hundreds of varieties at Kaahumanu Shopping Center on Maui. The Kauai Orchid Society brings out amazing varieties of orchids at the War Memorial Convention Hall in Lihue at the **Kauai Orchid Show** ((808) 247-8335. And at the **Greenthumbs Orchid Show** ((808) 247-3345, orchids are displayed at Club 100 on Oahu.

Betsy Nagelsen, Kapalua touring pro, holds court during the annual gathering of Women's International Tennis Association professionals, the **Kapalua Tennis Invitational** ((808) 669-5677. Avid amateurs rally with the professionals during a week of pro-am and pro doubles competition at Kapalua Tennis Club.

DECEMBER

The people of Hilo celebrate a **New England Christmas** in memory of the missionaries with **A Christmas Tradition**, held at the Lyman House Memorial Museum, Hilo ((808) 935-5021.

Bodhi Day is ushered in with ceremonies at Buddhist temples to commemorate Buddha's day of enlightenment.

At the Mauna Kea Beach Hotel's **Annual Invitational Golf Tournament** ((808) 882-7222, men and women play at this fabulous golf course on the Kohala Coast.

The premier juried craft fair of Hawaiian-made arts and crafts in Honolulu, the **Holiday Craft Fair** ((808) 531-0481 is held annually at Mission House Museum in Honolulu. The fair includes entertainment, food, workshops and demonstrations.

The Ritz Carlton Kapalua has a **Gala Tree Lighting Ceremony on Maui** ((808) 669-6200, and Christmas lights are on display for the entire month.

Cooking demonstrations, signature dinners and wine pairings and tastings are all part of the **Grand Chefs on Tour**: Kea Lani Hotel, Suites and Villas, on Maui.

Na Mele O Maui ((808) 661-3271, Kaanapali Resort, Maui, aims to perpetuate Hawaiian culture with a children's song contest, hula festival and arts and crafts fair.

Experience the magic of Christmas with **A Candlelight Christmas at Mission House** ((808) 531-0481. Take in the aroma of holiday foods being prepared and discover traditions from Christmas long ago in a nineteenth century holiday celebration at Mission Houses Museum in Honolulu.

On New Year's Eve hold onto your hat, because they do it up big in Hawaii. The merriment flows all over the islands. Firecrackers are illegal, but they go off everywhere. The Maui Arts and Cultural Center hosts **First Night Maui** ((808) 879-1922, an alcohol-free, family-style festival to celebrate the New Year on Maui.

Hawaiian Food Specialties

Hawaii's cosmopolitan nature makes eating here both a pleasure and a great adventure. The population's tremendous ethnic mix has given rise to an expansive range of foods and restaurants reflecting the preferences of the Asian and European communities that now call Hawaii home. The choices range from Japanese inns and sushi houses to elegant Thai, Chinese, Korean and Filipino restaurants serving authentic native foods, often prepared by native chefs.

The art of the lei. OPPOSITE: A crown for gray tresses TOP, a colorful hat topper BELOW, and a festive wreath of blossoms ABOVE for the family vehicle.

Outside of this cornucopia of Asian foods, there exists a cuisine that is uniquely Hawaiian; and just as the language of the islands echoes the many groups that have made Hawaii home, Hawaiian cooking speaks a delicious blend that incorporates the subtleties of Asian cooking with the lusty dining preferences of the native Hawaiians. This marriage has produced the "mixed plate," an eating tradition not to be found anywhere else in the world.

As the name implies, a mixed plate is little bit of this and a little bit of that — Japanese and Chinese and Korean and Hawaiian and anything else for that matter, served with scoops of rice at either a restaurant or a lunch wagon. The results are often unexpected but almost always delicious.

HAWAIIAN LUAUS

Dining authentic Hawaiian style is something else again. While it can be as casual as tossing a hamburger on a barbecue grill, the true Hawaiian luau is much more than that. It encompasses the traditions of a native feast with the relaxed ambiance of the Hawaiian lifestyle.

There are numerous luaus, many organized purely for tourists. Not all serve the traditional kalua pig (baked in an *imu* or pit oven), the stamp of an authentic native feast.

When the first Polynesian adventurers landed in these islands, they brought their pigs ashore. Pork is still a favorite meat of Hawaiians today, when they can afford it.

Most of the Hawaiian restaurants sell kalua pig along with other favorite native dishes such as *lomilomi salmon* (salted salmon kneaded, chopped and mixed with tomatoes and green onions), the taro root staple *poi* (which comes in varying degrees of thickness or fermentation), *poke aku* (Hawaiian raw fish), and *laulaus* (a delicious blending of pork, rice and salted butterfish steamed in ti leaves). But the *pièce de resistance* of any luau remains the kalua pig.

The pit oven is what gives the luau ritual its stamp of authenticity. The imu

is a trench about 18 inches (45 cm) deep, dug into the ground to accommodate a pig that weighs about 90 lb (40 kg) dressed. A fire of hardwood logs is started in the pit, and about two dozen imu stones are placed on the fire. The pig, meanwhile, has been eviscerated, skinned and shaved of bristles. It is rubbed inside and out with rock salt and soy sauce and left to soak in a marinade until the stones are red hot. The pig is then laid on a square of chicken wire. Hot rocks are placed in the throat cavity and between the legs and body. The chicken wire is wrapped around the pig and the pig is placed in the pit. Fresh corn husks or banana leaves, sweet potatoes, bananas and fish

wrapped in ti leaves are piled on top of the pig. The mound is covered with burlap bags and soaked with water to keep it steamproof. Earth is then piled on the mound to prevent the steam from leaking. Four hours later, the earth is cleared away, and the pig is unwrapped. The aroma of roasted meat, fruit and ti leaves assails the senses. Pig done this style is succulent and totally Hawaiian.

There are numerous commercial luaus on all the islands, arranged with tourists specifically in mind. Finding an authentic native luau may be a bit of a problem. Most of the commercial luaus serve a distinct purpose — they give the visitor a glimpse of the real thing without actually being the real thing.

The visitor is left with many choices, but we recommend the luaus organized by the major hotels on the neighbor islands. On the Big Island try the Hale Hookipa on Friday nights at the **Kona Village Resort**, or the "Drums of Polynesia" luau at the **Royal Kona Resort**. On Maui it's the "Drums of the Pacific" luau at the **Hyatt Regency**, or the Royal Lahaina luau at the **Royal Lahaina Resort** in Kaanapali.

For visitors on Oahu, there are two good commercial luaus: **Germaine's** ((808) 9949-6626 or 941-3338, near Barber's Point, where the spectacular Polynesian show matches the food, and

Preparing the roasted pig at a Big Island luau.

the **Paradise Cove** luau ((808) 973-5828, on 12 beachfront acres (five hectares) near the Ko Olina Resort. Both luaus give the visitor a real Polynesian experience, capturing the lifestyle of the Polynesian people — their music, dance, games and feasts. The Paradise Cove luau features a traditional sunset imu ceremony at Hawaii's only Imu Amphitheater, where the kalua pig is unearthed from the steamy underground oven. Both luaus have true atmosphere, down to the flaming torches, the beachfront settings and the superb entertainment.

SHAVE ICE

Shave ice is legendary in Hawaiian food folklore. It is nothing more than crushed ice with flavored syrups, yet the humble shave ice — or the snow cone, as it is known in other parts of the world — has taken on a mystique all its own. There are shave ice stores all over the islands, but two of the best are on Oahu. For Waikiki tourist traffic, try the **Waiola Store** in the district of Moiliili. It may be the best there is. But what makes it the best? Perhaps it's the quality of the ice that's so finely crushed it's almost like powder. And they have an unbelievable variety of flavors.

For those of you cruising the island, stop in at **Matsumoto Shave Ice** in the town of Haleiwa on the north shore. On a hot summer day — and they can get quite hot in Hawaii — there isn't a better place to break a journey. Matsumoto's is located in a colorful general store that's a holdover from plantation days — seedy, yet charming. And the shave ice is almost as good as that at Waiola Store. Other good shave ice places, when you are in the neighborhood, are **Hawaiian Island Ice** at Aloha Tower Market Place and **Tropicana** in Manoa.

Special Interests

HEALING THE HAWAIIAN WAY

The resurgence of interest in Hawaiian culture and the arts has also spawned a revival in spirituality and the traditional healing powers of the islands.

The ancient Hawaiians are believed to have been among the healthiest people on earth. They believed that all living things are connected. In the same way, the whole person is connected in all his or her physical and emotional aspects.

From Kauai to the Big Island people from across the globe now come in search of relief, and native Hawaiian healers are willing to support, nurture and share their abilities.

A typical restorative session might include a steam bath and a body scrub with sea salt, aloe and red clay, for which the western side of the island of Kauai is famous. This may be followed by lomilomi massage, which was used by ancient Polynesians to soothe pain and relax or limber up stiff muscles. This form of massage is often accompanied by chanting.

On Kauai, the **Association of Healing Practitioners** ((808) 823-8088 TOLL-FREE (800) 599-5488 FAX ((808) 823-8088 E-MAIL heal-hi@aloha.net WEBSITE http://lauhala. com/ahap, P.O. Box 160, Kapaa, HI 96746, is an good source for health and healing. Dozens of practitioners offer reiki, meditation, acupuncture, herbal and nutritional therapy, hypnotherapy, yoga, tai chi, chiropractic medicine, psychotherapy, sound therapy, astrology, psychic counseling and more.

Helping Hands ((808) 822-1715 E-MAIL helping@pixi.com, 4-1579 Kuhio Highway, Suite 210, Kapaa, HI 96746, offers courses in guided imagery, meditation, yoga, and qi gong — a classical Chinese method of gentle invigorating movement. Helping Hands also offers massage therapy combined with spiritual healing.

Some of the finest spas in the Pacific region are in these islands, in particular on the sun-drenched **Kohala Coast**. It could be argued that the entire Kohala region on the Big Island of Hawaii is itself a natural spa with its warm and cool, dry and wet microclimates, freshwater pools and its warm salt sea. Hawaiian traditions of lomilomi massage and a variety of health and fitness approaches reflect the multiculturalism of the island.

In the words of Isabela Bird, who visited Kohala in the nineteenth century:

"I was traveling for health, when circumstances induced me to land in Hawaii, and the benefit which I derived from the climate tempted me to remain for nearly seven months. During that time the necessity of leading a life of open air and exercise as a means of recovery, led me to travel on horseback to and fro through the islands..."

The proximity of the new North Hawaii Community Hospital and of a wide range of clinics offering both mainstream and alternative therapies make this region an outstanding health and healing destination.

As an important part of the Five Mountain Medical Community, several resort spas are developing significant health and fitness facilities and programs.

The **Kohala Spa** at the **Hilton Waikoloa Village**, for instance, offers total relaxation. This tranquil yet invigorating environment offers seaweed body masques, aromatherapy, tai chi classes and lomilomi Hawaiian-style massage.

The **Orchid at Mauna Lani** Wellness Program and Health Quest at **Spa Hapuna** at the **Mauna Kea Resort** are two other respected health vacation destinations.

GARDENS OF SPLENDOR

Hawaii is a treasure house of extraordinary tropical plant life. Native and introduced flora flourish in the perfect climactic conditions nurtured by an abundance of rain and sun. Within the islands are five major ecosystems. This diversity is to be seen in Hawaii's botanical gardens.

There are many superb gardens, but to give visitors a taste of what to expect, we feature 13 of the best. Three of these gardens are on Kauai; seven on Oahu; one on Maui; and two on the Big Island.

KAUAI

The 252-acre (101-hectare) **Lawai Garden** in the Lawai Valley and the 100-acre (40-hectare) **Allerton Garden** ℂ (808) 742-2623 are on Kauai's south shore. Lawai specializes in native Hawaiian plants, palms, heliconia and erythrina. It is the headquarters of the National Tropical

Botanical Garden. Allerton Gardens which lies next door is a masterwork of landscape design that marries dramatic topography with the sights and sounds of water and the color and texture of foliage.

Limahuli ℂ (808) 826-1053, on Kauai's North Shore in the Haena district, also contains a wide range of habitats for native plants, and features some of the earliest traces of Hawaiian culture to be found anywhere in the islands.

By comparison to the other gardens on these islands, **Olu Pua Gardens and Plantation** ℂ (808) 332-8182, Kalaheo, is small — only 12 acres (five hectares). But these acres compass a unique collection of heliconia, orchids, bromeliads, anthuriums and palms. The rolling hills of this site once served as the retreat for Hawaii's ruling chiefs. Later it was taken over by the Alexander family which developed Kauai's largest pineapple plantation. The garden still contains the historic plantation residence designed by one of Hawaii's foremost architects, C.W. Dickey. Guided tours of the residence and gardens take visitors past rare and exotic plants, fountains and groves of eucalyptus, and a tropical rain forest.

MAUI

Black lava flows form a dramatic backdrop to the plant life at **Kahanu**

Shave ice, in dozens of flavors, is an island favorite.

Garden ((808) 248-8912, on the Hana Coast. The 122 acres (49 hectares) of this garden encompasses ethnobotanical collections and the Piilanihale Heiau.

OAHU

The **Waimea Arboretum and Botanical Garden, Halweiwa** ((808) 638-8511, is situated in historic Waimea Valley in a 1,800-acre (720-hectare) nature park. Waimea Falls is part of this park system. The arboretum and botanical garden concentrate on rare and endangered tropical and subtropical plants. Unique plant collections include those of the Hawaiian, Mariana, Mascarene and Ogasawara islands. There are also exceptional plants in other floral regional collections.

The **Harold L. Lyon Arboretum, Honolulu** ((808) 988-7378, deep in lush Manoa Valley, is an active research facility and academic resource for the University of Hawaii as well as an enchanting tropical public garden. Its 194 acres (78 hectares) hold one of the most important collections of tropical plants and one of the two largest palm collections in any botanical garden. It has also established the United States' largest and most successful program for propagation of endangered plants by tissue culture.

A 14-acre (five-and-a-half-hectare) oasis almost in the heart of downtown Honolulu, **Foster Botanical Garden, Honolulu** ((808) 522-7076, includes a palm collection, an orchid garden and a prehistoric glen.

Once the favorite picnic ground of Hawaii's Queen, the seven-acre (three-hectare) **Liliuokalani Botanical Garden, Honolulu** ((808) 522-7060, is now devoted to native Hawaiian plants.

The 200-acre (80-hectare) **Koko Crater Botanical Garden** ((808) 522-7060, Hawaii Kai, is being developed as a xeriscape in which plants suitable to desert-like surroundings thrive and flourish. The garden is inside an extinct crater (not far from Hanauma Bay) which it shares with an English riding stable. Much of the arid crater is planted in frangipani (plumeria) which blooms in shades of pink, yellow

and white throughout the year. It is also the home of an ancient grove of wiliwili trees, the wood of which was used to make surfboards for Hawaiian royalty in pre-Cook Hawaii. Various legends are attached to their gnarled growth.

The sprawling 400-acre (160-hectare) **Hoomaluhia Botanical Garden, Kaneohe** ((808) 233-7323, on Oahu's windward side, includes picnic and camping grounds.

Wahiawa Botanical Garden, Wahiawa ((808) 621-7321, is a relatively small (237-acre or 95-hectare) garden situated between two mountain ranges in Oahu's central highlands. It features plants that thrive in cooler climates.

HAWAII

The **Amy B.H. Greenwell Ethnobotanical Garden** ((808) 323-3318, Kailua-Kona, is a small yet fascinating garden on the slopes above Kealekekua Bay. On display are Hawaiian plants and Polynesian crops set in ancient agricultural stonework. Visitors learn about traditional Hawaiian farming techniques and the diverse use of natural and cultivated plants in Hawaiian agricultural known as the Kona Field System.

The gorgeous **Hawaii Tropical Botanical Garden** ((808) 964-5233, in Onomea Bay, is set in a valley that opens out onto the ocean. Streams and waterfalls flow through a tropical rain forest, easily navigated along meandering trails. Over 2,000 species of tropical plants from many parts of the world are featured. Visitors may also see the garden's collection of Japanese koi and tropical birds such as the African lessor flamingo and colorful giant macaw.

TREASURED TREES

Among Hawaii's most treasured possessions are its trees — stately palms, towering Norfolk pines, spreading banyans, exotic sausage trees, royal poinciana and many, other varieties.

On Oahu alone, over 102 of nature's best have been designated "exceptional" and are protected under a 1975 ordinance. Many of the trees on this list can be seen

in **Foster Botanical Gardens**. In an island filled with trees, the concentration of unusual and majestic trees is a result of research and an extensive plant importation program during the early twentieth century. Among the celebrated trees at this site is the 62-ft (19-m)-high Queen Flower Tree which spreads nearly 50 ft (15 m) from limb to limb. It is the largest of its kind in the United States. From May through September, this stunning native of Asia wears a crown of lavender flowers clustered on long, thin branchlets that rise above the green foliage.

A bo tree, revered by Buddhists, also has pride of place in this garden. The tree, rooted from a cutting taken from the oldest known historical tree (circa 288 BC) in Sri Lanka, was planted here at the turn of the century.

One of the oldest trees in the gardens is the 117-year-old false olive tree. But the most photographed tree in the gardens is a century-old kapok tree which spreads 1,612 ft (491 m) across the lawn and has a 20-ft (six-meter)-thick trunk.

Among the more exotic trees on the island is the banyan at **Iolani Palace**. The tree was originally two trees, wide enough apart for a carriage to pass between. But over the years, as aerial roots touched the ground, new trunks were created, forming a massive roots "forest" comprising a single trunk.

Another grove of exceptional trees is the kamani growing at **Kualoa Beach Park** in windward Oahu. The low branching trees, aside from their natural beauty, were prized by Hawaiians for their oil and fragrant flowers.

The island of Kauai also has several protected trees. The most magnificent examples are to be found at its famous **Tree Tunnel** formed by long rows of swamp mahogany which flank the road to Koloa and Poipu Beach.

THE LEI

The lei is a gift from the heart, given in the spirit of love.

There are probably less than 100 truly great lei makers in Hawaii. Among this distinguished group are the sisters Marie McDonald and Irmalee Pomroy. Being masters of their trade, their services are in constant demand. And for 30 years,

Picking orchids.

they have taken the art of lei making to new heights. McDonald has been designated a "Living Treasure of Hawaii."

The sisters developed their passion for flowers from their mother while growing up on the island of Molokai. And McDonald tells it all in her book, *Ka Lei, The Leis of Hawaii.*

In ancient times, a lei was more than a mere ornament, it was interwoven into every aspect of life. Yet a lei need not be an extravagant creation. A simple strand of flowers or aromatic leaves may be sufficient to convey its message.

The lei accompanied the Polynesians on their journey to the islands; it was there to commemorate great events, honor the gods, celebrate joys or ease sorrows. Leis were used for symbolic reasons rather than personal decoration. They were an important part of everyday life.

Hawaiian lore tells us the lei was the favorite token of the gods and demigods. A lei was given in the hope of evoking a blessing from the deity in question. A fisherman might seek a big catch, the farmer a good taro crop and the dancer an inspired performance. To ensure a favorable response, the lei would be made of the deity's favorite flowers. For example, Pele (goddess of the volcano) preferred a lei made of feathery lehua blossoms. Laka, when she reigned as goddess of the dance, favored a lei of fragrant maile leaves. But when provoked, she became Kapo (bearer of ill tidings) and sought leis of hala fruit.

Worn sparingly, even in the dance, they also served chiefly as symbols of rank, but were, and still remain primarily, a declaration of love and sometimes lovemaking.

In the broadest terms, leis can be divided into two categories — permanent and temporary. Permanent leis are made of durable materials such as feathers, shells, seeds, bone, paper or ribbon. Temporary leis are made primarily of flowers, but may also include vines, or tree bark.

Ancient trees dwarf picnickers in Foster Botanical Gardens.

The Permanent Lei

The most spectacular of the permanent leis was the ancient lei niho palaoa or lei palaoa, used on some islands as a symbol of royalty. The lei was composed of a single pendant, carved from a sperm whale's tooth, suspended on a thick rope of human hair, woven into thin plaits.

Hawaiian royalty also favored garments and ornaments — including leis — made entirely of feathers, plucked from exotic birds by the po'e kahai manu (a guild of professional bird catchers). Yellow was the most popular color, followed by red and, to a much lesser degree, green and black. Some fine examples of this royal raiment are on permanent display at the Bishop Museum on Oahu.

Leis of bright feathers or lei hulu manu were reserved exclusively for the alii or ruling class. The feather lei was considered to be the most valuable possession of a woman of rank; she wore it to denote her lofty position.

For sheer beauty, however, it is the shell lei from the island of Niihau, or lei pupu o Niihau, which commands the highest honors — and price — today. A single strand has more than 200 tiny shells, which must be gathered from along the island's western beaches, matched for pattern, color (20 types and colors are commonly used) and then strung. One lei requires a dozen or so of these strands.

The Temporary Lei

Though they are evanescent, it is the temporary leis for which Hawaii is best known. They come in a profusion of colors, styles and scents. Much of the greenery and most of the flowers used in the modern lei were not available to pre-Cook Hawaiians. But some popular materials — principally the leaves of the maile vine and the fruit of the *hala* (pandus) — can be traced back to Hawaii's earliest beginnings. Both these plants produce a rich fragrance, which once was believed to rival the finest French perfume. To some, the hala was a symbol of love and was thought to arouse passion.

Maile is the oldest and most popular material for leis. The bark and tender leaves of the vine-like shrub are stripped from the young plant in one swift motion (if you know what you are doing). Several lengths of maile are knotted together to form a single strand, which is worn as an "open lei," draped around the neck. Maile grows on all the islands, but there are subtle differences in the exotic fragrances of each lei.

Styles and Care of the Lei

There are five basic styles of leis: *kipuu* or knotted leis, *hilo* and *haku* (braided leis), *wili* or wound leis, and *kui* or sewn leis, in which flowers are strung with a long lei needle and strong thread.

As you travel through the islands, you will discover the vast variety of beautiful flower leis available. Don't let the term "temporary" dissuade you from purchasing one. It will keep for several days, if you treat it with care. Wear it during the day, then sprinkle it with water (some lei makers recommend soaking it for a few

OPPOSITE: Native Hawaiians sport a variety of beautiful leis. ABOVE and OVERLEAF: Perpetuating the art of lei making.

minutes), shaking off the excess and placing it in a plastic bag, and putting it inside the refrigerator overnight to freshen.

For those who want to learn more about the history and tradition of the lei, Bishop Museum has an excellent exhibit titled *Ka Lei, Continuation of a Tradition.* This exhibit — using photographs, audiotapes illustrations and text panels — offers an appreciation of the important island tradition of giving leis and a context for understanding the development of the Hawaiian lei. It includes wide varieties of examples covering the range of leis in Hawaii from pre-Cook to the present day.

Galloping Gourmet

COOKING'S CAVALIERS

Until recently Hawaii didn't have much of a reputation as a center of the culinary arts. For years it prided itself on its "local" foods — a blend of Japanese, Korean and Chinese dishes mixed with Hawaiian ingredients called "the mixed plate" or "plate lunch."

There were good ethnic restaurants serving a variety of Asian and European cooking styles, not to mention American-style steak houses. For the most part food was prepared traditionally, but often without much imagination.

Then along came Roy Yamaguchi — and many believe that his entrance into the culinary arena helped turn Hawaii into a culinary hotspot.

From his training in French cuisine, Yamaguchi's blended French cooking with the flavors of his native Asian cuisine. Purists of European cooking may have thought this was sacrilege, but Yamaguchi didn't think so. He embarked on a course that eventually helped coin the term "Hawaii regional cuisine" or "Pacific rim" cooking.

Some may challenge Yamaguchi's place in culinary history, but few question the publicity that put him in the spotlight. The publicity, was good for all those chefs, both new and yet to be discovered, who profited from Yamaguchi's fame.

Born in Japan and trained at the Culinary Institute of America, Yamaguchi began his experiments with French and Oriental cooking in California. After a stint in Hollywood, where he earned his title of executive chef, Yamaguchi came to Hawaii where his family had roots and opened Roy's in the suburban Oahu district of Hawaii Kai. And the rest is history — Hawaii regional cuisine, or Pacific Rim fare became the rage.

This spawned a slew of Hawaii-based chefs who emerged to be acknowledged for their extraordinary culinary skills. Among the best known practicing their art in these islands today are Frenchmen **Jean-Marie Josselin** (A Pacific Café), **Phillipe Padovani** (Manele Bay Hotel), and **George Mavrothalassitis** (Four Seasons Resort Maui), mainland Americans such as **Mark Ellman** (Avalon), **Roger Dikon** (Maui Prince Hotel), **Gary Strehl** (Hawaii Prince Hotel), and **Peter Merriman** (Merriman's), two women, also from the continental United States, **Amy Ferguson Ota** (Orchid at Mauna Lani) and **Beverly**

Gannon (Haliimaile General Store), and true local "lads" **Alan Wong** (Alan Wong's) and **Sam Choy** (Sam Choy's).

This cooking renaissance in Hawaii can be summed up in these words: freshness and the quality of the local produce (fruits, vegetables, and fish) and the unfettered imagination of the practitioners of this art.

Convention and caution are thrown to the winds as these cavalier chefs blend meat, fish and poultry and herbs and spices, creating sauces and marinades that at one time would have been unthinkable. All culinary boundaries have been crossed.

For example, a Yamaguchi favorite is curry-blackened Hawaiian swordfish with cucumber tomato and ginger relish. The recipe includes strong flavors of lemongrass (Thai), ginger (Chinese) and garlic (Italian) — all part of the marinade for the fish. The tomato, cucumber and ginger relish includes touches of olive oil, sesame oil, soy sauce and white pepper.

No matter which island you go to, you're going to find a restaurant run by one of these great chefs. We recommend that you spend at least one evening with them — wherever you may be (see WHERE TO EAT under each region or city).

GOURMET FESTIVALS

Several outstanding culinary events happen in Hawaii each year. One of the most important takes place on the Big Island at the Mauna Lani Bay Hotel and Bungalows. **Cuisines of the Sun** ((808) 885-6622 is a gourmet food festival that traditionally takes place in August.

Since its debut in 1989, Cuisines of the Sun has become one of America's most prestigious food and wine extravaganzas, highlighting the cuisines of sunny climates and emphasizing healthy cooking.

Each year a theme is featured, such as "The Spices of Life: Celebrating Fragrance and Flavor" where the focus was on pungent flavorings such as cardamom, cinnamon, ginger and others

OPPOSITE: A Japanese breakfast. BELOW: Pacific Rim cuisine graces tables throughout the islands.

that transform ordinary dishes into exotic journeys. Each year, cooking styles from around the world are represented. From Moroccan to Cajun to Hawaiian, talented chefs work their culinary genius to create exotic dishes enlivened with the perfect touch of spice. Top winemakers also make an appearance here.

The **Grand Chefs on Tour** program (See also LIVING IT UP, page 54) hosted by the **Kea Lani Hotel**, on Maui, takes place throughout the year. It pairs some of the most celebrated chefs in the world with local chefs in joint cooking demonstrations and signature dinners. Dinners and classes are combined with wines selected by the program's wine director, Anthony Dias Blue, who is also wine and spirits editor for *Bon Appetit* magazine.

The Kea Lani event generally consists of three days — Thursday, Friday, and Saturday. Each day features a cooking class and sampling, a wine tasting and a seminar followed by a signature dinner. Thursday features the Hawaii chef; Friday presents the "fusion" — the Hawaii chef and the visiting chef together, and Saturday showcases the culinary style of the visiting chef.

The **Orchid at Mauna Lani** ((808) 885-2000 on the Big Island is the venue for the **Annual Big Island Bounty Festival** over Memorial Day weekend. The three-day festival is the premier showcase for Hawaii regional cuisine, a nonstop immersion in the newest food developments in Hawaii and the mainland. Top chefs unveil their latest culinary creations. Farmers, ranchers, fishermen, and specialty food producers display their wares and invite samplings of their harvests. There are grill-outs, seminars, cooking demonstrations, and a lavish Sunday brunch.

The annual **Winter Wine Escape** is already an established tradition at the **Hapuna Beach Prince Hotel** ((808) 880-1111, on the Big Island. This event invites the public to meet top winemakers from around the world, and top chefs who place the perfect wine with the best of Hawaiian regional cuisine.

Wine experts from around the world gather at Maui's Kapalua Resort in June for the annual **Kapalua Wine and Food Symposium** ((808) 669-0244. Formal tastings and discussions and the Chef's Kapalua Seafood Festival are all part of this event.

VEGETARIAN DINING

There is a growing vegetarian movement in Hawaii, which has led to a rise in health food stores and what are described as "vegetarian-friendly restaurants."

Asian cultures, of course, have been practicing vegetarianism long before the Europeans got into the act, so it isn't surprising that some of the best places serving vegetarian food are Asian restaurants. All of the restaurants listed below are in the moderate-price range.

OAHU

Honolulu has a good selection of vegetarian places. The **Buddhist Vegetarian Restaurant** ((808) 532-8218, Chinese Cultural Plaza, 100 North Beretania Street, is a Chinese vegetarian eatery with outstanding imitation meat dishes. The best bet here is the vegetarian "pork" made from bean curd. **Pali Gardens** ((808) 263-5500, Castle Hospital Cafeteria, 640 Ulukahiki, is an moderately-priced vegetarian spot. Healthy, low-fat gourmet fare with a Pacific Rim flair is served at **Pacific Vegetarian Café** ((808) 536-6565, Aloha Tower Marketplace. **Crêpe Fever Restaurant** ((808) 521-9023, Ward Center, 1200 Ala Moana Boulevard, offers natural foods and all-vegetarian dinners. **Chiang Mai** ((808) 941-1151, 2239 South King Street, a Thai restaurant, has a full vegetarian menu. The food is very good and reasonably priced. Nearly all the dishes at the **Indian Bazaar Madras** ((808) 949-4840, 2320 South King Street, are vegetarian. And they are reasonably-priced. **Fresh Garden Deli** ((808) 524-8242, 212 Merchant Street, is California-style eating, with the accent on vegetable dishes and sandwiches.

KAUAI
The **International Museum and Café**
((808) 338-0403, 9875 Waimea Road, is a
primarily vegetarian restaurant serving
international food.

MAUI
The little seaside town of Paia on Maui
has the **Vegan Restaurant** ((808) 579-9144,
115 Baldwin Avenue, that serves
international–Thai food. The restaurant
is run by members of a vegan commune,
many of whom have been together since
the Woodstock Festival in 1969. The
restaurant has a small but varied menu
of tasty vegan dishes, served occasionally
to the accompaniment of live music.
Vegetable lovers give this restaurant
high marks for quality and taste.

HAWAII
Tony's Vegetarian Restaurant ((808) 966-
8091, Keaau, is an almost completely
vegetarian eatery.
   Huna Ohana ((808) 965-9661,
Akebono Theater Complex, Pahoa,
conjures up images of "flower power"
and the age of Aquarius. It's a vegan-
friendly café that serves a variety of
dishes and jellies using fresh island
produce, susch as Puna papaya, organic
strawberry jam, and tofu dishes.

Shop till You Drop

Every island has its shopping centers,
shopping malls, farmer's markets and
flea markets. Almost every name brand
and designer item available in London,
Paris, Tokyo, Milan or New York is also
available in Hawaii. But the fun of
shopping in a new place is discovering
what is unique to that place in the way
of arts and crafts or other goods not
available in the high-priced boutiques
and malls of the world.
   The islands have lovely wood,
particularly koa and milo, and the bowls
and boxes turned out by artists working
in this medium are quite special. There
are artist colonies on all the islands.
In addition to wood, artists, local and

expatriate, work in glass, palm fronds,
paper, silk and cloth.

CLOTHING
Classic **aloha wear** is available on all the
islands. There are tropical prints on silk
shirts, hand-painted scarves, sarongs
and other items of clothing. Several local
designers turn out high-fashion garments.
You can even buy antique aloha shirts,
but one of them could set you back as
much as $2,500. A good place to start
looking is **Avanti Fashion** in Waikiki.
   Hilo Hattie's is a chain of stores
selling all manner of local products
and perhaps is best known in the tourist
trade. It specializes in local garments for
the mass market.

BOOKS
There are many secondhand bookstores
around the islands, but one that
specializes in Hawaiiana is **Tusitala
Bookshop,** at 116 Hekilli Street on
Oahu. This store has everything from
out-of-print books to Hawaiian sheet
music and old menus. There's also a
fine collection of books on Hawaiian
culture.
   Lisa Louise Adams is the creator of
handmade miniature books filled with
writings and hand-colored drawings. She
also produces handmade papers from
local plants that grow near her house in
the village of Volcano.

HAWAIIANA
Old Waikiki postcards and photo
reproductions are available at the **Bishop
Museum** and the **State Archives**. There
are also illustrated song sheets from the
1920s, and plenty of Hawaiian music
available on tapes and compact discs.

ART
The paintings of **Herb Kane** capture a
vision of ancient Hawaii. Kane is part
artist, part historian. He creates works
rich in detail and color, and many hang
in museums around the world. Prints
and books stemming from Kane's fertile
imagination are available at bookstores
and art galleries.

Fire Mountain is **Jane Chao**'s vision of the 1986 Kilauea eruption that destroyed 28 houses in the Kapaahu and Kalapana districts. Originally watercolor on silk, now an 18.5- by 21-in (46- by 53-cm) print. Another of Chao's works, *Under the Sun*, depicts peacocks and anthuriums captured in a profusion of light and color.

Ira Ono's *Hawaiian Fishermen* is a lovely old-style reproduction print framed in a mat hand-stamped with petroglyph figures. Ono has also created masked pendants, pit-fired in the volcano forests using koa wood and packaged in a lovely gift box.

Inspired by the beauty of Kauai, several artists from that island are making names for themselves. **Dawn Traina**, who works out of the town of Hanapepe, concentrates on pen and ink images of Hawaiians at work and play; Hanalei's **Laka Morton** produces portraits of the people of the islands; and **Evelyn de Buhr** turns out oils of brilliant tropical flowers.

The oils, watercolor originals, and fine prints of environmental artist **Wyland** are on display at the Kapaa shopping center on Kauai, in his own gallery in Haleiwa on Oahu as well as other select outlets. Also in Kapaa, **Margaret Ezekial** showcases her own original artworks as well as those of other talented artists at **Treasures of Kuan Yin**.

Raymond Massey's splendid paintings, scrimshaw, sculptures and other accent pieces on the theme of Polynesian sailing vessels and Polynesia are to be found in galleries in Poipu and the Coconut Marketplace on Kauai.

ARTS AND CRAFTS

Paula Kokomo Kamanu specializes in images of volcanoes and other one-of-a-kind paintings on canvas, as well as sand paintings.

Elizabeth Hicks creates original handcrafted dolls. Each doll is made from antique materials and captures the spirit and culture of the islands.

Exquisite Hawaiian quilts are available from **R.K. Creations**. Made of 100 percent cotton, these are one-of-a-kind works of art suitable for wall hangings.

Ronald Puakukui Kanakanui Sr. learned the art of carving from his grandfather and today is recognized as one of the islands' premier wood carvers. He designs for Kukui Woodworks on the Big Island.

Crater Rim Ceramics produces beautiful ocean and volcano landscapes in ceramic that are inspired by the natural beauty of the Big Island. Each piece is hand built and wheel thrown, then fired twice in a gas kiln.

JEWELRY

Hawaiian heirloom jewelry is based on jewelry favored during the monarchy period. Designers work in gold and silver, etching floral patterns and names onto pendants, bracelets, earrings and charms. Heirloom jewelry is expensive, but it is elegant and a reminder of Hawaii's royal past.

The other jewelry much prized by local residents is that made from the beautiful **Niihau shells** — tiny seashells collected from the beaches of the equally tiny island of Niihau that sits off the coast of Kauai. Niihau shell jewelry is designed and made by the women of this island. This jewelry has a certain amount of intrigue because visitors are not permitted on this island which is inhabited by a small colony of Hawaiians.

There was a time when the Hawaii islands produced some remarkable jewelry fashioned out of whalebone, known as scrimshaw. But since the whale became an endangered species, artisans, such as those on Molokai, have turned to carving on **deer horn**, which most agree is a good substitute for whalebone. First of all, there is no reason to kill the animal to acquire the antler. During the season, they drop their antlers, and Molokai carvers forrage and collect the antlers from around the kiawe groves, which the deer frequent. The horn is carved and made into pendants for both men and women. The pendant is ivory or cream colored and is usually suspended from a lightweight circlet of brown twine or black leather. They weigh about half an ounce (14 g) and cost about $35.

The fishhook pendant is based on the fishhooks ancient Hawaiians carved out of bone and actually used for fishing.

This is an attractive piece, and very delicate, being only about three quarter by three quarters of an inch (four by four centimeters). Other pendants depict turtles, canoe paddles, dolphins, geckos and whale's tails.

The natural **flower essences** of Hawaii's beautiful and unique flowers are rare and unusual gifts. Soaps, shampoos and lotions scented with the perfumes of flowers and made from coconut and kukui nut oil make interesting gifts.

RIGHT and ABOVE: Shells and coral make lovely necklaces and plant hangers. OPPOSITE: Handpainted coconuts make playful and unique souvenirs.

FOODS

Jams, jellies, relishes and chutneys made with island fruits such as pineapples, papaya and bananas are wonderful gifts. There are also tropical cordials and a variety of superb Kona coffees available. Many of the islands also have a variety of candies made from coffee, macadamia nuts and fruit. And of course, there are Hawaii's unique wines that come from the Tedeschi vineyard on Maui and the vineyard at Volcano on the Big Island.

WHERE TO SHOP
OAHU

An international mall with 200 shops, several large department stores, 11 restaurants and nine snack shops, **Ala Moana Center** has two levels, with a nice outdoor feel to the place. It attracts about 56 million visitors each year.

Borders Bookstore and Music and the Crazy Shirts outlet are among the 120 unique shops at **Victoria Ward Center** and **Ward Warehouse**. Among the 65 specialty stores featuring locally made goods are **Blue Ginger**, which sells cotton prints, and the **Nohea Gallery,** which specializes in wood bowls and boxes, stained glass, jewelry, ceramics and fine arts and crafts. **Mamo** is the store of local fashion designer Mamo Howell whose aloha wear has found international appeal. The two complexes also have several excellent restaurants.

Waikele Center, H-1 Freeway west to Exit 7, has over 75 discount factory outlet stores and several restaurants.

Kahala Mall is a classy place with 86 shops. Stop by **Following Sea** if you are looking for an unusual gift. It has an excellent inventory of gifts from around the world. One of the hottest selling items is the Wolford oil lamp. The **Corner Loft** sells jewelry, antiques and Hawaiiana, while **Jeffrey Barr's** clothing store is worth a visit.

For a taste of the real Hawaii, the **Aloha Flea Market** at Aloha Stadium on a Wednesday, Saturday and Sunday, is the place to be. The market is held in the parking lot of the stadium and there are sometimes as many as a thousand

vendors plying their trade, selling everything from eelskin wear, to leather goods, seashells, baskets, flowers, clothing and exotic produce.

Aloha Tower Market Place is a two-story series of galleries housing shops and restaurants built around walkways filled with flowers and fountains overlooking Honolulu Harbor. If you are looking for local handmade furniture and woodcraft, check out **Martin and McArthur**.

In addition to good restaurants, **Restaurant Row** has a variety of interesting small stores. A favorite is **Opal Fields**, a jewelry store that features the craft of local woodwork artists.

MAUI

Kahana Gate is a new shopping center north of Kaanapali with everything from fast foods to fine dining — even a jazz club. They also have souvenir, gift and children's fashion stores.

Lahaina Cannery Mall, Maui's only enclosed, fully air-conditioned mall, is situated between Lahaina and Kaanapali. Designed along the lines of an old pineapple cannery, the mall has an arty feel. There are more than 59 shops and restaurants.

Little Polynesia has shops for children featuring puppets, stuffed animals, toys, games and swim and aloha wear.

KAUAI

Hanapepe is the art center of the island where several galleries are found. They include **Village Gallery, Lele Aka, 8 Bells** and the **Kauai Fine Arts and Artsphere**.

Kapaia Stitchery has unique island needlework designs, and quilts in tropical fabrics. The quilt selection is particularly appealing. Located in Lihue.

The **Kiahuna Shopping Village**, located in Poipu, has 33 specialty shops, art galleries and restaurants built around an open-air garden. You'll find everything here from fine jewelry and art to sports gear.

The **Kela's Art Gallery**, in Kapaa town, is the state's only glass gallery, and features the work of over 35 artists.

Kauai's largest shopping center, **Kukui Grove Center,** sprawls over 35 acres (14 hectares) in Lihue. The center contains 50 specialty stores, 13 restaurants, two movie theaters and an outdoor recreation area. You might want to check out the Kauai Products Council Store that promotes local craft, art and agricultural products.

Barbie and Ken's Hawaiian Wear, in Waimea Canyon Plaza in Kekaha, specializes in cotton garments and other natural fibers that hold their color, wear well and stay cool in tropical climates.

Old Koloa Town is a restored plantation town shopping area, complete with storefronts dating back 150 years — quaint, charming, colorful and full of interesting merchandise.

Princeville Shopping Center is another plantation-style center with 33 businesses.

Ship Store Galleries, in Poipu Shopping Village and the Coconut Marketplace, feature art on the theme of sailing ships and Polynesia.

HAWAII

Kamaaina Woods is located in Honokaa on the Big Island's Hamakua Coast. Its shelves are stocked with museum-quality pieces made of native Hawaiian and other hardwoods. Most of its wooden bowls have been hand-turned. Other items for sale include boxes, poi pounders and accessories in koa, milo, monkeypod, mango and Norfolk pine.

The **Punaluu Bake Shop** doubles as the visitor center in the town famous for the green sea turtles that inhabit its waters. The bakery is famous for its macadamia nut products, garments, Hawaiian sweetbread, sandwiches, coffee and ice cream.

MOLOKAI

Artists of Molokai ((808) 553-3461 is a network of professionals creating contemporary and traditional Hawaiian works, including fine jewelry, woodcraft, paintings, sculpture, quilts and clothing. Visits to various studios can be arranged.

Jewelry designer **Carol Klein** specializes in distinctive work in gold and silver. Her handcrafted necklaces and earrings with Hawaiian themes are one-of-a-kind creations.

OPPOSITE: Brilliant blossoms spill out of a farmer's market stall. ABOVE: Exquisite and rare Niihau shell necklace adorns an island woman.

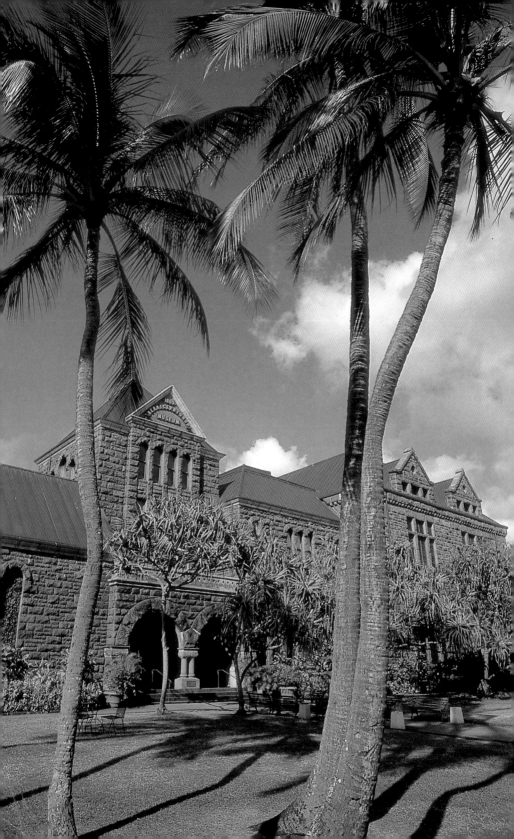

Watercolor artist **Julie Patten** of **Designs Pacifica** creates papercast Hawaiian quilt designs on cards, clothing and glassware, as well as floral and spirit paintings.

At **Basket Creations**, Molokai designers create unique gift baskets of Molokai products.

LANAI

Heart of Lanai Art Gallery, in Lanai City, specializes in Hawaiian jewelry, paintings, sculptures and local arts and crafts. Owner Denise Hennig's own works are featured alongside those of other local artists such as Pamela Andelin, Macario Pascual and John Young.

Maunalei Gifts is also worth checking out for its interesting collection of local arts and crafts. The store is located in the town's only mini-mall.

Cultural Kicks

MUSEUMS, MEMORIALS AND GALLERIES

For its size and remoteness, Hawaii has an extraordinary diversity of cultural and art exhibits at excellent museums on almost every island. From the ancient to the modern, there's something for everyone with an appreciation for beauty and learning.

OAHU

The **Bishop Museum and Planetarium** ((808) 847-3511, 1525 Bernice Street, Honolulu, HI 96817, has an international reputation as one of the world's finest museums on Hawaiian and Polynesian art, culture and history. On display are ancient Hawaiian feather cloaks, weapons, clothing, koa calabashes and jewelry. The first Sunday of every month is Family Sunday, a cultural celebration with Hawaiian entertainment, food, displays and demonstrations. From time to time the museum also has special interactive exhibitions.

The museum's departments include: The **Herbarium Pacificum** with 500,000 Pacific Basin plant specimens, has the largest and most comprehensive assemblage of vascular plants in the world. The **Gressit Center for Research in Entomology** conducts research on the insects and arthropods of Hawaii and the Pacific. Because of its volcanic and tectonic setting, Hawaii is an ideal place to study geological and volcanological events. The museum's **geology section** conducts projects including an oceanographic research expedition to the southeast Indian Ocean to study the formation of the Indian Ocean Basin as India, Australia, and Antarctica separated starting 150 million years ago.

Finally, the **Planetarium** ((808) 847-8201 offers a variety of entertaining and educational programs. The "Journey By Starlight" program is presented daily at 11:30 AM, 1:30 PM and every Friday and Saturday evening at 7 PM. On the first Monday of each month at 7 PM the museum presents "The Sky Tonight". Reservations are recommended for evening shows and can be made by calling during business hours. At the conclusion of all evening programs, the museum observatory is open to the public for exciting views of the universe.

The **Contemporary Museum** ((808) 526-1322, 2411 Makiki Heights Drive, Honolulu, HI 96822, has one of the loveliest settings of any of the islands' many fine museums. Formerly the private residence of Alice Cooke Spalding, the museum sits in the midst of three and a half acres (one and a half hectares) of magnificent gardens, with superb views of the city and the ocean.

Initially designed as a retreat in which to meditate and experience the harmony of nature, the gardens provide a natural setting for works of art and a quiet place for contemplation. The museum consists of five galleries as well as the Milton Cades Pavilion. Selections from the museum's permanent collection are shown in the exhibition schedule. A highlight of this collection is David Hockney's works inspired by the Ravel

The Bishop Museum is internationally recognized as a leading museum on Polynesian art and culture.

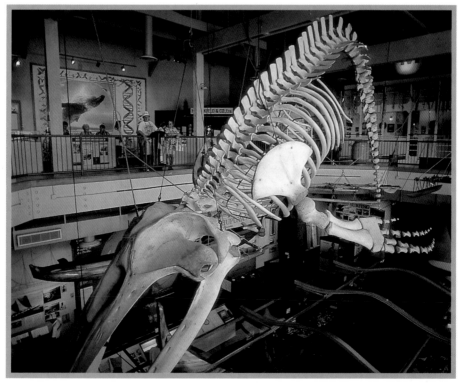

opera *L'Enfant et les Sortileges* (The Child and the Bewitched). Free garden tours are offered by appointment. The museum also has a café and a gift shop.

Much of Hawaii's history is tied to the ocean. It has its roots in the great voyages of exploration by the early Polynesians, and has depended for generations on shipping to sustain it. The **Hawaii Maritime Center** ((808) 536-6373, Pier 7, Honolulu Harbor, Honolulu, HI 96813, presents an exciting guided tour through all the different eras in Hawaii's maritime development.

Fifty displays focus on a variety of themes — from the first Polynesians to land here in their canoes to the boisterous whalers who made Hawaii the center of the whaling industry, to the legends of surfing, and finally to the service provided by ocean liners since the 1930s. Among the major attractions are the *Falls of Clyde*, the last four-masted, fully rigged vessel in the world, and the Polynesian voyaging canoe, *Hokulea*, that retraced the steps of the original voyaging groups which discovered these islands centuries ago. An admission is charged.

Dedicated in 1927, the **Honolulu Academy of Arts** ((808) 532-8701, 900 South Beretania Street, Honolulu, HI 96814, is noted for its fine collection of Asian and Pacific art as well as American and European masterpieces. Its regular program of exhibitions, films, concerts and educational and community activities make it the most comprehensive art center in the islands. An admission is charged.

One of the city's great attractions is also a place of tragedy. The **Arizona Memorial** ((808) 422-0561, 1 Arizona Memorial Drive, Pearl City, HI 96818, marks the watery grave of 1,102 officers and enlisted men who died in the Japanese attack on Pearl Harbor on December 7, 1941. The huge American battleship sank five

minutes after being hit, entombing almost its entire crew. The white monument with its smooth, clean lines was designed by local architect Alfred Preis and is today a national shrine. From 8 AM to 3 PM, navy launches shuttle tourists from the shore to the memorial. Entrance to the site is about one half a mile (just under one kilometer) east of Aloha Stadium on Highway 90. An admission fee is charged.

The **USS Bowfin Submarine Museum and Park** ((808) 423-1341, USS Arizona Memorial Visitor Center, Pearl Harbor, HI 96818 E-MAIL bowfin@aloha.net, is located adjacent to the USS Arizona Memorial Visitor Center at Pearl Harbor. The Bowfin is a World War II submarine that was launched on December 7, 1942, and completed nine successful war

OPPOSITE: The USS *Bowfin* TOP, a World War II submarine, the splendid Maritime Museum OPPOSITE BOTTOM and the Arizona Memorial RIGHT, attract streams of visitors to Pearl Harbor, site of the infamous attack on the American fleet in World War II. ABOVE: An ancient sailing vessel, the *Falls of Clyde* is a major tourist attraction on Honolulu Harbor.

patrols. Opened to the public in 1981, it was designated a National Historic Landmark by the Department of the Interior in 1986.

Visitors to Bowfin Park are given a portable cassette player that narrates their tour as they explore this historic submarine, imagining life on board for the 80-man crew. In addition to the submarine tour, there is a 10,000-sq-ft (929-sq-m) museum whose exhibits include an impressive collection of submarine-related artifacts such as submarine weapon systems, photographs, paintings, original recruiting posters, and detailed submarine models, all illustrating the history of the United States Submarine Service. New exhibits include a Poseidon C-3 missile that allows visitors to examine the inner workings of a missile. It is the only one of its kind to be on public display. A mini-theater screens submarine-related videos.

In Bowfin Park stands a public memorial honoring the 52 American submarines and the more than 3,500 submariners lost during World War II.

The park is open daily from 8 AM to 5 PM and the last tour of the submarine begins at 4:30 PM. Children under the age of four are not permitted on the submarine for safety reasons, but are allowed to tour the museum and mini-theater at no charge. The fee for the submarine and Museum tour is $8 for adults and $3 for children ages 4 to 12.

MAUI

The **Alexander and Baldwin Sugar Museum** ((808) 871-8058, 3957 Hansen Road, Puunene, HI 96784, in a former sugar superintendent's house, is an historic, award-winning museum exhibiting photographs, artifacts and a working model of sugar processing machinery. The museum is located next to Hawaii's largest sugar mill. The museum is open daily from mid-June to the end of August; an admission fee is charged.

The **Hale Kohola Whale Museum** ((808) 661-9918, Whalers Village, 2435 Kaanapali Parkway, Lahaina, HI 96761, is devoted to the evolution of the humpback

whale and features "touch and see" displays — computer terminals where visitors may punch up whale facts, a theater showing videos on whale migratory patterns, and impressive whale models, including a 16-ft (five-meter) model of the skeleton of a baby humpback.

The compact, quaint **Hana Cultural Center** ((808) 248-8622, Box 27, Hana, HI 96713, tells the story of the Hana Coast. Its displays include rare Hawaiian artifacts such as a 100-year-old fishing net, baskets, quilts, and shells as well as photographs and bottle collections. The latest addition to the complex is Kauhale O Hana, an Hawaiian Living Complex complete with ethnobotanical gardens. There is no admission fee, but donations are accepted.

Hui Noeau Visual Arts Center ((808) 572-6560, 2841 Baldwin Avenue, Makawao, HI, occupies the historic upcountry estate designed in 1917 by internationally acclaimed Hawaii architect C.W. Dickey for the Baldwin family, who made their money in sugar. The center is set amidst 12 acres (five hectares) of beautiful garden on the cool slopes of upcountry Maui. Still under development, it is already enhancing Maui's reputation as a cultural center. Along with art and craft classes, Hui Noeau provides visiting artists' workshops and outreach programs for the community and courses for teachers. Visitors to the center will often see a printmaker at work in the print studio, and several potters at their wheels in the open-air ceramics area.

Situated at the foot of dramatic Lao Valley overlooking Kahului Bay is the **Maui Arts and Cultural Center (** (808) 242-7469, Maui Central Plaza, P.O. Box 338, Kahului, HI 97732, Hawaii's first and finest comprehensive arts facility. The center's 12-acre (five-hectare) site in central Maui is the island's hub, a gathering place for a broad range of artistic and social events. The $56 million complex features two theaters, an outdoor amphitheater and a gallery. Also featured is an outdoor *pa hula*, a rock-faced mound dedicated to Hawaiian culture.

Gracious arcades, classrooms, dance studios and a grassy courtyard are among the creative spaces where public and private events are held.

Some of the entertainment industry's biggest stars have performed to sold-out audiences at the center. Cultural events such as the center's *Tales of Maui*, which chronicles the legend of the demigod Maui in chant and in hula, and the premiere of *Holo Mai Pele*, a hula epic performed in its entirety for the first time in 200 years, are also on the list of sold-out shows.

KAUAI

At the **Kauai Museum (** (808) 245-6931, 4428 Rice Street, Lihue, HI 96766, the culture and history of Kauai unfold in the museum's artistic, geological and ethnic displays, providing insights into the island's social and natural history. Kauai was once home to the most mysterious tribes from central Polynesia, the menehune, who inhabited Kauai and none of the other Hawaiian islands. The menehune legend is documented at the Kauai Museum, aong with the arrival in 1778 of British Captain James Cook, which started an era of irrevocable cultural and social change for the island. An admission fee is charged.

OPPOSITE: Sugar machinery, dying relic of a once thriving industry. BELOW: Maui's sugar train is now a tourist attraction.

Grove Farm Homestead Museum

((808) 245-3202, P.O. Box 1631, Lihue, HI 96766, is the former house of George Wilcox, son of missionaries and founder of one of Kauai's largest sugar plantations. Touring this gracious residence and its 80-acre (32-hectare) garden recalls what life was like on a nineteenth century sugar plantation. It is also a reminder of how the birth of the sugar industry changed Kauai and what it was like to be a pioneer in the island's development. An admission fee is charged.

BIG ISLAND

The **Lyman Mission House and Museum** ((808) 935-5021, 276 Haili Street, Hilo, HI 96720, was built in 1839 for the first Christian missionaries to arrive in Hilo. In 1973 an adjacent museum was constructed to showcase rare Hawaii artifacts. An admission fee is charged.

The **Parker Ranch Visitor Center and Museum** ((808) 885-7655, P.O. Box 458, Kamuela, HI 96743, documents the history of the Parker family and the largest individually owned ranch in the United States through displays, photographs, memorabilia and a 15-minute video. Tours are given at nearby Puuopelu and a replica of Mana, the Parker family houses. An admission fee is charged.

MOLOKAI

The historic **R.W. Meyer Sugar Mill Museum and Cultural Center** ((808) 567-6436, P.O. Box 986, Kaunakakai, Molokai, HI 96748 now serves as both a research center and a museum housing artifacts collected by the pioneering Meyer family. An admission fee is charged.

Short Breaks

Visitors to Hawaii have an almost infinite number of vacation choices. But when your time is limited, these choices may seem overwhelming. Here are three-day itineraries for the best destinations for travelers on a tight schedule:

BIG ISLAND

Our number one destination for a short vacation is the Big Island, including a visit to **Hawaii Volcanoes National Park**. Make your bookings for accommodation and car rental in advance. Plan to fly to Hilo and pick up the car in Hilo, and arrange to drop the car at Kona on the western side of the island. It will probably cost you more to do this, but it pays for itself in time saved and convenience.

Three days is sufficient to see the highlights of the Big Island. Here's how to go about it: First, book lodgings at Kilauea Lodge or Volcano House in Volcanoes; next, book accommodation in the town of Waimea (or Kamuela as it is otherwise known). Finally, make a booking for accommodation on the Kona Coast at one of the resorts in the town of Kailua-Kona. Fly into Hilo in the morning and pick up your car. Drive to the park (it's about 40 minutes from the airport). The park is huge. Tour it at your leisure for the entire day, then check in at your accommodation in the late evening. Dine at Kilauea Lodge.

The next morning, get up early and take a leisurely drive to the black sand beach at **Punaluu** and watch the turtles at play. Retrace your steps and make your way back to Hilo. Have lunch there, explore Hilo town, and then proceed down the **Hamakua Coast Road** (Highway 19, going north). This is a beautiful drive. Take the scenic route, which is clearly marked. It leaves the main highway for several miles and wanders along backroads, hugging the coast, with dramatic views of forests and ocean. After you get back on the highway, your next diversion should be to go to **Waipio Valley** — The Valley of the King. Leave Highway 19 and get onto Highway 240, following it until it ends up at the Waipio Valley Lookout. Gradually make your way back to the Hamakua Coast Road and on to **Waimea**. There are several excellent restaurants in this small town.

On the third day, again, start early and head off along Highway 250 through rich pasture land and quaint towns to the **Pololu Valley Lookout**, near the northernmost tip of the island. From here you can look into one of those lovely, mysterious Hawaiian valleys. On the way back, catch Highway 270 and travel through the town of Kawaihae and then along the Kona Coast. Stop in and check out some of the superb resorts along this coast (see KAILUA-KONA, page 268). Plan to have lunch at one of the hotels. If you have kids with you, the **Hilton Waikoloa Village** is fun. Take a dip in the hotel's huge pool or watch the dolphin show before your lunch break. Proceed to Kona International Airport, check in your rental car and catch the flight back.

MAUI

Three days on Maui could be turned into an exciting adventure — depending of course on the time of the year. If you happen to be visiting any time between October and April, then you have an extraordinary range of choice. Book a hotel or condominium on Maui's south or west shore. Swim or snorkel in the ocean's clear waters in the morning, but make sure you spend the afternoon whale watching. This is the season when the humpbacks come into the channel between Maui and its neighboring islands to spend the winter months.

The next day, cruise upcountry Maui, checking out the coastal town of **Paia** en route. Check into Kula Lodge or Silver Cloud Upcountry Ranch (a bed and breakfast in the cool hills on the slope of Haleakala). Silver Cloud has a separate guest cottage fully equipped and very private, as well as the Plantation Home with two suites ($125 per night) and four bedrooms ($85 to $105 per night). The Paniolo Bunkhouse is a U-shaped building with five suites ranging in price from $105 to $145. Dine at the **Haliimaile General Store** near the town of Pukalani off Highway 37, or at

New lava builds up the Big Island coastline.

Kula Lodgè, or in one of the many fine restaurants in the cowboy town of Makawao. Rise early on the third day, about 4:30, and drive to the summit of Haleakala to watch the sun rise over the great crater. It's an experience you won't forget. After coming down the mountain, spend the day at the beach in **Kihei** before setting off for the airport.

KAUAI

If you're going to Kauai and have only three days to spare, find accommodation at **Poipu** on the island's southern shores. It's roughly halfway between the spectacular north shore and its lovely beaches, and the grandeur of **Kokee State Park** and **Waimea Canyon** (see THE HIGHLANDS, page 197–199). If you have the spirit of adventure, join a kayaking expedition from Poipu (see OCEAN PLAYGROUND, page 21) or a Captain Zodiac ocean expedition to the magnificent sea cliffs and caves of the **Na Pali Coast**. This is an all-day event. For a different dining experience, try Kilohana Plantation, just outside Poipu.

On day two travel along the southern shoreline (Highway 50, going west) and then catch Highway 55 to Highway 550 into the hills and Kokee State Park. Spend the day in the park exploring the lush forests and the canyon from many different perspectives. Return to Poipu.

On the third day, plan a trip to the north shore via the eastern route

(Highway 50 to 56). This will take you through the many little picturesque towns of Kauai all the way to the fabulous **Princeville Resort**, and then on to the **Na Pali Coast State Park**, where the road ends.

OAHU

Three days on Oahu should let you see much of the island. On day one, drive over the Pali Highway to the **Pali Lookout**. Take in the great view of the windward coast. Resume your journey down the Pali Highway to **Kailua**. Pick up something to eat in Kailua town, and proceed to beautiful **Lanikai Beach**. Early in the afternoon, set off along Highway 72 going south and drive through the town of **Waimanalo** and up the cliffs to **Hanauma Bay**. Spend the rest of the afternoon here — it's one of the finest marine sanctuaries in the world. End the day by dining on the terrace of **Roy's Restaurant**. The sunset, looking across the bay to Diamond Head, is fabulous.

Make day two of your Oahu stay a cultural one. Spend the morning at the **Arizona Memorial**, and then visit one of the Pacific's great museums, the **Bishop Museum** at 1525 Bernice Street. Drive to the waterfront for cocktails at **Gordon Biersch Brewery and Restaurant** in the Aloha Tower Marketplace. Catch the **Society of Seven** in concert at the Outrigger Main Showroom in Waikiki.

Confine day three to visiting the north shore. You may want to start very early. Drive through the town of **Haleiwa**. Take a break at **Waimea Bay** and watch the big rollers pound the shores. Cruise a little further down the coast to **Sunset Beach** and swim and watch the surfers attack the famous Banzai Pipeline. Have lunch at the **Turtle Bay Hilton**. Spend the afternoon at the **Polynesian Cultural Center**. You can tour this fine cultural center at your leisure and dine and watch the evening Polynesian show here. Or you can set off down Highway 83 to the **Crouching Lion Inn** in Kaaawa if you want a more intimate dining experience.

YOUR CHOICE

Taking a Tour

There's more than one way to see the islands. Some parts are best viewed from the ocean. Other areas are remote and difficult — or impossible — to reach by road or sea and, therefore, are best viewed from a helicopter or small plane. In these flights you will be transported into secret valleys laced with waterfalls, or over lava flows rushing to the ocean. Tour companies offer a mind-boggling assortment of daily coach tours on every island. The cost of the neighbor island tours include air fares and transportation from your hotel to the airport and back.

SEA ADVENTURES
OAHU
There are all manner of cruises to choose from on each of the islands. Some of the

OPPOSITE: For artists the islands offer endless inspiration. ABOVE: The rolling range of the Big Island's Parker Ranch. OVERLEAF: Hanauma Bay, where snorkelers and fish swim in perfect harmony.

best are provided by **Navatek** ℂ (808) 848-6360. The company has developed a patented technology that provides stability in the roughest of waters; Navatek can cruise fairly far out to sea in quest of whales, for example, while providing guests with the smoothest of rides. Cruises are conducted at all times of the day, with on-board naturalists providing educational insights into curious whale behavior. There's even a sunset whale watching cruise that includes dinner. Navatek claims that its whale sightings have risen steadily since the boat was first introduced to Hawaiian waters. In 1992, recorded sightings were 253; in 1996 sightings had risen to 845. Navatek also does daily cruises along the Oahu coasts.

If you are looking for a romantic cruising adventure, check out **Windjammer Cruises** ℂ (808) 537-1122 TOLL-FREE (800) 367-5000, which operates the 282-ft (85-m) tallship, the *Rella Mae*. This big, beautiful and graceful sailing vessel offers an evening of fun and romance to go along with spectacular scenery. Magical sunsets and good food are guaranteed.

KAUAI

The Na Pali Coast on Kauai is the perfect venue for an ocean tour. The grandeur of the sea cliffs and the magnificent sea caves will leave you in awe. The inflatable rafts of **Captain Zodiac** ℂ (808) 826-9371, the motor-driven catamarans of **Na Pali Adventures** ℂ (808) 826-6804, or the kayaks of **Kauai Outfitters** ℂ (808) 742-9667 can take you under waterfalls and into lava tubes or sea caves. These vessels are small, fast and maneuverable. They're good for viewing tours, or for transporting you to snorkeling and SCUBA diving sites. Or you can just cruise ocean within sight of land and see whales (in season), dolphins, turtles and flying fish.

If you'd like to take a fascinating ocean or river tour while getting in a little exercise, then try kayaking. The **Na Pali Sea Kayak Tour** conducted by Kauai Outfitters is a one-day 15-mile

guided sea kayak adventure of one of the most beautiful and remote shorelines in the world. These tours are available in the summer, between the months of May and September. The launch site is Haena on the north shore. An hour's paddling will take you to the famed sea caves of the Na Pali Coast. The first stage of this trip is about 11 miles. You'll view plunging waterfalls, hanging valleys and secluded beaches. You'll come ashore for the first time at Milolii, the site of an ancient Hawaiian fishing village, where lunch will be served. After lunch, there will be a paddle to Polihale, generally in calm waters. Some hours will be spent snorkeling in waters teeming with reef fish and green turtles. The journey ends at Polihale State Park. A van will transport you back to the store at Poipu. Groups depart at 6:30 AM and return at 6:30 PM. The cost per person is $130.

Kauai Outfitters' **Kipu Kai Sea Kayak Adventure Tour** takes you to a beautiful, isolated beach on Kauai's southern shores accessible only by sea. Kipu Kai is best visited during the winter months, when high surf pounds the island's northern shores but the south remains protected. This is the season of the humpback whale. It is likely you'll see these creatures up close, together with a variety of marine life such as flying fish, dolphins, sea turtles, and if you're lucky, the monk seal. The one-day exploration of Kipu Kai is launched from Nawiliwili. From here, the first stage of the 11-mile (18-km) paddle will be six miles (nine and a half kilometers) in typically heavy seas along the base of spectacular 2,000-ft (600-m) sheer sea cliffs. The tour reaches Kipu Kai, a mile-long white sand beach set in a natural amphitheater at the foot of 3,000-ft (900-m) Mount Haupu in late morning. Here a picnic lunch will be served and there will be an opportunity to snorkel in pristine waters. A four-mile (six-and-a-half-kilometer) paddle in calm waters will take you to your destination on the shores of Poipu. The cost per person is $115.

The three-hour **Blue Lagoon** TOLL-FREE (800) 437-3507 snorkel tour of the Hanalei River and the National Wildlife Refuge and Bay is a family adventure that begins and ends at Hanalei. The tour drifts lazily along the scenic Hanalei River and the Bay Reef Lagoon, with interesting facts about the land, water, flora and fauna explained by historians. You'll get a chance to wade on a sandy beach, snorkel with reef fish, and view the bird life on this island. The cost per person is $55.

MAUI

There are numerous whale watch cruises available from various Maui ports from Lahaina to Kihei, but one of the best may be the **Pacific Whale Foundation's Ultimate Endangered Species Adventure** ((808) 879-8811, a two and three-quarter hour whale watch and reef tour out of Lahaina aboard a glass-bottomed Chinese junk, the *Lin Wa II*. The vessel is a Chinese junk right up to its red sails and is equipped with 10 viewing ports on the lower deck, while her upper deck consists of a dance floor and a cocktail bar at the rear of the boat. The *Lin Wa* first explores the coral gardens along the Lahaina Coast where

a variety of reef fish and other creatures dwell. Next it visits the habitat of the green sea turtle before heading out to the blue water in search of the humpback whale. There aren't many more thrilling sights than to see a whale up close, or watch it cruise beneath your boat as you view it through the glass bottom of the *Lin Wa*. Cruises departure three times a day at 8:30 AM, noon and 3 PM; cost of the tour is $49.95 for adults and $24.95 for children.

BIG ISLAND

There is no shortage of choice for whale watching tours off the Big Island. If you are fortunate enough to vacation on the Kona-Kohala Coast during the winter season, you are almost certain to see these giant mammals swooping and diving and thumping the waters with their tails. One of the great viewing sites is the footpath along the Mauna Lani golf course. And if you are lucky to be around on the night of the full moon when the whales are very active, it's a sight you'll never forget.

A romantic sunset cruise off Waikiki is an unforgettable part of many Hawaiian vacations.

For a closer look, sign up with **Captain Dan Mcsweeney's Whale Watch Learning Adventures** ((808) 322-0028. Captain Dan is a marine biologist with 20 years experience studying the humpbacks. And he knows where to find his quarry in Kona's calm and deep offshore waters. Because of the conditions here it is easier to see the smaller whales and the larger migrating humpbacks. The Big Island's Wild Whale Research Foundation, of which McSweeney is a founding member, is trying to find out all it can about these creatures and their migratory patterns. Researchers have discovered to date that humpbacks travel between the islands and cover 50 to 100 miles (80 to 160 km) a day. During their stay here, they mate and calve. Researchers are still trying to find out what whales in these waters eat — and how much.

In addition to McSweeney, there are quite a few other groups that offer whale watching tours, including **Body Glove** ((808) 326-7122, **Captain Zodiac** ((808) 329-3199, **Fairwind Rafting Adventures** ((808) 322-2788, **Kamanu Charters** ((808) 329-2021, **Living Ocean Adventures** ((808) 325-5556, and **Sea Quest Rafting Adventures** ((808) 329-RAFTS.

AIR ADVENTURES

OAHU
Rainbow Pacific Helicopters ((808) 834-1111 offers a variety of tours on all the islands. They can get you to all sorts of remote and secret places, but on Oahu they also do a night tour of the city which is breathtaking.

Pappilon Hawaiian Helicopters ((808) 367-7095 will carry you high over the Koolau mountain ranges, or sweep you low through valleys over some of the most beautiful beaches in the island chain.

KAUAI
It is estimated that over 80 percent of Kauai's terrain is inaccessible. Viewing the interior of the island with its deep verdant valleys, spectacular waterfalls,

rain forests, swamps, and secluded beaches from the air will remain forever etched in your memory. **Island Helicopters** ((808) 245-8488 TOLL-FREE (800) 829-5999, one of several helicopter companies operating on Kauai, offers an hour-long Deluxe Kauai Grand helicopter tour. Your high-flying adventure begins at Lihue then soars over magnificent landscapes that include Manawaiopuna Falls, featured in *Jurassic Park*, Hanapepe Valley, Olokele Canyon, through Waimea Canyon, over Alakai Swamp, Kokee State Park, and of course the Na Pali Coast. The cost per person is $166 (see also SEA CAVES AND SECRET COVES, page 16).

MAUI
Hawaii Helicopters TOLL-FREE (800) 994-9099 offers three excellent air tours that take off from Kahului Airport. The 45-minute Rainbow Special explores east Maui, taking in Haleakala Crater, the lush rain forests of Hana and the waterfalls that cascade off Maui's rugged north shore. The cost per person is $129

The hour-long Valley Isle Deluxe tour takes you from one end of the island to the other, encompassing all of the Rainbow Special plus the West Maui Mountains, Iao Needle and the Waihee Valley. The cost per person is $179.

The hour-long West Maui and Molokai tour explores sea cliffs and waterfalls, lush valleys and the historic Kalaupapa Peninsula where the legendary priest Father Damien worked among victims of Hansen's disease. The return journey is over the West Maui Mountains. The cost per person is $179.

BIG ISLAND
Legend has it that the goddess of the snows, Poliahu, an enemy of Pele, the goddess of fire, resides in the snows of Mauna Kea. She is credited with being the only deity ever to vanquish Pele, cooling her lava and driving her away from the top of the White Mountain. If you want to see the interplay between

these two goddesses, then you must take a helicopter tour of the eastern side of the Big Island. The Volcano Isle Deluxe tour offered by **Hawaii Helicopters** TOLL-FREE (800) 994-9099 is a thrilling flight over soaring lava flows, lush rain forests and the spectacular Big Island waterfalls. The tour tracks the lava flow to the ocean. The hour-long flight costs $169 per person.

Two other flights are offered by Hawaii Helicopter on the Big Island: The Waipio Valley flight soars over the beautiful north shore valleys of Waimanu, Waipio and Pololu. You'll also get a bird's-eye look at Parker Ranch, the largest privately owned cattle ranch in the United States. This 50-minute flight costs $129 per person.

The Ultimate Volcano Isle Adventure combines the best of the volcano tour with the best of the valley tour. You'll never forget the experience as you soar over Saddle Road and over the snow-capped peaks of Mauna Kea to Kilauea's fiery Puu Oo vent. You'll trace the lava flow on its journey to the ocean and black sand beaches. This two-hour flight costs $290 per person.

YOUR CHOICE

ROAD ADVENTURES

OAHU

The 120-mile (193-km) Circle Island Beach and Picnic Tour shows off some of the island's favorite destinations such as Diamond Head Crater, Hanauma Bay, and the great windward and north shore beaches. There are swimming and sunbathing options as well. The highlight of the tour is a visit to Waimea Falls Park on the north shore and a picnic at fabulous Waimea Bay. The price is $55 for adults; $40 for children aged six to 12; and $36.50 for children aged four to five. For more information call **Polynesian Adventure Tours** ((808) 833-3000.

E Noa Tours ((808) 591-2561 offers short historic tours of the downtown area or of the Arizona Memorial, Pearl Harbor and a shopping excursion to the outlet stores at Waikele. The Pearl Harbor and Historic Honolulu Tour takes in the Arizona Memorial plus Punchbowl National Cemetery, Chinatown, the State Capitol and Iolani Palace. The price is

A Big Island helicopter operator flies sightseers high over a remote coastline. OVERLEAF: A new highway curves its way through the palis on the island of Oahu.

$22 for adults; $19 for children aged 11 and under.

Most tour companies offer excursions to the **Polynesian Cultural Center (** (808) 293-3333 for a whirlwind tour of the Pacific islands. You'll come in touch with the cultures of Tahiti, Fiji, Tonga, Samoa, New Zealand, the Marquesas and old Hawaii. You'll dine and be entertained at a traditional Polynesian luau. The 42-acre (17-hectare) center is a series of South Sea villages designed around lagoons that includes restaurants, theaters and an IMAX Polynesian theater. High point of the evening's entertainment is a Polynesian revue featuring over 100 talented performers. There are fire eaters and fire-knife performances to go with great singing and dancing. Check with your travel agent or local tour companies, or call the Polynesian Cultural Center to arrange a visit.

Polynesian Adventure Tours (see above) also packages some interesting neighbor island tours. On Kauai, the entire Garden Isle is covered in a tour which takes in everything from Waimea Canyon in the west to the Fern Grotto and the north shore. On Maui, you can combine a visit to the summit of Haleakala with a scenic tour of Iao Valley and the town of Lahaina. Or embark on a guided tour down the Hana Highway to Hana. Visitors to the Big Island can take a 260-mile (419-km) Grand Circle Island tour which includes 20 of the most visually interesting and historic sites on the island, including Hawaii Volcanoes National Park.

Iolani Palace, America's only royal residence.

A Fiery
Birth

FORGED BY FIRE, blessed by rain, kissed by the sun, and carved by wind, the Hawaiian islands are among nature's most beautiful creations, encircled by leis of beaches set amidst the bluest of oceans.

The eight main Hawaiian islands rose from the depths of the ocean millions of years ago and constitute one segment of a long chain of volcanoes which once extended all the way to Siberia.

The islands' landscape has a fascinating and violent geological history. The earth's surface or crust is composed of 12 large plates

Kahoolawe, Maui and Hawaii, also called the Big Island.

The northern part of the chain is composed of a series of sunken volcanic peaks known as the Emperor Sea Mounts. The northwestern Hawaiian islands, the central section of the chain, is a national wildlife refuge.

The islands lie 2,390 miles (3,846 km) west of California, 3,850 miles (6,196 km) east of Japan, and 2,400 miles (3,862 km) north of the Marquesas Islands, home of the first seafaring Polynesian adventurers who came and discovered the islands.

made up of solid rock more than 50 miles (80 km) thick. These plates move less than one inch (two and a half centimeters) per year. Volcanoes and earthquakes are common where they come together. The Hawaiian chain is located on the Pacific Plate and was formed as the plate moved across a stationary "hot spot" or magma well (liquid lava) over a period of about 80 million years.

As the outpouring of magma piled up, a new island began to form from the hardened lava, eventually pushing its way above the surface of the ocean. Even as you read this, such an island is taking shape near the Big Island of Hawaii.

The major islands in the Hawaiian chain are Kauai, Niihau, Oahu, Molokai, Lanai,

Initially ruled by Polynesian warrior chiefs and kings, Hawaii today is populated by people of diverse races who bring with them their cultures, customs and religions.

Hawaii's early prosperity was founded on the whaling industry and in later years on sugar and pineapple production. Today it is the tourist industry that dominates and fuels the economy.

EIGHT UNIQUE ISLANDS

The islands are famed for their volcanoes, mysterious valleys, beautiful beaches and

OPPOSITE: Wild surf pounds Oahu's North Shore.
ABOVE: Signs of life in a desolate field of hardened lava on the Big Island.

A Fiery Birth

warm Pacific Ocean waters. Snow fields are less than 62 miles (100 km) from deserts, and deserts stand on the fringe of green forests.

Below are some facts which demonstrate Hawaii's uniqueness:

Measured from its base on the ocean floor to its snow-capped summit, Mauna Kea on the Big Island, at 33,476 ft (10,203 m), is the world's highest mountain.

Mauna Loa, whose summit is 13,677 ft (4,169 m) high and occupies 10,000 cubic miles (41,680 cubic km), is recognized as a perfect shield volcano and the largest volcanic mass in the world.

Mount Waialeale on Kauai with an annual rainfall of more than 450 inches (1,143 cm) is the wettest location on earth.

The Hawaiian islands claim some of the driest areas in existence, such as the Kau desert, and the most active volcano, Kilauea, both on the island of Hawaii.

The Alenuihaha Channel between Hawaii and Maui, which drops to a depth of 6,300 ft (1,920 m), is one of the deepest areas of the Pacific Ocean.

The islands have probably the balmiest, most beautiful weather in the world — right in the midst of hurricane tracks.

THE ISLAND CLIMATE

It's Hawaii's weather, along with all the state's attractions, that draws the million plus visitors to the islands each year.

Why are the islands so blessed? Much has to do with the manner in which they are aligned in a slanting pattern from northwest to southeast across the path of prevailing winds known as the northeast trades. These winds are generated out of an area of high pressure north of the islands, above which at a height of 35,000 ft (10,500 m) lies the subtropical jet stream. Winds are created when the jet stream interacts with the high pressure area, creating the cooling trades which blow at a constant 15 to 25 mph (25 to 40 kph). Without the trades, Hawaii would probably suffocate in humidity, as temperatures in summer range from 80°F (27°C) to above 90°F (32°C).

Remnants of old volcanoes and mountains stand in the path of the trades. At certain heights, when they strike these volcanic

mountains, the winds cool and condense to create rain. The rain belts on mountains are to be found at elevations of 1,970 to 2,950 ft (600 to 900 m), which is why the summits of Haleakala on Maui and of Mauna Kea and Kilauea on the Big Island are so dry. This is also why weather patterns vary so dramatically over the distance of a few miles.

Some islanders refer to the seasons not by spring, summer and fall, but as the "season of the winter storms," which falls between November and March, and the "season of the tropical storms," from April to November.

The winter storms bring cool, wet weather fairly consistently to Hawaii when the trade wind patterns are interrupted. This breakup takes place in high pressure belts and the

storms sweep in from the southeast to the leeward side, hence the term "Kona winds." During this period, surf runs high on the northern shores of the islands, influenced by areas of intense depression across the northern Pacific which sets up large wave patterns and draws the world's greatest surfers to these shores.

April to November is the season of the tropical storms when there are limited interruptions to the trade wind patterns. Beaches on the southern side of the islands are affected by winter storms in the southern hemisphere, and surf often runs high in these areas.

However, don't be put off by the thought of these storms and winds, for there is no bad time of the year to visit Hawaii; rarely does the poor weather lock in and ruin a vacation.

This makes it the ideal holiday destination, and by virtue of its colorful history and culture, truly unique — one of America's most fascinating states.

Waikiki sunset.

A Fiery Birth

Welcome
to Hawaii

ON A MORNING OF FINE MISTY RAIN, two huge rainbows arch across Manoa Valley on the island of Oahu in the Hawaiian islands chain. Commuters marvel at the shimmering pastel beauty of nature's handiwork.

The perfect rainbow requires a curious mix of sun and rain, ingredients with which the islands are amply blessed. And so common a phenomenon are they that the people of Hawaii have adopted the rainbow as a symbol; Hawaii is known as the Rainbow State.

If paradise is cornflower blue skies, warm Pacific waters which range from aqua to deep

the determination that the old ways must be preserved has taken root. The islands and their people are in the midst of a renaissance of Hawaiian art, music and culture which Western influences, promoted by the missionaries, once threatened to eradicate.

THE POLYNESIAN CONNECTION

Historical evidence indicates that the earliest inhabitants of these islands came from the Marquesas chain northeast of Tahiti. Perhaps they undertook these hazardous

blue tinged with lilac, sunsets which splash the skies and ocean with fiery oranges, reds and soft pinks, or beaches of white, black or green sand, then this is indeed Eden. Add to this riot of beauty exotic flowers that bloom in vibrant tropical shades, tranquil lagoons and beaches frothing with wild surf, soaring sea cliffs sculptured by centuries of battering by ocean swells—and we may have taken paradise to another dimension.

In the minds of millions, Hawaii remains a land of legend and fantasy — a land of gently waving palms and gorgeous maidens and strong, handsome men living idyllic lives. But the quickening pulse of modern Hawaii has meant a change in lifestyles for many. At the same time, in recent years,

voyages because of tribal wars or overcrowding on their islands, or both. Whatever the reasons, they braved the elements in sturdy double-hulled canoes, navigating by the sun, the stars, ocean swells, currents, and the migratory patterns of birds and marine life. It is not known how many voyages they undertook or how many lives were lost in this vast ocean often whipped by sudden and ferocious storms, before they sighted the lovely new land of wind and fire which was the island of Hawaii. It wasn't until several hundred years later that other Polynesian fleets from Tahiti landed here.

The Tahitians are said to have named the Big Island "Hawai'i," which later became the name of the entire island chain. Polynesians, like explorers throughout history, gave many of their discoveries names of their homelands. In Polynesia, the name "Hawaii" appears, with dialectical differences, as Savai'i in Samoa; as "Ra'iatea" in the Society Islands; and as "Havai'i" in Tahiti. In the ancient legends of the New Zealand Maoris, the homeland of their ancestors was called "Hawaiki."

CAPTAIN COOK AND HIS LEGACY

Westerners were unaware of the existence of these islands until the British explorer Captain James Cook sighted Oahu and landed on Kauai in January 1778. He named the group the Sandwich Islands after John Montague, the Fourth Earl of Sandwich and First Lord of the Admiralty.

Cook's command consisted of two British ships, *HMS Resolution* and *Discovery*; sailors from these vessels soon began to trade with the natives at Waimea, Kauai. Tragically, European diseases, including sexually transmitted diseases such as syphilis and gonorrhea, took their toll on the island. Historians note that from a population of about 300,000 at the time of Cook's visit, only 60,000 remained 80 years later.

Cook continued his voyage in search of the northwest passage linking the Atlantic to the Pacific Ocean, but he returned to Hawaiian waters in November 1778. After cruising off the islands for two months, the ships finally dropped anchor in Kealakekua Bay on the western, or Kona, side of the Big Island, at the height of an annual religious celebration honoring the deified ancestor Lono Ikamakahiki. A huge crowd greeted the British explorer and his crews, and Cook was honored and lavished with gifts.

Cook was at first thought to be Lono, who had sailed from Hawaii several generations earlier, promising to return.

On February 4, 1779, Cook set sail again, only to run into a fierce storm which was to change the course of history. The British explorer and his ships were forced back to the safety of Kealakekua Bay, but the mood this time was anything but festive. A brooding hostility prevailed due to several incidents that had occurred while the British were there earlier. The ruling chief, Kalaniopuu, after seeing so many of his female subjects

being taken by the sailors and kept on board, had imposed a *kapu* or ban, on the ships, making it punishable for the women to go on board. But the sailors were not to be denied and came ashore for the women, respecting neither the kapu, pertaining to the religion, nor the high chiefs. They also had no qualms about tearing down religious structures for firewood. Before their last departure, Cook and his men had also seriously depleted the district's food supply in provisioning their ships, and this had not been forgotten by the natives.

As antagonism between the foreigners and the Hawaiians grew, the ships and the sailors found themselves subjected to petty thievery. Matters came to a head when the cutter from the *Discovery* was stolen and a high chief was killed in the process of recovering it. Cook blocked the bay and went ashore with a party of marines to take Chief Kalaniopuu hostage, and in so doing broke the kapu forbidding the touching of the high chief by any but his own close relatives or retainers.

OPPOSITE: Painted escarpment LEFT of Haleakala Crater, Maui. Carved icons RIGHT at Puuhonua O Honaunua — The City of Refuge — Kealakekua Bay, Big Island. ABOVE: Sparse signs of life on Devastation Trail, Hawaii Volcanoes National Park.

A scuffle broke out between the landing party and the Hawaiians, and the marines were attacked by a large number of armed Hawaiian warriors. Using stones and clubs, they set upon Cook and his sailors, killing five of them including Cook himself who died in the bloodstained waters of Kealakekua Bay.

KAMEHAMEHA: WARRIOR KING

Upon the death of Kalaniopuu, somewhere around 1780–81, his son Kiwalao was de-

meha's victory at Nuuanu also won for him the islands of Molokai and Lanai.

Kamehameha planned at least two expeditions to conquer Kauai and its satellite island, Niihau, and to this day Kauai's people will tell you he was repulsed and sent back to Oahu. Others say he never reached Kauai because storms swamped much of his fleet.

Not until 1810 did Kaumualii, ruling chief of Kauai and Niihau, come to Oahu at the invitation of Kamehameha. It was agreed that Kaumualii would remain ruler of those

clared chief. But several other chiefs, dissatisfied with the manner in which Kiwalao was redistributing the land, convinced Kalaniopuu's nephew, Kamehameha, that he should try to wrest control of the island from his cousin.

For more than five years thereafter the islands were gripped by tribal wars. By 1796, Kamehameha had defeated his rival chiefs on Hawaii, Maui and Oahu. The turning point of the campaign occurred at Nuuanu Valley in 1795, where Oahu chief Kalanikupule and his allies attempted to make a stand. Kamehameha drove the defending forces up the Nuuanu Pali, where many soldiers of the Oahu army were driven over the cliffs by Kamehameha's warriors. Kameha-

islands, but be tributary to Kamehameha, until "the black tapa cloth [death] covered Kaumualii." When he died, his islands became part of Kamehameha's kingdom.

Kamehameha strengthened his hold on the islands by the wise application of the ancient feudal kapu system by which the chief held absolute power over his subjects, including that of life and death. Kamehameha gained a reputation as a wise, just and peaceful ruler. At his side during this period was his favorite wife, Kaahumanu. Kamehameha remained ever faithful to his ancient gods, never forsaking the religion of his forefathers even in the face of pressure and influence from the ever-increasing presence of Western civilization in Hawaii.

THE MISSIONARY INFLUENCE

When the great king died in 1819, Kaahumanu declared herself Queen Regent and ruled the land with her foster son Liholiho (Kamehameha II). Kaahumanu's influence on the history of the islands was considerable. Supported by Kamehameha II, she set about eliminating the kapu system by the simple act of dining together, which under the old laws had been forbidden.

Destruction of sacred temples and idols followed. Since the culture of Hawaii was deeply intertwined with religion, this had a profound effect on the people. Suppressive as it may seem to twentieth century Western thinking, the kapu system was one which had been perfected more than 1,000 years before the first contact with Europeans. It was a system which fitted the needs of, and was accepted by, the people.

Kaahumanu also came under the influence of American missionaries and spearheaded the drive to spread the gospel throughout the islands. This era marked the beginning of Hawaii's first period of modernization.

In 1823, Kamehameha II and his wife Queen Kamamalu embarked on a long voyage to Britain at the invitation of King George III. It proved to be tragic. After being royally entertained in London but before meeting King George, Kamehameha II and the Queen contracted measles and died. Their bodies were brought back to Hawaii.

Kamehameha's 10-year-old brother Kauikeaouli (Kamehameha III) succeeded him as king, but for the greater part of his 30-year reign, it was Kaahumanu who wielded the greatest influence on the people of the islands. In a development of considerable significance, Kaahumanu converted to Christianity, and many other Hawaiian leaders followed suit. The void which had been created by the banning of the kapu laws and a disavowing of the ancient gods was being filled by the new religion which swept the islands.

THE END OF A DYNASTY

Under the rule of Kamehameha III and Queen Kaahumanu, a new form of government began to take shape, and the capital of the nation was moved from Lahaina on Maui to Honolulu on Oahu. Kamehameha III earned a permanent place in Hawaiian history by bringing about a constitution and enacting new laws. When he died in 1854, leaving no legitimate heir, he was deeply mourned by his people. His successor, nephew and foster son Alexander Liholiho (Kamehameha IV), assumed leadership at the height of an economic boom in the islands set off by the whaling industry, of which Hawaii was one of the centers. Lahaina and Honolulu had become major whaling ports.

Kamehameha IV's nine-year reign was one of mixed fortunes for the people of the islands. The whaling industry soon went into decline as whales were indiscriminately killed and fuel other than whale oil began to appear on the market. The dreaded disease leprosy, brought in, it is said, by Chinese immigrants, spread like wildfire. Kamehameha IV died of an asthma attack in 1863 and was succeeded by his elder brother Lot (Kamehameha V). Kamehameha V ran the islands with dictatorial authority. He did away with the old constitution, which he felt had placed too much power in the hands of

OPPOSITE: A painting depicts Kamehameha the Great surrounded by his chiefs. ABOVE: Coat of arms guards the Iolani Palace gate in Honolulu.

the white business community, and had a new constitution drawn up. He also established a bureau of immigration which in turn began encouraging laborers to come to the islands to assist the growing sugar industry. Because Kamehameha V never married, his death signaled the end of the Kamehameha dynasty.

THE MERRIE MONARCH

And so began a new dynasty under an elected king or *alii* (nobleman). Prince William Ka-

naina, a descendant of a half brother of Kamehameha I, took the name Lunalilo. Lunalilo had many noble traits and may have become a fair and just ruler, but unfortunately he was partial to drink, brought about by a broken romance, and died 13 months into his reign.

Lunalilo was loved by the people and was known as the Citizen King. He requested that he be buried with his people. His tomb is on the grounds of Kawaiahao Church in Honolulu, the only monarch of the modern Hawaiian kingdom not to be buried at Mauna Ala (the royal mausoleum) in Nuuanu Valley, Oahu.

The man who succeeded Lunalilo was the man whom Lunalilo defeated in the election — Colonel David Kalakaua.

Kalakaua set about developing a British-style monarchy and, in the process, established royal standards in spending taxpayers' money. He had extravagant tastes, but he also had a vision of the world which was rare in his time. Kalakaua was a man of great intelligence and charm, and while he built a reputation as the Merrie Monarch, he also achieved several diplomatic triumphs. He was the first monarch from a foreign kingdom to visit Washington, and while there negotiated a reciprocal treaty with the United States, enabling Hawaii to sell its sugar cheaper by eliminating a tariff.

In 1881 he embarked on a world tour, the first monarch of any nation to do so. His first stop was Japan where he was feted by Emperor Matsuhito. From Japan, Kalakaua and his entourage went on to China, then through Asia to Europe. In London he was received by Queen Victoria and the Prince of Wales. Inspired by the pomp and pageantry of the British court, Kalakaua decided to have a coronation in Hawaii. It was a lavish and colorful affair.

The political scandals which followed the coronation weakened Kalakaua's grip on the nation he ruled. At the center of the trouble was the acquisition of much of Hawaii's prime land by a group of *haole* (white) businessmen. Hawaii's land problems today are a spill-over from this period in its history.

Kalakaua was keenly aware of the common ancestry of the Polynesian race and visited Samoa as a first step to establishing a United Kingdom of Oceania. He was hampered, however, by bad advisors at home, chiefly those in the American sugar community, and the efforts of such European powers as Germany and Great Britain that were determined to see that his dream would never come true. He was a man whose visions were far ahead of his time and far beyond the means of his small, young kingdom.

Kalakaua died in San Francisco in 1891.

THE FIFTIETH STATE

Kalakaua's sister, Liliuokalani, brought to the throne a passion for the rights of native Hawaiians and a determination to take power away from the white minority in the government. The task was to prove too great for her. Powerful business forces marshaled quickly against her, and with the assistance of sailors and marines from a visiting United States naval ship, they established a provisional government under Sanford B. Dole. They took control and forced the queen to abdicate.

It was an era of great bitterness in the islands and much political maneuvering. While President Grover Cleveland sought to reinstate Queen Liliuokalani, Dole and his supporters declared Hawaii a republic, with Dole as its president. Liliuokalani was placed under house arrest when she supported a counter-coup.

In 1898, Hawaii became a possession of the United States, with the backing of the new President McKinley, through the signing of the Joint Resolution of Annexation — an act which left native Hawaiians bitter and former President Cleveland "ashamed."

In 1900 Hawaii became a United States territory through the Organic Act.

In 1941 Hawaii survived the Japanese attack on Pearl Harbor that shifted United States awareness of the war to the Pacific. Following Japan's surrender in 1945 and the end of the war, there were moves to have Hawaii accepted into the union. This finally came about in 1959 when Hawaii — once a kingdom, then a republic, and finally an American territory — became the 50th state of the United States. Only the tiny island of Niihau, populated then, as it is now by people of Hawaiian ancestry, rejected statehood.

In the same year, the first commercial passenger jet touched down at Honolulu International Airport, opening Hawaii as a cultural, economic and political pathway between East and West. Modern Hawaii was born.

The post-statehood years were marked by the political leadership of Governor John Burns (1962–1973) and by a booming economy. Governor Burns was followed by his Lieutenant Governor, George Ariyoshi, who stood at the state's helm through 1986.

On a national level, Hawaii's most notable leader is World War II hero Daniel Inouye, who was first elected to the United States Congress in 1962 and today is still one of the United States' most accomplished senators.

Another local hero was Ellison Onizuka, Hawaii's first astronaut, who died when the space shuttle Challenger exploded on January 28, 1986.

Hawaii's location, blend of cultures, extraordinary natural beauty, and rich human resources give a unique distinction to the islands and add weight to its political standing. As Governor Burns stated in his 1966 inaugural address: "Our heritage and *aloha* spirit uniquely qualify us for Pan-Pacific leadership, and a new destiny. Our people have already stepped into the van-

guard of Pacific affairs. But there is much more we can do and which we must do to assume our rightful place in the Pacific sun."

King David Kalakaua would surely have agreed.

OPPOSITE: Hula, Hawaii's native dance is unique to the islands. ABOVE: Beloved Queen Liliuokalani is immortalized in this statue on the grounds of the state capitol.

Hawaii's Culture and Its People

A PANTHEON OF GODS

The culture of ancient Hawaii was once deeply entwined with religion. Life was lived according to sacred laws, or *kapu*, and religion, with its pantheon of gods, pervaded every aspect of life.

The religion was based on gods major and minor. The four major Hawaiian gods were also major gods in most of the southern Polynesian groups. Kane, known in the south as Tane, was revered as a god of creation, light and fresh water. He was the ancestor of chiefs and commoners alike. As the chief god of life-giving forces, no human sacrifice was ever made to him. Kanaloa, known in other parts of Polynesia as Ta'aroa, Tangaroa and Tagaloa, was god of the sea and constant companion of Kane. The freshwater springs in Hawaii were said to have been created by them. Ku, or Tu, was associated with the rising sun and was the god of masculine virility. He was appealed to in his various forms for many diverse favors, from rain to powers of sorcery. He was best known as the god of war. Lono, known as Rongo or Ro'o elsewhere, was said to be the last of the four great gods to arrive from Kahiki, one of the Hawaiians' ancient homelands. He was the god of agriculture, clouds, winds and fertility.

Of equal stature with these four major gods was Hina, probably the most well known of Polynesian goddesses. She and her mate Ku were said to have come to Hawaii before either Kane or Kanaloa. Hina was associated with the sunset and possessed all the female attributes complementing the ones of Ku. Together these two had the whole world as their realm along with all generations of mankind born and unborn.

There were many gods, all taking different forms—fish, birds, animals and humans. Their particular realms encompassed the whole world of the ancient Hawaiians. There were also demigods, part human, part god, who possessed supernatural powers and who committed many feats of strength and endurance.

Among the most famous of Hawaiian and Polynesian folk heroes was Maui, sometimes nicknamed the Trickster. He is credited throughout the Pacific with fishing up whole islands, slowing down the sun by snaring it, discovering fire, and other wondrous things. He, like the other demigods, was not worshipped or prayed to for help. But deeds of these legendary figures inspired and held men in awe for generations.

Of all the gods and demigods in the Hawaiian pantheon, perhaps the most feared and most revered is Pele, goddess of fire. Pele is believed to be an *'aumakua* or ancestor who lives on as a guardian spirit. Many modern Hawaiians still pay tribute to her and believe in her powers.

KAPU AND THE POWER OF LIFE AND DEATH

To appreciate Hawaii, not merely for its physical beauty but for its traditions and historic past, one must probe the mysteries of its culture, which were almost forgotten but are now being revived.

The kapu system, which Christian missionaries found too harsh and were determined to eliminate, had a fixed purpose in Hawaiian life which was little understood by Westerners. It was repressive and often appeared illogical, but it was designed for environmental, economic and ecological reasons, at the hub of which was the love and preservation of the land and the sea. In this system, ruling chiefs held the power of life and death over all their subjects. Human sacrifice was common.

As an example of the kapu system, let us look at the simple act of going fishing, as beloved by the Hawaiians today as it was by their ancestors. In order to fish, a fisherman had to know which fish were under kapu and therefore unavailable to him until such time as that kapu was lifted by the priest or high chief, a direct descendant of the gods. He had to know which type of fish, if any, were personifications of his *'aumakua* or family guardian spirit; such fish, of course, could never be eaten. And he had to ask the gods for permission to fish, reading their answer in signs such as the weather and waves. There were also certain items and foodstuffs he wasn't permitted to carry in his canoe to the fishing grounds. A portion of his first catch

Young dancers from the Polynesian Cultural Center, Laie, Oahu, garbed in feather capes.

had to be returned to the sea to appease the god of the sea. On reaching the shore, he was required to leave part of his catch at the *ku'ula* or local fishing shrine. Once home he had to know which types of fish the female members of his family were allowed to eat and which ones were strictly for males.

This scenario was enacted, to one degree or another, in every aspect of daily life, from the manufacturing of tools and weapons to the hewing of a canoe, from the planting of crops to the building of a house. Restrictive as it may seem, it was a system perfected for almost 10 centuries before Hawaiians first met Westerners.

The kapu system ensured the protection of natural resources. When it was eventually done away with, Hawaiians, with no god of the sea to answer to, overfished; in the forests they depleted the bountiful supply of sandalwood, so prized in the China trade. The chiefs used it to barter for Western tools, weapons and bolts of cloth from Western sea captains.

This trade signaled the end of the manufacture of local goods, and the ancient crafts began to disappear. Gardens and farms were neglected as people moved from their ancestral homes to be nearer the centers of commerce and trade. Indeed, neglect of the land or *'aina*, perhaps more than anything else, almost destroyed the Hawaiian race.

THE SELLING OF A HERITAGE

From time immemorial, each island was ruled by an aristocratic class of warrior-nobles called *alii*. Each alii could trace his lineage back dozens of generations through one or more lines to the founding godlike parents of the Polynesian race. These founders, Wakea the sky father and Papa the earth mother, were themselves traced back in time to the very beginning of life on earth.

The sovereign lord of each island was termed the *alii nui* (great chief). Generally this chief was the senior male member of the ruling family of the island. Under him were district chiefs, *alii 'ai moku*, literally "chiefs who eat the land." These chiefs were

appointed by the alii nui from younger members of the ruling family, or other favorites of his among the other alii families. When an alii died or was overthrown, and after his successor was settled upon, new district chiefs were appointed or the old ones were reconfirmed in their positions.

As a general rule, the common people, *maka'ainana*, were not affected by changes in rulers. As long as their taxes were paid in the form of produce from land or sea and/or craft work (mats, bowls, tapa cloth, etc.), they and their descendants were permitted to stay where they were.

The maka'ainana were also expected to answer the call to arms in times of war. The main difference between the Hawaiian maka'ainana and the serf class of medieval Europe was that the Hawaiian was free to leave his district or island if he thought living under a chief somewhere else would be better. Once proving himself loyal to his new chief, he could apply for a plot of land to work. His European counterpart, however, was tied to the same place from generation to generation and could leave only with the consent of the hereditary lord of the land.

In 1848, Kamehameha III, on the advice of *haole* (white) advisors, opened up the land for "fee simple" ownership, meaning that it became possible to purchase the land. One-third of the land was to be held by the king; one-third of the land was set aside for the chiefs and awarded on an individual basis. These lands could be sold. The last third was set aside to be applied for and awarded to the maka'ainana. To be awarded the land, one had to show cause based on living and working on the plot or *kuleana* in question for some length of time. Each applicant was interviewed individually with corroborating witnesses. Once he was awarded land in fee simple, the individual was free to do what he wished with his property.

Undoubtedly the king enacted this law with the welfare of his people in mind and with the intent of bringing the Hawaiian in line with modern Western culture. Instead, this act, coming before Hawaiians learned the western concept of land ownership, along with the overthrow of the monarchy, is regarded by native Hawaiians as one of the lowest points in Hawaiian history.

Carved icon guards Kamakahonu Heiau (temple) on the Big Island.

Title to property was practically given away to foreigners who were "crazy" enough to pay a few dollars for it. The average Hawaiian didn't know that by selling his land he was forever barring himself and his family from returning to the land he and his ancestors had lived on for so long. Family unity was eroded, ancestral roots lost, and the culture all but wiped out.

No segment of the culture was as hard hit by the interference of Christian missionaries as the dance or ancient hula. Considered sensual and indecent, public and private performances of hula were banned. As recently as 25 years ago, only the sedate kneeling hula was permitted to be performed by students of the Kamehameha Schools, a Protestant-oriented educational institute founded in 1887 by a Hawaiian princess exclusively for the purpose of educating children of native Hawaiian blood. Then, as now, teachers had to be Protestants. Thirty-five years ago, no course in the Hawaiian language or history was offered in this school's secondary grades. Fortunately, most of the school's puritanical thinking has since been left behind, and the school today is a prime collector and dispenser of Hawaiian artifacts and culture.

A CULTURAL RENAISSANCE

After nearly 200 years of erosion, Hawaiian culture is in the midst of a renaissance. Spurring this movement are many young college-educated Hawaiians who identify with their roots. Balancing this cultural equation are a small number of *kupuna* (grandparents or relatives from a generation of grandparents), who, having retained knowledge of Hawaiian culture passed down from their kupuna, have joined forces with the younger generation to lead this resurgence. Hawaiians in ever-increasing numbers are immersing themselves in the movement to relearn the old ways. Featherwork, wood carving and *lei* (garland) making in the ancient style are some of the traditional arts making a comeback. Interest in the Hawaiian language has never been higher.

But none of these skills has matched the passion for the hula that the renaissance has brought about.

The origin of the hula has been obscured by time. What was recorded by early European visitors to Hawaii and what has been passed down by Hawaiians show that its roots lay in religious ceremonies. To become a dancer one had to be chosen young by the *kahuna* (priest of the temple) and turned over to a *kumu hula* (dance master) for years of training. When the kuma hua determined that the student was fully versed and prepared in all aspects — religious, mental and physical — an *'uniki* or graduation ceremony was held.

The Protestant missionaries from New England, who first arrived in 1820, pressured the chiefs to abolish the "lascivious native dances," but it was Queen Kaahumanu, who became a Protestant in 1830, who issued an edict against public performance of the hula. In the 20 years that followed, the teaching and performing of the hula went underground.

In 1851, public performances were once again permitted, but strictly controlled by licensing and the levying of heavy fees for each performance. Private performances

There is some disagreement among scholars about what happened after a student graduated. Some say that all dances were performed for purely religious reasons, such as in supplication or worship of the gods. Most formal religious ceremonies were held within the confines of the *heiau* (temple) grounds, and since these grounds were considered *kapu* (in this sense sacred), this would have barred female dancers from participating; women were not allowed within confines of the heiau.

Since it has been recorded by early visitors that women did participate in dances, it is believed by other scholars that the hula was performed not only for religious purposes, but also for entertainment and enjoyment.

were another matter altogether. By the 1860s, clandestine schools were operating throughout the islands, much to the chagrin of Hawaiian and haole Protestants alike.

In 1863, Lot Kamehameha ascended the throne as Kamehameha V, following the death of his brother Alexander Liholiho, Kamehameha IV. Lot has often been referred to as "the last great chief of the olden type."

Being true to the ideals of his grandfather, Kamehameha I, he believed in the king's right to rule firmly and justly over the people of Hawaii. He also viewed the constitution as too liberal, especially in areas promoting the business interests of a handful of foreign-born people, and refused to take the oath maintaining the constitution of 1852 — a gesture which earned him the hostility of the foreign business community.

It is not surprising then that during his reign the chiefs openly reverted to the old custom of having *po'e hula,* people associated with Hawaiian dance, in their retinues, both at home and during their travels between islands. This, of course, did not do much for the king's popularity among the Christian community.

It was during the reign of King Kalakaua that the hula regained full, if not enthusiastic, acceptance. Before his coronation ceremo-

Today, just as in the times of the ancients, the hula student goes through rigorous and careful training of mind and body. No two kumu hula teach exactly in the same manner. What is emphasized in one *halau* (dance school) may not be strictly adhered to in another.

Usually when the po'e hula are arguing over the styles of the various halaus, someone will repeat the old Hawaiian admonishment — *"A'ole i pau ke'ike i ka halau ho'okahi"* (All knowledge is not taught in one school), and the bickering stops.

nies in 1883 and again before his 50th birthday "jubilee" in 1886, various kumu hula spent months teaching chants and dances to their students.

Much of the art of ancient hula was lost during the early half of the nineteenth century through religiously inspired repression. Consequently most of what is known and performed today in the ancient style of dance is what was passed down from the mid-to-late 1800s.

If the interpretive movements of today's *kahiko* or ancient dance have not been passed down in a strictly unadulterated manner, it has not lessened the oneness the modern Hawaiian feels with his forebears when witnessing or participating in hula kahiko.

Students in a halau learns about Hawaiian language and culture as they learn the movements of the dance. The student learns of Laka, the goddess of the dance, and what plants are sacred to her. They also learn the names and stories of the ancient chiefs and heroes of the Hawaiian people. Pele, the fire goddess, and her sister, Hi'iaka, are prominent in the legends learned through chants and dances.

Pele and her family are said to have come to Hawaii from Kahiki well after these islands had been originally settled by southern Poly-

OPPOSITE: No mistaking the message at a special show for island visitors at the Waikiki Shell, Oahu. ABOVE: For over three decades, the hula was banned by Christian missionaries. Now it is in the midst of a revival.

nesians. She is referred to by older Hawaiians as a *malihini* (newcomer) among the old gods. Nevertheless, she is remembered today in chant and dance much more than some of the more powerful gods. Many island-born people, Hawaiian and non-Hawaiian alike, claim either to have seen her spirit or to know a friend or relative who has.

Pele sometimes appears as an old woman in white hitchhiking on a deserted stretch of road, who, after being picked up, disappears from the back seat of the car. At other times she appears in the countryside as a

beautiful young woman in red, often preceding a volcanic eruption on the Big Island. She has appeared to more than one family just before a lava flow has suddenly and inexplicably been diverted around their house. Pele lives!

Her home at Kilauea Crater on the Big Island is visited regularly by people bearing gifts of ohelo berries, pork or her favorite brand of gin, which are tossed into the crater. Chief among those who go to Pele's home to do her honor are various hula halaus. They make their pilgrimage every year before participating in the Merrie Monarch Festival dance competition in Hilo.

The hula kahiko is danced to the accompaniment of *oli* (chanting), and only traditional Hawaiian instruments are used such as the *pahu* (large shark skin-covered drum), the *puniu* (coconut shell drum tied to the leg), *kala'au* (sticks usually used by dancers), *ipu* (gourd used as percussion instrument), *'uli 'uli* (seed-filled gourds with feather tops used by dancers), *'ili 'ili* (small smooth stones used like castanets by dancers) and the *pu'ili*

(lengths of bamboo, roughly one and a half feet (half a meter) in length, partially split and used by dancers).

The *hula 'auana* (literally the moving from place to place or wandering dance—the term today usually means "modern hula") was born in the years immediately following the overthrow of the Hawaiian monarchy in 1893. Its conception, however, probably occurred some 20 to 30 years earlier, during Kalakaua's reign. During that time, many traditional dances were coupled with the dances of Europe, such as the minuet and flamenco. New foreign musical instruments were used as accompaniment together with traditional Hawaiian instruments. Today, many of the instruments introduced during the Kalakaua era, such as the ukulele (from Portugal), the guitar, and the bass viola are looked upon as "Hawaiian."

In the mid-1880s a young Hawaiian boy by the name of Joseph Kekuku discovered that by pressing a length of smooth metal to the strings of a guitar and sliding it from fret to fret, it produced a beautiful sound. Thus was born the steel guitar, still popular in Hawaiian music and adopted in American country and western music. The unique style of dancing during this period was called *hula ku'i* (joined or spliced together dancing).

By the beginning of the twentieth century, after the overthrow of the monarchy, what little of the original culture, *mele* (song), and hula that had been retained was discarded or went underground again.

To fill the musical void of this period a new breed of Hawaiian entertainment took root. As tourism increased, musicians began writing songs, mostly in English, with a ragtime beat, to meet the demand for "exciting native dances." The lyrics shallow, and the dancer's movements became nothing more than a blur of exaggerated hip swaying, shimmying torsos and undulating abdomens, accompanied by rolling eyes, waving arms and "come up and see me sometime" smiles (enough to make the missionaries turn in their graves).

Hula troupes began touring the globe performing this pseudo-Hawaiian style of entertainment. By 1920, "Hawaiian" music was all the rage. All-white troupes were the toast of Broadway and the ukulele was the college fraternity man's status symbol. The grass skirt (born in this era) began to give way to brightly colored cellophane skirts, as Hollywood promoted lavish "South Sea" movies.

At the end of World War II and into the 1950s and 1960s, hula 'auana, as we know it today, was perfected. The modern Hawaiian dance began to take on a deeper meaning and the movements became more fluid and stately, with only a hint of sensuality. True hula kahiko was still in hibernation, but the Hawaiian people were beginning to reclaim the hula as an art form, not just entertainment.

However, due to the subtleties of style that modern dances were taking, the tourists were getting bored. No more would Hawaiian girls wiggle their way through such popular numbers as "Yacka Hula Hickey Doola!" To hold the tourist trade together, Samoan knife dancers began doing their thing alongside their female Hawaiian cousins. "Female" is stressed here, as public male dancing, an important part of the old culture, had died out by the turn of the century, with the exception of a few comic hula dancers such as Sol Bright and Sterling Mossman.

By the early 1960s, troupes of Tahitian dancers were also added, and Polynesian revues were being presented at many Waikiki hotels and nightclubs. The Tahitian dancer brought back to the tourist his ever-abiding delight in gyrating hips and grass skirts. Everybody was happy.

It was the mainland civil rights movement which prodded Hawaiians to ask themselves: "If African Americans, Hispanic Americans and Native Americans are making themselves heard, and in doing so regaining their self-esteem, what about Hawaiian Americans?"

In search of a cause to use as a rallying point, the Hawaiians turned to the hula kahiko. There's a wide divergence of style and teaching methods, and much of what is taught as hula kahiko is mainly what has been handed down in a diluted form from that which was known 100 to 140 years ago — a lot has had to be improvised due to lack of verifiable knowledge. But this improvisation has never been haphazard. Instinct and spiritual inspiration have guided the Kumu hula.

These days there are a handful of kumu hula kupuna left, but there are many more young, promising kumu hula carrying on the revered traditions (see also FESTIVE FLINGS, page 59).

THE PEOPLE OF THE ISLANDS

Look at the faces of the people on the streets of the Hawaiian islands. The racial and ethnic mix that you see are in a sense what Hawaii is all about. Nations around the world pay lip service to racial harmony, but

few have achieved it on the grand scale that Hawaii has. It is the strength of the state.

While the North American continent owes much of its vitality to the European migrant, Hawaii derives its ethnic uniqueness from the many ethnic groups of the Asian subcontinent. The people of the islands take pride in what they have achieved through racial and religious tolerance.

Ask a resident of the islands what his ethnic background is, and you may have to leaf through a geography book to understand the answer. Try this for size: "Chinese, Japanese, Portuguese, Irish, and of course, a little bit of Hawaiian." You'll hear that last line often: Many Hawaiians are proud of the Polynesian blood which flows through their veins.

Individually, the various nationalities that make up the racial and ethnic mix of the islands are proud of their heritage. Collectively, it is

OPPOSITE: Modernized and admittedly garish versions of the hula are mixed with high technology for the enjoyment of tourists. ABOVE: The ritualistic fire-knife dance lives on, a standard stop of the tourist trail.

the acceptance of all peoples and their cultures that makes Hawaii so remarkable.

The influx of migrants from the far-flung corners of the Pacific and Asia filled a vital need for laborers to work the sugar and pineapple plantations. Most who came stayed, and their children perpetuated the bloodline.

The first great wave of immigrants was the Chinese in 1852. They were followed by the Japanese (1885), the Koreans (1903), the Filipinos (1906, although a group of musicians are said to have settled here in 1888), and the Samoans (1952).

JAPANESE

Today, the Japanese Americans probably wield the greatest influence in the islands, particularly in politics. But they paid for this right with blood, sweat and tears. Thanks to their stoicism, patience and hard work, and that of other migrant Asian labor, the sugar and pineapple industries prospered.

In 1985, the Japanese community celebrated the 100th anniversary of the arrival of the Kanyaku Imin, the first contract labor-

HAOLES

The largest racial group in the islands today are the Caucasians, or *haoles*. They include descendants of many European settlers, particularly the Portuguese, who were the first European migrants to set foot in these islands in 1878. Around 1830, Spanish-Mexican cowboys were imported from California to work and train native cowboys. They came to be known as *paniolo* (from the Hawaiian pronunciation of "español," Spanish). Next came the Puerto Ricans in 1900. The sugar and pineapple plantations also imported labor from Austria, Russia, Spain, Italy and Germany, but few stayed long enough to make an impact on the demography of the state.

ers hired to work on sugar plantations. The initial boatload numbered 700 laborers, many accompanied by their families. They were selected from 30,000 applicants. The rush to volunteer was spurred by economic depression in their homeland. Food and work were scarce and poverty was widespread.

So they came to Honolulu aboard the *City of Tokyo*, bringing with them their customs, traditions, and modes of dress. They were the first of a wave. In the next nine years more than 28,000 Japanese laborers came to work in the plantations of Hawaii for $15 a month ($9 wage and $6 food allowance).

Plantation life was brutally hard. Men and women hacked their way through cane field after cane field under a pitiless sun, their skin left split and bleeding by the sharp-edged cane leaves. Cane was cut into huge bundles and then hoisted on bruised shoulders to be dumped into waiting carts for transportation to the mills. Conditions at the mills were not any better. If it was hot outside, it was hell indoors, and boiler operators suffered the most, afflicted by the terrible heat and the head-splitting noise of the machinery.

The plantation workers' day began at 4:30 AM. Twelve hours later their day ended, and for most of that day they were at the mercy of the *luna*, or foreman, armed with

obliged to cook in their rooms. At other plantations several hundred persons of both sexes are also mixed up and kept in one large, square house without any partition in it. Their sleeping bunks are long shelves of rough wooden boards, consisting of four stories. These shelves run in a row about 35 or 40 ft [10.5 or 12 m] long. Six or eight rows of these shelves constitute sleeping apartments of several hundred laborers in a single room. Each bottom shelf in every row is given to one married couple, the other three upper shelves being given to single men."

a whip which he was not slow to use if he thought his charges were flagging. Brutality became a way of life on the plantations, and the lunas were spoken of in the folk songs of the labor gangs, such as:

"Wonderful Hawaii, or so I heard
One look and it seems like Hell
The manager's the Devil and
His lunas are demons."

Living quarters on the plantations were so squalid that in 1899 Japanese Consul General Miki Saito filed this complaint after visiting plantations on Maui and Hawaii: "At one camp six families are forced to stay in a house of 12 by 30 ft [three and a half by nine meters] without any partitions, and there is no cook-house furnished for them, they being

Eventually the Japanese began to resist the mistreatment in subtle ways, sometimes by refusing to obey orders, by slowing down production and by acts of sabotage. When all else failed, the workers resorted to arson. Plantation profits suffered.

Desertion became commonplace. Riots broke out among Japanese and Chinese laborers. Joji Nakayama, the Immigration Bureau's chief inspector of Japanese workers, clamped down hard on the workers in an effort to please plantation owners, and even succeeded in reducing the wage contract from $15 to $12.50 a month for which he was rewarded with a $2,000 bonus.

Four faces of modern Hawaii reflect its diversity.

Plantation owners imported 26,103 Japanese contract laborers in 1899, the most in a single year. As things got rougher, many Japanese laborers escaped to the West Coast of the mainland United States. Those who stayed worked even harder to make a life for themselves and their families. Conditions and wages improved somewhat after the 1900s, though the scourge of the luna and his whip remained on some plantations.

Amidst soaring plantation profits (sugar barons netted $22 million in 1908), the clamor for higher wages reached a fever

being paid $22 with the promise that a bonus system would be instituted. The strike and its aftermath gave the Japanese in Hawaii self-respect and a newborn dignity.

CHINESE

Although there are records of Chinese living in Hawaii as early as 1802, the first group of around 2,000 laborers from China, mostly Hakkas and Puntis, arrived January 3, 1852. They were followed seven months later by a group of 100.

pitch, culminating in the formation of the Higher Wages Association, which called for a wage increase from $18 to $22.50. The Sugar Planters Association flatly refused the demand.

In June 1909, some 7,000 Japanese workers from the leading plantations on Oahu went on strike. This led to an eviction order by the Sugar Planters Association, and Honolulu was turned into a vast "refugee" camp. Eventually the strike leaders were jailed for four months and the strike crushed, but it cost the plantations $2 million and it eventually accomplished what it set out to do — improve the wages and living conditions of Japanese plantation labor. Less than three months after the strike, sugar workers were

The Chinese, for the most part, worked hard, saved their money and married Hawaiians. Through the generations, they have totally integrated, yet have managed, perhaps more than other ethnic groups, to preserve their language, their religion, and their culture. Their festivals, such as Chinese New Year, are observances in which all residents of Hawaii seem to participate.

As the Chinese community grew in affluence and influence, many left to take up residence on the loftier slopes in the better residential districts of Honolulu. Yet old habits die hard, and when the urge for dim sum, snake soup, salted eggs, salted fish or herb tea grips the soul, even the wealthy succumb to the temptation and gravitate to the narrow, sometimes dingy back streets of Chinatown.

The back streets haven't changed from the days when the Chinese revolutionary movement took shape under Sun Yat Sen, the founder of modern China. Sun Yat Sen graduated from Iolani School in Honolulu in 1882 at the age of 16. The youthful Sun returned to China to study medicine, but came back to Hawaii seeking support for his revolution. That is why China's history books credit Hawaii as being "the Cradle of the Chinese Republic." Sun's brother, Sun Ah Mi, owned an 800-acre (324-hectare) ranch in Kula, Maui, and Sun Yat Sen was a frequent visitor there. When the revolution proved successful, there were celebrations in many Chinese communities around the world. The community in Kula was no exception.

FILIPINOS

The majority of Filipinos in Hawaii today are Ilocanos, from Ilocos Norte. Many of the earliest Filipino immigrants had macho reputations as "hell raisers," brought about, it is said, by a shortage of women. Fights over women were common, most settled with knives rather than fists. But the reputation they established in the old days as good labor union organizers prevails.

The Filipinos have made a niche for themselves in the islands, their contributions being in areas of business, politics, and music.

KOREANS

The first party of 100 Koreans arrived in Hawaii in 1903. They were hired by the Hawaiian Sugar Planters' Association. By 1905, their numbers had risen to more than 7,000.

It was in Honolulu that Syngman Rhee, the Korean patriot, fostered his revolutionary plans. Following Japan's defeat in World War II, he became the Republic of Korea's first president. Deposed by a military coup in 1960, Rhee lived in exile in Hawaii until his death five years later.

The Korean community continues to thrive in Hawaii. They are a strong, passionate people who love parties. Korean restaurateurs and businesspeople often hold prominent positions in local communities.

SAMOANS

Since Samoans are Polynesians, it was relatively easy for the first big group of Samoans, who arrived in 1952, to adapt to the lifestyle here, even though the pace was faster than they were used to in American Samoa. There were, however, some cultural differences.

Many of the new wave of Samoans coming to the islands are Mormons and gravitate to Laie on the North Shore of Oahu, site of the Mormon Temple and the Polynesian Cultural Center, run by Mormons.

While some members of the Samoan community find it hard to get jobs in a limited job market, the is not true for Samoan athletes who have already made names for themselves in professional football. There are several Hawaiian Samoans playing in National Football League teams on the mainland and in colleges throughout the country.

PORTUGUESE

Most of the Portuguese immigrants came to Hawaii from the Azores and Madeira islands, after an arduous sea voyage. They brought their families with them, intending to stay. A total of 17,500 were recruited between 1878 and 1887. By 1910, it is said, the Portuguese population had exceeded the Chinese. Portuguese contributions to the Hawaiian lifestyle include the ukulele and wonderful Portuguese food, including *malasada* (a light doughnut), Portuguese bean soup and spicy sausage. But there is little architectural evidence of the Portuguese presence such as you find in Macau, 40 miles (65 km) from Hong Kong, and Melaka in Malaysia.

SOUTHEAST ASIANS

The latest wave of immigrants have come from the war-torn nations of Southeast Asia — Vietnam, Cambodia, Laos and Thailand. They have brought with them their religious beliefs, customs and cuisines. All have been made welcome and are integrating into the Hawaiian lifestyle and making their own contributions to it.

Entries in the Miss Chinatown pageant and their escorts parade down a rainy Honolulu avenue.

Oahu
The Gathering Place

OAHU

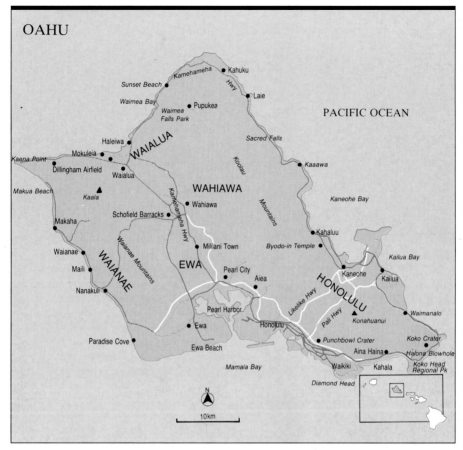

PACIFIC OCEAN

Kahuku
Sunset Beach
Waimea Bay
Pupukea
Laie
Kamehameha Hwy
Waimea Falls Park
Sacred Falls
Haleiwa
WAIALUA
Kaena Point
Mokuleia
Dillingham Airfield
Waialua
Kaaawa
Koolau
Makua Beach
Kaala
WAHIAWA
Wahiawa
Kaneohe Bay
Schofield Barracks
Mountains
Kahaluu
Makaha
Waianae
Waianae Mountains
Mililani Town
Byodo-in Temple
Kailua Bay
Maili
EWA
Pearl City
Kaneohe
Kailua
Kamehameha Hwy
Nanakuli
Aiea
HONOLULU
Pearl Harbor
Likelike Hwy
Waimanalo
Paradise Cove
Ewa
Honolulu
Pali Hwy
Konahuanui
Koko Crater
Ewa Beach
Punchbowl Crater
Aina Haina
Halona Blowhole
Mamala Bay
Waikiki
Kahala
Koko Head Regional Pk
Diamond Head

N
10km

Population: 836,231
Capital city: Honolulu
Area: 607.7 sq miles (1,574 sq km)
Length: 44 miles (71 km); *width:* 30 miles (48 km)
Highest elevation: 4,020-ft (1,225-m) Mt. Kaala
Coastline: 112 miles (180 km)
Airport: Honolulu International
Seaports: Honolulu Harbor, Ala Wai Harbor, Kewalo Basin
Flower: Ilima

He Ahiahi Kapu No Kuihewa
It is the evening sacred to Kuihewa
I Kukaniloko, I Lihue, Ilaila Ka Pa Awaawahia O Ke Kapu
At Kukaniloko, at Lihue, there is the terrible enclosure of the Kapu
O Ko Kuihewa Awahia I Malania
Kuihewa's strict kapu that was declared
O Kuihewa, Kakuihewa, Kuihewa O Ka Uauapena
Kuihewa, Kakuihewa, Kuihewa of the colored garment
O Ko Lakou Ahiahi I Lihue
For them the evening at Lihue
Oahu: The Gathering Place

FROM THE DAYS of the first tourists to these islands, the two images most identified with Hawaii have been Waikiki Beach and Diamond Head. For almost a century nothing has occurred to change this. Every island has marketed its attractions with a passion, but if you were to survey the traveler and ask the question: "What landmark do you associate most with Hawaii?" chances are that the response would be one or the other of these two Oahu landmarks.

Despite competition from its neighbor islands, Oahu continues to attract tourists and the international business community to its shores. Its commercialism notwithstanding, Oahu is still a fun place to visit. While it may not have the scenic drama of some of the other islands, it has 112 miles of coastline, the world's greatest surfing beaches on its north and west shores, and a wonderful marine

---

Reclining at dusk at water's edge in Waikiki.

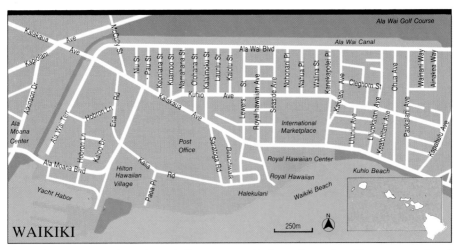

WAIKIKI

life park in Hanauma Bay. Best of all, it remains the entertainment and cultural center of the state. Oahu is today what it has been from the days of Hawaiian royalty: the Gathering Place.

WAIKIKI

Fun and entertainment combined with great weather and fabulous beaches bring the tourists to Oahu, and it's to the district of Waikiki Beach that most of them gravitate.

Waikiki, a subdivision of Honolulu, covers an area about two miles (three kilometers) long and less than half a mile (one kilometer) wide. It is bounded along its width by the ocean on one side and the Ala Wai Canal on the other, and is sandwiched on its flanks by two lovely parks, Kapiolani on its eastern boundary and Ala Moana on the west.

Waikiki's points of interest, in addition to its beach and luxury hotels, are its fine little zoo and aquarium. Behind the zoo is the **Waikiki Shell**, where watching the moon rise above Diamond Head while listening to a great performer is one of this island's special pleasures. **Kapiolani Park** has become internationally famous as a venue for kite flying competitions. You can buy or rent kites at a nearby store, and even get a lesson in the art.

Waikiki was once mostly swamp. Then it made a natural transition to agriculture and rice paddies; taro patches and duck ponds flourished. The beach, however, had long since been discovered by Hawaiian royalty who considered it their playground.

Today, where the alii once surfed and frolicked, the commoner now languishes, soaking up the sun's rays in the sometimes painfully obsessive quest for a tan.

Waikiki is exciting, loud, and sometimes garish. But for all that, its tree-lined streets and beach walks remain charming. The pulse of the place quickens as the sun starts to go down, for Waikiki offers front row seats to the some of the world's most memorable sunsets. And when the lights finally come on, a broad range of entertainment unfolds until dawn.

While the bustle and liveliness of the area can be a bit confusing, Waikiki is easily navigable. All that one has to bear in mind is that it has three streets running parallel to the ocean. **Kalakaua Avenue** is a one-way street running west to east towards Diamond Head; **Kuhio Avenue** is a two-way street running the length of the district. **Ala Wai Boulevard** runs one way, east to west. These three streets are connected by a network of side streets.

WHERE TO STAY

As befits its reputation as a premier tourist destination, Waikiki has a hotel to suit every taste and every pocketbook. At the basic level, a standard double room comes with a continental breakfast but no other hotel services. Medium-priced hotels have a coffee shop but not always room service. At major hotels, in the three-digit dollar category, you can expect more comprehensive room and valet service, additional restaurants, discos, fitness rooms and ready advice on events on the premises and off, such as helicopter tours, big game fishing, and seasonal events. "Resort" indicates a luxury hotel with more extensive grounds in which a combination of aquatic activities, golf, tennis and jogging paths are available to guests.

Staying in Waikiki has the virtue of convenience, and indeed some of the finest hotels on Oahu are there, in excellent locations often right on the beach.

The first hotel on Waikiki's Kalakaua Avenue opened in 1901 amid much fanfare. Then called the Moana, it was created by succession. Among the long list of those who have stayed at the Moana are the Prince of Wales, the late Lord Louis Mountbatten, Amelia Earhart and Alice Roosevelt Longworth.

In 1989, the Moana underwent a $50 million facelift, merged with its sister Sheraton hotel, the Surfrider, and was renamed the **Sheraton Moana Surfrider ℂ** (808) 923-2800 TOLL-FREE (800) 325-3535 FAX (808) 923-5984, 2365 Kalakaua Avenue, Honolulu, HI 96815 (expensive to luxury). It remains what it always was, the "First Lady of Waikiki," an

renovating the house of Walter C. Peacock and adding guest cottages.

Oliver Traphagen, a well-known Minnesota architect of that period, created the hotel in the colonial style using only wood. Each guest floor was furnished in a different fine wood — oak, mahogany or maple. A feature of the old hotel was its roof garden, a place to dance the night away or take in the sweeping views of Diamond Head and the ocean that literally rolled onto the doorstep of the hotel. The elegance of the building, combined with its fine service, brought guests back time and again.

The hotel's first guests were said to be a group of Shriners who paid $1.50 per night for their rooms. Celebrities followed in quick

elegant, classic hotel. All who walk through the hotel's grand columns are instantly reminded of its gracious past. From the striking Palladian windows that frame the ocean, to the sweeping Banyan Verandah, guests are never far away from nostalgic comfort. The centerpiece of this beachfront property is the ancient banyan tree beneath which Robert Louis Stevenson once wrote his famous lines.

The hotel has 791 rooms, including 44 suites, three restaurants, two cocktail lounges, a two-tiered outdoor verandah and an oceanfront beach bar.

The Waikiki skyline and beach with the outline of the "Pink Lady" in the foreground.

The **Ship's Tavern** (very expensive) is the hotel's signature restaurant — widely acclaimed for its seafood. Favorites include the New England-style Moana classic clam chowder and opakapaka with papio.

The National Trust for Historic Preservation lists the Moana Surfrider in the National Register of Historic Places.

The **Halekulani Hotel (** (808) 923-2311 TOLL-FREE (800) 367-2343 FAX (808) 926-8004 WEBSITE http://www.halekulani.com, 2199 Kalia Road, Honolulu, HI 96815-1988 (expensive to luxury), located on Gray's Beach, was

built in 1917 as a private residence and converted into what many believe is today the finest hotel on the island. It is the second oldest hotel on the strip. Plush and elegant, the Halekulani is recognized internationally for its good taste and personalized service. Check-in is done in your room, extra-deep bathtubs (and complimentary bathrobes) with separate showers await you, and fresh flowers adorn every corner of these flawless and exquisitely designed rooms.

At sunset the Halekulani's **House without a Key** has the best view in Waikiki and serves cocktails from 5 PM to 8:30 PM daily to the accompaniment of Hawaiian guitar music. In addition, hula is performed every night between 6 PM and 8 PM.

La Mer ((808) 923-2311 (very expensive), the Halekulani's French neoclassic restaurant, echoes the hotel's high standards. The influence of consultant French chef Philippe Chavant of the well-known La Tour Rose in Lyon is reflected in the artistry of the presentations, as well as the excellence of La Mer's cuisine. Chef de Cuisine Yves Garnier conjures up a seasonal menu, including exotically flavored salads and superb fish entrées. La Mer is one of only 15 restaurants in the United States to be awarded five diamonds by the American Automobile Association. It is also a winner of the Travel–Holiday Award and was chosen as one of the 10 most romantic restaurants in the world by Robin Leach, host of the television program, *Lifestyles of the Rich and Famous*.

The adjacent **Waikiki Parc Hotel (** (808) 921-7272 TOLL-FREE (800) 237-9666 FAX (808) 923-1336, 2233 Helumoa Road, Honolulu HI 96815 (mid-range to expensive), is a well-situated and lower-priced alternative to the Halekulani.

The **Royal Hawaiian (** (808) 923-7311 TOLL-FREE (800) 325-3535 FAX (808) 924-7098 WEBSITE http://www.royal-hawaiian.com, 2259 Kalakaua Avenue, Honolulu, HI 96815 (expensive), a sumptuous hotel built in 1927, and the grande dame of Hawaiian hotels certainly deserves its native nickname, "The Pink Lady." Its Spanish–Moorish-style architecture, coral-pink stucco, and French provincial decor make it one of Waikiki's most charming attractions. The Royal Hawaiian has 527 rooms and 49 suites, a lovely tropical garden, the **Surf Room** restaurant (expensive), and a beachfront bar.

The **Hyatt Regency Waikiki (** (808) 734-0000 WEBSITE http://www.hyatt.com, 2424 Kalakaua Avenue, Honolulu, HI 96815 (expensive to luxury), has a glamorous image with a wide range of offerings. A block-long labyrinthine complex, it contains several shops, restaurants and a waterfall.

Outrigger Hotels ((303) 369-7777 TOLL-FREE (800) 688-7444 FAX (303) 369-9403 WEBSITE http://www.outrigger.com E-MAIL reservations@outrigger.com (mid-range to luxury), is the chain that Californian Roy Kelley launched with just a few dollars in his pocket. The Kelley family went on to become Waikiki's biggest landlords, the family empire now totaling 20 hotels on Oahu alone, two on Kauai, two on the Big Island, and four on Maui. The flagship hotel of the group is the 530-room **Outrigger Waikiki** on the beach. Situated in this property is the legendary Duke's Canoe Club restaurant (inexpensive), named after the great Hawaiian swimmer and surfer Duke Kahanumoku. You don't have to be a tycoon yourself to book a room in the Outrigger chain.

The **Hilton Hawaiian Village (** (808) 949-4321 TOLL-FREE (800) HILTONS FAX (808) 947-7898 WEBSITE http://www.hilton.com/hawaii/hawaiianvillage/index.html, 2005 Kalia Road, Honolulu, HI 96815 (expensive), is Waikiki's only self-contained resort. You can come here, spend several days and never leave the resort, yet experience that dreamed-of Hawaiian holiday. From the hotel's rooms in multiple high-rises — Diamond Head, Tapa and Rainbow Towers — there are views of three pools, a private lagoon, and the largest beach in Waikiki. There's also a great shopping center.

The **Colony Surf Hotel,** Colony Hotel and Resorts **(** (808) 922-1928 TOLL-FREE (800) 367-6046 FAX (808) 526-2017, 2895 Kalakaua Avenue, Honolulu, HI 96815 (mid-range to luxury), is an intimate, tastefully decorated hotel where the accent is on personalized service. The lavish 1,000-sq-ft (93-sq-m) suites have expansive views and come with full kitchens and twice-daily maid service. Most of the guests return year after year.

Condé Nast Traveler rated the **Hawaii Prince Hotel (** (808) 956-1111 TOLL-FREE (800) WESTIN-1 FAX (808) 946-0811 WEBSITE http://www.westin.com/listings/index.html, 100 Holomoana Street, Honolulu, HI 96815 (expensive to luxury) among the 500 best hotels in the world. It's not difficult to understand why. Located at the gateway to Waikiki overlooking the picturesque Ala Wai Yacht Harbor, it compensates for its lack of real gardens by making the most of great design elements in its 33-story rose-colored, Italian marble and glass edifice. The fifth floor is a luxury terrace that includes a pool, sundeck and terraces for sunset viewing and drinks. The Prince has several dining facilities including the **Promenade Deck** for poolside dining and cocktails; the **Hakone** (moderate) and **Takanawa** (moderate), two Japanese restau-

rants, and the **Prince Court** (expensive), which specializes in Hawaii regional cuisine.

The **Hawaiian Regent Hotel (** (808) 922-6611 TOLL-FREE (800) 367-5370 FAX (808) 9921-5222 WEBSITE http://hoohana.aloha.net E-MAIL hwnrgnt@aloha.net, 2552 Kalakaua Avenue, Honolulu, HI 96815 (mid-range to luxury), is a huge complex located directly across from the beach and designed around a pleasant courtyard decorated with fountains and waterways. Though it is luxurious, its deluxe rooms do not approach those at the Halekulani or Kahala Hilton. But the Regent

has the best lower-priced rooms around, with two swimming pools, tennis courts and extensive convention facilities thrown into the bargain.

SHOPPING

Shopping is one of Waikiki's main attractions and a pleasurable alternative to languid sun worship. Many shops remain open until 9 PM, and some until 11 PM. Most of Waikiki's shops are concentrated in centers and malls.

In Waikiki, the enormous **Ala Moana Shopping Center** is situated near Ala Wai

OPPOSITE: Waikiki's historic Moana Surfrider Hotel. ABOVE: "The Pink Lady", Royal Hawaiian Hotel, is a Waikiki landmark.

Yacht Harbor at the gateway to Waikiki. Spread over 34 acres (14 hectares), it is said to attract over 54 million people each year. In 1989, Ala Moana added a collection of high-class boutiques carrying some of the world's hottest brand names. Palm Boulevard is the most elegant section, housing Chanel, Gucci, Christian Dior, Escada, Waterford-Wedgewood, Fendi, Cartier, Adrian Bittadini, Lancel, MCM, Loewe, Emporium Armani, Ann Taylor and Etro.

The largest shopping center in Waikiki is the **Royal Hawaiian Shopping Center**, 2233 Kalakaua Avenue. Retailers include Louis Vuitton, Chanel, Celine, Van Cleef & Arpels, and Sonia Rykiel.

The **Waikiki Shopping Plaza**, 2270 Kalakaua Avenue, is a five-story water show of fountains and Plexiglas sculpture. The plaza has three floors of shops, a food court, and two floors of restaurants.

One of the attractions of the **Atrium Shops**, 2424 Kalakaua Avenue, is a three-level waterfall with a miniature lagoon.

King's Village, 131 Kaiulani Avenue, is a split-level complex designed in the architectural style of nineteenth century urban Honolulu. Though some may find it a touch overdone, its shades of browns and greens contribute to a pleasing effect overall.

International Market Place, 2301 Kalakaua Avenue, is a bustling bazaar of Asian and Polynesian shops, stalls, restaurants and bars that appeals to budget shoppers — just the place for that Hawaii souvenir. There is not much here that can't be bargained for if you stick to your guns. In fact, if you don't haggle you'll probably be paying too much.

Just behind the market is the **Waikiki Town Center**, 2301 Kuhio Avenue. Its lack of crowds — though not of attractions — provides a welcome change from the bustle of most shopping centers. The mall has 38 specialty shops as well as a serene atmosphere, provided in part by its vined terraces, carp stream and two waterfalls.

The **Rainbow Bazaar**, Hilton Hawaiian Village, 2005 Kalia Road, is worth strolling through to admire the mixture of Chinese, Japanese and Polynesian architecture. It also has more than the usual number of shops specializing in Asian jewelry crafts and antiques. The **Ali'i Plaza** adds upmarket boutiques (Benneton, Esprit and Georgio Armani) to the Hilton Hawaiian Village.

Victoria Ward Centers, 1200 Ala Moana Boulevard, is a popular shopping and dining center with 120 outlets, including Borders Books and Music.

Ward Warehouse, 1050 Ala Moana Boulevard, has 65 unique shops and eight restaurants with harbor views.

WHERE TO EAT

There was a time when one despaired at the overall quality of the food served in Hawaii's restaurants. A great deal has happened in the past 10 years. New faces, new talent and fresh inspiration have brought sophistication to the eating habits of the islands. What has been dubbed "Pacific Rim" cuisine, or "Hawaii regional" cuisine is very much in vogue.

Not all expensive restaurants can be applauded for the excellence of their fare. However, the **Secret** ((808) 922-6611 (very expensive, formerly called the Third Floor), at the Hawaiian Regent Hotel, 2552 Kalakaua Avenue, is considered by many to be among the better restaurants in Honolulu. Specialties of the house include rack of lamb and pink snapper.

Chez Michel ((808) 955-7866 (expensive), at Eaton Square, 444 Hobron Lane, is an excellent French restaurant. It received an award from the International Association of Food Critics as "one of the finest restaurants of its kind in the country." Try the veal chops in Normandy sauce. Located in the northwest corner of Waikiki, Chez Michel is a welcome alternative to the restaurants of Kalakaua and Kuhio avenues.

A new establishment with a trendy menu is **Ciao Mein** ((808) 923-2426 (expensive), which replaced the once popular Bagwell's in the Hyatt Regency, 2424 Kalakaua Avenue. **Sergio's** ((808) 926-3388 (expensive), 445 Nohonani Street, remains one of the better Italian restaurants in Waikiki. The house specials change daily (depending on what Sergio has brought back from the mainland on his latest gourmet expedition).

Situated in the Hilton Royal Hawaiian Village, **Bali by the Sea** ((808) 949-4321 (expensive) is an open-air restaurant overlooking bustling Waikiki, with an elegantly understated atmosphere. The menu is continental with seafood dishes featuring fresh island fish.

If you would like a complete evening under one roof and are prepared to pay the rather high price, the **Hanohano Room** ((808) 922-4422 (expensive), in the Sheraton Waikiki Hotel, is the place to go. It has the best early evening view of Waikiki on the Diamond Head side and a gorgeous sunset view on the downtown side. The food is excellent and a pianist performs nightly from 6:30 PM to 11 PM.

Prominent among the newcomers is **Singha Thai Cuisine** ((808) 941-2898 (moderate), Canterbury Place, 1910 Ala Moana Boulevard. In addition to the fine food, Singha Thai provides Royal Thai dancers as entertainment.

A restaurant that consistently receives critical acclaim for Chinese-style cooking is the **Golden Dragon** ((808) 949-4321 (expensive), in the Hilton Hawaiian Village, 2005 Kalia Road. The Chinese chefs tend to be traditional, but the venerable Dai Hong Chang, who has been a chef at this restau-

Nick's Fishmarket ((808) 955-6333 (expensive), Waikiki Gateway Hotel, 2070 Kalakaua Avenue, is the place for a romantic seafood dinner, though the lighting is so dim you might find the candles a necessity rather than an aesthetic pleasure. Try the Maine lobster and *onaga* (red snapper). A band plays from 8:30 PM until 1 AM.

The region has a growing number of Japanese, Thai and Chinese restaurants from which to choose. At the Hyatt Regency's **Furasato Japanese Restaurant** ((808) 955-6333 (very expensive), 22424 Kalakaua Avenue, the style is authentically Japanese with most of the seating on tatami mats, though there are small areas set aside for those who wish to be seated Western style.

rant for over 30 years, has created new flavors by introducing ingredients from Southeast Asia and Europe. Clearly the recipes work, for the restaurant continues to attract diners in large numbers. There's also a touch of showbiz in this place — from the decor and gimmicks, such as the tea lady who also tells fortunes, to the striking table settings.

NIGHTLIFE

Clubs

On and off the strip, Waikiki has a proliferation of nightclubs, discotheques and video-

LEFT: Waikiki's Kalakaua Avenue. RIGHT: Night shopping at the International Marketplace.

theques that appeal to both the sophisticated and the college crowd with clubs perpetually opening, closing and reopening, it is difficult to keep track of what's hot and what's not, but there is always plenty from which to choose.

A new hot spot, **Eurasia** ((808) 921-5335, 2552 Kalakaua Avenue, in the Hawaiian Regent, is one of the few places in town where you can listen to good jazz.

The **Captain's Room** ((808) 956-1111, Hawaii Prince Hotel, 100 Holomoana Street, overlooking the Ala Wai Yacht Harbor has

the Imperial Hotel, where the preference is for Top 40 music. The club is closed Monday and Tuesday.

One of the "in" places with the mandatory state-of-the-art sound and light is the **Maharaja Hawaii** videotheque ((808) 922-3030, located in the Waikiki Trade. It is open from 8 PM to 4 AM daily and has a cover charge. **Rumors Nightclub** ((808) 955-4381, in the Ala Moana Hotel, attracts disco dancers who generally swing until the early hours of the morning. The **Hard Rock Café** ((808) 955-7383, 1837 Kapiolani Boulevard,

built a steady clientele since its opening. The art deco-style room is unique to the city, and entertainment leans heavily to jazz. Many jazz greats have passed through, including Dizzy Gillespie, Herbie Mann, and Ramsay Lewis. On nights when jazz isn't being performed, you can listen to contemporary Hawaiian music.

The **Jungle** ((808) 922-7808, on Lewers Street, restaurant and nightclub go full blast — and the operative word is blast — until 4 AM. Located in the Waikiki Marketplace, at 2310 Kuhio Avenue is **Scruples Beach Club** ((808) 923-9530 where the disc jockeys play Top 40 and alternative music from 8 PM every night. A favorite hangout of the college crowd is the **Cellar** ((808) 923-9952, 205 Lewers, in

is as popular as ever. It's a good place to eat, and if you like classic rock, it's a good place to roll. If you want even more action, then try the **Wave Waikiki** ((808) 941-0424, 1877 Kalakaua Avenue. It remains the most popular of all Waikiki dance establishments, with live new wave music. At 2 AM live music gives way to disco until closing at 4 AM.

There are three new clubs within a couple of miles of each other, just outside Waikiki: **Studio 1 Hawaii** ((808) 531-0200, at Aloha Tower Marketplace is a nightclub and showroom unlike anything that's existed in Hawaii before. By any standards, this is a huge place. The stage is vast and in its first week a big band was churning out Sixties sounds, supporting three vocalists. Studio 1 Hawaii has 85 video screens throughout the establishment.

The **Mixx** is situated at the Waikiki end of Queen Street. The disk jockeys here concentrate on contemporary and hip hop music for dance patrons. An adjacent room is crowded with video games. There are alcoves where you can retreat for a drink and quiet conversation.

Ocean Club ((808) 526-9888, in Restaurant Row is a happy addition to that complex. The emphasis is on sophisticated music that is clearly aimed at the professional crowd.

costumes for the "big" numbers, superb comedic timing and an almost psychic understanding of their audiences has generated a host of adoring fans around the world. The Society of Seven performs Monday through Sunday at 8:30 PM and 10:30 PM (Wednesday only an 8:30 PM show). The dinner show price is $47.50 and the cocktail show is $25.

Highly recommended for an evening of pure fun and laughter is the **Frank De Lima-Glenn Medeiros Show**, at the **Polynesian Palace Showroom** ((808) 923-

Stage Shows

For almost three decades, one show has been the talk of Waikiki: the **Society of Seven**. This colorful show band, whose original members were prominent Filipino musicians playing the Asian circuit, has been a fixture at the **Outrigger Waikiki** ((808) 922-5777, 2335 Kalakaua Avenue, since moving to Hawaii from Hong Kong in 1970. With its mix of zany humor and musical talent, the band blends contemporary music with show tunes and comedy skits for a show that leaves the audience demanding more. Their longevity may be traced to the group's willingness to keep pace with the times and to present a show that has both nostalgia and passion. Great

7469, in the Outrigger Reef Towers. De Lima's forte is ethnic humor, and his jokes are derived from the cultural hodgepodge that is Hawaii. A Portuguese who once studied for the priesthood, De Lima is a kindly, gentle man with a wicked sense of humor. No one escapes his barbed wit (with perhaps the exception of the Samoans, who he claims are too big to joke about!). De Lima takes on everyone — Portuguese, Chinese, Filipino, Korean, Japanese, *haole*

OPPOSITE: Sunrise over the Ala Wai Canal, Waikiki. ABOVE: Torches and tropical drinks are the accompaniment to Waikiki evening hours. OVERLEAF: A variety of vessels, new and old, traditional and modern, drift on the tranquil waters off Waikiki Beach.

(Caucasians), and sometimes even the Samoans. If you want a taste of the real flavor of the islands, catch this very funny man in action with his partner, Glenn Medeiros. Pop singer Medeiros has a fine lyrical style and also plays keyboards. Together they put on a show that is thoroughly entertaining.

Karaoke Bars

A 15-minute walk or a five-minute cab ride out of Waikiki will allow you to experience the karaoke phenomenon.

behind Ala Moana Center. (Be aware, however, that many of the bars in this area, including several of the karaoke places, are hostess bars.)

It is well to remember a few simple guidelines when visiting karaoke bars. Most karaoke bars have dim lighting and seating in high-backed booths. People who sing in the karaoke bars often do so for a group of friends. In general, they don't want anyone else to pay any attention to them. So even if you hear a good voice (and there are usually many), try to refrain from discovering the

Karaoke bars started in Japan and have been an enormous success there. Naturally, they have found their way to Hawaii because of its large indigenous and visiting Japanese population. The term *karaoke* has no intrinsic meaning, but can be freely interpreted as "sing-along." In a karaoke bar, you'll find a large video screen linked to a laser disc player, public address system, an echo machine and microphones. From a play list, you choose a song, and a microphone is brought to your table. Each song is accompanied by an MTV-style video that flashes the words on the screen. All you have to do is sing. It costs about a dollar.

There are several of these bars (which get going around 11 PM) on Kapiolani Boulevard

face behind it by peering over the tops of the booths. The best way to show that you are not just slumming is to sing yourself. If you need some liquid courage, try some hot sake (Japanese rice wine). English songs are usually limited to around 60 standards, so be prepared to attempt "New York, New York" or "You've Lost That Lovin' Feeling." The chances are that once you've sung you'll find the atmosphere a good deal friendlier. You'll probably also be hooked.

Cocktail Bars

Bustling clubs and karaoke bars are not for everyone, though. You may want after-dinner liqueurs and a quiet corner to share them. If so, the place to go is the **Mai Tai Bar (** (808)

923-7311, at the "Pink Lady," Royal Hawaiian Hotel, 2255 Kalakaua Avenue, the most serene spot you will find outdoors in Waikiki. The bar is tucked away in a corner of the hotel's courtyard, literally a step away from the beach. On moonlit nights, with the sound of waves gently breaking, the Lady regains much of its glory as one of the state's architectural landmarks.

Also recommended for after-dinner drinks (or predinner cocktails) is the **Library** ((808) 922-6611, 2552 Kalakaua Avenue, Hawaiian Regent Hotel. Seating comes in various combinations of leather, velvet, and chrome, with tastefully subdued lighting. A smoked glass-enclosed fireplace creates an intimate ambiance.

DOWNTOWN HONOLULU

There is an abundance of historical, cultural and architectural points of interest on Oahu that won't be found in the tourist strip of Waikiki. To get a real sense of the gracious days of old Hawaii, you must visit downtown Honolulu.

As business districts go, downtown Honolulu is charming. Old buildings stand next to modern skyscrapers on streets lined with a variety of ancient trees. Among the many distinguished buildings are the **C. Brewer Building** (1930), 827 Fort Street, the **Alexander & Baldwin Building** (1929), 822 Bishop Street, and the **Hawaiian Electric Company** (1927), 900 Richard's Street.

WHAT TO SEE AND DO

The dominant feature of the city's business district still is **Iolani Palace**, the only royal palace in the United States. This was the home of King David Kalakaua and his wife Queen Kapiolani. Kalakaua was clearly impressed by the pomp and pageantry surrounding European royalty, and the palace he built in 1882, at a cost of about $360,000, reflects his obsession. The palace has been refurbished and restored by the nonprofit Friends of the Iolani Palace ((808) 538-1471. This is a relatively small palace measuring just 140 by 100 ft (42 by 30 m) on each of its two floors. The magnificent gilded throne room occupies half of the first floor. The rest

of the floor is taken up by the reception area and dining room. The upper floor was the royal family's living quarters. Through an architectural flaw, the king and queen's bedrooms were not connected. The first telephones on the island were installed in these bedrooms. In a symbolic gesture, the queen's bedroom remains devoid of furniture and personal belongings, a constant reminder to all that Kalakaua's sister, Queen Liliuokalani, was imprisoned here during the revolution that led to the overthrow of the monarchy.

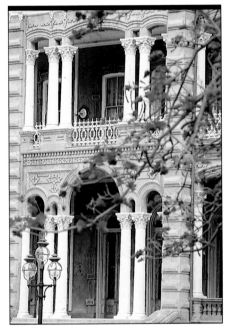

In the palace grounds is the copper-domed Coronation Bandstand where King David Kalakaua and his queen were crowned. Indeed, history records that Kalakaua, like Napoleon, placed the crown on his own head. The Friends conduct tours of the palace. Reservations are required.

In front of the main gates of the palace on King Street is the magnificent gold and black statue of the warrior king, **Kamehameha the Great**. On King Kamehameha Day (June 11) the statue is wreathed in long leis that stretch from the neck of the statue all the way to the ground.

OPPOSITE: Downtown Honolulu. ABOVE: Iolani Palace, Honolulu, is a reminder of a royal past.

A block away going towards Diamond Head down King Street is the **Kawaiahao Church** (at the corner of Punchbowl Street), completed in 1842 and constructed entirely of blocks of coral cut from Hawaii's reefs. The church was founded by the first company of New England missionaries to come to these islands. When the church opened its doors on July 21, 1842, 4,000 to 5,000 people attended the service. Today, services are conducted in English and Hawaiian. In 1874, a little chapel on the grounds of the church became the final resting place of King Lunalilo, a beloved monarch who asked to be buried with the people rather than at the Royal Mausoleum in Nuuanu.

Immediately behind Kawaiahao Church is the **Mission Houses Museum** ((808) 531-0481, 552 King Street, which includes the first frame house built in the islands in 1821. Later, two coral block houses were added and collectively represent the oldest North American-style buildings in Hawaii.

Behind the Palace is the **State Capitol** with its sweeping high-roof and fine collection of artworks. Here the state's politicians meet to debate the issues of the day. In front of the capitol, across Beretania Street, is the nine-foot (three-meter)-high **War Memorial** and eternal flame dedicated to the men and women who fought for the United States in World War II. On a cool, quiet spot on the Richard Street side of the capitol grounds is a more recently dedicated memorial to those who fell in the Korean and Vietnam wars.

To the left and across the street is **Washington Place**, the official residence of the governor of Hawaii and an architecturally interesting building with a colorful history. It was built by an American sea captain named John Dominis whose son married Princess Liliuokalani, who went on to become Hawaii's queen.

Ghosts and Spirits
If you want some totally unconventional tours of Oahu and old Honolulu, then take an evening tour with master storyteller Glen Grant. Grant specializes in the supernatural — tours with a ghostly twist.

First, there's "Ghost Walk through Old Honolulu." As Grant tells it, Honolulu has a tradition of haunted buildings, lonely grave-

yards, and eerie supernatural occurrences. Hawaii's ghosts are as multi-ethnic as the people who live here — Polynesian, Asian and Caucasian. Grant will regale you with tales of faceless women, fireballs and other apparitions as he walks you through the historic downtown district of the city. "Haunted Oahu" is offered once a month. Head off into the night in a small touring van with Grant, visiting sites that have bizarre histories. Finally there's Grant's "Haunted Trolley Tour" that combines the best ghost stories from his walking tour and bus tour. Your transport to the world of the supernatural is on a trolley as Grant guides you through sites in districts from Kaimuki, Makiki and Manoa to some old-fashioned Irish hospitality at O'Toole's pub in downtown Honolulu. This is a wonderful, entertaining and unusual way to see the city and its sights. And Grant is a great weaver of tales. If you want to join one of these tours, book early; space is limited and bookings go fast. Contact **Honolulu Time Walks** ((808) 943-0371, 2634 South King Street, Suite 3, Honolulu, HI 96826.

Chinatown
No visit to downtown Honolulu would be complete without a stroll through **Chinatown**. Head northwest along prosperous King Street, and suddenly modern Honolulu is transformed and the air is thick with the language, sounds and smells of Hong Kong.

Chinatown has a special fascination and remains a historic landmark in the city. The people who helped create Chinatown are a hardy breed. Their ancestors came to plant sugar and pineapple and stayed to become some of the wealthiest men and women in the land.

While the old ways still exist in Chinatown — you see it in the fish and vegetable markets, in the goldsmith shops and in the jewelry stores — you also see what a new generation of Chinese are doing as they acknowledge their roots and return to make their contribution to the neighborhood. Many historic buildings are being renovated and restored, and there is confidence that a facelift will revitalize this corner of the city. **Daily walking tours** of Chinatown ((808) 923-1811 are offered by several groups.

WHERE TO EAT

As befits a resort destination, Honolulu and the other major towns on the island abound with restaurants and eateries. Outside Waikiki and Chinatown, there are restaurants to suit everyone's pocketbook. But you have to be selective. Remember, the state thrives on tourism, and you can expect to find some restaurants where the quality of the food leaves much to be desired. The fast food restaurants are exactly what you would expect.

yard is fascinating—reminiscent of a garden in a traditional Chinese village — with its huge iron gate leading nowhere, open lanai and rattan blinds.

Chu describes his cooking style as "Eurasian." His dishes are based on the techniques and tastes that his grandmother taught him, but the rest he learned during his college days in Detroit and from his travels in Europe and Asia. On the menu, you'll find delectable dishes such as goat cheese won tons with fruit sauce, or Thai beef salad with chili lime vinaigrette, and of course the very popular

To appreciate what culinary Oahu has to offer, you should get out of the Waikiki area and explore the restaurants that proliferate there.

Chinatown

Typical of the generation of Chinese who are helping to revitalize Chinatown is Glenn Chu, who owns and operates **Indigo** ((808) 521-2900 (expensive), 1121 Nuuanu Avenue, one of several excellent nontraditional Chinatown restaurants. Indigo is located in a charming old building that once housed several shops. The inside of the restaurant has a main dining room with high ceilings that is a showcase for the works of well-known local artist Pegge Hopper. The court-

Peking duck with imperial plum sauce and green onions.

On a street parallel to Nuuanu Avenue are two fine restaurants influenced by the Vietnamese-French style of cooking, both owned and operated by Duc Nguyen: **A Taste of Saigon** ((808) 947-8885 (moderate), 2334 South King Street, serves traditional Vietnamese food with distinctive Western overtones. The food and service is excellent and the price is right. The more upmarket **Duc's Bistro** ((808) 531-6325 (expensive), 1188 Maunakea Street, is an elegant little restaurant that specializes in French–continen-

Honolulu's Chinatown: A bakery LEFT displays a mouth watering array of pastries, and a dragon dance RIGHT winds through narrow streets.

tal food with a hint of Vietnamese. The menu is imaginative. For starters, you can have gravilax — that wonderful Scandinavian dish of raw salmon with dill and aquavit served with mustard-dill dressing, or aromatic beef *la lot* — minced beef tenderloin wrapped in la lot leaf, broiled and served with pineapple anchovy sauce. There are a variety of salads, but duck salad *beaulieu* — sautéed breast of duck with raspberry vinaigrette — is especially good. For your main course, try *steak au poivres flambé au VSOP* (black angus New York steak sautéed with pink, green and black peppercorns). Most evenings, a very good jazz singer, Azure McCall, entertains.

Restaurant Row

Restaurant Row is a dining, entertainment and shopping complex developed on a site that once housed the Honolulu Iron Works. Within walking distance of downtown Honolulu, Restaurant Row attracts the lunchtime crowd and is particularly lively on Friday and Saturday night. The complex has seven five-story buildings set amidst nine acres (three and a half hectares) of landscaped gardens. Outdoor seating at some of the restaurants gives a continental atmosphere to the place. The **Row**, an outdoor bar located in a central atrium, enjoys good patronage.

The **Sunset Grill** ((808) 521-4409 (moderate) offers some "San Francisco-style" dishes. Try their smoked salmon or roasted garlic with goat cheese. Their fish is cooked imaginatively with a wonderful array of garnishes. They'll also pack gourmet picnic baskets for you, put together from any items on the menu.

Changes continue to ripple through Restaurant Row, with some operations closing and others opening up just as quickly. A new establishment which looks as though it's here to stay is **Payao Thai Cuisine** ((808) 961-6100 (moderate), an excellent Thai restaurant.

Two clubs bracket Restaurant Row — the **Blue Zebra** is on the eastern side and **Ocean Club** ((808) 538-0409, a ritzier affair that occupies the west end of the complex.

On Monday, Wednesday and Friday a farmer's market is spread out over the Restaurant Row complex with everything from food to arts and crafts.

The Old Town Honolulu Trolley runs from Waikiki to Restaurant Row and on to the Aloha Tower Market Place on the city's waterfront, starting each day from 11:20 AM and running throughout the day.

The Seaport

For over a century, one edifice has stood as a lasting monument to Honolulu's stature as a world seaport. Because the tourist industry has been so important to the islands for so long, the city fathers completed a structure on the edge of the harbor that was meant to create a lasting impression on all those who arrived or departed these shores. The **Aloha Tower**, One Aloha Tower Drive, completed in 1926, 10 stories tall and for four decades was the highest building in Hawaii. Around its base the facilities of the harbor expanded rapidly, and the arrival of passenger ships became a festive celebration with streamers and bands and hula dancers greeting or saying farewell to island visitors.

In the Nineties a world-class marketplace was developed that retains the character of the city's waterfront: **Aloha Tower Marketplace**, a shopping complex that captures the leisurely, colorful style of a bygone era. Buff-colored rectangular buildings with green-tiled roofs house 120 apparel stores, gift and specialty shops, restaurants, bars and entertainment venues. Here you'll find an astonishing array of art, jewelry and apparel. Among the places to dine are the **Big Island Steak House** ((808) 537-4446 (moderate), a steak and seafood restaurant on the water's edge, **Hongkong Harbor View Seafood Restaurant** ((808) 524-3600 (moderate), a gourmet Chinese restaurant that serves an excellent dim sum lunch, and **Scott's Seafood Grill and Bar** ((808) 537-6800 (moderate), where there is live jazz on Friday night. For drinks there's **Gordon Biersch Brewery Restaurant** ((808) 599-4877 (moderate), Hawaii's first microbrewery restaurant serving Pacific Rim food and freshly brewed lager beer. There's also live music here Wednesday through Saturday.

Moiliili and Kapahulu Districts

The hottest restaurant in Honolulu is **Alan Wong's** ((808) 949-2526 (very expensive), 1857 South King Street, Fifth Floor, in the

Moiliili district, just a stone's throw away from Waikiki. Wong's opened in 1995, and in the first year it was honored in a magazine poll as the best new restaurant, and restaurant of the year. The following year it repeated the honor as restaurant of the year. National honors followed in 1996 when Wong flew to New York to receive the prestigious James Beard Foundation Award as best chef in the Northwest. He has received numerous other culinary awards and continues to carry the flag as one of the founders of Hawaii regional cuisine.

Alan Wong figured out early in life that there was more to good food than a couple of scoops of rice and macaroni salad (a local favorite). After going to community college in Hawaii, he was accepted as an apprentice at the Greenbrier Hotel in West Virginia. His ambition, however, was to work in New York, and when he finally made it to the Big Apple he was determined to work for the internationally famous André Soltner of Lutèce restaurant. Soltner eventually hired the enthusiastic young Asian chef, and Wong stayed three years learning all he could from the master chef. When he returned to Hawaii in 1985, he was classically trained in French and European cuisine. This knowledge, in the hands of the imaginative Wong, translated into the new style of cooking which has become known as Hawaii regional. It combines the solid foundations of the French school with the ethnic influences of Hawaii and its local products and ingredients. Wong's team of sous chefs are drawn from many different parts of the world — as is his growing clientele. And Wong has not forgotten how it all came together for him.

Chef Sam Choy is a larger-than-life figure whose joy in cooking is an inspiration to many. Choy now owns and operates two highly successful restaurants on Oahu — **Sam Choy's Diamond Head** ((808) 732-8645 (expensive), 449 Kapahulu Avenue, and the latest in his chain, **Sam Choy's Breakfast, Lunch and Crab** ((808) 545-7979 (expensive), on Nimitz Highway. Choy grew up sampling the food of his Hawaiian–German mother and working at his father's restaurant, Sam's Place, in Laie on the north shore. Choy's dishes are as international and as hearty as the man himself. His ingredients have the

be the freshest, and he avails himself of all the fine homegrown produce. Out of this passion for food has evolved what some have described as Choy's "nouvelle tropical culinary style." A sampling of Choy's food tells all: for starters, baked shiitake mushrooms stuffed with crabmeat and water chestnuts; and for an entrée, Chef Sam's Kona cuisine combo — macadamia nut breast of chicken with jumping barbecue shrimp.

All Choy's restaurants are well patronized, but Breakfast, Lunch and Crab, a spacious 380-seat restaurant lined with miniature aquariums, with a central fountain for washing your hands, and paper tablecloths, is wildly popular. Breakfast and lunch prices are reasonable; dinner is more expensive, with entrées for Sam's 18 different crab dishes hovering around the $30 mark. Book well in advance.

Keo's Thai Cuisine ((808) 737-8240 (expensive), 625 Kapahulu Avenue, was Honolulu's first Thai restaurant and has remained one of the very best. The restaurant is regularly named in local fine dining polls and continues to attract visiting celebrities to its orchid-filled rooms.

In a city filled with many good Chinese restaurants, three of the best are **Dynasty I** ((808) 947-3771 (expensive), 1778 Ala Moana Boulevard, **Dynasty II** ((808) 596-0208 (expensive), 1057 Ala Moana Boulevard, Ward Warehouse, and **King Tsin** ((808) 946-3273 (moderate), 1110 McCully. All three serve authentic Chinese food. The two Dynasty restaurants serve an interesting blend of northern and Cantonese food, and King Tsin specializes in Szechuan-style cooking.

DAY TRIPS FROM HONOLULU

WAR AND PEACE

The **National Memorial Center of the Pacific** ((808) 566-1430, 2177 Puowaina Drive, situated in Punchbowl Crater overlooking downtown Honolulu, is the final resting place of 20,000 American men and women who gave their lives in service to their country. This is a beautiful and serene place, well worth visiting. The Memorial Building houses a chapel and a gallery of maps of the

Pacific conflicts of World War II and Korea, and it includes the series of stairways bordered by massive marble walls called the "Courts of the Missing." Here marble slabs inscribed with the names of more than 26,280 servicemen missing in action from World War II and the wars in Korea and Vietnam lead up to Lady Columbia, a 30-foot statue symbolizing all grieving mothers.

From the rim of Punchbowl Crater, visitors get one of the great panoramic views of the city, from Diamond Head all the way to the Waianae mountains. The Hawaiian

name for this place is Puowaina, meaning "Hill of Sacrifice."

Another historical site not far from the city center, and not to be missed, is the **Arizona Memorial** (see WAR AND REMEMBRANCE, page 18).

MANOA VALLEY

Ten minutes from downtown Honolulu is the University of Hawaii campus at Manoa. The campus covers the lower half of Manoa Valley, one of the oldest and most elegant residential neighborhoods on the island.

Tucked away in a corner of Vancouver Drive in the valley is one of Oahu's best kept secrets, the **Manoa Valley Inn ℂ** (808) 947-6019

TOLL-FREE (800) 634-5115 FAX (808) 946-6168, 2001 Vancouver Drive, Honolulu, HI 96822 (mid-range to expensive). Built in 1919, the inn was restored to its former glory in 1982, all the way down to the hardware fixtures and chandeliers. It is listed on the National Register of Historic Places. Eight bedrooms are furnished with four-poster, antique iron beds, marble-topped dressers and patterned wallpaper. Five of the rooms have attached bathrooms; three share bathrooms. On the shady lanai of the inn, white wicker chairs invitation you to sit and sip a glass of fresh fruit juice or savor a cup of Kona coffee. There's an enchanting garden filled with flowers and neat lawns, and from the lanai at night you have a view of Honolulu's city lights.

POLYNESIAN CULTURE

Be sure to include time in your intinerary for a side trip to the **Bishop Museum and Planetarium ℂ** (808) 847-3511, 1525 Bernice Street, Honolulu, HI 96817. Founded in 1889 by Charles R. Bishop in memory of his wife, Princess Bernice Pauahi, the museum began as a repository for the royal possessions of this last direct descendant of King Kamehameha the Great. It has since achieved international recognition as a center for Polynesian archaeology, ethnology and history (see CULTURAL KICKS, page 95).

EXPLORING OAHU

Because Waikiki gets so much publicity, the island's other attractions often don't receive the attention they deserve. But Oahu offers numerous choices, and it has the best stretch of coastline in the islands for fine surfing and safe swimming.

You can drive round the island in one day, but it is not advised. Take your time and split up your exploration of the island into three excursions. The first takes you east and then all the way around the northern (windward) shores and back through the sugarcane and pineapple fields to Waikiki. On your second outing, head west along the Waianae Coast to Kaena Point State Park. The road goes no farther. Your third outing should be into the hills around Nuuanu and Manoa, site of the University of Hawaii campus.

THE EASTERN SHORES

If your time is limited, cross the Ala Wai Canal and join the H1 Freeway going east. But if you can afford a more leisurely pace, head east down Kalakaua Avenue until you reach Kapiolani Park. Proceed down the avenue of tall trees in the direction of Diamond Head with the ocean on your right. Turn right at the stop sign and make your way to the Diamond Head Lookout. The ocean below the lookout is a favorite with surfers and wave jumpers, and the myriad colored sails racing over the shallow waters are striking. A bit farther on is the picturesque **Diamond Head Lighthouse**, one of the oldest in the Pacific region.

Once you've had your fill, though the temptation to linger is great, continue on this road until you reach Kahala, a small but significant district of Waikiki.

KAHALA

Before going farther afield, check out this corner of Oahu — the district of Kahala — where the island's wealthy seclude themselves in huge mansions on opulent estates, behind walls and high fences. Properties on Kahala Avenue are valued in the millions of dollars. Some houses have played host to heads of state and presidents.

Where to Stay

Kahala Avenue ends at the **Kahala Mandarin Oriental (** (808) 739-8888 TOLL-FREE (800) 367-2525 FAX (808) 739-8800 E-MAIL mohnl @aol.com, 5000 Kahala Avenue, Honolulu, HI 96816 (expensive to luxury), a holiday retreat that has welcomed kings, queens, prominent politicians, and entertainment stars. A $75 million restoration by the Hong Kong-based Mandarin Group enhanced the resort's reputation. The Kahala reputedly keeps records of the preferences of its guests in terms of room choice and views. There is a main 10-story structure, but the choice accommodations are the cottages on the edge of the lagoon. The 370 rooms and 32 suites are designed with turn-of-the-century motifs, mahogany furniture, teak parquet flooring over which are scattered Tibetan rugs. Grass

cloth wall coverings and rich fabrics accent the rooms.

The Kahala Mandarin's 26,000-sq ft (2,415-sq m) private lagoon has a fine collection of marine animals, including dolphins, tropical fish and sea turtles. The landscaped gardens are replete with waterfalls.

At night, beams of light dance on the ocean waves, creating an atmosphere of perfect harmony that adds to the dining pleasure of those patronizing **Hoku's (** (808) 739-8777 (very expensive), the Kahala Mandarin's signature oceanfront restaurant. This is the

domain of Chef Oliver Alther, who, like so many of his peers, is European trained but versed in the culinary arts of Asia. The hotel also has an open-air restaurant, the beachfront **Plumeria Beach Café** (moderate), which serves a variety of buffets for breakfast, lunch and dinner. Guests are entertained by nightly Hawaiian music and dance performances from 5:30 PM to 7:30 PM.

ALONG THE KALANIANAOLE HIGHWAY

Continuing your eastern tour, Kalanianaole Highway runs parallel to the ocean, skirting the residential communities of Aina Haina, Niu Valley and Hawaii Kai. Some small, but pretty beach parks line the ocean side of the highway.

As you drive beneath an elevated pedestrian bridge, you'll see **Koko Crater** on your left. The road to **Hanauma Bay**, everyone's

OPPOSITE: The Bishop Museum, custodian of Hawaii's cultural history. ABOVE: The Arizona Memorial, Pearl Harbor. OVERLEAF: Oahu's Kahala Beach.

favorite private aquarium, branches off to the right (see PALETTE OF EXOTIC COLORS, page 18).

Exiting Hanauma Bay, Kalanianaole Highway continues downhill with towering, sculptured cliffs on the left and more sparkling views of the ocean on the right. At the first scenic lookout you'll get a view of the **Halona Blowhole** geyser where ocean water surges through a lava tube into the tidal basin. Thrill seekers have attempted to ride this rush of water and some have perished. The undertow here can be deadly.

There are several superb beaches in this area and they never become truly crowded because there are no hotels east of the Kahala Oriental Mandarin. The surf off **Sandy Beach** and further up the coast at **Makapuu** can be ferocious, so take care.

The cliffs above **Makapuu** are a favorite launching point for hang gliders. On days when the winds are brisk and clouds are but a memory, the sight of these daring pilots suspended beneath colorful sails will take your breath away.

In the shadows of the cliffs is **Sea Life Park** ((808) 259-7933, Makapuu Point, 41-202 Kalanianaole Highway, where there are daily performances by trained marine creatures and a wonderful multilevel aquarium. This unique oceanside setting is home to penguins, turtles, dolphins, sea lions and sharks. The park's imposing 300,000-gallon (1,140,000-liter) reef tank holds a marvelous cross section of the ocean's creatures. It's a good way to get a feel for what you'll be seeing should you decide to go snorkeling.

Where to Eat
On the mountain side of the highway are three outstanding restaurants.

The **Swiss Inn** ((808) 377-5447 (moderate) has been a fixture in this neighborhood for many years. It is run by the husband and wife team of Jeanie and Martin Wyss and is a family-style restaurant in every sense of the word. It serves excellent Swiss fare at a reasonable price. Martin is the chef and Jeanie acts as hostess throughout the evening. Dining here is rather like being invited guests in a friend's house.

Cliquo ((808) 377-8854 (expensive), in the Niu Valley Shopping Center, at 5730 Kalanianaole Highway, is owned and operated

by two French chefs, Yves Menoret and Bruno Chemel. It's a good traditional French restaurant. Cliquo gets its name from the flower that abounds in Brittany, the homeland of Menoret. And flowers dominate this restaurant, which is intimate without being crowded. In addition to the regular menu, Cliquo offers the patron a choice of five fixed menus. The items are intriguing — fish poached in court bouillon, turbans of leeks and a saffron velvet sauce; an organic mesclun salad with vanilla vinaigrette, followed by roast duck à l'orange, accompa-

nied by turban of linguini with pistachio butter drops.

Further along the road is Hawaii Kai, a residential district built around ancient fish ponds. Magnificent Maunalani Bay, a water sports playground, is on the doorstep of **Roy's** ((808) 396-7697 (expensive), located in the Hawaii Kai Corporate Plaza, Kalanianaole Highway, the flagship restaurant of Roy Yamaguchi. Many believe it to be the finest restaurant in the state. Fusing the flavors of East and West, Yamaguchi has created a menu whose magic is in the sauces — a subtle combination of Hawaiian fruit, nuts and vegetables, exotic spices of Asia, and smooth California wines. Roy's has excellent service and a superb location with a wonderful view of Diamond Head and the sunsets for which Hawaii is famed.

If you decide to dine at Roy's, book early or arrive early and enjoy a cocktail in the bar downstairs or on the patio. In the open-plan restaurant you can watch the artistry of a team of top chefs in action (see GALLOPING GOURMET, page 86).

TREE-LINED BEACHES

The drive along the highway gets increasingly beautiful as the road passes through

stretch of the coast as Kalanianaole Highway winds through the suburban towns of **Kailua** and **Kaneohe**.

KAILUA

If you weren't looking for Kailua, the chances are you'd probably drive right through it. But despite its modest manner, this Windward community has a great deal to offer. To begin with, Kailua is where people escape the bustle of the city — it's a wonderful alternative to Waikiki. Not only does it have

Waimanalo. On the left is an area referred to as the **Hawaiian Homelands** and reserved for those of Hawaiian descent. On the right is a stretch of perfect beach, the start of Waimanalo Bay.

Bellows Air Forces Base, a major military installation, occupies a large area of the shoreline on the right. Before you reach the main gate of the base, however, there is a gate leading to one of the loveliest beaches on the island. Tall pines stretch to the edge of white sand caressed by the waters of Waimanalo Bay. This is **Bellows Field Beach Park** which locals refer to as "Sherwood Forest," though it rarely appears in guidebooks as such.

This combination of tree-lined beach and clear blue waters is characteristic of this

magnificent Kailua Bay — a five-mile (eight-kilometer) stretch of white sand beach that curves tantalizingly from Mokapuu Point all the way to Lanikai — but it also has protected waters where you can swim in safety, paddle a kayak or race across the bay on a sail board when wind conditions are right. In fact, wind conditions here are so good that Kailua Bay is considered one of the world's premier windsurfing sites. It is here that world champion Robbie Naish cut his teeth in the sport he helped popularize. Kailua is green and clean, and the air, whether it is blowing off the rugged Palis or coming in off the ocean,

Dolphins and seals are among the popular attractions at Sealife Park, East Honolulu.

is fresh and invigorating. Also in the area is the **Heeia State Park** and 88 acres (35 hectares) of fish ponds meticulously developed by ancient Hawaiians.

Lanikai Beach is another of Oahu's spectacular seashores. An exclusive community has grown around this attractive area. To reach Lanikai, you continue past Kailua Beach Park to Mokulua Drive. Access to the beach is by public trails adjacent to many of the area's elegant beachside residences. On a clear day you can see the islands of Maui and Molokai from this beach.

(luxury) is on the superb white sand beach at Kailua Bay. It has three bedrooms, plus modern conveniences, including a large swimming pool.

The enclosed lawn of **Lanikai Sunrise** ((808) 261-2106 (luxury) opens onto the beach at Lanikai Bay. Two of the four and a half bedrooms in this large house open onto views of the Pacific and Mokulua Island. Other rooms overlook the mountains. All rooms are finished with eucalyptus hardwood floors. A neat white picket fence surrounds the property.

Where to Stay

There are no hotels on the Windward side of the island, but there are some exceptional vacation rentals and bed-and-breakfast establishments around Kailua from which to choose.

Two houses occupy the superb beachfront property of **Pua O Lanikai** ((808) 261-2106 (expensive to luxury): an A-frame Polynesian beachfront villa with four bedrooms and five bathrooms, and a two-bedroom, one-bathroom guesthouse. The main house has been recently remodeled and decorated in the Balinese style. There's a great swimming pool on the property.

The tastefully decorated, very private beachfront **Hale Maluhia** ((808) 261-2106

Two large and comfortable rooms are available at **Paradise Palms** ((808) 254-4234 FAX (808) 254-4971 (inexpensive). The Banyan and Maile rooms come with kitchenettes, private bathrooms, shower, and private entrances. The Banyan Room has a queen-sized bed and the Maile Room, a king-sized bed. The property is within walking distance of the many fine beaches in the area as well as restaurants and grocery stores for self-catering. Your hosts are Jim and Marilyn Warman.

Home in Paradise ((808) 254-1076 or (808) 263-4373 FAX (808) 262-8502 has private, spacious and modern rooms set amidst tropical landscaped gardens in the heart of Kailua. There are three accommodations to choose from — a large studio, a one-bed-room or a two-bedroom unit. All modern conveniences are provided. The beach is just a few steps away. This family-owned bed and breakfast has been in business since 1978. The hosts speak Dutch, French and Spanish.

Where to Eat

People used to complain that you couldn't find a decent restaurant in Kailua. But that has changed. There are now a number of good restaurants in the district.

Assagio Ristorante Italiano ((808) 261-2772 (moderate), Kailua Business Center, 3454 Uluniu Street, is a reasonably priced spot with an extensive menu and very tasty food. **Jaron's** ((808) 261-4600 (moderate), 201A Hamakua Drive, specializes in a variety of cooking styles including American, Japanese, Pacific Rim and Thai. The huge menu includes hot sandwiches, pizzas and salads. **El Charro Avitia** ((808) 263-3943 (moderate), 14 Oneawa Street, is a very good Mexican restaurant. **Cisco's Cantina** ((808) 262-7337 (moderate), 123 Hekili, also serves good authentic Mexican food. This restaurant's claim to fame is that it serves a 40-oz (over one-liter) margarita affectionately known as the "megarita."

TEMPLES AND RANCHES

Kalanianaole soon turns into Kahekili Highway. Set deep in the **Valley of the Temples Memorial Park** is the **Byodo-In** ((808) 239-5570. Built in 1968, it is a replica of the 900-year-old Buddhist temple in Uji, Japan. As you cross the bridge over a stream, the entrance to the temple is dominated by an enormous three-ton bronze bell. The centerpiece of the temple is a sitting Buddha, almost nine feet (three meters) high. Thousands of

carp create a moving tableau of color in a huge pond, and peacocks roam the temple grounds. The temple is a place of rare serenity, and is beautifully situated with the majestic Koolaus as a backdrop.

Leaving the temple, Kahekili Highway soon becomes Kamehameha Highway. The road hugs a magnificent coast with towering palis on the left, in whose shadows lie horse and cattle ranches.

One of the ranches sprawled in these sacred valleys is **Kualoa Ranch** ((808) 237-8515

OPPOSITE: Jagged palisades form a rugged backdrop to the expanse of Waimanalo's palm-fringed beach. ABOVE: A bridge LEFT leads to the serene Byodo-In Temple. Visitors enjoy a canal cruise RIGHT at the Polynesian Cultural Center.

TOLL-FREE (800) 231-7321, P.O. Box 650, Kaawa, HI 96730, a 4,000-acre (1,600-hectare) spread that doubles as both a ranch and a holiday resort for weary tourists. It even has a secret island to which visitors are transported in a double-hulled Hawaiian canoe across an ancient fish pond. You can absorb the culture of this quiet and beautiful place while at the same time participating in a host of activities ranging from dune cycling and helicopter rides, to SCUBA diving, jet skiing and snorkeling. Nearby, private trails wind through the 2,000-acre (800-hectare) **Kaawa**

Valley where parts of *Jurassic Park* were filmed.

Across from the ranch is **Kualoa Regional Park**. There's not much of a beach here, but the waters are great for swimming and snorkeling. The currents, however, can be tricky, so be careful. This area has an ancient and sacred history. Locals will tell you, for instance, that according to legend, Mokolii, the little offshore island, is the lopped-off tail of a dragon. Most residents refer to this island as Chinaman's Hat.

Your journey then continues past the Crouching Lion and its famous inn. It is a pretty setting, but the inn's popularity stems from the fact it also is one the few eating places on this segment of the road.

Laie is the last town of any significance on the windward side of the island. It is the site of the Brigham Young University, the Polynesian Cultural Center and the Mormon Temple. As with Waikiki, the **Polynesian Cultural Center** ((808) 293-3333 has its critics because of its commercialism, but it does give the visitor more than a passing glimpse of various Polynesian lifestyles. The center is composed of several villages representing the main Polynesian cultures. Students from the Pacific islands, in native garments, demonstrate arts and crafts techniques employed in their island homes. The Pageant of the Long Canoes, held in the afternoon, is a popular attraction with visitors, as is the fine evening performance of singing and dancing by the students, most of whom pay for their education by working at the center.

Tickets to the Polynesian Cultural Center and its variety shows are not cheap, but most visitors enjoy the experience. The center offers a variety of packages that range from $27 for a general admission ticket for adults to $16 for children, all the way up to an Ambassador package that costs $95 for adults and $63 for children. The center is closed on Sunday.

Leaving Laie, you pass the community of Kahuku and round the northernmost tip of the island. In front of you is the **Turtle Bay Hilton Golf and Tennis Resort** ((808) 293-8811 TOLL-FREE (800) 445-8667 (mid-range to expensive), easily the biggest resort on the island. It has fine golf and tennis courts, a large pool and an atmosphere designed for relaxation.

The road journey now takes you parallel to one of the most famous series of surfing beaches in the world: **Sunset**, **Ehukai** and **Waimea** beaches. For the less than skilled, the waves at this site remain a form of purgatory. Take, for instance, the **Banzai Pipeline** at Sunset, a great curling tube of a wave that has been described by those who have dared ride it as being on a roller coaster ride through a black tunnel (see OCEAN PLAYGROUND, page 21).

Passing Sunset Beach, the seemingly endless white sand is interrupted by the tide pools of the **Pupukea Marine Life Conserve**. The pools are fun places to lie in, paddle around in or observe marine life. Around the

outer fringes of the rocks, the coral formations and fauna in the clean, clear waters
make Pupukea among the favorite SCUBA
diving and snorkeling sites on these northern shores.

Pupukea Drive, across the street from the
conserve's parking lot, leads to an exceptional
heiau (temple). **Puu O Mahuka** (Hill of Escape) is on the National Register of Historic
Landmarks and is one of the finest examples
of an ancient culture's place of worship.
Archaeologists haven't pieced together the
puzzle which lies in the stones. They have
been able to ascertain that human sacrifices
took place here. Among the victims were
three seamen from a British vessel who were
captured while drawing water at the mouth
of the Waimea River.

The terraced heiau is dominated by what
looks like an altar at the far left of the ruins.
Follow the walk around this end of the heiau
and you will find yourself gazing out over
an unforgettable landscape — the **Waimea
River** and the **Waimea Falls Park** on the left,
cane fields stretching out to the distant hori-
zon above it, and immediately below you to
the right, **Waimea Beach Park**. Where the
Waimea River enters the ocean is a swimmer's delight in the summer, when the waters
of the bay are placid. Only the greatest surfers, however, challenge the mountainous
winter surf which pounds these shores. If you
are visiting Oahu in summer, experience the
beauty of this bay after leaving the heiau by
stopping for refreshment on the grassy banks
of the river or on the beach. If it's winter, watch
out! Waves sometimes reach up to 30 ft (nine
meters) in the bay.

For a cultural experience in more serene,
less glitzy surroundings than the Polynesian
Cultural Center, **Waimea Valley,** home of
Waimea Falls Park ((808) 638-8511, is recommended. Here the foliage is lush and green
and the flowering plant life spectacular.

The **Falls at Waimea** are unspectacular,
but the high divers who plunge into the chilly
water compensate for any disappointment
at having come so far to see what some tourists have described as "a mere trickle." The
1,800-acre (730-hectare) park has outstanding flora (particularly its hibiscus garden), a
fine arboretum, beautiful birds (including
peacocks) and a collection of Hawaiian arti-

facts. Many who have visited both the
Polynesian Cultural Center and Waimea Falls
Park prefer the performances of ancient hula
performed in the natural settings of the park,
in grassy vales, under stately trees. There are
also exhibitions of the old Hawaiian games.
Visitors are encouraged to participate.

The road out of Waimea leads to one of
the most interesting little towns in the state.
Haleiwa resembles a Western cow town,
yet its proximity to the ocean makes its atmosphere unique. This north shore community has, over the years, developed into very

much an artist's enclave. Neat art galleries,
antique shops, some excellent sandwich
shops, and a couple of very good restaurants
are attracting visitors to Haleiwa in increasing numbers.

Across the street from the courthouse is a
little eatery called **Kua Aina Sandwich** ((808)
637-6027 (inexpensive), 66-214 Kamehameha Highway. Its specialty is charbroiling.
Whether it's large, juicy burgers or tender
breasts of chicken, the Kua Aina does it well.
Try the mahimahi sandwich with lettuce,
pepper and cheese.

OPPOSITE: Bountiful foliage at the lovely Waimea
Falls Park. ABOVE: Early morning strollers on a
Maui beach.

Cholo's Homestyle Mexican II ((808) 637-3059 (moderate), North Shore Marketplace, serves a good Mexican breakfast and is fast earning a reputation with locals as a good place to dine.

Jameson's by the Sea ((808) 637-4336 (expensive), 62-540 Kamehameha Highway, is conveniently located as you enter Haleiwa from the northeast. It has a comfortable bar, patio dining at lunch, and an elegant dining room for dinner. Prices are reasonable and the food is admirable. The restaurant is noted for its seafood — and there's no charge for the famed north shore sunset. While at Jameson's, try the north shore fudge.

Exiting Haleiwa at its western extremity, the road forks to the right at Thompson's Corner, taking the traveler to **Mokuleia**. The way is somewhat rutted, but press on, for Mokuleia is a very interesting and attractive place. Here Kamehameha Highway gives way to Farrington Highway and runs through sugar cane fields and ranches.

On your way back to Honolulu, Highway 99 runs through miles of pineapple fields. Stop at the **Del Monte Pineapple Variety Garden**, where you can get a crash course in the history of this prickly fruit which once played such an important role in the state's economy.

Coming off the highway on your left is the town of Wahiawa, which attracts more native Hawaiians than it does tourists because of two historic sites. In north Wahiawa are the **Wahiawa Birthing Stones** where the wives of chiefs came to give birth on the curved surfaces of the stones. The **Healing Stones**, in a building at 108 California Street, are said to have great powers of healing. Believers come bearing ritual offerings of ti leaves and flowers, convinced the stones can cure them of their pain.

The H2 from Wahiawa connects with the H1 and will take you back to Honolulu past the towns of Pearl City and Aiea.

WEST ALONG THE WAINAE COAST

There is an exterior toughness to the Wainae Coast that reflects the economic circumstances of the people who live here. This corner of the island is one of the last bastions of Hawaiian culture. There is a determined

movement to preserve this culture, and from Makaha to Nanakuli, that movement appears to be growing.

Lanikuhonua, near Paradise Cove, could become the center of this renaissance. Now an 11-acre (four-and-a-half-hectare) institute for the sharing of Hawaiian culture, Lanikuhonua was the site where Queen Kaahumanu bathed and performed rituals. It is destined to become the prime venue for the flourishing Hawaiian art forms. A hula platform, the *pa hula*, has been built, blessed and dedicated. Hawaiian organizations are being encouraged to use it for functions and workshops and for exhibiting and learning the skills of old Hawaii.

Every night of the week, bus loads of tourists come here for a sampling of Hawaiian food and culture at the open-air luaus at **Paradise Cove** ((808) 945-3571 and **Germaine's** ((808) 941-3338. There, they eat and drink Hawaiian style and are entertained by dancers and singers from this part of the island.

The construction of a new resort hotel, the **Ihilani Spa and Resort** ((808) 679-0079 TOLL-FREE (800) 626-4446 FAX (808) 679-0295 WEBSITE http://www.ihilani.com, 92-1001 Olani Street, Ko Olina, HI 96707 (expensive to luxury), is giving this stretch of coast a much needed economic lift. It has a perfect swimming beach with little wave action. Its attractions include spacious guest rooms, a huge spa and fitness center and five restaurants. The 18-hole Ted Robinson championship golf course is nearby.

The hotel's **Naupaka Terrace** restaurant serves breakfast, lunch and dinner, blending fresh local ingredients with the flavors of Southeast Asia. **Ushio-Tei** is the hotel's specialty Japanese restaurant serving sushi and other authentic Japanese cuisine.

Because of its prime fishing waters, the Waianae Coast was once the center of island life. Waianae has some marvelous surfing beaches, particularly at Makaha, where international surfing contests are still held.

Three miles north of Makaha is the **Cave of Kane** (Kaneana), also known as Makua Cave. The cave is enormous, in some places 460 ft (140 m) deep and 100 ft (30 m) high. Legend has it that this was the home of Kamahoalii, half human, half shark, who feasted on passersby. Another mile down the road is **Makua Beach**, where much of James Michener's epic, *Hawaii*, was filmed.

Keawaula Beach (Yokohama Bay) is another beach favored by board surfers, body surfers and fishermen. Beyond this bay is **Kaena Point**, the extreme northwestern tip of the island and the end of the highway. To proceed any farther you need a four-wheel drive vehicle.

WAIANAE AFTER DARK

The ancient Hawaiians practiced the art of storytelling at night by torchlight. Modern-day storytellers **Glen Grant and Keone Nunes** ((808) 943-0371 try to recreate this atmosphere as they guide you through a Waianae that few tourists see. The pair will introduce you to the legends and history of this colorful and very Hawaiian community, stopping at interesting sites where you'll be entertained and feasted. At Pokai Bay, for instance, there's a performance of ancient hula kahiko near the remains of the Kuiliola heiau. An informal Hawaiian-style meal will be served as you relax on woven mats. After the sun has gone down, the tour will continue to Keawaula near Kaene Point, the northernmost point on the island, where Hawaiians believe the ghosts of the dead depart this world. Here Grant and Nunes will share legends about life after death. Next it's on to Makua Valley, where at Kaneana Cave there will be more tales of this spirit-filled region.

HEADING INLAND

For one of the greatest views on the island of Oahu, visit the 985-ft (300-m) **Nuuanu Pali Lookout** along the Pali Highway. From this windswept vantage point you can look down the Koolau Mountain Range to the windward side of the island. The cliffs here have been finely chiseled and carved by wind and water. It was here, in 1795, that the warriors of Kamehameha the Great routed the Oahu army, under Kalanikupule, and his allies under Kaiana. Defeated warriors who were unable to escape down the steep trails were driven over the cliffs.

Nuuanu gets plenty of rain, and the landscape is dominated by thick, dark green forest. While in this area, take the opportunity to dine at a genuine Japanese teahouse and visit a number of historic sites. The **Nuuanu Onsen** ((808) 595-2885, 87 Laimi Road, Honolulu, HI 96817, tucked away in a residential corner of Nuuanu, will transport you to old Japan. The restaurant is a split-level affair with tatami mat floors, sliding shoji screens and lanterns. Kimono-clad waitresses pad their way to the various rooms, serving food, sometimes entertaining, while you dine on Japanese delicacies. Be sure to book well in advance because Nuuanu Onsen is very popular.

Not far from Nuuanu Onsen is **Queen Emma's Summer Palace and Museum** ((808)

595-3167, 2913 Pali Highway, once home of Kamehameha IV and his wife Emma. The palace stands amid huge shade trees and remains a quiet, cool retreat from city life. It is open daily and there are tours of the premises.

Located at 2261 Nuuanu Avenue is the **Royal Mausoleum**, the most important burial site in Hawaii, where Kings Kamehameha II, III, IV, Kalakaua and Queen Liliuokalani are interred. About three blocks down Nuuanu Avenue is **Foster Botanical Gardens** ((808) 533-3214, 180 North Vineyard Boulevard, where some of Oahu's extraordinary protected trees grow.

Pineapple harvests will soon be a thing of the past in Hawaii.

Oahu: The Gathering Place

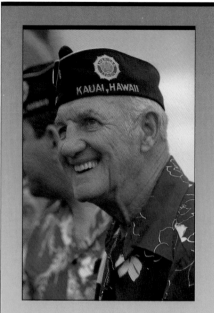

Kauai
The Garden Isle

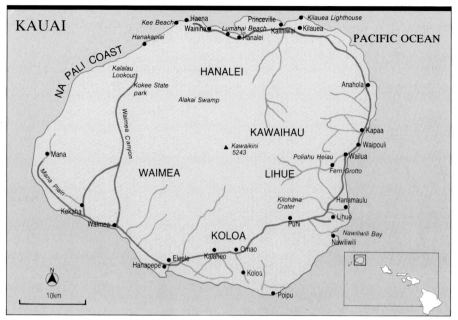

Population: 51,177
Main town: Lihue
Area: 553 sq miles (1,432 sq km)
Length: 33 miles (53 km); *width:* 25 miles (40 km)
Highest elevation: Kawaikini, 5,243 ft (1,598 m)
Airports: Lihue; Princeville
Harbors: Nawiliwili; Port Allen; Hanalei Bay
Coastline: 90 miles (145 km)
Products: sugar, bananas, papayas, guava, taro, livestock
Flower: Mokihana

E Pi'i I Ka Nahele
Climb to the upland forest
E Ike Ia Kawaikini
Let us visit Kawaikini
Nana Ia Pihanakalani
And gaze upon Pihanakalani
I Kela Manu Hulu Ma'ema'e
Its birds of plumage so fine
Noiho Pu Me Kahalelehua
Be comrade to Kahalelehua

THE PEARL IN THE CHAIN

Everyone who visits Hawaii has a favorite island. For many, it's Kauai, long the inspiration of poets and artists. Kauai is shaped and replenished by the waters that run off the towering rock faces of Mount Waialeale from whose crater once poured the great lava

flows that built the island. Today, Kauai resembles a lustrous South Sea pearl in the Hawaiian necklace.

The volcano is silent now, but the mountain remains the source that triggers nature's irrigation system — a system that, for millions of years, has carved the magnificent canyons and valleys, fed the lush rain forests and watered the plains, giving the island its unique topography.

Born nearly 10 million years ago, Kauai is the oldest island in the chain. A volcanic eruption some 14,800 ft (4,500 m) in the depths of the Pacific Ocean began the process, with lava piling on lava and, over millions of years, creating the island.

Geologists estimate that most of the surface portion of Kauai is 5.6 million years old. Its basic shape, almost round, is said to have been formed by the initial eruption. At the center of all the activity was the volcano that came to be named Mount Waialeale (Rippling Waters). Waialeale is the largest shield volcano in the islands. It has a volume of about 1,000 cubic miles (4,200 cubic km) and a diameter at the top of 10 to 12 miles (16 to 19 km).

Its crater, the Alakai Swamp, is some 30 sq miles (78 sq km) of seeping bog and mud

Dappled waters and palms of Haena Point on Kauai's lovely northern shores.

almost always shrouded in mist and pelted by rain—a treacherous place where sunlight is scarce and where moss and ferns flourish and trees grow only to knee height. But the swamp is a botanist's Aladdin's Cave and a fascinating, endless source of discovery.

Alakai Swamp is also the source of seven rivers and innumerable waterfalls that have gouged spectacular canyons, sharpened knife-edged cliffs, and fed the valleys and the plains. Indeed, Kauai is the only inhabited island in the chain with navigable rivers.

Waialeale's peaks rise to 5,243 ft (1,598 m), just the right height to draw the rain clouds like a mantle. The resulting rainfall of 450 inches (1,143 cm) each year makes Waialeale the wettest place on earth. Add rich volcanic soil and ample sunshine and you have the ideal conditions for a vast tropical garden—which has earned Kauai its sobriquet "the Garden Isle."

The rich mix of sun, rain and fertile land causes hillsides to come alive with wild bougainvillea in flaming reds, purples, oranges, pinks and whites, encourages water lilies which open in bursts of rich burgundy and mauve and turns the grass in the grazing meadows an iridescent green.

It was this abundance of rain and sunshine that attracted planters to create the islands' first sugar cane plantation at Koloa in 1835. This plantation, in south Kauai, spawned an industry.

Kauai's people are a hardy breed, having weathered the wrath of nature and charted their own course. Kauai was the one island King Kamehameha the Great never conquered, and to this day, the island retains a fiercely independent streak.

A TURBULENT PAST

Kauai's early history is as turbulent as that of any of the other islands in the chain. Armed combat often occurred between the chiefs and the alii. The vanquished were shown little mercy. Defeated warriors not slain in battle were sacrificed to the gods at the heiaus. Even women and children were not spared.

In the midst of such turmoil a chief named Kaumualii — born to the hereditary ruling chieftess of Kauai, Kamakahelei, and Kaeo, high chief of Maui and King of Kauai — rose

to be king of Kauai. Kamakahelei is said to have given birth to Kaumualii at the Birthstones in Wailua on the island of Oahu, where royalty traditionally came to give birth. Kaumualii, who was also the grandson of the great Maui warrior-king Kekaulike, was only 16 when he became king, but even at that age believed that because of his royal blood he was a superior being to Kamehameha and refused to heed Kamehameha's call for a united Hawaii.

In the spring of 1796, Kamehameha decided to end the impasse once and for all and assembled an enormous fleet of 1,500 canoes and an army of warriors totaling 10,000. This impressive armada set sail at midnight from the beaches of Waianae, Oahu. Halfway across the Kaieie Waho Channel that divides Kauai from Oahu, a sudden storm swamped the canoes. To prevent his entire fleet from being destroyed, Kamehameha gave the order to return to Oahu.

It was to be almost eight years before Kamehameha would try to conquer Kauai again. This time his forces included 7,000 warriors and about 50 Europeans armed with muskets. He also had some heavy artillery cannons, swivel guns and mortars, as well as several armed schooners to support his fleet of canoes.

Just as he was about to launch his attack from eastern Oahu, Kamehameha's forces were struck by what scholars now believe was typhoid fever. Among the hundreds of warriors who died were many loyal and powerful chiefs.

Kamehameha had not given up hope of bringing Kauai into his kingdom, but he decided to resort to diplomacy in order to do so. Finally, in 1810, he and Kaumualii met in Oahu, and it seemed as though the islands would be entering a period of genuine peace. But when Kaumualii was told of a plot to poison him, he returned in haste to Kauai.

When Kamehameha died, his son Liholiho (Kamehameha II) succeeded him. In 1821 Liholiho set sail for Waialua from Honolulu, ostensibly to inspect the gathering of sandalwood. En route he ordered the vessel to change course and headed for Kauai, where he met Kaumualii. The two kings made declarations of peace and then left on a 45-day tour of the island of Kauai. On a Sunday in September, the two kings met once more in Waimea Harbor where Kaumualii joined Liholiho on his yacht, the *Pride of Hawaii*. That night, Liholiho gave orders for the vessel to set sail for Oahu and in so doing, kidnapped the Kauai king.

The brains behind this deception was Kamehameha's widow, the imperious Kaahumanu. Four days after landing on Oahu, Kaahumanu forced Kaumualii to become her husband, and a short time later, married Kaumualii's son, Kealiiahonui. After her conversion to Christianity, Kaahumanu released Kealiiahonui from his forced marriage.

In 1824 Kaumualii fell ill and died suddenly, and Kauai was plunged into mourning. His death divided the kingdom of Kauai between those loyal to Liholiho and those who still wished for the independent days of Kaumualii. A rebellion, led by George Kaumualii, son of the former king, supported by Deborah Kapule, favorite wife of the late king, ended in a disastrous rout for the rebels after troops under Governor Hoapili of Maui were brought in.

In the aftermath of this defeat, the island was looted and the chiefs deported to Oahu, Maui and Hawaii.

History records that the nobles of Kauai always worked in the best interests of the people, who loved and honored them. This unity may still characterize the people of Kauai more than it does the people of the other islands.

That pride and sense of independence survive even today and stand the people in good stead in times of crisis. Evidence of the character of the people of this island has been seen in the wake of two devastating storms — one in 1982, the other 10 years later. The 1982 Hurricane Iwa brought the island to its knees. Then, in September 1992, Hurricane Iniki struck the island an almost lethal blow. It was the strongest storm to strike Hawaii in a century. The hurricane's eye, fifteen miles (25 km) in diameter, leveled almost everything in its path. Winds, waves and rains battered the island. Houses, apartments and hotels were left in ruin. Almost none of its once burgeoning tourism facilities were left standing, and residents were left with nowhere to go. The hurricane caused

an estimated $1 billion dollars in structural damage and left the island's tourism industry in shambles.

Today, Kauai's revival continues to gather momentum. Much of what was destroyed has been rebuilt, and the industrious people of Kauai have once again made their beautiful island a pleasure to visit.

LIHUE

Planes land at its airport and liners dock in Nawiliwili Harbor disgorging tourists, but Lihue is far more than a mere gateway to Kauai. It's a lively town. The island's business and government seat, as well as a residential center, Lihue boasts venues for live entertainment, and has become the cultural focal point of the island.

WHAT TO SEE AND DO

Not far from the Lihue town center, on Maalo Road (Route 583), is **Wailua Falls**, an 80-foot (24-m) cascade that drops into a pool once regarded as the private playground of the nobility. The falls were featured in the television series, *Fantasy Island*.

A major attraction in Lihue is **Kilohana** ((808) 245-5608, 3-2087 Kaukualii Highway, the old plantation house of Gaylord P. Wilcox, nephew of one of the island's legendary sugar kings, George Wilcox. The Wilcox family also owns **Grove Farm Homestead** ((808) 245-3202 in Lihue, now a museum complex. Lying empty since the early 1970s, Kilohana has recaptured its 1930s grandeur. Many of the fine antique pieces which once decorated this gracious old house have been recovered and restored to it.

Set amidst 1,704 acres (690 hectares) of cane fields, Kilohana in its heyday attracted political and religious leaders, businessmen and intellectuals who gathered to socialize and discuss the events of the day. The magnificent open horseshoe-shaped lanai has been converted into a restaurant appropriately named Gaylord's (see below). Most of the smaller rooms on the ground floor, with the exception of what was the main living room, and the dining room have been turned into a variety of retail shops selling everything from island crafts and fine jewelry to Niihau shell necklaces and scrimshaw, high fashion and fine art. In the restored guest cottages around the complex, Hawaiian food products, a fragrance store and a plant shop are found.

Visitors to Kilohana can tour the plantation in a 106-year-old horse-drawn carriage shipped from Fairbanks, Alaska.

WHERE TO STAY

Sitting on the edges of Kalapaki Beach and Nawiliwili Harbor is the **Marriott Kauai Resort and Beach Club (** (808) 245-5050 TOLL-

FREE (800) 220-2925 FAX (808) 245-2993, 3610 Rice Street, Kalapaki Beach, Lihue, HI 96766 (expensive), the largest hotel on the island. It has a golf course, swimming pool, tennis complex, and 40 acres (16 hectares) of freshwater tropical lagoons that serve as a sanctuary for exotic wildlife.

The family-owned and operated **Garden Island Inn (** (808) 245-7227 TOLL-FREE (800) 648-0154, 3445 Wilcox Road, Kalapaki Beach,Lihue HI 96766 (inexpensive to mid-range) is near the Kauai Marriott. This quaint and intimate hostelry has all the comforts of home in a tropical setting. The inn is a short walk to beach, shops and restaurants.

Kaha lani means "heavenly place," and the **Aston Kaha Lani** TOLL-FREE (800) 922-7866,

4460 Nehe Road, Lihue, HI 96746 (mid-range to expensive) is certainly that. This property sits amidst lush tropical landscaping and miles of sandy white beach. The spacious one-, two- and three-bedroom suites come with fully equipped kitchens. Amenities include pool and tennis courts.

The **Outrigger Kauai Beach (** (808) 245-1955 FAX (808) 246-9085, 4331 Kauai Beach Drive, Lihue, HI 96766 (mid-range to expensive) is an oceanfront resort hotel on Kauai's Royal Coconut Coast.

WHERE TO EAT

The presence of the Marriott has improved tourist traffic through Lihue and helped popularize a string of good restaurants in the area.

Gaylord's ((808) 245-9593 (expensive) looks across the sweeping lawns of the Kilohana plantation to the majesty of the Kilohana crater. This is an elegant, expensive restaurant, where you will enjoy both the quality of the food and the experience.

One of the better restaurants on the island, and certainly in Lihue, is **Café Portofino (** (808) 245-2121 (expensive), Pacific Ocean Plaza, 3501 Rice Street, Nawiliwili. Master chef Christian Risos was trained by both French and Italian chefs and restaurateurs. His forte is northern Italian cuisine, and the meals are light and fresh. Try *coniglio al vino bianco olive nere* (rabbit sautéed in white wine or black olives and herbs). His *osso buco all'arancio* (veal shank in orange sauce) and eggplant *parmigiana* are also tasty. Café Portofino also offers the best lunch deal in town: an all-you-can-eat buffet of hot and cold pastas, frittatas, salads and desserts. **Duke's Canoe Club Barefoot Bar and Restaurant (** (808) 246-9599 (moderate), at the Marriott Kauai, has great atmosphere and good food. Situated on Kalapaki Bay, Duke's serves excellent seafood and prime rib. Their hula pie is well worth trying.

Not many tourists take the trouble to seek out the **Tip Top Motel and Bakery (** (808) 245-2333 (moderate), 3173 Akahi Street, Lihue, but if you do, your effort will not be in vain. This unpretentious restaurant, family run for 75 years, serves one of the better breakfasts in town. Specialties include pineapple and macadamia nut pancakes and fresh-baked bear claws. On Wednesday, Friday and Sunday, their lunch menu includes a fine ox tail soup. Prices are very reasonable.

EXPLORING KAUAI

Kauai can be divided into five touring zones as follows: the east coast; the north coast and Princeville; the Na Pali Coast; the south coast including Poipu to Kekaha; and finally — Kauai's biggest attractions — Waimea Canyon State Park and Kokee State Park in the highlands.

river is the Mount Waialeale watershed, which feeds all seven of the island's rivers. Going upstream from the ocean, the river splits, the northern fork going far inland to the base of the mountain range, the southern fork going past the famed **Fern Grotto** and onto **Opaekaa Falls**.

Fern Grotto is one of the most photographed and publicized caves in the world. This huge subterranean amphitheater with its emerald glow and cascading ferns has been the scene for numerous weddings. The Fern Grotto is only accessible by boat on tours

THE EAST COAST

A journey tracing the eastern seaboard takes you along the Kuhio Highway (Highway 56), past Wailua and Wailua Bay, Waipouli, Kapaa, Anahola and Anahola Bay.

Exit Lihue Airport Road and turn right onto Kuhio Highway (Highway 56), and you are on the Royal Coconut Coast. Just before you reach the little town of Wailua, you'll come across **Lydgate State Park**, situated behind the Kauai Resort Hotel. Kids love this spot not only for its swimming, but for its great playground designed by the children of Kauai and built by residents.

The town of **Wailua** is situated at the mouth of the Wailua River. The source of the

conducted by **Waialeale Boat Tours (** (808) 822-4908. Singers entertain tourists on these river cruises. The tour office is located just inside Wailua River State Park. Features on the river's north fork include Kamokila, a recreated Hawaiian village in a beautiful setting that captures the lifestyle of an ancient past. Further upriver is the Keahua Arboretum, the perfect place for picnics and a cool dip on a hot day in the nearby swimming hole.

OPPOSITE: The evening festivities might begin with the sound of the conch shell horn. ABOVE: An antique outrigger canoe adorns the lobby of a luxury resort.

Kauai: The Garden Isle

WHERE TO STAY

There are several bed-and-breakfast places in this area, but if you want a quiet, secluded hideaway, you may want to try **Kauai Vacation Cottage** TOLL-FREE (800) 822-9565 (inexpensive), behind Sleeping Giant Hill and above the Wailua River. Your hosts are Steven and Tracy Bauman. The cottage on their property offers panoramic views of numerous waterfalls and the rain forests of Mount Waialeale. The accommodation includes a bed-

room and living area with high vaulted ceilings and ceiling fans, plus a kitchenette. The cottage comes equipped with color television and a private phone. Some of the island's best hiking trails are on your doorstep. The hosts live on the property in the main residence and can advise you on beaches, shopping and entertainment.

COCONUT PLANTATION RESORT

The Coconut Plantation Resort in **Waipouli** is a crowded complex of hotels and resorts laid out on a stretch of Waipouli Beach. The seashore at Coconut is better for strolling than swimming because of the reef which lies just offshore.

One of the better hotels in the complex is **Kauai Coconut Beach Resort** TOLL-FREE (800) 22-ALOHA, Coconut Plantation, P.O. Box 830, Kapaa, HI 96746 WEBSITE http://www.kcb.com (mid-range to expensive), a sprawling multi-winged building with large, airy guestrooms with lanais, garden-like public areas, and a 40-ft (12-m) waterfall cascading into a reflecting pool in the lobby. There are good tennis courts, a swimming pool, and live music in a couple of the restaurants. The hotel's most popular attraction is the luau, rated by many as the best on the island.

The **Islander on the Beach** TOLL-FREE (800) 822-7417 FAX (808) 822-1947, 484 Kuhio Highway, Kapaa, HI 96746 (mid-range) is a Hawaiian plantation resort set in six acres (two and a half hectares) of tropical garden and 500 ft (150 m) of perfect beach. Activities include swimming, SCUBA diving and snorkeling.

Formerly known as the Kauai Resort Hotel, the **Wailua Bay Resort** ((808) 245-3931 TOLL-FREE (800) 272-5275 FAX (808) 822-7339, 3-5920 Kuhio Highway, Kapaa, HI 96746 (mid-range to expensive) is situated on a splendid beachfront setting in the Coconut Plantation Resort. A protective cove fronts the beach, making it ideal for snorkeling. Two swimming pools, a restaurant and tennis courts are among the amenities.

KAPAA TO ANAHOLA BAY

Not far from Coconut Plantation is **Kapaa**, a quaint and characteristic Kauai small town. Flowers decorate windows, and planters hang outside restaurants and shops. Kapaa's narrow streets invite you to walk and browse. Don't forget to visit Old Kapaa Town. There you'll find a variety of interesting merchandise and art, from glass to batiks, handpainted silk to Hawaiian crafts and rare books.

The further you get from Lihue, the greener and more rural the countryside becomes. Past Kapaa you come across some of the finest beaches on the eastern side of the island. **Kealia Beach**, for example, is a favorite with the locals. Kapaa Stream exits near this beach and can create strong currents, so be careful.

ABOVE: Fern Grotto, a lush hideaway on the Wailua River. OPPOSITE: Wailua Falls tumbles into deep clear pools.

Kauai: The Garden Isle

Further north, the water is calmer. Surfers love this spot, and the beach is a great place to watch the action.

Canefield dirt roads lead from the highway to **Donkey Beach,** but since private vehicles are not permitted on these roads, the only way to reach this beach favored by nudists is on foot. This is an undeveloped stretch of coast that is quite beautiful. From Donkey Beach you can see the migration of the whales each winter.

Still further north is **Anahola Bay**. It's a wide sweeping bay, at the south end of which lies a reef-enclosed pool that's perfectly safe for swimming.

Where to Stay and Eat

For the budget-conscious traveler, the reasonably priced **Aston Kauai Beachboy Hotel** TOLL-FREE (800) 922-7866, 4-484 Kuhio Highway, Kapaa, HI 96746 (mid-range to expensive) has guest rooms and one-bedroom suites. Amenities include a pool, tennis courts and a restaurant.

French chef Jean-Marie Josselin of **A Pacific Café-Kauai (** (808) 822-0013 (expensive), 4-831 Kuhio Highway, in the Kauai Village, combines the flavors of Japan, China and other East Asian countries with those of his native land. Try the deep-fried ahi sashimi with wasabe lime sauce, or the baked potato soup with smoked marlin and sour cream. Main dishes include stir-fried chicken with garlic peanut sauce, or grilled swordfish with coconut basil curry sauce.

There are Mexican restaurants all over the islands, but a good choice is **Norberto El Café (** (808) 822-3362 (moderate), 4-1373 Kuhio Highway. Prices are reasonable and the food is excellent. Try their outrageous burrito or fresh fish taco.

If you're into omelets and big breakfasts, then the **Kountry Kitchen (** (808) 882-3511 (moderate), 1485 Kuhio Avenue, Kapaa, is the place. The Kitchen boasts an 18-item omelet bar and claims to serve the finest banana pancakes on the island. The hungryman's breakfast is served on a huge tin plate. At lunchtime, the Kitchen specializes in mixed plates, a Hawaiian tradition (see HAWAIIAN FOOD SPECIALTIES, page 73). These include complete meals featuring everything from grilled mahimahi to "Kountry" chicken

served with hot corn bread. There's also a wide variety of burgers and sandwiches to choose from. At dinner, Kountry Kitchen offers down-home country-style dining. It's a good place to take hungry kids.

THE NORTH COAST

From Kilauea, the north shore tour carries you through the superb Princeville Resort and Hanalei, with its gorgeous bay, all the way to where the road ends at Ke'e Beach. Ahead is the Na Pali Coast.

A few hundred yards past the 23-mile marker on Kuhio Highway, a sign directs the traveler to Kilauea Lighthouse, the northernmost point in the Hawaiian islands. To reach the lighthouse and bird sanctuary drive through Kilauea.

KILAUEA

When the large sugar plantation on which the economy of Kilauea depended shut down, the people rallied. Supported by the International Longshore Workers' Union to which most of the townspeople belonged, the residents and the plantation owners put together a deal enabling most of the workers to buy their houses. A new job training program was started, and the people did the rest.

Kilauea prospers today. There is a complex of little shops and a charming Italian restaurant built around the old Kong Lung Company and general store. These buildings date from 1881 and were recently given a facelift. The complex includes a jewelry store and a flower shop, in addition to the restaurant. There's also a wine store called Farmers' Market with a fine selection.

After stocking up on goodies at the Kong Lung Center, proceed down Kilauea Road to **Kilauea Lighthouse** and **bird sanctuary**. The lighthouse, built in 1913, stands stark and lonely on the lip of a high cliff. It once housed the largest lens of its kind in the world. When an automated light was installed in 1967, the old lighthouse became obsolete and was taken over by the United States Fish and Wildlife Service, which also oversees the sanctuary surrounding the lighthouse. The sanctuary consists of 31 acres (12.5 hectares) of cliffs and headlands rising 200 ft (60 m) above the surf. It is home to red-footed boo-bies, shearwaters, frigatebirds, red-tailed and white-tailed tropicbirds, Laysan albatrosses and brown boobies. The sanctuary is open daily from 10 AM to 4 PM, except national holi-days. The entrance fee is a maximum of $2 per family.

On the road back to the highway, note **Christ Memorial Church** with its English stained glass windows. The church also fea-tures a handsome hand-carved altar.

Where to Stay

Pavilions at Seacliff ((808) 828-6615 TOLL-FREE (800) 292-6615 FAX (808) 828-1208, P.O. Box 3500-302, Princeville, HI 96722-3500 is a seven-acre (three-hectare) private estate adjacent to Kilauea Lighthouse, with tennis and volleyball courts, putting green, Jacuzzi, gym and three master suites. Call for cur-rent rates.

Just outside the town of Kilauea and 10 minutes from Princeville is **Makai Farms** ((808) 828-1874 FAX (808) 828-1048 (mid-range), a little slice of paradise in a country setting. This private two-story cottage is a vacation hideaway with mountain views set amidst tropical fruit trees such as avocado, mango, banana, papaya, lychee and star fruit. The property has majestic Cook pines, un-usual tropical flowers and an orchid nurs-ery that can be explored at leisure. The bed-room is upstairs and can accommodate four people. The kitchen is on the ground floor. There's a private sitting area outside with a shower for when you come in off the beach.

The **Kilauea Lakeside Estate** ((808) 312-379-7842 is a gated retreat on a three-acre (1.2-hectare) peninsula surrounded by a private 20-acre (eight-hectare) freshwater lake with over 1,000 ft (300 m) of frontage and a secluded white sand beach nestled in a cove. Forty varieties of fruit trees dot the property. The lake offers a variety of water sports in-cluding boating, kayaking and fishing. Chil-dren love the treehouse overlooking the lake and the rock-filled freshwater stream mean-dering through a rain forest. The house has three bedrooms, three baths and soaring cathedral ceilings with windows that open onto magnificent views of the property. Rates vary by season, but Christmas rates, for example, are $2,500 per week.

Where to Eat

The Kong Lung Center on Lighthouse Road may be an unlikely place for one of the best Italian restaurants and pizza places on the island, but this is the home of the **Kilauea Bakery and Pau Hana Pizza** ((808) 828-2020 (inexpensive). The Bakery turns out superb breads and pastries. As for the pizzas, they'd pass any taste test. It's good food at a good price.

Casa di Amici ((808) 828-1555 (expensive) can be recommended for its setting and some of the most authentic Italian food this side of Napoli. Veal, beef and fish dishes are pre-pared in a variety of Italian styles with subtle herb and spice flavors. Casa di Amici is a highly rated restaurant that attracts patrons from all over the world.

KALIHIWAI ROAD TO PRINCEVILLE

From Kilauhea, continue your journey on Kuhio Highway and turn right on **Kalihiwai Road**. Guava trees line this byway and their heady scent is in the air. The fruit is deli-cious when ripe and there's plenty of it. When you can drive no further, you'll find yourself facing Kalihiwai Bay and one of the loveliest beaches on the island. This great swimming beach with its fine white sand and warm clear waters may be one of Kauai's best kept secrets. Stately ironwood trees line the arc of the beach, and dunes fringe the point where the Kalihiwai River empties into the ocean.

At one time, Kalihiwai Road looped its way down to the beach, crossed the river and came up on the far side of Kuhio Highway, but in 1957 a tidal wave lashed this coastline and washed away the bridge and the road across the river. It was never rebuilt.

If you take the second Kalihiwai Road you'll end up at **Annini Beach Park**. The waters here are considered among the safest on the island for swimming since a reef 200 yards (182 m) offshore provides perfect protection. Novice windsurfers love it here because the winds are constant and the bot-tom is shallow. Underwater experiences are as great as those above the surface because of the variety of marine life that exists in and around the reef. As for the beach itself, beach-combers think its the best because of the variety of seashells that wash up on its sandy shores.

Kuhio Highway leads through the **Kalihiwai Tree Tunnel**, a glorious canopy of green — all but destroyed by the winds of Hurricane Iwa and battered again by Iniki — but slowly regaining its glory. From the scenic lookout shortly after exiting the tunnel, you'll see the valley and the waterfalls that feed the Kalihiwai River.

The road now drifts inland, though the ocean is never far away. On the left is **Princeville Airport** where most of the helicopter tours to the Na Pali Coast and Waimea Canyon depart (see TAKING A TOUR, page 103).

PRINCEVILLE

The 11,000 acres (4,450 hectares) of the Princeville region was once a ranch owned by one of the most charismatic westerners to serve the Hawaiian kings. Robert Wyllie, in fact, served three kings and represented the islands in their dealings with foreign powers. Princeville is named after Prince Albert Edward Kauikeaouli, the two-year-old son of King Kamehameha IV and Queen Emma who captured the heart of Wyllie while on a visit to the ranch. Two years later the little prince was dead, a victim of a terrible fever. Kamehameha IV died a year later, many said from a broken heart.

The views across the bay from Princeville are nothing short of breathtaking. The bay, once a busy harbor for whalers and traders, is today used mostly as a harbor for pleasure boats and tour boats which ferry tourists to the diving sites and on water tours of the Na Pali Coast.

Where to Stay and Eat

Two miles (three kilometers) from the entrance to Princeville and perched on a spectacular site overlooking the wide expanse of Hanalei Bay is the **Sheraton Princeville Hotel** ((808) 826-9644 TOLL-FREE (800) 826-4400 FAX (808) 826-1166, 5520 Ka Haku Road, Princeville, HI 96722-3069 (expensive). From almost every angle in the hotel, guests are afforded breathtaking views of Hanalei Bay. Pastel shades of Italian marble, fireplaces and overstuffed couches and chairs, seventeenth and eighteenth cen-

tury antiques and the original piano built about 1730 by L. Simonette grace the public areas. Some of the old Hawaiian quilts that adorned the former property have been retained, but much of the original collection has been donated to museums.

The rooms of the Princeville Hotel are built into the cliffs and descend to the beach in a series of steps. Each floor has butler service.

One of Princeville Hotel's fine restaurants is **La Cascata** (expensive), overlooking Hanalei Bay. Emerald mountains paint a backdrop to the sparkling ocean below. La Cascata specializes in Mediterranean food with the accent on fish dishes and light sauces. The menu is extensive, but here are a couple of items to whet your appetite: baked island snapper with Kauai sweet basil, and sautéed veal medallions with lemon butter and capers. La Cascata also has an excellent wine cellar. The Friday night seafood buffet is a treat not to be missed. The chefs create a remarkable variety of imaginative dishes for this weekly event.

For a special evening, have a romantic candlelight dinner on the beach below the hotel. You can order your meal from either La Cascata or the **Café Hanalei** (moderate) dinner menu.

The **Hanalei Bay Resort and Suites** ((808) 591-2235 TOLL-FREE (800) 367-5004 FAX (808) 596-0158, 5380 Honoiki Road, Princeville, HI 96722 (mid-range) is one of several fine hotels and condominiums in this area.

The **Bali Hai** restaurant (expensive) at the Hanalei Bay Resort has an expansive open-air lanai providing unrestricted views of the mystical mountain Makana — known as Bali Hai ever since *South Pacific* was filmed there. Watching the sunset strike this lovely peak from the restaurant named in its honor, is a real joy. And the food is good too. The chefs create wonderful fresh tastes with their homegrown herbs and spices. Try the chicken creole, a blend of chicken, herbs, spices and Drambuie.

HANALEI

Despite catering to a rush of tourists in recent years, Hanalei has managed to retain its plantation town atmosphere. Cozy restaurants do a thriving business, as do shops and stores which supply campers, hikers, hunters, fishermen or aquatic sportsmen. An art gallery, surf shop and a clothing store add color to an old schoolhouse. From Hanalei there are deep-sea fishing excursions, river cruises, Zodiac boat trips to the Na Pali Coast, sunset catamaran cruises, and almost any outdoor activity.

Hanalei Trader and the nearby **Ching Young Village Gas Station** are the last two places on the north shore where you can buy gasoline for your car or any other essential

a primal landscape of volcanic rock festooned with rain-drenched forests. White sand beaches, featured in classic movies such as *South Pacific, King Kong,* and more recently, *The Thornbirds,* and *Jurassic Park,* line the edges of these forests.

LUMAHAI BEACH

Leaving Hanalei, Kuhio Highway crosses the Waioli Stream. Note in the meadow on the left the grove of plum trees; they grow profusely on the north shore. Your journey takes

item for a day out in the woods or on an isolated beach. The **Ching Young General Store**, a family enterprise, has been a part of the Hanalei community for almost a century. When a new store opened its doors just down the street in 1981, the old store seemed doomed. It closed, only to reopen a few months later as the island's cultural center.

Before proceeding along the highway, make a point of exploring the town's inner roads leading to the beach. **Black Pot** and **Pine Trees Beach Park** are both lovely.

Further down Highway 56 on the left are the **Waioli Hui'ia Church** and the **Waioli Mission Home**, now a museum.

The eight miles (13 km) from Hanalei to the beginning of the Na Pali Coast remains

you around the edges of Hanalei Bay as you head for **Ke'e**. It is quiet in this rural area, and so it comes as something of a surprise when, after passing the 32-mile marker, to come upon the buzz, hum and traffic of **Lumahai Beach,** made famous as the locale for many of the great scenes in the movie *South Pacific.*

To reach Lumahai, take the small trail which begins at the second stone wall. Despite its natural beauty, Lumahai's waters can be deceptive. It is easy to be dazzled by the combination of lava rock, blue waters, white sand fringed by hala trees, and forget the dangers which lie offshore. Lumahai's

A rainbow adds to the color and serenity of the verdant Hanalei Valley.

currents have a habit of turning nasty. In the winter months, waves 20 to 30 ft (six to nine meters) high pound these shores. Even on a good summer's day, and even if you are a good surfer or swimmer, approach Lumahai with caution; swimmers have perished here.

WAINIHA

The next little community down the road is **Wainiha** with its pretty valley on the left and the bay on the right. The bay will probably be empty, which may prompt the obvious question: "Why?" The answer is that this particular bay is a nursery for young tiger sharks and hammerheads. The parents stay further out, but locals decided long ago that discretion was the better part of valor. They fish in this bay, but few dare to swim in it. Wainiha means "fierce water." Now you know why.

Two of the most photographed buildings on the north shore are the Wainiha General Store and Snack Shop and the small house nestling on the edge of a taro patch near the banks of the river.

Wainiha, incidentally, is one of many secluded sites to lay claim to being the birthplace of hula, but with no written record, it is impossible to substantiate this claim or any other.

Haena, which is down the road from Wainiha, was struck by two devastating tidal waves in April 1946 and March 1957 with a high cost in lives and extensive property damage.

The mountains above Haena used to be the domain of the ancient kings of Kauai. From these vantage points, lookouts were stationed to warn people on the plains and in the valleys below of the approach of raiders from the other islands. Kings don't live in Haena anymore, but it continues to attract the rich and famous, such as tennis star Billie Jean King and members of the rock group Crosby, Stills and Nash, all of whom own property here.

Shortly after passing the geodesic house, a road on the right leads to Ke'e and **Tunnels,** one of the most popular beaches on the island. Tunnels gets its name from the numerous small holes and caves in the lava

rock below the waterline carved by centuries of battering by ocean swells. Tunnels also is the breeding ground for a dazzling array of fish, making its waters a paradise for snorkelers.

THE CAVES

As you proceed towards the Na Pali Coast, your journey takes you past three caves, which legend says were dug by the fire goddess Pele in her desperate quest for fire. She eventually gave up in frustration and went looking elsewhere, finally locating that source of energy on the Big Island.

The first cave you'll come to is **Manniholo Cave,** which extends almost 76 yards (70 m) into the base of the mountain. The white sand you'll see was deposited there by the 1957 tidal wave. Water drips from sections of the cave's roof, but it is generally dry inside.

Drive the last two miles (three kilometers) to the end of the road in the shadows of the imposing mountain known as **Bali Hai,** immortalized as Bali Hai Island in the film *South Pacific.*

A rushing stream fills a dark, cold pool on the edge of the highway near **Haena State Park.** A dip in this pool on a hot and humid day will bring the color back to your cheeks in a hurry.

The wet caves just past this point are within walking distance of each other. The first, **Waikapale,** has two large "rooms" tucked away in the recesses of the mountain. One of these caverns extends almost 98 yards (90 m) into the base of the mountain.

The entrance to **Waikanaloa Cave** is off the road and up a gradient. An equally steep gradient takes you down to the water's edge.

If you decide to explore the wet caves, bring a flashlight.

KE'E BEACH

Finally you're at Ke'e Beach, site of one of the most sacred Hawaiian hula heiaus. It was here that male dancers were trained from a young age in the meanings and techniques of the hula, for only male dancers were permitted to learn the art of the old ways. It was here that Pele is said to have first set eyes on Lohiau, the handsome king of Kauai, and decided she wanted to be his wife. Pele, however, told the king she couldn't live with him until she had found fire. Pele journeyed to many islands before striking fire at Kilauea on the Big Island, but by this time, unknown to Pele, Lohiau had died. Pele, yearning for the young king, sent her sister Hiiaka to escort the king back to the Big Island, but warned her not to kiss Lohiau. Accompanied by a woman she found making leis in a forest above Hilo, Hiiaka journeyed to Kauai only to learn of the king's death. Seeing the spirit of Lohiau above the peaks behind the sea, she captured the spirit in a flower and brought him back to life.

Hiiaka, her companion and Lohiau returned to Kilauea. At the crater's rim, Hiiaka's companion left to tell Pele of their arrival. As Pele came to greet them, Hiiaka in a moment of emotion kissed the king, a gesture which enraged Pele. Using her powers, she buried Lohiau in a sea of lava. Pele's brothers, however, brought the king back to life for a second time and took him back to Kauai, where he went into hiding. Here Hiiaka discovered him and they lived happily in Haena for many years. Near the heiau today are what seems to be the remains of a house which legend says was Lohiau's house.

It was on the beach near this site that aspiring dancers camped in the hope of gaining admittance to the famous halau. The school demanded the ultimate in effort and discipline, whether in dance or *meles* (chants). The heiau Ka Ulu A Paoa is named after the hula master Paoa, who was a friend of Lohiau. The dancing pavilion and shrine of Lohiau once stood behind the heiau. In Hawaiian custom, the shrine was dedicated to Laka, goddess of the hula.

Strict rules governed all those fortunate enough to be selected to train here. Graduation was a time of celebration. Hundreds of canoes would be drawn up on the beach, for people came from all the islands to witness the rituals associated with graduation. One of these rituals called for a warrior to climb the heights of the nearby mountain, Makena, and hurl shafts of fire which spiraled, trailing smoke, into the ocean below.

The heiau is tucked away behind the house belonging to Chicago industrialist John Gregg Allerton. You'll have to walk through a gate with a "No Trespassing" sign to get to the site. Treat the area with respect, for the heiau is revered by Hawaiians, particularly by the dancers who come to pay homage to Laka and the spirits of the old dance masters.

Where to Stay

The **Pali Ke Kua Princeville** ((808) 826-9066 TOLL-FREE (800) 535-0085 FAX (808) 826-4159,

5300 Ka Haku Road, Princeville, HI 96714 (mid-range to expensive) has luxury one- and two-bedroom suites perched on the cliffs at Princeville overlooking Hanalei Bay and the mountains. Amenities include full kitchens, a restaurant and pool. It's adjacent to one of the finest golf complexes in the country, Princeville Resort Golf Course (see GOLF: THE ULTIMATE DESTINATION, page 289).

The **Hanalei Colony Resort** ((808) 826-6235 TOLL-FREE (800) 628-3004, P.O. Box 206, Hanalei, HI 96714 (mid-range) has 52 two-bedroom condominiums with private lanais and fully equipped kitchens. Amenities

Kauai's high annual rainfall creates ideal conditions for cultivating taro, a staple of the Hawaiian diet.

include maid service and a pool, but there are no televisions, stereos or phones in the units. This is a secluded beachfront hideaway where you can get away from it all.

The **Hanalei Land Company Ltd.** ((808) 826-1454 FAX (808) 826-6263, P.O. Box 81, Hanalei, HI 96714 is an historic plantation house with guest cottages on the beach at Hanalei Bay. Call for current rates.

Pacific Paradise Properties ((808) 826-7211 TOLL-FREE (800) 800-3637 FAX (808) 826-9884, P.O. Box 3195, Princeville, HI 96722 has beautifully appointed condominiums and a house with all amenities. They offer premier oceanfront and golf course locations. Call for current room rates.

Where to Eat

North shore dining is restricted to Princeville and Hanalei. But there's plenty to choose from in addition to the fine dining at the resorts. The seafood dinners at the **Hanalei Dolphin Restaurant** ((808) 826-6113 (moderate) are particularly good. The bonus here is the view of the Hanalei River. The swinging **Tahiti Nui** ((808) 826-6277 (moderate) presents a family-style luau and show with lots of good local food and plenty of family fun. There's a trendy and expensive Italian restaurant in the Hanalei Center called **Café Luna** ((808) 826-1177 (expensive).

THE NA PALI COAST

Towering and awesome in their wild grandeur, the famous sea cliffs of the **Na Pali Coast** are best seen from boat or helicopter. You can hike the trails of this fabulous wilderness coastline, but cannot explore it in a vehicle (see SEA CAVES AND SECRET COVES, page 16, and HITTING THE TRAIL, page 33).

THE SOUTH COAST

Beginning your southern explorations from Lihue, Highway 56 turns into Highway 50, or Kaumualii Highway. Exit 50 onto Route 520 to explore the former plantation town of Koloa and the resorts of Poipu, then head west to the sugar towns of Hanapepe and Waimea, and on to 15 miles (24 km) of white sand beach at Kekaha. Further along this stretch of coast is Polihale, then Barking

Sands, site of the Pacific Missile Range Facility. Beyond this point is the rugged Na Pali Coast.

The fertile lowlands of south Kauai were an agricultural base for the earliest Polynesian settlers. It was at **Koloa** that the first plantation in Hawaii was started in 1835. Sugar brought a new prosperity to Hawaii with Koloa and Lihue plantations setting the pace. Today, the industry has fallen on hard times, and many plantations and mills have been forced to close. But the enterprise of the sugar barons left a legacy which the people of Kauai continue to build on. Descendants of the Japanese and Filipinos who came to work the plantations now make up the largest percentage of the population, and their skills are dispersed in new industries, chiefly tourism: Towns have been turned into tourist attractions, and plantation houses have been turned into quaint and colorful lodgings, museums, restaurants and specialty galleries.

On leaving Kilohana, continue along Kaumualii Highway, then turn left on Route 520 for **Poipu**, and you find yourself traveling through the beautiful **Tunnel of Trees** on the road to Koloa and the picturesque complex of **Old Koloa Town**. This was Hawaii's original plantation town and also served as the mercantile and retail center for the south side of the island. Within its three acres (1.2 hectares) today, in a setting of monkeypod trees and neat courtyards, is a collection of restored old buildings housing a variety of shops, services and restaurants. At night, the town is gripped by a carnival atmosphere. Driving down the darkened highway, the fairy lights of Old Koloa Town, first seen through the trees, are a welcome sight to the traveler.

POIPU

Poipu, not far beyond Koloa, is Kauai's resort playground. The wonderful beach led to the construction of superb hotels and resorts boasting every luxury the pampered tourist could ever wish for. Unfortunately, the last hurricane to strike Kauai, Hurricane Iniki, was especially severe in this area. Three of the most glamorous of these resort hotels — Poipu Beach Hotel, Sheraton Kauai, and

Stouffer Waiohai Beach Resort — have yet to reopen after closing down for repair and renovation. The Hyatt Regency Kauai Resort and Spa was also forced to shut down but recently reopened. Other hotels and condominiums survived the battering and are running as usual (see WHERE TO STAY, below).

The south shores offer the best swimming, surfing and windsurfing waters in Kauai. Not just Poipu, but the beaches all the way to Kalapaki Beach at Lihue, Hanamaulu to Wailua and Kapaa are ideal for water sports. For surfing, however, Poipu is the best. The most spectacular windsurfing site is **Shipwrecks**. All varieties of water sports from snorkeling to sport fishing are available here.

If you get as far as Shipwrecks, then you must make the extra effort to walk or drive over to **Mahaulepu,** east of the golf course. This rugged coastline differs from almost everything else on the southeastern shores of this island. The limestone cliffs here stand out dramatically against the blue waters. Centuries of pounding by huge ocean rollers has caused deep chasms in the cliffs. You can walk for miles on the trails above the bluffs and watch whales languishing in the waters below. You can also join a trail ride at the nearby stables, or rent a mountain bike and explore the coastal trails and the cane haul roads.

A favorite Poipu attraction is **Spouting Horn** geyser at the end of Lawai Road. This geyser of water shoots out of an ancient lava tube, emitting a sigh as it does so. According to legend, the sound you hear is that of a lizard trapped in the tube. There's a full-scale bazaar in this most unlikely of spots, where you can purchase a wide variety of interesting souvenirs from an equally interesting group of vendors.

There are excellent tropical gardens in the vicinity of Poipu, Lawa and Kaleheo. From Highway 50, take the Lawai turn-off to Lawai Valley, which will bring you to the **Pacific Tropical Botanical Garden**, P.O. Box 340, Lawai, HI 96765. This former vacation home of Queen Emma, wife of Kamehameha IV, was transformed into one of the most beautiful botanical gardens in the state by Chicago cattleman Robert Allerton and his adopted son John Gregg Allerton. The gardens are next to the younger Allerton's estate, which he has requested be joined with the

botanical gardens upon his death. Visitors are allowed to tour both estates.

On Kaumualii Highway, going west again, keep an eye out for **Olu Pua Botanical Garden and Plantation,** just after passing the town of Kalaheo on the mountain side of the road. Olu Pua's name translates as "floral serenity." Once the manager's estate for the Kauai Pineapple Plantation, it has been converted into a botanical showplace for an outstanding collection of tropical plants, fruits and trees gathered from around the world. There's the Kau Kau Garden (edible

plants), Hibiscus Garden, Front Lawn with flowering shade trees, Jungle (shaded paths among exotic foliage and flowering plants), and the Palm Garden. Olu Pua is open on Monday, Wednesday and Friday, with guided tours scheduled at 9:30 AM, 11:30 AM and 1:30 PM.

Where to Stay

There's a wide range of accommodation available on the south shore. These accommodations take many forms, from cozy and luxurious bed-and-breakfast places to condominiums and private houses.

Bougainvillea adorns the paths of the Pacific Tropical Botanical Garden, Lawai.

The **Hyatt Regency Kauai Resort and Spa** ((808) 742-1234 TOLL-FREE (800) 233-1234 FAX (808) 742-1577, Poipu Road, Koloa, HI 96756 (expensive to luxury) may be the last major development in the Poipu Beach Resort area for some time. The 600-room, $220 million resort opened late in 1990. Generous use of wood, high ceilings and open courtyards with public areas displaying modern Hawaiian art and ancient artifacts give the hotel a special appeal.

The hotel's 50 acres (20 hectares) are situated on the shores of Keoneloa Bay, known to residents as Shipwrecks, after an ancient sampan that was wrecked on the beach east of Poipu. A replica of that shipwreck now graces the fringe of the Regency's five-acre (two-hectare) lagoon. The hotel's "pool" is in reality a man-made estuary replete with rivers that let guests float away from the main pool into hidden grottoes and inlets. One of the hotel's many restaurants, **Tidepools** (expensive) — specializing in steaks, chops and seafood — is perched in the midst of the lagoon. The hotel's other restaurants include **Dondero's**, (expensive; northern Italian dishes), the **Ilima Terrace** (moderate; Pacific Rim fare) and **The Dock** (inexpensive; quick snacks). A golf course with driving range, tennis courts and a 25,000-sq-ft (2,300-sq-m) spa with its own 83-ft (25-m) lap pool are among the hotel's recreational amenities.

A program of guest activities called "Discover Kauai" is conducted under the auspices of the Kauai Historical Society and Na Hula Kaohikukapulani, one of the island's most respected hula halaus. Incorporating the traditional Hawaiian "talk story" form, guests are taken on conducted tours of the property's numerous archaeology sites and introduced to the lore and legends of the island, including the hula, the history of the Koloa region and a dunes walk at Keoneloa Bay that features an explanation of native plants and sea life.

The Hyatt Regency Kauai also organizes some off-the-beaten-track experiences, including an exploration of the Waimea Canyon rim on horseback and a sunset sail aboard the *Lady Leanne II* that will take you to pretty and secluded Wahiawa Bay. There are other organized excursions up the Hanalei River by kayak, and a hike through Kokee State Park to spectacular Waipo'o Falls.

One of the nicest of the nonhotel accommodations is the **Poipu Kai–Suite Paradise** ((808) 742-1234 TOLL-FREE (800) 367-8020 FAX (808) 742-9121, 2827 Poipu Road, Koloa, HI 96756 (inexpensive to mid-range). The properties are completely furnished vacation houses, most within walking distance of great beaches, golf courses and shopping facilities. The low-rise condominiums are built in clusters, each with its own pool. They are set amidst gardens of ginger, bird of paradise, banana trees and tall palms. The resort has nine tennis courts (free to Poipu Kai guests) and a resident tennis professional.

Colony Poipu Kai Resort ((808) 742-6464 TOLL-FREE (800) 777-1700 FAX (808) 742-7865, 1941 Poipu Road, Koloa, HI 96756 (mid-range to expensive) has one-, two- and three-bedroom condominiums with lanai and ocean or garden views. Amenities include six pools, nine tennis courts and a resident tennis professional.

Coastline Cottages ((808) 332-9688 FAX (808) 332-7620, Poipu Beach, Kauai, P.O. Box 287, Kalaheo, HI 96741 has plantation-style bungalows on a secluded beach, nestled between the sea and a sugar cane field. A romantic, tropical setting.

Kiahuna Plantation ((808) 742-2200 TOLL-FREE (800) 367-7052 FAX (510) 939-6644, P.O. Box 1120, Koloa, HI 96756 (expensive) has furnished one- and two-bedroom condominiums with kitchens. Lush gardens are a feature of this property, which is right on the beach. Other amenities include pool and tennis courts. There is a two-night minimum stay.

The privately owned **Poipu Plantation** TOLL-FREE (800) 733-1632 FAX (808) 822-2723, 1792A Pe'e Road, Koloa, HI 96756 (mid-range) has one- and two-bedroom deluxe oceanview units.

Contact **Bed-and-Breakfast, Kauai** ((808) 822-1177, 6436 Kalama Road, Kapaa, HI 96746, for more information and listings.

Spouting Horn TOP, on the southern coast near Poipu, is a geyser which shoots water out of an ancient lava tube. A placid pool BOTTOM at the Pacific Tropical Botanical Garden, Lawai.

Where to Eat

As the number of vacationers has increased, so too has the choice of restaurants in this busy tourist zone. First, there's **Roy's Poipu Bar and Grill (** (808) 742-5000 (expensive) in the Poipu Shopping Village. By now you should be familiar with the talented Roy Yamaguchi, whose innovative style helped define much of Hawaii's great modern cooking. His talent, it would seem, is only matched by his fame and business acumen. This restaurant is one in a chain in the islands and in Japan. It's good.

There are a couple of very good beachfront restaurants in Poipu. One of the older and better establishments is **Brennecke's (** (808) 742-7588 (moderate), overlooking Poipu Beach Park. This good-value restaurants serves tasty yet simple fare in pleasant surroundings. Brennecke's is open for lunch and dinner.

At **Beach House Restaurant (** (808) 742-1424 (expensive), 5022 Lawai Road, a branch of A Pacific Café, they serve up uniquely Hawaiian food to go with the uniquely Hawaiian sunsets. A new menu is created daily with dishes such as Pacific snapper local style with ginger, scallions and hot oil, tumbleweed shrimp, Caesar salad, or Chinese pesto with mustard dressing.

In **Keoki's Paradise** (moderate), in Kiahuna Shopping Center, waterfalls and fish ponds add to the ambiance. Apart from the fresh fish, try the Koloa barbecue ribs and taco bar.

Exiting Poipu and Koloa, head west and you'll come across the town of Kalaheo. There's nothing noteworthy about Kalaheo except that it boasts two of the finest little food places on the island: the **Bread Box (** (808) 332-9000 (inexpensive) and the **Kalaheo Coffee Company and Café (** (808) 332-5858 (inexpensive). Locals will tell you that the Bread Box makes the finest macadamia nut sweet rolls and croissants this side of heaven, while the Kalaheo Coffee Company, in addition to turning out a superior cup of Kona, specializes in great salads.

WAIMEA COAST

The charming towns of the Waimea Coast, with names such as **Eleele, Hanapepe** and

Kekaha, could have been torn from the pages of an Old West chronicle. The dominant color of the landscape in this scenic region is red — red clay, red dust.

On the drive to Hanapepe (Crushed Bay), a pattern begins to emerge. Waving green cane fields start to form a mosaic with the rich red earth for which Hanapepe is so famous. Stop at the **Hanapepe Canyon Lookout** over a once prosperous valley. Old taro terraces are still discernible beneath the undergrowth. It was this exotic, seemingly wild valley that Steven Spielberg used for parts of his blockbuster film, *Jurassic Park*. Directly opposite the lookout is the site of the final Kauai revolt against Kamehameha by Kaumualii's son George, which was put down by the governor of Maui.

Hanapepe, situated on the banks of the Hanapepe River, is one of the prettier plantation towns on the island. Although residents like to refer to it as "the biggest little town in Kauai," Hanapepe has obviously seen better days, and there is a sense of decay about the town. But artists love it for that very reason. It remains charming and true to what it was in days gone by. Natural and unspoiled, it's a reminder of a more leisurely paced era. Many artists have took up residence in the store fronts on the town's main street, helping to keep the town alive after the demise of the sugar industry.

It is easy to understand why the artists love Hanapepe. For all its run-down appearance, the town is awash in color. Pastel and brown tones of the old wooden buildings reflect in the waters of the river; bougainvillea explodes in vibrant colors amidst the red earth on the hillsides — all this against a backdrop of vivid blue ocean and cloud-enclosed mountains.

Lolokai Lele Road will take you to Salt Pond Beach Park. This is a safe swimming beach year round as the crescent-shaped beach is protected by a reef. A small lagoon created by rocks is a perfect bathing pool for kids. The tidepools are also worth exploring, and the sunsets from Salt Pond are superior. This lovely beach gets its name from the salt pans that exist in this area. Salt is still harvested by descendants of ancient salt makers who worked these pans as far back as the 1700s. Salt makers mix the salt with the red earth called *'alaea* and sell this red salt, which is highly prized. You have to receive permission from the salt makers to enter the pan area.

There are some interesting eating places in Hanapepe. **Green Garden (** (808) 335-5422 (inexpensive) is tucked away at the end of the main street. It is as popular with local folks as it is with tourists. Many local patrons descend on the place for Sunday breakfast immediately after church. Lappert the Ice Cream Man is well known in Hawaii. The treats at **Lappert's Factory (** (808) 335-6121, in Hanapepe, are rich and flavored with the delicacies of the island, such as macadamia nut, guava and mango.

WAIMEA

The town of **Waimea** has a special place in Hawaiian history and folklore. It was here that the British explorer Captain James Cook first set foot on Hawaiian soil in January 1778. Mistaken for Lono the Hawaiian god and treated with great respect, Cook remained on Kauai for less than two weeks. He was to return the following year only to meet his death (see CAPTAIN COOK AND HIS LEGACY, page 123).

Every February the townspeople of Waimea stage a carnival commemorate the Cook expedition's historic visit to the island and this town. There are mule and horse races, mountain bike and foot races, carnival rides and, of course, great food.

Just outside Waimea town is the old **Russian Fort**, built by a charismatic Russian doctor named George Scheffer, who was sent to the islands to establish a colony. Scheffer sailed to the Big Island in November 1815 and gained the confidence of Kamehameha through his medical skills. Later he came to Kauai and established an excellent rapport with Kaumualii. So good was this relationship that eventually the two men — Hawaiian and Russian — plotted the conquest of Oahu, Molokai, Lanai and Maui.

Part of the plan called for Scheffer to build a fort on every Hawaiian island, under the command of a Russian. But at this point Scheffer overplayed his hand. The Russians began construction of a blockhouse on Oahu and had raised the Russian flag — much to the ire of the Americans, who informed Kam-

ehameha. The Hawaiian monarch ordered the blockhouse attacked and the Russians were driven from it. This isolated Scheffer, who was on Kauai at the time. Nevertheless, most of the fort at Waimea was completed by late 1816 and named Fort Elizabeth. It was an impressive structure with 17-ft (five-meter)-thick walls which rose to heights of 20 ft (six meters). But Scheffer's days were numbered, and he left Kauai in 1817 for Macao on the China coast before eventually migrating to Brazil. Little remains of the fort except for some of its star-shaped foundations.

Waimea River, which began its journey as Waialae Stream, meanders through the town on its way to the ocean. A lane called Menehune Road runs parallel to the river shortly before it empties into the ocean. *Menehune* are the legendary "little people" of the island, a kind of Hawaiian leprechaun, who according to Hawaiian legend did most of their work at night. Though shy forest dwellers, the menehune were also said to be master builders capable of creating complicated irrigation systems in a single night. Nearby Menehune Ditch, or *Kiki A Ola*, is pointed to as evidence of their work. It is an unusual construction said to have been built

Hanapepe Overlook. Once sugar was king in this part of Kauai.

by the little people for High Chief Ola of Waimea, who paid them in shrimp. To many Hawaiians, the menehune were no fairytale, but were among the first settlers here. The menehune are said to have had a great love for the fragrant mokihana berry, which only grows on Kauai. They also thrived on a diet of sweet potatoes, squash and taro leaves. The densely jungled valley of Honopu on the Na Pali Coast is thought to have been the last home of the menehune and is still referred to as the "Valley of the Lost Tribe." Some people insist the menehune exist still in the deep forests of the island.

Where to Stay and Eat
The **Waimea Plantation Cottages** ((808) 338-1625 TOLL-FREE (800) 922-7866 FAX (808) 338-2338 (mid-range to expensive) are an extraorinary hideaway far removed from the other tourist activities on the island. Set amidst a 27-acre (11-hectare) coconut plantation on the ocean's edge, these former sugar worker's cottages were built in the early 1900s by owners of the flourishing Waimea Sugar Mill Company. Extensively renovated, the rooms have ceiling fans and period furniture of mahogany, rattan and wicker, plus all the modern comforts. Amenities include a swimming pool and tennis courts, as well as facilities for more sedate sports, such as croquet and horseshoe pitching. A host of activities are available, such as whale watching, sunset sails, and biking. Cottages come in several sizes, from the one-bedroom, one-bathroom variety to the five-bedroom, four-bath cottage that accommodates up to nine people, all the way up to the six-bedroom, three-bath cottage that can sleep up to 12.

An interesting and reasonably priced restaurant to visit in Waimea is **Wrangler's** ((808) 338-1218 (moderate), at 9852 Kaumualii Highway. The menu includes steaks, fresh fish and Mexican food. There is live music every Saturday; closed Sunday.

KEKAHA

The last town on this stretch of coast is **Kekaha**, home of a still prospering sugar plantation. The humble plantation houses are alive with flowers. The people of Kekaha love a

party and stage major festivals here several times a year. If you can get to the ukulele jam and hula festival, you'll be glad you did. They're a blast.

If you are looking for adventure, keep going past Kekaha along Kaumaulii Highway to the Pacific Missile Range Facility at Barking Sands. The beach here is generally opened to the public, but you will be required to show your license and auto insurance card to get past the guard gate. Major's Bay Beach is rarely crowded, the waves are great, and the sunsets are fabulous.

The remote **Polihale State Park** lies at the end of the road. The going is rough, but it's worth the effort. Polihale Beach is the longest beach in all the Hawaiian islands. It's a dramatic, lonely place where the wind sighs

across vast open stretches of sand and huge waves crash onto the shoreline. Use extreme caution when wading and swimimg here; the waves are powerful and the undertow can be lethal. At the base of the Na Pali Range in the Polihale State Park lies the Polihale heiau, where ancient Hawaiians believed that the spirits of the dead departed the island.

THE HIGHLANDS

The interior of the island is a network of rivers feeding sugar plantations and ranches. Most of the land is private, some of it inaccessible by motor vehicle. One of the best ways to see the island is by helicopter. Most helicopter companies operate out of Lihue Airport (see TAKING A TOUR, page 103).

Access to Kokee State Park is from Waimea town, and there are two possible routes. The first goes along **Waimea Canyon Road** and joins Highway 550. The other, **Kokee Road**, is heavily used and rutted in many places. Once into Kokee Park, however, the going gets better.

WAIMEA CANYON

Your ascent along Kokee Road leads to a spectacular panorama: Waimea Canyon — "the Grand Canyon of the Pacific" — one mile (1.61 km) wide, 14.5 miles (23.3 km) long and 2,750 ft (833 m) deep. The canyon was created

Waimea Canyon is a place of spectacular natural beauty.

by a fault in the earth's crust and has been eroding for centuries due to weather and rivers. It's a mighty canvas in shades of brown, red, ochre, and green with here and there a splash of purple (see CANYON OF RED WATERS, page 16).

KOKEE STATE PARK

Eight miles (13 kilometers) from the canyon lookout, in a vast green meadow deep in the 4,345 acres (1,758 hectares) of Kokee State Park are **Kokee Mountain Lodge** ((808) 984-8109 and the **Kokee Natural History Museum** ((808) 335-6061, 3600 Kokee Road. Here, at an elevation of 3,600 ft (1,100 m), the air is cool and invigorating.

Soon after the park at Kokee was officially established in 1952, construction began on four rental cabins, a natural history museum and a small grocery store, built mostly from surplus salvaged from the United States Army. The country store eventually became Kokee Lodge. Initially it consisted of what is now the cocktail lounge and kitchen; the two dining wings were added later, as were six more housekeeping units — two duplexes built in 1962, and four six-person cabins completed in 1978.

The cabins vary in size from one large room sleeping three, to two-bedroom cabins that will accommodate six. They are furnished with stoves, hot showers, refrigerators, eating and cooking utensils, linen, towels and blankets. Wood for the fireplace is also available. Maximum length of stay is five days. Call for current rates.

The lodge is the support system for the 12 cabins that dot the park. It serves hot meals and acts as the check-in point for the cabins.

The museum is small, quaint and informative and is devoted to the flora, fauna and natural history of the area. It also has an interesting collection of shells and Hawaiian artifacts. It's opened daily from 10 AM to 4 PM. Guided hikes are offered during the summer for $3.

Kokee State Park has a network of 45 miles (72 km) of hiking trails (see HITTING THE TRAIL, PAGE 33) and freshwater fishing streams. Hunting is permitted in certain areas. Hunters can go after wild boar, feral goats, black-

tail deer and numerous game birds during certain times of the year. The only rainbow trout season in the state opens each August in Kokee. There's also a plum season each summer when the succulent wild methley plum is ripe for the picking.

For information about hunting and fishing, contact the Hawaii State Department of Land and Natural Resources, P.O. Box 1671, Lihue, HI 96766.

KOKEE LOOKOUT

A few miles further into the park will take you to **Kokee Lookout,** elevation 4,000 ft (1,220 m), and a glimpse into one of the more mysterious valleys on the island. The lookout is often shrouded in-mist. Patience is required if you are to get a glimpse of Kalalau for it too is often obscured. The magnificent valley slopes like a massive green carpet towards the ocean, bounded on three sides by cliffs which once isolated and protected the Hawaiians who first settled here.

For more than 1,000 years, native Hawaiians lived an idyllic existence here, cultivating the fertile land for their taro crops. With the coming of the Caucasians, new centers of civilization were established at places such as Lihue, and the country people gradually drifted away until the valley was deserted.

In the mid-1950s Bernard Wheatley stood at Kokee Lookout gazing into Kalalau. This physician from the Virgin Islands had lost his young wife and child in a tragic car accident. Wheatley walked the 10 hard miles (16 km) into the valley carrying his lunch in a paper bag, and settled in a cave beneath the cliff near the beach. He remained there for 23 days before falling ill, and was picked up by a passing fishing boat and taken to hospital. When he recovered, he hiked back to Kalalau and set up residence in his cave.

Wheatley asked nothing of anyone, only to be left in peace. He ate the fruit in the valley, showered in the waterfalls, swam at the beach and reveled in the glorious sunsets and the magnificent night skies. When he needed food, he walked to Kilauea town for supplies and walked all the way back. For more than 10 years he lived here, writing poetry and philosophy. Visitors were always welcome and invited to stay in a guest cave near his own. He lived a civilized existence even in the wilderness, always marveling at the beauty that surrounded him. He came to be known as the Hermit of Kalalau. One day he disappeared and hasn't been seen since. He wrote:

"There is more here than just quietness. There is big peace. There is music in the wind and the surf. I like sundown best and the moonlight on the ripples in the sand. I like to sit in my cave and watch Venus in the night sky." His words capture the essence of Kauai.

NIIHAU

For more than a century, the tiny island of **Niihau** has been the last bastion of Hawaiian culture. Situated off the coast of Kauai, Niihau is shrouded in mystery—populated by approximately 200 Hawaiians and off limits to visitors. The island is owned by the Robinson family who have jealously guarded and protected this refuge. Today Niihau remains a pristine slice of an ancient lifestyle that has all but disappeared from other islands.

The 72-sq-mile (186-sq-km) island, basking just 17 miles (27 km) off the western end of Kauai, has no paved roads and therefore no motor vehicles and no electricity except for some independently owned generators. Inhabitants of the island get about on horseback or bicycle. The most populated area of the island is the village of **Puuwai**, which consists of tiny wooden houses, a church and a school. Bougainvillea splashes the village with color.

The island's main source of revenue has come from the selling of shell necklaces made from the rare Niihau shells found on the island's beaches.

Niihau has a fascinating history. Captain James Cook and one of his lieutenants, the infamous William Bligh of *Bounty* fame, are said to have stepped ashore here. The island was sold by King Kamehameha IV to Eliza McHutcheon Sinclair, a New Zealand sea captain's widow, for $10,000 in gold. For 127 years, descendants of Mrs. Sinclair—the current owners of the island are Bruce and Keith Robinson, sons of the fourth-generation matriarch, Helen Matthew Robinson—have controlled the destiny of the island's inhabitants.

Niihau, unlike its neighbor Kauai, is for the most part an arid island of volcanic rock. A plateau of scrub grass and a few shallow lakes relieve the landscape. About 1,200 short-horn cattle and some 12,000 merino sheep roam the island, sharing their habitat with wild turkeys, pigs and pheasants.

The waters around Niihau abound with dolphins, green turtles and Hawaiian monk seals. The beaches are strewn with delicate Niihau shells of which there are two types —*kahelelani*, which resemble brown and pink grains of rice, and the *momi*, which are small,

lustrous snail shells. Of the two types, the fine-grained kahelelani is more highly prized. A long necklace of this variety can sell for as much as $2,000—provided the maker of the necklace wishes to part with it.

In recent years the residents of Niihau have begun to come and go more freely and have made more contact with the outside world.

A Niihau weaver sports a Polynesian frond hat.

Maui

The Valley Isle

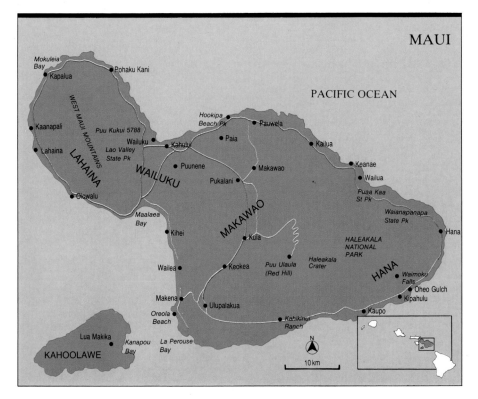

MAUI

PACIFIC OCEAN

Mokuleia Bay
Kapalua
Pohaku Kani

WEST MAUI MOUNTAINS
Kaanapali
Puu Kukui 5788
Lahaina
LAHAINA
Lao Valley State Pk
Wailuku
Kahului
Puunene
Olowalu
WAILUKU
Pukalani
Maalaea Bay
Kihei
Kula
MAKAWAO
Wailea
Keokea
Makena
Ulupalakua
Oreola Beach
Kahikinui Ranch
Lua Makika
Kanapou Bay
La Perouse Bay
KAHOOLAWE

Hookipa Beach Pk
Pauwela
Paia
Makawao
Kailua
Keanae
Wailua
Puaa Kaa St Pk
Waianapanapa State Pk
Hana
HALEAKALA NATIONAL PARK
Puu Ulaula (Red Hill)
Haleakala Crater
HANA
Waimoku Falls
Oheo Gulch
Kipahulu
Kaupo

N
10 km

Population: 100,374
Main cities: Kahului and Wailuku
Area: 729 sq miles (1,887 sq km)
Length: 48 miles (77 km); *width:* 26 miles (42 km)
Highest elevations: Haleakala, 10,023 ft (3,055 m); Puu Kukui, 5,788 ft (1764 m)
Coastline: 120 miles (193 km)
Airports: Kahului; Hana
Products: sugar, pineapple, livestock
Flower: Lokelani

O Hana, Aina Ua Lani Haahaa
Hana the Land of Low Heavens
Nei O Kauiki, Mauna I Ka Lani,
Kauiki is victorious, mountain towering high
O Kapueokahiu, O Mokuhano, I Kai O Kaihalulu
Kapueo and Mokuhano are down at Kaihalulu
O Manianiaula, O Hamalewa, O Kauiki
Manianiaula, Hamalewa and Kauiki
Mauna I Ka Lani, Ka Mauna
Mountain soaring to heaven
I Ka Paipai
Mountain at the threshold

MAUI SEEMS TO HAVE STRUCK the perfect balance: It's both a terrific tourist destination
Maui: The Valley Isle

and remains true to its roots — its Hawaiian face is always there, ready to be greeted. Other islands struggle to find this equilibrium. Some suggest Oahu has gone too far in catering to the tourist trade. Others say the island of Hawaii may not have gone far enough. Not so with Maui. The blend of quiet sophistication and serene beauty is unique.

So far, at least, Maui has successfully isolated its tourist belt to a sweeping stretch of coastline which extends from **Makena** in southwest Maui to **Kapalua** in the northwest without interfering with the charm of upcountry Maui, the lush grandeur of the East Haleakala Range, and its ruggedly beautiful coastline. First-class resorts are not in short supply here, but many prefer the small towns of Haiku and Hana, Hawaiian settlements such as Kahakuloa and Keanae, or the plantation life to be had in small cottages with tin roofs, replete with lanais and gardens. Still others favor the cool climes, ranches and farms of upcountry Maui. Here and there in these secluded communities, small pockets

A spectacular sunset on the Maui coast is the perfect romantic setting.

of artists have taken up residence, adding to the eclectic mix.

DOMAIN OF THE THUNDER KING

Maui was formed by two volcanoes. Where their lava flows together is today the isthmus or valley from which Maui derives its nickname, "The Valley Isle."

The greater part of the island's history is turbulent. Around 1700, a warrior chief named Kekaulike, "The Just," established control over the island. His son and succes-

sor, Kamehamehanui, ruled Maui for 29 peaceful years. On his death bed, he handed the reins of power to his brother Kahekili, "The Thunder King."

Kahekili was aptly named. During the next 25 years, he was constantly at war, either with the chiefs on his own island or with his mortal enemy, Kalaniopuu, fighting chief of the island of Hawaii, who also happened to be Kahekili's brother-in-law.

Kahekili succeeded in conquering the islands of Molokai, Lanai and Oahu. He even managed to establish his brother Kaeo as ruling chief of Kauai, but he was never able to conquer Hawaii and fulfill his dream of a united kingdom.

When Big Island chief Kalaniopuu died, his nephew Kamehameha the Great became chief of Hawaii and the enemy of Kahekili. The battles between the forces of these two chiefs were terrible. The carnage is described as being the worst in the history of the islands. The climax of this blood feud came at Maui's Iao Valley in 1790. Kamehameha the Great sailed across from the Big Island and beached his huge fleet of war canoes at Kahului. His army was engaged there by forces led by Kalanikupule, the son of Kahekili. But Kamehameha now had the advantage of Western weapons, a cannon and swivel guns, two Western advisors and a small sloop captured from the Americans by an ally of Kamehameha. The Maui warriors were no match for Kamehameha's army. They were driven back from the coast and up into Iao Valley, where those who weren't slaughtered had to flee for their lives.

The defeat of Kalanikupele's forces was to change the course of Hawaiian history; it represented a major step in Kamehameha's master plan to unite the islands under one monarch.

After this battle, Kamehameha sent a message to Kahekili, who was on Oahu at the time. The message was in the form of two stones — one white, one black. Kahekili, correctly interpreting the message, responded by sending one back to Kamehameha: "Go back and tell Kamehameha to return to Hawaii. When the black tapa covers Kahekili and the black pig rests on his nose, then is the time to cast stones." (When I die, the kingdom shall be yours.) Kahekili died on Oahu in 1794 at the age of 87. Kamehameha, meanwhile, had fallen in love with Kaahumanu, granddaughter of Kekaulike, and made her his queen, thus establishing a royal line that lasted 100 years.

Kaahumanu, born in a cave in Hana, was as intelligent as she was beautiful. She stamped her name indelibly on the history of these islands — first as favorite wife of Kamehameha the Great and later as wife of both Kaumualii, chief-king of Kauai, and his son and heir, Kealiiahonui. In this one act of double-marriage, Kaahumanu accomplished what Kamehameha could not — the conquest of Kauai.

Kaahumanu was immensely popular with the people. With another of Kamehameha's wives, Keopuolani (the sacred wife), she led Hawaii into the era of Christianity after first breaking the sacred kapus of the old ways.

The legacies of both these extraordinary women can be seen at the many historic sites throughout the islands.

SUGAR, PINEAPPLES AND PROSPERITY

Maui's prosperity was founded on the sugar industry. The early Polynesians brought the cane to the islands, where it grew wild. Many attempts were made to turn it into a cash crop. Some plantations were started, and several failed, but the history of Maui is sprinkled with the names of businessmen who helped found the industry—none more famous than Claus Spreckels, who came to be known as the Sugar King.

Spreckels formed the Hawaiian Commercial and Sugar Company (HC&S) and made an initial investment of $500,000 to construct a ditch to carry water from the northern slopes of Haleakala across 30 miles (50 km) to the plains and the cane fields. Spreckels had a reputation for wheeling and dealing and political meddling, but he contributed greatly to the development of Maui's economy. Sugar has since fallen on hard times, but the great plantations remain; many today are in the process of diversification.

It was the Baldwins, who while developing sugar plantations, discovered that pineapples would flourish under similar conditions to sugar. Henry Perrine Baldwin, who succeeded Spreckels as Maui's Sugar King, established the Maui Pineapple Company at Kapalua on the northeast coast of Maui. The company was later bought by the heirs of J. Walter Cameron, who had married Baldwin's granddaughter. Maui Land and Pineapple Company soon went into real estate, constructing a luxury resort complex at Kapalua.

Their timing was obviously right. Today tourism fuels the economy of Maui as it does the economy of the entire state. It is this island which, after Oahu, attracts the most visitors on an annual basis.

KAHULUI–WAILUKU

Maui, viewed from above, has the appearance of a kneeling figure—the "neck" dominated by the twin towns of **Kahului** and Wailuku. This is the business center of the island and one of its major residential districts. **Wailuku** is the commercial center and the seat of the county government, yet there's a homespun feeling to the place. Its hilly streets reflect that unique balance of Maui. Family-run stores and shops rub shoulders

with glitzy emporiums, producing in the process a wonderful mélange of products and services. Some of these family operations have been in business for generations. The people who run them have something money can't buy — a genuine warmth and spirit of aloha. Homegrown and crafted products proliferate on Market Street, where Mark Twain once lived. Are you an adventurous eater? Then try local palate pleasers such as mochi, manju, sushi and manapua all made fresh — and with a great deal of traditional pride.

OPPOSITE: Sugar cane factory equipment near Paia. ABOVE: Pineapples sprout from red earth in neat furrows, but economic conditions are gradually forcing the disappearance of Maui's plantations. OVERLEAF: Coconut pruner at sunset.

About three miles (five kilometers) from Wailuku is **Iao Valley State Park**, the centerpiece of which is the famous Iao Needle, a unique 2,250-ft (685-m) cinder cone. A natural amphitheater lies at the head of the valley, the caldera of the original volcano that formed the island. The valley is laced with trails lined with ohia, ti and giant tree ferns. Wild orchids grow on the edges of streams, and if you're lucky, you'll see the occasional moonstone sparkling on the bed of a clear stream.

Also at Wailuku are the **Kepaniwai Heritage Gardens**, where the island's various

a Western movie, house some quaint restaurants and bars.

Finding good ethnic restaurants in Wailuku isn't easy. **Tokyo Tei ℂ** (808) 242-9630 (moderate), situated at 1063 Lower Main Street (enter through the parking lot), though, fits this description, offering excellent Japanese cuisine at modest prices.

EXPLORING MAUI

Maui can be divided into four distinct touring zones. The main coastal touring artery

cultures are represented, and **Maui Historical Society Museum ℂ** (808) 244-3326. Nearby is Maui's oldest church, the **Kaahumanu Church ℂ** (808) 244-5189, 103 South High, which was built in 1837.

Where to Stay and Eat

Kahului's main hotel, **Maui Beach Hotel ℂ** (808) 877-0051 (mid-range) is a 10-minute drive from the airport. This hotel is ideal for budget-conscious travelers.

Tucked away in the industrial section of Kahului are some fascinating places in which to dine. These back streets, infrequently visited by tourists, are worth exploring if only to get the true flavor of local city life. Old wooden structures, reminiscent of a set from

consists of Maui's western shores extending all the way from Makena in the southwest up to Kapalua in the northwest. This area can in turn be divided into two other major areas: One that stretches from Makena, through Wailea and Kihei all the way to Maalaea; the other that extends from the town of Lahaina to Kapalua and encompasses one of the island's great resorts at Kaanapali.

The third zone is upcountry Maui and Haleakala Crater. This is cowboy country, with an atmosphere all its own.

Finally there's Hana — "Heavenly Hana" as the natives like to refer to it — on Maui's eastern seaboard, where the spirit of old Hawaii lives on.

Maui: The Valley Isle

THE SOUTHWEST COAST

Heading south after leaving Kahului or Wailuku, Highway 37 turns into 380 and then into 30 as you go north past Maalaea or 31 as you head south towards Kihei, Wailea and Makena.

Maalaea Bay lies at the crossroads of tourist activity. Here you will find a splendid little boat harbor, a smattering of condominiums and a couple of very good restaurants. Maalaea sits on the doorstep of whale sanctuary waters and the start of a stunning beach that doesn't end until it reaches Oneloa at Makena. During the season, whale sightings become almost commonplace. Even so, these magnificent mammals remain a never-ending source of fascination, and short of riding out in a boat, there a few better places to observe them in their natural element than from the Maalaea shoreline as the sunset turns from pink to fiery red.

The 10-mile (16-km) ribbon of road from Maalaea to Makena runs parallel to one of the longest and most beautiful beaches in the world — pure white sands, aquamarine waters, safe swimming, and a staggering choice of hotel and condominium rentals at a variety of prices.

KIHEI

South of Maalaea is **Kihei**, once the haunt of Hawaiian royalty. The Hawaiians loved it for its superb beaches, and a few little villages lie scattered about its shoreline. Descendants of the warrior kings still frequent Kihei, but they have been joined by large numbers of visitors from other islands and from overseas.

Kihei exploded rather than grew in popularity. Today it rivals Lahaina down the coast as a center of tourist activity and entertainment. Hotels, condominiums, restaurants, night spots, and sports and karaoke bars have proliferated. And you don't need to have a king's ransom to be able to afford a stay in Kihei. Prices are reasonable, and the sun, the moonlight and the ocean are all free.

Where to Eat

Kihei has a restaurant in every price range with choices from gourmet establishments

to pancake houses that serve wholesome, hearty food.

Jean-Marie Josselin's **A Pacific Café Maui** ((808) 879-0069 (expensive), another in this Frenchman's highly successful chain of island restaurants, is a distinctive restaurant serving clever blends of Indian, Mediterranean and Hawaiian flavors. Try the wok-charred mahimahi with garlic sesame crust and lime ginger sauce. This restaurant also has a wood-burning grill and a tandoori oven for those great Indian breads and spicy chicken dishes.

There's a surprisingly good Greek restaurant in Kihei. We say "surprising" because there aren't many authentic Greek restaurants anywhere in the islands. But the **Greek Bistro** ((808) 879-9330 (moderate) makes up for that. With its series of terraced open-air cabanas, this restaurant has a pleasant atmosphere, as well as tasty and moderately priced food. In contrast, the fare at **Stella Blues Café** ((808) 874-3779 (inexpensive), 1215 South Keihi Road, is a simple affair. This is where to go for a quick, satisfying and inexpensive meal served amidst bright decor and high ceilings. A good choice here is the grilled egg-

OPPOSITE: Rugged grandeur of the northwest Maui shoreline. ABOVE: The Iao Needle remains one of the most visited sights on the Valley Isle.

plant sandwich accompanied by cucumbers, feta, sweet peppers and pesto mayonnaise.

WAILEA

The further south you go from Kihei, the larger your wallet should be; but if you care to spend the money, it won't be wasted in this splendid resort region.

Wailea is deep in golf country. It boasts 54 championship holes on courses that are as good as any anywhere in the world (see GOLF: THE ULTIMATE DESTINATION, page 289).

and exceptional service. The 380-room hotel, built at a cost of $160 million, sits on 15 acres (six hectares) of beachfront property. It also has one of the premier chefs in the country — George Mavrothalassitis, who presides over the **Seasons** restaurant (very expensive), a dramatic open-design establishment with great ocean views and a distinctly Mediterranean cuisine. One of the favorite dishes among regular patrons is baked onaga with rock salt crust.

The **Kea Lani** ((808) 875-4100 TOLL-FREE (800) 882-4100 FAX (808) 875-1200, 4100

Where to Stay

Within Wailea's lush 1,450 acres (590 hectares) are dozens of magnificent resort hotels and condominiums.

Travelers rate the **Four Seasons Resort Maui at Wailea** ((808) 874-8000 TOLL-FREE (800) 334-MAUI FAX (808) 874-2222 WEBSITE http://www.fourseasons.com/locations/Maui/index.html, 3900 Wailea Alanui Drive, Wailea, HI 96753 (expensive to luxury) one of the best in the world — high praise for any destination resort in these days of luxury travel and extraordinary choice, but the acclaim is justified. All of Hawaii's fine resorts have one thing in common — superb scenery. What sets the Four Seasons apart is its understated elegance

Wailea Alanui Drive, Wailea, HI 96753 WEBSITE http://www.kealani.com (expensive), Hawaii's only luxury all-suites resort, is ranked in *Condé Nast's* Top 50. It sits on 22 acres (nine hectares) of prime Wailea oceanfront with views across the water to the islands of Lanai, Molokai and Kahoolawe. The startlingly white Mediterranean architecture of the hotel is in sparkling contrast to the brilliant variety of bougainvillea and other flowers, shrubs and trees that dress the landscaped gardens. Seven waterfalls and four cascading fountains enhance the ambiance of this enchanting place. Kea Lani offers 413 one-bedroom suites, as well as 37 exclusive one-, two- and three-bedroom villas, each with its private plunge pool and sunning lanai. The villas are separated from the beach by a lawn shaded with coconut palms.

Kea Lani has a bakery and deli as well as three restaurants — the **Kea Lani Restaurant** (very expensive), serving Euro-Pacific cuisine, **Caffe Ciao** (moderate), a gourmet Italian delicatessen with oven-fresh pizzas, and the **Polo Beach Grille and Bar** (moderate), famous for its kiawe burgers. Between the buildings and the ocean is a 22,000-sq-ft (2,000-sq-m), split-level lagoon-style swimming pool and water slide.

Grand Wailea Resort and Spa ((808) 875-1234 or (808) 874-2355 TOLL-FREE (800) 888-6100 WEBSITE http://www.maui.net/~gwr, 3850 Wailea Alanui Drive, Wailea, HI 96753 (expensive) is a spectacular addition to the luxuries offered at Wailea. Over $500 million was spent on this 787-room hotel set in 42 acres (17 hectares) of oceanfront. The Grand Wailea consists of five wings plus the Napua Tower, an exclusive resort within a resort. The average guest room in the Napua Tower is 715 sq ft (66 sq m); the Grand Suite is 5,500 sq ft (511 sq m).

Everything at this hotel is large and dramatic — such as the lovely beachside 15,000-sq-ft (1,400-sq-m) formal pool and 2,000-ft- (600-m)-long river pool. Even the name of its "floating" restaurant (expensive), the **Humuhumunukunukuapuaa** (Hawaii's state fish) hints of extravagance.

Renaissance Wailea Beach Resort ((808) 879-4900 TOLL-FREE (800) 992-4532 FAX (808) 874-5370, 3550 Wailea Alanui Drive, Wailea, HI 96753 (expensive) is the only Hawaiian resort to have received the prestigious AAA Five-Diamond Award for 14 consecutive years, and it is ranked in *Condé Nast's* Top 50. It's a resort of quiet elegance with the accent on intimacy and exceptional service. The Renaissance has 347 units, its own beach and a pool surrounded by waterfalls. Its award-winning restaurant, **Raffles** (expensive), is recognized as one of the finest on the island.

Destination Resorts' **Wailea Villas** ((808) 879-1595 TOLL-FREE (800) 367-5246 FAX (808) 874-3554 WEBSITE http://www.maui.net/ ~drh/index.html E-MAIL drh@maui.net, located at 3750 Wailea Alanui Drive, Wailea, HI 96753 (mid-range to expensive) offer

luxurious accommodation in four distinct townhouse villages. These are one-, two- and three-bedroom condominiums, each with a kitchen and lanai. Each village has its own swimming pool, barbecue grill and other amenities, including golf and tennis facilities. In this resort rich in dining and entertainment pleasures, try the **Set Point Café** (moderate) at the Wailea Tennis Club. This is a place for breakfast and lunch where, apart from the fine food, you can enjoy a spectacular aerial view of the ocean and nearby islands.

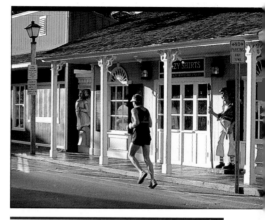

MAKENA

At the end of Maui's southern shoreline is **Makena**, one of the driest areas on the island. The **Maui Prince Hotel** ((808) 874-1111 TOLL-FREE (800) 228-3000 WEBSITE http://www. westin.com/listings, 5400 Makena Alanui, Makena, HI 96753-9986 (expensive), with its splendid golf course, is the only development of any significance in the area. The V-shaped hotel sits on the edge of a pretty and secluded quarter-mile (half-kilometer) white sand beach, with views of either the ocean or Haleakala from each of the hotel's 310 rooms. This is an idyllic spot, perfect for honeymooners (see LIVING IT UP, page 54).

The Maui Prince Hotel has a variety of restaurants including the highly rated **Prince Court** (expensive) and the **Hakone** (inexpensive), an authentic Japanese restaurant and sushi bar.

Makena is not far from major tourist attractions such as the **Puu O Lai Cinder**

OPPOSITE: A stroller enjoys the solitude of a Maui beach. ABOVE: Jogging on Front Street in the picturesque town of Lahaina.

Cone, a red-earth hillock that juts out to sea just beyond the hotel. Puu O Lai is one of Haleakala's craters, beneath which is a large cave said to be the sacred dwelling of the shark god Mano. During the whale-watching season, the Pacific Whale Foundation sets up a lookout station on top of the cinder cone.

Nearby are **Big** and **Little Beach**, favorites with swimmers and body surfers.

Further down the Makena Trail is the **Ahihi-Kinau Natural Preserve**, probably the finest body of water for snorkeling and SCUBA diving on this side of the island. **La Perouse**

Bay, named after French explorer Admiral Jean Francois Galaup, Comte de la Pérouse, is the last bay accessible by car. The Frenchman, believed to be the first Caucasian to set foot on Maui, anchored his two frigates in the bay in 1786.

The beaches at the end of the road are a reminder of the old Maui — and the people of this island would love to keep it that way. There are, in fact, two beaches here of which **Oneloa** (Long Sands) may be the best undeveloped beach in all of Hawaii.

THE NORTHWEST COAST

Retracing your route back up the southwest coast, you sweep north past Maalaea Bay and

are soon in **Lahaina**, a little town steeped in Hawaiian history. Lahaina was once the capital of the islands and one of the most famous whaling ports in the world. Members of the Kamehameha dynasty resided here. Later came the whalers, who turned it into a wild seafarers' town. History records that at times as many as 400 ships were berthed in the little port. The arrival of the missionaries led to confrontations with the sailors, and the missionaries introduced Western-style schools, installed Hawaii's first printing press and helped change the course of Hawaiian history.

Lahaina has continued to reflect its colorful past while developing into an elegant little town much loved by visitors to this island. It has become a retreat for the island's artists, and now its narrow streets are lined with sophisticated specialty stores, restaurants, art galleries and interesting hotels. But it hasn't lost touch with its roistering past; Lahaina still swings, especially when the sun sets.

But before you go out on the town, avail yourself of the Lahaina Historical Guide (at the visitor center kiosk) and tour the many sites of historical interest.

At the edge of the town square is a replica of the brigantine *Carthaginian II*, a floating museum and a reminder of the days when Lahaina was a great whaling port. Other historic buildings include the waterfront courthouse, the old jail, the Seamen's Hospital, and the Baldwin Mission House.

When you tire of strolling, take the little sugar cane train on a six-mile (10-km) ride through the cane fields. The journey between Lahaina and the resort of Kaanapali will give you a glimpse of what plantation life was like in the old days as the vintage steam locomotive chugs its way past old houses and a golf course.

Lahaina is a good base for numerous aquatic activities, from snorkeling and SCUBA diving at Molokini Atoll (see OCEAN PLAYGROUND, page 21) to sunset cruises, surfing and water skiing.

WHERE TO STAY

The **Puunoa Beach Estates (** (808) 667-5972, 45 Kai Pali Place, Lahaina, HI 96761 (luxury), feature 10 beautifully furnished townhouses, minutes outside Lahaina. Set amidst three acres (1.2 hectares) of landscaped beachfront property, these townhouses boast etched glass and koa wood decor, plus Jacuzzis. Two- and three-bedroom units range in size from 1,700 sq ft (158 sq m) to 2,100 sq ft (195 sq m).

Lahaina Shores Beach Resort ((808) 661-4835 TOLL-FREE (800) 628-6699 FAX (808) 661-1025, 475 Front Street, Lahaina, HI 96761 (mid-range to expensive) is a perfect place to vacation if you want to absorb both the history and the culture of this old whaling port without sacrificing holiday excitement. You're on the ocean, in the heart of Lahaina, in a resort which boasts 199 studio and one-bedroom apartments. Each unit features a full kitchen and spacious lanai. It's not a typical resort because the beach isn't private and there's no golf or tennis, but the price is reasonable.

You'll fall in love with **Plantation Inn** ((808) 667-9225 TOLL-FREE (800) 433-6815 FAX (808) 667-9293, 174 Lahainaluna Road, Lahaina, HI 96761 (mid-range to expensive), a Victorian-style hostelry noted for its grace, elegance and old world charm. Its wicker chairs, broad lanais and large airy rooms are reminders of an age past. **Gerard's Restaurant** (expensive) on the ground floor of the hotel has a distinctive atmosphere.

In addition to the condominiums and resorts in the area Lahaina also has a variety of reasonably priced bed-and-breakfasts establishments.

The **Aloha Lani Inn** ((808) 661-8040 TOLL-FREE (800) 57-ALOHA FAX (808) 661-8045 (inexpensive), is a Hawaiian-style guesthouse located across from a neighborhood beach, and within walking distance of Lahaina town with its shopping, dining and nightlife. Your host is Melinda Mower.

Blue Horizons ((808) 669-1965 TOLL-FREE (800) 669-1948 (inexpensive to mid-range), is an upscale residence located between Kaanapali and Kapalua with great panoramic views and only minutes from the ocean and golf courses. You can choose between an apartment with a separate bedroom and living room, a studio (both with kitchens), or the traditional bed-and-breakfast room with a queen-sized bed. All units have private bath facilities. There's a lap pool on the property. Your hosts are Jim and Beverly Spence.

A little oasis minutes from the beach, the **Garden Gate** ((808) 661-8800 FAX (808) 667-7999 (inexpensive to mid-range) includes a garden with fountains and a waterfall. Choose from the Garden Studio with queen-sized bed and sofa–sleeper, sitting area, kitchen, and private deck; or the Molokai Room with double bed and private bath. There's a hot tub too. Your hosts are Ron and Welmoet Glover.

Perched above Lahaina town, the remodeled 7,000-sq-ft (650-sq-m) **House of Fountains** ((808) 667-2121 TOLL-FREE (800) 789-6865

FAX (808) 667-2120, 1579 Lokia, Lahaina, HI 96761 (mid-range) offers six spacious bedrooms, all furnished island style with queen-sized beds and all conveniences. Amenities include a swimming pool, Jacuzzi, barbecue area, and outdoor showers. The views of Lahaina and the islands of Lanai and Molokai from this elevation are inspiring. Your hosts are Thomas and Daniela Clement.

Just a few steps away from a quiet beach, yet two blocks from Lahaina town, **Old Lahaina House** ((808) 667-4663 TOLL-FREE (800) 847-0761, P.O. Box 10355, Lahaina, HI 96761 (inexpensive to mid-range) is tucked away in a tropical garden with local tropical birds and plants and a good-sized pool. You have a variety of accommodations to choose from and can elect to have either a private or shared bath. Your hosts are John and Sherry Barbier.

Wai Ola ((808) 661-7901 TOLL-FREE (800) 4WAIOLA, P.O. Box 12580, Lahaina, HI 96761

Lahaina attractions: The *Carthaginian II* OPPOSITE, an ancient sailing vessel, is as beloved by visitors as is the historic Pioneer Inn ABOVE.

(inexpensive to mid-range) is an elegant, tastefully furnished private house between Lahaina and Kaanapali a stone's near Wahikuli Beach. There are two apartments for rent: a spacious 1,000-sq-ft (93-sq-m) one-bedroom flat with living room full kitchen,/ pool, and Jacuzzi that faces a lush private garden; or a 500-sq-ft (46-sq-m) studio in a private courtyard, also with pool access.

The 50-room **Pioneer Inn (** (808) 661-3636 FAX (808) 667-5708, 658 Wharf Street, Lahaina, HI 96761 (inexpensive), across from the harbor, is a hotel whose architecture reflects the

town's seafaring history. Reserve well in advance if you want a room here.

WHERE TO EAT AND NIGHTLIFE

Lahaina has an astounding variety of restaurants, bars and places to dance the night away.

Avalon ((808) 667-5559 (expensive) is the domain of Chef Mark Ellman, another of those elite gourmet chefs of the new but fashionable school of Hawaiian regional cuisine. The teenager who flipped burgers in a Los Angeles suburban restaurant has come a long way indeed. Ellman's cooking is always an adventure for the palate. He has combined his affinity for the curries of Asia with the soul food of America and comes up with combinations which constantly surprise and delight his growing circle of devotees. Like other practitioners of Hawaiian regional cuisine, he works with local homegrown produce. Ellman's specialties include wok-fried opakapaka with a spicy black bean sauce, shrimp and green papaya salad, and skillet-roasted clams,

Assuming you take the incredible views for granted, then the reasons for visiting the **Chart House (** (808) 661-0937 (moderate) are the freshest seafood on the market and great prime rib and steaks.

The **Hard Rock Café (** (808) 667-7400 (moderate) has great food at a great price, along with music and dancing nightly.

There's a party going on at **Kimo's (** (808) 661-4811 (moderate), most nights of the week. You may start with a tropical cocktail, then opt for any of the delicious Hawaiian fish dishes.

One of the most honored chefs on Maui is David Paul of the **Lahaina Grill (** (808) 667-5117 (expensive), voted "Best Maui Restaurant" in a local magazine poll three years in a row. Paul specializes in what he calls "new American cuisine." The popularity of this exceptional restaurant attests to Paul's culinary skills.

Situated at the far end of Front Street is the European-style **Longhi's (** (808) 667-2288 (moderate), founded by New Yorker Bob Longhi in the mid-Seventies. Since then the restaurant has gained a reputation for style, quality and atmosphere. There are no menus at Longhi's; the staff describes what's available, such as fresh strawberries, country-style ham and eggs and Kona coffee for breakfast. And while you enjoy your meal, you can watch the whales frolic in the waters below Lahaina.

Adding to the excitement of Lahaina is another in the worldwide chain of **Planet Hollywood (** (808) 667-7877 (moderate) establishments, those highly stylized entertainment centers designed to give you a steady diet of motion picture nostalgia mixed with music, dancing and food at a reasonable price. You can't miss this Planet Hollywood — it's smack in the middle of Front Street in the historic Pioneer Mill Building. As is usual with Planet Hollywoods all over the world, the Lahaina branch is packed with movie memorabilia. For instance, there's Mel Gibson's motorcycle from *Lethal Weapon III*, the creature from *Alien* and the Joker's heli-

ABOVE: Amateur astronomers and heaven watchers get a chance to view the stars through some high powered equipment at the Hyatt Regency at Kaanapali. RIGHT: The torch-lighting ceremony is a nightly ritual at the Sheraton Hotel in Kaanapali.

copter from *Batman.* There is also a wide
assortment of souvenirs on sale, including
limited-edition items.

The appearance of Roy Yamaguchi on the
scene has enhanced the reputation of the
Lahaina area as a great place to dine. Yamaguchi has opened two restaurants: **Roy's
Kahana Bar and Grill** ((808) 669-6999
(expensive), and right next door, **Roy's Nicolina** ((808) 669-5000 (expensive). Both
places are founded on Yamaguchi's philosophy and traditions, but the styles of their
executive chefs — Tod Kawachi of Kahana

Grill and Jacqueline Lau of Nicolina—make
each place unique. These chefs create nightly
specials of 20 "Euro-Asian" treats.

KAANAPALI BEACH RESORT

A colorful ritual takes place at Kaanapali
Beach Resort each evening as the sun begins
to set. A lone Hawaiian lights the torches
leading to the edge of Black Rock at the
Sheraton Hotel property situated at the northern end of the resort, and then plunges into
the ocean below. Ancient drums and the
haunting sound of shell horns summon the
hula dancers to the beachside luaus. For visitors the ritual merely adds to the enchantment of the evening, but this ritual has great

cultural significance as well, for it reenacts
the feat of much-loved Maui ruler, King
Kahekili, who dove into the waters off the
rock at a time when the spot was considered
the jumping-off point for spirits entering the
nether world.

Kaanapali, with its three-mile (five-kilometer)-long white sand beach, was a favorite of Hawaiian royalty. These days hoteliers,
restaurateurs and entrepreneurs have come
to recognize what the royal Hawaiians loved
and admired about this place, and they've
turned it into a mecca for those seeking escape
from the pressures of the modern world.

Where to Stay
Kaanapali Beach Resort, the state's first
planned resort, is a collection of luxury hotels
and condominiums on a 1,200-acre (480-
hectare) property. This resort is big, busy and
exciting but not brassy. It offers many choices,
and there's something to suit the budgets of
most travelers. Supplementing the usual
attractions are numerous tennis courts and
two 18-hole golf courses, one designed by
Robert Trent Jones Sr., the other by Arthur
Jack Snyder (see GOLF: THE ULTIMATE DESTI-
NATION, page 289).

At one end of this "tourist alley" is the
very lovely **Hyatt Regency Maui** ((808) 661-
1234 TOLL-FREE (800) 233-1234 FAX (808) 667-
4498, 200 Nohea Kai Drive, Lahaina, HI
96761 (expensive), rated a *Condé Nast* Top
50 resort. This 815-room facility was built
at a cost of $80 million and recently under-
went an $11-million renovation. The Hyatt
has numerous restaurants, bars and a spectacular Polynesian dinner show, "Drums of
the Pacific." One restaurant you should certainly try is the **Swan Court** (expensive).
This airy, elegantly appointed room opens
onto an ocean view and a miniature lake
and Japanese garden inhabited by flamin-
gos, peacocks and swans.

At the other end of the beach are the **Royal
Lahaina** ((808) 661-3611, 2780 Kekaa Drive,
Lahaina, HI 96761, and **Sheraton Maui** ((808)
661-0031 FAX (808) 661-0458 WEBSITE http://
www.sheraton-hawaii.com/maui/
index.html, 2605 Kaanapali Parkway,
Lahaina, HI 96761 (expensive to luxury). The
Sheraton, located on what is perhaps the best
beach in Kaanapali, recently went upscale

Maui: The Valley Isle

and upmarket after undergoing a major facelift. Guest rooms combine tropical furnishings, Hawaiian art and deluxe amenities. It is a particularly interesting hotel with a variety of elevations. Tourists love Black Rock (see above). Seven-story guest units and the **Discovery Room** (expensive), a classy dining facility, are perched on this piece of landscape.

Sandwiched between the Hyatt and the Sheraton (the Royal Lahaina is further north of the Sheraton and somewhat isolated) are the **Kaanapali Beach Hotel (** (808) 661-0011

667-5821 WEBSITE http://embassy-maui.com, 104 Kaanapali Shores, Lahaina, HI 96761 (expensive), an all-suites condominium resort built on seven acres (three hectares) of gardens. The suites are spacious and have all the conveniences.

Where to Eat

Dominating the center of the Kaanapali Beach Resort is the **Whalers' Village**, a shopping complex with over 100 shops, two whaling museums and two fine places to eat on the beachfront — **Leilani's on the Beach (** (808)

FAX (808) 667-5978, 2525 Kaanapali Parkway. Lahaina, HI 96761 http://www.maui.net/~jstark/kanapali.htm E-MAIL mauikbh@aloha.net (mid-range to expensive), the **Marriott Maui (** (808) 667-1200 TOLL-FREE (800) 763-1333 FAX (808) 667-1200 WEBSITE http://www.travelweb.com/TravelWeb/mc/common/marriott.html, 100 Nohea Kai Drive Lahaina, HI 96761 (expensive), and the **Westin Maui (** (808) 667-2525 TOLL-FREE (800) 228-3000 FAX (808) 661-5764, 2365 Kaanapali Parkway, Lahaina, HI 96761 (expensive).

The latest addition to the luxury accommodation available in the Kaanapali Resort area is **Embassy Suites Resort Maui (** (808) 661-2000 TOLL-FREE (800) 669-3155 FAX (808)

661-4495 (expensive), and the superb establishment of master chef Peter Merriman called the **Hula Grill Restaurant (** (808) 661-1148 (expensive). Merriman, who also owns a restaurant in the hill town of Kamuela, belongs to that band of fine young chefs who have given modern Hawaiian cooking such a mark of distinction. At the Hula Grill, he specializes in seafood dishes. For starters, have the Tahitian *poisson cru* (raw fish marinated in lime and coconut with Maui onions and tomato). For a main course try the baked opakapaka in parchment paper, with green bananas and spicy coconut sauce.

OPPOSITE: The pool area at the Hyatt Hotel in Kaanapali. ABOVE: Clouds form over the West Maui mountains.

KAPALUA BAY

A few miles further down the road from Kaanapali is the **Kapalua Resort**, a more upscale destination. Set amidst 1,500 acres (600 hectares) of lush tropical gardens, it is arguably the finest resort on the island. Like other Maui properties it was developed with an aesthetic eye as well as a respect for the culture and history of the island.

Two significant scenic features make Kapalua special. First, there's the five splendid bays that lie sheltered by an imposing lava peninsula. Then there's the grandeur of the West Maui Mountains looming behind the 23,000-acre (9,200-hectare) pineapple plantation of which the resort is a small part.

The **Ritz-Carlton Kapalua** ((808) 669-6200 TOLL-FREE (800) 262-8440 FAX (808) 665-0026, One Ritz-Carlton Drive, Kapalua, HI 96761 WEBSITE http://www.maui.net/~mauiritz/index.htm (expensive), has 548 guest rooms and suites overlooking the ocean or tropical gardens. All rooms have private lanais and marble bathrooms with separate showers. The grounds sport three championship golf courses, 10 tennis courts, a pool, whirlpools, sun deck, spa and fitness center.

The **Kapalua Bay Hotel and Villas** ((808) 699-5656 TOLL-FREE (800) 367-8000 FAX (808) 669-4690 WEBSITE http://www.maui web.com/kapalua, One Bay Drive, Lahaina, HI 96761 (mid-range to expensive) is currently closed for renovation, but if you're lucky enough to visit when it reopens, you'll find that it is situated on what has been described as "the best beach in America" — an accolade bestowed by the University of Maryland's Laboratory of Coastal Research, which surveyed 650 of the finest beaches in the nation. Kapalua was voted number one for beauty, swimming conditions, water and air temperatures, color of the sand and solitude.

At Kapalua, solitude is guaranteed. You can lose yourself in a native rain forest, a protected marine life sanctuary, or golf courses that double as wildlife sanctuaries. There are also historic sites such as native burial grounds and the old Honoluas Store.

With 194 rooms, the Kapalua is modest in size when compared to the hotels of Kaanapali, but its size contributes to its intimacy — and its chic. From its impressive, vaulted lobby which captures the ocean breeze, to its black-marbled waterfall, the Kapalua Bay Hotel emphasizes luxury.

Villas which may be rented by the day, week or month are scattered around the hotel complex and on the fringe of the two Arnold Palmer-designed golf courses, are the . These huge, well-appointed houses are

beautifully designed — all with stunning ocean and mountain views.

If you enjoy golf, you must play at Kapalua, where the challenges of the Palmer courses, plus the new Kapalua Plantation Course designed by Ben Crenshaw and Bill Coore, are matched only by the spectacular panoramas.

Adjacent to the Kapalua Resort is **Fleming's Beach**, access to which is gained by walking through a thick grove of trees. The beach has more pebbles than sand, and while the clear waters and range of marine life make it a tempting place to snorkel and dive, caution should be exercised.

Two views of House of the Sun, Haleakala Crater.

BEYOND KAPALUA

Once past the Kapalua Resort, the road gets narrows and starts to hug the contours of the cliffs as it winds its way towards Honolua and Mokuleia Bay.

The longer you continue on this road, the rougher it gets. Black lava gives way to red earth. The land is arid, barren, windswept and sparsely inhabited. It is an area of rock slides, and there are frequent warnings to this effect. Be advised that the best way to traverse this road is by four-wheel-drive vehicle. The scenery, however, improves in inverse proportion to the quality of the road. Keep an eye out for evidence of ancient Hawaiian culture.

The heiau at **Pohaku Kani** is a place of solitude. You may decide to turn back here, for the next few miles are still more rugged. The road winds past Nakelele Point and the blowhole, and soon Highway 30 gives way to "Highway" 340 — an extremely narrow, heavily rutted road which demands reduced speeds, sometimes less than five miles per hour (eight kilometers per hour). Just when you think you are surely lost, you'll come across a hamlet with a quaint green church, a bridge across a rushing stream, where children are playing, and a few tiny houses. The road gradually improves after this as it climbs into the high country before beginning its descent once again into Kahului.

If you have the time, the courage and a sturdy four-wheel-drive vehicle, it is worth navigating this 18-mile (29-km) stretch of road.

UPCOUNTRY MAUI

The drive from Kahului to the crater of Haleakala at an elevation of 10,023 ft (3,050 m) is one of the finest in the islands, taking you through pretty, rustic towns such as **Pukalani**, **Makawao**, and **Kula**, often through mist and light rain, always through regions of scenic beauty and charm.

As you climb, tropical vegetation gradually gives way to grasslands and then groves of eucalyptus and verdant meadows where cattle and horses graze. If you make this drive in May, June or July, the jacaranda will be in full bloom, their purple flowers adding to the vibrancy of the landscape.

HALEAKALA CRATER

In this high country, where the temperatures run from cool to cold in the evenings and the sun warms the land during the day, grapes and flowers such as carnations and giant protea all thrive. From sea level at Kahului to the crater's edge is a distance of 40 miles (64 km), which should take you no longer than two hours to negotiate. The higher you go, the drier the landscape becomes, and if it's drizzling or pouring rain at lower altitudes, chances are that when you break through the clouds, **Haleakala Crater** will be there—in all its glory, bathed in sunshine.

At dawn or dusk, the great crater is an awesome sight. Within its 21-mile (38-km) circumference lie caves and caverns, walking trails, patches of verdant forest, grassy plains and desert sands. The bowl of the crater looks as if it were fired by a sensitive potter. The sands are in muted shades, from chocolates and tones of beige, to pinks, blues and greens with an occasional burst of violent orange. Native legend has it that the demigod Maui lassoed the sun here in order to lengthen the day so that his mother Hina could dry her tapa cloth.

The grandeur of Haleakala is best appreciated by walking its trails and camping overnight, by observing the sun creep over the edge of the rim. It's at sunset that the "Specter of the Brocken" occurs—and other

than in Scotland and Germany, Haleakala is the only place you can experience it. This optical illusion — created by a rare combination of sun, shadow and fog — is the reflection of a person's shadow on the face of a cloud. The image forms at sunset about 100 ft (30 m) from the crater's edge and 1,000 ft (300 m) above the ground, as clouds billow up the crater's face. A photograph of this phenomenon may reveal a rainbow-tinted halo. As many as seven distinct rainbows may appear within a single image.

If you have the time, book one of the three cabins available in Haleakala Crater through **Maui National Park ℓ** (808) 572-9177, P.O.

Visions such as this one over Maui have earned Hawaii its title as the "Rainbow State".

Box 369, Makawao, HI 96768. The cabins are assigned by lottery three months in advance of your visit. If your time is limited, try one of the shorter hikes (see CRATER OF MANY COLORS, page 12; HITTING THE TRAIL, page 33.)

VILLAGES OF THE HIGH COUNTRY

Coming down the mountain, your first landmark is the interesting little town of **Kula**. There's more to Kula and its surrounding environs than meets the eye. Portuguese

immigrants were among the earliest foreign settlers in the area, and in 1894 they built a pretty little church here. Today the octagonal church, recently restored and painted a bright white, is one of Kula's landmarks. If you visit the church, pay special attention to the magnificent altar, a gift to the Portuguese plantation workers of Maui from the king and queen of Portugal.

Well known to devotees of upcountry Maui, **Kula Lodge (** (808) 878-1535, Haleakala Highway, is a romantic hotel and restaurant where the views of the Kihei Coast and the West Maui Mountains are matched by the hearty food served there. At the lodge, the fires are lit in the hearth at night. A smart way to see Haleakala at sunrise is to stay

overnight at the lodge and set out at about 4:30 AM for the crater.

Nearby is the village of **Keokea** that attracted many Chinese immigrants in the island's early days. Reminders of that era, and of the Chinese influence, are to be seen in the Kwock Hing Society Temple. Keokea is dotted with little farms growing a variety of flowers, such as the magnificent protea, roses and carnations, and vegetables such as the famous Maui onions. If you are interested in visiting one of the many flower gardens or flower farms in the area, then try **Cloud's Rest Protea Farm (** (808) 878-2544 or the **Enchanting Floral Garden of Kula (** (808) 878-2531. There's also the 34-acre (13.5-hectare) **University of Hawaii Experimental Garden (** (808) 244-3242.

About 15 miles (24 km) from the Kula Lodge on Highway 37 is the **Ulupalakua Ranch**, now famed not only for its dairy herds, but also for the quality of the wines produced in its vineyard, a relatively new venture. The **Tedeschi Vineyard and Winery (** (808) 878-1213 produces an excellent red wine named La Perouse in honor of the French sea captain who sailed into the bay near Makena. More recently it began to make a fine brut champagne. Tedeschi's pineapple wine is also popular and is served in restaurants from Lahaina to Kaanapali. You can tour the vineyard and sample wines.

Makawao (Forest Beginning) is the liveliest of the upcountry towns and the site of the annual **Fourth of July Rodeo** (see FESTIVE FLINGS, page 59), one of the island's biggest attractions and one of several rodeos held upcountry every year.

Makawao was once purely a "cow town." Hawaiian *paniolos* (cowboys) from nearby ranches used to ride their horses down the little main street in search of a drink or some action. Today, while a slice of that atmosphere remains, Makawao has become something of a contradiction. Behind its cowboy veneer lurks sophistication, created, no doubt, by the infusion of middle- and upper-middle-class dollars which have been brought into the district. Makawao's shops and restaurants reflect this prosperity. Juxtaposed with saddle shops or feed and grain stores are thriving art galleries and exquisite crafted glass boutiques. Some of these new galleries lie tucked away in picturesque courtyards that are worth seeking out. At the center of much of this activity is the **Hui Noeau Visual Arts Center** ((808) 572-6560, 2841 Baldwin Avenue, which organizes and holds classes, exhibitions and workshops by prominent artists on elegant estates in the area.

There's also good eating in Makawao. Try the **Makawao Steak House** ((808) 572-8711 (moderate), 3612 Baldwin Avenue, where the setting is rustic yet elegant. The chops, ribs and fish are done to perfection, while the steaks may be the best in Maui.

house Restaurant ((808) 572-1325 (inexpensive), 360 Pukalani Street, which serves Hawaiian food, ribs and steaks and offers a delightful view of the Valley Isle across a beautiful golf course. Early bird specials are available from 5 AM to 6:30 AM.

Not far from Pukalani, just off Highway 37, a road bisects the vast acreage of sugar cane and pineapple fields. This nondescript country road, not particularly well signposted, and not lit at all, is Haliimaile Road, or Route 371. Several miles down this stretch of road — driving it in the dark is something

Across the street is **Kitada's KauKau Corner** ((808) 572-7241 (inexpensive), a favorite with locals. The storefront is not inviting because it hasn't been redecorated in years, but Mrs. Kitada serves a fine breakfast and lunch in pleasant surroundings.

Situated on a busy intersection, **Polli's Mexican Restaurant** ((808) 572-7808 (inexpensive), 1202 Makawao Avenue, is a favorite with residents and tourists alike. The vegetarian fare is very good. Try the sapodillas with ice cream and honey to top off a meal of a light salad or stuffed potato.

Not far down the hill from Makawao is the residential neighborhood of Pukalani (Heavenly Gate). A little difficult to find but worth the effort is **Pukalani Country Club-**

of an adventure — you'll find the **Haliimaile General Store** ((808) 572-2666 (expensive), 900 Haliimaile Road, an equally nondescript building with plantation-style architecture. Don't be fooled by the exterior. On closer inspection what looked like your basic country store turns out to be an elegant, well-designed restaurant — one of the best in all of Hawaii — with beautiful decor and great art adorning the walls. The ambiance is matched by the food, superbly prepared by chef Beverly Gannon, a Texan who co-owns this eatery with her husband Joe. Beverly is one of the new wave of local chefs specializing in

OPPOSITE: This church in Kula is the legacy of early Portuguese settlers. ABOVE: Maui ice cream in Paia, the last major town on the way to Hana.

Hawaiian regional cuisine, but she leans less towards Asian flavors than do her peers. The emphasis is on local produce, which she turns into surprising and exotic dishes. For an example, duck salad with warm goat cheese and chive crêpes, or opakapaka baked in parchment with leeks, herbs and lobster. The menu is extensive. Make sure you book early.

HANA

There are two ways you can get to Hana — by road and by air. The latter choice is the

lazy, though luxurious, way to do it. But to fly to Hana would be to miss much. The true adventurer sees Hana from ground level.

Before undertaking the journey, you should decide whether to make this round trip of about 100 miles (160 km) in a day, or stay overnight. If you opt to stay overnight, your choices are one of the many bed-and-breakfast places, camping out in one of the lovely state parks, or parking yourself at Hana's resort hotel — the beautiful, secluded Hotel Hana-Maui (see below). But, make your plans well in advance if you want to stay at the very popular Hana-Maui.

Day trippers can do the drive comfortably if they start early. This lovely corner of Maui is so well known and so often written

about that it has taken on nearly mystical proportions. Hana itself, however, is not the only attraction; what you encounter en route is equally as fascinating.

The most sensible way to make the journey to Hana is to let someone else drive — the road has almost 15 curves to the mile, 617 curves in all and 56 one-lane bridges to negotiate. To get to the Hana Highway (Highway 360) from West Maui, take Highway 30 to 32 and then to 36. If you are coming from Makena, you'll want to be on Highway 31 until it connects with 30. The last chance to stock up with provisions and gasoline is at the little town of **Paia**.

If you are making a very early start, contact **Picnics Restaurant (** (808) 579-8021 (inexpensive), 30 Baldwin Avenue, where you can pick up some tasty food at a reasonable price for a quick getaway to Hana.

Exiting Paia, the road meanders along the coast, passing by **Mama's Fish House (** (808) 579-8488 (moderate), 799, Poho Place, a large private residence converted into a restaurant where the food is good but pricey.

The waters off **Hookipa State Park**, on the same stretch of road, are usually rippled with wind and teeming with windsurfers. If time permits, stop and watch. Soon after passing Hookipa, the scenery changes, and as the road begins a gentle ascent away from the sand dunes and around the eastern flanks of Haleakala, the traveler enters a zone where the eerie quiet is broken by the soft sound of rain on thick foliage and the rush of waterfalls.

Replenished by over 100 inches (255 cm) of rain annually, this area is lush with vegetation, the air heavy with the scent of wild flowers and tropical fruit. Wild heliconia, red, white, pink and yellow ginger and a variety of orchids are showcased against varying shades of green. Mountain apples, mango and guava grow alongside bamboo groves. In the summer, tulip trees, their scarlet blossoms in proud bloom, stand tall off the hillsides, often in the midst of thick carpets of moss and fern.

At the nine-mile marker the forest surrounds you. This is Waiakmoi Ridge where slender groves of bamboo compete with eucalyptus, gingers, heliconia and vines for the dappled sunlight. Here and there, pockets of ferns thrive in the dampness of miniature waterfalls.

Drive another two miles (3.2 km) and you're at **Puohokamoa**. Take a break, stretch your legs and plunge into one of the cool, deep pools in the area. Here the vines mingle with impatiens, ti leaves and kukui nut trees.

Yet another 1.2 miles (1.9 km) later, the **Keanae Peninsula** lies stretched before you. This may be the best place of all to break journey. The peninsula is a place of utterly wild beauty. Raging surf crashes on a shoreline of lava rock, or throws a tantrum, pounding the sea cliffs halfway up their sides — a scene which is even more dramatic by moonlight. Exercise caution if you're walking on the cliffs on the point or on the shoreline; the ocean can be dangerously unpredictable. It is sometimes difficult to measure the heights of these waves.

Keanae Peninsula also boasts an arboretum where both native and non-native plants grow to extraordinary sizes.

At the summit of the hill leading away from the Keanae Peninsula is **Wailua Valley Lookout**, with views of one of the prettiest towns on the island.

As the road begins its ascent up to 1,275 ft (383 m), you'll hear before you actually see the many waterfalls cascading down Haleakala's flanks. Nearby **Waikani Falls** is one of the most romantic sites on this stretch of highway. After this, an imperceptible shift in scenery begins to take place. The tropical foliage gives way to lush meadows sloping down to the ocean. Horses and cattle graze in the sunshine.

There are numerous state parks on this stretch of road. Both **Kaa**, with its waterfalls and cold pools, and **Waianapanapa**, famous for its black sand beach and sea caves, are popular attractions. Waianapanapa also has a thick native coastal forest, blowholes and hala trees that seem to sing in the wind. Signs on the road take on a commercial slant with advertisements for country kitchens and food stalls.

Three miles (five kilometers) before Hana is a five-acre (two-hectare) slice of heaven that includes the **Hana Gardenland Café** (moderate) — specializing in dishes made from organically grown produce — and a botanical garden and gift shop. All the pro-

duce used on the menu here comes from local farms, so the food is as fresh as possible. It is now part of Hana legend that First Lady Hillary Rodham Clinton discovered the Gardenland Café in 1993 and liked it so much that she returned on two other occasions to dine there.

HANA TOWN

You'll sweep into **Hana** almost without warning. Signs indicating the airport, the **Heavenly Hana Inn**, the **Hotel Hana-Maui**,

the gas station and **Hasegawa's General Store**, a family-owned landmark since 1910, are indications that you have arrived. While the district of Hana is enormous, the town is only a couple of blocks long. If you are seeking serenity and peace of mind, you've come to the right place.

Celebrities looking for privacy have also discovered Hana. Don't be surprised to see Carol Burnett, James Garner, Richard Pryor or Kris Kristofferson strolling into Hasegawa's. They all have homes here and they all shop at Hasegawa's — for two reasons: There aren't many choices for grocery shop-

The road to Hana reveals many quiet spots such as Red Sand Cove OPPOSITE and the beach near Hana-Maui Hotel ABOVE.

ping in Hana, and it's a wonderful little store, crammed with almost everything you could dream of needing.

Hana's population numbers about 1,000 and most of these people either work for the 7,000-acre (2,834-hectare) Hana Ranch with its 9,000 head of cattle, or the Hotel Hana-Maui. The **Hotel Hana-Maui** ((808) 248-8211 FAX (808) 248-7202, P.O. Box 9, Hana, HI 96713 (expensive) was originally built by Paul Fagan, owner of the San Francisco Seals. Fagan bought the sugar plantation owned by August Una, the Danish consul in Hawaii, and turned

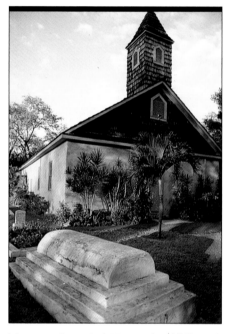

it into a cattle ranch. A 10-room hotel followed. It was here that the Seals came for spring training at the Hana Ball Park, the home field today of the Hana baseball team.

The Hana-Maui has since gained an international reputation as the most romantic hotels in the world. Once Hawaiian chiefs repaired to Hana to recover from the rigors of battle. Today, the world's celebrities find their way here to escape the glare of publicity. And they find it at this hotel and its one-story Sea Ranch cottages that are spread out over the property's 66 lushly planted acres (27 hectares). The cottages, located on a coastal bluff, feature generous decks, most with hot tubs, and floor-to-ceiling glass with views of the shoreline and mountain top.

Most of the cottages feature pretty, private gardens. The interiors of the cottages have oversized tropical furniture with original Hawaiian art and quilts.

The **Dining Room** (expensive) is where guests take most of their meals. A 35-foot (10.5-meter)-high exposed-beam ceiling and a covered outdoor lanai give this restaurant a wonderful blend of country elegance and modern sophistication. The food served here is equally intriguing — a mélange of Pacific Rim, American and Oriental cuisine prepared with great flair. Three miles (five kilometers) away, on Hamoa Beach, which author James Michener called "the most perfect crescent-shaped beach in the world," the hotel serves a buffet lunch daily. Once a week this beach is also the site of a luau.

Most visitors come to Hana to luxuriate in one of nature's most primitive and beautiful hideaways. The silence is engulfing, broken only by the gentle slap of waves on the beach at Hana Bay.

At Hana, you can sit on the old wharf and let your imagination roam, recalling the battles fought here by rival chiefs from Maui and the Big Island.

OHE'O GULCH

If you haven't got room at one of the hotels or the little lodges which take in guests, make your way down to **Ohe'o Gulch**, site of the famous **Seven Sacred Pools** and a favorite tourist destination. The 10 miles (16 km) to the pools can be hard going because of the tourist traffic on these country roads. Watch out for the Virgin by the Roadside, a pretty Catholic shrine.

Ohe'o Gulch is an extraordinary place, a reward for the rigors of the long journey from Kahului or Kaanapali. This corner of Hana once supported a thriving Hawaiian population. Picnic on the grassy cliffs above the crashing surf where you can look across the Alenuihaha Channel, at 6,300 ft (1,920 m), one of the deepest in the Pacific. Strong currents and sharks make swimming risky, but swimming in the pools is fun.

Take some time to explore the more than 20 pools in the system and plunge into the cold waters. On a clear day, it's an experience you won't forget. Camping is permitted on the bluffs near the ocean, and while there are chemical and pit toilets, no drinking water is available.

Ohe'o Gulch offers many outdoor experiences. One of its best trails winds through an exotic bamboo forest to **Waimoku Falls**. It begins across the street from the car park. For further advice, seek out the park ranger (see HITTING THE TRAIL, page 33; HORSEBACK RIDING, page 47).

WHAT TO SEE AND DO

Many visitors to Hana are taken to Ohe'o Gulch and then whisked back to the resorts in Maui. But there's plenty to do in Hana. Here's a sampling:

Take a stroll down Ulaino Road through forests of mango, guava, ilima, ferns, ginger, heliconia and impatiens to a 150-foot (45-m) waterfall tumbling down to **Blue Pond**. Dive into this gorgeous freshwater pool and enjoy the clean, invigorating water.

In the Hotel Hana-Maui, you'll find the **Hana Coast Gallery**. This splendid gallery features the work of over 50 of the state's finest artists, including everything from native featherwork and lau hala jewelry to oil paintings and bronze sculptures.

The **Hana Cultural Center** is a fascinating little museum dedicated to the preservation of the region's history. For a museum of its size, it displays an extraordinary range of Hawaiian artifacts including Hawaiian quilts, turtle shell fishhooks, koa canoe paddles, stone lamps, and woven fishing traps.

Legend has it that the demigod Maui hauled a mass of land off the bottom of the ocean using a magic fishhook. When the landmass shattered and formed the Hawaiian islands chain, what was left was a small shard, **Alau Island**, now standing off the Hana coast. A lane leading off County Road 31 a few miles south of Hana will take you to a spot from which to view the island.

Of the people who have come to Hana seeking to escape public attention, no one was as famous as aviator **Charles A. Lindbergh**. In the end of his years — marked by triumph, and later the tragedy of the kidnapping and death of his young son — he chose to live out his years in Hana. He was laid to rest in Kipahulu, 10 miles (16 km) south of

Hana in the beautiful little churchyard of Palapala Hoomau Congregational Church.

There are also a variety of ocean tours to spice up your stay in Hana. Among the best is a two-hour **kayaking tour** of Hana Bay that finishes at a cove where you can see exotic fish in beautiful coral gardens, as well as sea turtles and dolphins at play.

BEYOND HANA

It's possible to complete your Hana journey by proceeding in the direction of Ulupalakua

and upcountry Maui using a four-wheel-drive vehicle. But caution is advised. The road is narrow, unpaved and unstable in parts. On the way you'll pass through the hamlet of **Kipahulu** and **Kaupo Ranch**, where beef cattle have been raised since the 1800s. Kaupo was a site favored by the ancient Hawaiians because of its dry climate, the rich supply of marine life in its waters and the fruit and timber from its rain forests.

At Ulupalakua, the roughest part of the drive is over.

OPPOSITE: Aviator Charles A. Lindbergh is buried in this pretty churchyard in Kipahulu, East Maui. ABOVE: Hawaii's indigenous protea.

Maui: The Valley Isle   227

Molokai
The Friendly Isle

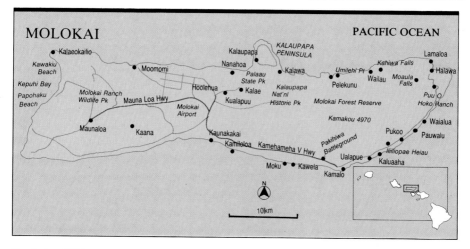

Population: 6,700
Main town: Kaunakakai
Area: 261 sq miles (676 sq km)
Length: 38 miles (61 km); width: 10 miles (16 km)
Highest elevation: Kamakou Mountain, 4,970 ft (1,515 m)
Coastline: 88 miles (140 km)
Airports: Hoolehua; Kalaupapa
Harbor: Kaunakakai Harbor
Products: bread, watermelon, honey
Flower: white kukui

A Molokai nui a Hina
Famed Molokai, island child of Hina
Ma Kaunuohua He Pali
There Kaunuohua, a cliff
A Kukui O Hapuu
When Hapuu was a fire
Hapuu Ke Akua
Hapuu the God
Paka Mai Pele Ke Akua Nui
Pele the great goddess came forth

THERE IS AN unhurried grace to Molokai. Oahu is face-paced, modern and bustling; Maui, Kauai and the Big Island have accelerated their drive to develop their tourist industries but Molokai remains relatively unspoiled, clinging tenaciously to an honored past.

Molokai is genuinely old Hawaii, laid back and free from the traumas that some-times afflict the tourist centers of the other islands. Many Molokai residents fear that increased tourism will dilute and destroy a traditional and beloved lifestyle. The island has none of the trappings of a modern com-munity — no movie theater, no shopping center or fast food chain— and the people who live here like it that way.

Locals create their own entertainment with family parties, luaus and backyard bar-becues — and the art of conversation is alive and well. Molokai's population has the high-est percentage of native Hawaiians among those of the major islands in the chain, and many of them guard their heritage jealously. Efforts to modernize the island have run into fierce resistance. While some residents may favor development, they don't want to pay the price other islands have had to pay in terms of the impact on the Hawaiian culture.

Molokai is an island whose potential as a tourist destination has only been scratched. It has a charming atmosphere that is differ-ent from all of the other islands. To see it now in its pristine state is an opportunity not to be missed. One day Molokai could become a major, rather than a minor, stopover on Hawaii's tourist trail.

A RICH HERITAGE

The island of Molokai, fifth largest in the Ha-waiian chain, has a unique history. Like Maui, Molokai's main body was formed by two vol-canoes which flowed together to create a common plain. But Molokai, created by lava spewing from the ocean floor over one and a half million years ago, is much older than Maui. Over the centuries rain and seas have

Lone jogger beside the creamy surf of Kepuhi Beach at Kaluakoi Resort.

Molokai: The Friendly Isle

worked on the land, smoothing its jagged peaks, forming profound gorges along the eastern plains, and carving immense sea cliffs, the world's highest, on her northeastern flank, which render the island inaccessible from her windward shores.

Much later in its history, another eruption produced a remote and forbidding stretch of land along the base of the sea cliffs on the island's northern shores. This isolated peninsula was to become a prison for thousands of people afflicted with Hansen's disease, then known as leprosy.

On the eastern tip of Molokai is Halawa Valley which, until recently, was regarded by some historians and archaeologists as the earliest recorded Polynesian settlement in the Hawaiian chain. But this remains in dispute, for others believe that Kau on the Big Island, where the first canoes are said to have landed at South Point is older still (see HAWAII, TO KONA VIA SOUTH POINT, page 263).

Polynesians from the Marquesas were the first to arrive on Molokai, with Tahitians emigrating many years later. These early residents grew taro, sweet potato and other staples which had been introduced from the South Pacific. They fished extensively and developed an early aquaculture, thought to be unique to the Hawaiian islands. On Molo-

kai, as many as 58 fish ponds were constructed of lava rock and coral along the shallow waters of the southern coast, possibly before the thirteenth century, though no record exists to confirm the date. The fish in these ponds were reserved exclusively for chiefs and kings. Commoners, though responsible for keeping the ponds stocked, fished in the open sea.

In the days of the first Hawaiian kings, Molokai was noted for its learned and powerful *kahunas* (priests), some said to have extraordinary powers. One of the most respected and powerful was Lanikaula, who lived during the last half of the sixteenth century. Lanikaula chose to live in seclusion, but he was eagerly sought by people from all islands for advice on important matters. Under his influence, the island was unofficially declared a retreat and was thus spared of the warring of the other islands. Legend has it that during the seventeenth century, the *kalaipahoa* (poisonwood gods) appeared on the island, stepping forth from a grove of trees that had mysteriously grown overnight. Whereas Lanikaula had protected Molokai with his gift of wisdom, the kalaipahoa were said to be endowed with supernatural powers of sorcery, and used their magic to guard Molokai against warring neighbors. During this period, Molokai was regarded as far from being a "friendly isle," and the people of other islands avoided it.

Evidence of the island's rich religious heritage remains; Molokai's heiaus include some of the largest and most impressive to be found in the Hawaiian islands.

The Western world had little interest in Molokai during the eighteenth century when the other islands were being explored. On November 26, 1778, Captain Cook sailed by the island without stopping. Eight years later, the islanders had their first meeting with foreigners — on a British ship captained by George Dixon. He must have found little to interest them, as the next recorded visit did not occur until 1832, when Protestant missionaries arrived and established a mission at Kaluaaha.

Foreigners, however, were ultimately to play a major role in Molokai. Widespread change came with the Great Mahele, brought about by Kamehameha III in 1848, which provided for private ownership of land in Hawaii. Kamehameha III sent Rudolph Wilhelm Meyer, an immigrant from Hamburg, Germany, to Molokai to survey the land for native claims. It became the first of 18 positions Meyer ultimately held in the Molokai government.

Aside from his official roles, Meyer is credited with turning much of Molokai's idle acreage into fertile pasture lands, which he managed for the alii (Hawaiian nobles). During the 1860s, several large tracts of land were united into the Molokai Ranch, Kamehameha V's favorite holiday retreat. That too was managed by Meyer.

King Kamehameha V willed the ranch to Princess Bernice Pauahi Bishop, a Hawaiian princess who was the last of his line. Her husband, Charles Reed Bishop, enlarged the ranch through the purchase of 43,000 acres (17,400 hectares) extending from Ahupuaa to Kaluakoi and the leasing of additional government lands. Meyer managed the Molokai Ranch from its formation until his death in 1897.

The industrious German married a high chieftess of Molokai, Dorcas Kalama Waha, and maintained a homestead in Kalae where he grew his own food, milled sugar and raised 11 children. He is buried in a private cemetery next to his home.

A year after Meyer's death the Molokai Ranch was sold to a group of Honolulu businessmen who turned it into the American Sugar Company. But the water used for irrigation proved too salty to support a viable sugar crop. In 1908 the land was sold to one of the partners, Charles M. Cooke, and became a ranch once more.

Large portions of the ranch in central and western Molokai were leased out to Libby, McNeil & Libby and later to the California Packing Corporation for the cultivation of pineapple.

Pineapple became Molokai's principal industry for the next 50 years. During its heyday, the towns of Maunaloa and Kualapuu were built to support the swelling number of laborers brought in to work the fields. In 1939, the ranch became Molokai Ranch Ltd. Today the ranch spreads over 53,000 acres (21,000 hectares), or more than 37 percent of all the land on Molokai.

During the latter half of the nineteenth century, Molokai entered a period of notoriety following a royal decree by Kamehameha V: In 1864 Molokai's remote Kalaupapa Peninsula was designated as a dumping site for islanders afflicted with leprosy.

KAUNAKAKAI

Kaunakakai is Molokai's largest town — all three blocks of it. This former canoe landing hasn't changed much over the past half century. Though small, the village has some

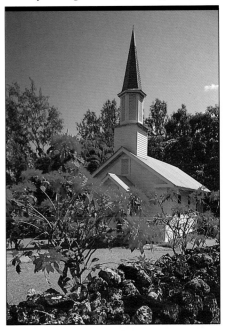

well-stocked grocery stores, restaurants, and bakeries to supply all your needs. **Kanemitsu's Bakery** ((808) 553-5855 has a statewide reputation for its produce. They make delicious Molokai bread and pastries and sells fresh fish. Neighbor island visitors to Molokai rarely go home without delicacies from this family bakery.

In recent years, the town has also become the center of the island's arts and crafts activities, and designers specializing in native jewelry, art in glass, quilt making, silk screening and leis have all taken up residence here.

OPPOSITE: Early morning fishing off Molokai's rocky coastline. ABOVE: Siloana Protestant Church on the remote Kalaupapa Peninsula.

Molokai: The Friendly Isle

Exiting Kaunakakai's main street, make a turn in front of the elementary school and you'll arrive at the **Pau Hana Inn (** (808) 553-5342 FAX (808) 553-3928, P.O. Box 540, Kaunakakai, HI 96748 (inexpensive), where accommodation is reasonably priced. The **Banyan Tree Terrace Restaurant** (moderate), under the eponymous tree, becomes a rendezvous at night for Molokai residents. There's usually live music here on weekends, and the food is good.

EXPLORING MOLOKAI

Molokai has four distinct touring zones to explore: the southeastern portions of the island from the town of Kaunakakai via Kamehameha V Highway to Halawa Valley; western Molokai; central Molokai; and finally the Kalaupapa Peninsula, which must be reached by helicopter, on foot (for which a permit is required) or on the back of a mule.

KAUNAKAKAI TO HALAWA

The 30-mile (48-km) drive east from Kaunakakai along the southern coast to Halawa is exceptionally beautiful. But the distance is deceptive. It will take you the better part of a day to negotiate the road, so start early.

The journey to Halawa takes you through areas rich in history. On an inaccessible ridge above Kawela Plantations, just out of sight on your left, stands the **Puuhonua Place of Refuge**, a fortress where defeated warriors once sought sanctuary.

On the right, along the beach, is the **Pukuhiwa Battleground**, site of a savage battle during Kamehameha the Great's campaign to unite the islands. Kamehameha's war canoes are said to have lined this beach for four miles (six and a half kilometers). Piles of sling stones from the battle remain. Windsurfing is said to be good in this area.

Just east of **Kamalo**, on the right-hand side of the road, is **Saint Joseph's**, constructed in 1876. It was the second church built on the island by Father Damien. Less than a mile past the church, also on the right, is the spot where pilots Smith and Bronte crash landed in 1927 after completing the first commercial, nonstop trans-Pacific flight. The journey took more than 25 hours to complete.

All along the southern shores are scenic beaches and ancient fish ponds such as **Keawanui**. On the right is **Wavecrest Resort (** (808) 558-8103 FAX (808) 558-8206, HC 1, P.O. Box 541, Kaunakakai, HI 96748, the last accommodation on these shores until you reach Halawa. Approximately 13 miles (21 km) out of Kaunakakai on the left you will find the ruins of **Kaluaaha Church**, once one of the largest Western-style structures in the islands. Built in 1844, the church was used for worship until the 1940s. Further down on the left is **Our Lady of Seven Sorrows Church**, Father Damien's first church, built in 1874.

The **Mapulehu** area has great religious significance for native Hawaiians dating from well before first contact with westerners.

Hidden from sight in the hills on the left is **Iliiliopae Heiau**, an important Hawaiian temple dedicated to the highest gods. The **Molokai Horse and Wagon Ride** (/FAX (808) 558-8132, P.O. Box 1528, Kaunakakai, HI 96748 organizes excursions to the heiau.

Measuring 310 ft (95 m) by 210 ft (64 m), Iliiliopae Heiau is one of the largest in the islands and was a place of human sacrifice. Legend says that an evil priest ordered the sacrifice of nine of 10 sons of a villager, whereupon the bereaved father appealed to the shark god for vengeance. A violent storm flooded the heiau and washed the priest and his followers into the ocean, but left the heiau intact. The site is on private land.

Nearby is also the beginning of the rugged **Wailau Trail**, which cuts clear across to the northern coast of Molokai. The Neighborhood Store at **Pukoo** is the last "watering hole" before you reach Halawa Valley, so don't forget to stock up.

Once past this little oasis, the beaches get prettier. This stretch of road is lined with wild ilima, and streams flow into the ocean through narrow valleys. The water in the little bays shines many different shades of blue. Then, almost imperceptibly, the road begins to climb and the rocks and white sand give way to the grazing land of the **Puu O Hoku Ranch**. At the crest of the hill you will see **Kaulukukuiolanikaula** on the right, the sacred grove of kukui where the prophet

Bathers enjoy the sun-dappled waters near Pukoo on the southeastern cost of Molokai.

Lanikaula is said to be buried. At the 25-mile mark, the road improves, and the run into Halawa Valley begins.

HALAWA VALLEY

When you spot Halawa Valley, stop the car at a suitable vantage point and take in the view. This large and beautiful northern valley is one of the most stunning areas on the island. Lantana flowers and hale koa bushes line the hillsides, which sweep down into the fertile valley where houses snuggle

in little coppices against the base of jungly slopes, almost hidden from view.

Halawa Valley was home to the island's earliest settlers, and the beach was a favorite playground of the chiefs because of its excellent surfing conditions. A tidal wave struck the valley in 1946 causing extensive damage. These days only about 20 people live here, without electricity or telephones. The population is supplemented temporarily by the tourists and townspeople who camp here and enjoy the serenity of an all but forgotten lifestyle.

Once in the valley itself, you can hike to **Moaula Falls** in about one hour. This is private property, however, so you'll need to hire a guide from **Molokai Action Adventures (** (808) 558-8184. The falls feed a deep, clear pool. Legend has it that a giant *mo'o* (lizard) resides there in an underwater cave. Before you dive in, Hawaiians suggest you first drop a ti leaf into the pool. If it floats, then it is safe to swim. But if the ti leaf sinks, it means that the mo'o is annoyed and will not welcome intruders.

The great sea cliffs stretch from Lamaloa past Wailau, Pelekunu Valley and Waikolu, all the way to Kalaupapa. The cliffs are spectacular, but must be viewed from the sea or air to be appreciated. Near **Umilehi Point**, these cliffs drop nearly 3,300 ft (1,000 m) to the ocean, descending at an average gradient in excess of 55 degrees.

For first-rate overview of the sea cliffs, take an air tour that will fly you past the cliffs, the 1,765-ft (535-m)-high **Kahiwa Falls**, Hawaii's tallest waterfall, and on to **Kalaupapa**.

WHERE TO STAY

An exceptional bed-and-breakfast establishment now operates in East Molokai where there were not many options for accommodation previously. **Kamueli Farms (** (808) 558-8284 FAX **(** (808) 558-8281 E-MAIL dcurtis @aloha .net, P.O. Box 1829, Kaunakakai, HI 96748 (inexpensive to mid-range) is tucked away at the base of the legendary Kaapahu Mountain. This is country living at its finest. The property is situated in the middle of an eight-acre (three-hectare) orchard of grapefruit, bananas, papaya, mango and breadfruit. Axis deer wander in the nearby pastures; trails behind the house lead to ocean vistas and fish ponds. The islands of Lanai, Maui and Kahoolawe can be seen a few miles offshore. Great beaches and snorkeling waters are just 10 minutes to the east of Kamueli Farms. The guest suite has a private entry and is separated from the main house by a large deck. The rooms open onto great views of the mountains, the gardens and a 75-ft (22.5-m) swimming pool. Breakfast is served either on the deck or in a sunny dining room in the main house. All sorts of recreational activities are available, including horseback riding. Your hosts are Dorothe and David Curtis.

(800) 367-6046 FAX (808) 552-2821, P.O. Box 26, Maunaloa, HI 96770 (mid-range to expensive). Of the 700 accommodations on Molokai, 500 are in Kaluakoi. The resort is superbly situated on a 6,800-acre (2,750-hectare) oceanfront property.

Most of the rooms and cottages have superb views of the ocean and the 18-hole championship **Kaluakoi Golf Course**. The cottages are luxuriously appointed and decorated in Polynesian style. The 30-ft (ninemeter) ceilings keep the rooms cool, while sliding doors open onto private lanais. The

cottages consist of a master bedroom, which opens up onto a living room, a dining area and kitchenette.

The resort has five and a half miles (nine kilometers) of beautiful coastline, with an ample supply of white sand beaches, though not all are recommended for swimming. Kepuhi Beach faces the resort's golf course. The **Ohia Lodge** restaurant (moderate) is the resort's main dining room.

WESTERN MOLOKAI

Ancient teachings speak of lush forests in this area, where ohia trees bore lehua blossoms so beautiful that a lei of the flowers would inspire love. Now the land is nearly devoid of trees.

Within the Kaluakoi Resort is the imposing Kaiaka Rock and further on, the vast expanse of Papohaku Beach, Hawaii's largest white sand beach. Past Kepuhi Beach to the north lies the **Pohakumauliuli Cinder Cone**, formed in the vent of a volcano. The cone changes hue with the shifting sunlight, from a dull black to chocolate to reddish brown.

KALUAKOI RESORT

Where to Stay and Eat

At the far western end of the island, just a 25-minute drive from the airport, is Kaluakoi Resort, encompassing the **Kaluakoi Villas** ((808) 552-2721 FAX (808) 552-2201, (mid-range to expensive) and the **Kaluakoi Hotel and Golf Club** ((808) 552-2555 TOLL-FREE

OPPOSITE: Post Office LEFT and Big Wind Kite Factory RIGHT in the sleepy plantation town of Maunaloa. ABOVE: Houses of worship LEFT on "Church Row" leading into Kaunakakai, where restaurants such as the Hop Inn RIGHT offer unpretentious and good dining.

If you are planning an extended stay in western Molokai, a condominium might suit your needs. The **Ke Nani Kai** ((808) 922-9700 FAX (808) 552-0045, P.O. Box 126, Maunaloa, HI 96770 (mid-range) is a block from Kepuhi Beach. The **Paniolo Hale Resort Condominiums** ((808) 552-2731 FAX (808) 552-2288, P.O. Box 146, Maunaloa, HI 96770 (mid-range to expensive) has garden- and ocean-view studios, one- and two-bedroom condominiums with private lanais, and a pool.

Just beyond Kaluakoi Resort lies **Kawakiu Beach**, one of the best swimming beaches

552-2681 TOLL-FREE (800) 254-8871, P.O. Box 259, Maunaloa, HI 96770. The preserve was developed in part to curb unwanted brush and grasses which were encroaching on cattle pasture lands. In the 1970s the Molokai Ranch imported a few exotic antelope and sheep to feed on 400 acres (160 hectares) of brush. The first animals included African eland, Indian black buck and Barbary sheep. Besides controlling the vegetation, the ranch also succeeded in creating an environment where rare species of animals could live and multiply without fear of predators.

on the island. The beach also has some important archaeological ruins. Look along the shoreline and you can see the remains of house platforms and a temple structure that mark the location of an ancient fishing village.

At the far northwestern tip of the island is **Kalaeokailio** (Ilio Point). On one of the dunes nearby early Hawaiians built a fishing *koa* (shrine). However, during World War II, the area was used for bombing practice. Access to the area is now prohibited.

MOLOKAI RANCH

A five-minute drive from Kaluakoi is the famed **Molokai Ranch Wildlife Park**, operated by the **Molokai Ranch Outfitters** ((808)

The preserve proved ideal for the animals, as it duplicated many of the conditions present in their natural habitat. Other species introduced included axis deer, oryx, giraffe, zebra, and crowned cranes. Local spotted deer invited themselves. Camera safaris are conducted through the park.

There are no paved roads in the preserve, but transportation is provided by comfortable vans. The safari drivers traverse rutted hill tracks and follow meandering gulches, seeking wildlife and attempting to get as close as possible to the animals.

In addition to the safari tour, the ranch now offers a new lodging and recreation program called the **Great Molokai Ranch Trail** for which visitors design their own travel adventure choosing from a variety of campsites and activities in the Molokai Gulch. The gulch offers great views of the ocean and the surrounding countryside. This is the type of outdoor adventure where you can rough it in style. A total of 40 one- and two-unit tents on elevated wooden platforms are furnished with wooden chairs, tables and comfortable beds. There's even a private lanai, as well as hot and cold running water and a composting toilet. The idea is to create an ambiance replicating the paniolo lifestyle, but with all the comforts of home. Within this paniolo camp

reation activity per person per day, an ice chest stocked with cold drinks and snacks, and airport transportation.

The Molokai Ranch also offers year-round hunting of axis deer and Barbary sheep. The fee is $1,000 per animal plus an additional $400 daily hunting fee (whether you sight any game or not). Only 10 hunters are admitted per day. From November through January, on weekends and holidays, the ranch also permits the shooting of game birds. The fee is $300 for the season, and hunters must bring their own gear. The ranch will furnish maps

is an open-air dining pavilion, swimming pool, and fire circle.

For recreation, there's horseback riding and wonderful hiking trails. And if you still have energy left after a day of hiking and riding, you can play volleyball at the camp or pitch horseshoes.

Other adventure vacations offered by the ranch include the **Paniolo Trail Adventure**, a guided tour of the island that explains its rich cultural heritage; **Paniolo Round-up**, where visitors are taught horsemanship and experience the thrill of traditional cowboy competition; and **mountain biking**, with guided tours of a network of trails. Rates for these adventure packages start at $185 per person and include all meals, one major rec-

but not guides. A guide service is provided, however, by Walter Naki, who runs **Molokai Action Adventures** ((808) 558-8184. Naki also takes visitors on hiking, snorkeling, SCUBA diving, spearfishing and kayaking trips. To obtain a hunting permit, contact the Department of Fish and Wildlife in Kaunakakai.

MAUNALOA

Eight miles (just under 13 kilometers) from the Kaluakoi turn-off, down the road to the right, is the old pineapple plantation town

OPPOSITE: Wild surf pounds the edges of the Kaluakoi Resort Golf Course. ABOVE: Molokai Ranch Wildlife Park provides an ideal habitat for a variety of island deer.

of **Maunaloa**. Much has changed here in the past few years — and the changes continue. The town is undergoing a major facelift with the construction of new modern houses by the landowners of Molokai Ranch. Plans are also underway for a 60-room lodge, a museum and cultural center, a movie theater and new retailers.

Clinging to the past, however, are Jonathan Socher and his wife, designer Daphne Socher, who operate the **Big Wind Kite Factory** out of one of the original old buildings. The store has a wonderful ambiance. Kites in all shapes and sizes turn the interior of this charming store into a blaze of color. The reputation of the Big Wind Kite Factory for quality design and workmanship has brought the creations of other great kite makers into the store. There are daily tours of the factory and free kite-flying lessons.

The store adjacent to the Big Wind Kite Factory, once a restaurant, has been transformed into the **Plantation Gallery**, which sells delicate deer horn and coral scrimshaw souvenirs and gift items created by Molokai's finest artists and craftspeople. Ex-surfer Butch Tabanao, for instance, creates magnificent deer horn cribbage boards (measuring less than four inches, or 10 cm long), notebooks, cards and paintings.

CENTRAL MOLOKAI

A 20-minute drive east from Maunaloa, back along the Maunaloa Highway (Highway 46), will bring you to central Molokai and on to Kaunakakai. Just past the Kalae Highway turn-off is the State Forest Reserve Road leading off to the left to the **Kamakou Preserve**, a refuge for rare and endangered forest birds. The roads are accessible only by four-wheel drive-vehicle, but occasional tours are conducted by the **Nature Conservancy of Hawaii** ((808) 553-5236 FAX (808) 553-9870. For information on the Kamakou hiking trails, see HITTING THE TRAIL, page 33.

KAANA

Atop Maunaloa's neighboring hill, **Kaana** is said by some to be the birthplace of hula, the site where the goddess Laka was taught to dance by her sister Kapo. From this lofty stage, Laka traveled through the islands teaching hula to the islanders.

Molokai's hula masters have recently taken advantage of the legend of Laka by organizing a spectacular hula festival that takes place every year in May, at the Papohaku Beach Park at Kaluakoi. The annual **Molokai Ka Hula Piko** attracts hula halau, musicians and singers from Molokai as well as the other Hawaiian islands and Japan. It also provides a showcase for Hawaiian crafts such as deer horn scrimshaw work, featherwork, woodwork and quilting. For more information call the **Molokai Visitors Association** ((808) 553-3876 TOLL-FREE INTERISLAND (800) 553-0404.

PALAAU STATE PARK

Running along the bluff above Kalaupapa is the **Palaau State Park**. This cool, beautifully wooded area is ideal for a picnic and casual strolls. The **Kalaupapa Lookout** provides an aerial view of the peninsula and the colony below.

A short walk away from the lookout is the phallic stone of **Nanahoa**. Hawaiians believe that a stone has certain powers related to its form. Thus, the phallic rock was a place of pilgrimage for barren women seeking children. It was said that if a woman sat at the base of the stone, where rain water collected, she could absorb the power of the rock and become fertile.

At **Kalae** is the site of **Molokai Museum and Cultural Center** ((808) 567-6436, Kalae Highway, and the **R.W. Meyer Sugar Mill** ((808) 567-6436. This historic mill has been restored by the Friends of the Meyer Sugar Mill. Powered by steam and animals, the mill was built in 1878. It is, today, the only mill of its kind remaining in the United States. Meyer Sugar Mill is open for guided tours.

KUALAPUU

Kualapuu is the site of a relatively new industry on Molokai — coffee. The bean has been grown with such success in Kona on the Big Island that it was inevitable that other islands would be encouraged to experiment. At the **Malulani Estate** ((808) 567-9241 TOLL-FREE (800) 709-BEAN, some 450 acres (180 hectares) are under cultivation. The coffee produced here — described as "delicious, full-bodied, low in acidic content and rich in taste and flavor" — is planted, harvested, roasted and packaged at the Coffees of Hawaii plantation. Wagon tours of the plantation are available twice a day during the week and once on Saturday.

In Hoolehua on Lihipali Avenue is **Purdy's Natural Macadamia Nut Farm** ℂ (808) 567-6601, P.O. Box 84, Kualapuu, HI 96757. The farm sells fresh fruits, nuts, and Molokai's famous Macadamia-blossom honey.

At Kualapuu a road leads to the west, past Hoolehua and part way to the northwestern coast. Most of the beaches on the northwestern coast, such as **Moomomi Beach**, are inaccessible by car but may be reached by hiking along the coast.

THE KALAUPAPA PENINSULA

The **Kalaupapa Peninsula** is an isolated strip of land on the northern shores of Molokai. Here, 20-ft (six-meter) breakers thunder in from the open sea, past the tiny islands of Mokapi and Okala, dashing themselves in a frenzy on the pebbly shores at the feet of towering sea cliffs. The cliffs are too high to climb and the waters too rough to swim.

BACKGROUND

Standing on the bluff high above the ocean, you may imagine hearing in the wind the ghostly cries of anguish from the thousands of sufferers of leprosy — or Hansen's disease, named after the Norwegian scientist who discovered the bacillus causing the condition, which was then believed to be highly contagious. They were sent here in 1866 following an act signed into law by King Kamehameha V. Shipped to Molokai in cages, these unfor-

tunate men, women, and children were cast into the raging waters of Waikolu Bay and left to sink or swim to the forbidding shore. If they survived this ordeal, they faced an inhospitable environment and the predatory tendencies of their fellow sufferers.

It took a man of immense courage to draw the attention of the world to the horrors of Kalaupapa leper colony. This man was a young Belgian priest named Father Damien Joseph de Veuster, who came to the colony in 1873 and gave back to the people both their dignity and their will to live. The patients assisted in building a settlement at Kalawao which included a primitive hospital and a

Youngsters examine a statue LEFT of Father Damien. RIGHT: Kalaupapa muleteer.

church. During the nineteenth century, the settlement shifted from Kalawao to the town of Kalaupapa on the leeward side of the peninsula.

Father Damien eventually contracted the disease. In 1889 at the age of 49, after living 16 years in the colony and weakened by his condition, he died of pneumonia. His work, however, continued. Eventually, Hansen's disease on the island was halted by the drug sulfone.

Once you reach Kalaupapa, you must have a guide because this remains a restricted area. **Damien Tours** ℂ (808) 567-6171, run by Richard Marks, has the only blanket permit to bring the general public to the peninsula. On the tour you'll be taken to Kalawao, site of the first settlement, and the church of **St. Philomena's**—now a pilgrimage shrine —which Father Damien began, and patients completed after his death. Sitting in this tidy church, in the same pews in which the sufferers of Hansen's disease sat, and listening to the guide describe the work of this beloved priest, it isn't difficult to understand why Father Damien is destined for sainthood.

With the advent of sulfone treatment, many former patients moved back to live with their families in a free society. But not all chose to go. Only a handful of residents remain, all voluntarily, in the colony. For them, Kalaupapa is home, and they prefer to live their final days in the tranquillity of this beautiful place which once knew such great sorrow and suffering.

Today, through the efforts of current and former Kalaupapa residents, the peninsula has become a retreat from the pressures of modern life. The State of Hawaii administers the settlement jointly with the National Park Service. The settlement, along with the rest of the peninsula, has been designated as a National Historical Park, though it is not yet open to the public.

The spectacular cliffs lining the peninsula served two purposes: They kept victims of the disease in and unwelcome visitors out. Patients trying to escape Kalaupapa by scaling the cliffs were shot at by guards—if they made it to the top.

In a feat far removed from the peninsula's unhappy past, a European athlete set a record by racing up the mule trail (see below), from

the base of the cliffs to the top, a distance of just over three miles (five kilometers), in 38 minutes.

THE MULE TRAIL

Thousands of tourists, lured by its history, its scenic beauty and the marvelous serenity of Kalaupapa, visit the peninsula each year. Some are flown in on small aircraft or helicopter to the Kalaupapa airstrip. Others hike in with a permit. But the most popular way of reaching Kalaupapa is on the back of a mule, down the rugged mule trail with its 26 switch-backs.

The mule trail was cut by a Portuguese immigrant named Manuel João Farinha in 1886. In some places, Farinha and his fellow

workers had to be suspended by ropes secured to the cliff's face in order to complete their Herculean task. Thanks to the courage and tenacity of Farinha and his fellow workers, the modern tourist can enjoy an exhilarating journey down this remarkable trail.

The trail down the 1,800-foot (540-m) cliff meanders through a forest splashed here and there with wild flowers and fruit trees. Each bend in the trail opens up vistas of the ocean below and the cliffs above.

The **Molokai Mule Ride** ((808) 567-6088 FAX (808) 567-6244, Mule Route 1, Box 200, Molokai, HI 96757 began in the 1970s and became the must-do adventure for tourists visiting this island. The ride shut down in 1992 while the National Park Service rebuilt the trail. The Molokai Mule Ride reopened for business in 1995 under a veteran muleteer named Buzzy Sproat. The mule tour and unguided trail hike is open every day except Sunday.

There is only one mule trail ride each day. It begins at the Mule Barn at Kalae at 8:30 AM and concludes at approximately 3:30 PM. No horseback riding experience is necessary to take this ride. The mules are well-trained veterans of this trail, and they are under the guidance of experienced muleteers. The cost of the mule ride is $75 per person; children under 16 are not allowed.

The Molokai Mule Ride snakes down the sea cliffs on the way to the settlement far below.

Molokai: The Friendly Isle

Lanai
The Private Isle

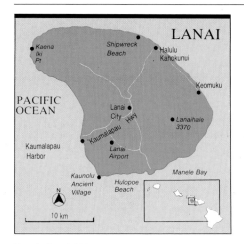

LANAI

Population: 2,800
Area: 140 sq miles (363 sq km)
Length: 18 miles (29 km); *width:* 13 miles (21 km)
Highest elevation: Lanaihale: 3,370 ft (1,027 m)
Product: pineapple
Coastline: 47 miles (76 km)
Airport: Lanai
Main harbors: Kaumalapau Harbor; Manele Bay
Flower: kauna'oa

A Lana'i Kaulahea
At Kaulahea, Lana'i
A Maunalei, Kui Ka Lei
At Maunalei, twine the wreath
Lei Pele I Ka 'Ie'e La
Pele is wreathed with the 'ie'e
Wai Hina Po'o O Hi'iaka
Hi'iaka oils her head
Holapu Ili O Haumea
Haumea anoints her body

THE SIXTH LARGEST ISLAND in the Hawaiian chain, Lanai is a 30-minute flight from Honolulu. But it's another world — that of the old Hawaii, quiet, slow paced, mystical. Lanai has only 30 miles (48 km) of paved road that were once used primarily for the pineapple industry. Within this tropical paradise are magnificent beaches and secluded coves, mountains rising to 3,400 ft (1,020 m), exotic flora and wild game, spectacular vistas, and enchanting and friendly people.

A SLEEPY RETREAT AWAKENS

For seven decades Lanai was the sleepiest backwater in the Hawaiian chain. Its only

town, Lanai City, and its surrounding residential district consisted of neat, somewhat weather-worn but gaily painted buildings, one hotel, one public golf course, and lots of stately Norfolk pines. Almost everywhere you went you could smell the sweet scent of pineapple in the air.

The prickly fruit became the island's only industry starting in 1922, when Boston businessman Jim Dole bought the island and planted 15,000 acres (6,070 hectares) of pineapples. Later, the Dole Company, a subsidiary of Dole Food Company Inc., purchased the island and expanded the pineapple acreage. In its prime, Lanai was the world's largest pineapple plantation.

In 1985, David Murdock purchased 98 percent of the company, but eight years later the pineapple industry ran into tough economic times, and Castle & Cooke Properties of Honolulu took over the company, with Murdock remaining at the helm. Castle & Cooke has since developed two high-class resorts on the island.

Making the transition from an agricultural economy to a tourist-based economy hasn't been easy for the people of Lanai. But there are signs that the friendly people of this unusual island are adapting. The majority of the people who worked the pineapple fields have switched to the hospitality industry and its support services. Arts and crafts skills and entrepreneurship have been encouraged, and there's a great deal of confidence in the air. But most important, what made Lanai such a wonderful place to visit is still deeply ingrained in the people, and that is their spirit of aloha. You still see it in the smiles on the faces of the many races who make up the population of Lanai and whose ancestors came to plant and harvest pineapple — the Japanese, Filipinos, Koreans, Chinese, Puerto Ricans, Caucasians, and of course, the native Hawaiians.

LANAI CITY

Most of the residents of Lanai live in or around Lanai City, in actuality a plantation village, in the upper elevations of the island.

Bougainvillea adds a splash of color to the Lanai brush on an island where tourism has replaced pineapple cultivation as the main industry.

Lanai: The Private Isle

The streets are lined with charming old stores and houses, many with tin roofs. Where once there were mainly traditional grocery and small goods stores, there are now some nice art galleries such as the **Heart of Lanai Art Gallery**, which features the works of local artists Pamela Andelin, Macario Pascual and John Young. Owner Denise Hennig also has on display a collection of Hawaiian jewelry, paintings, sculpture and local arts and crafts.

Maunalei Gifts, another new store, is located in the town's only "mini-mall" alongside the town's only health food store, **Pele's**

the old hunting lodge and has opened a fine restaurant, **Henry Clay's Rotisserie** (moderate) in this classic inn. This sophisticated addition to the island's dining choices has helped bring an upscale clientele to Lanai City. Richardson describes what he serves as "simple American country cuisine," but this simple fare gets rave reviews. Pine furnishings, hardwood floors and patchwork quilts help to enhance the character of this fine old inn, where in the days of the hunter, there were always convivial gatherings on the open verandah (since enclosed), but

Garden, and the only health food deli, **Pele's Other Garden** (inexpensive).

The Lanai Company, which literally owns the island, tries to support this spirit of entrepreneurship among the local people, so large corporations are not encouraged to enter this market. In addition to the new stores, the town has three restaurants open for breakfast, lunch and dinner, a couple of banks and a police station with a wooden jail in the yard.

The center of the town's social activities is the 11-room **Hotel Lanai (** (808) 565-4700 FAX (808) 565-4713, P.O. Box 520, Lanai City, HI 96763 (mid-range). It has been the gathering place of the town for countless years. Henry Clay Richardson recently took over

where the atmosphere for camaraderie and good fellowship has never changed.

LANAI'S RESORTS

Two resorts provide the other accommodation on Lanai — the **Lodge at Koele (** (808) 565-3800 TOLL-FREE (800) 321-4666 FAX (808) 565-3858 (expensive to luxury) and the **Manele Bay Hotel (** (808) 565-3800 TOLL-FREE (800) 321-4666 FAX (808) 565-3868 WEBSITE http://www.lanai-resorts.com, Lanai Company Inc., P.O. Box 310, Lanai City, HI 86763 (expensive).

The Lodge at Koele, patterned after an English-style hunting lodge, is situated in the highlands. Manele Bay Hotel has Mediterranean-style architecture and occupies a prime site on the edge of Hulopoe Bay's lovely white sand beach. Since both resorts have world-class golf facilities, the choice a tourist makes will be purely a matter of taste. But since the resorts are but a few miles apart and linked by a regular shuttle service, one should be able to experience the pleasures of both resorts without missing a beat.

The 102-room **Lodge** sits at over 1,700 ft (500 m) in the island's cool highlands, up the hill from Lanai City. Groves of Cook Island pine trees, banyan, eucalyptus, jacarandas and lush formal gardens surround the property.

The extensive use of timber and high-beamed ceilings give the Lodge a comfortable atmosphere. Visitors can take afternoon tea on a spectacular verandah or relax in the library, music room, or the Great Hall with its huge stone fireplaces and high-beamed ceilings. The fireplace is not just for show; it can get quite cold here in the winter months.

Leisurely sporting activities in addition to golf include croquet, lawn bowls, hunting, skeet shooting, horseback riding, jeep tours, archaeological tours and garden walks. A regular shuttle service connects to Hulopoe Bay for deep-sea fishing, snorkeling, SCUBA diving and swimming alongside the Manele Bay Hotel.

Much of the fresh food is local, coming from a 10-acre (four-hectare) organic garden which nurtures such exotic plants as chamomile, arugula, as well as legumes and vegetables such as fava beans and Italian tomatoes. Imagine starting your day at **The Terrace** (moderate) with Palawai sugar pineapple, fish caught fresh that morning, a sweet rice waffle with *lilikoi* (passion fruit) coconut chutney with warm Vermont maple syrup, and a steaming mug of macadamia nut coffee. For lunch you might want to start with fresh pineapple cider and dine on grilled pastrami of striped marlin served with pineapple salsa, or seared *ahi* (yellow tuna) on a bed of greens with cilantro dressing.

Dinner is in the cozy comfort of the **Formal Dining Room** (expensive), where the style of cooking is described as "modern American cooking with an upcountry flair." This means it's wholesome, tasty and very

fresh. For starters, the specialty here is "marble" of ahi and snapper with radish, fennel and mustard seed. Fresh venison is usually in abundance on this island, and so for the main course, the Formal Dining Room offers roasted venison with a marinade of lilikoi. There are also omelets filled with Japanese and Chinese vegetables, accompanied by sausage made of Lanai axis deer meat.

The **Manele Bay Hotel** blends old Hawaii's kamaaina-style living with Mediterranean elegance. A total of 250 luxury suites and villas with private lanais overlook spectacular ocean views. The centerpiece at Manele is beautiful **Hulopoe Beach**. Hulopoe was once a bustling Hawaiian fishing village where people worshipped native gods, and worked the land.

Traces of an ancient past at Hulopoe are being carefully preserved. Nearby is the tomb of Pehe, and just offshore is the rocky islet of Puu Pehe, also known as Sweetheart Rock, which played a role in a bittersweet romantic legend.

One of the most visually striking aspects of Manele is its theme gardens designed to incorporate and reflect the lushness of the islands. The landscapers cleverly blended aspects of Hawaii gardens with those of Japan and China, countries with which the islands have close ties.

At **Hulopoe Court** (moderate), one of several fine restaurants at this property, Hawaiian regional cuisine is alive and well. The menu includes such dishes as fennel cured salmon and green lentil salad, buckwheat pasta with vegetable vermicelli, tiger prawns in tangerine olive oil with garlic cloves and Italian parsley, and roast saddle of rabbit with porcini mushrooms, fava beans and olives.

Manele Bay's specialty restaurant, the **Ihilani** (very expensive), is designed in the style of a grand salon of the Hawaiian monarchy. Here, at tables set with silver and crystal, you will be served by staff in period attire. The cuisine is French-Mediterranean.

VISITING ARTIST PROGRAM

Lanai's **Visiting Artist Program** ((808) 548-3700 TOLL-FREE (800) 321-4666 is fast gaining a reputation as one of the finest programs on

Tranquil antiquity surrounds the Lodge at Koele.

culture and the arts in the country. First introduced in 1993, the Visiting Artist Program brings together guests of the island's two resorts and members of the local community with artists of national renown who share their talents in an informal, living room setting.

Here's how it works: Each of the literary and performing artists offers an evening lecture or performance. Each visiting chef presents dinners for two nights as well as complimentary cooking demonstrations. Guests get an opportunity not only to listen to or see a world-class performance in an intimate setting, but to talk to the celebrity artist.

Many guests plan their visits to Lanai to coincide with a visiting artist. Those who have participated to date include novelist Paul Theroux, Pulitzer prize-winning writer Jane Smiley, humorist Garrison Keillor, pianists Andre Watts and Roger Taub, jazz singer Cleo Laine, composer, author and satirist Peter Schickele, television producer David Wolper, humorist Dave Barry, classical guitarist James Russell Hunley, Brazilian classical pianist Ciao Pagano, and chef Bradley Ogden, recognized as one of the top talents in the western United States. The program runs throughout the year; the resorts can provide a performance schedule.

EXPLORING LANAI

Lanai is small and can be explored easily on foot (see HITTING THE TRAIL, page 33), or at a faster clip in a four-wheel-drive vehicle.

Two hours by motor vehicle is all you'll need to see Lanai's scenic and historic places. Take the Hoike turn-off and continue on to the top of Lanaihale, then come back through Hookio Gulch to Koele and Lanai City. On the way you'll see **Hookio Ridge**, an ancient battlefield and the island's only fortifications.

Ancient Hawaiians regarded Lanai as a sinister place because it was reportedly inhabited by malevolent spirits. Legend has it that a mischievous young prince banished from Maui by his father killed off the ghosts and opened the island for migration from Maui and Molokai.

Lanai's children still tell ghostly tales, but the island evokes pleasant memories too, particularly for plantation workers who remember the good old days when pineapple was the king of fruit.

Lanai was one of Kamehameha the Great's favorite islands, and he built a summer residence at **Kaunolu Bay**, the ruins of which are regarded as the most complete archaeological site in Hawaii. The site includes the **Halulu Heiau**. Kaunolu Village is close to **Kahekili's Jump** where the monarch's warriors are said to have tested their courage by sprinting down a narrow path and leaping more than 60 ft (18 m) into the sea after clearing a 15-ft (4.5-m) ledge which protrudes from the cliff's base.

Garden of the Gods is an area of eerie rock formations which give the impression of having been dropped from a great height. The red earth looks as though it has been seared, creating a landscape of pinnacles and canyons. At sunrise or sunset, the stones glow in tones of amber. Garden of the Gods is situated northwest along the Awalua Highway, seven miles (11 km) from Lanai City.

Shipwreck Beach gained its reputation not from the single wreck of a World War II vessel offshore, but because of all the sailing ships that came to grief here, driven ashore by lusty trade winds.

Branching east from Shipwreck Beach, a dirt road meanders along the coast past isolated beaches to the site of what was once the Maunalei Sugar Company. All that remains of the little village of **Keomoku** is its old Hawaiian church and a grove of coconut palms.

Overlooking the stunning white sand Hulopoe Beach from Manele Bay Hotel.

Hawaii
The Big Island

Population: 120,300
Capital city: Hilo
Area: 4,038 sq miles (10,457 sq km)
Length: 93 miles (150 km); *width:* 76 miles (122 km)
Highest elevations: Mauna Kea, 13,796 ft (4,205 m);
Mauna Loa, 13,677 ft (4,169 m).
Active volcanoes: Kilauea, Mauna Loa
Coastline: 266 miles (428 km)
Major airports: Hilo International (Hilo); Keahole-
Kona International (Kona); Waimea-Kohala
Products: Kona coffee, macadamia nuts, cattle,
sugar, cut flowers
Flower: red lehua

Ua Hanau Ka Moku
Born was the island
A Kapu, A Lau, A Loa, A Ao, A Mao
It budded, it leafed, it grew
Ka Moku Iluna O Hawaii
The island arose, it was Hawaii
O Hawaii Nei No Ka Moku
This Hawaii was an island
He Pulewa Ka Aina, He Naka Hawaii
Unstable was the land, tremulous was Hawaii

LAND OF CONTRASTS

HAWAII, OR THE BIG ISLAND, is larger than all
the other Hawaiian islands put together. It
has the highest mountains, the most active
volcanoes, an abundance of desert, and lush
rain forests. It even has snow, which during
the winter months drapes the summits and
shoulders of Mauna Kea — which native Big
Islanders refer to as the White Mountain —
and Mauna Loa.

This combination of fire and ice has helped
create a wealth of scenery on Hawaii that is
nothing less than astonishing. Beaches with
sand as soft and white as talcum powder contrast with beaches that are black or even
green, all washed by waters so blue and clean
as to look supernatural. Providing the backdrop are the deep chocolate fudge-colored
and ebony lava fields, a constant reminder
of how this island was created and why it
continues to grow.

The Big Island's magic lies in its contrasts.
The east coast is very wet. The vegetation
here is rampant, including flowers in a riot
of color. On the opposite side of the island,
it is very dry. There are secluded tropical
valleys where time has virtually stood still,

mountain pastures reminiscent of Switzerland, and sprawling resorts that rank among
the best in the world.

If you want to fish, hunt or hike trails
which traverse lunar landscapes and rain
forests draped in mist, plunge into the waters
of a marine wonderland, or witness the dancing curtain of fire which only a volcano such
as Kilauea can kick up, then you've come to
the right place.

But it's not just the scenery and the drama
of Kilauea which have made Hawaii famous.
Because of the clarity of the skies above
Mauna Kea, the mountain has become the
center of an international astronomical research program, while the perfect blend of
soil conditions and the hot dry climate have
enabled the Kona region on the west side of
the island to produce high-quality macadamia nuts and arguably the finest coffee in
the world.

And here's one other remarkable fact
about this island: over 90 percent of its native
flora and fauna is found nowhere else on
earth. Bearing in mind that this was once a
barren island, the astounding diversity of life
that now flourishes here is testimony to the
force of evolution — and the tenacity of
nature.

HILO

Travelers familiar with the small towns of
Asia and Southeast Asia find Hilo nostalgic.
There are images of old Portuguese towns
such as Melaka (Malacca) in Malaysia and
Kandy in Sri Lanka. Others may compare it
to Singapore in the days before it became a
republic. The reminders are in the architecture — some preserved buildings date back
to the turn of the century — in the awnings
that protect the older buildings from the rains,
in the scent of flowers that hang in the air. In
fact, Hilo is a classic tropical town where the
tempo of life hasn't changed much in the last
50 years.

Occasionally the moan of a ship's foghorn
will remind you of Hilo's other role in Hawaii's history — as a major port.

Hilo's bay front has been ravaged by two
tsunamis (tidal waves), the first in 1946, the

A hala tree clings to the barren earth of Lapakahi
State Park.

Hawaii: The Big Island

second in 1960. Many lives were lost. A man-made hill called Kaikoo (rough seas), 26 ft (eight meters) above sea level, was built to ensure that the ocean won't win a third time.

In recent years, charming, laid-back Hilo has begun to spruce up its image, thanks to the care and concern of its citizens who have renovated the old town while retaining what has always made Hilo so beloved — its quaintness and warm hospitality. But Hilo is also undergoing a very subtle change in-fluenced no doubt by the newcomers who have taken up residence here—it has grown in sophistication. Alongside the mom and pop stores, you now find art galleries, gift shops and some fine restaurants. At night,

the discos, bars, and restaurants on Main Street are crowded and lively. At certain times of the year,—Mardi Gras, for instance, and the Black and White Night in late Octo-ber — a carnival atmosphere takes over. In April each year, the Merrie Monarch Festi-val draws an international crowd for a rich celebration of the art of hula (see FESTIVE FLINGS, page 59).

Good things continue to happen in Hilo. With the support of federal, state and pri-vate sector grants, the Main Street Program has helped merchants and landowners to plan and implement improvements, particu-larly to the old buildings in the town. This renewed interest in the town as a center for the arts led to the restoration of the 65-year-old **Palace Theater**, a grand old building that once served as the town's premier movie house. A team of dedicated volunteers donated many hours of time and energy to help the theater regain its glamorous past. On October 25, 1990, the playhouse opened with a production of *13 Rue de L'Amour* by the Hilo Community Players. It was the forerunner of many other performances by theater companies and entertainers, both from Hilo and from overseas.

This new spirit has attracted several hundred businesses to this small corner of Hilo. Gift shops, old bookstores and quaint bars rub shoulders with an collection of snack shops, tasty take-away joints and fancy restaurants. The older barber shops remain, but the new look of the old town is refreshing. Typical of the new generation of businesses is **Sig Zane Design**, at 122 Kamehameha Avenue, which sells contemporary Hawaiian clothing and interesting arts and crafts, such as lauhala hats and bags.

Many of the businesses that moved here established themselves on and around the town's two main streets, Kilauea Street and Kinoole Street. Kilauea merges with Keawe Street and runs one way toward the Wailuku River. Kinoole runs one way away from the river and feeds into Kilauea creating a large loop. Running along the bay in front of the town is Kamehameha Avenue.

People say the daily **Suisan Fish Auction**, on Lihiwai Street, is the best free show in town. In a warehouse near the waterfront, restaurant chefs gather to bid on the day's catch. It's a colorful ritual that has been going on in Hilo for generations.

Every Wednesday and Saturday, the **Hilo Farmer's Market** sets up under canvas on a lot bounded by Kamehameha and Mano streets. Here you can buy everything from arts and crafts to fresh fruit and vegetables, a dazzling variety of cut flowers, and food products such as goat cheese.

The Big Island is renowned for its orchids and anthuriums, and the best place to see them is at one of the many tropical gardens in the city. These gardens include the **Nani Mau Gardens**, **Hilo Tropical Gardens**, **Akatsuka Orchid Gardens**, **Hawaiian Flower Garden Nursery**, and **Anthuriums**

of **Pahoa**, all of which display some of the finest examples of these exotic flowers. The best selections of all, however, are at the **Hilo Orchidarium**, at 524 Manono Street, or **Orchids of Hawaii**, at 575 Hinano Street. The Orchidarium is the headquarters of the Hilo Orchid Society.

You might also want to visit Rainbow Falls in the **Wailuku River Park**, which is located along Waianuenue Avenue.

WHERE TO STAY

Hilo's only first-class accommodation is the **Hilo Hawaiian Hotel** ((808) 591-2235 TOLL-FREE (800) 367-5004 FAX (808) 596-0158, 71 Banyan Drive, Hilo, HI 96720 (mid-range to expensive). It has 283 well-appointed rooms overlooking the bay and is within walking distance of the town, its shopping center, golf courses and parks.

The oceanfront **Hawaii Naniloa Resort** ((808) 969-3333 TOLL-FREE (800) 367-5380 FAX (808) 969-6622, 93 Banyan Drive, Hilo, HI 96720 (mid-range to expensive) features two swimming pools, a golf driving range, a very fine spa and fitness center, and seaside dining and entertainment. With 325 rooms, the Naniloa is the largest hotel on this side of the island.

For something different as well as reasonably priced try **Maureen's Bed-and-Breakfast** ((808) 935-9018, 1896 Kalanianaole Street, Hilo, HI 96720 (inexpensive). This 1932 mansion was built by a Japanese banker and his Hawaiian wife. Maureen Goto took over the mansion and completely restored it, decorating it with oak, mahogany and koa wood antiques. There are four rooms upstairs, with master bedrooms overlooking the mountains. A Japanese garden, a carp pond and a flower garden full of gardenias, bromeliads, jasmine and torch ginger add to the beautiful ambiance of this house.

WHERE TO EAT

Many new restaurants have arrived in the wake of Hilo's renaissance. **Pescatore** ((808) 969-9090 (inexpensive), 235 Keawe Street, caters to both the lunch and dinner crowds. Their dinner menu includes an excellent *cioppino classico*, a stew of clams, mussels, scallops and lobster, served with garlic bread.

High ceilings and neat tile floors contribute to the pleasant atmosphere of the **Café Pesto** ((808) 969-6640, South Hata Building, 130 Kamehameha Avenue (inexpensive). It specializes in excellent open-faced sandwiches, "provocative" pizzas and organic salads. The shrimp Milolii is good value. The restaurant is famous for its calzones — folded pizzas full of inventive fillings such as Japanese eggplant and artichokes, or lime-marinated fish. For those with big appetites, try the paella with lobster and calabrese sausage.

Reubens ((808) 961-2552, 336 Kamehameha Avenue (moderate), is an earthy restaurant specializing in Mexican cuisine. Colorful cloth paintings give Reubens the feel of a tavern, but it is more than that. The portions here are lavish and matched only by the size of the margarita pitchers.

Nihon Cultural Center ((808) 969-1133, 123 Lihiwai Street (inexpensive), is an affordable Japanese restaurant that overlooks Hilo Bay and Liliuokalani Gardens. The atmosphere is great, the food is good, the view is just right. The fish dishes are particularly tasty. Full dinners start at $15. The sushi bar is open until 10 PM.

Slightly away from town, **Ken's Pancake House** ((808) 935-8711, 173 Kamehameha Avenue (inexpensive), is a Hilo institution. This restaurant is open 24 hours a day and specializes in local as well as standard American fare. The food is inexpensive and very good. As its name implies, pancakes are a specialty, but there's a large menu to choose from. Ken's serves breakfast, lunch and dinner — and a late supper.

You could easily miss **Harrington's** ((808) 961-4966, 135 Kalanianaole Avenue (moderate). It is tucked away in an unassuming timber building about a mile out of town overlooking Reeds Bay. But don't be fooled — the food is surprisingly good here. For starters, try the escargot in casserole. Main dishes run from $16 to $20 and include some excellent seafood creations such as calamari meunière, Cajun prawns and scallops Chardonnay. There's live music at Harrington's from Wednesday to Saturday.

EXPLORING THE BIG ISLAND

There was a time when tourists automatically flew into Hilo. Then came the resort developments in North and South Kohala, Kona and Keauhou on the western side of the island, and the habits of arriving tourists changed dramatically.

Hawaii has two major airports capable of accommodating the big jets: Keahole-Kona International Airport, the gateway to the west or Kona side of the island; and Hilo International Airport, the entry point to the wetter eastern side of the island. The latter is closest to Hawaii Volcanoes National Park and Mauna Kea.

For the purposes of guiding you around the Big Island, we'll take some liberties with compass directions and consider eastern Hawaii as being from Hilo all the way to South Point, including Mauna Kea and Hawaii Volcanoes National Park. From Puuhonua O Honnaunau National Park to Kawaihae is the west coast. The northern part of the island begins with the Kohala Coast Resorts just north of Keahole-Kona International Airport, extending onward to Lapakahi State Historical Park, Upolu Point, and includes the hill country of Waimea. Finally the road takes you along the Hamakua Coast to Pepeekeo, not far from Hilo.

One road — Highway 11 or 19 — circles the entire island. Going south from Hilo, it's Highway 11. On the west coast it changes to Highway 19 as it cuts across the pass to the beautiful mountain town of Waimea from which Highway 19 continues along the Hamakua Coast until Hilo.

EASTERN HAWAII

MAUNA KEA

Whether you are scientifically inclined or just wish to view the heavens from one of the best vantage points anywhere, you should make the journey to the summit of Mauna Kea and the Ellison Onizuka Center for International Astronomy — best reached from Hilo (see WINDOW TO THE HEAVENS, page 14).

Besides the observatory, Mauna Kea has other attractions. Tucked out of sight over the next ridge line lies one of the mysteries of the mountain. At an elevation of 13,020 ft (3,968 m) is **Lake Waiau**, one of the highest permanent lakes in the world. It is a small body of water, 150 by 300 ft (45 by 90 m), and only eight feet (two and a half meters) deep. The source of this lake remains a mystery. Scientists speculate, however, that permafrost may contribute to the lake's constant water supply. Early Hawaiians believed that the lake had magical properties, and that a baby would be guaranteed long life by having its *piko* (umbilical cord) thrown into the

years ago and then worked her way down to Hawaii.

Hawaiians past and present believe that the domain of the fire goddess is in the bowels of the fiery volcanoes and, at this epoch, these are the volcanoes of the Big Island. You feel Pele's presence in the cathedral-like silence of the vast, smoldering lava fields, sense her impatience in the hissing steam vents and see her wrath in the sudden eruptions of Kilauea.

The Big Island was formed by five volcanoes, three of which have erupted in recorded

lake. The fringes of the ice-blue lake are lined with grassy banks, the perfect spot for an afternoon picnic.

Snow is common on Mauna Kea, even in summer. In the winter (December to about March) it snows heavily enough to generate a lot of activity and excitement on the ski slopes. Mauna Kea has no ski lifts, so a four-wheel-drive vehicle is necessary to get you to the snow fields or any elevation above 9,000 ft (2,799 m).

VOLCANOES NATIONAL PARK

Formed 800,000 years ago, the island of Hawaii is the youngest in the chain. Pele is said to have first touched Kauai five million

history. The oldest, **Kohala Mountain**, makes up the northern tip of the island. The highest volcano, at 13,796 ft (4,205 m) above sea level, is **Mauna Kea**. It is second in age and is capped by many cinder cones. Both Kohala and Mauna Kea are dormant. If measured from the ocean floor, the summit of Mauna Kea tops out at 33,476 ft (10,203 m), which makes it is the highest mountain in the world (Mount Everest is 29,028 ft or 8,848 m).

Hualalai, another dormant volcano, looms over the town of Kailua-Kona. It last erupted between 1800 and 1801. The lava from this eruption contained a mineral thought to have come from an extraordinary

The summit of Mauna Kea.

depth in the earth's crust and is of world-wide scientific interest.

Mauna Loa and **Kilauea** are two of the world's most active volcanoes. Mauna Loa has built up a mass of 10,000 cubic miles (41,680 cubic km), the largest volcanic accumulation on earth. At the rate that lava poured out of Mauna Loa in historic times, it would take little more than one million years to produce the entire mass of this volcano. From 1934 to 1950, Mauna Loa was more active. Since that time, Kilauea has provided most of the fireworks.

Kilauea, about 4,500 ft (1,370 m) in height, is on the southeast flank of Mauna Loa, but is a completely independent volcano. The chemical difference in their lavas and their difference in elevation are generally believed to preclude a common magma chamber at shallow depths. Magma chambers are usually found about a mile (one and a half kilometers) beneath a volcano's summit.

Some connection between the two, however, is possible. Several times in the past, the level of lava in Halemaumau Lake, in the inner crater of the Kilauea Caldera, dropped abruptly when Mauna Loa began erupting. Halemaumau Fire Pit was a molten lava lake for most of the period between 1823 and 1924.

Since January 1983, volcanic activity on the Big Island has been going on almost uninterrupted. Intermittent bursts of energy have developed into a series of violent outbursts. Pele's deadly dance holds everyone spellbound.

For the past several years, lava has poured out of Kilauea's Puuo'o vent in an orange and red river of fire, scorching the terrain and destroying all before it. In 1990, lava snaked its way towards the southern end of Chain of Craters Road, buried part of the road, then destroyed the picturesque little town of Kalapana, and houses in some subdivisions, including Kalapana Gardens, Royal Gardens, and Kalapana Shores. To date, over 160 houses have been destroyed.

Some residents reacted before the lava reached their properties, lifting entire houses onto trailers and transporting them away. But most had no choice but to watch in stoic silence, resigned to their fate, as lava crawled to the foot of houses causing the timbers to explode in sheets of flame.

Several tourist attractions were buried under the huge flows, including the famous Kaimu Black Sand Beach, which was completely covered over. The Star of the Sea Painted Church (built in 1931) was saved, though, when members of the congregation, along with area residents, mounted a campaign to save the church. It was eventually jacked up onto a trailer and transported out of Pele's path. The church can be visited at its new location, off Highway 130 at about the 20-mile marker at the bottom of the Kalapana-Pahoa Road—just a few hundred yards away from the original lava flow.

Seeing the Park
Hawaii Volcanoes National Park ((808) 967-7184 is huge. Explore it leisurely. To rush through the park would be to miss out on an experience which could be the most memorable of your Hawaiian vacation.

For a 24-hour eruption message call ((808) 967-7977.

The entrance to the park is about 28 miles (45 km) or 40 minutes away from Hilo. It's a comfortable drive on Highway 11 through a forest of tall ohia trees and giant ferns.

No matter how many times you visit the park—a box seat above one of nature's most magnificent shows — the sights remain awe inspiring. Within the 377 sq miles (610 sq km) of this majestic park exists a seemingly extraterrestrial landscape fringed by forests and extraordinary plant life.

Before exploring the park, view the film of volcanoes either at the **Kilauea Visitor Center** or at Volcano House. You can also rent a portable cassette tape which thoroughly explains points of interest along **Crater Rim Road**. You'll learn, for example, that two types of lava create the brooding landscapes found throughout the island. Pahoehoe has

banks, creates the illusion of a dead planet. It is a landscape of trees singed by the heat of a Kilauea eruption — bleak yet fascinating.

In addition to the Crater Rim drive, there are several walking trails worth taking. The most challenging is the 18-mile (29-km) hike to the summit of Mauna Loa. It can take two days to get there, but the rewards for those who make the effort are a feast of shapes and colors created by the intermingling of lava and snow, found nowhere else in the islands.

No less fascinating, and certainly much less taxing, is the **Halemaumau Trail** into the

the appearance of dark chocolate fudge that has been smoothed out and then seemingly raked over with a fork. A'a is a rough-edged lava which looks like coal slag and usually trails off into channels.

Throughout the park a startling contrast of lava and plant life can be found. Fern forests populate the slopes above the lava fields, fed by year-round rainfall. Red lehua blossoms cling to ohia trees. Here and there, within the lava itself, some plants take root.

Other phenomena in the park include the **Thurston Lava Tube**, formed when magma flowed through a crust of hardened lava; and "tree molds," created when molten lava encompassed a tree and burned it away in the process. **Devastation Trail**, with its sulfur

Kilauea Caldera (6.4 miles or 10.2 km round trip); and the 3.6-mile (5.8-km) round-trip **Mauna Iki Trail** (Footprints Trail) across the Kau Desert — so called because of the footprints embedded in lava by 80 fleeing warriors who were trapped by the 1790 eruption and died six miles (10 km) southwest of the summit. These warriors were returning to the Kau district to defend it from an attack by Kamehameha. Their death was seen as a sign that Pele favored Kamehameha, who ultimately united and ruled the islands.

Every day, hundreds of visitors make their way down **Chain of Craters Road**, a spec-

OPPOSITE: Lava eruption and fire pit of Kilauea Caldera, Mauna Kea. ABOVE: The rugged Halemaumau Trail.

tacular drive across a landscape that reveals in detail the various eruptions that have occurred in the park. There are great lookout points over old craters and from atop the mountain down to the plains and ocean far below. The road ends abruptly after a run along the coast to a point where a recent flow surged across the road on its way to the ocean.

From there it's a walk across the freshest lava on the island to a point where magma continues to tumble into the ocean creating huge clouds of yellow-white steam. The sometimes swirling, often chocolate mousse-smooth lava is liberally laced with patterns of brilliant blue and gold crystals which glint in the hot sun. In the last 12 years, the lava from Kilauea has created several acres of new land on the Big Island.

It was once possible to complete the circular route from Hilo, through Hawaii Volcanoes National Park, along Chain of Craters Road, through Kalapana and back to Hilo. The town of Kalapana no longer exists. Gone are Walter Yamaguchi's Kalapana Store — a landmark in the town for so many years — and the Harry K. Brown Park. The route to Hilo has been closed.

Where to Stay
One hotel, several excellent inns and some great bed-and-breakfast establishments are available within or in close proximity to Hawaii Volcanoes National Park.

It began as a grass hut built on the crater rim by a sugar planter in 1846. If you wanted to spend the night in this shelter, the owner charged you a dollar. Today the **Volcano House** ((808) 967-7321 FAX (808) 967-8429, P.O. Box 53, Hawaii Volcanoes National Park, HI 96718 (mid-range) occupies this site. It has played host to kings, queens and writers such as Mark Twain. This hotel has the warm atmosphere of a large inn. It's perched on the lip of Kilauea Caldera providing some of the most dramatic views of the great crater. The rooms are cozy and well appointed. The main lobby has a huge fireplace where you can kick back, read or enjoy a drink on those cold, misty evenings. The tradition here is that the fire never goes out. Volcano House also has a restaurant that is earning an excellent reputation. It recently earned the AAA Five Diamond Award.

There are some great hiking destinations near Volcano House, or you can walk across the road to browse at the Volcano Art Center, where the works of the island's finest artists are on display.

Kilauea Lodge ((808) 967-7366 FAX (808) 967-7367, P.O. Box 116, Volcano, HI 96785 (mid-range) is only a mile from the entrance to Hawaii Volcanoes National Park, making it a perfect base from which to explore the park and its surroundings. Its spacious, beautifully appointed rooms with attached baths, Hawaiian country furnishings, and native art make the lodge a slice of heaven in the midst of one of nature's most spectacular settings. Six of the rooms have fireplaces, and the main lounge is a great place to sit around a roaring fire and enjoy a predinner or after dinner drink.

The lodge's main building houses one of the island's finest restaurants (expensive), operated with obvious pride by owner-chef Albert Jeyte, who runs the lodge and restaurant with his wife Lorna. Jeyte's cooking style reflects his European training. Homemade soups, superb main courses ranging from duck to fish and venison, and wonderful desserts complemented by an excellent wine list make for a memorable meal. When you make your lodge reservations, remember to book a table at the restaurant also, for there aren't too many other fine dining establishments for miles around, and this room fills up quickly.

Forest Haven (Contact Joan Early at the Country Goose) ((808) 967-7759 TOLL-FREE (800) 238-7101 FAX (808) 985-8673 (mid-range) is a lofty three-bedroom, two-bath chalet with cathedral ceilings, tucked cozily away in the forest. A covered deck catches the first rays of the morning sun, and soaring glass windows bring the splendor of the forest into the living room. This is modern country living at its finest, with natural wood and folk art textiles from Asia and original photographic art. A wood-burning stove spreads warmth around the house on chilly winter evenings.

Nestled among huge ancient trees on the grounds of one of Volcano's oldest family residences, **Volcano Country Cottages** ((808) 967-7960 TOLL-FREE (800) 967-7960, P.O. Box 545, Volcano, HI 96785 (inexpensive to mid-range) offers comfortable, well-appointed accommodation in the Artist's House and Ohelo Berry Cottage. The gardens are lovely and if you like country living, this is the place for you. It's only a mile from here to the park, and the property is within distance of some excellent forest walks. The charming Volcano Village is on your doorstep, and you have access to stores where you can buy fresh produce and good wines. Your host is Kathleen Ing. There is a two-night minimum stay.

WESTERN HAWAII

There are two routes you can take from Hilo to get to the west coast of the island. The shorter route carries you north along the picturesque Hamakua Coast through towns with names such as Papaikou, Honomu, Laupahoehoe, Honokaa and Waimea. The other route is to proceed along the edge of Hawaii Volcanoes National Park around the southern end of the island via South Point. Follow along as we take the latter route to coffee country.

TO KONA VIA SOUTH POINT

If you exit Hawaii Volcanoes National Park and join Highway 11 going left, or west, you'll continue to drive through lava fields and scrub forest until you reach the **Punaluu Beach Park**. This is a beach composed mostly of lava rocks and black sand that is a popular spot from which to view the green sea turtles. Every year the turtles nest and lay their eggs in the sands on this beach. Beware of strong offshore currents if you swim here.

Highway 11 now enters the massive Kau district, in the shadow of Mauna Loa, stretching from the slopes of the volcano through forest and pasture to a section of coastline. The town of Waiohinu, where author Mark Twain planted a monkeypod tree in 1866, is close to South Point Road. Twain's tree was blown over in a 1957 storm, but a new tree is now sprouting from the original trunk.

The residential community of Oceanview is your landmark for the turn-off for **South Point (Ka Lae)**, the southernmost tip of the United States, where the first Polynesians are said to have landed around AD 140. It's 11 miles (18 km) of rough riding from High-

way 11 down a straight-as-an-arrow road to the ocean. On the way you'll pass a wind farm that generates electricity. Finally you'll reach the rugged cliffs and the ancient canoe mooring site carved out of the rock. The right fork in the road takes you to a favorite fishing spot where fishermen haul their catch up the cliff by rope. There's also a huge blowhole in the vicinity. The **Kalalea Heiau** is the other landmark of interest in this area.

Going east from South Point, a three-mile (five-kilometer) hike will take you to **Green Sand Beach (Papakolea)**, which gets its dis-

tinct color from a cinder cone of olivine that poured into the ocean. The large grains of this semiprecious mineral have a beautiful, glassy luster. This is one of the most exposed beaches in the world and it is pounded by heavy seas and rough surf. Use extreme caution when swimming or surfing in this area.

PUUHONUA O HONAUNAU AND KEALAKEKUA BAY

Back on Highway 11, head west and then north into South Kona. Shortly after Keokea is an area that contains three of the best known

South Point, the windswept and sea lashed southernmost point in the United States.

historical sites on the island — **Puuhonua O Honaunau** (the City of Refuge), **Kealakekua Bay** — where Captain James Cook, the British explorer and navigator, met his death, and **St. Benedict's Church**, also known as the **Painted Church**.

Exit Highway 11 to Highway 160, which begins with a swift descent to the coast and ends at **Puuhonua O Honaunau National Historic Park** ((808) 328-2326, P.O. Box 129, Honaunau, HI 96726.

When ancient Hawaiians broke one of countless *kapus*, or sacred laws, or were on the run from an enemy, the system decreed that if they could reach a designated refuge, their lives would be spared provided they also did the penance handed out by the resident kahunas (*priests*). Reaching such a sanctuary was never easy. Apart from avoiding their pursuers, the hunted had to contend with wild waters and sharks.

Puuhonua O Honaunau is one of the best examples of such a sanctuary. Built in the twelfth century, this six-acre (two-and-a-half hectare) site includes heiaus, petroglyphs, thatched huts and giant wooden idols—startling, frightening symbols of an ancient and sometimes violent culture. The Hale O Keawe Heiau here has particular historical significance. The original heiau is believed to have been built around 1650 and housed the bones of at least 23 chiefs of Kamehameha's family. These remains are believed to provide the spiritual power that gave sanctity to the City of Refuge. Puuhonua O Honaunau is open from 7:30 AM to 5:30 PM. Admission is $1 for adults; free for children under age 17. Seniors in a car enable all passengers to get in free.

If you proceed along Puuhonua Road heading north, you'll come to **Kealakekua Bay**. It was here that explorer Captain Cook, the first European to land on the islands, dropped anchor. The Hawaiians heralded Cook as a reincarnation of the shark god Lono and greeted him with much respect. But an altercation on the beach led to Cook's untimely death at the hands of the Hawaiians. Across the bay, a white marker indicates the site where Cook was slain.

Kealakekua Bay is one of the island's best SCUBA diving and snorkeling sites. Tour operators offer a morning of snorkeling and lunch in this bay, or night diving.

If you double back around Puuhonua Road, you'll come across the **Painted Church** which Father John Berchmans Velghe decorated with biblical stories for the benefit of illiterate parishioners. Puuhonua Road links up again with Highway 160 near this point, which will bring you back to Highway 11.

COFFEE COUNTRY

Travelers have enjoyed the pleasures of the Kona Coast for the past half century. The resorts which began to develop in the wake of the Mauna Kea Resort earned Kona this notoriety. But internationally, this stretch of coastline played second fiddle to Waikiki Beach—that is, until the world became aware of a humble coffee bean.

Wherever gourmet coffee drinkers gather, Kona coffee is saluted for its sweetness and intense aroma. It is an arabica variety that rivals similar gourmet arabica coffees such as Jamaican Blue Mountain. It is grown and marketed in controlled quantities and is so prized that an international scandal developed in 1997 when distributors were caught packaging and marketing inferior coffee with the Kona brand name on it.

Kamehameha the Great's Spanish interpreter, Don Francisco de Paula y Marin, is credited with having brought a coffee tree into Honolulu in 1813. But it was Samuel Ruggles, a missionary, who in 1828 first took cuttings from trees planted on Oahu and planted them in Kona's rich, volcanic soil.

The Kona coffee industry has had its ups and downs in the last century and a half. But it has survived thanks the endurance of native Hawaiians and Asian laborers — Chinese, Japanese and Filipinos — who first came to work the sugar cane fields of the Big Island and then stayed to become coffee farmers.

Coffee generally blooms from March to May, when the trees are covered with the white blossoms that coffee farmers call "Kona Snow." These blossoms turn to green beans, and ultimately a dark cherry red when they are harvested from September to January.

LEFT: Giant wooden idols stand watch at Puuhonua O Honaunau, the City of Refuge. OVERLEAF: Vestiges of the ancient Kamakahonu Heiau, at Kailua-Kona, tower over a modern hotel.

Today coffee farms, large and small, exist on a 15-mile stretch of hill country above the coast, starting from the town of Honaunau all the way to Kailua-Kona. If you love coffee you'll need little encouragement to explore this part of the island; but even if you aren't an aficionado, you will enjoy a driving tour of this coffee belt.

A tremendous variety of coffee exists in this small belt because each farm has its own way of turning out its coffee. Stop and taste the coffee and find which bean you like best. Coffee tastes run from hearty, robust flavors

to the sweet. Remember, some of the finest coffee comes in the plainest packages. Hard-to-find private estate labels are available at several tour stops. You'll find these coffees on sale at places such as the Bad Ass Coffee Company and Kona Jack's Last Stop Coffee Shop, as well as farms big and small. Here's a buying tip: all Kona coffees are graded by the Hawaii Department of Agriculture. Kona Extra Fancy, for example, passes the most stringent tests, followed by Kona Fancy, Kona Nº 1, Kona Prime, Kona Nº 1 Peaberry and Kona Peaberry Prime.

An historic walking tour of the **Uchida Coffee Farm** will show you how a coffee farm operates. Built in 1925 by Japanese immigrants, Uchida is listed on the National Reg-

ister for Historic Places. The tour puts the accent on the unique coffee farm lifestyle of that period as visitors are shown the farm house, Japanese bath house, coffee processing mill and drying platforms. The tour costs $15 per person.

One of the fascinating little towns in the heart of coffee country is **Holualoa**, which sits above Kona along Highway 180. This former plantation town has changed dramatically since the prime years when sugar was king in this part of the country. The houses along Holualoa's main street are weather-beaten shacks with corrugated tin roofs. There's a seedy seen-better-days charm to the village, and it's in a wonderful location high on the hills overlooking the resort town of Kailua-Kona, with great views of the ocean and the lava fields of the Kona-Kohala Coast. The climate at these higher elevations make life in Holualoa very agreeable, and for these reasons the town has attracted a colony of artists. Holualoa has several galleries selling some of Hawaii's best woodwork and pottery. One of the older stores on the street is Kimura Lauhala Store, specializing in arts and crafts made from coconut fronds and the hala tree. In the heyday of sugar, this was the town's general store.

In comparison to the town, the **Holualoa Inn** ((808) 324-1121 FAX (808) 322-2472 (mid-range) is a polished establishment set amidst a 40-acre (16-hectare) coffee estate. The inn has six elegant rooms with Polynesian and Asian themes. The building is framed and finished entirely in cedar, with vaulted ceilings and 900 sq ft (84 sq m) of lanais. Floors are of eucalyptus wood milled on Maui. The main living room has a fireplace. For an alternative to the beach, there's a large swimming pool and deck where the view is as stunning as it is from the inn's rooftop gazebo. Holualoa Inn also has a lovely quiet garden.

KAILUA-KONA

The resort town of Kailua-Kona is something of a contradiction. It is quaint and picturesque, yet it radiates a garish energy; it also offers the budget-conscious traveler alternatives to the expensive resorts along the Kona Coast.

In the days of the ancient Hawaiians, Kailua was more than a leading fishing village; it was the seat of the government of Kamehameha the Great. Evidence of the royal past can be found at the **Hotel King Kamehameha**, at the beginning of Alii Drive. On the grounds of the hotel is **Kamakahonu**, a compound of thatched-roof huts and fish ponds which has been declared a National Historical Monument. It was here that Kamehameha united the islands, and it was here that he died in 1891. Also in the compound is the **Ahuena Heiau** from where Kamehameha ruled during the last seven years of his kingdom. The hotel offers guests and visitors free tours of this complex as well as access to the little museum in its mall, which has an excellent collection of artifacts.

Kailua's main street, Alii Drive, runs parallel to Kailua Bay. It is lined with restaurants, hotels, motels and shops selling everything from high-quality art and jewelry to inexpensive clothing and vacation souvenirs.

Not far down Alii Drive is **Mokuaikaua Church**, the first Christian church in the islands, built in 1836. Its lava rock and coral structure have weathered the years well.

Across the street is the **Hulihee Palace** ((808) 329-1877, 75-5718 Alii Drive. Built in 1838 by the island's governor, John Adams Kuakini, the palace served as King David Kalakaua's summer residence through the 1880s. There are daily tours through this two-story building. Admission is $4 for adults, $1 for children aged 13 to 18, and $.50 for children under age 13. It is open daily 9 AM to 4 PM.

The drive to the district of Keauhou takes you past more hotels and beach resorts. Along the way you pass "the little blue church." **St. Peter's Catholic Church** at Kahaluu was built in 1889 on the site of a heiau. Blue is the dominant color both inside and outside this church. It has seating for a congregation of 26.

The waters off the Kona Coast are the favorite hunting grounds of the world's big game fishermen. Every year around early August, fishing teams from around the world assemble in Kona for the **Pro Am Billfish Tournament** (see FESTIVE FLINGS, page 70). So rich in fish are these waters that big ones can often be caught just minutes after your boat leaves the shore.

Where to Stay

Most of the Big Island's hotel and condominium rooms are located in a five-mile oceanfront stretch along Alii Drive. There's accommodation here to suit a wide range of budgets.

On a massive lava field at the mouth of Keauhou Bay is the **Kona Surf Resort and Country Club** ((808) 322-3411 TOLL-FREE (800) 367-8011 FAX (808) 322-3245, 78-128 Ehukai Street (mid-range), probably the best hotel on the Kailua-Keauhou Coast. Its lack of a beach is compensated for by two swimming pools, sweeping lawns and gardens where wild surf constantly pounds the lava rocks of the property. The terraced design and open-air lobby make the Kona Surf one of the most visually exciting hotels in the islands. Keauhou Bay has plenty of aquatic activities, and golf buffs can enjoy the Keauhou-Kona golf course (see GOLF: THE ULTIMATE DESTINATION, PAGE 289).

One of the town's upmarket hotels, **King Kamehameha's Kona Beach Hotel** ((808) 329-2911 FAX (808) 329-4602, 75-5660 Palani Road (mid-range), is located on Kamakahonu Beach. The hotel also has a fine pool. Hawaiian music performances and craft shows, as well luaus, are held in the hotel's beautiful gardens.

The **Royal Kona Resort** ((808) 329-3111 TOLL-FREE (800) 774-5662 FAX (808) 329-9532, 75-5852 Alii Drive (mid-range) was formerly the Kona Hilton. The name has changed, but not much else has; the handsome white edifice remains a landmark in the area. Each room has a private balcony, most with ocean views. Its **Tropics Café** (moderate) has a reputation for excellent Pacific Rim food, and its Drums of Polynesia luau continues to attract travelers.

Kona Bay Hotel ((808) 329-6488 FAX (808) 935-7903, 75-5739 Alii Drive (inexpensive) is noted for its friendly service. It is located in the heart of town, and the rooms are simple, comfortable, air conditioned, and have attached bathes. A small pool graces the center of the complex. The **Banana Bay Buffet Restaurant** (inexpensive) near the pool is famous for its all-you-can-eat buffets ($4.95 for breakfast; $8.95 for dinner).

OPPOSITE: St. Benedict's Painted Church, Kailua-Kona.

If you're looking for luxurious accommo-dation with the coziness of a bed and break-fast, you might want to try **Kailua Planta-tion House** ((808) 329-3727 WEBSITE http://www.Ernstallen.com/tr/hi/Kailua PlantationHouse, 75-5948 Alii Drive (mid-range to expensive). The house stands on a promontory with unobstructed views of the ocean. The individually decorated suites have a private lanai, bath, color television, telephone, refrigerator and maid service. There's elegance and privacy at Kailua Plan-tation House—yet you're only minutes away

Hale Maluhia also has a Japanese stone and tile spa and a Zen garden with a stream. The proprietors are as knowledgeable about the island as anyone in the business. This inn also serves one of the best breakfasts on the Kona Coast: fresh baked breads, muffins, rolls, fresh local fruits, juices, smoked ham, eggs, strawberry crêpe suzette or pancakes with whipped cream and fresh biscuits, tea and, of course, Kona coffee. Your hosts are Ken and Ann Smith.

Sleepy Hollow ((808) 325-5043 FAX (808) 325-0653, 73-1530 Apela Place, Kailua-Kona,

from all the action in Kailua-Kona. Your host is Danielle Berger.

There are several very good bed-and-breakfast places on this side of the island. **Hale Maluhia Country Inn** TOLL-FREE (800) 559-6627 FAX (808) 326-5487 WEBSITE http://www.hawaii-bnb.com/halemal.html E-MAIL hawaiian@interpac.net, 76-770 Hualalai Road, Kailua-Kona, HI 96740 (inexpensive to mid-range) is a lush, tree-shaded estate 900 ft (270 m) up in Holualoa coffee coun-try. Set amidst tall trees, koi fish ponds and waterfalls, the property has four spacious bedrooms, a cottage and a house that's just right for families. Exposed-beam ceilings de-signed with local woods, family antiques and original oil paintings make the place homey.

HI 96740 (mid-range) is a romantic hideaway with breathtaking ocean and forest views. The three bedrooms have a variety of pleas-ant features that include picture windows, large patios and Hawaiiana from the own-ers' collection. Pele's Studio is a charming little apartment with a private entrance and a fully furnished kitchenette. Your hosts are Mike and Cindy Vidal.

Merryman's Bed-and-Breakfast ((808) 323-2276 TOLL-FREE (800) 545-4390 FAX (808) 323-3749 WEBSITE http://www.ilhawaii.net/merrymans E-MAIL merryman@ilhawaii.net, P.O. Box 474 Kealakekua, HI 96750 is a dream house on a breezy hillside in the Kealakekua–Captain Cook area. With large rooms in a country atmosphere, set amidst flowering gardens and sweeping lawns, the Merrymans has a large deck which overlooks the gardens and great views of the ocean. The property has four rooms, each tastefully decorated with beautiful linens and fresh flowers. It's within easy access of diving sites and other Kona Coast activities. Or you can stay close to home and unwind in a Jacuzzi. Your hosts are Don and Penny Merryman. Call for current rates.

Reggie's Tropical Hideaway ((808) 322-8888 TOLL-FREE (800) 988-2246 FAX (808) 323-2348, P.O. Box 1107 Kealakekua, HI 96750 (inexpensive to mid-range) is an unusual bed-and-breakfast lodging right in the midst of an authentic tropical fruit farm and coffee plantation. Relax in a hot tub in your private sunbathing garden surrounded by banana, papaya and mango trees. This is the place to get away from it all.

Where to Eat

Sam Choy of **Sam Choy's Restaurant** ((808) 325-7641 (expensive), 73-4328 Malu Place, Kailua-Kona is a local whose distinctive style combines the subtleties of Italian cooking with the ingredients of Hawaii and the flair of Asian cuisine. Try, for example, Papa's Island pig's feet soup with wild mountain mushrooms, mustard cabbage, peanuts and ginger. Or if you're not so adventurous, try the South Pacific seafood stew with Tahitian spinach-dill cream. This is delicious food (see GALLOPING GOURMET, page 86).

La Bourgone ((808) 329-6711, Kuakini Plaza South, 77-6400 Nalani Street N°101, (expensive), three miles (five kilometers) south of Kailua on Highway 11, is an intimate and authentic French restaurant. Its excellent appetizers include escargot and baked brie. On its soup menu are the traditional French onion and lobster soups. Entrées — which range in price from $20 to $30 — include the customary fish dishes, as well as saddle of lamb with garlic and rosemary.

Huggo's ((808) 329-1493, 75-5828 Kahakai Street (moderate), is a pleasant restaurant with good atmosphere and a large lanai on the water's edge. The Pacific Rim cuisine includes island-bred Maine lobster, fish stuffed with prawns, and grilled lamb chops. Prices range from $20 to $30 for a main course. There's live entertainment most evenings.

Palm Café ((808) 329-7765, Coconut Grove Marketplace, 75-5819 Alii Drive (moderate), is a comfortable restaurant with sweeping views of the bay and a sophisticated Pacific Rim menu. The chef here favors Thai spices and other Asian ingredients; the fish dishes are especially inventive.

There are some surprisingly good Thai restaurants in Kona, and **Bangkok Houses** ((808) 329-7764, King Kamehameha Mall, 75-5626 Kuakini Highway (inexpensive), is one of them. Dinners include a variety of fine curries made with or without coconut milk. At lunch time, the restaurant offers several $5 specials.

Tucked away in an industrial area, **Su's Thai Kitchen** ((808) 326-7808, 74-5588A Pawai Place (inexpensive), may be the best Thai restaurant in this town. It isn't elegant and there's no view, but it more than compensates for the lack of atmosphere with the quality of its food. Dinner includes a variety of Thai soups, excellent vegetarian dishes and tasty pad Thai noodles.

Facing the pier and with superb views of the bay, the old-style Hawaiian **Ocean View Inn** ((808) 329-9988, 75-5683 Alii Drive (inexpensive), offers dinner plates, lunches and good breakfasts. The food is unpretentious and tasty.

Ricos ((808) 885-0654, Alii Sunset Plaza, 75-5799 Alii Drive (inexpensive), is an intimate Mexican restaurant with no views, but with a pleasing decor and good food. Tamales, tacos and chimichangas cost between $6 and $8.

NORTHWEST HAWAII

Legend says the trinity of powerful Hawaiian gods — Kane, Lono and Ku — created Kohala, the northwest coast of the island. *Ho'okamaha'o* — something wondrous that takes on a new and more splendid form — is the word used to describe the northwest's **Kohala Coast**. Kohala is all that, and more. Once the playground of Hawaiian royalty, their legacy remains; you see it in the trails they carved, the fish ponds they created for their pleasure, and the heiaus they built for worship and sacrifice.

ABOVE: Colorful Alii Drive in downtown Kailua-Kona. OVERLEAF: Rainbow Falls, near Hilo.

KOHALA COAST RESORTS

If you land at Keahole-Kona International Airport in Kona and turn left going north up the coast, your route along Queen Kaahumanu Highway (Highway 19) will take you past seven exceptional resort hotels on a stretch of coastline from eight miles (13 km) north of the airport to Kawaihae, 28 miles (45 km) further up the coast.

The remarkable thing about these resorts is that unless you saw a sign, you would never know that they exist. Viewed from the highway, they blend discreetly with the landscape. Very little interrupts the magnificent expanses of lava fields and the variegated blue of the ocean.

The first in this strand of luxurious lodging is the **Four Seasons Resort Hualalai** ((808) 325-8000 TOLL-FREE (888) 340-5662 FAX (808) 325-8053 WEBSITE http://www.pierre hotel.com/locations/Hualalai/index.html, 100 Kaupulehu Drive, Kaupulehu-Kona, HI 96740 (expensive to luxury). The resort gets its name from the ancient volcano that looms over it, the same volcano that created the land on which the resort is situated.

The 243-room Four Seasons sprawls over 625 acres of lava fields, with the white-capped ocean in front and a new Jack Nicklaus golf course in back. Architect Riecke Sunnland Kono has created a place with the spirit and feel of old Hawaii, yet she hasn't compromised on luxury. Her design is based on a typical Hawaiian coastal village, or *kauhale*. The two-story, 600-sq-ft (56-sq-m) units are arranged in horseshoe configurations around four distinctive features of the hotel — the palm grove, the pool, the children's pool and the King's pond. The units each have earthtone stucco walls, Hawaiian-style roofs and floor plans that bring the outdoors inside. In addition to the units, there are 20 luxurious golf villas on the 18th fairway with unrestricted ocean views.

A special feature of the resort is its art collection, which spans from 1775 to the present and is almost entirely Hawaiian. The collection includes feather helmets and gourds, textiles and 100-year-old wooden paddles. Guests who want to know more about the culture should visit the Hawaiian

Interpretive Center which is staffed by a cultural historian.

Four Seasons has a marvelous approach to health and fitness. Its sports club and spa facilities, for instance, include 17 indoor and outdoor body treatment rooms, outdoor saunas and steam rooms, a sports gym and suspended-wood-floor aerobics gym. They also have a courtyard for yoga and meditation.

Three exceptional restaurants cater to the Four Seasons' patrons. The **Pahuia** (expensive) — it means aquarium— is an elegant oceanfront restaurant. The food served here is that magical blend of East and West, and features an extensive range of fish dishes. The Asian dishes are particularly good. The **Beach Tree Bar and Grill** (inexpensive) is a casual dining option adjacent to the pool and right on the beach. Again, there's an interesting blend of cuisines ranging from crispy chicken spring rolls with Vietnamese dipping sauce to California chopped salad sandwich. A bar on the beach serves exotic drinks, and it's a wonderful place to have an apéritif and watch the sun go down. The Hualalai's third restaurant is the **Hualalai Club Grille** (moderate) which is located above the golf clubhouse overlooking the 18th green. It specializes in brick-oven pizza and pastas.

The Four Season's new golf course is certain to gain in fame. It is the first in Hawaii to be designated a PGA Tour facility and will be the site of the Senior PGA MasterCard Championship for the next 10 years.

Adjacent to the Four Seasons Hualalai is the **Kona Village Resort** ((808) 325-5555 E-MAIL krv@ilhawaii.net, P.O. Box 1299, Queen Kaahumanu Highway, Kailua-Kona, HI 96745 (expensive). The two are as different in concept and mood as day is to night. Patrons of the Kona Village are sometimes reluctant to talk about it. It's the kind of place one wants to keep to oneself. This place could be the last genuine Polynesian retreat in the islands, one that has introduced with understated elegance all the luxuries modern civilization has to offer. The blend is so subtle that one is left wondering where ancient culture ends and the today's world begins.

Kona Village begins where the lava flows from the volcano Hualalai ended—at the edge of Kaupulehu Bay. One hundred Polynesian

274   *Hawaii: The Big Island*

hales (houses) representing the building styles of Tahiti, Tonga, Fiji, the New Hebrides, the Marquesas, New Caledonia, New Zealand and Hawaii dot the lava fields, the edges of ancient fish ponds, or are hidden in secluded groves or coves on black- or white-sand beaches.

In an atmosphere as close to the traditional Polynesian style as you are likely to find anywhere on the islands, each hale is spacious and exquisitely furnished. All have lanais or verandahs, some facing private beaches, all with views. There are no telephones or televisions at the Kona Village. In fact, this hotel does not even have room keys.

It all started when Californian contractor Johnno Jackson sailed his schooner *New Moon* into the shimmering waters of Kaupulehu Bay in 1959 and realized he had found his corner of paradise. By 1966 he had completed 46 hales after shipping all his building materials in by barge. When it first opened, guests flew in to land at the resort's own airstrip and taxied up to the reception hale. Today, a road leads off Queen Kaahumanu Highway, past a guard hut, and through the lava fields. Nothing much else has changed other than the ever-improving quality of comfort and the excellent food. Guests are on the American Plan, which means the price of a room includes food and the hire of all recreational equipment, including boat trips. Guests can snorkel just off the white sand beach or near the reef, visit the resort's petroglyphs, have a drink at the **Shipwreck Bar**, or enjoy one of the best hotel luaus in the islands. On a moonlit night, after dining by the soft glow of the lamps in the **Hale Ho'okipa Restaurant** (moderate), it may be possible to stroll across the path to the beach to watch a school of manta rays at play. Such moments of primitive beauty may stay with you for a lifetime.

The **Royal Waikoloan** TOLL-FREE (800) 688-7444 FAX (303) 369-9403 WEBSITE http://www.outrigger.com E-MAIL reservations@ outrigger.com, 69-275 Waikoloa Beach Drive, Kamuela, HI 96743 (mid-range to luxury) and the **Hilton Waikoloa Resort (** (808) 885-1234 TOLL-FREE (800) HILTONS FAX (808) 885-2902 WEBSITE http://www. hilton.com/hotels/ koahwhh, 425 Waikoloa Beach Drive,

Kamuela, HI 96743 (expensive) are located on Anaehoomalu Bay.

The Royal Waikoloan's name is derived from its proximity to the King's Trail, used by Hawaiians for centuries, and the royal fish ponds found on the property. In keeping with the style and standards of resorts on this coast, it is lovely. Its petroglyph fields are well preserved, and its golf course, designed by Robert Trent Jones Jr., is another masterpiece of lava field architecture.

The **Hilton**, by contrast, is an odd mix of Disneyland and old Asia. The theme park atmosphere is reflected in the modes of transport: a monorail and a boat depart from the lobby, which serves as both station and wharf. These two modes of transport carry passengers to the residential towers, which are some distance away from the main restaurants and shops that make up the complex. The resort occupies 62 acres (25 hectares) of prime land on the edge of the ocean. In this lush setting is a hotel complex whose sheer grandeur boggles the mind. Colonnades, palm trees, aqueducts, and four interlocking swimming pools are the exterior trappings of luxury. A key attraction at this hotel is the dolphin pool where several trained dolphins interact with fascinated visitors. There are two shows daily. You can even get into the water with these highly intelligent creatures (for a fee). Art from Asia and the Pacific is scattered about the beautifully landscaped property.

The Hilton's two main restaurants are the **Kamuela Provision Co.** (moderate), which specializes in fish dishes such as charred ahi, and the Japanese **Imari** restaurant (expensive), which offers everything from a sushi bar to a teahouse.

The **Mauna Lani Bay Hotel and Bungalows (** (808) 885-6622 TOLL-FREE (800) 367-2323 FAX (808) 885-1484 WEBSITE http://www. maunalani.com/home.html, 68-1400 Mauna Lani Drive, Kohala Coast, HI 96743 (expensive) is a truly superior hotel.

The Mauna Lani Bay incorporates 27 acres (11 hectares) of historic park and 15 acres (six hectares) of fish ponds which have been set aside as archaeological preserves. The land area of the complex is extensive, covering around 3,300 acres (1,226 hectares) on the edge of a beach lined with coconut palms and milo trees, and a series of small lagoons.

Undulating black lava fields provide a startling contrast to the greens and fairways of the **Francis I'i Brown Golf Course** (see GOLF: THE ULTIMATE DESTINATION, page 289), which many rank as the finest on the Big Island, not merely for the challenge it affords, but also for the unending series of ocean and mountain vistas that it offers. These amenities and a $7 million racquet club place the hotel in league with the world's most distinguished hotels. The Mauna Lani's living quarters comprise 80 luxury units surrounding the Terrace Lagoon and Mauna Lani

Point; and 116 luxury residences along the fairways and the ocean.

One of the better dining experiences on the Kohala Coast is a meal at the **Canoe House** ((808) 885-6622, extension 7986 (expensive), one of the Mauna Lani's fine restaurants located on a beautiful site just steps from the sea. At night, the soft lights from the restaurant cast a dramatic glow on the waters. You can dine by candlelight or the light of the moon, and savor great food.

The **Orchid at Mauna Lani** TOLL-FREE (800) 845-9905 FAX (808) 885-1064 WEBSITE http://www.sheraton-hawaii.com/

Petroglyph field ABOVE on the edge of the Sheraton Waikoloa Golf Course. OPPOSITE: A page-turner at the Mauna Lani Hotel Beach.

hawaii/orchid.html, One North Kaniku Drive, Kohala Coast, HI 96743 (expensive) has a rare intimacy. The lobby, with its colorful floral arrangements, sets the hotel's tone for style and elegance. Part of its charm are the many places you can find within the main section of the hotel to kick back, read a book, meditate or indulge in quiet conversation. There are carp pools, rushing waterfalls, and neatly arranged, cozy corners that encourage romance. Modern and beautifully designed, it has nevertheless managed to keep its finger on the pulse of Hawaiian history. They are subtle effects, but all around the resort's 32 acres (13 hectares) one perceives a sense of history and the mythical past of Hawaii. Learn about Hawaii's history through the Orchid Beach Boys, a group of fellows well versed in the ancient ways of their ancestors. These storytellers are part of a Hawaii beach tradition of a bygone era, when ocean-wise local men gathered on the beach to weave stories. The Orchid Beach Boys share their knowledge of the ocean and Hawaiian culture with visitors from all over the world. You can learn how to make fishhooks from bone, drums from coconut trees or accessories from palm frond. Or you can take a lesson in Hawaiian canoe paddling or just listen to the Beach Boys fill the air with the sound of the ukulele and song.

Within the Puako Petroglyph Preserve on the Orchid at Mauna Lani are 3,000 rock carvings, one of the earliest forms of communication and one in which the Hawaiians specialized. In a region so rich with history and culture, the hotel's owners made a conscious decision to preserve historic and natural sites with "enlightened stewardship." For this the guests, who come to this hotel to stay in its 485 rooms and 54 suites, are grateful.

For your dining delight, the Orchid offers a variety of choices. David Reardon is director of culinary services overseeing three excellent restaurants and six lounges. The **Grill** (expensive), the hotel's elegant top-of-the-line restaurant, has a distinct Hawaiian flair. The warm koa wood interiors make this an elegant place for a candlelight dinner.

The **Mauna Kea Beach Resort** ((808) 882-7222 TOLL-FREE (800) 882-6060 FAX (808) 880-3112 WEBSITE http://www.westin.com/listings/index.html, 62-100 Mauna Kea Beach

Drive, Kohala, HI 96743 (expensive to luxury) is the legacy of one man's extraordinary vision. Recognizing the need to encourage tourism in the islands beyond Waikiki, Hawaii's authorities in 1960 invited millionaire hotelier Laurence Rockefeller to tour the islands in the hope that he would choose a site for a hotel to add to his chain. Rockefeller selected a remote lava field with two lovely beaches. He spared no expense in creating the Mauna Kea. The house that Laurence Rockefeller built stands today as a testament to his energy and good taste.

Opened in 1965, the Mauna Kea has since set the standard for other resorts. It remains a work of art among resort hotels, enhanced by the 1,000 or more works of art from Asia and the Pacific which decorate almost every corner of the 310-room complex. But buildings age, so a facelift was carried out, not to remodel but to restore the hotel to its original glory. The changes were subtle. The terraced wings, the open-air lobby — trademarks of this hotel — remain, providing guests uninterrupted views of the ocean and sunsets. The landscaped gardens blend with the architecture to create the sense of outdoor living. One major change has been the addition of a second golf course to go with the superb course designed by Robert Trent Jones Sr., in the midst of lava fields (see GOLF: THE ULTIMATE DESTINATION, page 289.)

As befits a hotel of this eminence, the dining facilities are excellent. Its premiere restaurant is the **Batik** (expensive), where the style of cuisine is influenced by Provence. Many of the meals here are cooked at your table. The **Pavilion** (inexpensive) is a casual

open-air restaurant that specializes in Mediterranean and Pacific Rim fare. The **Terrace–Copper Bar** (moderate) serves the luncheon buffet for which the Mauna Kea has become internationally famous.

The second beach on the Mauna Kea property is the best on the Big Island. Early Hawaiians called this stretch of Kohala coastline Hapuna (Springs of Life) in reference to the spring flowing into the ocean in this area.

On the bluffs above spectacular Hapuna Beach has risen the **Hapuna Beach Prince Hotel (** (808) 880-1111 TOLL-FREE (800) 882-6060 FAX (808) 880-3112 WEBSITE http://www .westin.com/listings/index.html, 62-100 Kaunaoa Drive, Kohala Coast, HI 96743 (expensive), which completes Rockefeller's vision.

The Hapuna Beach Prince Hotel has a contemporary feel, unlike the Mauna Kea. Low-rise structures blend with the natural surroundings, trapping tradewinds and providing unimpeded ocean views from each of the 350 rooms and suites. The 1,200-sq-ft (111-sq-m) luxury suites — there are 36 of them — are superbly appointed. The Hapuna Suite, an 8,000-sq ft (743-sq m) house tucked away on the side of the hotel, has three master bedrooms with private baths and lanais, a massive living room, a dining room, pool, and butler service.

The Hapuna Beach Prince Hotel has four restaurants, and a beach bar and a coffee bar. The **Coast Grille** (expensive) is the hotel's top restaurant. It's a sophisticated place to dine, with a view from every table and Mediterranean specialties prepared at your table.

NORTH KOHALA

Leaving luxury behind, you rejoin the workaday world on Queen Kaahumanu Highway. Near the Kawaihae crossroads going north is the enormous **Puukohola Heiau** built in the 1550s and rebuilt by King Kamehameha in 1791 as a tribute to the god Ku. This god, Hawaiians believed, filled the ponds with fish to sustain the coming of man. Puukohola was a place of human sacrifice.

At the Kawaihae junction, you have the choice of bearing right and going cross country to Waimea, or continuing on Highway 270, which loops back to Waimea through North

Kohala via the Kohala Mountain Road. If you are not in a hurry, we recommend the North Kohala drive.

North Kohala is the birthplace of the warrior king Kamehameha, and the original statue of the Great One is in the town of Kapaau. (It is the replica of this statue opposite Iolani Palace in Honolulu that most visitors see and photograph.)

Kawaihae, once an important harbor for Big Island cattle and later for the sugar industry, lapsed into neglect when the sugar industry declined. But now as tourist traffic

well-forested bluffs, and the entire area of North Kohala is punctuated by forests, waterfalls, and pretty streams. Tiny wooden churches and small communities dot the area.

Highway 270 ends at the 28-mile marker in **Pololu Valley**, about 54 miles (87 km) from Kailua. From the lookout, a steep trail leads into a heavily forested valley hemmed in by a high-walled canyon. A stream runs through grassy banks into the ocean, past a beautiful black sand beach lined with eucalyptus and ironwood trees. Be cautious, however, about hiking into the valley if it has been raining.

through the town grows, drawn by the beauty of the North Kohala district, interesting shops and restaurants are sprouting up.

Enjoy the panoramas of rolling pastures and ocean as you climb the rise past Kawaihae, and keep a lookout for **Lapakahi State Historic Park**, a fishing village preserved as it was 600 years ago. Park your car at the top of the village, pick up a brochure at the gate, and walk its trails, reflecting on the lives of the people who lived here.

Picnic and camping grounds abound in this area. One of the best is at **Keokea Beach Park**, which will evoke memories of the Monterey Bay Peninsula for those who know that corner of California. Ocean breakers thunder into caves carved in the cliffs below

Backtracking west on Highway 270, at the town of **Hawi**, proceed along Highway 250 towards Waimea. The road begins to wind and climb past picturesque cottages bright with flower gardens. Soon you are deep in ranch country. At an elevation of approximately 3,000 ft (about 900 m), you pass **Kahua Ranch**. Stately ironwood trees shade the road, and the panorama of mountain pastures on one side and the deep blue of the ocean on the other is magnificent to behold. At an elevation of 3,567 ft (1,087 m) the road begins to descend into the town of Waimea.

OPPOSITE: The Orchid at Mauna Lani's pool and beyond it, the beach. ABOVE: Old West-style stores line the streets of Hawi, North Kohala.

WAIMEA

Waimea is no ordinary mountain town. At first it prospered because of the Parker Ranch, developed by John Palmer Parker, a ship's clerk from Massachusetts who jumped ship in 1809 in the harbor at Kawaihae. Parker came to the attention of King Kamehameha who hired the clerk to maintain his fish ponds. But Parker was restless: he joined a merchant ship and sailed away for several years. When Parker returned in 1814, the king

had another job for him. A gift to the king from Captain George Vancouver of six cows and a bull had multiplied into a herd of wild cattle that was now running rampant and destroying crops and terrorizing villagers. Parker was given permission to shoot the cattle, and this translated into a nice little business of supplying fresh beef and hides to the visiting whaling ships. Parker managed this business for the king, taking his reward in live cattle and quickly building a herd of his own. Parker later married the king's granddaughter, Kipikane, and moved to the village of Waimea in 1835.

As his herds of cattle and horses grew, Parker brought in Native American, Mexican and Spanish cowboys to work the ranch. The Hawaiians who were also recruited quickly adopted the trappings of the cowboys — the bandannas, ponchos and lassos — and called themselves *paniolos*, after *españoles*, Spaniards. By 1846, it was estimated that 10,000 domesticated cattle and 25,000 wild cattle roamed the hills. When the opportunity presented itself, Parker also began

to buy land. What he didn't buy he leased. Today, Parker Ranch sprawls over 227,000 acres, the largest privately owned ranch in the United States. The ranch occupies much of North Kohala, the Hamakua side of Mauna Kea and another 40 miles (64 km) up the western slopes of the mountain. Some 50,000 head of cattle now graze these ranges.

The name Parker is therefore much in evidence in the town of Waimea (sometimes referred to as Kamuela). There's the Parker Ranch Shopping Center, Lodge, Broiler and School. And then there's the Kahilu Theater, built by Parker Ranch owner Richard Smart, for $2.5 million, that stages performances by talented actors and musicians.

Half a mile (just under a kilometer) out of Waimea on Highway 190 going towards Kailua are the old Parker houses, Puupelu and the Mana House. About 500 yards (455 m) from these historic houses is **Paniolo Park** ((808) 885-7655, where every July 4 the Parker Ranch Rodeo takes place (see FESTIVE FLINGS, page 62).

Today, the mist-draped town of Waimea has an air of affluence, much of it brought about by a group of mainland artists who discovered it and came to stay. They brought with them their skills and sophistication, and they transformed this farming town into a charming enclave where antique shops, art galleries and excellent restaurants rub shoulders with feed and grain stores and shops selling fresh farming produce.

On good days, Waimea residents and visitors have the best of all worlds. Imagine being able look out of your window and see, on one side, the snow-capped top of Mauna Kea, and on the other, the cobalt blue of the Pacific Ocean.

Where to Stay

There are some lovely bed-and-breakfast establishments in Waimea and a splendid, comfortable inn.

Kamuela Inn ((808) 885-4100 FAX (808) 885-8857, P.O. Box 1994, Kamuela HI 96743 (inexpensive to mid-range), a former motel, has been renovated, its original rooms modernized, and a new wing added. Rooms are comfortable and clean. The inn is in walking distance of two of the best restaurants on the island.

Waimea Gardens Cottage ((808) 262-9912
FAX (808) 885-0559 WEBSITE http://www.
planet-hawaii.com/hea/bestbnb E-MAIL
bestbnb@interpac.com, P.O. Box 563,
Kamuela, HI 96743 (inexpensive to mid-
range) is about two miles (about three kilometers) west of the center of Waimea town.
On the property are two large and comfortable guest cottages beautifully furnished and
decorated with fine antiques. One of the cottages has a kitchen. The cottages have splendid views of the Kohala Hills. Your host is
Barbara Campbell. There is a three-night
minimum stay.

The **Hawaii Country Cottage (** (808) 885-
7441 TOLL-FREE (800) 262-9912 FAX (808) 885-
0559, P.O. Box 1717, Kamuela HI 96743
(inexpensive) is about two miles (about three
kilometers) west of Waimea. It is a well-fur-
nished, modern and comfortable apartment
that is attached to a private house. There is a
three-night minimum stay.

With wonderful views of the meadows of
Mauna Kea, **Puu Manu Cottage (** (808) 262-
9912 FAX (808) 885-0559, P.O. Box 563, Kamuela
HI 96743 (inexpensive to mid-range) is a
former horse barn that has been converted
into a delightful cottage. It's about three miles
(just under four kilometers) east of the town.
There is a three-night minimum stay.

Where to Eat

The quality of the restaurants in this little
town is remarkable. Just across the street from
each other as you approach the town from
the west are two of the finest restaurants in
the state. **Merriman's (** (808) 885-6822, Opelo
Plaza, 65-1227A Opelo Road (expensive) chef
and owner Peter Merriman emphasizes
organic produce in his cooking. His dinner
appetizers include wok-charred ahi and
steamed clams. Entrées feature fresh fish
done in a wide variety of styles, steak and
veal T-bones, and a superb dish of king
prawns. Main courses run from $22 to $25.
Lunch is a simpler yet no less tasty affair with
grilled shrimp salad among the choices.

It is not entirely out of character to find
an alpine chalet in this Hawaiian town. It
certainly gets cold enough in the months of
December through April to enjoy German
and Austrian fare at **Edelweiss (** (808) 885-
6800, opposite Kamuela Inn, Highway 19

(moderate), in a room of dark-hued woods.
This is a very good restaurant with a history
of quality. You can order a simple yet tasty
lunch of bratwurst and sauerkraut, or sandwiches and burgers for between $5 and $6.
Dinner runs between $17 to $20. Don't be
fooled by the limited menu. The specials are
seemingly endless. Edelweiss specializes in
wiener schnitzel (breaded veal cutlets) filet mi-
gnon, sautéed calf's liver and the finest green
peppercorn steak this side of the Rocky
Mountains. It is open Tuesday to Saturday
from 11:30 AM to 1:30 PM for lunch and 5 PM
to 9 PM for dinner. Reservations are not taken.

Paniolo Country Inn ((808) 885-4377,
next to Parker Ranch Lodge (inexpensive),
serves large meals at reasonable prices, so
bring your appetite. Breakfasts are particularly good — try the eggs benedict. The inn
serves good Mexican burritos and quesa-
dillas for dinner. A large porterhouse steak
costs $21. You can get a meal here at just about
any time of the day or night.

Mean Cuisine ((808) 885-6325, 65-1227A
Opelo Road, Opelo Plaza (inexpensive), is a
charming little bakery that serves wholesome
country-cooked meals and snacks with the
accent on freshness. Their stews, breads,
sandwiches and soups are quite good and
reasonably priced. Have a slice of homemade
cake with a nice cup of coffee.

Su's Thai Kitchen ((808) 885-8688, Parker
Ranch Center (inexpensive), is no ordinary
Thai restaurant. In the morning Su's serves
a very good American breakfast. After that,
the accent is on Asia, with the menu listing
a variety of Thai, Japanese and Chinese
dishes. Average price for a good curry is
around $6.

THE HAMAKUA COAST

Highway 19 runs through Waimea and along
the Hamakua Coast, past misty rolling meadows and vast expanses of ocean. The road
runs east to **Honokaa**, a town founded by
Chinese immigrant labor.

Honokaa is a charming old town of quaint
and colorful timber-framed stores on wooden
boardwalks along Mamane Street. Once the

OPPOSITE: A cowboy at the Waikoloa Rodeo near
resort areas on the Kona Coast. OVERLEAF: Cattle
dot the green expanse of the Parker Ranch lands.

town's economy depended on the Hamakua Sugar Company, but since the plantation shut down, the town has spruced up to attract more tourists.

The **Honokaa People's Theater**, built in 1930, has been restored over the last decade and has become the focal point for a Hawaiian music festival. Organizers are hoping it will become an annual event to support the town's Western week, the highlight of which is the rodeo. There are many gift and antique stores in this town, but the **Hawaiian Shop** of the venerable James Rice is definitely worth browsing. It's a sort of musty treasure trove, with items from all over the world.

Honokaa, incidentally, was the site of the first macadamia nut orchard that was started in 1881 with cuttings brought from Australia. These days, macadamia nuts and macadamia products are an important Big Island export.

WAIPIO VALLEY

Leave Highway 19 at this point, and branch left onto Highway 240, which will take you past the town of Kapulena to the **Waipio Lookout**. From this vantage point you get your first view of the legendary valley where King Kamehameha the Great lived until he was 15 years old.

It isn't merely the history of Waipio that makes it worth visiting. It is one of those idyllic, secret valleys for which the Hawaiian chain is so famous. Halawa, on Molokai, has the same mystique. But Waipio may be the best of all, in spite of the growing tourist traffic on the steep road that plunges down to the valley floor. Historians have evidence that a lot of bloodletting went on in this verdant and serene place, particularly at the heiaus which date back to about 680 AD. Little wonder that some native Hawaiians believe, even to this day, that a section of Waipio Beach is the entrance to the nether world, and that once a year a long line of ghosts stalk through this valley to enter their secret domain. But fear of the Night Marchers does not prevent nature lovers from exploring Waipio.

Tucked deep in the furthest recesses of a horseshoe-shaped canyon are the 2,000-ft (610-m) twin falls of **Hiilawe**, the tallest in the Big Island. The waters of Hiilawe feed a crystalline pool — refreshing on hot, humid days when clothes cling to the body, as they often do in this valley.

Waipio Valley is a giant orchard. Guava, mango, mountain apple and java plum trees grow wild, and the air is alive with bird song. A river meanders through the valley and spills out past the black sand beach into the ocean.

The only way down into the valley is by four-wheel drive, traversing a steep one-lane road. If you don't want to risk the drive, the guides and drivers of the **Waipio Valley Shuttle** (808) 775-7121 will be happy to take you on a tour for about $15 per person.

On the lower road to Kukuihaele village is **Waipio Woodwork**, a little Aladdin's cave of a gallery which sells the works of some of the most talented artists in the island chain. You can make your reservations here in person for the Waipio Valley Shuttle.

The drive from Honokaa to Hilo along further stretches of the Hamakua Coast offers more picturebook scenery. Places of interest include the **Akaka Falls State Park** and its 442-ft (135-m) waterfall, which is signposted shortly after passing through the town of Honomu.

If you happen to be on the Hamakua Coast road in April or thereabouts, be on the lookout for **Ononea Bay**, an area between Honokaa and Hilo. In springtime the hillsides and valleys in this area leap out at you, so rich are they in colors and textures. Giant palms and tulip trees, their red blossoms vibrant against the lush green of the foliage, reach for the sky through the tangle of vines and other tropical plants. Waterfalls tumble over rocks polished by centuries of pounding. The roar of the falls on one side of the highway blends with the crash of waves on rocks on the other side. Torrents of water pour downhill under old bridges, tributaries meet and then join the ocean.

Rich and colorful tropical foliage surrounds the spectacular Akaka Falls not far from Hilo.

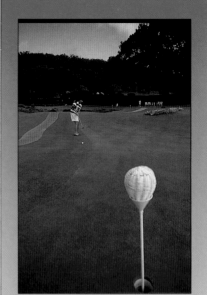

Golf

The Ultimate Destination

IN THESE ISLANDS, sprawled across some 300 miles (500 km) of ocean, there are so many beautiful golf courses, any three would be the envy of most Mainland states: Where but in Hawaii can an undulating field of rock-solid lava be transformed it into an oasis of rich greens, cool pools, tall trees and flowering hedges?

It is with some degree of pride, then, that the State of Hawaii can rightfully claim to be the ultimate destination for golfers. A remarkable mix of sun and gentle trade winds and an astonishing range of designer golf courses give the islands this reputation.

Some of Hawaii's courses can justifiably be described as being out of this world. There are courses high on the slopes of volcanoes, in lava fields, on old plantation lands, in affluent residential districts. There are private courses, resort courses and public courses. All have one thing in common: They are well designed, well maintained and a joy to play.

While it is expensive to play most of these courses — a round is likely to cost in excess of $100 at hotel and resort courses — there are many good packages. Tour operators or hotel representatives can provide information on these discounted golf vacations. Also, public courses are much cheaper, though getting onto them may be difficult since they are so heavily used by residents.

OAHU

Oahu has more golf courses than any other Hawaiian island. Most of them are open to the public. One of the most popular facilities is **Ala Wai Golf Course** ((808) 296-2000, 404 Kapahulu Avenue, Honolulu, HI 96815. This public course is on the fringe of Waikiki and may be the most played-on course in the world. It's not a difficult course. It's flat and generally friendly, but it will test you on occasion, especially if you're not used to playing on dry, hard fairways. This par-70 course is approximately 6,020 yards.

The 6,350-yard, par-72 **Hawaii Kai Championship Course** and the neighboring 2,386-yard **Hawaii Kai Executive Course** ((808) 395-2358, 8902 Kalanianaole Highway, Honolulu, HI 96825, were designed by Robert Trent Jones. The latter course, a par 54, is for golfers who want to test their short game.

Ocean winds and cleverly protected greens make these courses more challenging than they may appear.

On the sunny Ewa Plain 40 minutes out of Honolulu, the **Hawaii Prince Golf Club** ((808) 689-2213, 91-1200 Fort Weaver Road, Ewa Beach, HI 96706 incorporates three courses with 27 holes in total: the nine-hole, par-36 A Course is 3,138 yards; the nine-hole, par-36 B Course is 3,099 yards; and the nine-hole, par-36 C Course is 3,076 yards. Spread over 270 acres (109 hectares), this facility offers splendid views of the Waianae Mountain Range tests the skills of beginners and old pros alike. Its 27 dramatic holes, designed by Arnold Palmer and Ed Seay, make the only golf course of its kind in Hawaii.

West Oahu rarely sees rain, so the greens can be fast at **Ko'Olina Golf Club** ((808) 676-5300, 92-1220 Aliinui Drive, Kapolei, HI 96707. This is a gorgeous par-72 course with 6,867 yards. Ko'Olina is part of the Ihilani resort. Plan to stay overnight.

Rated the most difficult course in the United States by *Golf Digest*, **Koolau Golf Course** ((808) 236-GOLF or (808) 236-4653, 45–550 Kionaole Road, Kaneohe, HI 96744, in windward Oahu is a challenge worth accepting. At the base of the Koolau Mountain Range, this 18-holer has 6,324 yards and tests the range and skills of the best. The spectacular views may take some of the pain away.

The Koolau Mountains also frame the fairways at the **Olomana Golf Links** ((808) 259-7926, 41-1801 Kalanianaole Highway, Waimanalo, HI 96795, in the Waimanalo countryside. This is a popular course with locals. The front nine holes of this par-72 championship course are at the end of relatively flat fairways, but golfers shouldn't be deceived — the water hazards make it a real challenge. Characteristic of the back nine are tight fairways and small greens, which make this 6,326-yard course interesting.

Also known as Makaha West, **Sheraton Makaha Resort and Country Club** ((808) 695-9544, 84-626 Makaha Valley Road, Waianae, HI 96792 is recognized as one of the top five courses on Oahu. This course is long and flat, guarded by eight water hazards and 107 bunkers. Long drivers love to play here.

Ala Wai, on the edge of Waikiki, is the most heavily used public golf course in the world.

Nestled in the beautiful Makaha Valley, bounded by the ocean and the Waianae Mountain Range, the course is a par-72 with 7,077 yards. Reservations are required.

The beautiful, oceanfront **Turtle Bay Hilton and Country Club, Links at Kuilima** ((808) 293-8574, 7091 Kamehameha Highway, Kahuku, HI 96731 is located on the famous North Shore of Oahu where the spectacular high winter surf lures the world's greatest surfers. In fact the sound of the surf is ever present on this Arnold Palmer-designed course. Noted for its skillfully placed

bunkers which test golfers' accuracy, it is a very interesting and challenging 7,199-yard, par-72 course. It is highly rated by *Golf Digest* and *Golf Magazine*.

The 6,663-yard, par-72 **Waikele Golf Club** ((808) 676-9000, 94-200 Paioa Place, Waipahu, HI 96797 is a new course in west Oahu, near the shopping outlets of Waipahu, Oahu's second city. Waikele is on the plains in what was once sugar country. It's almost always sunny here, and the fairways get quite hot.

Oahu's newest course, the **West Loch Golf Course** ((808) 296-5624, 91-1126 Okupe Street, Ewa Beach, HI 96706 has added a new twist to the driving range. Here, you don't drive the ball into a dust bowl or a patch of green — you drive it into a lake. The balls used at this "watery" range float. The yard markers are buoys. On the par-four eighth, you have to bisect two lakes and avoid a sandtrap on the right of the green. The finishing holes are especially tough. The 17th is a par-three 210-yard nightmare from the championship tee. A timberline, a range of bunkers and a water hazard protect the green.

You drive the 400-yard-long 18th into the wind to an elevated green guarded by a small lake. The left-hand side of the fairway is out of bounds. This 18-holer is par 72 with approximately 6,480 yards.

MAUI

The first challenge of golfing in Maui is keeping your mind on the game. You can't ignore the views. **Kapalua Golf Club** ((808) 669-8044, 300 Kapalua Drive, Lahaina, HI 96761 has three gorgeous 18-holers: the Bay Course, the Village Course and the Plantation Course. The Bay Course, designed by Arnold Palmer, is the venue for the Kapalua International Championship, one of the premier events on the Hawaiian golf calendar. The long, wide fairways make this par-72 course of 6,600 yards popular with high-handicap players. The back nine meanders through what was once a pineapple plantation, with views of the ocean. For the serious golfer, the par-five first hole is a hint of things to come. Apart from the traps, the strong wind is always a factor. The par-71 Village Course, with 6,632 yards, was also designed by Palmer and has an even more spectacular setting than the adjacent Bay Course. From the fifth and sixth holes, the views of west Maui are stunning. The 18th is 453 yards from tee to green. This par-four has a 40-yard green guarded by a pond. The 7,263-yard, par-73 Plantation Course is equally beautiful and the most expensive of the three.

About 40 minutes from the Kahului Airport are the two courses of the **Makena Resort Golf Club** ((808) 879-3344, 5415 Makena Alanui, Makena, HI 96753. The North Course was completed in 1981. It's a par 72 with 6,914 yards and has great views on one side of the ocean the island of Lanai in the distance, and in the other direction, the imposing summit of Haleakala. The fairways are narrow and the fast greens are protected by 64 bunkers and four water hazards. The par-three 15th and par-four 16th face the ocean, with views as distracting as the holes are challenging. The par-71 South Course was designed by Robert Trent Jones Jr., who used 64 traps and four ponds on this lava landscape to create a 7,017-yard masterpiece. Two of the most difficult holes come late in the round.

It is 165 yards from the tee at the 15th to the green. You have to gauge your shot carefully here or end up in a sand trap so deep it looks like a dry well. Overshoot the green, and you're in the ocean.

Maui's most famous, the **Royal Kaanapali** ((808) 661-3691, Kaanapali Beach, Lahaina, HI 96761, also has two 18-holers, both par 71. The North Course has rolling fairways with the 541-yard, par-five first hole and the 438-yard, par-four 18th hole creating problems because of the water hazards. The South Course tests golfers' accuracy with an

Orange Course with 6,405 yards is entirely different. Many of the holes are doglegs, making it more challenging than the Blue. On some of the short holes, for instance, the play is downhill, which requires accuracy and control. Trees and lava rock walls serve as obstacles.

THE BIG ISLAND

The Big Island of Hawaii is well known for its oasis-like courses spread over mounds of dark lava. Rated as one of the world's great

extremely difficult 537-yard, par-five eighth close to the sugar cane fields and exposed to strong winds. The green is protected by three bunkers. This is a wonderful course.

There are remarkable views of the ocean throughout the two courses at **Wailea Golf Club** ((808) 879-2966, 100 Wailea Golf Club Drive, Wailea, HI 96753. Designed by Arthur Jack Snyder, the grounds incorporate ancient lava formations and heiaus. The par-72 Blue Course with 6,327 yards is spacious but tricky. Particularly difficult are the par-three second hole and the fourth hole. The second hole is guarded by two ponds with skillfully placed bunkers. If you don't make a good tee shot here, you'll run into trouble. The fairways are narrow. The layout of the par-72

courses, the **Mauna Kea Resort Golf Course** ((808) 880-3480, 62-100 Mauna Kea Beach Drive, Kamuela, HI 96743, is a Robert Trent Jones Sr. masterpiece. Carved out of the lava fields of beautiful Kona, every hole in this par-72 course is a gem, affording sweeping views of ocean and mountain ranges. Jones was determined to make this a challenging course—and he succeeded. Throughout the 7,114 yards, undulating fairways, steep greens, uphill holes, doglegs and strategically placed bunkers—20 in all—make this course both a golfer's dream and nightmare.

OPPOSITE: The Kaluakoi Resort course, Molokai. ABOVE LEFT: The popular Mauna Lani course. RIGHT: A golfer plays an intimidating hole at Mauna Kea.

Golf: The Ultimate Destination

The most dramatic hole is the par-three third where the water hazard is a surging inlet of the Pacific Ocean.

The **Hapuna Golf Course** ((808) 880-3000, Mauna Kea Resort, 62-100 Kaunaoa Drive, Kamuela, HI 96743 is Mauna Kea's magnificent new neighbor. Designed by Arnold Palmer and Ed Seay, the course opened for play in September 1992 and almost immediately was named one of the top 10 new courses in the nation by *Golf Magazine*. Hapuna is a links-style par-72 championship course with 6,534 yards set on a lava hillside and landscaped with grasses and shrubs.

The magnificent Jack Nicklaus-designed **Hualalai Golf Club** ((808) 325-8480, Queen Kaahumanu Highway, Kailua-Kona, HI 96740, at historic Kaupulehu has been

designated as the site for the annual Senior PGA MasterCard Championship for the next 10 years. Nicklaus designed this 7,117-yard, par-72 course taking advantage of the remarkable natural features of the landscape. The first hole, for instance, is a par-four 385-yard masterpiece that plays directly at the Hualalai Volcano bordered by the lava flows. Other holes weave around lava formations and deep bunkers, play over ancient Hawaiian fish ponds and skirt the shoreline. The 17th, the course's signature hole, is a challenging par three which, at high tide, is played to the accompaniment of thundering surf.

Designed by William Bell and featuring sloping fairways in the midst of lava fields, the **Kona Country Club** ((808) 322-2595, 78-7000 Alii Drive, Kailua-Kona, HI 96740, is

a 27-holer which is par 36 for nine holes. The 6,800-yard course overlooks Keauhou Bay in Kailua-Kona. It is not a course for the faint-hearted. On the short par-three 17th hole it is necessary to negotiate the lava.

Here are two more courses sculpted out of a lava field from a design by famed golf course architect Homer Flint. At the **Mauna Lani Resort, Francis I'i Brown Golf Course** ((808) 885-6655, 68-150 Hoohana Street, Kohala Coast, HI 96743, fairways are narrow, so accuracy is the key. The par-five first hole is a dogleg to the right. A feature of the front nine is that there is little rough and no trees to speak of, but there is lava on both sides of the fairway, and if you end up in the lava... watch out! Three holes stretch along the oceanfront, but the par-three sixth is the most talked about

because of the green, which fringes the edge of the ocean. The back nine meanders through groves of kiawe trees, interspersed with lava. One of the trickier holes is the 136-yard 17th, which must be played directly over a huge lava boulder. The South Course is a par-72 with 6,938 yards; the North Course, a par 72 with 6,913 yards.

Built in 1974, the 6,500-yard, par-72 **Sea Mountain at Punalu'u Golf Course** ((808) 928-6222, Highway 11, Pahala, HI 96777 has 22 bunkers, five water hazards, strategically placed lava rocks, and views of majestic Mauna Loa. It's a challenging course. In the middle of the sixth fairway is an island of lava rock. This hole has tested even the most confident of professionals. The 135-yard, par-three 14th has a valley 15 ft (four and a half-meters) wide in the middle of the fairway.

A Scotsman saw the potential of developing a course on the natural slope of Mauna Loa, in the shadow of the volcano, creating it in 1922 as a nine-hole course. In 1967, Jack Snyder turned it into an 18-hole course. In 1983, Bill Hayashi added 30 bunkers and four ponds, making the **Volcano Golf and Country Club** ((808) 967-7331, Golf Course Road, Hawaii Volcanoes National Park, HI 96718 even more challenging. This par-72 course of 6,505 yards has many doglegs and fast greens. Because of the high altitude, the ball tends to fly. Carry a sweater here — it gets quite cool.

Robert Trent Jones Jr. designed the **Waikoloa Beach Golf Club** ((808) 885-6060, 1020 Keana Place, Waikoloa, HI 96743, recognized as one of the finest in the islands. Completed in 1982, it is built around the historic King's Highway, on the edge of which are fish ponds and rock carvings. There are 76 bunkers, three water hazards, narrow fairways and lava interspersed with beautiful flowering bushes and shrubs. The greens on this 6,566-yard, par-70 course require technique.

The 7,074-yard, par-72 Tom Weiskopf/Jay Morrish-designed **King's Golf Course** ((808) 885-4647, 600 Waikoloa Beach Drive, Waikoloa Beach, HI 96743 is a special facility. From the hand-cut greens and tees to the manicured bunkers and foliage and some 150 acres (60 hectares) of black lava rock —

Some of the Mauna Lani's greens and surrounding hazards are laid out like Japanese gardens.

this course is a serene oasis. Weiskopf and Morrish have designed more than 15 golf courses, but they consider Waikoloa to be one of their more challenging. The fifth hole is a short par four with a left-hand dogleg. A 100-yard-long fairway bunker, one of 50 on the course, zigzags down the left-hand side of course. To test your nerves even further, two enormous lava boulders are positioned at the right corner of the bunker. You have the option of trying to carry the corner of the bunker with a 240-yard drive. If you miscalculate, it's trouble with a capital "T".

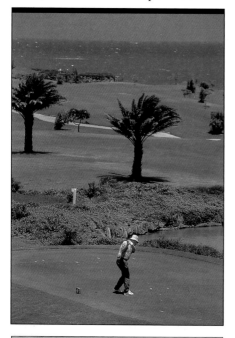

KAUAI

The Garden Isle has a healthy crop of golf courses — many with fine views. The 6,353-yard, par-70 **Kiahuna Plantation Golf Course** ((808) 742-9595, 2545 Kiahuna Plantation Drive, Koloa, HI 96756 is located at the resort of Poipu. This Robert Trent Jones Jr.-designed course — noted for its cleverly placed lava rocks — is one of the finest in the state. The most talked-about holes are the 12th and 16th, both pins being set at opposite ends of a single oval-shaped green. Don't leave Kauai without playing this course. It's an experience to be treasured.

Two courses are laid out at the **Kauai Lagoons Golf Course** ((808) 241-6000, 3351

Hoolaulea Way, Lihue, HI 96766. The 7,070-yard, par-72 Kiele Course combines the natural beauty of Hawaiian landscapes with dramatic views along cliffs that overlook the Pacific Ocean. The Lagoons Course — a par 72 with 6,942 yards — is a softer, gentler course than Kiele, but it's still a tough one. The front nine comprises two par-three holes, a mixture of par fours and two par fives that will test the longest hitters. All the holes — with the exception of the first and the 18th — are named after animals. The par-four fourth, the par-three fifth, and the par-five sixth, are named, dauntingly, the Ox, the Eagle and the Gorilla. The Ox may be the most difficult par four on the course. The tee shot has to carry a deep bunker on the left to a bowl-shaped green set between two mounds.

Since opening, the Princeville Resort on Kauai's northern shores has been rated as one of the best resorts in the world. The centerpiece of this first-class resort is its two courses, Makai and Prince. A 27-hole, par-72 course with 10,345 yards, the **Makai Course** ((808) 826-3580 is considered the most beautiful course in all Hawaii. Designed by Robert Trent Jones Jr., it has of three nine-holers: Ocean, Lakes and Woods. The par-three third hole on Ocean eptomizes all that is remarkable about this course. You have the illusion of driving your tee shot straight into deep blue waters. Woods has a unique layout. A feature of the par-three eighth hole is the huge lava rock positioned in the middle of the bunker guarding the green, creating the effect of a Japanese garden. Lakes, with its rolling fairways and scattered ponds, is as picturesque a course as you'll find anywhere.

Jones did such a great job with the Makai course, he was invited back to design the Princeville Resort's **Prince Course** ((808) 826-5000. This is an 18-holer; a par-72 course with 7,309 yards. While Makai is a "fun" course, Prince is for the serious. The course covers 390 acres (65 hectares) of forest and orchard, flowering trees and shrubs. One of the most fascinating holes on this course is the par-three 17th, "the Pali." It's a relatively short hole, only 205 yards to the pin, but you have to clear both water and heavy foliage to do get there. The 10th, or "Burma Road," is no easier. The way to the green is over a jungle bisected by a stream and ringed with bunkers. The distance from tee to green is 588 yards.

Lovely but treacherous **Poipu Bay Resort Golf Course** ((808) 742-8711, 2250 Ainako Street, Poipu Beach, HI 9675, on the south shores of Kauai, has rolling terrain and deceptive greens which will test the patience of the best golfer. If these obstacles don't challenge you, then the wind, always a factor here, will. You'll have to navigate a succession of bunkers, mounds and doglegs to get to the 18th. A fun time is guaranteed at this 6,959-yard, par-72 course.

Many consider the **Wailua Municipal Course** ((808) 241-6666, 3-5351 Kuhio Highway, Kapaa, HI 96746 to be the finest municipal course in the islands. Built alongside the ocean, it is full of doglegs, fast greens and large trees. This 6,918-yard, par-72 course was venue for the 1975 and 1985 USGA Amateur Public Links Championship.

MOLOKAI

Ted Robinson designed the **Kaluakoi Golf Resort** ((808) 552-2739, Kepuhi Beach, Maunaloa, HI 96770. Some consider it the most unique and spectacular course in the islands because of the mix of scenery and challenging holes. The verdant fairways are fringed by a rocky

shoreline on one side. Five holes are played along the coastline. Among the occasional hazards are wild deer, turkeys and pheasants. This is a par-72 course with 6,564 yards.

LANAI

The **Experience at Koele** ((808) 565-4653, Lanai Avenue, Lanai City, HI 96763, was designed by Greg Norman, the Australian professional, with Ted Robinson. It was Norman's first course and, based on what he achieved here, it won't be his last. Seven holes are located on a plateau 2,000 ft (600 m) above sea level, with the first and second facing west and the third, fifth and sixth holes facing the islands of Maui and Molokai. Nine of the holes meander through a mountain valley surrounded by pines. At Koele, Robinson's penchant for water is obvious. On the eighth golfers play from an elevated tee 250 ft (75 m) above the green, which is guarded by a lake on the right and dense trees and shrubs on the left. The 17th green doesn't leave room for error as it sits on an island. Koele is a par-72 course with 7,014 yards.

The Jack Nicklaus-designed 7,039-yard, par-72 **Challenge at Manele** ((808) 565-2222, One Manele Bay Road, Lanai City, HI 96763 is ranked among the top 100 courses in the United States. Golf addicts compare it to Pebble Beach. This course is unique because it's built on several hundred acres of natural lava outcropping, among wild ilima and kiawe trees. The course winds itself along the Lanai coastline and features dramatic over-the-water holes. Open fairways end on small, fast greens. The signature hole is the 12th, a fine par three. Golfers drive from a cliff above the ocean to a green positioned on another cliff — a distance of about 185 yards. There's little room for error. The 17th demands a 215-yard carry over the ocean to reach the green. The course has many changes of elevation which — together with an assortment of canyons, blind tees and approach shots — makes it a true challenge.

OPPOSITE: A golfer lines up a shot on a course at Poipu on Kauai, where the fine views can distract even the most practiced players. ABOVE: The course at Lanai's Lodge at Koele presents a delightful challenge to both the casual golfer and the professional.

Travelers'
Tips

GETTING THERE

The airlines service Honolulu International Airport on Oahu and Kahalui Airport on Maui:

MAINLAND CARRIERS

American Airlines ((808) 833-7600
Continental Airlines TOLL-FREE (800) 523-3273
Delta Airlines TOLL-FREE (800) 221-1212
Northwest Orient TOLL-FREE INTERNATIONAL (800) 447-4747 TOLL-FREE DOMESTIC (800) 225-2525
TWA TOLL-FREE (800) 221-2000
United Airlines TOLL-FREE (800) 241-6522

INTERNATIONAL CARRIERS

Air Canada TOLL-FREE (800) 776-3000
Air New Zealand TOLL-FREE (800) 262-1234
All Nippon ((808) 838-0173
Asiana Airlines TOLL-FREE (800) 227-4262
Canadian Airlines International ((808) 681-5000
China Airlines ((808) 955-0088
Garuda Indonesia TOLL-FREE (800) 342-7832
Japan Airlines TOLL-FREE (800) 525-3663; ((808) 521-1441 (Oahu)
Korean Airlines TOLL-FREE (800) 438-5000
Philippine Airlines TOLL-FREE (800) 435-9725
Qantas Airways TOLL-FREE (800) 227-4500
Singapore Airlines TOLL-FREE (800) 221-4750

INTERISLAND CARRIERS

Most travelers to Hawaii fly to Honolulu and connect with interisland shuttles:

Aloha Airlines
Oahu ((808) 484-1111
Molokai ((808) 836-1111
Maui ((808) 244-9071
Lanai ((808) 244-9071
Hawaii ((808) 935-5771
Kauai ((808) 245-3691

America West Airlines
TOLL-FREE (800) 235-9292

Hawaiian Airlines
TOLL-FREE (800) 367-5320
Oahu ((808) 838-1555
Molokai ((808) 553-3644
Maui ((808) 871-6132
Lanai ((808) 565-7281
Hawaii ((808) 326-5615
Kauai ((808) 245-1813

Island Air
TOLL-FREE (800) 652-6541
Oahu ((808) 484-2222

Mahalo Air Inc.
Other islands TOLL-FREE (800) 227-8333
United States and Canada TOLL-FREE (800) 4-MAHALO
Oahu ((808) 833-5555

TOURIST INFORMATION

The best source for tourist information on Hawaii is the **Hawaii Tourist Bureau**. The bureau publishes three useful booklets: a *Calendar of Events*, an *Accommodation Guide*, and a *Restaurants Guide*. The Bureau has branches on each of the islands:

Big Island ((808) 329-7787
Kauai ((808) 245-3971, 3016 Umi, Kauai, HI 96766
Lanai ((808) 565-7600, P.O. Box 700, Lanai City, HI 96763
Maui ((808) 244-3530, 1727 Wili Pa Loop, Maui, HI 96793
Molokai ((808) 553-3876, Kaunakakai, Molokai, HI 96748
Oahu ((808) 923-1811, 2250 Kalakaua, Suite 514, Honolulu, HI 96815

CONSULATES

The following foreign consulates are on Oahu:
American Samoa ((808) 847-1998, 1427 Dillingham Boulevard, Suite 210
Australia ((808) 524-5050, 1000 Bishop Street
Austria ((808) 923-8585, 1314 South King, Suite 1260
Belgium ((808) 533-6900, 745 Fort Street Mall, 18th Floor

Boogie boarders exit the surf on an isolated Maui beach.

Brazil ((808) 235-0571, 44-166 Nanamo-
ana
Chile ((808) 949-2850, 1860 Ala Moana
Boulevard, Suite 1900
Chinese Cultural Service ((808) 538-3725,
100 North Beretania, Suite 302
Denmark ((808) 545-2028, 1001 Bishop
Street, Suite 2626
Germany ((808) 946-3819, 2003 Kalia
Road, Suite 11
Hungary ((808) 377-3637, 631 Puuikena
Drive
India ((808) 262-0292, 307 Hahani

Italy ((808) 531-2277, 735 Bishop Street,
Suite 201
Japan ((808) 523-7495, 1742 Nuuanu Av-
enue
Kiribati ((808) 521-7703, 850 Richards
Street, Suite 503
Korea ((808) 595-6109 or 595-6274, 2756 Pali
Highway
Malaysia ((808) 525-8144, P.O. Box 3200
Mariannas Liaison ((808) 592-0300, 1221
Kapiolani Boulevard, Suite 730
Mexico ((808) 524-4390, 677 Ala Moana
Boulevard, Suite 920
Micronesia ((808) 836-4775, 3049 Ualena,
Suite 408
Papua New Guinea ((808) 947-3100, 1357
Kapiolani Boulevard
Philippines ((808) 595-6316, 2433 Pali
Highway
Sweden ((808) 528-4777, 737 Bishop, Suite
2600
Switzerland ((808) 737-5297, 4231 Papu
Circle
Taipei ((808) 595-6347, 2746 Pali Highway
Thailand ((808) 845-7332, 287A Kalihi

TRAVEL DOCUMENTS

When arriving in Hawaii, Canadian and Mexican nationals need only show proof of citizenship and residence. A driver's license will suffice. British and most European (EEC) citizens need a valid passport. Visitors from other counties must have a valid passport and a United States visa. Get in touch with the United States embassy or consulate in your country for details on obtaining a visa.

CUSTOMS

You are allowed to bring into the United States, duty free, gifts valued at no more than $100. Two hundred cigarettes, or 50 cigars, or three pounds (1.35 kg) of tobacco are allowed, as is one quart (one liter) of alcohol. Nonprescription narcotics are, of course, strictly prohibited.

CAR RENTAL

The following is a list of toll-free numbers of national car rental agencies in Hawaii:
Alamo TOLL-FREE (800) 327-9633
Avis TOLL-FREE (800) 321-3712
Budget TOLL-FREE (808) 537-3600
Dollar TOLL-FREE (800) 800-4000
Hertz TOLL-FREE (800) 654-3011 WEBSITE http://www.hertz.com
National TOLL-FREE (800) 227-7368
Thrifty TOLL-FREE (800) 357-2277

BASICS

TIME

Hawaiian Standard Time is eleven hours behind Greenwich Mean Time, six hours behind Eastern Standard Time (United States East Coast) and three hours behind Pacific Standard Time (United States West Coast).

MONEY

It is advisable to purchase some travelers' checks in United States currency. Not many Hawaii banks offer foreign currency exchange services. Credit cards are accepted by many establishments. Some Hawaii stores and restaurants do not accept travelers' checks.

TAXES

Hawaii has a 4.16 percent excise tax on all goods and services. This tax applies to gifts, clothing, medical services, hotel rooms, rental cars, and all other goods and services. In addition, there is a separate six percent room tax on hotel and resort accommodations and a $2-per-day road tax on rental cars.

ELECTRICITY

The electric current in the United States is 110–115 volts AC. Unless you have dual-voltage electronics or appliances, chances are they won't run unless you buy a transformer.

TELEPHONES

Calls within an island cost 25 cents. Calls between islands are considered long distance and are charged accordingly. To place long-distance calls, dial 1 + the area code and the number you are calling. All calls between Hawaii islands are preceded by 808.

Toll-free numbers within the United States begin with area code 800 or 888. Local information is reached by dialing 411. United States nationwide information is reached by dialing 1 + (area code) 555-1212. For direct dialing of international numbers, dial 011 + country code + city code + telephone number. For local operator assistance dial 0.

MAIL

Most post offices are open Monday through Friday from 9 AM to 5 PM. Some postal branch offices are open on Saturdays until noon. At present time, first-class letters sent within the United States require a $0.32 stamp and postcards a $0.21 stamp. International rates vary according to country.

WEIGHTS AND MEASURES

The United States uses ounces, pounds, gallons, miles, etc. It's an antiquated system, and if you're used to metric, it can be a bit confusing. Here are some conversions to help you along:

Distance and Length
1 inch = 2.54 centimeters
1 foot = 0.305 meters
1 mile = 1.6 kilometers

Weight
1 ounce = 28.35 grams
1 pound = 0.45 kilograms

Volume
1 gallon = 3.78 liters

Temperature
To convert Fahrenheit to centigrade, subtract 32 and multiply by $5/9$.

To convert Centigrade to Fahrenheit, multiply by 1.8 and add 32.

OPPOSITE: Detail of the palace gate at Kailua-Kona on the Big Island with the Mokuaikua Church in the background. ABOVE: The garden at Lanai's Lodge at Koele.

HEALTH

DANGEROUS ANIMALS

Although Hawaii is fortunate to have few problems with the more dangerous and aggressive marine creatures which inhabit its waters, some are potentially harmful and should be avoided. Eels are frequently found in crevices and under coral. They are normally not aggressive, but if threatened can be dangerous. Observe them

from a distance and never reach into holes or crevices where you may risk being bitten. Above all, never try to feed an eel.

Another potential danger is the Portuguese Man-of-War, a bubble-shaped creature whose long tentacles contain poison cells that can inflict painful stings on anyone venturing too close. They are uncommon in island waters, but if encountered, they should not be handled, dead or alive.

Other hazards include cone shells, which can shoot off a poisonous dart used to capture prey, and spiny sea urchins (or *wana* as they are locally known), which can inflict painful puncture wounds through their brittle spines. Remember too that coral cuts and abrasions are slow to heal and often become infected; therefore, be sure to wear adequate protection such as gloves and wet suits when handling coral.

TANNING

Since the difference between a suntan and a sunburn can be the difference between a

happy vacation and an unhappy one, it is well to remember that the Hawaii sun is intense and should not be taken lightly if you want to go dark pleasantly. To begin with, from 11 AM to 2 PM you are best advised to stay inside. Second, you must wear sunscreen, at least for the first few days, and you must be patient, increasing your exposure to the sun only gradually. Depending, of course, on the type of skin you have, you should only be out in the sun for half an hour (or less) the first few days, slowly increasing your exposure time to a couple of hours by the end of the first week. After that you should be ready for some serious sunbathing.

Another point to bear in mind is that some parts of the body are more sensitive to the sun than others. Your nose, knees, and the tops of your feet should be particularly well protected by sun lotion, and your eyes should be protected by proper sunglasses — ones that are UV coated to keep out harmful ultraviolet rays, and ones that preferably also have polarized filters if you plan to spend much time on the water, where your eyes are vulnerable to the reflected light.

EMERGENCIES

If you are seriously ill or critically injured, dial 911, the emergency hot line, for help. In addition to the hospitals listed below, many fire stations have paramedics on hand who can administer emergency first aid.

The following hospitals offer 24-hour emergency service:

OAHU

Castle Medical Center ((808) 263-5500, 640 Ulukahiki Street, Kailua

Kapiolani Medical Center ((808) 486-6000, 98-1079 Moanalua Road, Pearlridge

Kapiolani Medical Center for Women and Children ((808) 973-8511, 1319 Punahou Street, Honolulu

Queen's Medical Center ((808) 538-9011, 1301 Punchbowl, Honolulu

Straub Clinic and Hospital ((808) 522-4000, 888 South King Street, Honolulu

Wahiawa General Hospital ((808) 621-8411, 128 Lehua Street, Wahiawa

BIG ISLAND
Hilo Medical Center ((808) 969-4111, 1190 Waianuenue Avenue, Hilo

North Hawaii Community Hospital ((808) 885-4444, 67-1125 Mamalahoa Highway, Kamuela

Kona Community Hospital ((808) 322-9311, Kealakekua

LANAI
Lanai Community Hospital ((808) 565-6411, 628 Seventh Street, Lanai City

MAUI
Maui Memorial Hospital ((808) 244-9056, 221 Mahalani, Wailuku

MOLOKAI
Molokai General Hospital ((808) 553-5331, Kaunakakai

KAUAI
Wilcox Memorial Hospital ((808) 245-1100, 3420 Kuhio Highway, Lihue

West Kauai Medical Center ((808) 338-9431, 4643 Waimea Canyon Road, Waimea

ACCOMMODATION

Hawaii is generally recognized as an expensive state. In fact, based on the price of residential accommodation and the price of food, Hawaii is one of the three most expensive states in the country. From the tourist's point of view there are few goods and services that can be categorized as "inexpensive." Whether it's accommodation or food, prices tend to range from moderate to very expensive or luxury. But when compared with prices in parts of Europe or in Asian countries such as Japan, prices in Hawaii are not unreasonable.

The budget-conscious tourist — and most of us are — would be well advised to check out tour packages from home countries that include the price of air fare, accommodation and American-plan meals. There is a wide range of options in this respect; check with your travel agent for prices.

To give you an idea of what prices are like if you travel independently, here are some guidelines:

Rates for accommodation run the gamut from $60 for a clean and comfortable room in a bed-and-breakfast establishment to over $4,000 for a luxury suite in a resort hotel. Where possible, we have noted price ranges in the text. All prices are calculated at the cost of a standard double room, double occupancy during high season. **Inexpensive** accommodation will cost under $70; **mid-range** hotels will tend to

charge between $70 and $170; hotels listed as **expensive** will cost between $170 and $450; **luxury** means you can expect to pay over $450.

Condominiums are a popular option in Hawaii for longer stays. Most of these apartments are well appointed, with full-sized kitchens, but the number of bathrooms may vary, so this is something you should enquire about before committing. Recreational amenities in the complex may also influence the price. Many condominiums have large pools, well-equipped weight rooms, and the occasional racquet-

OPPOSITE: Woodcarving, Oahu. ABOVE: Kauai cowboy, or *paniolo.*

ball court. Most important in the price equation is the proximity of the complex to the beach, and of course the view from the apartment. As with hotel rooms, if the apartment has a ocean view, expect to pay more.

EATING OUT

There are many inexpensive fast food and local eateries that cater to the budget-conscious tourist. Participating in the Hawaiian ritual of the plate lunch will get you a

complete meal, in a variety of cooking styles ranging from Japanese to Chinese to Hawaiian, for between $5 and $8. There are also American fast food chains such as McDonald's, Burger King, Jack in the Box, Subway, and a good local fast food chain, Zippy's. Noodle shops are another low-cost alternative.

We have divided restaurants into four categories according to the range of prices you can expect. Restaurants listed as **inexpensive** cost up to $15 per person; **moderate** restaurants will generally charge between $18 and $30; an **expensive** meal cost between $30 to $60; and **very expensive** means that your meal, including wine, will cost $60 or more.

LANGUAGE

Spoken Hawaiian is a beautifully melodic language for which there was no written form until after the eighteenth century.

As part of the renaissance of Hawaiian art and culture, spoken and written Hawaiian is in midst of revival.

Hawaiian is not to be confused with pidgin, a dialect spoken widely by locals. Whereas Hawaiian is a Polynesian language which has its roots in the languages of Southeast Asia, pidgin evolved out of English, Japanese, Samoan and Chinese.

Hawaiian words are pronounced precisely as they are spelled. There are no silent letters, and ⬤ds can be easily broken down into syllables as in "Waikiki" (Wai-ki-ki) or "aloha" (a-lo-ha).

Below are some of the words you'll hear in day-to-day conversations while in the islands:

ahaiaina   feast

A hui hou   Until we meet again.

aina   land, earth; that from which plant food (*'ai*) comes

alii   chief, chieftess, the nobility

Souvenir shoppers cruise the Kona streets.

alii nui   paramount ruling chief of an island
alii 'ai moku   ruling chief of a district
aloha   lover; hello; good-bye
'aumakua   family or personal god, said to be deified ancestor
ewa   on the side nearest ewa beach; used to give directions
halau   longhouse such as used in hula instruction
haole   white person, Caucasian; formerly any foreigner
hula   the Hawaiian dance
kai   sea, salt water
kamaaina   old-time resident; literally "child of the land"
kahakai   seaside
kahiko   ancient, old; generally meant today as the time prior to the arrival of Captain Cook
kahuna   priest or minister of old religion; expert in any profession
kane   man, male
keiki   child
kuleana   small piece of property; right to, title, portion, responsibility, jurisdiction
kumu   base, foundation, bottom; teacher
kupuna   grandparent, relative of grandparent's generations; ancestor
luau   taro leaves; term used for Hawaiian feast
mahalo   thank you
makai   towards the sea
malihini   stranger, newcomer; one unaccustomed to a place or its customs
mauka   towards the uplands
mele   song, poem; to sing
moana   ocean; deep sea
pau   the end; finished, completed
pau hana   finished for the day
po'e   people; group of pec ico
'uniki   ceremony of graduation
wahine   woman, female
wai   fresh water

Recommended Reading

SIR PETER BUCK, *Arts and Crafts of Hawaii*, Honolulu, Bishop Museum, 1957.
Atlas of Hawaii, Honolulu, University of Hawaii Press.
VON TEMPSKI, *Born in Paradise*, New York, Duell, 1940.
MARY KAWENA PUKUI, *English-Hawaiian Dictionary*, Honolulu, University of Hawaii Press, 1964.
Place Names of Hawaii, Honolulu, University of Hawaii, 1966.
ROBERT SMITH, *Hawaii's Best Hiking Trails*, Wilderness Press, 1985 (new edition).
JAMES MICHENER, *Hawaii*, New York Random House, 1959.
JOSEPH R. MORGAN, *Hawaii*, Boulder, Westview Press Inc., 1983.
ROBERT SMITH, *Hiking Oahu: The Capital Isle*, Boulder, Wilderness Press, 1980.
GRANT KUHNS, *On Surfing*, Rutland, C. E. Tuttle Co., 1963.
JOHN AND BOBBY E. MCDERMOTT, *Our Hawaii: What We Tell Our Friends to Do in the Islands*, Honolulu, Orafa Publishing Company.
Selections from Fornander's Collection of Hawaiian Antiquities and Folklore, University of Hawaii Press, 1959.
FRED HEMMINGS, *Surfing — Hawaii's Gift to the World of Sports*, New York, Zokeisha Publishing Company, 1977.
GARY FAIRMONT AND R. FILOS II, *The Surfers' Almanac: An International Surfing Guide*, New York, Dutton, 1977.

Photo Credits

Robert Holmes: pages 13, 17, 32, 33, 35, 37, 39, 41, 51, 55, 57, 61, 69, 80, 83, 84, 86, 87, 90, 91 (top and bottom), 92, 93, 96 (top and bottom), 97 (top), 99, 103, 104, 110, 113, 167, 173, 180, 181, 187, 195, 208, 209, 212, 214, 217, 278, 285, 294.

Quick Reference A–Z Guide
to Places and Topics of Interest with Listed Accommodation, Restaurants and Useful Telephone Numbers